A True and Exact

DESCRIPTION

OF THE

Moft Celebrated Eaft-India Coafts

OF

MALABAR AND COROMANDEL,

As also of the Isle of Ceylon.

PHILIPPUS BALDÆUS DELPHENSIS V.D.M.
PRIMO ANNUM IN PUNTE GALE. POSTEA
IN REGNO IAFFNAPATNAM IN INSULA CEY:
LON 8 Annos. Iam in Geervliet 2. Ætatis 38. A. 1671.

A True and Exact
DESCRIPTION
OF THE
Moft Celebrated Eaft-India Coafts
OF
MALABAR AND COROMANDEL,
As also of the Isle of Ceylon.

With all the adjacent Kingdoms, Principalities, Provinces, Cities, Chief Harbors, Structures, Pagan Temples, Products, and living Creatures. The Manners, Habits, Oeconomies and Ceremonies of he Inhabitants; as likewife the moft remarkable Warlike Exploits, Sieges, Sea and Field-Engagements betwixt the *Portu-guefes* and Dutch; with their Traffick and Commerce.

The Whole adorn'd with new Maps and Draughts of the chief Cities, Forts, Habits, Living Creatures, Fruits, &c. of the Product of the *Indies*, drawn to the Life, and cut in Copper Plates.

Alfo a moft Circumftantial and Compleat Account of the Idolatry of the Pagans in the *Eaft-Indies*, the *Malabars*, *Benjans*, *Gentives*, *Brahmans*, &c. Taken partly from their own Vedam o Law-Book, and Authentick Manufcripts; partly from frequent Converfation with their Priefts and Divines: With the Draughts of their Idols, done after their Originals.

By PHILIP BALAAEUS, Minifter of the *Word God in* Ceylon.

Tranflated from the *High-Dutch* printed at *Amfterdam*, 1872.

GYAN

Published by

Gyan Publishing House
5, Ansari Road
Daryaganj, New Delhi-110002
Phone: 011-47034999, 9811692060
E-mail: books@gyanbooks.com

Distribution Network
gyanbooks.com
India, USA, Canada, UK, Australia, France

ISBN : 978-81-212-4553-1 (HB)

2nd Impression 2020

Printed at: Gyan Press, Delhi.

The book at your disposal is the edition of an old book originally published long back. The Text quality of this book may not be at par as compared to our other books but many readers approached us to reprint this important book so that it could satiate their hunger. We request all the readers of this book to help us to improve its quality by providing the necessary text of those pages which are not properly visible. Your valuable support in this case will be highly appreciated and acknowledged and our future readers will be benefitted immensely.

A True and Exact DESCRIPTION OF THE Most Celebrated *East-India* Coasts OF MALABAR AND COROMANDEL, As also of the Isle of *Ceylon.*

With all the adjacent Kingdoms, Principalities, Provinces, Cities, Chief Harbors, Structures, Pagan Temples, Products, and living Creatures. The Manners, Habits, Oeconomies and Ceremonies of the Inhabitants; as likewise the most remarkable Warlike Exploits, Sieges, Sea and Field-Engagements betwixt the *Portugueses* and *Dutch*; with their Traffick and Commerce.

The Whole adorn'd with new Maps and Draughts of the chief Cities, Forts, Habits, Living Creatures, Fruits, *&c.* of the Product of the *Indies*, drawn to the Life, and cut in Copper Plates.

Also a most Circumstantial and Compleat Account of the Idolatry of the Pagans in the *East-Indies*, the *Malabars*, *Benjans*, *Gentives*, *Brahmans*, &c. Taken partly from their own *Vedam* or Law-Book, and Authentick Manuscripts; partly from frequent Conversation with their Priests and Divines: With the Draughts of their Idols, done after their Originals.

By PHILIP BALDÆUS, *Minister of the Word of God in* Ceylon.

Translated from the *High-Dutch* printed at *Amsterdam*, 1672.

LONDON
*Printed for Awnsham and John Churchill,
at the Black Swan in Pater Noster Row 1703.*

THE PREFACE TO THE READER.

MOST of the Modern East-India *Voyages that have been published of late years, being very defective either in respect of the many fabulous Relations that are inserted frequently, rather to please the Reader, than to pursue the strict Rules of Truth (not to mention the Errors in the Computation of the distances of Places, and frequent unnecessary Digressions) it is no wonder if the most curious in History have conceiv'd a very indifferent opinion, if not an entire aversion to them. It was upon this Consideration, that the ensuing Treatise coming to our hands, we thought it absolutely worthy the publick view, it being agreed by all who have had the opportunity of travelling in those Countries, that the same may in respect of its sincerity and exactness challenge the Prerogative before any other hitherto publish'd upon the same Subject. For, considering that the Author thereof liv'd not only in the* Station *of a* Minister *in divers places of* Malabar *and* Coromandel, *and especially for several years in the Kingdom of* Jafnapatnam *in the Isle of* Ceylon, *but also assisted in Person in divers Sieges and Expeditions, and thereby had more than ordinary opportunity to be inform'd concerning the Nature and Constitution of those Countries, their Products, Inhabitants, Manners, Customs, Religion, Ceremonies, Oeconomy, Traffick, Manufacturies, Civil and Military Exploits, and what else may be requisite for the accomplishment of a good History, founded upon the Faith of one who had been an Eye-witness of those Transactions; consequently he might challenge the Preference before many, who relate matters chiefly upon hearsay. As to those things which are not grounded upon his Ocular Testimony, the same were taken from Authentick Records and Manuscripts, and illustrated with Maps and Draughts of those several Countries, Cities, Nations, &c. done to the Life. What relates to the Idolatry of these* Pagans, *we are convinc'd by his own Testimony, that besides the opportunity he had of visiting their* Pagodes, *or Temples (a thing rare-*

ly allow'd there) *one of their most learned* **Brahmans** *liv'd with him in the same House for a considerable time, from whom he by constant Conversation, as well as out of their own Records, learn'd the most secret Recesses of their Religion, and had the exact Draughts of their Idols, much beyond what* Abraham Royerius *(who writ upon the same Subject) can pretend to upon that account. As for our part, we have made it our chiefest care to give you an exact* Delineation *of the before-mention'd Draughts in the best Copper Plates that could be procur'd, and that with all imaginable exactness according to the true Originals, contrary to what is practis'd by many, who study to represent matters of this kind, rather according to their own Fancy, than to Truth. We have only this to add, that to avoid all unnecessary Prolixity, it was judged requisite to omit many Digressions, tending not so much towards the Elucidation of the History, as (we suppose) to shew the Author's Criticism in the Holy Scripture.*

An

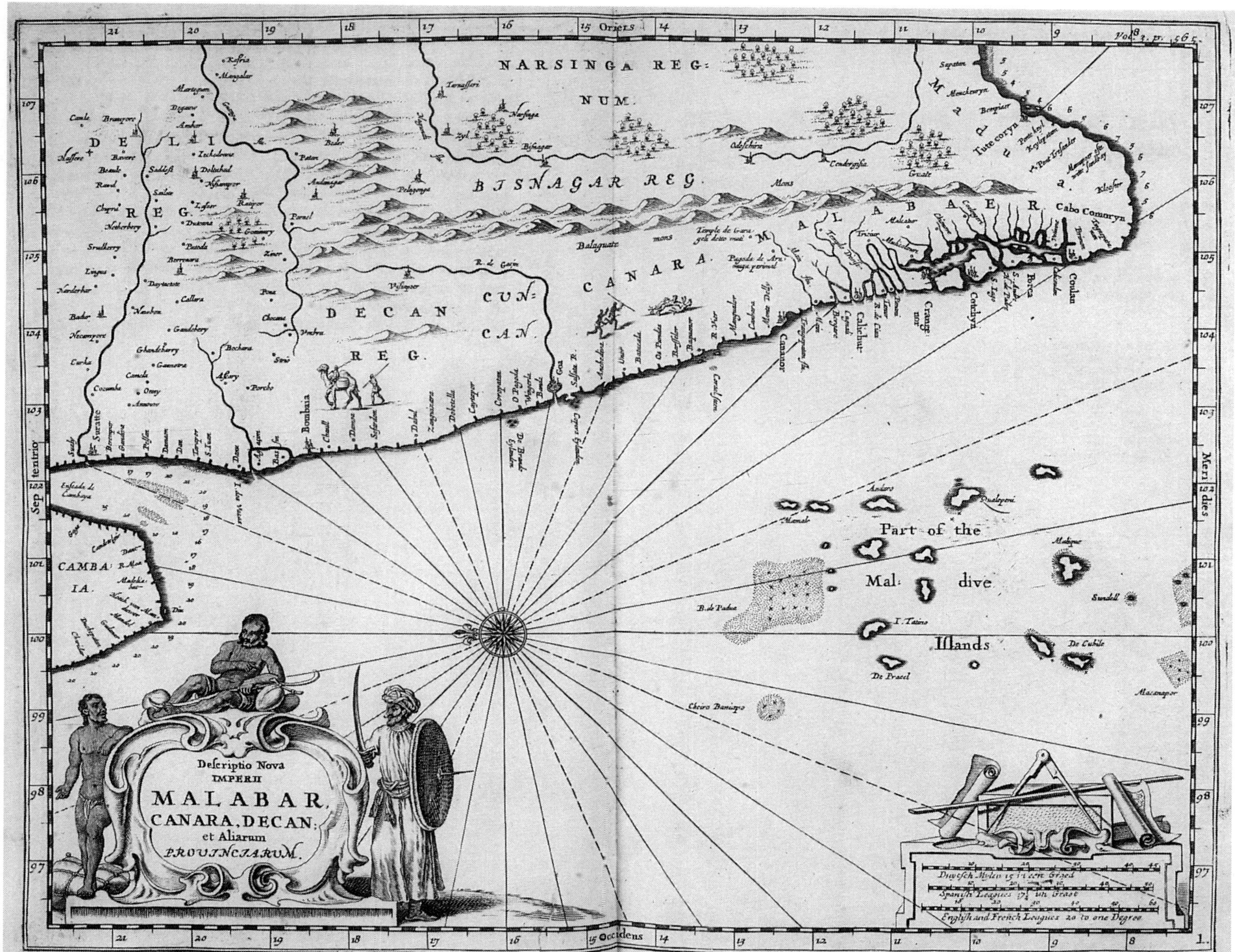
Vol. 2. pr. 565.
Descriptio Nova
IMPERII
MALABAR,
CANARA, DECAN;
et Aliarum
PROVINCIARUM.
NARSINGA REG:
NUM.
BISNAGAR REG.
MALABAER.
CANARA.
DECAN
REG.
CUN:
CAN.
DELI
REG.
CAMBA
IA.
Part of the
Mal dive
Islands
Cabo Comoryn
Coulan
Porca
Cotchyn
Crange nor
Calichut
Cananor
Goa
Bombaia
Suratte
I. dos Vacas
De Brando Eylanden
Duytsch Mylen 15 in een Graed
Spanish Leagues 17½ in Grado
English and French Leagues 20 to one Degree
Meri dies
Sep tentrio
15 Oriens
15 Occidens

Baldæus.

An Exact Description of the Coasts of *Malabar* and *Coromandel* in the *East-Indies*.

CHAP. I.

The Division and Limits of the Indies. *The Author's purpose in the ensuing Treatise. A Description of* Cambaja *and* Suratte. *The Treaty with the* Great Mogul, *by Mr.* Van Teylingen.

THE main Design of the ensuing Treatise being to give an exact Account of the *Indies*, as far as is come to our knowledg, either by our own Experience, or the constant Conversation with People of unquestionable Credit, *viz.* the Coasts of *Malabar* and *Coromandel*, together with the Isle of *Ceylon*, and places thereunto belonging; we thought it not beyond our scope to insert the true Limits and Division of the whole *Indies*, whereby the Reader (together with the annexed Map) may form to himself the more clear *Idea* of the Situation of these Places.

The Limits of the Indies. *India* therefore borders to the West upon the River *Indus*, towards the *Arabian Sea*; to the North it is inclosed by the Mount *Taurus*, on the East-side by the vast *Eastern Ocean*, and to the South by the *Indian Sea*. *India* was antiently divided into two Parts by the River *Ganges*; thence the more Eastern Part was call'd *India* beyond the *Ganges*, and the Western Part *India*, on this side of the *Ganges*, now known by the Name of *Indostan*; and according to the opinion of some Authors, is the same mention'd in the Scripture by the Name of *Havila*.

India is besides this divided into several Kingdoms and Provinces, to wit, The Empire of the *Great Mogul*, *Decan*, *Malabar*, *Coromandel*, *Crika*, *Bengale*, *Pagu*, *Siam* and *Cambodia*, besides the *Maldive Isles* (of which there is a vast number) the Islands of *Ceylon* (of which in the second Book) of *Sumatra*, *Borneo*, *Celebes*, *Amboina*, *Banda*, and the *Molucque Isles*, viz. *Termate*, *Machian*, *Bachian*, *Tidor*, *Motir*, *Potbacker*, and divers others.

As it is not my Intention to treat of the whole *Indies*, but to confine my self to those parts I have for the most part seen my self, and to give you a relation of such remarkable Transactions both of Peace and War as have happen'd there; so I will begin with the Kingdom of *Cambaja*, and its Capital City having the same Name, and end with *Bimilipatam* upon the Coast of *Orixa*, bordering upon *Bengale*. *The Author's Intentions.*

Cambaja is a different Province from *Gusuratte*, situate at 22 deg. of Northern Latitude; it has got its Name from its Capital City nam'd *Cambaja*, (formerly the *Indian Cayrus*) seated at the mouth of the River *Indus* (or *Sandus*) known by different Names among divers Nations: it rises among the Mountains of *Paramisus*, and being augmented by at least nineteen other Rivers (among which are the *Hydaspes* and *Hypasis*, whither *Alexander* the Great carried his Arms) it falls by seven different Channels, or as some will have it by five, into the Sea; two of which pass through and exonerate themselves into the Sea in this Kingdom of *Cambaja*. It borders to the East upon the Country of *Mandoa*, to the West upon the Country of the *Nautakers* or *Gedrosiers*, to the North it has the Kingdoms of *Sanga* and *Dulcinga*, and to the South that of *Decan*. It is one of the most fruitful Provinces of the *Indies*, which furnishes the circumjacent places with Corn, Wheat, Rice, Pease, Butter, Oil, and divers other Provisions. The Inhabitants are generally either *Gusurattiens* or *Benjans*, being much addicted to Traffick, and very quick in their dealings. They make here the best Calico's of all sorts; and the Country abounds in Indigo, Granates, Hyacinths, Ame-

The Province of Cambaja. *The River* Indus *was formerly also call'd* Sandus *and* Pangab, *from its five Branches.* *The Limits and Fertility of* Cambaja.

Baldæus.

Amethists, and divers others precious Commodities. According to *Cluver's* Computation *Cambaja* is 150 *German* Leagues long, and as many broad.

Its Extent.

A Description of the City of Cambaja, *formerly a rich City, but somewhat decay'd since by the ill Conduct of the* Moors.

The City of *Cambaja* (call'd the *Benjan Paradise*) lies according to the common Computation 16 Leagues to the West of *Brochia*, seated at the Entrance of one of the largest Channels of the River *Indus*. About three Leagues thence on the opposite Shore is a great Village, inhabited by the Rebellious *Raspoutes*, a perverse Generation, living for the most part upon Rapine. This River is almost dry all the Winter, tho at high Tide it rises several Fathoms deep, so that then Ships may come up to the very Walls of the City, where at low Tide it is fordable. This City is reckoned as big again as *Suratte*, being well built, and fortify'd with a triple Wall. It has three *Bazars*, or great Market-places, for the sale of all sorts of Merchandises, and twelve Gates, besides that almost every Street has a peculiar Gate, which is shut up every night to prevent Disorders: Its whole Circuit is about six or seven English Miles; and without the Gates are four very delicious large Cisterns or Ponds, and fifteen Gardens, for the Diversion of such of the Inhabitants as are pleased to divert themselves there with walking in the cool of the Evening. They are for the most part Pagans, and addicted to Traffick, especially in all sorts of Stuffs for clothing, which they transport to *Diu*, *Goa*, *Atchin*, *Mecha* and *Persia*.

A Description of Amadabath.

Amadabath the Capital City of the Province of *Gusuratte*, lies 18 Leagues from *Cambaja*, about 23 $\frac{1}{2}$ deg. Northern Latit. and consequently directly under the Tropick of *Cancer*: It is seated in a great and most delightful Plain, just on the Bank of a very fine River; it is both strong and populous, being fortified with a goodly Wall with round Turrets and twelve Gates.

The Streets are very broad, the Houses very handsom, and the Pagan Temples stately built. In the Center of the City is the Castle, the Residence of the Governor, surrounded with a very high Wall, the Gates whereof are guarded by a certain Body of Troops, who let nobody pass or repass without leave: This being formerly the ordinary Seat of their Kings. The Commodities found at *Amadabath* are Girdles, Turbants, Gold Tissues, Silk Stuffs, Satins, Damasks, Tapestrys, Suchar, *Amspien* or *Opium*, *Gummi Lacca*, *Borax*, preserv'd Ginger, Mirabolans, Sal-Armoniack and Indigo. Under the Jurisdiction of *Amadabath* are 25 considerable Towns, and 2998 Villages.

The City of Suratte.

The City of *Suratte* is a place of great Traffick, both the *English* and *Dutch* having Factories here: It lies open to the Water-side, except that the Castle is well provided with Cannon brought from the Ship *Middleburgh*, which was lost there 1617. But on the Land-side it is fortified by a Wall of Stone, the old Fortifications being only of Earth: It has no more than three Gates, but two Governors independent on one another, one of the Castle, the other of the City. Next adjacent to the Palace of the last stands the Custom-house, where all Goods imported or exported pay 3 $\frac{1}{2}$ *per Cent.* Custom, except Gold and Silver, which pay only 2 *per Cent.*

Differences about the Customs.

These Custom-house Officers are very troublesome and injurious to Strangers, and have often given great cause of Complaint to our Company, as will appear from the following Petition, and the *Mogul's* Patent (or *Firman*) granted to the said Company, and dated the 15*th* day of the Month *Ramnasay*, in the 16*th* year of the King's Reign, and since that of *Mahomet* 1052.

The Dutch petition the Great Mogul.

"The *Dutch* are approach'd to the "Gates of your Majesty's Court, expecting at the feet of your Majesty's "Throne (whose Brightness is like that "of the Sun, and reaches to the Skies) "the happiness of seeing the Eyes of the "greatest Monarch, to offer their just "Complaints against the Officers of your "Majesty at *Suratte*, who have been extremely troublesome to them, in exacting from them illegal Duties of their "Goods bought at *Agra* and *Amadabath*, "and thence brought to *Suratte*: They "humbly request your Majesty to send "your Orders by your *Duwan* or *Commissioner* to the Custom-house Officers "at *Suratte*, with strict Command to regulate themselves accordingly, as they "expect to be accountable for it to your "Majesty.

The King did immediately dispatch his Orders, that the Custom-house Officers should not take from the Commodities bought at *Agra* and belonging to the *Dutch*, from 10 to 12 *per Cent.* and those bought at *Amadabath* 10 or 10 $\frac{1}{2}$ *per Cent.* that they should be oblig'd to rest satisfied with the Bills of Loading given them by the *Dutch* Merchants, and exact no more Custom under any other pretence: That furthermore all Commodities bought at *Brodera* and *Suratte* should pay according to

The City of
AMADABATH

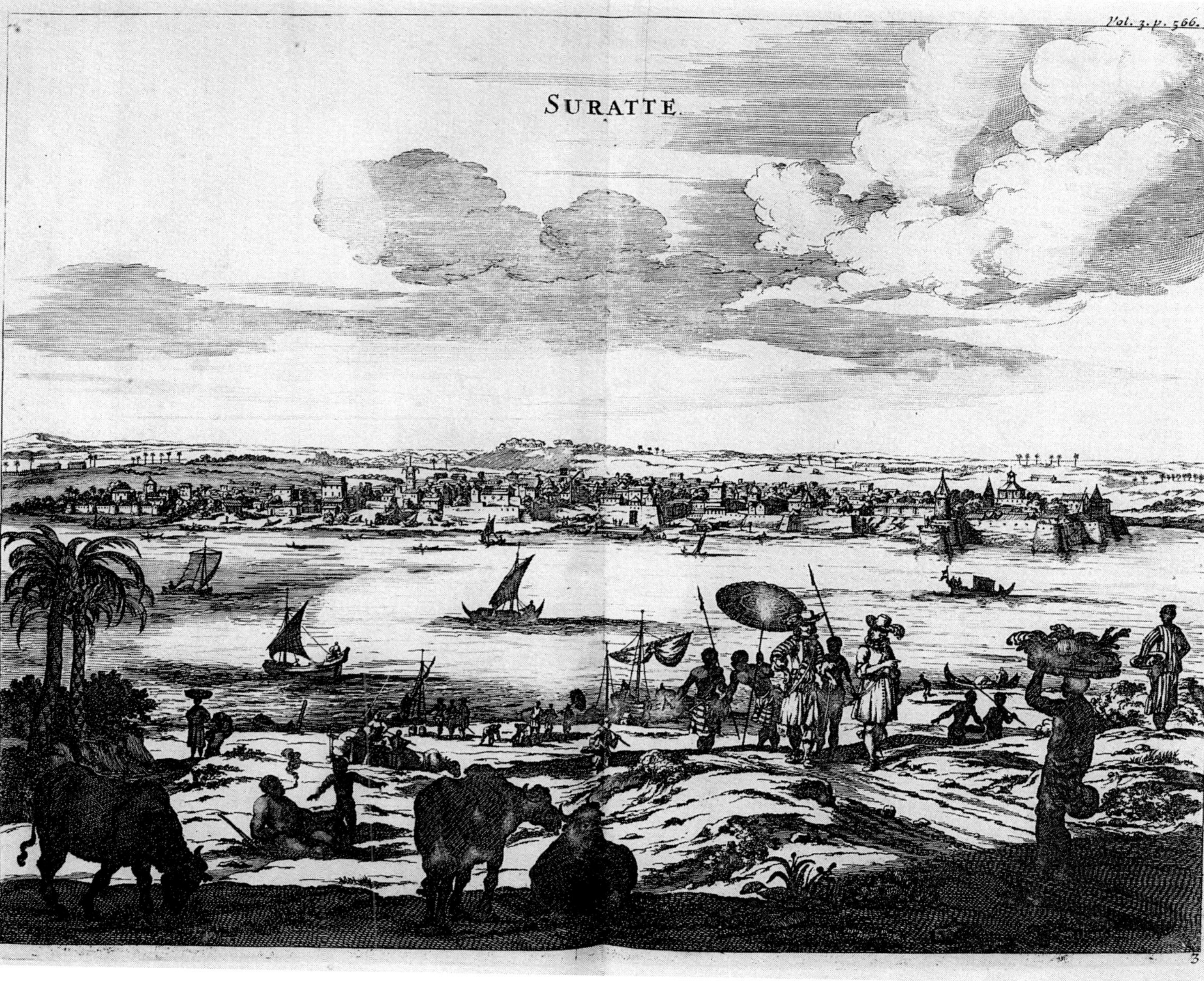
SURATTE

to the Price they were bought for, and that they should avoid giving any just reason of complaint to the *Dutch*. But these Promises had not the desired Effect, as will appear out of the next following Letter of Mr. *John van Teylingen* President and Governor of the *Dutch* Factories in *Gusuratte*, *Indostan*, and *Mocha*.

Mr. Van Teylingen's Letter.

'Whereas by the manifold Exactions 'and Injuries, the robbing of the 'Factory of our Company, the Detenti'on of *Daniel Massouw* Barber's Mate, 'and divers other enormous Proceedings; 'the Persons in the Service of the Com'pany, in the Empire of the Great *Mo'gul*, have received considerable Detri'ment from divers of the Great *Mogul*'s 'Officers (contrary to the intent of his '*Firman*, or Letters Patents) which must 'needs tend to the great damage of the 'Company in general: It has, after ma'ture deliberation, been thought expe'dient, by Mr. *Cornel. van der Lijn* Gover'nor-General, and the rest of the Mem'bers of the Council of the *Indies*, to 'redress the said Affronts and Injuries 'by Force of Arms. The Yachts, the '*Larck*, the *Sluice*, the *Lillo*, and the '*Eight-Churches*, being equipped lately 'for that purpose, and to be join'd by 'divers other Ships from *Batavia*, we 'give the Command thereof, during my 'absence from the Fleet, to the Head 'Factor *Gerard Pelgrim*, which how'ever shall cease that Minute, when I 'come aboard any one of these Ships in 'Person. To prevent all Disorders, Ra'pine, and other Enormities, I do by 'these Presents give a strict Charge to 'all the Officers, of what degree soever, 'and to all the Soldiers and Seamen a'board these Vessels, not to hurt the '*Moors* either in their Lives or Estates '(this being contrary to the Intention of 'the Council) but only to seize upon 'their Ships, Mony, and Goods, and to 'secure them, till Satisfaction be obtain'd 'by the Company upon their just Preten'sions. We therefore once more com'mand all the Officers, Soldiers and Sea'men, without exception, not to injure 'or rob (after the seizing of any of these 'Ships) the *Moors* in their Persons or 'Goods, under the penalty of corporal 'punishment, and (according to the na'ture of the Crime) of the loss of their 'Lives, as they will answer the same to 'the contrary at their peril.

Given at the *Dutch* Factory at *Suratte*, Feb. 10. 1649.

John van Teylingen.

Baldæus.

The following Order was likewise directed to the Head Factor *Gerard Pelgrim*, and the Factor *Peter Ruttens*.

Secret Orders to Mr. G. Pelgrim, and P. Ruttens.

"It being firmly resolv'd in Council, "the 25th of *Octob.* to prosecute with "the utmost vigour the Design laid "formerly by the Governour General "and the Council of the *Indies* (which "was delay'd by our long stay) with the "first opportunity; the Yachts the *Sluice*, "*Larck*, *Lillo*, and *Eight-Churches*, are cho"sen for that purpose: But two of them "being now at *Mocha*, and the other two "ordered to stay there the Winter at "*Dabul*, we constitute the Head Factor "Mr. *Gerard Pelgrim* Commodore over "the said Ships, as soon as they are re"join'd aboard the *Larck*, or any other "of these Ships he shall be pleased to "chuse, where he shall carry the Flag, "with Authority to call on board the "Council of War, when Occasion re"quires. In his absence, or separation "of the Ships, the Factor, *Petter Ruttens*, shall exercise the same Autho"rity as *Gerard Pelgrim*, both which "however shall cease, with the arrival "of the President Mr. *John van Tey"lingen*. Whether the two beforemen"tioned Yachts shall leave *Mocha* toge"ther or not, is not yet determined; "but in the mean while we strictly "charge you, that so soon as you have "notice that the *Chasirovan* (a Ship of "a vast bulk) or any of the other Ships "belonging to *Suratte*, are preparing to "depart, you set sail some days before "them, under pretence of being bound "(according as we used to do) for *Gam"ron*. All which is to be understood, "provided Matters be not brought to a "happy conclusion before that time; for "if that were, you have nothing to do "but to prosecute your Voyage in good "earnest thither, unless you had a sure "prospect of gaining considerably by "your stay, and increasing the price of "your Cargo. For the rest, it is to be "your main concern, to take effectual care "that none of the Great *Mogul*'s Ships, "nay even such as trade thither from "*Diu*, escape your hands; and especially "to keep a watchful Eye over the *Chasi"rovan*, which commonly sails sooner "than the rest, and has more ready Mo"ny aboard. In case it should happen "(which we hope it will not) that the "Yacht the *Eight Churches*, which is to "return from *Gamron*, should, by some "Accident or other, be detain'd in her "Voyage,

Baldæus.

"Voyage, we have provided against it, "by dispatching to the Commanders "thereof a Copy of these Orders for "their direction upon occasion; which "after the return from their Voyage "they are to deliver sealed up into your "custody, where the same is to remain "till you set sail again, which is to be "redelivered to them to serve for a sure "direction, in case you should be separated at Sea. Silence ought to be your "most peculiar care in this case, for fear "the Secret coming to the Ears of the "*Moors*, they should stop the departure "of their Ships. The *Larck* and the "*Lillo*, and in default of those the *Post*, "after their first appearance here, shall "be sent to *Gamron*, whence they shall "sail pretty late, as if bound for *Batavia*, but, under pretence of being unable to prosecute their Voyage, come to "an anchor in the Road before *Dabul*, "from whence they shall sail *Aug.* 15. "steering their Course directly for the River of *Suratte*; where they are to stay "till the arrival of the President Mr. *John* "*van Teylingen* aboard them; and in the "mean while seize upon all the *Moors* "Vessels coming from *Mocha*; yet so, "as not to commit any further Outrages "against them, except only to keep them "in safe custody till the Company shall "have received Satisfaction from the "King *Chastiaan*. So soon as they have "retaken a Vessel, they shall take the "*Nachodas* Merchants and Seamen over "in their Ships, and keep them under a "good Guard, yet without any molestation, rather shewing them all the "marks of Respect and Civility that "can be; and shall put as many Soldiers and Seamen of ours aboard such a "Ship as shall be thought sufficient to "keep her: and Proclamation is to be "made, enjoining every body to abstain "from doing the least injury to the seized "*Moors*, either in their Persons or Goods; "and Officers are to be appointed to see "the same put in execution. After we "have got all, or most of the *Moorish* "Vessels into our hands, you shall take "care to embark all the *Facquiers* and "other loose People in one Ship, and to "let them sail their ways where they "please, they being not worth our keeping. This done, you shall take the "first opportunity of fair Weather to "transport, first the ready Mony, and "afterwards the Merchandizes aboard "our Vessels; but so, as that they be "well pack'd and seal'd up first, and exact Inventory made, with the Names "or Marks of the respective Owners: "Each Parcel is to be mark'd with a peculiar Letter; a Copy of which is to be "given to the Owners, and a written "Acknowledgment to be taken from the "*Nachodas* of what is thus taken, and to "be redelivered, in case Matters be adjusted hereafter, that so every one may "know where to look for his own; the "Factor being to be careful in this Point "in the Transportation, as well as the "Master of the Ship in receiving, as "they will answer for the loss at their "peril. The *English* Yacht coming from "*Mocha* you are to let pass unmolested, "for weighty Reasons, pursuant to the "Resolution taken in Council the 14*th*. "The same is to be done in respect of all "*French*, *Danish*, and all other Ships in "amity with the States, provided they "don't attempt any thing upon the "*Moors* in your custody; in which case "you shall defend your selves to the last "Extremity. Lastly, If the Matter "could be so contriv'd, that our Vessels "coming from *Mocha* might intercept "and seize the Ships of *Cambaja*, and "carry them to the River of *Suratte*, it would be a singular piece of Service, and much hasten the Accommodation. I conclude, wishing you "Health and Happiness in your Voyage "and Undertaking, for your own Glory, "and the Interest of the Company.

Signed,

From the *Dutch* Factory at *Suratte*, Febr. 20. 1649.

Arent Barentsz.
John van Teylingen.
Joost Dirik.
Adrian van der Burgh.
Daniel van der Hagen.
Gerardo Pelgrim, and
Elias Boudaan.

CHAP.

Baldæus.

CHAP. II.

The Treaty carried on. What Articles were propoſed by the Dutch, *and agreed to by the King. His Patent or* Firman; *and Ratification of the Treaty.*

FOR fear of exaſperating the Great *Mogul* beyond redreſs, it was thought fit to diſpatch the following Letter to his Majeſty.

"Moſt Renown'd, moſt Potent, and "moſt Illuſtrious King, and Lord, fill'd "with Majeſty and Wealth, the brighteſt Princes among the moſt Powerful: "As an unjuſt War is deſervedly deteſted by all Nations, and ſeldom comes to "a happy Concluſion; ſo our being oblig'd to act againſt your Majeſty (purſuant to the Command of our General, "and the Council of the *Indies*) is founded upon very juſt and legal Pretenſions. Had your Officers thought fit to "treat us according to the Tenour of "your Majeſty's Patent, or *Firman*, granted to us, we ſhould never have attempted to raiſe any Differences betwixt your Majeſty and us, much leſs "have had recourſe to open Hoſtilites. "But when we were forced to ſee our "Traffick, not only in this Place, but "alſo at *Bengale*, interrupted and ſpoil'd "by moſt injurious Monopolies (to the "great Detriment of the Company) "by intolerable Affronts, and refuſing "our juſt Requeſt, and humble Petitions, to have the two Fugitives, and "ſince circumciſed Servants of the Company, delivered into our hands; and "to have due reparation made for the "Damage ſuſtained by the Company in "the Robbery committed upon their "Factory: All theſe injurious Proceedings have obliged our Governor-General, and the Council of the *Indies*, to have Recourſe to the Law of "Arms, to procure us reaſonable Satiſfaction; and having for this purpoſe "ſent us four Ships from *Batavia*, we "did the 12*th* and 16*th* of this Month, "ſeize your Majeſty's Ships the *Genjawer* and *Sababbi* (coming from *Mocha*) and after having taken out of "them all the ready Mony they had aboard, and underſtanding that the "ſaid *Genjawer* and *Sababbi* belonged "properly to your Majeſty, we thought "fit (out of reſpect to your Perſon) to "have them carried by our Seamen into "the River, and under the Caſtle of *Suratte*, not queſtioning but what we have "been forced to undertake upon this account for the maintaining of our Juſt "Rights, will meet with a favourable "conſtruction from your Majeſty. The "Mony ſeized by our Veſſels, ſhall not "ſuffer the leaſt diminution, but be kept "with all ſecurity, till ſuch time that "your Majeſty ſhall grant us a new Patent in due Form, purſuant to ſuch "Articles as we have Orders from our "Superiors to repreſent to your Majeſty, and are as follows.

'I. It is deſired that leave be given to 'build a Warehouſe for our own Uſe, 'either in or near the Square of the Caſtle, where we may lay up ſafely our 'Merchandizes at the firſt hand, free 'from thoſe Diminutions and Loſſes we 'ſuſtained yearly in the *Alphandigo*, paying exactly the uſual Cuſtoms; that 'done, we ſhall be at liberty to carry on 'our Traffick, as formerly, undiſturbed 'and unmoleſted. *Articles propoſed by the* Dutch *to the Great* Mogul.

The Governour's Anſwer was, 'That 'either a Place or Houſe ſhould be granted us juſt without the Caſtle, not far 'from the *Alphandigo*, for our proper uſe 'only. *The Anſwer.*

'II. We deſire that our Traffick may 'be carried on without diſturbance at '*Bengale*, and in the circumjacent Places, 'free from paying any Dutys, except 'what is paid uſually at *Pipeli* (the 'place where Goods are embark'd, purſuant to the Patent formerly granted by 'his Majeſty, but contravened by the 'avaritious Governours.

Hereunto it was anſwered, 'That the 'Governour *Miermoſa* ſhould endeavour 'to obtain this Point from the King.

'III. Reſtitution was required of ſuch 'Sums of Mony as of late Years had been 'unjuſtly detained, both at *Suratte* and '*Amadabath*, and full Satisfaction deſired for what Cuſtoms had been extorted from our Ships betwixt *Agra* and '*Amadabath*, contrary to the expreſs 'Words of his Majeſty's Patent; the 'whole Sum amounting to 41479 *Ropias*.

'IV. His Majeſty was requeſted to 'iſſue his Orders for the full reſtitution 'of what Mony was taken out of our 'Factory at *Suratte*, and that a certain 'Sum (as his Majeſty ſhould direct) 'might be allotted in lieu of Satisfaction 'for

Baldæus. 'for the Robbery committed upon the 'said Factory, the murdering of the 'Company's Servants, and the Injuries 'and Affronts put upon us: The Sum of 'the Mony taken away from thence a-'mounting to 66000 *Ropias*.

Unto these two Points the answer was made; 'That the restitution of what 'was taken from us, was a reasonable 'Request, but to give satisfaction, for 'that other Enormities were committed 'by Robbers (since fled from Justice) 'was not in their power; but if any of 'these Criminals could be taken, they 'should be delivered into our hands.

'V. That for the future none of his 'Majesty's Ships, or any others belong-'ing to those of *Suratte*, *Bengale*, or o-'ther places, should traffick to *Achin*, '*Pera*, *Queda*, *Oedjang-Salang*, *Malac-'ca*, &c. and in case they should, they 'might be seized and declared as good 'Prizes by our Vessels, by reason that the 'Company being then ingaged in a War 'against these places, were resolved to 'block up their Rivers, and to keep 'all Foreigners from trafficking with 'them by Sea, till they have received 'entire Satisfaction at their hands.

'VI. It was desired that his Majesty 'Majesty would deliver to us the (be-'forementioned) two circumcised Ser-'vants of the Company; and if they 'were at present out of reach, to depo-'sit into our hands in lieu of them '400000 *Ropias*; which Sum shall be re-'stored immediately after the delivery 'of these two Persons.

The Answer was; 'That one of these 'circumcised Fellows was retreated ma-'ny Years before into *Persia*, and the 'last died in his flight about eight 'Months before: But if they would have 'his Bones, they would endeavour to pro-'cure them.

'VII. That if ever any of the Companys 'Servants shall run away hereafter, they 'shall not be protected, much less be cir-'cumcised; and in case any of the infe-'rior Officers should notwithstanding 'this detain any of them (contrary to 'your Majesty's knowledg) they shall be 'obliged to deliver the same to us.

'This Article was granted, provided 'they did not take refuge among the '*Raspoutes* then in rebellion against the '*Mogul*.

'VIII. That Satisfaction should be gi-'ven for what Expences the Company 'had been forced to be at both by Sea 'and Land, since the Robbery committed 'upon their Factory.

'This Article was rejected, a general 'Satisfaction being promised already.

'IX. That for the future a sufficient 'Guard should be kept to protect the 'Servants and Goods of the Company 'from the like danger; and that in case 'any such thing should ever happen a-'gain, the Governor shall be obliged 'to make satisfaction.

'It was promised that for the future a 'Guard should be kept to secure the Com-'pany against all danger.

'X. If our *Caffila*, or Caravan (which 'God forbid) should be plundered by 'the way, that the Governour shall be 'obliged to find out the Goods; and if 'found, restore them to us, and in case 'of neglect, to make satisfaction for 'them.

It was answered; 'That we must sue 'for a *Firman*, or Patent, on that ac-'count, which would without question 'be granted.

'XI. That in all the Citys, Towns and 'Teritories under his Majesty's Jurisdic-'tion, we shall be exempted from paying 'any Dutys, Customs, or Impositions, 'except the Customs at *Suratte* and *Bro-'chia*; and in case any Mony should be 'exacted from the Servants upon that 'account, the Mony shall be made good 'by his Majesty's *Duwan*, or Commissio-'ner, at *Suratte*.

'XII. That the Custom payable from 'such Goods as are to be exported, shall 'continue on the same foot as settled 'by the King's last *Firman*, or Patent.

'This Article was granted without the 'least limitation.

'XIII. That the Customs of the Mer-'chandizes imported, shall (as former-'ly) be satisfy'd with Merchandizes 'each in its kind.

'This was also granted.

'XIV. That we shall be at liberty to 'dispose and sell our Cargo's and Goods 'where and when we please, without be-'ing controuled therein by the Governor, 'or any other Merchant.

'This was likewise agreed to.

'XV. That no Governor, of what 'quality or degree soever, shall obstruct 'us in the buying up what Commodities 'we have occasion for, or employing of 'Brokers and other Servants for that 'purpose, such as we judg may be most 'serviceable to us; neither shall they be 'taxed or otherwise molested on that 'score.

It was answered; 'That doubtless his 'Majesty would grant that Article, and 'that in the mean time no body should

'in-

'intermeddle with the Traffick belonging to the Company.

'XVI. That no body of what degree or quality whatever ſhall pretend to obſtruct us in the ſending away of our Goods, or ſtop our *Caffilas* (Caravans) or Carts, and Camels thereunto belonging, much leſs to endeavour to detain the ſame after they have been hired.

'Unto this it was anſwer'd, that the King would doubtleſs grant this Requeſt.

'XVII. In caſe of any Conteſts ariſing betwixt both the Nations, whereby Murder or Manſlaughter may enſue (which God forbid) the Governors ſhall have power only to puniſh the Criminal, if he be one of his Subjects; but if he belong to the Company, he is to be put into the hands of our Directory, in order to be puniſh'd according to the Laws of our Country; and if any of our People engage with any of the *Indian* Women, the ſame ſhall be deliver'd up to us to ſuffer condign Puniſhment.

'Unto this it was anſwer'd, that this Article muſt be referr'd to the King's Determination; but that further Satiſfaction ſhould be given upon this Head to the *Dutch* Company at *Suratte*.

'XVIII. If by Tempeſts or other Accident ſome of our Ships ſhould be ſtranded, or otherwiſe be loſt on theſe Coaſts, the Goods ſav'd by your Majeſty's Subjects ſhall be reſtor'd to the Owners.

This was granted.

'XIX. That we ſhall be maintain'd and protected in the quiet enjoyment of the propagating and refining of the Salt-peter; and that we ſhall meet with no oppoſition from the Governors in tranſporting the ſame, or be burdened with new Exactions, as it happen'd two years before, when the Prince of *Zaatſchan* ſqueez'd 600 Ropias out of the Company.

This Article was refer'd to the King.

'XX. That ſuch as ſhall be injurious in words to any of our Nation, ſhall be puniſh'd by the Governor, in the preſence of the affronted Party, to prevent further Inconveniences, which otherwiſe might ariſe from thence.

This Article being very juſt, was agreed to.

'XXI. That we ſhall have full liberty to keep and maintain the Yatch we always have had upon the River of *Suratte*, and (in caſe this becomes uſeleſs) to build another, and uſe it as formerly, for our Diverſion, or other occaſions.

'We don't in the leaſt doubt, but that your Majeſty, according to your wonted Bounty, will take into ſerious Conſideration this our humble, but nevertheleſs juſt and equitable Requeſt; it being our conſtant wiſh, that matters may be brought to a ſpeedy Accommodation; and we promiſe that immediately on the receipt of your Majeſty's *Firman*, or Letters Patent, we will diſcharge what Mony and Perſons are in our Cuſtody, and carry on our Traffick in your Majeſty's Dominions, as before: But in caſe your Majeſty (which we hope not) ſhould refuſe our Petition, we deſire notice may be given us thereof, that we may in time (with your Majeſty's Conſent) remove our Effects, and quit your Territories; it being our firm Reſolution not to ſtay here, unleſs your Majeſty will be pleaſed to grant our juſt Requeſt; notwithſtanding which we live in hopes of a favourable Anſwer from your Majeſty's Goodneſs. *Baldæus.*

Unto this was affix'd another Paper, as follows.

Moſt Potent King!

'JUST upon the Concluſion of our humble Petition, the Deputies impower'd by *Miermoſa* the Governor, to treat with us concerning the Differences on foot betwixt us, *viz. Mierſia Mamoeth, Hagie Siasbeecq, Zabandaar*, and ſeveral other Perſons of Note, have promiſed us to give ſatiſfaction for the Mony (purſuant to your Majeſty's Orders) taken from us, to ſtop all Traffick from *Bengale*, and this place, *&c.* to *Aetchin, Pera, Queda*, and *Oetjang-Salang*, &c. till the Differences betwixt us and thoſe Places be brought to a Concluſion; concerning which we expect further Orders from our Governor-General of the *Indies*. It was further promiſed us, that a Place ſhould be aſſign'd us for the building of a Warehouſe near the *Alphandigo*; which as well as the other Articles being confirm'd to us by Oath of the before-mention'd Deputys, we were on our ſide willing to releaſe the Goods ſeiz'd by our Ships, which we have done accordingly, and reſettled our Traffick at *Suratte*, as before: All which we hope will not be unacceptable to your Majeſty; humbly begging your Majeſty to be pleaſed to take our further Propoſals into Conſideration, and to favour us with your Royal *Firman*, to avoid all further Differences, 'and

Baldæus. 'and to establishish a mutual, firm and 'everlasting Correspondence betwixt us, 'which we shall very religiously observe '(as long as your Majesty's Governors 'don't act contrary to the said *Firman*) 'without the least interruption on our 'side. We wish your Majesty a prosperous 'and long Life, and Victory over your 'Enemies.

Dated in your Majesty's City of *Suratte*, 28 *Sept.* in the year 1649 after the Birth of Christ.

The King's Letter was thus.

The King *Chaasjan* sends the following Directions to *Miersia Arep* his Governor of *Suratte.*

King's Letter, or Firman. 'JUst as the *Sajetes* are esteem'd among 'the Saints, so is *Miersia Arep* re'spected in his Family. I would have 'you rest secure of my Royal Favour: 'Besides what Dignities you were pos'sess'd of before, we have thought fit 'to bestow upon you the Reward of '*Paans Zeddi*, and 300 Horses for your 'Services, in the Government of the 'open Country; and since the departure 'of *Miermosa* have put you into his 'place; and for the better maintaining 'of your Grandeur, have allotted you the 'Royal Revenues of both your Govern'ments, in the Administration of which 'you shall be very vigilant and courteous; 'towards the chief Merchants you shall 'comport your self very obligingly, and 'give a helping hand to all the foreign 'Nations trafficking there, as tending to 'the no small increase of our Treasury. 'Your Authority shall not extend to ex'act more than the usual Customs, even 'of the meanest Persons, but you shall act 'in every thing as a Man of Honour and 'Conscience: What Rarities you hap'pen to meet with coming from foreign 'places, you shall (like your Predecessor '*Miermosa*) send to my Daughter *Sa'bebbejen*, who twice a month pays her 'Respect before my Throne; whatever 'is extraordinary fine and rare, let it be 'valued, and purchase it of the Owner 'accordingly; but if you can't agree, 'send him hither, that he may be satis'fied in his just Demands. So soon as 'my Royal *Firman* comes to your hands, 'you shall endeavour to list 10 Christian 'Constables, well versed in their Art, into 'our Service, and you shall spare no Cost 'to have some great Cannon cast for our 'use. We have been inform'd, that a'bout two years ago the *Dutch* Factory 'was robb'd of 50000 *Ropias*, for which 'they have seiz'd divers Sums of Mony 'belonging to our Merchants, and 'coming in their Ships from *Mocha*, and 'have thereupon declar'd their Senti'ments to the Governour *Miermosa*; it 'is therefore that I command you to ob'lige the *Hollanders* to restore the said 'Mony to the Owners, who have nei'ther the least share or knowledg in what 'relates to their loss: And in case you 'should not be able to bring things to 'an agreement with the *Hollanders*, we 'command you to demand the said Sums 'of Mony of *Miermosa* and *Ommerchan*, 'and pay the same to the said Merchants '(whose Effects are seiz'd) in recom'pence of their Loss. *He makes it less than it is.*

These are the Contents of the King's Letter, as it was translated from the *Persian*.

CHAP. III.

The *Chom* of *Suhali*, or the Road before *Suratte.* Traffick of the *Dutch*, *English*, *Moors* and *Portugueses* to *Suratte*, *Gusuratte*, *Brochia*, *Goga*, *Pattepatane*, *Mangerol*, *Brodera*, and other places.

Description of Suratte. THE City *Suratte* did (pursuant to their antient Records) pay a yearly Tribute of 2000000 *Mamoidys*, or 1000000 Livres, or 400000 Crowns, to their King *Achabaar*, one *Ganna Ganna* being then their Governour, who had 1800 Villages under his Jurisdiction. All about *Suratte* are abundance of very pleasant and stately Summer-Seats, and magnificent Burying-places (a thing much in request among the *Moors*) besides several large Cisterns, or rather Ponds, fac'd with Freestone. Among the rest one deserves particularly to be taken notice of, as having no less than a hundred Angles of 28 yards each, with Stone Steps to lead you down into the Cistern; in the midst of which stands the Tomb of the Founder.

About an hour and a half to the North from the Mouth of the River of *Suratte* (named *Tap-gyly*) is a Road, where Ships may ride at anchor near a ridg of Sand-banks, which, together with part of the Continent, breaks the force of the Winds. This Road, commonly call'd *Chom Subali*, or *Sualicom*, lies at 21 deg. 50 min. North Latitude, extending from North-East to North, and again South-West to South: The entrance of it is but narrow, and at high Water not above 7, but at low Water scarce 5 Fathoms deep, with a hard sandy bottom: The North-North-East, and South-South-West Winds make here the highest Tides. The Harbour of *Subali* is not above a Musket-shot broad: The South-South-West Winds make this Road unsafe, the Land-Shelves lying then almost dry. The *English* settled their Factory there 1609. and the *Dutch* 1616. who carry their Merchandizes upon Waggons drawn by Oxen from the said Road 4 Leagues to the City.

The Chom of Subali.

Traffick of Suratte.

It is to the Settlements of those two Nations, *Suratte* owes its chief increase in Trade, many rich Merchants and Artisans having been drawn thither since that time, who send their Commodoties thence by the *Red-Sea* to *Arabia*, *Aden*, *Mocha*, *Hideda*, *Juda*, *Mecca*, *Chihiry*, *Catziny*, *Doffer*, and *Souakin* (in *Ethiopia*) consisting in fine and coarse *Indian*, *Gusuratte*, *Decan*, and *Bengale* Stuffs and Cloths, Callicoes, Indigo, Sugar, Gums, Ginger, Tobacco, Wheat, Rice, Butter, and other Provisions, in which this Country abounds. Besides that, two or three of the King's Ships trade into these Parts, and transport certain precious Commodities belonging to some peculiar Merchants and Persons of the first Rank; these are generally obliged to the Company, for furnishing them with some able Seamen and Constables (the *Moors* being but ill versed in these things) especially while they were at enmity with the *Danes*.

One of the Kings Ships, named *Saby*, arrived here 1618. in its return from the *Red-Sea*; the Cargo whereof consisted in Coral, Camlets, Sattins, Velvets, Woollen and Linen Cloths, Tin, Quick-silver, Cinaber, Leather, Saffron, Slaves, (both Black and White) Gum Arabic, Aloes of *Socotora*, Amber, Civet, *Sanguis Draconis*, Myrrh, Raisins, Almonds, Dates, Coffee-Berries, and about six or seven hundred Passengers returning from *Mahomet*'s Tomb at *Mecha* and *Medina*; the whole valued at 2500000 *Ropias*, each *Ropia* being about half a Rix-Dollar.

The Value of a Ropia.

Baldæus.

These Ships set sail in *March* and *April* for the *Red-Sea*, and return in *September* or *October*; they seldom spend above 25 days in their passage. The Inhabitants of *Goa*, *Dabul*, *Bassain*, *Daman* and *Diu*, do also send their Ships to *Mocha* and some other places in the *Red-Sea*; and the *Benjans* and *Armenians* used to come thence to *Suratte* in their light Ships loaden with all sorts of Trifles, which they exchange for Wheat, Linen, Rice, and Coffee-Berries.

Traffick of the Red Sea.

Towards the latter end of the *Mousson*, *viz.* in *March* and *April*, abundance of *Malabars* resort hither: these being mortal Enemies of the *Portugueses*, are commonly well arm'd with Fire-locks and Scimeters, and formerly used to be very mischievous to them. The Commodities they bring to sale here, are coarse Sugar, Cardamon, Pepper, and *Cayr* (of which they make Cables and Ropes) and Coco-Nuts.

The Malabars Enemies of the Portugueses.

Formerly the Inhabitants of *Suratte* used to send yearly one or two Ships in *May* or *June* (when the *Portuguese* Ships were in harbour) to *Achin*, *Tanasseri*, *Queda*, and the *Maldive* Islands, laden with Stuffs, and Cloths, and Callicoes; and return'd with Pepper, Camphire, Cloves, Nutmegs, Mace, Sandel-wood, Porcelain, *Chinese* Silks (brought thither by those of *Malacca*) Tin, Benzorn, Elephants Teeth, and Coconuts, the last being almost the only product of the *Maldive* Isles.

The Men in Power here are generally very haughty and fierce; and tho sufficiently curb'd by the King's absolute Sway, yet by reason of the distance of the Provinces from his Residente, commit many Enormities; his Territories bordering upon *Persia*, *Auwa*, the River *Ganges*, and *Bengale*, thence to *Decan*, and to the West by the Sea.

Extent of Gusuratte.

The Province of *Gusuratte* (in which all the beforementioned Citys lie) extends in length from South to North; it begins at *Damana*, and reaches 40 *Cos* beyond *Amadabath*, bordering upon the Country of *Pathane* inhabited by Pagans, so that its whole length is 180 *Cos*, or 90 *Dutch* Leagues: to the East it borders upon the Country of *Parta Basia*, or at least within 40 *Cos* or 20 Leagues of it, extending further Eastward for three days journey towards *Amadabath*, and to the West to the Sea, and the Kingdom of *Suadi*, which is divided from *Persia* by a great Desart. It was a most fruitful and populous Country, before it was reduced by the *Great Mogul*.

One Indian Cos two Dutch Leagues.

About

Baldæus. *The City of* Brochia. About 12 Leagues to the North of *Suratte* lies the City of *Brochia* about 9 or 10 Leagues from the Sea, and 21 deg. 56 min. upon the River *Nardabath*, which coming down by *Decan* and *Mandouw*, affords a good Passage for Ships, about half way from the Sea towards *Brochia*, the passage being stopt up there by a Sand-bank, which has not above 9 or 10 foot Water. The situation of this City is both very convenient and pleasant, upon a Hill, being surrounded by a strong stone Wall: This place is famous for its Manufactories of Linen and Cloths, of which they make more here than in any other place of the *Indies*; and they have the best way of whitening the first. The *Malabars* used formerly to come hither every Year with 9 or 10 Ships. The *Dutch* and *English* have had their Factories here a considerable time ago. Its Inhabitants are for the most part *Benjans*, who are very expert in managing the Linen Manufactury: The two Suburbs of the City are chiefly inhabited by Callico-weavers and Merchants; *Brochia* is reckoned to contain 87 Villages in its Territories, the Country round about being all low Grounds, except that about five or six Leagues to the South-East the Mountains of *Vindat* have their beginning, which are very rich in *Achatstens*. All Merchandizes passing through *Brochia* pay 2 *per Cent*. Custom.

Goga 30 *Leagues from* Cam- *Goga* is a small City seated in the Bay of *Cambaja*, where it grows so streight, that it rather resembles a River than an Arm of the Sea: It has neither Walls nor Gates to the Land-side, but is defended by a stone Wall towards the Sea. Here all the Ships designed for *Arabia*, and the Southern parts (by the Merchants of *Cambaja* and *Amadabath*) are careen'd and victuall'd, there being a safe Road here, tho somewhat shallow: Here also the *Portuguese* Convoys used to keep their station, to expect the coming of their Merchantmen.

Pattapatane *and* Mangerol, Brodera. There are besides these several other Places of less note belonging to this Province, as *Pattapatane*, *Mangerol* (mentioned by some under other Names) the Inhabitants whereof live upon Husbandry, and managing of Cotton; *Brodera* an inland Town, inhabited by Husbandmen and Clothiers; the Company used to keep some Factors there, to buy up coarse Cloth for the *Arabians* and *Ethiopians*. Not to mention here its Fortifications, Gardens, Tombs, *&c.*

Mamadabath. *Mamadabath* was for its pleasant situation sometimes honoured with the Residence of its Kings, but is since come to decay to that degree, that it is no more than a poor Village now. We will also make mention only of *Nariau*, *Wasset* (a very antient Castle) *Issempour*, *Batona*, and their Products, such as Indigo, Saltpeter, *Borax*, *Asa Fœtida*, *Amfion* or Opium, *Gummi Lacen*, and divers other Commodities.

But before we leave the Province of *Gusuratte*, and take our way thence over *Diu*, *Daman*, &c. to *Goa*, and so to the *Malabars*; we must say something of its Traffick. It is beyond all dispute that the Traffick of *Suratte*, and adjacent Places, is of great consequence, provided there be no want of ready Mony, and the management thereof be committed to Persons of understanding. I remember that the College of XVII give these following By-rules to their Factors: To inform themselves of the Constitution and Manners of the Inhabitants, what Commodities are vented, and best to be vented there; who, and how potent our Enemies are; what Religion and Coin is most regarded, and the true situation of the Place where they settle, in respect to its Northern or Southern Latitude. Certain it is, that the Inhabitants of the Province of *Gusuratte* are a cunning and settled Generation, who must therefore be managed with dexterity, and much reservedness, mix'd with a becoming gravity and outward splendor, wherewith these People are much taken, yet without ever attempting to lord it over them, a thing which after has proved detrimental, if not destructive to the Undertakers. It is to the wise Conduct of our Forefathers that we are obliged for the Establishment and Improvement of our Traffick at *Suratte*; where our Factory was no sooner settled, but we sent from thence 1624. *Jan.* 20. our first Ship call'd the *Heusden*, along the Coast of *Melinde* and *Soffala*, and thence to the *Cape of Good Hope*, and so to *Holland*. *Traffick of* Gusuratte.

This was follow'd the same Year, 12 *March*, by another call'd the *Peuca*, but was forced to winter on the Coast of *Coromandel*. These were follow'd 1625. *April* 23. by the Ship the *City of Dort*, and the *Wesop* Yacht, but were obliged to winter in the Isle of St. *Maurice*. In the Year 1626. the following Ships were sent to *Holland*, taking their way through the South Sea, *viz.* The *Golden Lion*, *Walcheren*, and *Orange*. 1628. The *City of Dort* was sent thence to *Holland* through the Straits of *Madagascar*, along the Coast of *Fussalia*.

Our

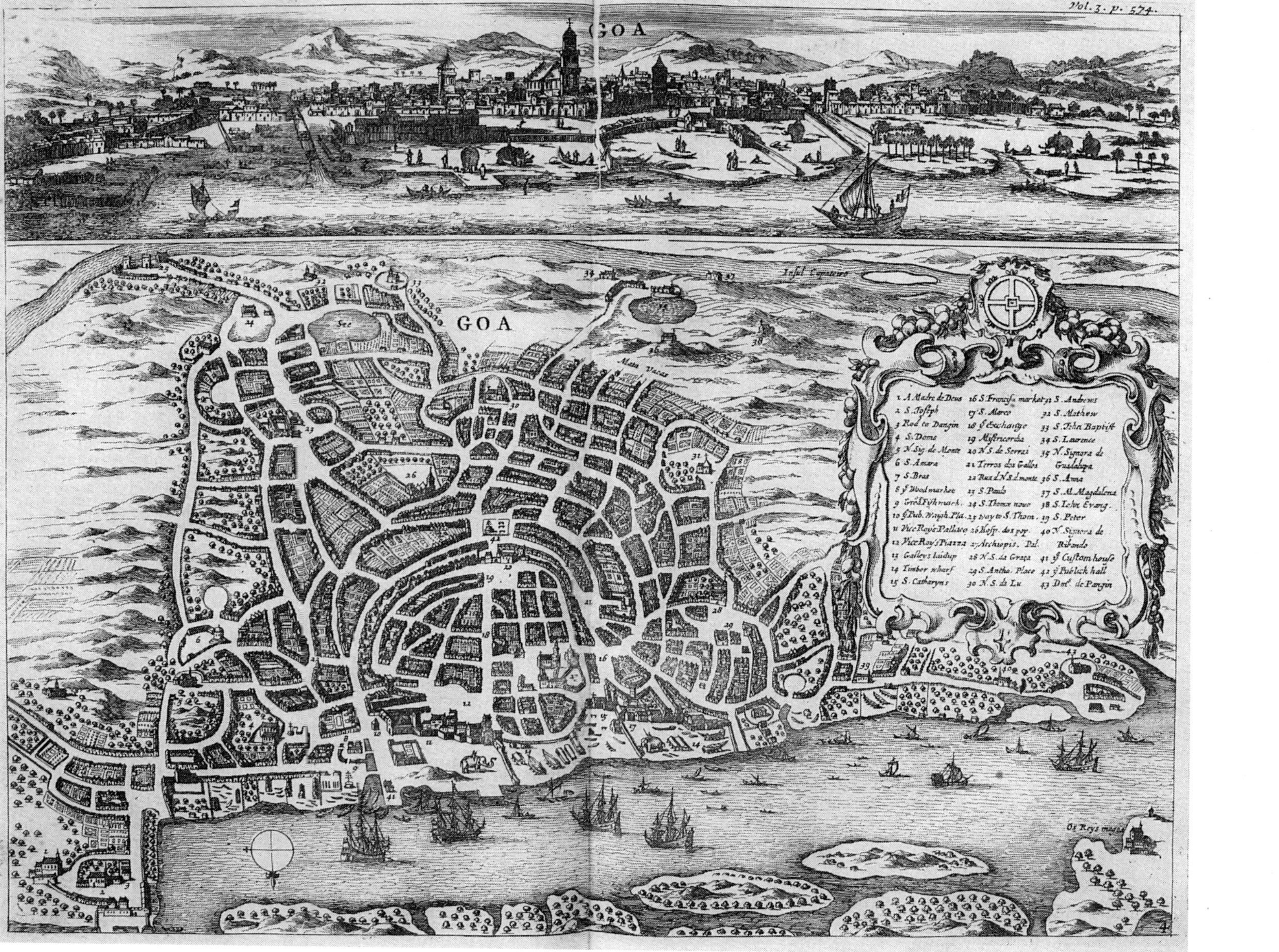
GOA
GOA
Mato Vacas
Os Reys magos
1. A Madre de Deus
2. S. Joseph
3 Rod to Dangin
4 S. Doms
5 N. Sig. de Monte
6 S. Amara
7 S. Bras
8 ye Woodmarket
9 Great Fyshmark.
10 ye Pub. Waygh. Pla.
11 Vice Roys Pallace
12 Vice Roy's Piazza
13 Galleys landing
14 Timber wharf
15 S. Catharyns
16 S. Francisse market
17 S. Marco
18 ye Exchange
19 Misericordia
20 N. S. de Serrai
21 Terros dos Gallos
22 Rua d N. S. d monte
23 S. Pauls
24 S. Thomas nova
25 way to S. Thom.
26 Hosp. dos pop.
27 Archiepis. Pal.
28 N. S. da Graça
29 S. Antho. Place
30 N. S. da Lu
31 S. Andrews
32 S. Mathew
33 S. John Baptist
34 S. Laurence
35 N. Signora de Gualalupa
36 S. Ama
37 S. M. Magdalena
38 S. John Evang.
39 S. Peter
40 N. Signora de Ribando
41 ye Custom house
42 ye Publick hall
43 Dre. de Pangin

Our *Dutch* Vessels generally arrive here from *Batavia* about the end of *August*, in *October*, or beginning of *November*, and sometimes towards the middle of *December*: The *Dutch* Factors at *Suratte* taking always care to send their Ships into *Persia* in *January*, or about the middle of *February* at farthest, that they may be at *Batavia* before the end of *March*. *Baldæus.*

CHAP. IV.

Of what consequence the Traffick of Suratte *is. A particular Description of the City of* Mocha, *and of its peculiar Customs. The City of* Agra, *and its Strength. The Descent of the Great* Mogul, *his Pomp and Riches.*

OF what Consequence the Traffick of *Suratte* is to the *Dutch*, they have been sufficiently made sensible by their Factors ever since 1616. The chief Commodities to be vented here, are, Lead, Quick-silver, Cinabar, Ivory, Tin, Copper, Cumeta's, Cloves, Nutmegs, Mace, Pepper, Porcelain, &c. And this Traffick is the more considerable in respect of the Communication it maintains with our other Factories in those parts, with *Agra*, *Mocha*, and divers other places upon the Coast of the happy *Arabia*, where our Traffick seems to be well establish'd, provided we take care to live in good Correspondence with those Nations, which must be maintain'd by all possible means, by avoiding such things as tend to the Dissolution thereof. Amongst these the seizing of the *Moorish* Ships has several times brought our Traffick into no small Jeopardy, as it happen'd 1621. when our Ships the *Samson* and *Wesos* having made Reprisals upon some *Moorish* Vessels, our Trade into *Arabia* was quite interrupted, and likely to have been quite lost. And we run the same danger 1628. after the Yacht the *Grottenbroeck* had taken a Ship of *Gusuratte* upon the Coast of *Coromandel*; and tho our late Seizure happen'd not to prove much to our disadvantage, yet can't we at all times promise our selves the same success, it being certain, that tho the *Moors* court our Friendship, yet are they on the other hand very stubborn, and not easily reconcil'd. *Some Remarks upon the Traffick in those parts.*

Another thing absolutely requisite for the carrying on of the Trade here, is, the King's *Firman*, or Patent, to keep the avaritious Governours of *Cambaja*, *Suratte*, *Brochia*, and other places, in awe; besides, that the *Portuguese* Priests are always busy to create an ill Opinion of us in the *Moors*: They must be carefully watch'd in their Measures and Weights, without which they will play you the same Game as *Godjanisan* and *Godjaassan* did many years ago to Sir *Henry Middleton*, an *English* Knight, who put them in Irons aboard his Ship till they had given him full satisfaction.

Our Traffick to *Mocha* is likewise of great Consequence to us: *Mocha* is seated in the *Happy Arabia*, at the entrance of the *Red Sea* at 13 deg. 28 min. Northern Latitude: It is of a considerable extent, without any Walls, in a barren ground, but well built with red and blue Stones, the Houses flat on the top like those of *Constantinople*; it has three very fine Pagodes, or *Pagan* Temples, two whereof have no Steeples, the third, in the midst of the City, being adorn'd with a very high Steeple. At the North end stands a small Castle like a Redoubt built, of blue Stone, for the Defence of the Harbour, 1612. *A Description of Mocha.*

Mocha was about 90 or 100 years ago no more than a Village inhabited by Fishermen; but since its Reduction by the *Turks*, is so encreased by degrees, that it is one of the chief Places on that Coast now; the Traffick of the *Indian* Ships that used to come to an Anchor at *Aden* (formerly a great Trading City) being transferr'd to *Mocha*, by reason of the Caravans which come thither with more conveniency at certain times of the year. Its Inhabitants are *Turks*, *Arabians*, *Benjans* and *Jews*: Here is constantly a great concourse of People from the beginning of *March* to the middle of *September*; about which time the great Ship call'd *Mansouri* (which is kept by the *Turkish Sultan* for the Transportation of the richest Commodities from the farthermost parts of the *Red Sea* hither) arrives here, its Cargo being generally esteem'd at 2500000 or 3000000 Reals, and consisting in Pieces of Eight, Golden Ducats, Italian Golden Tissues, Camlets, Saffron, Quick-silver, and divers other Commodities, besides Slaves of *Its Encrease.* *The Trade of Mocha.*

Baldæus. of both Sexes taken in the *Levant*, or thereabouts, being generally *Grecians*, *Hungarians*, or of the Isle of *Cyprus*; of all which they pay 10 *per Cent.* Custom. The same Ship sails back again the first of *January*, laden with Spices, Indigo, fine Callico's, Turbants, and such like *Indian* Commodities.

Besides this, there comes every year in *March* a *Caffila* or *Caravan*, consisting commonly of 1600 Camels, the Merchants being for the most part *Turks*, *Arabians* and *Armenians*; these come by the way of *Aleppo* and *Alexandria* hither, and spend commonly two Months in their whole Journy, because they travel not above three or four *Dutch* Leagues in a day. They bring along with them twisted Silk, Gold Wire, red Coral, Cinabar, Saffron, Myrrhe, divers sorts of small Wares, Needles, Spectacles, Knives, Scissars, Looking-glasses, &c. This *Caravan* leaves the place again in *December*, loaden with all sorts of *Indian* Commodities, and thus spends near a twelve month in their whole Journy.

Caravans over Aleppo *and* Alexandria.

At *Cayro* you see a vast multitude of Pilgrims towards the beginning of the year, who take the conveniency of this *Caravan* to travel to *Mocha*, eight Leagues from whence lies *Medina*, where is the Tomb of *Mahomet*, which is thus yearly visited by betwixt 30000 and 40000 Pilgrims.

Pilgrims going to Mocha.

Mocha has been so rich for many years past, that in Customs and Taxes it pays no less than 200000 Reals, or Pieces of Eight every year to the *Grand Signior*, being one of the largest and most considerable places under the Jurisdiction of the Bassa of *Yemak*. The Governour of the City sits sometimes in Person at the Custom-house visiting the Packs and Chests, he having a certain allowance out of every Chest or Pack. All *Indian* Ships coming to an Anchor here are oblig'd to pay, besides the ordinary Customs, Anchorage-mony, according to their Bulk, from 10 to 50 Reals, which with some other Exactions makes the whole amount to 15 *per Cent.* The *Turks* here have also another Invention of squeezing some Mony out of the *Moorish Nacbodes*, or Officers of the Ships; for the Governor having summon'd them immediately after their arrival to appear in his Presence, they are conducted thither in great State, attended by his Drums, Pipes, &c. and being reconducted to their Lodgings, the Clothes are taken away again. The same is repeated afterwards just before their departure, when they are reconducted to their Boats; and their Clothes being taken off again, each Officer is oblig'd to pay for this mock Dress 20 or 25 Reals each time.

Riches of Mocha.

Anchorage-mony.

No sooner are the *Moorish* Ships come into the Roads after they have dropt their Anchor, but they must carry their Rudder and Sails ashore, and unload the whole Cargo of the Ship (whether they sell it or not) of which they are oblig'd to pay the full Customs. After they are quite unloaden, they give a Signal with a Cannon for the Governor or his Deputies to come aboard, to see whether any thing be left behind; and then they have liberty to sell.

Rudder and Sails to be brought ashore.

In the Spring the *Portugueses* come hither with their Ships from *Goa*, *Goga*, and other places; their Cargo is commonly Indigo, Sarcaa, Callico's, Sail-cloth, all sorts of *Gusuratte* Stuffs and Clothing, Tobacco, Rice, and Medicines; most of which Commodities are sold to the *Turky* Caravans, except the Rice and Tobacco, which is consum'd in the Country. They carry back Reals or Pieces of Eight, Golden Ducats, a certain Root used by the *Indians* in dying red. A little before, or about the same time, used also to come to *Mocha* the Ships of *Daman*, *Cambaja* and the *Malabar* Coast, loaden with Pepper, Clothings of *Cambaja* and *Coromandel*, *Allegias*, *Taffacelas*, red and white *Cassen*, red *Jetas*, *Canekyns*, *Baftas*, fine Turbants, white and blue Girdles, painted Callico's, Rice, Tobacco, coarse and fine Porcelain, in lieu of which they carry back Horses, Raisins, Almonds, Camlets, Elephants Teeth of *Soffala*, red Roots for dying, which grow only in *Arabia*, *Chauru* or Coffee-berries. Besides these, the Inhabitants of *Achin*, of *Paty*, and other places on the Coast of *Melinda*, trade hither; they commonly set sail from home in *February*, or beginning of *March*, and return from *Mocha* about *August*, to take the conveniency of the *Mousson*.

Traffick of the Portugueses *at* Mocha.

The want of good Water and Fuel, which the Ships much purchase here at a dear rate, is a great defect in *Mocha*: However, not far from the City lies a small Isle, where the *English* used to lay up and careen their Ships; here you may have Provisions for old Clothes in abundance, as likewise Fuel and Water enough; whence it is evident that the Trade of *Suratte*, *Agra*, *Mocha* and *Libiry* (a City seated on the Red Sea at 14 deg. 50 min. fortified with four round Bastions, and adorn'd with three Temples) is one of the most considerable in those parts;

Water and Fuel scarce at Mocha.

parts; as the *English* have found by Experience.

The City and Castle of Agra.

But before we take quite our leave of *Suratte*, and the adjacent Territories, we must say something also concerning the City and Castle of *Agra*. This Castle, the ordinary Residence of the *Great Mogul*, is one of the most noble Structures of the East, seated upon the Banks of the River *Jemeni*, fortified with a strong Wall of red Stone, with large and deep Ditches, Draw-bridges, and four Gates. Here is also kept the King's Treasury, and the whole Court, or General Assembly of the Great Men of the Empire, who oftentimes are not refrain'd by the Absolute Authority of their Monarch, from committing most barbarous Enormities.

Murders committed in the presence of the King.

Thus it happen'd *August* 4. 1644. in the Evening after Sun-set, when all the Persons of Quality used to appear in the *Gosalchanna* to salute the King; among the rest, *Raja Ammersing* (a Commander over 5000 Horse, who had been absent some days by reason of his Indisposition) making his appearance there, was ask'd by *Sillabatchan* the King's chief *Bakia*, why he had not appear'd there in several days? He answer'd him, That he had been prevented by his Indisposition; wherewith the other being not satisfied, gave *Raja* some opprobious words, which so exasperated him, that without more ado he run *Sillabatchan* with his Scymeter thro the Body, laying him dead upon the gound. Another Lord named *Galichan*, seeing the other murder'd in the King's sight, cut almost off the Arm of *Raja*, and another Gentleman, the Son of *Raja Kittelda*, dispatch'd him quite. The King seeing this Tragical Spectacle, gave immediately Orders that the Body of *Sillabatchan* should be carried to his House in order to his Burial; but that the Body of *Raja Ammersing* should be thrown into the River: but scarce were they got with the Body without the Gate to execute the King's Command, when some of the *Rasboutes* (a rebellious Crew) who had serv'd under him, seeing their Commander's Body drag'd thus along, did fall upon the King's Servants, and kill'd above thirty of them, among whom was the King's Scepter-bearer; so that if the King would see his Orders put in Execution, he was oblig'd to send a conside-

Baldæus.

Baldæus.

rable Force to protect them against the *Rasboutes*.

Agra has four Gates, one on the North-side, cover'd by strong Works; the second on the West-side, where is the Market-place, and the Royal Court of Judicature; the third on the South-side leads to the Royal Palace, being always chain'd up to prevent any body from passing through it on Horse-back, except the King and his Children: The fourth faces the River, where the King every day salutes the Sun, and about Noon sees the Engagements of Elephants, Lions, and other wild Beasts.

The City of *Agra* therefore is now the Capital City (as *Labor* was formerly) of that part of the *Indies* on this side of the *Ganges*, which is under the Jurisdiction of the *Great Mogul*. The Castle is said to have been founded by King *Accabar* (descended from the Great *Tamerlan*) after the Conquest of *Gusuratte*.

Wealth and Strength of the Mogul.

I will not pretend to give you an exact account of the Wealth of the *Mogul*, but leave you to guess at his Strength by the Forces he brought into the Field 1630. against *Chasjaan*, which consisted in 144500 Horse, and 5000 Elephants; these last the *Mogul* also uses for his Diversions, and he is often seen in great State on the back of an Elephant richly accoutred, attended by a great number of Horse. When these Elephants are to engage against one another before the King, they pay their Reverence by bending their Knees, and shaking their Trunks to the King; which done, they fall on with a great deal of fierceness; but as soon as they are hotly engag'd, certain Persons are appointed to part them; which done, all Enmity ceases betwixt them, they touch one another with their Trunks, and are fed with Sugar Reeds, and *Arack*, or Strong-waters.

Combat of the Elephants.

As to the Wealth of the *Great Mogul*, the same appears in its Lustre on certain Festival days: The New-year's Feast kept on the day of the first New-Moon in *March*, which lasts eighteen days. On the young Prince's Birth-day every body brings his Offerings to the King, who in his turn makes Presents to his Courtiers, bestows new Places and Dignities upon such as have deserv'd well, and augments their yearly Salaries. The People flock on that day to the Queen's Palace (if she be living) where having likewise made their Offerings under the sound of their Musical Instruments, the Prince is weighed in a Golden pair of Scales against Gold and Silver, which (after the weight thereof is set down) is distributed the next day among the Poor.

Festival-days.

The Prince's Birth-day.

The King's Birth-day.

The present King's Birth-day is celebrated the second of *September*, when the King is weighed in the same manner, against Precious Stones, Gold, Silver, Gold Tissues, Silk Stuffs, Butter, Rice, Fruits, &c. which is afterwards bestow'd upon the *Brahmans*; and Nuts made so curiously of Gold Wire (as likewise Almonds, and other Fruits) are thrown among the People, that 1000 of them weigh not above 20 Ropias, and cost about 60 Ropias. The whole Ceremony is concluded with drinking to a great excess all the night long, notwithstanding *Mahomet*'s Law. Sir *Thomas Row* relates, that he had a Golden Cup beset with *Turquoises*, *Rubies* and *Smaragdes*, presented him by the Great *Mogul* on his Birth-day, but not till he had emptied it four or five times.

Another Feast.

The *Moors* also celebrate a certain Feast to the Memory of two Brothers, Servants to *Mahomet Raly*, who being on their way to *Coromandel* on Pilgrimage, were forced by the *Pagans* of the Country to seek for shelter in a certain Castle; but being distitute of Water, they sallied out courageously upon the Pagans, and after having killed many of them, were at last slain themselves. Their Memory is celebrated in *June* ten days after the New-Moon, when they carry a Bear along the Streets loaden with Turbants, Arrows, Bows and Scymeters, certain Priests singing doleful Tunes, and slashing themselves with Knives, till the Blood follows very plentifully. In the Market-place they set up the Figures of two Men of Straw, representing the Murderers of these two Saints, at which they let fly their Arrows, and at last burn them to Ashes. They keep also another Feast in *June*, when they kill abundance of He-Goats, and afterwards feast upon the Meat: This is said to be done in Commemoration of the Sacrifice of *Abraham*.

The *Great Mogul* being absolute Lord over 37 large Provinces and Kingdoms, the Persons and Estates of all which are at his sole disposal, besides the immense Presents of his Subjects (none of whom dare approach his Person without them) must needs be Master of immense Treasures. The King of *Visiapour* sent at one time 30 Elephants, two whereof were girded by Golden Chains, weighing 400 Pound weight, two others with Silver Chains, the rest of Brass, besides 500 Horses, the Saddles and

Bridles whereof were beset all over with Diamonds, Pearls and Rubies. Mr. *John Twist* has given the World an exact account of the Treasury of King *Accabaar*.

Baldæus.

CHAP. V.

The Title of the Great Mogul, *and of the Kings of* Achem *and* Siam. *The Origin of* Mahomet; *some of his pretended Miracles*, Alcoran, *&c.*

IT is most surprizing to understand what God-like Titles the Subjects of the *Great Mogul* bestow upon their Lord and Master! How all his Words are look'd upon as Oracles, and all his Actions receiv'd with a profound Amazement! Hence it is that the vulgar sort are really of opinion, that certain Rays dart from his Head and Turbant, which admit not of the near approach of indifferent Persons; and that they scarce ever mention his Name without the additional Titles of *the Most Potent upon Earth, Lord of the World, Great Monarch, The most exalted Majesty, The brightest of Princes among the Great Ones*, &c. 'Tis true, most of the *Indian* Kings affect most magnificent, or rather vainglorious Titles; but the Kings of *Achem* and *Siam* seem to outvie all the rest in this point: The first stiles himself 'King of the World, 'created by God, whose Body shines 'like the Sun at Noon-day: A King 'unto whom God has given the Lustre 'of Full-Moon; a King chosen by God, 'a King perfect as the North-star, King 'of Kings, of the Posterity of *Alexander* the Great; a King before whom all 'other Kings must bow their Heads, and 'pay Homage; a King as wise as a round 'Globe, and happy like the Sea; a King 'who is God's Slave and Servant; who 'sees God, and lets the World know 'the Justice of God; a Protector of 'God's Justice, a King blessed by God, 'a King who covers the Iniquities of 'Men, and forgives their Offences; a 'King, under whose Shade Slaves seek 'for shelter; a King perfect and infallible in his Councils; a King and Benefactor to his People; a just King, who 'maintains God's Justice; the most beneficial King upon Earth, the Soles of 'whose Feet emit a most odoriferous 'Scent, beyond all other Kings; a King 'whom God has blessed with his Gold 'Mines, whose Eyes are as bright as the 'Morning Star: A King who is Master 'of many Elephants of all sorts: A King 'unto whom God has given Riches to adorn his Elephants with Gold and precious Stones; besides a great number of 'Elephants of War, armed with Iron 'Teeth and Copper Shoos: A King upon 'whom God has bestowed Horses with 'golden Harnesses beset with precious 'Stones, and many thousand Horses for 'War; the choicest Stone-horses of *Arabia, Turky, Catti*, and *Balacki*: A 'King whose Territories extend from 'the South to North: A King who bestows his Favours upon all that love 'him, and rejoices such as are disturbed 'in Mind: A King who has in his custody every thing that God has created; 'A King whom God has placed above all 'things, to rule, and to shew the Lustre 'of the Throne of *Achem*.

The King of Achem's Titles.

The King of *Siam* goes still beyond it, as may be seen by his Letter written 1636. to the late Prince of *Orange, Frederick Henry*.

The King of Siam's Title.

"THIS is a Golden Letter of Friendship and Confederacy, replenish'd "with the Brightness of God, the most "Excellent, comprehending all that is "to be known; the most fortunate above what is to be found by Men; the "best and the most secure in Heaven, "Earth, and in Hell; the most magnificent, delicious, and most agreeable "Words; the Glory and irresistible Virtue whereof pass all over the Earth, "with the same Vigor, as if thro God's "Power the Dead were revived from "their Graves, and purify'd from all "their Iniquities, to the surprise, not "only of the Priests, but also of Merchants, and all the servile sort of Mankind. For what King can compare "with Me, who am the most Potent, "most Illustrious and Invincible? The "Master of 100 Crowns, adorn'd with "nine sorts of precious Stones: Supreme "Lord (*we pass by some blasphemous Expressions*) of the vast and most noble "Kingdom of *Siam*; the Brightness of "the most beautiful City of *India*, the

Baldæus. " Capital City of the World, the Streets " whereof are crowded daily with People; a City adorned with all the Beauties of the World, and irrigated with " delicious Brooks; whose Lord has a Palace of Gold and precious Stones; a " Master of gilded Thrones, of the white, " red, and round-tail'd Elephants, which " three sorts God has not bestowed upon any other Kings; a Divine Lord, " in whose Territories is deposited the " Victorious Sword, and who resembles " the God of War with four Arms.

The Mogul's Court. But to return to the *Great Mogul* and his Court: The *Persian* Language is the Court Language there, tho besides this there are at least three other Languages used throughout his Territories. The chief Lords of his Courts have their certain monthly Salaries allotted them, out of which they are obliged to maintain a certain number of Horses; among these are four who maintain 12000 Horses each (the King's Sons entertain 15000 Horse) others 1000, others 100, in proportion to their Salaries; the whole number of Horse maintained by his Courtiers, being computed at 100000 Horse.

The *Mogul* changes his Clothes every day for new ones, which he bestows upon his Courtiers. The *Mogul* entertains certain Officers of Quality, call'd *Nababes*, at *Suratte* and other places, whose business is, to enter upon Treaties with Foreigners, and to keep the Roads free from Robbers, by punishing them with the utmost Severity. The *Mogul* has also a laudable custom, to lay up vast Sums of Mony and Provisions in certain places, to be reserved for necessitous Occasions. He appears three times a day, and sits in Council, from seven till nine in the Evening.

Religion. The *Moguls* profess the *Mahometan* Religion, but are no great Zealots in it, as *Athanasius Kircher* has well observed in *Gelal Edim Mahomet*, the tenth of the *Moguls* descended from the *Great Tamerlan* the first, who call'd the *Jesuits* into his Empire; and their continual Debaucheries in strong Liquor (directly contrary to the Law of *Mahomet*) is an infallible sign of their indifferency in point of Religion: Besides, that throughout all the Empire they are not near so well versed in the *Alcoran*, and the Law of *Mahomet*, as the *Africans*, those of *Fez* and *Morocco*, &c. Notwithstanding all their Ignorance, this accursed Doctrine has spread it self within fifty or sixty Years, from hence all over the Isles of *Java*, *Borneo*, and *Celebes*, besides divers other Countries in those parts.

The Mahometan Religion. The *Mahometans* are obliged to pray five times every day, *viz.* in the morning, at noon, in the afternoon, after Sun-set, and at midnight; certain People being appointed, who from the Steeples of the *Mosques*, exhort them to their Prayers, by crying *Lailla illa illa, Mahomed Resul Lalla:* when they are going to pray, they stand upright upon a Carpet spread upon the ground, holding both their Hands to their Ears; sometimes bowing towards the ground, sometimes standing upright again. The *Alcoran* is the Law Book of the *Mahometans*, containing 114 Chapters, being a mixture of the *Jewish* and *Christian* Doctrine. *Mahomet* flourished about the Year of Christ 600, and died 632. His Companion was one *Sergius* an *Arian*. The Father of *Mahomet* was one *Abdalla*, and his Mother *Emine*, descended of the Illustrious Family of the *Koreishites*.

Mahomets Origin. *Mahomet* first served in the Wars under the Emperor *Heraclius*, and afterwards served a Merchant; after whose death he married *Chadiga* a rich Widow; and being addicted to Enthusiasm, he and his Companion *Sergius* compiled the *Alcoran*, pretending that he kept correspondence with the Arch-Angel *Gabriel*, who in his Trances (which were nothing but Epileptic Fits) had revealed to him these Secrets. He was born at *Mecca*, but being forced from thence fled to *Medina*, from which time the *Mahometans* take their *Epocha*, and call it *Medina Alnabi*, or the City of the Great Prophet. His Doctrine was first received by his Wife *Chadiga*, and his Servant *Seydin*; afterwards by *Hali*, *Abubeker*, *Omar*, *Otman*, and others his Followers, who were called *Caliphs*. The *Persians* prefer *Hali* before *Mahomet*, and the *Turks*, *Omar*. *Abubeker* reign'd two Years, *Omar* ten Years; it is he who regulated the *Alcoran*, and instituted the Fast in the Month *Rammedan*. *Otman* reign'd 12 Years, and conquered *Mauritania* and *Cyprus*. *Hali* was by *Mahomet* appointed his Successor; but the other three having usurped the Kingdom, with the exclusion of *Hali*, this is the reason the *Persians*, who adhere to the last, abominate the three former.

The hatred between the *Persians* and *Turks* (tho both *Mahometans*) proceeds from the different Interpretations of the *Alcoran*, and certain Ceremonies relating to their Prayers, covering their Heads, &c.

CHAP.

Baldæus.

CHAP. VI.

The Feasts, Sabbath, and some other things belonging to the Mahometans; *their Priests, Holy Orders, Manners and Customs.*

NOT to insist here upon the fabulous Trifles of *Mahomet's* Visions, contained in some parts of the *Alcoran*, we will proceed to give you a short Account of the most material Parts of the *Mahometan* Religion.

Their Circumcision. They commonly circumcise Boys and Girls at thirteen Years of Age, *viz.* so soon as they are able to say their Confessions; *There is but one God, and* Mahomet *his Prophet.* If a *Jew* turns *Turk*, he is not circumcised again, but only washed with Water. Their Washing, or Bathing, is performed upon a threefold occasion.

Washing. 1. After they have eased Nature, or cohabited with their Wives.

2. When they are to go to the *Mosque*, or to read the *Alcoran*. And,

3. After they have committed some enormous Sins.

Their High Priest is call'd *Mufti*, in great esteem with the Grand Seignior, and a Member of his Privy Council. Next to him are the *Cadilesheri*, or Provincial High Priests of *Europe*, *Natolia*, &c. These are followed by the *Cady*, *Seriphes*, *Santones*, *Hoggy*, *Talismans*, and *Dervises*.

Sabbath. The Sabbath of the *Mahometans* is on Friday, which they keep with the same strictness as the *Jews* do theirs on Saturday, at least with more devotion, as the Christians their Sunday. They have in each City, besides the other *Mosques*, one great *Mosque*, where they then assemble to perform their Devotion. Their Lent begins in *February* with the New Moon, and continues thirty days, with a great deal of severity, for they neither eat nor drink all the day long; but some make themselves amends at Night, tho the Zealots will not taste the least of Wine, or any other strong Liquor all that time, nor converse with their Wives. They are permitted to marry as many Wives as they please, tho the *Alcoran* allows no more than four Wives.

Churches or Mosques. Their Churches are flat on the top, commonly built on a rising Ground, so as to be seen at a distance above the other Houses. They have within nothing but bare white Walls, without Pictures or Hangings; tho on some of their Tombs we see certain Passages ingrav'd out of the *Alcoran*. On the South-East of the *Mosque* stands the Pulpit made of Brick-work, about three steps from the Ground, from whence their Teachers say their publick Prayers, and explain the *Alcoran*. Their Great *Mosques* are generally adorn'd with two high Steeples, each having Stairs within from the bottom to the top. Their Mosques have scarce any Revenues belonging to them, except what the Priest makes by letting some few Chambers belonging to them: Many of them are built by charitable Persons, and some of these have a settled Income. It is further worth observation, that if a *Jew* will turn *Mahometan*, he must first own Christ, before they will receive him among the *Musselmen*.

Divers Orders. They have many Ecclesiastical Orders among them, three whereof have no Possessions, or any other Propriety; and some pretend to such a degree of Purity, that they profess themselves born without manly Seed. Some make certain Vows, like the *Roman Catholick* Monks; some appear quite naked, others only cover their Privities. Some have vow'd perpetual Silence; some carry Water without Reward; some prick themselves with sharp-pointed Needles or Instruments; others carry a Ring of three pound weight in their Privy Members.

Tenets of their Religion. For the rest, they believe God a Corporeal Being, who is carried in a Throne by the Angels, and Christ to be only a Man, and *Mahomet* the Comforter mentioned by *John* 14. 16. They believe a third place besides Heaven and Hell, and therefore pray for the Dead; as also a General Judgment, but implicated in many fabulous Absurdities; for they tell you that two black Angels, one call'd *Munger*, the other *Quaregner*, will appear, the first with an Iron Club, the other with a large Fork in his hand; that every Man besides is to have two Angels to assist him; but if after all he cannot give a good account of himself, the Angel with the Club knocks him down, and so he is carried to Hell. And because they are of opinion that those Angels appear to them in their Graves, these are generally built hollow; whence also they often make the following Ejaculation: *Good God, preserve us from the Interrogating Angel, from*

Baldæus. *from the Pain of the Grave, and from the Evil Way.* They add many fabulous things concerning the Angel *Adriel*, who at the approach of the day of Judgment, is to kill all living things, and to hang himself at last, till after forty Years the Angel *Seraphiel* shall waken the Souls; and such-like Fables too long to be inserted here.

Paradise. Concerning Beatitude, and the Paradise, they believe it consists in a continued enjoyment of Pleasures there. They divide it into seven different Apartments; one whereof is of Gold, the second of Silver, another of Pearls, precious Stones, and so forth. Here they are to pass their time in Pleasures, with certain most beautiful Women, created for that purpose by God, whilst their Wives shall look through a Grate, and be Spectators of the Enjoyments of their Husbands with these most beautiful Women, who shall not be subject to the monthly times, or Child-bearing, and the Men as vigorous as *Mahomet* himself, who gloried in his having outdone by double the number *Ovid* himself; *Et memini, numeros sustinuisse novem.* They say they shall drink in Paradise of the Spring of *Alcazar* mentioned by *Mahomet*; they shall be delighted with the scent of the most odoriferous Citrons, which shall produce most beautiful Virgins that shall imbrace the *Mussulmans*, and delight them with their Charms for fifty Years together: and more such like Notions tending to elevate the Thoughts with imaginary corporeal Pleasures to be injoy'd in the next World, by such as have observ'd the following Rules in their life-time, which they reckon absolutely requisite to attain to this Bliss.

Rules to attain Eternal Bliss. To believe one God, and *Mahomet* his Prophet, and a Day of Judgment; to pray at certain times; to wash, bow, and observe certain other Ceremonies in praying: To pay the Tenths, to fast in the Month *Rammedan*; to go on Pilgrimage to *Mecca*; to abstain from Extortions, Wine, and Hogs-flesh, because they believe the Hogs to have been progenerated out of the Elephants and Mens Dung in the Ark of *Noah*. They are also forbid not to use Tables nor Dice, not to swear by God, not to be rash in our Judgment, or deceive a Brother either in publick or private; not to part from a virtuous Wife; not to be too forward to object and discover the Faults of a Brother, or to despise him; not to set the Fear of God and his Punishment out of our Eyes, or to calumniate our Neighbour, and spread what is heard upon slight Reports. On the other hand, they are enjoined to be thankful for God's Mercy; to be patient in Adversities, and not to despair of God's Mercy; and to believe that whatever happens to us does not come by chance (for the *Mahometans* maintain strongly God's Providence) not to deny a Brother's Request out of Avaritiousness, not to raise God's Anger out of love to his Creatures, or to prefer a Temporal Interest before that which is to come: In all Ghostly Affairs to have a respect to him that is above us, and in Temporal Matters to those that are below us: Not to enter into any Association with the Devils; to refrain from Vanity, allow Orphans and Widows their own; to instruct their Children in such things as relate to the Divine Service; to do good to your Neighbour, not to curse any of God's Creatures, but to praise him in his Works; to read the *Alcoran* (except when you are unclean) to appear at the publick Congregations, and to do as you would be done by. It is further their opinion, that the Souls of the Brutes are likewise to be reviv'd and join'd with their Bodies.

In relation to their Manners and Customs, I will begin here with the Character given them by a Person of extraordinary Learning, *viz. That in their whole Behaviour they are declar'd Enemies to Vanity, as well in their Words and Deeds as in their Clothing, which makes them look upon many of us Christians like Monkys, who are apt to imitate every thing they see; whereas the* Turks *of both Sexes, young and old, rich or poor, are as regular and decent in their Habits, as if they belong'd to one certain Order; and are so careful in the Education of their Youth, that their School-Masters prescribe every day a certain part of the* Alcoran, *which they learn by heart, and so in two years time pass through the whole* Alcoran. *Their Manners and Customs.*

In their Marriages, and the tokens of Marriageableness and Virginity, they observe the following Rules: As soon as the monthly Times begin to appear, they carry the Maiden for seven days together, adorn'd with Flowers, and as it were in Triumph, to the next Brook, during which time she is to eat nothing but what comes from the Coco-tree. The *Portugueses* (who perhaps have got it from the *Moors*) publish the Mariageableness of their Daughters by the sound of Trumpets, and invite their next Relations to a Feast. When a Marriage is to *Tokens of Marriageableness.* *Their Marriages.*

to be concluded, they bargain very hard for the Dowry; but this being past, and the Agreement made betwixt the Parents, Guardians, or other nearest Relations, the Day for the Consummation thereof is appointed: then the Bridegroom on Horse-back adorn'd with sweet-scented Flowers, under two Umbrello's, passes with his next Friends through the chiefest Streets under the sound of Trumpets, Hautboys, Drums, and other such like Instruments, to the Bride's House, where having stay'd half an hour at the door, and entertain'd his Bride with the Musick and the throwing of some Squibs, and other small Fireworks, he is admitted into the House; and being seated upon a Chair railed somewhat from the ground, and cover'd with Tapestry, the Bride is brought to him by her Parents and Relations, in the presence of a Priest and the Judg of the Place (without whose Consent no Marriage is valid): The Priest having read certain Passages out of a Book, the Bridegroom swears, that in case of a Divorce from his Wife, he will be ready to restore her Dowry; which done, the Priest gives the Benedictions, and they are married, the whole being concluded at that time with a Present of *Betel* and *Arack* to the Guests, yet not to any excess, tho afterwards they keep the Wedding for three, four, six, seven or eight days together, according to every ones pleasure and ability.

Divorces. However Divorces are very frequent among the *Moors* (or *Indian Mahometans*) which is soon done, if the Husband pursuant to his Promise returns the Dowry, which consists commonly in nothing else but the Woman's Apparel. A Man is at liberty to kill his Wife in case of Adultery, but a Woman may not so much as sue a Divorce upon the same score. When a Woman is divorced from her Husband, she takes generally her Daughters along with her, leaving the Sons to the Husband's disposal. The next morning after the Bridegroom has lain with his Bride, and found her a Virgin, publick Proclamation is made thereof throughout the whole Town (for the honour of her Parents) when the Bride's Mother hastening to her Daughter's Bed-Chamber, and finding the usual tokens of Virginity in the Sheets or Clothes laid for that purpose, she carries them to the Bridegroom's Parents, who rejoice with her at the Conquest of their Son over the Maiden's Virginity. But if these Tokens are not apparent, matters are carried off with less Pomp and more Silence.

Baldæus. *The Mahometans Enemies to Incest, but addicted to Sodomy.* The *Mahometans* in general are Enemies to Incest, so that even the Grand Signior's Son after the death of his Father never touches his Concubines, but shuts them up in a certain Castle; on the other hand, they are extremely addicted not only to Lust, but also to Sodomy it self, and Combination with Brutes. There are Instances, that two Prostitutes in *Persia* have been condemned, one to be occupied by a Horse, the other by an Ass; the first died, but the second escap'd with Life.

Their Food. The *Moors* feed generally upon Rice instead of Bread, which is well tasted here, and grows in great plenty in *Bengale*, and divers other Provinces; the same is in much request throughout the *Indies*, in *China*, *Japan*, in the Isles of *Formosa*, *Java*, *Celebes*, *Borneo*, *Ceylon*, in *Malabar*, and other places, tho *Japan* and *Bengale* produce likewise very good Wheat. The poorer sort, who can't get above 4 or 5 *d.* a day to maintain themselves, are forc'd to be contented with *Kitzery* (a mixture of Beanflower and Rice) boil'd in Water. *Habitations.* Their Habitations are also very low and mean, made of Clay, and their Houshold-stuff sutable to their Houses; for besides a few Vessels of Brass, and the two Bedsteds where the Man and Wife lie (who never sleep together) there is nothing to be seen there, they having neither Benches nor Chairs, but only Mats to sit upon. In some places they use Cording instead of Wood for Fuel: But the Houses of People of fashion are spacious, and divided into many Apartments, flat on the top, whereupon they take the cool Air in the Evening. They are very splendid in their Entertainments, Wives and Houses, but especially in Gold and Silver Plate.

Their Clothing. Their Clothing is very grave, and they scarce ever change the fashion thereof; the Men wear Coats of Callico, or rich Tissues and Silks; they are strait above, close to the Body, fastened with a Girdle round the Waste, and reach down to the Knees: their Breeches are wide above, and narrow at the bottom, reaching down to the Legs, and trimm'd with Fringes; their Shoos are of gilt Leather, which they turn down at the heels, for the conveniency of throwing them off upon occasion. When they salute one another, they touch the Turbant with the Hand only, but never move them as we do our Hats. They are girt about their Loins with a Girdle of some fine Stuff, over which they wear another of fine Linen, and a broad Dagger on the left side.

The

Baldæus. The Ornament of the Women consists chiefly in Bracelets about their Arms and Feet, Ear-pendants, Nose-rings, and other Jewels; when they are going abroad, they cover their Heads with a Veil, with several hair Locks twisted together, hanging down their backs.

Their Burials. They observe certain peculiar Customs in their Burials; for no sooner is the Breath out of the Body, but their Wives, Children and Neighbours make a most lamentable Outcry, asking ever and anon the Deceased, what made him die, whether he wanted any thing in his life-time? This they continue for three days successively; then they invite his Friends to a Feast in memory of the Diceased, whose Corps being in the mean while well washed, and sow'd up in some white Stuff, with all sorts of odoriferous Drugs, is laid upon a Bier, and accompanied by three Priests (who sing and read all the way) carried by ten or twelve Persons to the Grave: here they lay him upon his right side, with the Feet to the South, the Head to the North, and the Face to the West. This done, they lay Boards over the whole Corps to keep the Earth from touching it; and whilst they are filling up the Grave, the Standers-by mutter out certain Prayers, and then return to the House of the Deceased, with the Priests, who for several days after pray for his Soul, shorter or longer, according as they are able to pay them. During this time no Fire must be seen in the House, what Victuals they use being dress'd without doors. Upon the Grave they lay two Stones, one at the Head, and another at the Feet, the Interstice being of the same length with the dead Corps underneath it: upon these the Priests read certain Chapters out of the *Alcoran*, and distribute some Bread among the Poor: Upon the same at the Head, they set sometimes a Turbant, and if a Female be buried there, a kind of a Bonnet. Thus much of the *Mahometan* Subjects of the *Great Mogul*; of the Idolatry of the *Gentives* we shall have occasion to treat at large in the third Book.

CHAP. VII.

A Description of Diu. *A Sea-Engagement of the* Portugueses *with* Jazy *and* Hocenus. *The singular Bravery of* Laurence d'Almeyda, *and* Nonnius Vasques Pereria. *The Harbour of* Diu *taken by the* Portugueses. *The Flight of* Jazy *and* Hocenus. *Moorish Colours sent to* Portugal.

At the uttermost Southern Point of *Gusuratte* lies the City of *Diu*, the Draught whereof you see here annexed, where the *Portugueses* have three strong Forts. It's commonly call'd *Diu*, tho its right Name is believ'd to be *Tivo*, i. e. an Isle, in the *Malabar* Language, as may be seen in the Names of *Naynativo*, *Anchativo*, *Maltivo*, or the *Maldive* Islands, which being in all sixty in number, extend from the Cape *Commoryn* from the 7 deg. of Northern Latitude, to the third deg. of Southern Latitude, a Tract of 140 or 150 *German* Leagues.

Origin of Diu. As to the Origin of *Diu*, they relate, that one *Jazy*, a Native of *Sarmatia*, did settle in this Island; but being taken Prisoner and made a Slave by the *Mahometans* in these parts, he chang'd the Christian Religion for that of the *Turks*, and being sold into *Cambaja*, was at last for his singular dexterity in managing the Bow and Arrow, prefer'd to the Service of K. *Madrafakaon* the Father of K. *Mamudius*. *Jazy*, to give a Proof of his Skill, shooting one day a certain Bird of Prey flying, he gain'd thereby so much Credit, that the King not long after gave him his liberty, and restor'd to him the Isle of *Diu*.

This Isle, which at that time had nothing to shew but the Ruins and miserable Remnants of a once flourishing City, began to recover part of its former Splendor under *Jazy*, by reason of its convenient Situation, betwixt the *Arabian* Shoar, and the Kingdom of *Decan*. *Restor'd by Jazy.* Having provided for the security of the place, by erecting divers Forts and other Fortifications, and his Wealth increasing in a few years, he began to equip a Fleet, in order to attack his Enemies Ships at Sea. *Hocenus* (otherwise named *Mir Amirazem*) a *Persian* by Birth, and Commander in chief of the Ships that were to come from *Egypt* into the *Indies*, having lately had a smart Engagement with the *Portugueses*, *Laurence* and *Francis d' Almeyda*, and coming that way, *Jazy* thought fit to enter into a Confederacy with

He enters into a Confederacy with Hocenus.

with him, which was done accordingly: Whilst they were consulting by what means best to annoy their Enemies with their joint Fleets, News was brought, that *Laurence d'Almeyda* was with a few Ships come to an Anchor before *Chaul*, and had landed his Men (as being quite ignorant of the arrival of the *Egyptian* Fleet in those parts.) One *Nizamaluc* reign'd at that time at *Chaul*, for the great Persons of *Decan* having imprison'd their King, had divided his Kingdom among themselves, whereof this part was fallen to his share. *Nizamaluc*, tho no great Friend to the Christians, yet for Interest sake had order'd his Subjects to maintain a good Correspondence with the *Portugueses* trafficking in those parts; which *Almeyda* being not ignorant of, he thought he might stay here with safety enough, till he had the opportunity of convoying the *Portuguese* Merchant Ships to *Cochin*. It was indeed rumour'd abroad, that the *Egyptian* Fleet had been seen on that Coast; but the *Portugueses* imagining that the same might be occasion'd by the arrival of certain Ships coming about that time of the year from *Mocha*, they made no great account of it: One of the

The Portuguese *Fleet comes to* Chaul.

Ship's Crew at length espy'd a considerable Fleet from the top of the Main-mast, but could not discern their Strength, till at last they began to suspect the truth; for *Hocenus* was advancing that way, and *Jazy* preparing to follow him, in order to attack the *Portugueses*. Certain Intelligence being at last brought to *Almeyda*, that the Enemy was at hand, he order'd his Men aboard, which was scarce done when they saw the *Egyptians* advancing against them. These *Barbarians* had flatter'd themselves with hopes to surprize the *Portugueses*, but these having just had time enough to put themselves in a good posture of Defence, receiv'd their Enemies so warmly, that they thought fit to stay for the arrival of *Jazy*; however, they charged one another (but at a distance) all that day, but towards night *Hocenus* retreated with his Vessels to the other Bank of the River among the Sands, for his greater Security's sake.

The Portugueses *engage* Hocenus.

The Night being spent on the *Portuguese* side in preparing for the Combat against next day, when *Almeyda* being ignorant of the Confederacy betwixt *Hocenus* and *Jazy*, attack'd the first with

Baldæus. great fury, in hopes of boarding the Egyptian Ships; but not being able to come close enough up with them by reason of the Sands, he was forc'd to rest satisfied with plying them with his Cannon, which he did all the day long, notwithstanding the Enemy were much stronger in Ships and Men. The Engagement was very hot, *Laurence d' Almeyda* being himself wounded twice with an Arrow: The Combat continued thus with considerable loss on both sides, till towards night, *Jazy* came to the Relief of the *Egyptians* with 40 Ships, but not daring to engage with the *Portugueses*, came to an Anchor at the Entrance of the River, to be nearer to *Hocenus* in order to join with him the next day.

Advices of the Portugueses to their Admiral. The *Portugueses* being somewhat moved at this unexpected sight, represented to their Admiral *Almeyda*, that having gain'd sufficient Honour in the yesterday's Engagement, they ought now to consult Prudence, and to endeavour to bring their Ships out of the Harbour in the night time into the open Sea. *Almeyda* did not disapprove the Advice of his Sea-Commanders, but as he was of a haughty Temper, so he could not resolve to steal away by night, but determin'd to make the best of his way to *Is rejected.* morrow by day-light; with this Resolution he order'd all his Ships, as well Merchants as others, to be ready to set sail with the first Tide by break of day. The *Moors* no sooner perceiv'd his Intention, but they made towards them in order to intercept their Passage; in this Engagement a Bullet happening to strike through the *Portuguese* Admiral next to the Rudder, she took much Water, and *The Portuguese Admiral cast upon a Rock.* was cast upon the Rocks, whence she could not be got off: The *Portuguese* Commanders seeing the impossibility of saving the Ship, sent a Boat to the Admiral, desiring him to save his Person, and preserve himself for another occasion; but in vain, for he told them, *that he would never be guilty of such a piece of Treachery, as to leave those who had hitherto been his Companions in the Danger, in the* *His Bravery.* *lurch.* Accordingly he animated his Men both with his Words and Example to defend themselves to the utmost extremity; being thus animated by their Admiral, they fought like Lions, rejecting all Proposals offer'd them by the Enemy, resolving either to save the Ship, or die in the defence thereof.

Is wounded. In the mean while *Almeyda* having one of his Thighs shot off by a Bullet, lost however not his wonted Courage, but ordering his Men to place him upon a Chair near the Main-mast, he there gave his Orders as occasion requir'd; but whilst he was busy in incouraging his Men, another unfortunate Ball took away part of his Breast and Ribs, so that his Entrails falling out he gave up the Ghost immediately, and his dead Carcase was carried below Deck immediately. This was the end of the Brave *Almeyda*, who had signalized himself so often by his Bravery in the Service of his King and Country. *And kill'd.*

There were besides him two other brave Fellows, tho much inferiour in Rank, whose Names do well deserve a place in this History; one was *Laurentius Frerius Catus*, a Servant to the deceased Admiral, who being wounded with an Arrow in one of his Eyes, threw himself notwithstanding this upon his Master's Body, and when he saw the *Moors* enter the Ship, fell in pell-mell among them, and kill'd several of them with his Sword before they could dispatch him. The other was a Sailor, named *Andrew Van Portua*, who standing on the top of the Main-mast, and being wounded by a Musquet-Ball in his Shoulder, and having before lost the use of his Right-hand, defended himself from thence with his left hand for two whole days against those *Barbarians*, till at length they promised him his Life, upon which he surrender'd, and afterwards return'd safely into *Portugal*, where he was honourably rewarded for his Bravery. *Two other brave Exploits.*

The taking of the Admiral's Ship of the *Portugueses*, tho it cost the *Barbarians* 600 Men (140 being lost on the Christians side) yet occasion'd no small joy in their Fleet; as on the other hand, the loss thereof soon reach'd to *Cochin* by such Ships as were fled thither: However the *Portugueses* were so far from being dismay'd thereat, that resolving to be reveng'd upon those *Barbarians*, they left no stone unturn'd to gather a more formidable Strength at Sea; and *Albuquerque* after having settled matters at *Socotora* (an Isle at the entrance of the *Red-Sea*) did considerable mischief to the *Moors* near *Ormus*, as *Laurence d' Almeyda* (the Father of the Admiral lately kill'd) reveng'd himself for the Death of his Son, by the taking of *Dabul*, *Diu* and *Panane*, whereof we shall give you a more ample account anon.

For *Emanuel* King of *Portugal*, being inform'd concerning the convenient Situation of the Harbour of *Diu*, sent his Orders

Diu attack'd by the Portugueses. Orders to *Sequeria* to build a Fortress there, cost it what it would. Accordingly *Francis d' Almeyda*, after the taking of *Dabul*, steer'd his course for the Harbour of *Diu*. *Hocenus* was for engaging the *Portugueses* without the Harbour; but at the perswasion of *Jazy* laid aside that Design, it being thought much more expedient to expect the coming of the Christians with their joint Forces, and to annoy them at their approach both by Sea and Land; for which purpose they had besides the *Egyptian* Ships and those of *Diu* receiv'd 80 Brigantines of *Calecut*, and had planted their Cannon at convenient distances along the shore. The *Portuguese* Admiral was somewhat surpriz'd to see the Enemy keep so close beyond expectation; yet interpreting the same as a good Omen of his future Victory, he spent the remainder of the day in viewing the Posture of the Enemy, and Consultations what was best to be done.

He having declar'd his Resolution of attacking the Admiral's Ship of the *Egyptians*, aboard of which was *Hocenus*, the same was approved; but he desir'd not to expose his Person at this critical Juncture, but to commit the management of the Design to *Nonnius Vasques Pereria*: *They attack the* Moors *Ships in the Harbour.* Accordingly, every thing being got in readiness, they enter'd the Harbour the next morning with the first Tide, and a strong Sea-Wind, *Nonnius* leading the Van in his Ship with 200 chosen Men, being follow'd by the Admiral *d' Almeyda* to protect and cover his Rear. *Nonnius* advanced bravely under the thundering Noise of the Cannon (by which ten Seamen that were furling the Sails were kill'd at once) *10 Men kill'd by one Bullet.* and making his way through the midst of the *Barbarians*, at last boarded *Hocenus* in his Ship, tho not without great slaughter on both sides, he himself having the misfortune to be wounded in the Throat by an Arrow, of which he died three days after. Nonnius *wounded.*

The *Portugueses* not being dismay'd at the disaster of their Commander, but inflam'd with Revenge, redoubled their Fury, which the *Barbarians* being no longer able to withstand, they gave all over for lost, *Hocenus* himself narrowly escaping in a Boat to the shore, *Hocenus flies.* and (being somewhat diffident of *Jazy*) took Horse immediately, in order to fly to the King of *Cambaja*, where he was well receiv'd. *Baldæus.* Those of *Calecut* seeing the best of their Brigantines ruin'd by the Enemy's Shot, *So do those of* Calecut. thought it their best way to save themselves with the lightest over the Sands, and two of *Hocenus* his Gallies were carried off by *Roderic Zoares*; many of the *Barbarians* leap'd into the Sea, where they lost their Lives, the rest got ashore, and dispersed, *Jazy* not being able to stop their flight.

There was as yet remaining the Ship of *Jazy*, a Vessel of a vast Bulk, appearing like a Castle well provided with Artillery and Men, being besides this cover'd with Oxes Hides to keep off the Arrows, and hinder the Enemy from boarding by its slipperiness: The *Portugueses* made several attempts to master it, but being as often repulsed, at last sunk her with their Cannon. Jazy's *Ship sunk.* The loss of the *Barbarians* was computed at 3000 Men, the *Portugueses* had only 30 kill'd, but 300 wounded. The *Portugueses* relate, that *Nonnius* his Ship being very old, yet held out very well during the Combat, but immediately after was found leaky in many places; most of the *Mamaluques* or *Egyptians* were slain in this Engagement. How slenderly the *Portugueses* were provided with all manner of Necessaries, may be guessed from hence, that when *Nonnius* his Wound was to be dress'd, there was no Linen in the Ship to do it with, but they were forc'd to tear a Shirt for that purpose. Certain it is that the *Portugueses* can make harder shift than most other Nations, a thing of great consequence in time of War, Plenty and Luxury being often the ruin of the best Armies. The Booty got by the *Portugueses* in this Engagement was considerable; for besides four War-ships, and as many Merchant-Men, with their Artillery, they got a considerable quantity of Gold, Silver and precious Stuffs and Cloths, all which was given a Prey to the Soldiers and Ships Crew: Three of the *Sultan*'s Colours were sent to *Portugal* to be preserv'd there in memory of so remarkable a Victory; which made an ample amends to the *Portugueses* for the loss they had sustain'd some time before near *Chaul.*

Baldæus.

CHAP. VIII.

Peace made with Jazy. Ferdinand Coutinho *made Viceroy. Differences arisen betwixt* Almeyda *and* Albuquerque. *The* Portugueses *take* Diu, *which is refortified by* Jazy. Nonnius *goes to* Diu. *The Isle* Betel *taken.* Saldania *surprizes* Goga.

Jazy *sues for Peace.*

JAzy thought it now time to sue for Peace, to obtain which he was not sparing in his Promises, to endeavour to engage all the Neighbouring Princes into the Interest of *Portugal*; so the Peace was concluded under condition that he should surrender all the remaining *Egyptian* Ships to the *Portugueses*, release the Prisoners taken near *Chaul*, and provide their Fleet with all manner of Necessaries. *Jazy* being very willing, or rather necessitated, to comply with the Conditions, the *Portugueses* thought fit not to attempt any thing further against *Diu* for that time, as being unwilling to embroil themselves with the King of *Cambaja*. Thus *Almeyda* retir'd victorious to *Cochin*, having paid to *Nizamaluc*, as he passed that way, the usual Presents that were in Arrears.

Almeyda *is succeeded by* Ferdin. Coutinho.

But *Almeyda* did not long enjoy the fruits of his late Victory, for *Ferdinand Coutinho* a Person of Quality, was soon after sent with 15 Ships and 3000 Men to join with *Albuquerque* in order to attack the *Moors*, and especially the City of *Calecut*; for some Differences being arisen betwixt *Almeyda* and *Albuquerque*, which were fomented by some malicious Persons, the King of *Portugal* thought he could pitch upon no better Expedient to prevent the ill Consequences thereof, than by sending *Coutinho* to succeed *Almeyda*, who preferring the King's Interest before his private Interest, quietly surrendred his Charge, and at the same time was reconcil'd to *Albuquerque*, after he had managed the Government of the *Indies* with more than ordinary Conduct and Wisdom; a Person worthy of a much better Fortune than what happen'd to him afterwards. For in his return to *Portugal* having occasion to touch at the *Cape of good Hope*, to take in some fresh Provisions, some of his Men being got ashore, and falling into Differences with some of the Natives about the exchange of their Commodities; *Almeyda* running thither with Sword in hand, to see what was the matter, the Natives began to fall upon him and his Men; and being reinforc'd with fresh Numbers, set so hard upon the *Portugueses*, that they were not able to get to their Ships without fighting their way through them, which they did with a great deal of Bravery, but alas! not without the loss of their Commander *Almeyda* (who was run through the Body with a Stick pointed at the end) and twelve more of their best Soldiers; this was the unfortunate end of this great Man, so famous for his great Atchievements both in *Europe* and *Asia*, being forc'd to end his days upon the shore of *Africa*, which robb'd him both of the Rewards due to his Services, and even of a Christian Sepulture.

Differences betwixt Almeyda *and* Albuquerque.

The Death of Almeyda.

We told you before, that the *Portugueses* thought fit not to attempt any thing further against *Diu*; it is now time to shew you what further measures were taken to bring about their design to erect a Fort in that Island. They had so far agreed the matter with the King of *Cambaja*, that he favour'd their Intentions, or at least was not against them; but *Jazy* not only used all his Endeavours at Court to obstruct the design of the *Portugueses*, but also prepar'd every thing for a vigorous Resistance in case of need. In the mean while he was not sparing in fair Words or Promises, nay even in Deeds, to the *Portugueses*; for no sooner arriv'd *Sequeria* at *Diu* from *Ormus*, but he regal'd the Fleet with fresh Provisions, and the Officers with Presents, with a great many Protestations of Friendship to the Crown of *Portugal*: but when *Sequeria* began to talk to *Jazy* concerning the intended Fort, he declin'd the matter, alledging that it lay not alone in his power, and therefore they must obtain the King of *Cambaja*'s Consent, in which he would assist them with all his Interest.

Jazy *plays the Hypocrite with the* Portugueses.

Sequeria was not so stupid as not to smell the Rat, but thinking it best to repay him in his own coin, he dissembl'd the matter, and returning his Complements with much Civility, he prepar'd underhand for War; but *Jazy* who had a watchful Eye upon all his Actions, knew so well how to improve his time, and provide for his Security, that *Sequeria* thought it most adviseable to delay his Project

Is discovered.

Project till the next year, against which time he expected some considerable Reinforcement.

Jazy fortifies himself.

Sequeria was no sooner departed, but *Jazy* imbrac'd this opportunity of strengthning himself on all sides; he added several new Works to the place, and erected a Castle in the midst of the Entrance of the Harbour, and betwixt that and the City, defended it with a strong Chain: He kept several Ships loaden with Ballast ready to be sunk upon occasion, to stop up the Passage on the other side, and order'd vast pieces of Stones and Rocks to be sunk under the Walls, to prevent the *Portugueses* Gallies from approaching near to them: He also for the better Defence of the Harbour hir'd 180 Brigantines, and some Merchant-men, man'd with *Arabians*, *Persians* and *Turks* (profess'd Enemies of the Christians) leaving in the mean while no stone unturn'd to thwart the design'd Project of the *Portugueses* at the Court of the King of *Cambaja*.

Neither were the *Portugueses* idle on their side, but having made what Preparations they thought fit for such an Undertaking, *Nonnius Acunia* the chief Commander of the *Portugueses* in the *Indies*, set forward in order to put it in Execution: But being resolv'd to make use both of Cunning and Force at the same time, he had by Presents engag'd several bold and cuning Fellows, who were to pass to *Diu* in the Quality and Habit of Merchants, but in effect to serve for Spies, and to give notice of what they thought worth his knowledg. Thus prepar'd, the time and place of the Rendevouz of the whole Fleet being appointed at *Chaul*, he set sail from thence with 300 Sail great and small, well provided with Artillery and Ammunition, having aboard 3000 *Portugueses*, as many *Malabars*, and 2000 *Canarines*, for *Dabul*, a small City in the Confines of *Cambaja*; where the *Portugueses*, being much animated by the Presence and Speech of a certain *Franciscan* Frier, named *Anthony Petron*, declar'd that they would not desist, till they had forced the *Barbarians* from their strong Holds in those parts. But finding the Place deserted by its Inhabitants, they steer'd their course towards *Betel* (a small rocky Isle not above a League in compass, separated from the Continent only by a narrow Strait) about 80 Leagues from *Diu*. The Situation of this Isle being such, by reason of the Rocks which inclose the Isle near the shore, that it might easily be made defensible by an indifferent Force, the King of *Cambaja* had not long before sent thither a certain Commander, a *Turk* by Birth, with 2000 Soldiers, and 1000 Workmen, to erect certain Fortifications there; but having not had sufficient time to bring them into such a condition as to be able to resist such a Force as this, they thought it their safest way to capitulate.

Nonnius Acunia goes for Diu. *His Rendevouz.* *Sail for Dabul.* *Baldaeus.*

Betel begun to be fortified by the Cambajans.

The Commander in chief (having obtain'd a Passport for that purpose) had an Interview with the *Portuguese* General, offering to surrender the Isle, under condition that they might have liberty to depart with all their Baggage and Goods. *Nonnius* allow'd the first, but would not consent to their taking the least thing away with them, except what they had about them. This harsh Answer was no sooner known in the Isle, but they resolv'd to abide the utmost extremity, rather than comply with it. The King's Treasurer found means to have a Boat built, wherewith he transported all the King's Mony and Goods to the Continent: Many of the Garison enraged with Revenge and Despair, brought all their Horses, best Moveables, Wives and Children together, and burnt them and themselves. There were about 700 left, most of them Votaries, resolv'd to die with Sword in hand: These like mad Men fell upon the *Portugueses* with more fury than effect; for the *Portuguese* General having repulsed them, attack'd the next night by the light of the Moon their Intrenchments with so much Vigor, that after a most obstinate Resistance (in which the *Turkish* Commander was kill'd) they left them to the *Portugueses*, some running to the Rocks, from whence they precipitated themselves into the Sea; others endeavouring to escape the Sword by hiding themselves in the hollownesses of the Rocks, but being discover'd, some of them were cut to pieces, the rest made Slaves. A certain *Moor* having nothing left but his Sword, and seeing his Comrade slain just by his side, and a *Portuguese* advancing with his Pike towards him, in order to kill him, ran desperately towards him, and thrusting himself upon the *Portuguese*'s Launce, at the same time kill'd his Enemy with his Sword, so that they both died upon the spot.

They offer to surrender upon Conditions. *A most desperate Resolution.* *The Portugueses take the Isle.*

The *Portugueses* lost in this Action about 17 Persons of Note, and had 150 wounded, many of whom died afterwards. *Nonnius* thought fit to tarry here eight days, in hopes of receiving some Intelligence from his Spies at *Diu*; this prov'd of great advantage to those of *Diu*, for in the mean while *Mustapha* and

Loss of the Portugueses.

Sophar

Baldæus. *Sophar* (who had been at the Siege of *Aden*) coming to an Anchor with 600 *Turks* and 1300 *Arabians* before *Diu*, the Inhabitants thereof (who before that time thought of nothing else than how to come to a good Composition) being encouraged by this Reinforcement, were resolv'd to venture all for their Defence. *Mustapha* was no sooner enter'd the City but he order'd the Women, Children, and other defenceless People to be sent out of the Town; the rest being muster'd were found 11000 in number (without the *Turks* and *Arabians*) able to bear Arms; strict Watches were set in all places, to let nobody pass in or out of the Town without special licence; the Cannon were planted on the Walls, Mines dug and fill'd, Chains made across the Harbour, and the Entrance thereof defended by 73 well man'd Brigantines: To be short, nothing was omitted that was thought necessary to strengthen themselves either by Sea or Land.

Preparations at Diu. *Nonnius Acunia* in the mean time tarried at *Betel*, in expectation of the Tidings he waited for from his Spies there; but these being too narrowly watch'd to send any Intelligence, he resolv'd to take his chance, and so set sail for *Diu*, where he cast his Anchor in hopes to come to a Parley with the Inhabitants: but he was not a little surpriz'd when he heard the Cannon from the Ramparts thunder among his Ships, and three Bullets that pass'd cross the Admiral's Ship, gave him sufficient warning, that it was not safe staying there long, which made him give immediate Orders for the whole Fleet to weigh Anchor, and to secure themselves without the reach of the Cannon from the City. Being by this time sufficiently convinc'd (without consulting his Spies) that there were but little hopes of Peace or a Surrender, he took a full view of the Town, to see on what side it might be most conveniently attack'd; and finding more probability to succeed on the Harbour than on the Land-side (especially since he was better provided for a Sea than Land Enterprize) he order'd all his Ships and Artillery to be got in a readiness, in order to attack the Castle at the entrance of the Harbour, break the Chains, and to fall upon the Enemy's Fleet, from whence he might annoy the City with his Cannon on the North-side. *The Portugueses assault* Diu *in vain.* The Attempt was made accordingly, but without success, the *Portugueses* being so fiercely gall'd on all sides by the Enemy's Cannon, that they were forced to desist, and *Nonnius* thought fit to retreat to *Betel*, from whence he return'd with his Fleet to *Goa*, leaving *Anthony Saldania* with some Ships on the Coast of *Cambaja*, to watch the Enemy's Motions. *Saldania*, after having done considerable Mischief to the Enemy, by the taking of the small City of *Goga*, and burning 25 Brigantines, left *James Sylveria* behind him, and return'd afterwards to *Goa*, where having spent the greatest part of the Winter in refitting their Ships, *Nonnius* in the Spring set sail for *Chaul* about two Leagues from *Calecut*, to intercept the *Arabian* Ships trading in those parts.

CHAP. IX.

Nonnius *routs the* Mahometans, *takes* Bazain; *and* Martin Souza, Daman. Badur *King of* Cambaja *engages in a Treaty with the* Portugueses. *His Forces, and Expedition to* Citor. *The Destruction of that City.* Badur *twice defeated, flies to* Diu. *His End.*

Sylveria was in the mean while not idle, but took many Ships bound for *Diu*, burnt some Villages, and kept the place so block'd up on all sides, that in a little time they were within reduced to great scarcity of Provisions: The next following year *Sylveria* continued to play the same game, by destroying many Towns, Villages and Ships; he also took the Cities of *Pate* and *Patane*, as also *Mangalor* in *Cambaja*, with a vast Booty, and a great number of Prisoners; the new King of *Cambaja* being not in a condition to assist those of *Diu*, by reason of some intestine Troubles.

Nonnius at the same time keeping still in remembrance the Disgrace he had receiv'd before *Diu*, and being resolv'd to let slip no opportunity of revenging himself, he laid his Design against *Bazain* in *Cambaja*; accordingly he set sail with a Fleet of 80 Ships great and small, with 4000 Land-men aboard them (half *Portugueses*, half *Malabars*) he sent *Emanuel* Nonnius *his Design against* Bazain. *Albu-*

Albuquerque with some Ships before, to secure the Entrance of the Harbour, sent for *James Sylveria*, who had his Station on the other side of *Diu*, and follow'd himself with the whole Fleet.

Tocan the Chief of *Diu*, had, upon notice that the *Portugueses* were arming against him, intrench'd himself with a considerable number of Horse and Foot at *Bazain*. *Nonnius* on the other hand, being well inform'd of the Condition of the place by certain Deserters, divided his Troops into three Bodies: The Vanguard was led by *James Sylveria*, the main Battel by *Ferdinand de Za*, the Reer being commanded by *Nonnius* in Person.

The Portugueses attack it. As they were advancing towards the Town, they receiv'd several smart Salutes from the Enemy's Cannon, and whole showers of Arrows, *Tocan* having intrench'd himself with 10000 Men in the Out-works; notwithstanding which the *Portugueses* lost not so much as one Man whilst they were advancing towards the Enemy, whom they charg'd so briskly, that they were forc'd to betake to their heels; and the Inhabitants seeing themselves deserted by their Protectors, follow'd their Footsteps. Thus this City with all its Works fell into the hands of the *Portugueses*, with the loss only of six Men on their side; whereas the loss of the *Moors* was computed at 550. *And take it.* They found in it a considerable Booty of Provisions and Ammunition, as Bullets, Gunpowder, and Brimstone. *Nonnius* highly extoll'd the Bravery of *Sylveria*, who commanding the Vanguard, had behav'd himself so gallantly, that the main Battel did not as much as come to the Charge, and as an acknowledgment of his Services presented him and all his Officers. After they had destroy'd all the Fruits of the Field round about it, they destroy'd the City, and demolish'd the Fortifications, as thinking it not for their interest to spare a sufficient number of Troops to garison it. Thus *Nonnius* having taken an ample Revenge upon the *Barbarians*, return'd with his Fleet to *Goa*; and the *Mahometans* being convinc'd by this as well as the loss of the Isle of *Betel* (and afterwards that of *Daman*) of the Strength and Bravery of the *Portugueses*, began to remit much of their Fierceness, and were at last forced to submit to the building of a Fort upon the Isle of *Diu*, as will appear out of the sequel of the matter.

Soza attacks Daman. *Martinus Alphonsus Soza* being come lately from *Portugal* (in the quality of Admiral) to *Goa* with five stout Vessels, and being join'd by 35 Ships and 600 Land-Souldiers of *Nonnius* his Squadron, he set sail for *Daman*, a City of *Cambaja*, about 14 Leagues from *Bazain*: This being a Place of no strength, the Inhabitants had deserted their Habitations; but the *Rasboutes*, a daring and unruly Generation, being join'd by some *Turks* to the number of 5000 in all, had intrench'd themselves near the Harbour, and defended the Entrance thereof with a good number of great Cannon. *Baldæus.*

Alphonsus Soza took peculiar care in taking a view of the posture of the Enemy; and as he was going in his Boat from the Harbour along the shoar, having taken notice of a place in the City which was but ill guarded, he order'd scaling Ladders to be hung to the Walls, so that whilst they were scaling the Town the Defenders fled, and thereby gave an opportunity to the *Portugueses* to make themselves Masters of a Gate; here it was the Slaughter begun, the Fight being carried on with equal Obstinacy for some time, till the *Rasboutes* being forc'd to give way, many of them were cut to pieces by the *Portugueses*, who lost no more than ten Men in this Action, but had many more wounded. *Takes and demolishes it.* Three days were spent in demolishing the Fortifications, and laying the whole City level with the ground: Which done, *Soza* turn'd his victorious Arms towards *Diu*, and all along the Coast of *Cambaja*.

Badur King of *Cambaja*, being extremely nettl'd at the success of the *Portugueses*, whom he was not in a condition to oppose, at a time when he saw himself intangled in another War, thought it his best way to sue for Peace with *Nonnius Acunia*, offering not only *Bazain*, but also the adjacent Isles (among which were likewise the *Salsetes*) and a considerable Tract of Land on the Continent, thereby to engage the *Portugueses* in his Interest against his Enemies, *viz.* *Cremantina* the Queen Dowager of *Sanga*, and the *Mogores*, a Warlike Nation descended from the *Scytæ*, who are frequently at War with the *Persians*: Their King *Miramudius*, who boasted himself to be descended from the Great *Tamerlan*, having not long before made a powerful Irruption into *Cambaja*. *Peace betwixt the Portugueses and Badur.*

The Intention of *Badur* was first to vanquish the Queen of *Sanga*, and afterwards the *Mogores*: His whole Force consisted in 150000 Horse, and 500000 Foot, besides 15000 hir'd Foreigners, 200 Elephants train'd for the War, and a very good Train of great Artillery; *His Warlike Preparations.* with

Baldæus. with this Army he march'd to *Citor*, a very fine and populous City under the Queen of *Sanga*, who was not long before retreated thence with her Children. The Inhabitants of *Citor*, unable to resist so powerful an Army, resolv'd to follow the footsteps of those in the Isle of *Betel* (mention'd before) and having brought together all their Gold, Silver, and precious Stones, &c. burnt themselves with their Wives and Children, with the Treasure. It is said, that during the Conflagration, which lasted three days, more than 70000 Persons perish'd by the Flames. *Badur* enter'd victoriously into *Citor*, where having rewarded the Services of his Officers that behav'd themselves well with Presents, he march'd directly against the *Mogores*, but with very different success; for being twice put to the rout by them, and deserted by *Mustapha* his General, he was forc'd to fly to *Diu*, and being full of despair, would have taken a Resolution to leave his Kingdom, and to send his Treasure to *Mecca*; but being, at the earnest entreaty of his Friends, remov'd from that Resolution, he sent an Ambassador to *Soliman* the Grand Signior, to offer him 600000 Crowns, provided he would send a certain number of well-disciplin'd Troops to his Assistance; but fearing lest the desir'd Succours should come too late, he offer'd to *Soza*, who then lay before *Chaul*, as also to *Nonnius Acunia*, a proper place for the erecting of a Fort near *Diu*, provided they would assist him against his Enemies.

He takes Citor.

Sues for Peace.

The *Portugueses* willing to take the opportunity by the forelock, *Soza* sail'd to *Diu* immediately, and being follow'd by *Nonnius*, the Treaty was sign'd, and a place assign'd, *viz.* the Hill which overlooks the Harbour of *Diu*. This happen'd in the year 1535. The *Portugueses* went to work immediately, and laid the Foundation of a Triangular Fort, the Wall from the Sea-side to the Hill being 17 Foot thick, and 20 high, at the end whereof just upon a Hill near the City was erected a Redoubt, and on the other end a Stone Tower (such a one as the *Portugueses* have at *Cranganor* and *Cananor*) from whence extended another Wall to the other Corner of the Island: The Wall was defended by a deep Ditch as far as the Rocks would permit. In the midst whereof was a Gate defended by two Towers, named St. *Thomas* and St. *James*. Thus King *Badur* saw a goodly Fortress perfected by the *Portugueses* within 49 days, that part to the Sea-side being set aside till another opportunity.

The Portuguese Fort near Diu.

One *James Bottelho* a brave Commander, but fallen into Disgrace with *Emanuel* King of *Portugal*, being willing to court any opportunity of being restor'd to the King's favour, got a Brigantine built on purpose of 18 foot in length, and six broad; and having provided himself with as many Seamen as were requir'd to manage her at Sea, he set sail from *Diu*, without letting them whither they were bound, and prov'd so prosperous in his Voyage, that without any remarkable Accident, he arriv'd safely at *Lisbon*, and brought the kind Advice of their good success at *Diu*.

Boldness of James Bottelho.

The *Portugueses* left a Garison of 800 Men under *Emanuel Soza* in the Fort, and were no sooner retir'd from thence with their Fleet, but *Badur* began to repent of his having admittted the *Portugueses* into the Isle of *Diu* (especially since the promised Succours arriv'd but slowly) whereupon he order'd the Governor *Ninaar* to surround the City with a new Wall, and to enclose the Royal Square without the place, whereby their Fortifications must approach very near to, and lie directly opposite to those of the *Portugueses*. These being resolv'd not to permit a thing of this nature, which must needs tend to their Prejudice, *Badur* was much incensed thereat, exclaiming highly against their Proceedings, and endeavour'd to have surpriz'd them in their Fort, which not succeeding, he sought for Aid from the *Samoryn* of *Calecut*, and several *Malabar* Kings against them.

New Differences betwixt Badur *and the* Portugueses.

Nonnius being advertised of all these Treacheries, sets sail once more with 20 Ships, and 500 chosen *Portuguese* Soldiers for *Diu*, ordering *Martin Alphonso* to follow him from the *Malabar* Coast. No sooner had he cast Anchor before *Diu*, but feigning himself sick aboard, he sent certain Persons to compliment King *Badur*, and beg his Excuse for his not coming in Person: Whereupon *Badur* went aboard together with *Soza* the Governor of the Fort to give a Visit to *Nonnius*, who met *Badur* at the Door of his great Cabin, and saluted him with a great deal of Civility. For tho the Death of *Badur* was resolv'd on before-hand, yet that they might not seem to violate the Laws of Hospitality, they had thought fit to defer the Execution thereof till his return towards the shore: It was not long before *Badur* went into his Boat again in order to return, but was no sooner got into

Nonnius *sails once more to* Diu.

Badur *gives him a Visit aboard.*

into it, and making the best way to the shore, when *Nonnius* giving the Signal to his Men, and exhorting them to do their Duty, they leap'd into Boats kept for that purpose, and following that of *Badur* attack'd him on all sides. The King being grown desperate, exhorted his People to a brave Defence, encouraging both by his Words and Example, which made the Fight so obstinate, that the *Portugueses* were in danger of losing their Prey, *Soza* himself being slain in the first Attack. The Bravery of a certain Servant of *Badur* deserves our particular notice, he being observ'd to have wounded with 18 Arrows, as many *Portugueses*, till he was kill'd by a Musquet-shot himself.

Is kill'd.

The Bravery of a Servant of Badur.

In the mean while three Yachts arm'd with *Turks* were sent from the shore to succour the King; but being most of them kill'd, and the King's Galley struck upon a Bank, he leapt into the Sea, and tho sorely wounded, did swim to the Galley of *Tristan Pavia*, and discovering himself to be the *Sultan*, beg'd his Life, which *Tristan Pavia* would willingly have granted, but just as the King was entring the Vessel, he was slain by a Seaman, who knock'd his Brains out with a Club. This was the unfortunate end of *Badur*, one of the most Potent Kings of *Asia*, who not long before had been a Terror to all the circumjacent Countries.

Baldæus.

Badur *slain.*

CHAP. X.

Sofar *made a Prisoner. The* Portugueses *become Masters of the whole Isle.* Mamud *King of* Cambaja. *A considerable number of* Ottomans *sent to the* Indies. Diu *besieg'd by the* Turks. *A smart Engagement betwixt the* Mahometans *and* Portugueses. Diu *reliev'd.* Garzias Noronia *constituted Vice-Roy.*

BUT to return to *Diu*, and the Sea-Engagement, where *Sofar* being taken Prisoner, was kindly entertain'd by *Nonnius*. The Death of *Badur* (tho not very honourable on the *Portugueses* side) prov'd however of very great consequence, the *Portugueses* becoming thereby Masters of the whole Island without much opposition, the said *Badur* being deservedly hated by his Subjects, by reason of his Tyranny and Cruelty; 600 Foot were left there in Garison, and all necessary care was taken that the Customs both at *Diu* and *Rumenstadt* might be regularly paid. *Maffæus* in his 4th Book of the *Indian* History, says, that *Rumenstadt* or *Rumopolis* (lying not far from *Diu*) was built by *Jazy* (mention'd before) and got its Name from the *Constantinopolitan Turks*, that scour sometimes in the *Indies*, call'd by them *Rumes*.

Sofar *a Prisoner.*

Portugueses *Masters of the Island.*

Rumenstadt.

The *Portugueses* found no great Treasure of ready Mony at *Diu*, but considerable Stores of Ammunition and Provision, and the better to strengthen themselves, fortified the City on the Sea-side.

The Portugueses *fortify the Sea-side.*

Badur was succeeded in the Kingdom of *Cambaja* by *Mamud* his Sister's Son, who being an Infant, under the Tuition of *Driacan*, *Madremaluc* and *Alucan*, these were sollicited by *Sofar* (out of a hatred to the *Portugueses*) to engage in a War for the recovery of *Diu*. *Alucan* having got together a Body of 5000 Horse, and 10000 Foot, and *Sofar* 3000 Foot, and 1000 Horse, they pitch'd their Tents in *June* not far from *Rumenstadt*. *Sofa* attack'd the Town vigorously, but being in one of the Attacks wounded in both his hands, the *Portugueses* got a little breathing time, and in the mean while repair'd the Walls of *Rumendstadt*, which for some reasons they had demolished before: For *Anthonius Sylveria* having resolv'd to fortify and defend the whole Island against the *Indians*, was disappointed in his design by *Alucan*, who improving the loss of some *Portuguese* Ships by Tempest to his advantage, gall'd the *Portugueses* so sorely from his Ships in their Entrenchments, that they were forced to quit their Posts; so that *Alucan* landing his Men, soon became Master of the whole Isle and the Suburbs, where there happen'd frequent Skirmishes betwixt them, the *Indians* being not strong enough to attack the Fort, which was bravely defended by *Lupo Soza Cotinho*.

Mamud *King of* Cambaja.

His Tutors engage in a War.

The Portugueses *forced into the Fort.*

Whilst these things were transacting in *Cambaja*, the Grand Signior, to revenge the Murder of *Badur* (at the request of his Widow) had equipp'd a Fleet of 64 stout Gallies, which being join'd

Baldæus. join'd by 7 Ships of *Cambaja* and three *Moors* of *Malabar* with 3500 Land-men aboard them, under the Command of *Solyman* Bassa of *Egypt*, they set sail from *Aden*, not questioning but they would soon be masters of the *Portuguese* Fort, and consequently of the Island, from whence they might extend their Conquests into the Continent of the *Indies*. Matters being concerted beforehand betwixt *Solyman* and *Sofar*, the last went out to meet the *Turkish* Squadron about 15 Leagues at Sea; and *Anthonio Sylveria* being advertis'd of their appoach, took all imaginable Precaution for his Security, in disposing what Force he had to make a vigorous Defence, and at the same time gave notice thereof to *Goa*, to sollicite for prompt Succours from thence, encouraging his Men both by his Example and Exhortations. By this time *Solyman* having cast Anchor in the Road of *Diu*, he order'd 700 chosen Men to land, and attempt the Attack of the *Portugueses* Fortress, which they did accordingly, but were forced to retire to *Sofar*'s Fort with the loss of 50 *Janizaries* kill'd, and a greater number wounded; the *Portugueses* had also six Men kill'd, and 20 wounded.

Sylveria *prepares for a brave Defence.*

Solyman *lands, and attacks the* Portugueses.

About the same time the *Turkish* Fleet being in great danger of being forc'd by a strong South Wind upon the Coast, and much expos'd to the Enemy's Shot, he retreated to the Harbour of *Madrafaba* five Leagues from *Diu*; where having concerted new measures with *Sofar*, he sent back his Land Forces to renew the Siege of *Diu*. But *Alucan* one of the Tutors of King *Mamud* having conceiv'd a jealousy of the Design of the *Turks*, retir'd with his Forces from before *Diu*, and having represented their ambitious Projects to the King, he soon obtained of him a Prohibition in all his Territories not to furnish the *Turkish* Camp with Provisions.

Retreats to Madrafaba.

Alucan *leaves* Diu.

This prov'd no small disappointment to *Solyman*, who notwithstanding this did not lose Courage, but pursued his design of carrying the place, cost it what it would: For this purpose the *Turks* contriv'd a very large Fireship, which under favour of the Tide and the smoak of some burning Wood, they intended to send into the Harbour, and to fix to the Fortifications; and whilst the *Portugueses* were busied in quenching the Flames, they were to attempt the surprising of the Fort on the Land-side: but whilst they were staying for the Spring-Tide, *Francisco Goveano* a *Portuguese* found means to set it on fire, tho not without great hazard, being oblig'd to pass twice the Enemies fire; 20 of the *Turks* aboard the Fireship leap'd into the Sea, and were all slain. The *Turks* were so incensed at this disappointment, that they exerted all their Fury against *Rumenstadt*, the Walls whereof being so ruin'd as not to be maintain'd any longer against a vigorous Attack, *Patieco* the chief Commander thereof thought fit to quit it in time. The *Turks* flush'd with this Success, renew'd the Siege of *Diu* both by Sea and Land with more vigor than ever, leaving nothing unattempted, with Cannonading, Mining, or whatever might be attempted to reduce the place; whilst the *Portugueses* on the other hand with Countermines, Retrenchments and frequent Sallies endervour'd to stop their Fury. The *Turks* being at last by means of a Gallery advanc'd over the Ditch, and entring the Breach, a most furious Combat ensu'd for four hours successively, the *Portugueses* defending themselves like Lions. *Maffæus* relates, that a *Portuguese* having spent all his Balls, pull'd out one of his Teeth and charg'd his Musquet with it. At last the *Turks* were forced to retire with the loss of 500 Men slain, and 1000 wounded: The *Portugueses* also on their side had 14 of their best Officers slain, and so many of their Soldiers either kill'd or wounded, that they had scarce 40 Men left fit for Service. Besides this they began to be in such want of Provisions and Ammunition, that they were very near reduced to the last extremity. However they did not lose Courage, but incouraged one another rather to die upon the spot, than to submit to the most sordid slavery; the Women and Children were even not backward in giving all the Assistance they were able.

A Fire-Engine of the Turks.

Set a fire by the Portugueses.

Rumenstadt *left by the* Portugueses.

The Turks *renew the Siege of* Diu.

The Turks *storm the Place.*

Are repulsed.

In the mean time *Nonnius Acunia* being sufficiently sensible of the danger of the Fortress of *Diu*, had left no Stone unturn'd for the relief thereof; but the case admitting of no delay, he sent 16 *Patachos* or Yachts thither: these coming to an Anchor in the night time before *Madrafraba*, had each put four Lanthorns on their Sterns, with an intention to terrify the Enemy. This succeeded accordingly; for the *Turks* having by this time lost above 3000 Men, and fearing the Succour expected from *Goa* might be much stronger than really it was, set fire to the City, and leaving 500 wounded Men, and most of their great Cannon behind, reimbark'd the first of *November*, steering their Coast towards *Arabia*; and *Sofar*

Diu *reliev'd.*

*

Sofar with the Remnants of his Forces retir'd to the Continent, to the no small honour of the *Portugueses*, who with so small a number had defended themselves not against barbarous undisciplin'd *Indians*, but against a Body of warlike well-exercised *Turkish* Troops. It's said, that *Francis* I. King of *France*, was so highly pleased with this brave Action, that he desir'd and had an Original Picture of the brave *Sylveria*, the Governour of the place.

To the great Honour of the Portugueses.

Whilst *Nonnius* was busied in making all the necessary Preparations for the Relief of *Diu*, *Goa Garzias Noronia* was sent by *Don John* King of *Portugal* with 11 Men of War, and 7000 Land-Men to relieve *Nonnius*: Among these there was one Ship fill'd with Malefactors and Criminals of all sorts, who had obtain'd their Pardon from the King; but this being separated from the rest, was never heard of afterwards. *Nonnius Acunia* having surrender'd the Government to *Noronia* after a stay of ten years in those parts, set sail for *Portugal*, his Native Country, but before he could reach it died at Sea, near the *Cape of Good Hope* on the *African* Coast.

Baldæus.

Nonnius *reliev'd by* Garzias Noronia.

Nonnius *his Death.*

CHAP. XI.

Noronia *makes an Agreement with King* Mamud. Lupius Soza *constituted Governour of* Diu. Sofar's *sinister Designs against the* Portugueses. *He besieges* Diu *in conjunction with* Mamud: *Is slain in the Enterprise. The City is vigorously assaulted, and as bravely defended. An unsuccessful Sally made by the* Portugueses.

Noronia *sends his Deputies to* Mamud.

Noronia apply'd all his Thoughts to the Affairs of *Diu*; and having dispatch'd certain Deputies to *Mamud* to treat with him of a Peace, they at last, not without a great deal of difficulty, came to the following Agreement, in the Negotiation of which they met with no small opposition from the Grand-mother of *Mamud* and *Sofar*, who were continually inciting the young King to revenge the Death of his Uncle King *Badur*; *viz.* That the King of *Cambaja* should remain in the Possession of the City of *Deu*, and the *Portugueses* continue Masters of the Fort and Harbour thereof; that they should divide the Customs share and share alike, and that the *Cambajans* should be at liberty to erect a Wall to front the Castle, provided the same were done at a convenient distance.

Their Agreement.

Lupius *constituted Governour.*

Matters being thus settled, *Lupius Soza* was constituted Governour of the place instead of *Sylveria*, with a Garison of 900 Men. But it was not long before *Mamud*, at the Instigation of his Grand-mother, sent a considerable Body to attack *Bazain*; but *Laurentius Tavora* making a vigorous Sally upon them, constrained them to seek for Peace. *Sofar* in the mean time having recover'd himself, had for six years together bent all his thoughts upon the ruin of the *Portugueses*; and having found means to ingratiate himself into King *Mamud* his favour, they sent underhand their Emissaries to the neighbouring *Indian* Princes, to engage them against the *Portugueses*, who they told them did lord it over them, under pretence of trafficking in the *Indies*. The Affairs of the *Portugueses* were at that time but in a very indifferent condition in those parts, their Treasuries exhausted, their Naval Strength neglected, their Seamen very scarce; and the Land Soldiers deserted in such numbers, that of the 900 that were in Garison under the Command of *Lupius Soza*, there were not above 250 left in the Government of *Mascarenhas*; and what was worse, there was not above a month's Provision, and a slender share of Ammunition left.

Miserable state of the Portugueses.

Sofar was not unacquainted with these things, having learn'd them from divers *Portuguese* Merchants; so that looking upon this as a fit opportunity to execute their projected Design, they pitch'd upon the Winter-season, when they knew the *Portugueses* could not be so easily secured from *Goa*. *Sofar* being in the mean while not negligent to cajole *Mascarenbas* the *Portuguese* Governour by his Letters into a belief of his Sincerity, the same did not discover his real Intentions, till it was almost too late; but finding no other redress but in a brave Defence, he made all the necessary Preparations for it, by sending away all the useless Mouths, and fortifying himself after the best manner he could: and having bought up what

Treachery of Sofar.

Baldæus. what quantity of Rice, Flesh and dried Fish he could get of the *Portugueses*, he sent Advice of his approaching danger to *Bazain*, *Chaul* and *Goa*. This happen'd in the year 1546. *Sofar* took for a pretence the new Walls that were to be erected at one end of the City, which being built too near the *Portuguese* Fortress, these stopt the Progress thereof, which soon gave occasion to open Hostilities. *Mascarenhas* to animate his Soldiers told them, "That they ought to "remember the brave Actions of the "*Portugueses* in this very place, where "they had frustrated the Designs of the "*Turks*, of which the same *Sofar* who "now came to attack them had born his "share; that God would certainly punish the breach of Faith of this "Wretch; and that they ought not to "be dismay'd at the Winter-season, "there being no question but that the "*Portugueses* by their Skill in Maritime "Affairs, would overcome these Difficulties, and succour them in due time. The next thing he did, was to take care of all the Posts; the Water-Redoubt he committed to the care of *Martinho Carvalho* with 30 Men, and the Defence of the shore towards *Cambaja* to *Jacobo Leti*.

Breaks out into open Hostilities.

Sofar by this time had begun to carry on his Approaches a good way, and ply'd the place warmly with his Cannon, but could not without much difficulty attempt an Assault by reason of the Ditch, which being inlarg'd of late, was as broad again now as it was in *Sylveria* his time; however he ceased not to play with his Cannon, especially in the night time; and being sensible of what advantage it would be to him if he could make himself Master of the Harbour, by taking the Water-Redoubt, he contriv'd such another Engine or Fireship as the *Turks* had made use of in the former Siege, which they intended to set on fire, and to carry with the high Tide under the Fort: But the *Portugueses* having receiv'd Intelligence of this Design, sent out *Jacobo Leti* with 20 Men to burn her, which he did with incredible Bravery, and the loss of one Man only, being forc'd to carry the Vessel through the Enemy's Fire on both sides, till he brought her within a certain distance of the Fort, where she was set on fire, and consequently *Sofar's* Project vanish'd into smoak.

Sofar attacks Diu.

Sofar's Fireship burnt.

A Fire-ship burnt before it could do Execution

Nat

Not long after the *Portugueses* were rejoic'd with a fresh supply of Men, Provisions and Ammunition from *Goa*, under the Command of the young *de Castro*, a brave Gentleman, who, after he had been afflicted with very hard Tempests at Sea (in which several of his Vessels were separated from his Squadron) came with the rest, being eight in number, into the Road of *Diu*, and in spite of the Besiegers, landed his Men, Ammunition and Provisions, which increased the Number of the Garison to 450 Men. About the same time *Mamud* King of *Cambaja* came in Person with a good number of Troops into the Camp: *Mascarenhas* being willing to know their exact number, sent out several Desperado's, who engaging the Outguard of the Enemy, three of them were kill'd in the Skirmish, but the rest had the good fortune to carry off one of the Enemy's Sentinels, by whom *Mascarenhas* was inform'd of what he had a mind to know. *Mascarenhas* having order'd certain Signals of rejoicing to be made, the Enemy sent a Messenger to know the reason thereof, who was answer'd, that 'twas done on account of the King's arrival in the Camp, which put them in hopes that for the future they should fight against a great Prince, whereas hitherto they had been engag'd with Vagabonds and Rogues.

The Portugueses receive some Succours.

K. Mamud comes into the Camp.

Mamud immediately after his arrival levell'd his Cannon with great fury against the Walls of the Fortress, and having brought along with him an expert Gunner, he order'd him to cast certain fiery Balls into the place, tho without much success, till the said Constable being kill'd, another succeeded in his place, who was so unskilful in his Art, that his Fireworks did more mischief in the Camp than to the Enemy. However by the continual battering of the Enemies Cannon, a large Breach was made by this time in the Wall, which the Besieged repair'd to the best of their power; but their main Reliance was upon the breadth of the Ditch, which the Besiegers were endeavouring to pass by the help of their Galleries. To prevent this, the *Portugueses* had open'd an old Vault at the foot of the Wall, in which they spent several days and nights, but turn'd to their advantage, since from thence they could take away great part of the Materials the Enemy had brought thither for the filling up of the Ditch. From hence it was also that *Sofar* receiv'd his Death's wound, being slain by a Bullet which pass'd through his Hand and Forehead, which occasion'd no small disturbance in the Enemies Camp; and had it not been for *Rumecan* his Son, the Siege had been likely to have been raised at that time.

Makes a Breach in the Wall.

Sofar kill'd.

Baldæus.

The Joy the *Portugueses* had conceiv'd at the death of *Sofar* their mortal Enemy, was not a little allay'd by the perseverance of the Besieged in filling up the Ditch, and that with such success, that having stopt up the before-mention'd Vault, *Mascarenhas* began to be reduced to the utmost stress, of which he gave notice to the Viceroy at *Goa*, requesting immediate Succours. It was now about the middle of *August*, when the *Mahometans* were preparing for the general Assault: They visited their Mosques with a great deal of Devotion, and St. *James*'s day being appointed for this Attack, they advanc'd without the least noise in two Bodies before break of day towards the Breach, in hopes of surprizing the *Portugueses*; but finding 'em upon their guard, they enter'd the Breach with most terrible and dreadful Outcries, which however was so far from terrifying the brave *Portugueses*, that they were repulsed with great slaughter: Some of the *Indians* taking the advantage of the low Tide, got into the Water-Fort, where they pitch'd *Mahomet*'s Standard, which *Mascarenhas* no sooner perceiv'd, but flying thither, he gave them such a Reception, that after 30 of them were slain upon the spot, the rest were forc'd down headlong over the Wall. This done, he return'd to his Post, where both by his Words and Actions he so encouraged his Men, that *Rumecan*, after a hot Dispute of six hours, saw himself oblig'd to sound a Retreat. In this Action not only *Mascarenhas*, but also *Ludovico Soza*, *Ferdinando de Castro*, *Anthonio Passando*, and all the *Portugueses* in general acquir'd immortal Honour, several Women having exposed themselves in the midst of the Combat.

The Indians storm the Fort.

Are repulsed.

Notwithstanding this Repulse, the *Indians* did not cease to continue their Fire against the Fortress, which not succeeding according to expectation, they began to apply their Mines, not without some success. *Mascarenhas* having taken notice that the Enemy retreated sometimes without any necessity, near a certain Tower, gave notice thereof to *de Castro*, and some other Officers of note, commanding them to quit it; but these flush'd with their last success, refus'd to obey, for which they paid dear soon after: for the Enemy taking the opportunity, when they perceiv'd the Tower full of Soldiers, blew

Baldæus.

blew it up on a sudden with at least 100 *Portugueses* in it, and among them *de Castro*, and several others of Quality; and such was the Barbarity of the *Indians*, that they thrust their Swords through the half-dead Bodies of such *Portugueses* as were thrown up into the Air before by the Mine. They were for improving this opportunity, and during the Confusion occasion'd by this Disaster, attack'd the Fort with incredible Fury, but were so warmly receiv'd by *Mascarenhas*, that they were glad to retreat. To prevent the like for the future, the *Portuguese* Governour order'd his Men to act with more caution for the future, and the Tower of St. *James* to be blown up, which was executed; and not long after, finding the Enemy ready to attack the Tower of St. *Thomas*, he blew up the Mine underneath it, and with it 300 *Indians*.

A Mine blows up 100 Portugueses.

300 Indians blown up by a Mine.

The *Portuguese* Affairs in the Fortress began notwithstanding all this to grow worse and worse; for tho they had made Intrenchments within Intrenchments, yet had they (after a Siege of four Months) not above 150 Men left for the defence thereof; and being reduc'd to great extremity for want of Provisions, were forc'd to feed upon unwholesom things, which so discourag'd the Garison, that they were resolv'd to put an end to their Misery by fighting their way through the Enemy.

But being just upon the point of putting their Design in execution, they were rejoic'd with a most unexpected Relief from *Goa*, whence they had sent 50 Frigats under the Command of *Alvares de Castro*, and *Franciscus de Meneses*, who ariv'd happily at *Bazain*. *Alvares* sail'd straitways thence with part of his Forces (amounting to 900 in all) for *Diu*, and good store of Ammunition and Provisions, the rest follow'd before the end of *September*. You may easily imagine with what Joy the poor emaccrated Soldiers of the Garison receiv'd this welcome News, which however they would not improve to so much advantage as they might have done, out of a perverse Temper, peculiar to the *Portugueses*, who as they are soon dejected in Adversity, so are they insupportable in Prosperity: For now the Soldiery began to accuse *Mascarenhas* of Cowardice and Neglect, telling him in plain terms, that they were resolv'd no more to be shut up within the Walls, but to act like brave *Portugueses*, to attack the Enemy in their Works, and to make him once for all to repent that ever he had attempted the *Portugueses*, whose Glorious Name was dreadful all over the *Indies*; this they told him they were fully resolv'd to put in execution, and if he refus'd to head them, they would choose another, the first, the best they could. *Mascarenhas*, who knew very well the stubborn Pride of the *Portugueses*, when flush'd with Success, did what he could to divert them from their Design by all the mild Insinuations and most forcible Arguments he could invent, telling them that the securest Methods were always the best, and how dangerous it might prove to hazard the losing of the Fort, when they were in a condition to keep it till the approaching Spring, when they expected sufficient Succours from *Goa*; but finding them deaf to his Perswasions, he spoke to them in the following manner: "Soldiers, ye are not insensible that, if you would consider your Duty, you ought rather to follow my Commands than your own Directions; but since you have ty'd up my hands, and both by your Words and Actions, nay by your very Looks, give me sufficiently to understand, that instead of commanding, I must obey; go on and shew your Courage, your Knowledg and Experience in Martial Affairs: Go on, I say, I will instead of leading you on, follow you, with this Caution however, that I would have you remember to take care to return with the same marks of Bravery as you march out. Then dividing the whole Garison into three Bodies, he order'd *Alvares de Castro* to command the Van, the main Battel he gave in charge to *Francisco de Meneses*, himself remaining to guard the Reer: Thus they march'd towards the Enemy, but with far different success from what they had promised themselves; most of them after the first Charge retreating towards the Town, instead of pushing forward; the Body commanded by *Meneses* being charg'd in Front and Flank, betook themselves to their heels, and *de Castro* himself being sorely wounded by a Stone, was hardly sav'd by *Mascarenhas*, who crying out to the Soldiers, that it was now time to shew their Bravery they had so much boasted of before, would fain have stopt their Flight, but in vain; for they retreated with so much fear and precipitation, that for some time after they scarce durst look the Enemy in the face, or keep their Post; whereas the *Indians*, incourag'd by this Success, approach'd with their Engines nearer and nearer to the Walls of the Town.

Diu reliev'd with some Men and Provisions.

Mutiny among the Portugueses.

Mascarenhas his Speech to his Soldiers.

Their unsuccessful Sally.

CHAP.

Baldæus.

CHAP. XII.

De Castro *comes to* Diu. *Takes some* Arabian *Vessels. Routs the* Indians, *who leave the Isle.* Rumecan *kill'd.* Soliman's *Transactions before* Aden. *He causes the King of that place to be hang'd on his Mast, and makes himself Master of the City. A Description of* Daman, Dabul *and* Visiapour.

De Castro *sends* Acunia *to* Diu.

DE *Castro* Viceroy of *Goa* had no sooner receiv'd the unwelcome News of the Death of his Son, and the distressed Condition of *Diu*, but he sent at the beginning of the Spring *Alvares de Acunia* with five Men of War and 400 Land-Men thither, with strict Orders that they should keep within their Fortifications till the whole Fleet with the intended Succours should arrive there. *Alvares* in his Passage thither took several *Arabian* Vessels, aboard of which were several Persons of Note belonging to *Sofar*, who, tho they offer'd a great Sum of Mony for their Ransom, were all cut to pieces, and their Heads thrown into the River.

He takes some Arabian *Vessels.*

The Spring being pretty well advanc'd by this time, *De Castro* set sail for *Bazain* with 40 Yachts, having aboard 1400 *Portuguese* Land-Soldiers, and 300 *Canarins*. With these, after having for some time infested the Coast of *Cambaja*, he arriv'd in the *Ilha dos mortos*, whence he sent an Express to *Mascarenhas* with Orders to batter the Enemies Entrenchments near the Sea-side with his Cannon, to facilitate his landing; which being bravely executed by *Mascarenhas*, *De Castro* enter'd the Harbour without much opposition, and soon after landed his Men. *De Castro* being not a little surpriz'd to see the Fort appear more like a heap of Rubbish than a Fortification, the very Ditches being laid level with the ground, he call'd a Council of War to consult of the most proper means to put an end to the Siege: Some were of opinion, that some time ought to be allow'd to the Soldiers to refresh themselves after the Fatigues of the Sea; but *De Castro* telling them, that it would be a great disgrace for a *Portuguese* Viceroy to be lock'd up in a Fort, it was resolved to attack the Enemy next day.

De Castro *relieves* Diu *in Person.*

Accordingly they march'd out in good order, *De Castro* ordering the Draw-bridges to be drawn up, to cut off all hopes of retreating into the Fort, and leaving *Anthonio Correa* with some Men to guard it against any sudden Attempt. The better to distract the Enemy's Forces, *Nicolao Gonsalvo* was commanded to make a false Attack with some Ships on the backside of the Island. *Rumecan* on the other hand, trusting to his Number, took care to guard his Posts on all sides, against which *De Castro* marched with a much lesser Force, exhorting his Soldiers in a few words: *That they ought to remember that they serv'd a King, who never fail'd to reward such of his Soldiers as fought bravely for God's Cause, and the Defence of his Territories in the* Indies, *the Preservation whereof depended on this Battel; that therefore they should fight like Men, and consider that all their Safety lay in their hands, all hopes of retreating being cut off by the shutting up of the Gates of the Fort, and the removal of the Fleet to the backside of the Isle.*

The Portugueses *make a general Sally.*

De Castro's *Speech to his Soldiers.*

Things being thus dispos'd, *Gonsalvo* made his false Attack on the other side of the Island, which so alarum'd the *Indians*, that they hastned in whole Troops thither, which gave opportunity to the *Portugueses* (who were about 3000 strong) animated by the Example of *De Castro* and *Mascarenhas* their Leaders, to break in upon the *Indians* with such fury, that they were not able to resist them. *Rumecan* finding his Forces to give way, and imagining that the Fort was left destitute of Men to defend it, assaulted the same full of despair; but being repulsed by *Correa*, was forced to follow the rest, and being closely pursued by the *Portugueses*, quitted the Isle, and with the Remnants of his Forces passed over to the Continent. The *Portugueses* enter'd the City, where they kill'd all they met with, without any regard to Age or Sex, where they got an incredible Booty, and among other things the Standard of *Cambaja*, a prodigious quantity of Arms, and 35 Brass Cannon, one whereof being of an extraordinary size, is kept to this day in the Arsenal at *Lisbon*, with certain *Arabick* Characters upon it. The *Portugueses* lost not above 60 Men in this Action, whereas of the *Indians* were kill'd no less than 4000, and 600 taken Prisoners; *Rumecan* himself lost his Life as he was preparing to pass over to the Continent.

He routs the Indians.

Rumecan *slain.*

Baldæus. tinent. *De Castro* after having given the King of *Portugal* an account in his Letter of this glorious Victory, and the Bravery of his Officers and Soldiers, gave Orders for the repairing the Fortifications of the Fort, and return'd triumphant to *Goa*, where he was receiv'd with the general Acclamations of the People.

Castagnedo gives a somewhat different Relation of this Action; for he tells us that *Rumecan* wanted neither Bravery nor Conduct, and that he put the *Portugueses* so hard to it, that had it not been for *Mascarenhas*, who led in Person the Soldiers to the Charge, the *Portugueses* would in all likelihood have lost the day. He says further, that they had 150 Men kill'd, and among them divers brave Officers, *George de Souse*, *John Manoel*, *Francisco Azevedo*, *Cosmo de Paiva*, *Balthasar George*, *Eduardo Rodrigo*, *Juliano Ferdinando*, *Vasque Ferdinando*, and others; that the *Indians* loss amounted to 3000 Men, and that the whole Siege of *Diu* consumed the *Portugueses* at least 2000 Men.

Solyman's *Treachery with the King of* Aden.

We told you before, that *Solyman* did come with his Fleet before *Diu*, from *Aden*; about 20 Leagues thence coming to an Anchor to take in fresh Water, he sent certain Deputies with a Letter to the King of *Aden*, with the usual Present of a Brocado'd Vest of Tissue of Gold, offering him his Friendship, and requiring him in the *Grand Signior*'s Name to furnish his Fleet with Flesh and Fuel, if he could not assist in Person in the Expedition he was going upon, to extirpate the *Portugueses* (declar'd Enemies of the *Mahometans*) out of the *Indies*. The King of *Aden* was at that time a Tributary to the *Portugueses*, unto whom he paid yearly 10000 Ducats Tribute, notwithstanding which he gave a very honourable Entertainment to the Messengers, promising to furnish them with what Necessaries they wanted. About seven days after the whole *Turkish* Fleet entring the Harbour of *Aden*, was receiv'd with singular Demonstrations of Joy, the King sending one of his chief Courtiers aboard to congratulate *Solyman* upon his arrival, and to invite him ashore. *Solyman* return'd for Answer, That he should be glad to imbrace the King's kind Offers, but that the late Fatigues of the Sea had put him into such a disorder, that he could not stir at present; but as soon as he should be recover'd of his present Indisposition, he would not fail to pay his Respects to the King.

The King's Messengers were no sooner return'd to the City, but *Solyman* sent 300 Men after them, under pretence of refreshing themselves, and taking a view of the place (being all chosen Men) and the better to cover his Treachery, he sent word to the King, that to prevent any Disorders, he would send 100 Men the next day to bring them aboard again. The King of *Aden* was so credulous as to assign these 300 Men their Quarters in his Castle, which *Solyman* had no sooner notice of, but he sent the next day instead of the 100 Men, no less than 2000 *Janizaries*, to the no small Astonishment of the King, who now beginning to mistrust the matter, did not know what course best to take; but whilst he was considering what measures to take, News was brought, that a much stronger Body of *Turks* was advanting into the City, who had no sooner posted themselves near the Castle, but the Commander in chief told the King with a smile, that he would be pleased to give a Visit with two or three of his Courtiers to *Solyman*, who was indisposed aboard his Vessels. The King now began plainly to see the danger that threatned him, but not being in a condition to make any opposition, he was forced to submit; and being brought before *Solyman*, he as'd them with an unparallel'd Magnanimity, Under what colour he could presume to take in Custody a Prince in Amity with the Grand Signior, and to treat him no otherwise than as a Criminal? Unto which *Solyman* reply'd, *And are you not asham'd to let the Admiral of the Grand Signior stay three days in your Harbour without paying him a Visit?* The King return'd, *Had the Grand Signior been here in Person, I ought to have done no more than what I have done, and I am sure I should not have been treated thus. 'Tis true, I am now in your power, which I might have prevented had I not trusted my self and my Kingdom with those who now are going to betray both; without which* Aden *need not have stood in fear of your Strength: I am now, tho too late, sensible of my approaching Destiny, seeing my self in the hands of a treacherous Tyrant; but tho you may dispose of my Body, I hope the Bravery of the Inhabitants of* Aden, *and the Grandure of their Princes will outlast your barbarous Cruelties.* He had no sooner ended his Speech, but *Solyman* order'd him to be hang'd on the Main-mast Yard, with four of his chief Courtiers, and afterwards seized upon the City, excusing his Treachery with the Grand Signior's

The King of Aden *forc'd aboard the* Turkish *Fleet.*

The King of Aden *hang'd.*

Baldæus.

The King of Aden hang'd aboard Soliman Bassus Galley.

Signior's Order, to punish the King for his being a Friend to the *Portugueses*.

Diu being one of the chiefest places of the *Indies*, we thought it would not be unacceptable to the Reader to insert the entire History thereof here. We will now proceed to the Description of the other places: *Daman* was one of the most antient and noted Places of the Kingdom of *Cambaja*, which, as we told you before, was taken and destroy'd by *Martino Alphonso de Soza*. As to *Chaul* and *Bazain*, there is scarce any thing remarkable to be said of them, except what has already been mention'd in the account of *Diu*.

Daman.

Chaul. Bazain.

A Description of Dabul.

Dabul is a City seated at 17 deg. 45 min. of Northern Latitude upon a most pleasant River, arising out of the Mountain *Ballaguatte*, about two Leagues from the Sea, in former times much frequented by Foreign Merchants, and famous for its Traffick and Riches. *Sabajus* (a declar'd Enemy of the *Portugueses*) had surrounded this City with a Wall, and fortified the Harbour thereof with a strong Castle, which being garison'd with 6000 Men, (among whom were 500 *Turks*) he thought himself secure against any Attempts of the *Portugueses*.

But *D'Almeyda* the *Portuguese* Admiral, appearing with his Fleet (aboard whereof were 1300 *European* Land Souldiers, besides 400 *Malabars*) sent some of his Gallies to make a false Attack upon the Castle, whilst he took this opportunity of landing his Men at some distance from thence. The *Indians* perceiving their Error, march'd with all possible speed out of their Gates against the *Portugueses*, whom they gall'd sorely with their Arrows; but these advancing with Sword in hand against their Enemies, made such a havock among them, that they were glad to retreat towards the City, and being closely pursued by the *Portugueses*, these enter'd pell mell with them, and made a great slaughter, killing all they met with, without sparing Men, Women or Children. They got here a considerable Booty, tho a great part of the best Moveables were burnt with the City, which was set on fire by the *Portugueses*.

Is taken by the Portugueses.

We have hitherto given you an account of the most considerable Cities of the Kingdom of *Decan*, bordering to the

Limits of the Kingdom of Decan.

Baldæus. the South upon *Malabar*, upon *Bisnagar* to the East, upon the Sea to the West, and upon *Cambaja* to the North; it's divided into three parts, *viz.* into *Cuncan*, *Canara* and *Ballaguatte*, the last of which is a ridg of high Mountains flat on the top, with most excellent Pastures, extending even beyond *Goa*. The next in order is the Kingdom of *Visiapour*, the length whereof is no less than 250 Leagues, and its breadth 150. Its Capital City, which bears the same Name, lies 70 Leagues beyond *Goa*, 80 from *Dabul*, and is said to be five Leagues in Compass, with very strong Walls, and five noble Gates, on which are mounted above a thousand Brass and Iron pieces of great Cannon; they tell us, that among these there is one carrying no less than 540 Pound weight of Gunpowder, cast by a certain *Italian*, a Native of *Rome*, who being question'd by one of the King's Commissioners concerning the Mony he had disbursed upon this account, threw him into the same hole where he had cast the Cannon before. Some have reckon'd this City, but erroneously, among the Cities of *Cambaja*. The King of *Visiapour* was formerly absolute Sovereign of this Kingdom, but after a long and heavy War was forced with divers other Princes in those parts, to become a Vassal to the *Great Mogul*: He used also sometimes to be embroil'd with the *Portugueses*.

The Kingdom of Visiapour.

The King of Visiapour now a Vassal of the Great Mogul.

This Kingdom borders to the South of *Wingurla* upon the River *Mirsee*, the Boundary of the Country of *Carnatica*, in the Territory of *Sivipaneyk*. To the North of *Wingurla* lies the Sea-port of *Danno*, the Boundary of the Kingdom of *Visiapour* on the side of the Empire of the *Great Mogul*, about 10 Leagues from *Daman*. The River here has $4\frac{1}{2}$ fathom Water at high Tide, and $1\frac{1}{2}$ fathom at low Water. The second River is named *Terrapour*, having at low Water half a fathom, and with high Tide two fathoms depth. The third call'd *Chunam*, has generally two fathoms. The fourth call'd *Machyn*, has $2\frac{1}{2}$ fathom at high Water, and half a fathom at low Tide. The fifth Harbour is call'd *Quelleny*; the sixth *Bazain*; the seventh *Bombain*, (*Bombay*) where the depth is six fathom at high, and four at low Water: The eighth is call'd *Siouwel*, where at high Water there is six fathom deep. All these Rivers belong to the Kingdom of *Visiapour*, but are for the most part in the possession of the *Portugueses*, who have built their Forts upon them: As for instance, at *Bombain* (*Bombay*) a spacious Harbour (at 18 deg. 50 min. Northern Latit.) where Ships may lie safe at Anchor against all the Winds; here the *Portugueses* have built a very fine Castle, (the Draught whereof you may see in the next Cut) which commands the whole Road, and was in 1662 given in part of a Dowry, together with *Tangier* in the Straits of *Gibraltar*, to the Infanta of *Portugal*, upon her Marriage with *Charles* II. King of *England*; whereby the *English* thought to have got a great Booty from the *Portugueses*, whereas they are in effect Places of no considerable Traffick. The Rivers *Dabul*, *Radiapour* and *Carapatan*, are entirely possess'd by the Natives.

Its Limits.

Bombay.

For the rest, this Kingdom abounds in Saltpeter Works. The Royal Palace lies in the Center of the Capital City, defended by a double Wall and Ditch, with 100 battering Pieces, and a Garison of 2000 Men; the richest Merchants dwell in the Suburbs. The other Cities of note of this Kingdom are *Cintapour*, a Seaport Town, *Razapour*, *Banda*, *Rajebaag*, Inland Cities; *Arec*, *Mirdsy*, *Asta*, *Tamba* and *Wingurla*, where the *Hollanders* have a stately Factory; it is seated at 15 deg. 7 min. of Northern Latit. a place very considerable, not only for its plenty in Wheat, Rice, and all sorts of Provisions and Refreshments, but also for its situation near *Goa*, which stood the *Dutch* in no small stead, whilst they were engag'd in War with the *Portugueses*, and had block'd up that Harbour. The Forces of the King of *Visiapour* consists in 150000 Horse, and 8000 Foot, of which more anon in the Description of *Negapatan*. We will in the next place proceed to the Description of *Goa*, together with its Origin, and what afterwards happen'd most remarkable in those parts, betwixt our Nation and the *Portugueses*.

The Royal Palace.

Wingurla.

CHAP.

The English Fort of Bombay

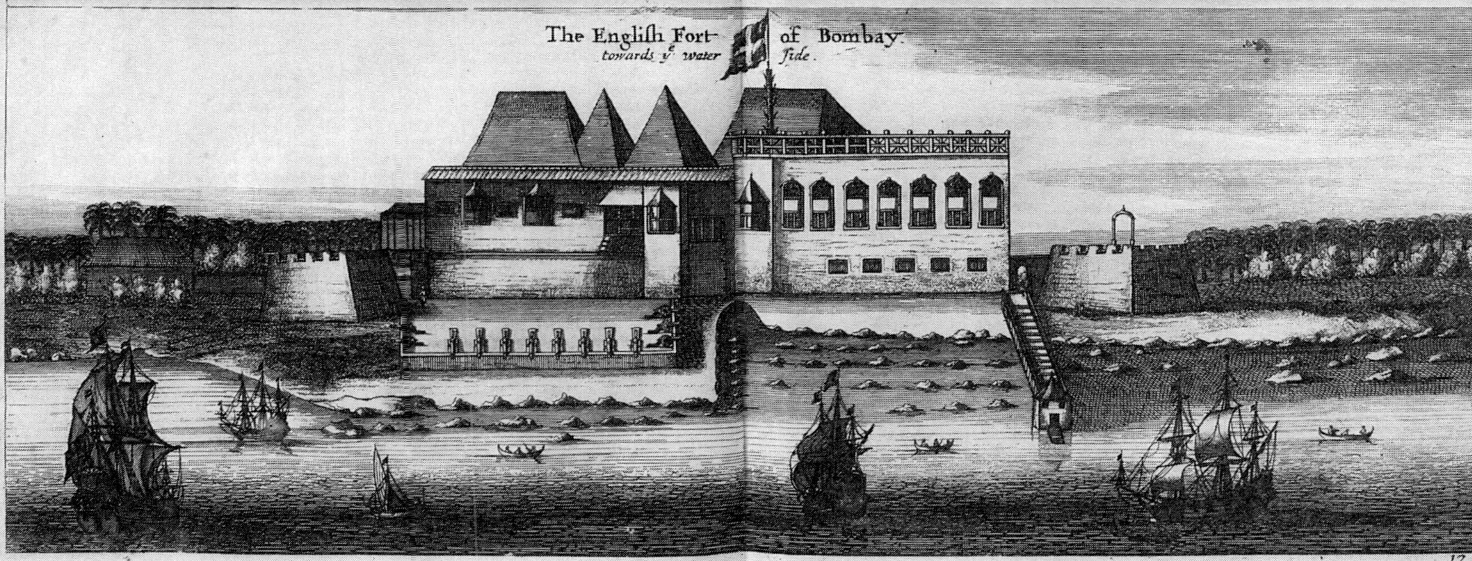

The English Fort of Bombay towards y^e^ water side.

Baldæus.

CHAP. XIII.

Goa taken by Albuquerque. The Death of Sabajus. Hidalcan comes before Goa. Albuquerque takes Goa a second time: Routs the Moors, and establishes Christianity in that City. The Life and Actions of Xaverius in the Indies, China and Japan. His Zeal and Piety.

Goa has a bad Air, and most of its Provisions from the Continent.

THE City of *Goa* is seated in an Isle of a considerable bigness, at 16 deg. of Northern Latit. The Air or Climat is not very wholesom here, so that the *Portugueses* have in this place (as the *Dutch* have at *Batavia*) their great Hospital of the *Indies*, because many of the *Europeans* die here immediately after their arrival, and many more fall sick by reason of the moisture of the Air, as it was formerly at *Batavia*, which has been remedied since in some measure, by draining the Fens thereabouts. *Goa* is the Capital City of the *Portuguese Indies*, the chief Residence of their Viceroy and Archbishop. The City is built after the *Portuguese* manner, each House having its peculiar Garden, as at *Cochin*, and other *Portuguese* Cities in the *Indies*.

Goa taken by Albuquerque.

The famous City of *Goa* was conquer'd for the *Portugueses* by *Albuquerque* in the following manner: One *Timoja* a famous Person in those parts, having possess'd himself of a small Isle belonging to the Kingdom of *Onor*, was a declar'd Enemy of *Sabajus* (of whom before) and the *Mahometans* of *Goa*, who interfering with him in their Commerce, he had destroy'd many of the Ships of the *Egyptians* and *Saracens* trading thither. Thus being link'd in point of Interest to the *Portugueses*, he had declar'd to *Almeyda* his readiness to do what Service he was able to perform to *Emanuel* then King of *Portugal*.

Albuquerque coming into those parts, sent for *Timoja*, to consult with him concerning certain matters of moment relating to those parts, who inform'd him, that *Sabajus* being a declar'd Enemy of the *Portugueses*, had after the taking of *Dabul*, bestow'd vast Sums of Mony in making Preparations against the Christians; but being prevented by Death from putting them in execution, he was succeeded by his Son *Hidalcan*, who being engag'd in a War with the neighbouring Kings, and *Goa* at this time embroil'd with intestine Divisions, which had made most of the Garison desert his Service, he was of opinion, that in case *Albuquerque* would for this time set aside his Expedition against *Ormus*, and attack *Goa*, he might make himself master of that City without much opposition: and to convince him of the sincerity of his Intention, he offer'd to go along with him in Person, and to take his share in all the danger. *Albuquerque* approving of the Counsel of *Timoja*, call'd together a Council of War, in which it being agreed to lay aside the Design upon *Ormus*, and in lieu thereof to attack *Goa*, *Timoja* listed a good number of Soldiers (under pretence that they were to be imploy'd against *Ormus*) and soon after having join'd *Albuquerque* with 14 Ships, they tarried near 11 days in the Isle of *Anchediva*: For some of the *Portugueses* began to question the success of this Enterprize, alledging that there were 4000 Men in Garison in the City, and that it was imprudence to rely too much upon *Timoja*; but *Albuquerque* persisting in his Resolution, set sail from the Isle, and came to an Anchor before the Bar of *Goa*.

Sabajus his Death.

Albuquerque sets sail for Goa.

From hence he detatch'd *Anthony Noronia* his Sister's Son, and *Timoja* with some light Vessels, to make themselves masters of the two Forts that defended the Entrance towards the City; which being done with all imaginable success, he sent his Messengers to *Goa*, to let the Inhabitants know, that if they would submit, they should be treated like Friends, and be discharged of one third part of the Tribute they were oblig'd to pay to *Hidalcan*; but in case of refusal they must expect no Mercy. The Inhabitants of *Goa* seeing themselves reduc'd to this nonplus, in the absence of *Hidalcan*, most of their Soldiers having deserted, and their Forts in the Enemies hands, thought it their wisest course not to abide the extremity, but to accept of the Offers of the *Portugueses*, which they did accordingly, and receiv'd *Albuquerque* with all the Demonstrations of Friendship, who rode triumphantly on Horseback into the City under the Acclamations of the People, a *Dominican* carrying an Ensign with the Cross in it, and another the Keys of the City (surrender'd to him) before him. He was very punctual in performing all the Articles agreed

Two Forts taken.

Goa surrender'd to the Portugueses.

Baldæus. agreed upon betwixt him and the Inhabitants, forbidding the Soldiers under the most severe Penalties, to commit the least Outrages. His next care was, to take a view of the condition of the City, where he found divers goodly Vessels, some lately built, others upon the Stocks; the Arsenal very well provided with Artillery, and the King's Stables with a considerable number of the best *Arabian* Horses. And finding by the situation of the Place, of what consequence it might prove to the *Portugueses* for the future, in carrying on the War upon the Continent of *Cambaja* and the Cape of *Corus*, and to keep the neighbouring Princes in awe, he left no stone unturn'd to provide for its Security.

Thus much for the first Enterprize of the *Portugueses* upon *Goa*. We will now also give you a short account of their further success, how they lost it again by Treachery, and regain'd it a second time the 25*th* of *Novemb.* 1510. where these following Persons signaliz'd themselves to their immortal Honour, *Manuel de Cunha*, *Manuel de Lacerda*, *Don John de Lima*, and his Brother *Don Jeronimo de Lima*, *Denys Fernandes*, *Diego Mendes de Vasconcelos*, with many others.

Lost again by the Portugueses.

For *Hidalcan* had no sooner receiv'd the surprizing News of the loss of *Goa*, but he made a Peace with the neighbouring Princes upon the best Conditions he could, with an intention to bend all his Forces towards the recovery of *Goa*. The better to compass his Design, he sent *Camalcan* his General, a brave Soldier, before with 8000 Foot, and 1500 Horse, to endeavour to pass a certain Branch of the Sea which incloses the Isle, he himself intending to follow with an Army of 5000 Horse, and 40000 Foot, as soon as he had made all the necessary Preparations for such an Enterprize.

Hidalcan *prepares for the recovery of* Goa.

Camalcan having pitch'd his Tents near the Sea-shore, this, together with the News of the approach of *Hidalcan* with a most powerful Army, caus'd no small Consternation in the Island. *Goa* was inhabited at that time by two sorts of People, *viz.* the Mahometans and Pagans; the first out of an irreconcilable hatred to the Christians, cry'd out for *Hidalcan* the Son of *Sabajus*, who was of the same Religion with them; and the Pagans fearing lest they should be severely chastised for their having surrendred the City upon such easy terms, were for purchasing *Hidalcan*'s favour by betraying *Albuquerque*'s Counsels to him. The worst of all was, that many even among the *Portugueses* began to upbraid *Albuquerque* with want of Conduct, who they said, out of Vain-glory only, without the least regard to the Interest of *Portugal*, had with a handful of Men ventur'd upon so desperate an Enterprize as the seizing of so populous a City.

Albuquerque nothing dismay'd at all these Obstacles, endeavour'd to appease the *Portugueses* by fair words and promises, took 100 of the chief Inhabitants into custody, and having intercepted a Letter directed to *Camalcan*, he punish'd the Author thereof with Death, with divers others who were convicted of a Correspondence with the Enemy. But as his chief aim was to dispute their Passage cross the Branch of the Sea, he had erected Batteries provided with Cannon, at convenient distances near the Sea-side, and secur'd all their Boats, by which means he had repulsed them several times in their Attempts. At last taking the advantage of a dark tempestuous night, they brought over both their Horse and Foot, without receiving any considerable damage from the *Portugueses*. Thus approaching to the City in Battel-array, most of the Inhabitants join'd with them, which oblig'd the *Portugueses* to retreat thither, tho without any great prospect of Security.

Albuquerque *endeavours to hinder their Passage into the Isle.*

Camalcan *passes into the Isle.*

Camalcan summon'd *Albuquerque* to a surrender under certain Conditions; but tho he was sensible of the approaching danger, and the difficulty there would be of receiving any Relief in the Winter-season from *May* till *September*, when the frequent Storms render the Seas thereabouts unnavigable, and choak up the Entrance of the Harbour of *Goa*, yet was he resolv'd to expect the arrival of *Hidalcan*, and to abide the utmost Extremities rather than to surrender the place, resolving if all fail'd to pass the Winter in his Ships in the Harbour in spite of the Enemy. *Camalcan*, astonish'd at the Resolution of the *Portugueses*, made several fierce Attacks upon them, but in vain, till at last *Hidalcan* appearing with all his Forces, he resolv'd to cut of all manner of Provisions from the *Portugueses*, by which means he did not question to become Masters of the Place without Bloodshed.

He resolv'd however to send a Herald to *Albuquerque* to offer him honourable Conditions if he would depart; but whilst they were treating upon that Head, he found means to have a Ship loaden with Ballast sunk below the City, where the Branch of the Sea is pretty narrow, and the Channel

Channel very ſtrait, with an intention to have another ſunk hard by it: *Albuquerque* was no ſooner advertiſed thereof, but he call'd a Council of War, in which it was unanimouſly agreed, that they ſhould embark the next night, before they had ſtopt up the whole Channel, that the Enemy might not intercept their Paſſage.

Accordingly they march'd out in the dead time of the night; but having ſet fire to their Magazine, they were diſcover'd and attack'd by the Enemy, ſo that with much ado they got to their Ships, when they weigh'd their Anchors, and with incredible difficulty paſs'd through the narrow Channel at ſome diſtance from the Town: By which however they were not freed from their Miſery or Danger; for by the continual windings of the River they were frequently expoſed to the Enemy's Fire, and being deſtitute of freſh Water, they were forc'd to drink ſalt corrupted Water; what Horſe-fleſh they had left being alſo conſum'd, they were reduc'd to feed upon Mice, Cats and Leather, which occaſion'd a great Mortality among the *Portugueſes*: Add to this, that they were continually annoy'd with the Enemy's Cannon from the two beforemention'd Forts (left by the *Portugueſes* for want of Men) and ſaw no way how to paſs them without a moſt manifeſt hazard.

The Portugueſes in great diſtreſs.

Albuquerque being put to theſe ſtraits, reſolv'd upon a thing which at firſt ſight appear'd rather to be a madneſs than founded upon ſerious Conſiderations: but the Event ſhew'd, that in Extremities the boldeſt and moſt hazardous Undertakings are often the beſt. Both theſe Forts were provided with good Gariſons, but being ſenſible of the Miſery of the *Portugueſes*, they regarded them ſo little, that they ſcarce thought it worth their while to guard their Poſts: *Albuquerque* having receiv'd ſome notice thereof, detatch'd 300 choſen Men, whom he divided into two Troops; theſe being animated with great Promiſes and Revenge, advanced towards the Forts at the ſame time, and finding the Centrys aſleep, kill'd them, and ſo entring the Forts ſoon put the reſt to flight, took poſſeſſion of the Fort, and carried off the Cannon aboard their Veſſels. *Hidalcan* was ſo ſurpriz'd at this bold Enterprize, that not thinking himſelf ſecure in the place where he was, he order'd his Tent to be pitch'd at a greater diſtance.

A hazardous Attempt of the Portugueſes.

The next thing the *Indians* attempted was, to endeavour to ſet fire to the *Portugueſe* Fleet by means of dry Bruſhwood and Faggots dipt in Pitch and Roſin; to prevent which *Albuquerque* man'd out certain Boats to burn them before they could come near enough: This occaſion'd a ſmart Engagement, wherein *Anthony Noronia* (a brave young Gentleman, declar'd Viceroy of the *Indies* after *Albuquerque*) being dangerouſly wounded in the Knee, died a few days after. The Enemy's loſs was alſo very conſiderable; but the Death of *Noronia*, together with the manifold Miſeries, Dangers, and Difficulties they had daily to ſtruggle with, made the *Portugueſes* reſolve to ſail to the Iſle of *Anchediva* to ſet aſhore their ſick Men, who ſtood in great need of Refreſhments for their Recovery.

Baldæus.

Anthony Noronia ſlain.

The Portugueſes ſail to Anchediva.

Whilſt *Albuquerque* was here ruminating with himſelf how to recover *Goa*, a Squadron of 10 *Portugueſe* Men of War arriv'd in the *Indies*. Strengthened with this Succour, and having new modell'd his Forces by purging them of ſome mutinous Spirits, he embark'd 1500 Land-Soldiers, and 300 *Malabars* aboard 34 Veſſels; and ſteering his courſe to the Iſle of *Onor*, he concerted new meaſures with *Timoja* for the Recovery of *Goa*: and having engag'd him to liſt as many Forces as poſſibly he could, he ſet ſail immediately towards *Goa* with ſuch an aſtoniſhing Confidence of ſucceſs, that the *Indians* upon his approach deſerted the Forts without firing a Cannon.

Advancing from hence to the City, a bloody Engagement enſued near the Royal Palace, which *Hidalcan*'s Soldiers pretending to defend to the utmoſt extremity, but being routed, the reſt threw down their Arms, ſome precipitating themſelves from the Walls into the Ditch, others ſeeking Refuge, or rather Death, among the Waves, whilſt the reſt diſperſed in the Iſland. This Engagement laſted above ſix hours. Immediately after *Timoja* coming to the Aſſiſtance of the *Portugueſes*, they enter'd the City, where they made a moſt miſerable havock among the *Moors*, whom they were reſolved to extirpate root and branch; 7000 whereof are ſuppoſed to have been ſlain in four days times; the Pagans themſelves being exaſperated at them for having diſpoſſeſs'd them of their Lands, cut many of them to pieces, and among the reſt the Treaſurer of *Hidalcan*, in whoſe Houſe they found a good Booty. Such of the *Mahometans* as were taken Priſoners, *Albuquerque* order'd to be encloſed in a *Turkiſh* Moſque, together with a certain Renegado Chriſtian, who had deſerted to *Goa*, and to ſet it on fire,

Attack Goa a ſecond time.

And take it.

Commit great Cruelties.

Baldæus.

fire, which was executed accordingly.

The next thing *Albuquerque* took care of, was to have Bricks and Lime made for the rebuilding and strengthening of the Fortifications; and (if we may credit the *Portugueses*) as they were digging under the Ruins of some old Walls, they found a Brazen Cross, which (considering no Christians were ever known to have liv'd there before) was look'd upon by them as a miraculous good Omen, presaging the Establishment of the Christian Religion there.

A Cross found in the Ruins of Goa.

Albuquerque having punish'd with Death such of the Inhabitants as had had a hand in the first Mutiny, order'd that the *Portugueses* should marry the young Women of the Country (after they had been baptiz'd) the better to people the City, which from that time began to encrease considerably: *Sequeria* having caused the first Church that was built, with the adjacent Houses and Convent, to be dedicated to S. *Francis*. And in the year 1548. the Church and Convent of *Dominicans* was erected of Brick-work, 12 Fathers of that Order being about that time introduced into the *Indies* by *James Bermudius* a *Castilian*. After the arrival of the Jesuits in those parts (who have also a fine College here) there were in four years time baptiz'd no less than 17290 *Indians*, without reckoning those converted by the *Franciscans* and *Dominicans* before. In the Jesuits Chappel lies intrench'd the Body of *Francis Xaverius*, of which the *Portugueses* relate strange Miracles, as well as of his whole Life; an ample relation whereof may be seen in *John de Lucena* in *Portuguese*, by *Daniel Bartholi* in *Italian*, and by several others in *Latin*; and in another Treatise of *Bartholi* printed at *Rome* 1653. concerning the Actions of the antient Fathers of the Jesuitical Order. It will be sufficient for us to touch upon some of the chief Heads related by the *Portugueses* of this Saint.

The Church of the Franciscans *and* Dominicans.

Increase of the Christians.

He died in the Isle of *Sanchan* in *China* 1552. the second of *December*, of a violent Fever, in the eleventh year of his Voyage over the *Indies*. His dead Carcase was laid in a Coffin with his Clothes on, fill'd with Lime, with an intention to transport his Bones thence after the Flesh had been consum'd by the quick Lime. Many days after the *Portugueses* opening the Coffin, found his Body not only uncorrupted, but also of a lively Colour, and most agreeable Scent: Thence being transported to *Malacca*, and the Coffin being opened a second time, above three Months after his Decease, they found neither the least signs of Corruption, or any nauseous Stench. After he had been buried here five Months, a certain Jesuit travelling that way from *Goa*, being desirous to see the Body of *Xaverius*, found not only the Body, but also his Clothes uncorrupted, and of a very odoriferous Scent.

The Death of Xaverius.

His Body uncorrupted.

Thus it being judged unseemly that his Body should remain any longer under ground, *Didacus Pereria* caused a magnificent Coffin adorn'd with Gold and Silk to be made, wherein the Body was deposited at *Malacca*, till it could be transported to *Goa*, where it was received with incredible demonstrations of Joy by the Viceroy, all the Persons of note, and especially by the Jesuits, and deposited with a great deal of Ceremony in the Chappel of S. *Paul*. And finding that the People were so eager to touch his Body, that it was to be fear'd they would in time consume it, or carry it away by piece-meals, it was inclosed in an Iron Grate; such being the Zeal of the People of *Goa* at that time, that they would imbrace the Body of *Xaverius* without intermission, lay their Beads upon it, rub it with their Hands, &c. and the whole City rung of the Praises of this Saint, of his uncommon Zeal, Piety, Charity, Mildness, his Dangers in his Voyages, his Chastity, Temperance, Fasts, Prayers, Miracles, Constancy, Prudence, and great Actions for the Honour of Christ.

Is transported to Goa.

The Speech he made upon his departure for *Japan* and *China* to his Friends, who were for disswading him from so dangerous an Undertaking, is so excellent in its kind, that it very well deserves a place in this Treatise.

Xaverius *his Speech.*

"I am surpriz'd to see you who spend "your days in the Praise of God Al- "mighty's Power and Mercy, should "now be so diffident thereof in regard "of my Person. Have you forgot who "is the Supreme Governour of the Uni- "verse, and that every thing is rul'd by "his Will? Can you be destitute of "Instances of this nature? Don't the "Waves of the Sea, who open'd a way "to the Servants of God through the "depth thereof, furnish you with an "undeniable Example? Don't the Winds "who allay'd their fury by his Com- "mand, proclaim his Power? Pray "look upon *Job*, who could not be af- "flicted by the Devil without God's "special Permission. The Mouth of "Truth himself tells you, that the Hairs "of

" of our Heads are number'd. As we " see Ambassadors of Temporal Princes, " relying upon their Characters, and the " Power of their Masters, pass unarm'd " and undisturb'd through an Enemy's " Camp; so it becomes us who bear the " Character of Interpreters of the Di- " vine Law, and of Teachers of the " Heathens, to rely upon nothing but " the Assistance and Power of the Di- " vine Majesty, which without any other " Weapons can carry us safely through " all Dangers both by Sea and Land, " through Fire and Sword, or what else " may seem to oppose the accomplish- " ment of his Will. And if it happen " that some of his faithful Ministers fall " into the hands of cruel Persons, if they " are devour'd by wild Beasts, suffer " Shipwracks, or are exposed to Hunger, " Thirst, Cold, Heat, Sicknesses, and " other Miseries, all these are to be " look'd upon as the Effects of the Di- " vine Pleasure, to try the Faith and " Constancy of his Servants: For were " it not so, we are sufficiently convinc'd " by many Examples, in what manner " our God has a careful Eye over them; " how he has sent the Ravens to feed " them, the Angels to feed them, how " the wildest Beasts have deposited " their natural Fury and become mild, " how the Flame it self has not been " able to hurt them, nor the greatest " Tyrants to execute their Cruelties " upon them. 'Tis true, the Victory " does not always incline on our side, " and we are often frustrated in the ex- " pectation of the fruits of our Labour; " but those Disappointments ought not " in the least stop the hand of a zealous " Minister, in attempting every thing " that may conduce to God's Honour, " and the Salvation of Souls. If a Sol- " dier in hopes of a small share of Ho- " nour, ventures his Life in the midst of " his Enemies; if the Seaman for the " hopes of an inconsiderable Lucre, leave " the shore, and commit his Life to the " merciless Waves, would it not be a " shame for a Minister of Christ to re- " fuse to hazard his Life for God's Ser- " vice, and to look upon every thing as " a trifle in comparison of the Kingdom " of Heaven, and its Increase? Let no " such thoughts enter our Minds, there " being nothing so precious, that ought " in this regard to hinder us from the " promoting of God's Service. *Baldæus.*

A most excellent Speech, worthy to be imprinted in the Hearts of all faithful Ministers of Christ, and the more valuable upon that score, that his Deeds were altogether agreeable to his Words: For embarking at *Goa* for *Malacca*, he thence set sail in a *Chinese Joncke* or Vessel for *Japan*, where he arriv'd happily at *Cangoxima*, where this great Man did not think it below himself to be instructed in the first Rudiments of that Language for Christ's sake. The next thing he applies himself to was, to have the chief Articles of the Christian Faith translated into the *Japonese* Language, making use for this purpose of an Interpreter, till he attain'd himself to the Perfection thereof, in which he ceased not to labour day and night; being mov'd by an uncontroulable Zeal of planting the Gospel among these Pagans. Truly a very commendable Zeal, not to be forgotten by all who bear the Name of Christians; and tho *Xaverius* his Religion differs in certain Points from ours, yet might his Piety and other commendable Virtues serve as an Encouragement to all pious Ministers, to follow his Footsteps in performing the Service of God to the utmost of their Power. It must be confess'd on all hands, that had not the active Spirit of the Jesuits awaken'd the *Franciscans*, and other Religious Orders from their Drousiness, the *Roman* Church had before this time been buried in its Ruins: And as for my self, I am very willing to own, that my Pen is not capable of expressing the worth of so great a Man; tho at the same time I am of opinion, that if *Xaverius* were alive now, he would disown many things, especially as to his Miracles, since publish'd by his Followers.

CHAP.

Baldæus.

CHAP. XIV.

Increase of the City of Goa. *Its Traffick, Manners, and way of living of the* Portugueses *there. The War betwixt the* Dutch *Company and the* Portugueses. *Their Ambassadors appear in the Great Council at* Batavia; *their Propositions and Transactions.*

THE City of *Goa* increasing every year in Riches and Traffick, increased also in Strength by the addition of several Forts near the Water-side; this being the Capital City of the *Portugueses* in the *Indies.* Its Traffick was much more considerable formerly than of late years, since by our blocking up the Bar of *Goa* they were not a little disturb'd by our Ships. Whilst *Goa* was in its flourishing State, they used to send their Ships to *Pegu, Siam, Japan, Persia, Cambaja, Arabia, Malabar, Coromandel, Bengale, Achem,* besides divers other places. It's well inhabited not only by *Europeans,* but also *Canarins, Moors,* and *Pagans* of all Nations, who live for the most part upon trading, or are Handicrafts Men. The great Street of *Goa* has many rich Shops well-stor'd with Silks, Porcellain, and other precious Commodities, Drugstery Wares, Manufactories, *&c.* Some of these as well as fresh Provisions are sold every day in the Market-places, where you hear a Crier, or Auctioneer (call'd by them *Lalang*) to sell in publick all sorts of Goods, both movable and unmovable, Cattle, Slaves, *&c.* to the fairest Bidder; but they leave off early, by reason of the excessive Heat about mid-day.

Increase and Traffick of Goa.

Inhabitants.

The manner of living of the *Portugueses* is the same here as in most other places of the *Indies*; they are distinguish'd into *Cazados, i. e.* married People, and *Zoldados,* single People; the last are most esteem'd. The *Portugueses* here are generally very idle, seldom applying themselves to any Employment, leaving the management of their business for the most part to their Slaves, even the Women committing the care of their Children to the Female Slaves, who also give them suck. The Men frequently marry with the Natives of the Country, yet not so much now as formerly: The Children begot betwixt a *Portuguese* and an *Indian* Woman are call'd *Mistices,* as the Children of these *Mistices* are call'd *Castices.*

The way of living of the Portugueses.

The Men are generally addicted to excessive Lust; and I remember to have seen three Women Slaves lie in at once, who were got with Child by their Masters; Fornication and Adultery being consider'd among them as Errors of little moment: but they are very averse to Drunkenness, notwithstanding which Quarrels and Murders are frequent among them.

The Men are also generally excessive proud, there being scarce any of them that thinks himself remov'd a little above the vulgar sort, but what has his Umbrello carried over his Head, another Servant to carry his Cloke after him, and another who holds his Sword: They use frequently Snuff, not excepting even the Maidens and Women; and as they walk along the Streets, they are continually stroking and setting up their Whiskers. The Women never appear abroad either a foot or in Chairs unveil'd, their Husbands being (and perhaps not without reason) very jealous of them; for which reason also they keep them at home in their Apartments above stairs, the Windows whereof are so contriv'd, that they can look upwards, but not downwards into the Streets.

Their Lust and Pride.

Their Jealousy.

The Distempers most in vogue at *Goa* are the burning Fevers, which the *Portugueses* cure by Venesection, sometimes five or six times aday, but they let but little at a time. The *French* or *Spanish* Pox are also so common here (as in most other parts of the *Indies*) that a *Fidalgo* or Gentleman here does not look upon it as a disgrace to have been afflicted with it twice or thrice in his life-time. For the rest, the *Portugueses* use much Sweetmeats, and take a Draught of cool Water after it, they being Enemies to strong Liquors, and moderate in their Diet, a small share sufficing for a good number of People. The Women feed much upon Rice, tho they have excellent Wheaten Bread; they also use frequently *Betel* and *Areek,* and all sorts of Pickles, which makes them have a pale Colour.

Distempers.

The King of *Visiapour* has more than once shewn his Inclination of attacking *Goa* by Land, especially at that time whilst *Cornelius Simonsz* commanded the *Dutch*

The King of Visiapour *willing to attack* Goa.

Dutch Fleet in thoſe parts, he being much reſpected among the *Mahometans* ever ſince his burning of the Galleons near *Mormagon:* But the Death of the ſaid Admiral prevented the deſign of that King, as much queſtioning whether his Succeſſor might be a Man of the ſame ſtamp. In the year 1641. the ſaid King promiſed a ſecond time to form the Siege of *Goa*, provided the *Dutch* Company would engage to let a certain number of their Ships winter at *Dabul*, *Ortzery*, or ſome other of his Majeſty's Harbours, which was no more than a neceſſary Precaution; it being certain, that in caſe the Siege ſhould miſcarry, the *Portugueſes* without our Aſſiſtance would have made themſelves Maſters of theſe Harbours. Formerly it was accounted dangerous to ſend our Ships to the Bar of *Goa* before *October*; but Experience has taught us ſince, that this Coaſt of the *Indies* is navigable towards the latter end of *Auguſt*, or in *September*, the exact time when the rich Ships come from *Moſambique*, *Maſcatte*, and divers other places, which have ſometimes been taken by our Ships; whereas if they come later, they have nothing elſe to do but to attempt the Galleons under the Caſtle. In the year 1640. the *Portugueſes* made ſhift to bring into the Harbour two *Caracks*, and as many Galleons, well provided with Men, and all other Neceſſaries, which gave them the opportunity to fortify the Iſle of *Mormagon*; ſince which time, to render the Blockade by Sea the more effectual, the *Hollanders* have order'd certain Frigots to cruiſe with a Sloop near the Cape and the *Burned Iſlands* (call'd *Ilhas quimadas*) whereby the *Portugueſe Caffilas*, which ſupply them with Proviſions, are prevented from going out or in.

How Goa *is to be block'd up by Sea.*

The Dutch *care not to be Maſters of* Goa.

It is ſufficiently demonſtrable, that the *Dutch* Company did at firſt judg it for their intereſt to be Maſters of *Goa*, but laid it aſide afterwards, thinking it more for their intereſt to block up the Bar of *Goa:* Certain it is, that both the Directors and the Governor and Members of the Great Council of the *Indies*, look'd upon the War betwixt them and *Portugal* as propitious to them, as is evident from the Petition deliver'd in *May* 1641. by the ſaid Directors in the *Hague* to the States General of the *United Provinces*.

The War betwixt the Dutch *and* Portugueſes *propitious to the firſt.*

The chief intent of this Petition was, to ſhew, That tho it was beyond all queſtion that the *Dutch Eaſt-India* Company was erected in its firſt beginning in the years 1601, 1602, and 1604. to carry on a peaceable Commerce in the *Indies*; but that ſince Experience had ſufficiently convinc'd them, that the *Portugueſes*, who had play'd the Maſters in the *Indies* for many years before, had left no ſtone unturn'd to diſturb the Commerce of the *Dutch*, by ſeizing their Ships, and imprinting very diſadvantageous Notions of them into the *Indian* Princes. That in 1602. when the *Dutch Eaſt-India* Trade was incorporated into one Society or Company, two peculiar Advantages were (among others) obtain'd thereby at that time: Firſt, Full Authority of protecting their Traffick jointly in the *Indies* by force of Arms: The Conſequence whereof had been, ſecondly, That the *Indian* Princes were enter'd into an Engagement with the ſaid *Dutch* Company, out of hatred and fear of the *Portugueſes*; that by theſe means the Ships of the *Dutch* Company having purged the Seas of the Pirats, had ſettled ſince the year 1604. their Factories and Traffick, not only in all the Iſlands from the Red Sea as far as *Japan*, but alſo in the Territories of the Grand Signior, in *Arabia*, at *Mocha*, in *Perſia*, even in the Capital City of *Iſpahan*, in the Kingdom of *Cambaja*, and the Empire of the Great *Mogul*, in *Decan*, in *Malabar*, *Narſinga*, *Coromandel*, *Golgonda*, *Bengale*, *Aracan*, *Pegu*, *Achin*, *Sumatra*, *Jambi*, *Palimban*, *Bantam*, *Cambodia*, *Siam*, *Cochin-China*, *Tonquin*, &c. That ſince the Eſtabliſhment of theſe Factories, the ſecurity of their Commerce was chiefly founded upon this Maxim, to maintain a War againſt the declar'd Enemy of theſe *Indian* Princes, their Engagements to us being founded upon their opinion of our Enmity with the *Portugueſes*. To prove this they alledg the following ten Reaſons.

Baldæus.

Factories of the Dutch *in the* Indies.

Ten Reaſons for the continuance of a War with the Portugueſes.

1. Becauſe the *Dutch Eaſt-India* Company was chiefly by means of the War with the *Portugueſes* arriv'd to that Greatneſs it is now at, their whole Traffick in the *Indies* being founded upon this Baſis, whence they draw yearly a return of 78910 Millions of Gelders; and if the ſaid Foundation were not ſhaken, they might expect every year larger Returns.

2. That in caſe of a Truce they ſhould not reap the fruits of the Victories, *viz.* to put a ſtop to their Power, a thing abſolutely to be conſider'd.

3. In caſe of a Truce the Equipment of many Ships of War would be laid aſide, by which means *Holland* would be depriv'd of the Strength of a conſiderable number of Men of War in caſe of neceſſity.

Baldæus.

4. That in case of an abatement of the Equipment of Ships of War for the *East-Indies*, and consequently of the diminution of our Trade in the *Indies*, and the return of our Ships from thence, the advantage accruing to *Holland* by the Convoys must also be necessarily diminish'd.

5. That many thousands of Families in the *Indies* would thereby be depriv'd of their livelihood.

6. That the whole *East-India* Trade, by which many Millions are gain'd yearly, would decay in proportion as the *Portugueses* should increase in the said Traffick.

7. That in regard of the Interest of the *Dutch* Company it ought to be consider'd, that since of late years they had been at vast Expences in providing Ships of War, and listing of Soldiers, they were (through God's Blessing) in a probability of making further Conquests upon the *Portugueses*.

8. That in case the *East-India* Trade should come to decay, and consequently their Profit be diminish'd, they would be in danger of being quite oppress'd by the heavy burden they lay under of providing Garisons and other Necessaries against the Attempts of the *Europeans* their Enemies.

9. That thereby the *Dutch* Company would be expos'd to the hazard of being depriv'd of all the advantages they had gain'd by right of Arms from the *Portugueses*, or otherwise.

10. In case of a Peace or Cessation of Arms betwixt the *Dutch* Company and the *Portugueses*, it was to be fear'd, that the good understanding betwixt the said Company and the *Indian* Princes, would soon decay, to the no small detriment and danger of the Company and their Servants, especially in *Japan*: which Traffick if it were lost, the Trade of *China* would be of little consequence; a Peace or Truce with the *Portugueses* being absolutely contrary to the Engagements they had with the *Indian* Kings.

In consideration therefore of the great detriment that would accrue to the said Company by a Peace with the *Portugueses*, the said Directors did most humbly petition their High and Mightinesses to take it into serious Consideration, whether the Damages their Subjects, and especially the Company, were likely to suffer thereby, would not in a great measure overballance the Advantages the States might promise themselves from a Peace with *Portugal*; and in case they judged the Peace with *Portugal* absolutely for their Interest, whether the *East-Indies* might not be excepted in the said Peace, as was done in the Truce concluded 1609. and whereof other Instances were in fresh memory betwixt *France*, *England* and *Spain*, who notwithstanding they were enter'd into Alliances since the Conclusion of the Peace in *Europe*, yet did continue the War in the *Indies*, as is evident from the *English* Squadrons appearing before *Mosambique*, *Goa* and *Maniba*, and the assisting of the *Persians* in the Conquest of *Ormus* against the *Portugueses*.

Lastly, They requested, that in case their High and Mightinesses did not judg their Reasons of such weight as to stop the Truce in the *East-Indies*, betwixt the Company and the *Portugueses*, who lately have shaken off the *Spanish* Dominion, and imbrac'd the Interest of K. *John* IV. their High and Mightinesses would be pleased at least to delay the Conclusion thereof till Advice could be had whether any of the Places belonging to the *Portugueses* in the *Indies* had declar'd for the new King, that the Directors might have the opportunity (in case of an ensuing Truce) to recal such of their Servants as were perhaps engag'd in the Service of some of the *Indian* Princes, without which they might be in danger of being surpriz'd and seiz'd there, to their irrecoverable Detriment.

Goa block'd up by the Dutch.

The Bar of *Goa* had for a considerable time been kept block'd up by a Squadron of *Dutch* Ships, the better to annoy the *Portugueses* in their Traffick. *James Cooper* kept the said Harbour block'd up for three years successively, as Commodore, who was succeeded by *Adam Westerwold* (of which hereafter in the Description of *Ceylon*) and he by *Anthony Kaan*. In the year 1639. commanded before that place *Cornelius Simonson Van der Veer* (mention'd before) a brave Commander; and 1641. *Matthew Hendriksz Quast* with 10 Ships, and 1147 Men: This Fleet took a *Carack* richly laden from *Portugal*; but he being kill'd in the Engagement, was succeeded by *Cornelius Leendertsz Blaau*, Reer Admiral.

Two Portuguese Ambassadors come to Batavia.

In the year 1642. two *Portuguese* Ambassadors, nam'd *Diego Mendes de Britto*, and *Gonsalvo Villoso de Sanct Joseph*, a Religious of the Order of S. *Francis*, being sent by the *Portuguese* Viceroy of the *Indies* to the General and Great Council of the *Indies* at *Batavia*. The same were order'd to be receiv'd with all marks of Honour and Respect: For which purpose Mr. *John Maatzuyker*, chief Pensionary,

*

Justus

Justus Schouten, a Member of the Great Council of the *Indies*, *Simon van Alphen*, Doctor of the Laws, Sheriff of the City of *Batavia*, *Sebald Wanderaar*, Receiver-General, *Peter Soury*, *Barent Wichmans*, *Dirk Snoek*, *Ewoud Spieringh*, head Factors, *John Lamoot*, Serjeant-Major, *Gerard Herbers*, Doctor of the Laws, head Factor, *Francisco de Souza de Castro*, and *Anthonio Fialho Fereira*, both *Portuguese* Gentlemen, were sent to conduct them from aboard their Vessel to the General's Palace, under the discharge of five pieces of Cannon; and being immediately introduc'd into the Apartment where the Great Council was then assembled, after the first Compliments on both sides, one of the Ambassadors began to make his Harangue: "That *Portugal* having withdrawn it self from the *Spanish* Jurisdiction, had chosen *Don John* Duke of *Braganza* their King; that the said King having soon after sent an Ambassador to their High and Mightinesses to treat of a Peace and an Alliance betwixt both Nations, they had all the reason to believe that the same was brought to a happy Conclusion before this time: In regard of which they were sent by the Viceroy of *Goa*, to treat with their Excellencies about a Cessation of Arms, as would more at large appear out of their Credentials, which they deliver'd at the same time to the Governor-General with this Superscription:

Their Reception.

Appear in the Council.

A. O. Senhor Anthonio de Diemen, Capitaon General de Nacaon Ollandesa n' este Oriente. On the other side was written, *De Conde d' Aveiras Viceroy e Capitaon d' India.*

The Letter was seal'd with the Arms of *Portugal*, and written in the *Portuguese* Language, as follows.

Their Credentials.

"IN the beginning of *September* arriv'd in our Fort *Onor*, a *Caravel*, sent from *Portugal*, whereby we were inform'd, that the *Portugueses* have proclaim'd and acknowledg'd a King of their own, by the general Consent of that Nation. His Majesty of *Portugal* did in one of his Letters give notice to us, that certain Ambassadors having been dispatch'd to their High and Mightinesses the States General, to treat about a Peace, it was not doubted, but the same would be soon concluded, a Truce having been already agreed upon betwixt the two Nations in *Europe*, whereof notice had been given by the said Majesty to the Commodore *Quast*, intimating, that as a Cessation of Arms was concluded in *Europe*, so the same might take effect in these parts, and that he had given orders to the Viceroy of *Goa* accordingly. After the Decease of the said Commodore, we gave notice thereof to *Cornelius Leendertsz Blaau* his Successor, who excusing himself with his want of Power, as being oblig'd to follow strictly the Orders of the Great Council of the *Indies*, we thought fit to send *Diego Mendes de Britto*, Gentleman of the King's Houshold, and Father *Gonsalvo Villoso*, to treat with your Excellencies concerning this Point; they being provided with Credentials from his Majesty, that whatever shall be agreed upon with them, shall be valid and kept inviolably. We wish all Blessings to the Crown of *Portugal*, and the *United Provinces*. Dated 6 *Decemb.* 1641.

Baldæus.

Subscribed, *Conde d' Aveiras.*

The Great Council having told them, that they would take the matter into serious Consideration, the Discourse began to turn upon indifferent matters, and among the rest concerning the *Caraque*, lately taken by the *Dutch*. The Ambassadors being ask'd whether the Captain did not present the Viceroy with two or three Casks of Wine; they answer'd, No: At which the Governor-General shew'd a great dislike, telling the Ambassadors, that they must pardon the matter, it being a common thing for the best Seamen to make the worst Courtiers. After the Ambassadors had din'd with his Excellency, they were conducted to their Lodgings at Mr. *James Harder*'s House. They were both Persons of a goodly Aspect, the *Franciscan* being betwixt 60 and 70 years of Age, the other of about 50. Their Train consisted in two Pages, and four *Portuguese* Footmen, besides the *Negroes* and *Mistices*, a Gentleman, a Secretary, Surgeon, and two Boys; their Livery was Orange Colour.

Their Age and Train.

The 8th of *February* the said Ambassadors demanded a second Audience, which being for weighty Reasons defer'd till the 10th, they appear'd a second time at Nine a Clock in the Morning in the Great Council, reiterating their former Propositions concerning a Cessation of Arms: And lest the Governor-General might not as yet have receiv'd a full account of what had been transacted in *Europe*, they produc'd certain Original Letters,

Their Second Audience.

Baldæus. Letters, sent by his *Portuguese* Majesty to the Viceroy; but these being only private Letters from certain *Dutch* Merchants living at *Lisbon*, and another Letter from the States-General to the Admiralty of that place, and consequently the same that were before sent hither from our Squadron at *Goa*, by the way of *Coromandel*, by the Sloop call'd the *Pipeli*: His Excellency the Governor-General reply'd, that the last being sent to the Council before by the Commodore *Quast*, they had perused the same, and found that in the Letter of the States-General, it was expresly said that the *Dutch should not molest the* Portugueses *on the other side of the Line*; which being to be understood of the North-side, the *Indians* were not comprehended therein; besides that they had not receiv'd any Instructions upon that account from the Governors and Directors of the *East-India* Company.

But to convince the Ambassadors that they were not enter'd into this War out of any other motive than to obtain an honourable Peace; they could not but put them in mind, that tho they had deliver'd their Credentials from the Viceroy, they had not brought along with them any positive Proof whether the said Viceroy were authorized by his Majesty of *Portugal* to treat concerning matters of such great consequence; and it was consequently to be doubted whether the same would be approv'd of and ratify'd by his Majesty.

One of the Ambassadors reply'd, that the Viceroy of *India* was always endow'd with a Power of making Peace and War, many Instances of which could be alledg'd upon divers occasions; which would leave no room to question his Authority in this case; but if they did, they were ready to remain as Hostages for the accomplishment of what should be agreed upon. His Excellency the Governour-General return'd, That he was satisfied of the Authority of the Viceroy in making Peace or War with the *Indian* Princes, but remain'd doubtful, whether the same did extend also to the *European* Nations: Neverthelefs, that he believ'd the Viceroy would not transgress his Commission, and that therefore they had been acknowledg'd as Plenipotentiaries; which being done, there remained nothing now to do, but to proceed to the Treaty it self, and to make their Propositions under what Conditions they would have the Truce settled.

The Ambassadors answer'd, that they look'd upon it as unnecessary to insist upon many Conditions or Limitations at this juncture, when they expected every day to hear of a Peace concluded betwixt both Nations in *Europe*, according to the Conditions of which, both Parties would be oblig'd to regulate themselves hereafter: That their only aim now being to obtain a Cessation of Arms, the main thing in question was, to fix a certain time of its beginning, which they thought ought to be taken from that very hour the Truce was agreed upon and sign'd betwixt them.

The Governor-General told them that he agreed with them in that point, that not many Conditions were requir'd at this time, but that it would be next to an impossibility the Truce should commence from the very hour the same was sign'd, it being very probable that the *Dutch* Squadron would in the mean while not let slip any opportunity of taking their advantage over the *Portugueses*; as the Forces lately sent to *Ceylon*, perhaps might have made an Enterprize upon *Negumbo* or *Columbo*; as on the other hand, the *Portugueses* might probably have undertaken something against *Gale*, or have obtain'd some advantages against the *Dutch* in other places: The Viceroy himself having commanded *Don Philippo Mascarenhas*, that he should (till the News of the Truce did arrive) act with his utmost vigor against the *Dutch* in *Zeylon*. He urg'd, that all these things consider'd, it was to be fear'd that in case the Truce commenced according to their desire, this might furnish occasion to new Misunderstandings, it being more than probable that neither of the two Parties would be willing to restore what they had conquer'd in the mean while; that therefore it was his opinion, that the beginning of the said Truce must be so fix'd, as that sufficient time might be allow'd for giving notice thereof to the Subjects of both Parties.

The Ambassadors made many Objections against this, insisting to have the beginning of the Truce settled from the Date of the signing thereof, alledging among the rest, that they could scarce imagine the Viceroy should have sent such Orders to *Mascarenhas*. The Governor-General reply'd, that he had certain advice of it from *Ceylon*, but that notwithstanding this, he hoped the Ambassadors should not leave *Batavia* unsatisfied. He at the same time invited them to dine with him, where they were splendidly entertain'd, and drank to the Health of the King of *Portugal*, and the Prince of *Orange*. The

*

Their third Audience. The 18*th* of *February* the ſaid Ambaſſadors had another Audience, wherein they deſir'd a poſitive Anſwer to their Propoſitions, the time deſir'd by the Governor to conſult with the Great Council being expir'd. They urg'd, that ſince the 14*th* of *February* ſome Yachts were arriv'd, which had brought the Confirmation of the News of the Peace lately concluded betwixt both Nations, therefore they did not queſtion but their Excellencies would no longer deny them the deſir'd Trade.

The Governour-General gave for Anſwer, That the ſaid Yachts had touch'd at *Fernambuco*, from whence they had brought the Articles of a ten years Truce betwixt his *Portugueſe* Majeſty *Don John* IV. and the High and Mighty the States General of the *United Provinces*, in reſpect of their Territories in *Europe*, with Exception however of the Places and Colonies belonging to the *Eaſt* and *Weſt-India* Companies; that they had alſo brought along with them the Articles or Conditions agreed upon betwixt their High and Mightineſſes and *Triſtan de Mendoza* the *Portugueſe* Ambaſſador, concerning the *Weſt-India* Company: whence it appear'd, that the ſame ought to be firſt ratified by his *Portugueſe* Majeſty, and ſent back to the States General; and that the ſame after that ſhould not take effect before notice be given thereof in *Brazil*: and the ſame being agreed upon in reference to the *Eaſt-India* Company, and our Ships which left *Holland* in *September* laſt, being expected every day in theſe parts with the Ratifications of the ſaid Treaty, it was thought convenient by the Great Council to expect their coming, and to regulate themſelves according to the Conditions agreed upon betwixt their reſpective Maſters, eſpecially ſince the ſaid Ships would probably arrive before the ſeaſon would permit the Ambaſſadors to depart for *Goa*, and conſequently there would be no loſs of time in this reſpect.

The Ambaſſadors told them that they could not but think it ſtrange, that ſince both Nations liv'd in Amity in *Europe*, they ſhould act in a hoſtile manner againſt one another in the *Indies*. The Governor-General reply'd, that ſince their reſpective Maſters had thought it convenient it ſhould be ſo, till the Ratification of the Treaty by his *Portugueſe* Majeſty, and that notice had been given thereof to them, they were oblig'd to take their meaſures accordingly. The Ambaſſadors anſwer'd, that they had promiſed themſelves a quite other Anſwer, tho in all other reſpects they acknowledg'd the Honours and obliging Entertainment they had receiv'd, deſiring that a Copy might be given them containing an exact account of all the Tranſactions during their ſtay here, betwixt their Excellencies and them, by which it might appear that they had not been defective in their Zeal and Induſtry to bring this matter to the deſir'd effect. This was promiſed by the Governour-General, with this addition, that to give them all imaginable Satiſfaction concerning the Truce, they would alſo give them a faithful Copy of the Articles thereof, not queſtioning but that the Ships would arrive in the mean while; but if they ſhould happen to ſtay longer, beyond expectation, they would conſult all proper means to give them what ſatisfaction they could. They thankfully receiv'd this Anſwer, extolling once more the obliging Entertainment they had met with at their hands; they din'd with moſt of the Members of the Great Council at the Governour-General's Houſe, and towards the Evening took the Air on Horſe-back. *Baldæus.*

Their fourth Audience. The 30*th* of *March* the ſaid Ambaſſadours had another Audience, in which they deliver'd a Memorial to the Great Council; which being read, the Governour-General told them, that what was alledg'd in the ſaid Memorial was a Matter of Fact, and agreeable to what had been enter'd in their Records; but that they would not have them deſpond concerning the arrival of the Ships, which he was ſorry ſtaid ſo long behind; but that notwithſtanding this, he hoped they ſhould not depart without Satisfaction. The Ambaſſadors reply'd, his Excellency would be pleaſed to remember his Promiſe, of not letting them depart without Satisfaction, or obtaining the end of their Commiſſion, in caſe the Ships ſhould not arrive.

The Governour-General return'd for Anſwer, That by ſaying ſo, he did not intend to conſent to the Truce, which was beyond his Power, at leaſt till the arrival of the ſaid Ships; but to give them all the poſſible marks of his Good-will and Eſteem, and that they ſhould be diſmiſs'd with all the marks of Reſpect they were able to pay them. That ſince his Maſters had thought fit to limit the beginning of the Truce to the time of its being ratified by his Majeſty of *Portugal*, and being return'd into *Holland*, and thence to the *Eaſt-Indies*, they were abſolutely oblig'd to wait for the arrival of it, leſt it ſhould ſeem as if they thought them-

Baldæus. themselves more understanding in this Point than the States-General.

One of the Ambassadors made Answer, That they were perswaded his Excellency the Governour-General, was sufficiently authorized to make Peace and War at his pleasure in these Countries, the same tending to the advantage of the *Dutch* Nation; and that this Cessation of Arms could not but be acceptable to the States-General, who had so lately concluded a Peace with the King of *Portugal*. He further told them, that the Viceroy of *Goa* was always authorized with such a Power, but in a more peculiar manner at this time, having receiv'd express Orders for that purpose by a *Caravel* from his Majesty.

At last the Ambassadors perceiving that the Great Council remain'd stedfast in their Resolution, they thought it unfit to push the matter any further for that time, reiterating their former Request of having a Copy granted them concerning their Transactions here, and desiring that since the Season began to open the Passage by Sea to *Coromondel*, they might be dismiss'd forthwith, in order to prosecute their Journy by Land to *Goa* before the Winter, the same being impracticable afterwards, by reason of the frequent Rains. The Governour-General promis'd them entire Satisfaction upon both these Heads, and that a Ship should be got ready for their Excellencies; but that however he could not forbear to tell them, that in his opinion they would do better to tarry a little longer, in expectation of the before-mentioned Ships, and the Ratification expected to be brought over by them. They reply'd, That having receiv'd express Orders from the Viceroy to return to *Goa* with the first opportunity, they were oblig'd to obey, unless his Excellency would lay his Commands upon them to the contrary. The Governour-General answer'd, That it was not in his power to command them, what he had said being only by way of Advice; but if they were resolv'd to the contrary, they should not be in the least detain'd: That if they thought fit, Advice might be sent thereof to the Viceroy by the Ship that was then just ready to sail for *Coromandel*; or if they disliked this Proposition, one of them might tarry at *Batavia* till the arrival of the Ratification, whilst the other return'd to *Goa*. This Expedient being approv'd by them, it was agreed that the *Franciscan* Father should go back to *Goa* by the way of *Coromandel*, and the other stay at *Batavia*, till the arrival of the Ratification.

Some particular Requests of the Ambassadours.

Then the Ambassadors desir'd the Releasement of certain *Mistices* and *Negroes* that were Prisoners among us; which being soon granted by the Governour-General, he ask'd the same favour in behalf of four other Persons who had been clapt in Irons on occasion of some Mutiny at *Batavia*, in which they were the Ringleaders; which was also granted, under Condition that they should depart the Country with the *Franciscan* Father. They also made the like Request concerning *Francisco de Souza de Castro*, who (at the request of the Governor-General) being releas'd out of his Prison by those of *Achin*, was deliver'd up to the *Dutch*; he had likewise leave given him to depart with the *Franciscan* Father, provided he paid his Debts before his departure.

Another Audience.

The first of *April* the two Ships call'd the *Tiger* and *Nassaw*, which had left *Holland* the 16th of *September* last, being arriv'd at *Batavia*, the said Ambassadours appear'd once more in the Great Council, intimating, that they being inform'd that at the time of the departure of these Ships out of *Holland*, the Ratification of the Articles of his *Portuguese* Majesty concerning the *East-Indies* was not arriv'd, at which they were much surpriz'd, as not knowing what might be the reason thereof: They desir'd to know whether his Excellency had not receiv'd any more particular Intelligence, which might induce him to grant the desir'd Cessation of Arms. The Governour-General reply'd, that he had put it beyond all doubt, that the Ratification would have been brought along with these Ships; but since it had happen'd otherwise, it was not in his power to grant the requir'd Truce. The Ambassadours ask'd whether they should both depart, or whether his Excellency thought convenient that one of them should stay behind: The Governour-General told them that they were at their own disposal; but that, since they expected every day the arrival of their Winter-Ships, which infallibly would bring over the said Ratification, he judg'd it might be best for them to continue a little longer at *Batavia*.

One of the Ambassadours returns to Goa.

Hereupon they resolv'd once more, that the *Franciscan* Father should go back over *Coromandel* to *Goa*, whilst the other should stay at *Batavia* for the arrival of the Ratification. Accordingly a written Certificate was given to the Ambassadors concerning their Zeal and Industry, in incompassing

compassing their Commission, sign'd by his Excellency the Governour-General *Anthony van Diemen*, by *Cornelius van der Lijn*, *John Maatzuyker*, *Justus Schouten*, *Cornelius Witzen*, and *Peter Boreel*, in the Castle of *Batavia*, *April* 9. 1642. To the *Franciscan* Father the Council gave the following Letter, directed to the Viceroy of *Goa*.

Most Illustrious Lord!

A Letter to the Viceroy of Goa.

" DIego Mendes de Britto, Gentleman " of the King's Houshold, and the " Reverend Father, Brother *Gonsalvo de S. Joseph*, your Excellency's Ambassadors, being come in our Road the 28*th* " of *January* aboard the *Dolphin*, were " honourably receiv'd by us the next day. " They have deliver'd to us your Excellency's Credential Letters, dated in " *Goa* the 6*th* of *December* of the last year, " as also the Letters of his *Portuguese* " Majesty to you, concerning the Truce " betwixt *Portugal* and the *United Provinces*. The before-mentioned Ambassadors have not been remiss in their " Zeal, Industry and Duty, to press in " their several Audiences the obtaining " of a Truce; which we would willingly have granted, had not we receiv'd " certain Advice by some Ships arriv'd " the 14*th* of *February* by the way of *Fernambuco*, and others arriv'd the first of " *April* here, of a Truce concluded betwixt his Majesty of *Portugal* and the " States-General of the *United Provinces*; " wherein it was expresly agreed with " his Majesty's Plenipotentiary *Tristaon* " *de Mendoza Furtado*, among other " Points, that the Truce agreed upon for " 10 years in *Europe*, should be of the " same validity in these parts, yet so that " the same should not commence before " that his *Portuguese* Majesty should have " sent back his Ratification into *Holland*, " and the same be publickly proclaim'd " afterwards in these parts, as will more " fully appear to your Excellencies out " of the enclosed Letters. Thus being " oblig'd to follow the Directions of our " Lords and Masters, we could not proceed further in this business till the " arrival of the next Ships from *Holland*; " which being expected daily, with the " said Ratification, we did advise your " Ambassadors to stay (or at least one " of them) for the coming of the said " Ships, as the only means not to render " your Excellency's Embassy altogether " fruitless: Accordingly Mr. *Diego Mendes de Britto* intends to hasten his " Journy to *Goa*, immediately after the " first further notice of the said Ratification, which we hope will prove " agreeable to your Excellency's Sentiments. We recommend your Excellency to God's Protection. Dated in " the Castle of *Batavia*, April 8. 1642.

Baldæus.

Subscribed,

The Governour-General for the *United Provinces* in the *East-Indies*.

CHAP. XV.

The Ratification of the 10 years Truce brought to Batavia. *A Protestation sent to the Count* d'Aveiras. *Treaty of Peace with the Viceroy. The Articles thereof. Agreements about the division of the Limits betwixt the* Portugueses *and* Hollanders *in the Isle of* Ceylon. *Agreement betwixt* Mascarenhas *and* Cornelius van Sanen.

The Ratification publish'd.

THE so much desir'd Ratification (signed at *Lisbon* the 16*th* of *January* 1642. and deliver'd at the *Hague* the 15*th* of *February* following) being at last brought to *Batavia*, the same was publish'd the 8*th* of *October* throughout the *Indies*.

" ANthony van Diemen Governour-" General, and the Members of the " Great Council of the *East-Indies* under the Jurisdiction of the *United* " *Provinces*, make known to all it may " concern; That whereas by two several Letters, dated the 22*d* of *February*, " and 15*th* of *March* 1642. brought over " by the Ship the *Salamander*, we have " been advertis'd, That the 12*th* of *June* " 1641. a firm Alliance and Truce has " been concluded for 10 years betwixt " the most Potent *Don John* IV. King of " *Portugal*, *Algerve*, and Lord of *Guinea*, " and of the Conquests made on the " Shoar of *Ethiopia*, *Arabia*, *Persia* and " *India*,

Baldæus.

“ *India*, on one ſide, and their High and
“ Mightineſſes the States General of the
“ *United Provinces* on the other ſide, in-
“ cluding all the before-mentioned King-
“ doms, Countries, Provinces, Iſlands,
“ and other places on both ſides of the
“ Equinoctial Line (without exception)
“ all ſuch as now actually are, or for the
“ future may be under the Juriſdiction
“ of the ſaid King and the States-Gene-
“ ral; during which ſpace of ten years
“ ſucceſſively all Hoſtilities betwixt their
“ reſpective Subjects ſhall ceaſe both by
“ Sea and Land, without limitation or
“ exception of any Places, Perſons or
“ Circumſtances, as by the Articles of
“ the ſaid Truce does more amply and
“ fully appear. It is therefore that we
“ are commanded to ſurceaſe all manner
“ of Hoſtilities from this day for the
“ next ſucceeding ten years, according
“ to which all our Subjects ſhall regulate
“ themſelves; and to take effectual care
“ that nothing may be tranſacted any
“ wiſe contrary to the true intent of the
“ Articles of the ſaid Alliance and
“ Truce, but to maintain the ſame in-
“ violably. And that nobody may plead
“ ignorance in this caſe, we have or-
“ der'd theſe Preſents to be publiſh'd,
“ enjoyning every body under ſevere Pe-
“ nalties, not to infringe any of the
“ before-mentioned Articles, as they will
“ anſwer the ſame at their peril. Dated
“ in the Caſtle of *Batavia*, *Octob.* 4. 1642.
“ and firſt publiſh'd the 7*th* of the ſame
“ Month, under the Great Seal of the
“ Company in red Wax.

Anthony van Diemen.

By Order of his Excellency,

Peter Mesdach, Secretary.

The Proteſt ſent to the Count d'Aveiras.

However this Truce was but ill obſerv'd by the Viceroy of *Goa*, eſpecially in the Territories of *Gale* in the Iſle of *Ceylon*, which induc'd the *Dutch* General and Great Council to ſend him this following Proteſt.

“ BY Letters from our Commiſſary
“ *Peter Boreel*, whom (after the
“ Ratification of the Truce betwixt
“ his *Portugueſe* Majeſty and the States
“ General of the *United Provinces*) we
“ diſpatch'd to *Goa*, to give notice there-
“ of to your Excellency, we have been
“ inform'd beyond all expectation, that
“ upon his arrival there, and his earneſt
“ requeſt to your Excellency (purſuant
“ to our Orders) to withdraw the
“ Army under the Command of *Don*
“ *Philip* of *Maſcarenhas*, from the Ter-
“ ritories of *Puntegale* under our Juriſ-
“ diction, your Excellency has been plea-
“ ſed to ſhew ſo much averſion to com-
“ ply with his Demands, tho founded
“ upon undeniable and juſt grounds re-
“ preſented to your Commiſſioners in the
“ ſeveral Conferences held upon that
“ Subject *, that he finding his Preſence
“ uſeleſs at *Goa*, he was forced to return
“ from thence without being able to en-
“ compaſs his juſt Deſigns, and (pur-
“ ſuant to his Orders receiv'd from us)
“ to denounce before his departure, the
“ Continuation of the War to your Ex-
“ cellency, till Satisfaction might be ob-
“ tain'd upon this ſcore. And ſince the
“ unjuſt detention of the Territories of
“ *Gale* tends to our conſiderable Detri-
“ ment, we declare, that upon peruſal
“ of the Writings ſent to us by your
“ Excellency by the hands of our Com-
“ miſſary, we can make no better Con-
“ ſtruction of the whole matter, than
“ that your Excellency's Intention is,
“ under this framed Pretext, to render
“ the Truce concluded betwixt our re-
“ ſpective Maſters, invalid and of no
“ worth. It is therefore that we think
“ our ſelves oblig'd to approve every
“ thing that has been tranſacted upon
“ this Head by our Commiſſary, and
“ to make uſe of ſuch means for the
“ Juſtification of our Rights, as God
“ has put into our hands, and are al-
“ together ſutable to the Laws of Na-
“ tions. And as upon theſe Conſidera-
“ tions, we have ſent back this Fleet,
“ by which your Excellency will at once
“ receive this *Proteſt*, and be made ſen-
“ ſible at the ſame time of our Reſo-
“ lution of maintaining our juſt Cauſe,
“ which will queſtionleſs prove the oc-
“ caſion of new Differences betwixt
“ his *Portugueſe* Majeſty and the States
“ General of the *United Provinces*, as
“ alſo of much Effuſion of Blood, of
“ vaſt Expences, and many other In-
“ conveniences; we call God to wit-
“ neſs, and declare and proteſt by theſe
“ Preſents, that we are innocent, and
“ are not anſwerable for the direful
“ Conſequences of this breach of the
“ Truce, which we were ready to have
“ punctually obſerv'd on our ſide, pur-
“ ſuant to the Intention of our Maſters,
“ had not your Excellency bereav'd
“ us of all hopes of adjuſting matters
“ by an amicable Compoſition, for the
“ recovery of our Rights in the Country
“ of

* *The Portugueſes pretended that the* Dutch *Juriſdiction did not extend without the Walls of* Gale.

"of *Gale*, unjustly detain'd by your "Excellency. Dated in the Castle of "*Batavia*, the 5th of *August* 1643.

Signed,

Anthony van Diemen,	*Cornelius van der Lyn,*
Francis Caron,	*John Maatzuyker,*
Justus Schouten,	*Salomon Sweers.*

Truce betwixt the Portugueses *and* Dutch *in the* Indies.

Thus matters remain'd in suspence betwixt the *Portugueses* and us till the year 1644. when Mr. *Maatzuyker* being authorized by their High and Mightinesses, as also by the General and Great Council of the *Indies*, to treat with the Count *d'Aveiras* Viceroy of *Goa*, concerning a firm Truce, and to adjust the remaining Differences for that purpose (yet upon approbation of their respective Masters) the same at last concluded a Truce the 10*th* of *November*, upon the following Conditions.

The Conditions.

"I. Both Parties declare, that this "present Agreement, intended for the "composing of such Differences as have "hitherto occasion'd much Bloodshed, "and obstructed the so long desir'd Peace, "shall in no wise be deem'd, or be prejudicial to the Rights and Sovereignties "either of the most Illustrious King of "*Portugal*, or of their High and Mightinesses the States-General of the *United* "*Provinces*, as the same are establish'd "(by the Truce agreed upon betwixt "his *Portuguese* Majesty and the said "States General) in their respective "Cities, Castles, Fortresses, Towns, Harbours, and Seas in the *Indies*; and that "this Agreement shall be inviolably observ'd on both sides immediately after "its second Publication at *Goa*.

"II. Since the happy Effects of the "Truce have been obstructed hitherto, "by certain Differences arisen about the "just Division of the Limits in the Isle of "*Ceylon*, it is agreed that the Decision "thereof shall be entirely remitted to "the respective Masters and Lords of "both Nations, and in the mean while "a full Cessation of Arms and all Hostilities to be kept inviolably, and all "Forts, Territories, and other matters "to remain in the same state as they "were at the day of the Publication of "these Presents at *Goa*; so that not the "least Alteration or Innovation is to be "made either in building, rebuilding, "or mending any thing, much less in "making any Preparations either for a "Defensive or Offensive War.

Baldæus.

"III. But that, whilst the before-mentioned Differences remain undecided, "the Products of the Country may not "be neglected, or lost, by reason of the "Differences betwixt the Possessors, it "is agreed that the same shall be divided into two equal shares betwixt "the *Portugueses* and the *Dutch*, yet so "that the same shall be deposited (remain in Custody) with the last, till the "decision of these Differences by their "respective Principals in *Europe*: whereby they oblige themselves at the same "time to a full Restitution in case the "same be agreed upon by the said Principals. And the said Ambassador declares and protests, that the word "*deposited*, inserted at the request of the "Viceroy (for the better adjusting of "matters) shall not in any wise be interpreted as prejudicial to the Possession and Title of the States General to "these Lands and their Products. And "to avoid all Contests concerning the "gathering of these Fruits, it is agreed "the *Portugueses* shall have full liberty "to gather, without any molestation or "hinderance, such Fruits as grow in one "part of the Lands in dispute, *viz.* that "part which is next adjacent to their "Fort; as on the other hand, the *Hollanders* shall enjoy the same freedom in "gathering the Fruits in that half part "adjoyning to their Fortress. The same "is also to be understood of equally "sharing the Administration of Justice "in these parts, lest Malefactors may be "encourag'd, and Crimes pass unpunish'd, by reason of the uncertainty of "the Administration of Justice; publick "Proclamation hereof being to be made "in this Isle by the respective Governours of both Nations.

"IV. *Raja Singa* the King of *Candy* "shall be comprehended in this Truce, "(according to the third Article) with "all his Kingdoms, Provinces and Possessions.

"V. All Proprietors, Owners, or Farmers in the Villages, shall have full "liberty to return to their Possessions "and Farms of what nature soever, "with their Families, provided they return within the space of six Months, "either in Person, or send their Deputies, and pay the usual Taxes and Duties to those under whose Jurisdiction "they live, without any trouble. And "that no Inconveniences may arise in "point of Conscience, it is agreed, that "Liberty of Conscience shall be allow'd, "and the free exercise of Religion in

"all

Baldæus.

" all Parishes or Villages, except in " the fortified Places belonging to the " *Hollanders*, till the before-mentioned " Decision be arrived out of *Europe*.

" VI. The Labourers of the Isle of " *Ceylon*, call'd *Schalias*, employ'd in peel- " ing of the Cinnamon, shall have liber- " ty to work with both Parties, yet not " without the consent of that Party un- " der whose Jurisdiction they live; and " the better to maintain the Truce, nei- " ther Party shall be permitted to en- " tice these Labourers of *Ceylon*, or any " other of the Natives out of one ano- " ther's Service, without mutual Con- " sent, but shall be oblig'd to send them " back to their respective Dwelling- " places.

" VII. All the Goods seiz'd on account " of or during these Differences, shall " be restor'd, or else the Value thereof " paid in Mony, provided they were " actually in the Possession of either " Party, and not otherwise; upon which " account the *Dutch* Ambassador pro- " mises to pay here at *Goa*, or at *Suratte*, " in the next following Month of *Janua-* " *ry* at farthest, the Sum of 100000 " *Spanish* Reals, to be accounted for ac- " cording to the true value thereof they " bear at *Batavia*, as the payment of the " Mony shall be made, according to the " course of Mony in those places where " these Goods were taxed; to be under- " stood of such Goods as notwithstand- " ing the payment of the before-said " Mony, are found to remain as yet un- " satisfied for from the 22*d* day of *Fe-* " *bruary* 1643. being a twelve-month " after the Ratification of his *Portuguese* " Majesty was sent to the *Hague*.

" VIII. In case during this Truce any " Differences should arise betwixt both " Parties, this Agreement shall remain " firm and inviolable, and every thing " remain in the same state, till the De- " cision of the respective Principals; " and in case the nature of the matter " admits of no delay, the same is to " be refer'd to the Determination of " certain Arbitrators, to be chosen by " both Parties; and whilst the same is in " agitation, the pretended Party to re- " main in Possession till the Point is de- " cided by the said Arbitrators.

" IX. This present Agreement is not " in the least to be prejudicial to such " Judgments or Decisions as have been " made or given betwixt contending " Parties, or may be given for the future " by our respective Principals; but the " same shall be regarded and taken as " valid in all respects by both Parties, " notwithstanding this Agreement, in- " tended only for the removing of Diffe- " rences till the same can be approv'd " of by our respective Principals. Which " Agreement for the ceasing of all man- " ner of Hostilities, and maintaining a " firm Truce in the Isle of *Ceylon*, is " promised by both Parties to be pub- " lish'd immediately, and inviolably ob- " serv'd both in respect of the Gover- " nours and Subjects: as his Excellency " the Viceroy engages the same for him- " self and his Successors, Generals, and " Governours; and my Lord Ambassa- " dor for the States of the *United Pro-* " *vinces*, and the *East-India* Company, " pursuant to the Authority granted him " by the most Noble *Anthony van Diemen*, " General-Governour of the *Indies*. In " Confirmation whereof this Agreement " is authoriz'd and confirm'd by a so- " lemn Oath taken upon the Gospel in " the presence of the most Reverend " Archbishop and Primate of *Goa*, *Don* " *Frey Francisco de Martyres*, and *Don* " *Alphonso Medis*, Patriarch of *Ethiopia*, " Members of the Privy-Council of his " Majesty; and in the presence of the " other Privy-Counsellors of *Goa*, who " have given their full Approbation and " Consent thereunto; as also in the Pre- " sence of *Wollebrand Gleynzen*, Chief " Director in *Persia*, *Abraham Fierens*, " Minister of the Gospel, *John Pottey* " Fiscal, *Andreas Frisius* Secretary, *Tho-* " *mas Kuyk*, head Factor; who together " with his Excellency the Viceroy, and " his Excellency the Ambassador, did set " their Hands to it; *Joseph de Chaves Co-* " *to Major*, his Excellency the Viceroy's " Secretary, having taken care to make " the Draughts thereof.

Signed thus,

Conde d' Aveiras,
John Maatzuyker,
Fr. Francisco de Martyres,
Alphonso Medis,
Francisco de Melo de Castro,
Don Manoel Pereira,
Anthonio Saria Mochado,
Anthonio Movis Baretto,
Joseph Pinto Pereira,
Wollebrand Gleynz the younger,
Abraham Fierens,
John Pottey,
Don Bras de Castro,
Lovis Mugilhaon,
Andreas Frisius,
Andr. Selem.

" Several

" Several Draughts of this Agreement " having been made both in *Latin* and " *Portuguese*, it is agreed betwixt the Vice- " roy and the Ambassador, that in case " any Doubt should arise about the In- " terpretation of certain words, recourse " is to be had to the *Latin*, which being " the Original, is to be interpreted ac- " cording to the plain signification of " the words, without any collateral Con- " struction, in Confirmation of which " this Declaration was thought fit to be " made: Subscribed a second time on " the same day by the under-written " Persons.

Conde d'Aveiras,
John Maatzuyker,
Fr. Francisco de Martyres, Archbishop and Primate;
Alphonso Medis, Patriarch of *Ethiopia*;
Francisco de Melo,
Don Manoel Pereira,
Anthonio Saria,
Anthonio Monis Baretto,
Joseph Pinto Pereira,
Wollebrand Gleynz the younger.

In the year 1645. *Jan.* 10. the Division of the Limits in the Isle of *Ceylon* was agreed upon in the City of *Columbo*, *Don Philippo Mascarenhas*, Successor to the Count *d'Aveiras*, being then Viceroy of *Goa*.

" The Countries betwixt *Columbo* and " *Negumbo*, shall be divided into two equal " shares, according to their several Di- " stricts (call'd *Corles*) as far as the same " can be done, to prevent the Confusion " which might otherwise arise from the " Division of the antient Jurisdictions; " but in such places where the same is " not to be done, this Division is to be " made by sharing the Villages: so that " considering there are 17 Districts be- " twixt the two before-mentioned Forts, " seven thereof are to be annexed to the " Jurisdiction of *Columbo*, viz. *Herra-corla*, " *Omapauduna-corla*, *Quatigora-corla*, *Bi-* " *ligal-corla*, *Galbare-corla*, *Apitigan-corla*, " and *Pernacur-corla*, lying altogether " towards that side. To the Fort of " *Negumbo* are to be annex'd eight Di- " stricts, *viz*. *Pitigal-corla*, *Diomede corla*, " *Vrupula-corla*, *Carvagal-corla*, *Vili-corla*, " *Madura-corla*, *Hieriela-corla*, and *Man-* " *gur-corla*; the rest to be divided into " two equal shares, *Alicur-corla* by the " River *Dandagan* to be the common " Boundary of both Nations; so that " part which lies to the North shall be- " long to *Negumbo*, and to *Columbo* what " lies on this side. The Province of " *Catugambala-corla* is to be divided by " the same River, together with its " three lesser Districts, *Vdacabapato*, " *Miendapato* and *Jetigalapato*; so that " *Jetigala* shall fall to the share of *Ne-* " *gumbo*, and *Vdacaba* to *Columbo*; but " *Miendapato* shall be divided into two " equal parts, in proportion to its Villa- " ges, such Villages as lie next *Jetigala-* " *pato* to be under the Jurisdiction of " *Negumbo*, and those on the side of *Vda-* " *caba* under *Columbo*. The *Portugueses* " shall remain in the possession of *Pu-* " *telaon* and *Calpentyn*; but the River of " *Alican* is to be the Boundary betwixt " *Columbo* and *Gale*: so that part lying " on the other side of the River shall " remain to the *Hollanders*, but the other " part on this side, together with the " River and Harbour to the *Portugueses*, " in the same manner as they were for- " merly possess'd of it, under this Con- " dition however, that the *Hollanders* " living here or in any other parts shall " have the free use of the said River " in fishing, or exporting and importing " their Merchandizes without paying any " Customs. And whereas by the 7*th* Ar- " ticle of the Agreement made at *Goa*, it " was agreed, that the Labourers (call'd " *Schalias*) who peel the Cinnamon, shall " be employ'd by both Parties to prevent " all further Differences for the future " upon this Head; it is agreed, that the " *Hollanders* shall every year in Harvest " time send one half of these Labourers " out of the Villages of *Bili* and *Cosgure*, " under their Jurisdiction on the other side " of the River *Alican*, to assist as former- " ly the *Portugueses* in peeling of Cinna- " mon, under condition that the Cinna- " mon thus peeled by them in the *Portu-* " *guese* Territories, shall be laid up in a " certain place upon the River *Dandagan*, " to be divided once every year in two " equal shares betwixt the two Parties, " provided that each Party pay the usu- " al Price to the *Schalias* for the peeling " of their share of Cinnamon. This Di- " vision is to take place, and to stand " firm till the same be otherwise de- " cided by our respective Principals in " *Europe*, with this reserve nevertheless " in regard of the *Hollanders*, who being " ignorant hitherto in the true situation " of the Country, may easily be deceiv'd " in this point, and therefore ought to " have the liberty to appeal to better " Judgment, and desire a recompensa-

Baldæus.

Baldæus.

"tion of their Losses: But in case the "Parties should disagree upon this Head, "this shall not occasion any Rupture, but "the Truce shall notwithstanding this "remain in its full force, according to "the intent of the 9*th* Article of the "before-mentioned Agreement. *Don* "*Philippo Mascarenhas* the present Vice-"roy, and Mr. *John Maatzuyker* do also "engage to cause this Treaty of the Di-"vision of the Limits to be publish'd "immediately, for the general benefit "of all such as have any concern therein, "that the Inhabitants of this Isle may "no longer remain in ignorance under "whose Jurisdiction they live; and for the "due performance thereof, have con-"firm'd the same with their Oaths, and "subscrib'd the Draughts thereof both "in *Latin* and *Portuguese*; yet so, that "in case of any doubt, recourse is to "be had to the *Latin* Original.

Agreement betwixt Philippo Mascarenhas, *and* Cornelius van Sanen.

In the year 1647. a provisional Agreement was made by *Don Philippo Mascarenhas*, the then Viceroy, and *Cornelius van Sanen*, head Factor and Director of *Wingurla*, for the adjusting of the Differences concerning the Fortress of *Malacca*.

"*IN the Name of God, Amen.* Be it "known to all who are concern'd in "this present Agreement, That 1647. "*April* 18. the following Agreement has "been made in the Castle of the City "of *Goa*, in the presence of his Excel-"lency *Don Philippo Mascarenhas* Vice-"roy of *Goa*, and *Cornelius van Sanen*, "head Factor and Director of *Wingurla*, "authorized by the Governour-General "and Great Council of the *Indies*, for "the adjusting of the Differences arising "concerning some pretended Rights of "the City and Fortress of *Malacca*, con-"cerning the Customs and Duties to be "paid at *Malacca*; several Conferences "having been held with the Merchants "of *Macau*, yet could not the same be "reduc'd to any just Equilibrium, or "settled upon a firm Basis, tho we made "as reasonable offers as possibly could "be expected: so that in case your Ex-"cellency thinks it convenient to pro-"ceed further in this matter, you may "treat upon this Head with *Cornelius* "*van Sanen*, our head Factor at *Win-*"*gurla*. By virtue of this Commission "I represented to the Viceroy, that in "point of Justice, such of our Ships as "pass by *Malacca* without unlading or "selling any of their Commodities, "ought to pay no Customs there: unto "which his Excellency having given for "Answer, that it appear'd out of the "Treaties and Writings agreed upon "betwixt both Parties, that they ought "to pay the same; it was thought fit for "the preventing of further Differences, "and maintaining a good Correspon-"dence betwixt both Nations, to agree "upon the following provisional Treaty, "till the full Decision of our respective "Principals, and with this Proviso, that "this Agreement shall not in the least "tend to the prejudice either of his "*Portuguese* Majesty, or of the States "General in their respective Rights and "Possessions. That his Majesty's Ships "as well as the *Dutch* Merchant-men "bound to *China*, or any other of the "Southern parts, coming to *Malacca*, "shall only be oblig'd to pay 6 *per Cent.* "for such Goods as they shall actually "sell there; the same to be paid to the "*Dutch* from all such Goods as they shall "sell in any of his Majesty's Harbours. "Pursuant to the Agreement made at *Ba-*"*tavia* by the Great Council with the "Merchants of *Macau*, in the presence of "the Reverend *Frey Gonsalvo de S. Joseph*, "each Vessel, whether small or great, "bound to *Macau*, whether it sells or un-"loads any Goods at *Malacca* or not, shall "pay two *Schutkens* of Gold for its Passage "thither and backwards; from which "Duties however are to be exempted "his Majesty's Ships, provided they may "be searched, and an Oath taken there-"upon, that they have no Merchandizes "aboard; and if any are found, the "Owners are to pay 4½ *per Cent.* That "such Ships as pass by *Malacca*, and are "not bound to *China*, shall pay 4½ *per* "*Cent.* whether they unload or sell any "Goods or not; then they may proceed "in their Voyage without any Molesta-"tion. Which Agreement is to be pub-"lish'd and strictly observ'd by both Par-"ties, and confirm'd by Oath, till the "Decision of our both sides respective "Principals.

Signed,

Don Philippo Mascarenhas,
Cornelius van Sanen,
Duarty de Fugeredo de Mello,
Frey Gonsalvo de S. Joseph.
Francisco de Melo de Castro,
Anthonio Souza Coutinho,
John van Teylingen, Head Factor,
Anthony Ondermeulen,
Jacob Roscam,
Leendert Johnson.

CHAP.

Baldæus.

CHAP. XVI.

A Description of Anchediva, Canara, Onor, Batecalo, Malabar. Cananor, *built and besieged by the* Malabars, *bravely defended by* Laurence de Britto; *besieged and taken by the* Hollanders.

The Isle of Anchediva.

THE Isle of *Anchediva*, not far from *Goa*, and about 50 Leagues from *Calecut*, is almost covered with Woods and Forests, but well stor'd with Fish; the *Portugueses* had formerly a Fort here: *Sebajus*, the Father of *Hidalcan*, sent a Fleet of 60 Ships to *Anchediva* (whilst *Glineyda* was at *Cananor*) to chase the *Portugueses* from that Island, under the Command of *Anthony Fernando*, a most impious Wretch, who having forsaken both his Religion, and the Service of his Native Country, turn'd *Mahometan*, assuming the Name of *Abdala*; and being well versed in Maritime Affairs, was in great Favour with *Sebajus*. This Renegado having landed a good Body of Men in this Isle, left no Stone unturn'd to make himself Master of the Fort, erected there by the *Portugueses*: But being bravely defended by *Emanuel Passangie*, a Native of *Genoa*, descended from a great Family, and famous for his brave Actions; *Abdala* hearing of the return of the victorious Fleet, was glad to leave both the Fort and the Isle. The Fort was not long after demolished by the *Portugueses* themselves, who had been taught by experience, that too great a number of Fortresses consum'd all their Profit, and exposes them besides to no small danger; like a Hen who has more Chickens than she can protect with her Wings, often loses one by the rapacious Kite.

The Portugueses Fort besieged.

Is demolished.

The Reason thereof.

Canara.

The Country of *Canara* is very fertile in Rice and other Necessaries of human Life; its Inhabitants, commonly called *Canarins*, are very robust, and fit for all manner of hard Labour. The chief Citys near the Sea-shoar, are the City and Kingdom of *Onor*, not far distant from *Goa*, where the *Portugueses* had also a Fort, it being formerly a Place of considerable Traffick. Next to *Onor* lies *Batecalo*, about 25 Leagues from *Goa*, the King whereof became tributary to the Crown of *Portugal* under the Reign of *Emanuel*; but refusing afterwards to pay the usual Tribute, *Sequeria* sent *Alphonso Menes* with some Ships to block up the Harbour, which soon reduc'd the King to Obedience. Afterwards the Queen of *Batecalo* entertaining the Pyrats in her Harbours, and refusing likewise to pay the Tribute, *Sosa* sailed thither with 49 Ships and 1500 Landmen; and after he had cast Anchor in the Harbour, sent his Messengers into the City to require the Payment of the Tribute, and the surrendring of the Pyrats: She being frightened at the Sight of so powerful a Fleet, surrendred four of the Pyrats Ships; but endeavouring for the rest to detain the *Portugueses* with fair Words, these landed their Men, not a little incommoded by the Arrows shot at 'em by the Inhabitants from the Coco Trees; but having put themselves in order of Battel, they advanced towards the City, where they were (in the Absence of the Queen) so warmly engag'd by the Inhabitants, that the Combat remain'd doubtful for some time, till these being worsted, they set the City on fire, with the Loss of 12 Men only on their side. In this Action one *Almeyda* a brave *Portuguese*, seeing his Comrade enclosed on all sides by the Enemy, fought his way thro 'em; and having rescued his Companion, withstood the whole Force of the Enemy, till he was relieved by a Body of the *Portugueses*. Afterwards they made Incursions into the Country, which soon obliged the Queen to consent to the Payment of the Tribute.

Onor.

Batecalo.

Barcelor, *Baranor* and *Mangalor*, being Places of no great consequence, deserve no particular Descriptions; wherefore we will proceed to the Country of *Malabar*, which (according to common Computation) begins about 50 Leagues to the South of *Goa*, and extends to the Cape of *Comoryn*, to the utmost Borders of *India*, on this side of *Ganges*. This whole Country being full of Rivers, is consequently of an easy Passage; tho most of the Rivers here are so shallow, that they are not capable of bearing any Ships of Bulk or Burden. The largest Rivers are *Bergera* (a great Receptacle for Pirats) *Panane* and *Cranganor*, the common Boundaries of the Kingdoms of *Calecut* and *Cochin*; these as well as the River of *Cochin* are about 18 or 19 Foot deep at High-Water. The whole Country of *Malabar* is divided into five Kingdoms, *viz.* *Cananor*, *Calecut*, *Cranganor*, *Cochin* and *Coulang*, unto which some add the Kingdom of *Trevancor*, the least fertile

Malabar.

Its Extent.

Its Rivers.

Baldæus. tile of all, and the two petty Kingdoms of *Porca* and *Calecoulang*.

The antient State of Malabar. In former Ages *Malabar* was subject to one Sovereign Prince, who kept his Court at *Calecut*, now the Residence of the Great *Sammoryn*. This King having at the Persuasion of some of his Courtiers, undertaken a Voyage over the *Red-Sea*, to visit *Mahomet's* Tomb, and to be thorowly instructed in that Faith, died in his return from thence; and leaving no Issue, the whole Empire was divided between his Esquire, Sword-bearer, and Scepter-bearer: The first taking for his share *Cananor*, the second *Calecut*, and the third *Cochin*.

Sammoryn, i.e. *Emperor.*

The Climate. The Nights are very cold all along the Coast of *Malabar*, with very thick Fogs, especially in *January*, *February*, and *March*, when the days are excessive hot. They have every day a Sea and Land Wind; the first begins every Morning at 9 or 10 a Clock, and holds till Sunset. This Coast is scarce navigable from *June* till *November*, the best time here being from *April* till *June*. Their Winter begins in *May*, and continues till *November*.

And Seasons.

Products. The chief Products of *Malabar*, are *Pepper* and *Cardamome*: *Cochin* affords great Quantities of Pepper, but *Cananor* yields the best; especially in the Inland Countries, whence the *Moors* and other Merchants from *Carnatica* and *Visiapour* use to fetch it in considerable Quantitys. The Pepper of *Calecut* is lesser of Grain than those of *Cananor* and *Cochin*. This Commodity is generally cheaper at one Place than another. They buy it by the *Canda*, at the rate of 390 or 400 *Fanams* a *Canda*, a *Fanam* being worth about 10 Pence of our Money. In the Year 1640. the Price rose to 450 *Fanams*. The Pepper delights in shady Places, the Stem is weak like those of the Vines, and uses to be upheld by Stalks like our Hops: Each Stem bears commonly 6 Bunches, every one a foot long, resembling in colour to our Grapes before they are ripe. They are gathered green in *October* and *November*, and dry'd in the Sun upon Mats, when they turn black. Besides the Pepper and Cardamome, this Country produces also *Ginger* and *Borborri* of a Saffron Colour. Formerly these two Commodities us'd to be sold for 5 *Fanams* a *Man*: It affords also some *Aloes*, but in no great Quantity. Besides these, *Malabar* affords very few Commodities, except a few *Bezoar*-Stones, * found about *Cananor*, Salt-peter, *Gummilacca* (tho none of the best, being sold for a *Fanam* (or 7 *Reals* a piece; some are as big as a Hen's Egg, and sold for 12 Reals a piece.) the *Man*) and abundance of Wax and Honey.

Pepper.

Man *is a certain Weight.*

* *Found in the Bezoars, and sold at 6 or 7 Reals a piece; some are as big as a Hen's Egg, and sold for 12 Reals a piece.*

The whole Country is covered with innumerable *Coco*-Trees, besides such other Trees as generally grow in the *East-Indies*. The Commodities carry'd to, and to be sold in *Malabar*, are *Amfion* or *Opium*, much in use here, especially among the *Nairos* when they are to fight, to intoxicate their Brains. *Ambergreese* also is in great Esteem among the *Malabars*, and transported thither from the *Maldive* Islands. I have seen an Ounce of it sold at *Cananor* for six *Reals*. *Malabar* consumes also abundance of *Cloves*, *Nutmegs* and *Mace*, as also *Allum*, *China-root*, *Lead*, *Tin*, *Brass*, *Copper*, *Brimstone*, *Cinnabar*, *Scarlet* and *Crimson Clothes*, red *Damasks*, *Benzorn*, and coarse *Porcellain*.

The whole Coast of *Malabar* abounds in Fishes, and at *Cochin* they have most excellent *Cods*. Belly Provisions are also here in great Plenty, and bought at an easy rate; for they abound in Oxen, Swine and Poultry. The Coco-Trees furnish them with Drink, which if not used to excess, is tolerably wholesome. Out of this Liquor they distil their *Arack*, much courted by the common Soldiers and Seamen, to their great detriment.

The first is the King of *Cananor*, not in respect so much of his Power, but of his Situation next to *Goa*. His Residence is about three or four Leagues in the Country from the River of *Balipatan*; the extent of his Kingdom is from *Montedely* to *Bergera*; he maintains a considerable number of Musqueteers and Archers, who are very expert in managing their Scymeters.

Cananor is a populous City, inhabited chiefly by rich *Mahometan* Merchants, who live without, yet under the Cannon of the Fortifications. They had formerly a considerable Traffick to *Suratte*, *Cambaja* and the *Red-Sea*, whither they used to send yearly 25 or 30 Ships; but this Place is much decayed in Trade of late Years, and is likely to be worse. Cananor.

About two Leagues to the South of *Cananor*, lies the City of *Termapatan*, under the Jurisdiction of a *Mahometan*; it is strengthened to the Land side by a good Wall. The rebellious Pirats of *Bergera* do considerable Mischief to the King of *Cananor* and his Subjects, who, as well as the other Nations trading in these Seas, are forced to buy Passports of them for their Security. They used formerly to infest these Seas with 40 Frigats at a time, but are not so potent of late Years, since the *Dutch* have frightened the *Portugueses* Termapatan. *Pirats of* Malabar.

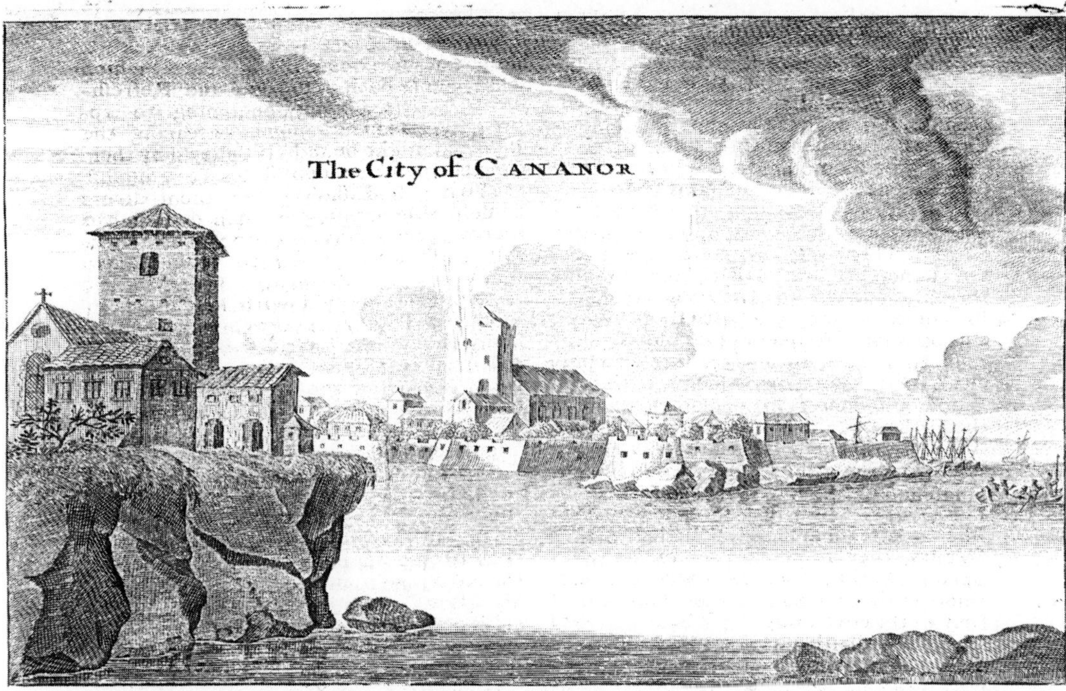

tugueses out of these Parts, since which time they have now and then attempted the *Dutch*, as they did with the Ship called the *Dolphin*, but got nothing but Blows. Their Chiefs are *Mahometans*, and the Soldiers partly *Moors*, partly *Pagans*.

Cananor lies about 40 Leagues to the North of *Cochin*, having a spacious and secure Harbour; the Country thereabouts abounding in *Pepper*, *Cardamom*, *Ginger*, *Mirabolans*, *Tamarinds*, &c. *Peter Alvarus Capralis*, Commander in Chief of the second Fleet sent by *Emanuel* King of *Portugal* into the *Indies*, after having given a Visit to the King of *Cochin*, and the Great *Sammoryn*, came also to *Cananor*, where being kindly received, the King sent an Ambassador along with him to the King of *Portugal*. *Almeyda* did erect here (with the King's Consent) a strong Fort, for the Security of their Commerce; which being afterwards most vigorously attack'd by those of *Calecut* and *Cranganor*, was bravely defended by *Laurence de Britto* to his Immortal Honour. And upon this occasion it will not be beyond our purpose, to give you the Reasons which induced the *Moors* to enter upon this War, which was accompany'd with many most remarkable Actions.

The Portugueses build a Fort at Cananor.

The *Portugueses* having made themselves Masters at Sea, not only on the Coast of *Æthiopia*, but also of *India* and *Arabia*, would not permit the Inhabitants of these Countries to send out their Ships, without Passports obtain'd from them; for which purpose they kept a strict eye over all the *Malabars*, in a most peculiar manner. A certain *Portuguese*, Captain of a Man of War, having attack'd a Vessel of *Cananor*, which he supposed to have come from *Calecut* without a Pass; he caused the Master thereof, and another Person of Note on board her, to be sowed up in a Cloth, and so threw them overboard; which being done not far from *Cananor*, the dead Carcases were cast ashore there. The Inhabitants knowing the Persons, and understanding their Fate, were so exasperated at the *Portugueses*, that they cry'd out for Vengeance, and assaulted the Fort: *Almeyda* offer'd them Satisfaction, and cashier'd the Captain, but in vain, the *Moors* continuing obstinate, and resolving to revenge the Death of their Countrymen upon the *Portugueses* in the Fort.

Reasons why the Malabars *entred into a War with the* Portugueses.

Lau-

Baldæus.

Britto sends to Almeyda.

Laurence de Britto being sensible that he must expect a formal Siege, resolved to stand the Brunt bravely, and sent his Messengers to *Almeyda*, to desire prompt Succours. In the mean time the King of *Cananor* was not idle, but having entrenched himself near the Harbour, all along the Sea-side he erected certain Forts, to cut off the Communication betwixt the City and Castle: At the same time being reinforced by 20000 Men, sent from *Calecut*, they now resolved upon a formal Siege. There was a certain Spring betwixt the City and Castle, which being the only one whence the *Portuguese* Garison could be supply'd with fresh Water, this occasion'd frequent and bloody Skirmishes, so that they were forc'd to purchase their Water with much effusion of Blood. *Laurence Britto* had with him in the Fort a certain Mathematician, named *Thomas Ferdinand*, by whose Advice they digged from the Fort underground to the Spring, and by Pipes conveyed it to the Place where they had occasion for it; so that after having supplied their own Wants, they stopt in the next Sally the Spring, so that the *Moors* were forc'd to remove their Camp from thence, but they in the Fort enjoyed the Benefit thereof. They then began their Attack on the other side, and by the help of Sacks filled with Cotton, advancing to the Ditch, fill'd it with Faggots, and made a fierce Assault; but being bravely repulsed by the *Portugueses*, and forc'd to retreat, these sally'd out upon them, and made a great Slaughter of the Barbarians.

The Spring was afterwards enclos'd within the Fortifications.

These finding that Force was not likely to do their Business, resolv'd to reduce it by Famine, knowing that the Winter Seasons would cut off all hopes of Relief to the Besieged. On the other hand the *Portugueses* made many successful Sallies upon them; in one of which a *Castilian*, nam'd *Guadalajara*, charg'd with 150 Men a strong Body of the Enemy, killing above 300 of them upon the Spot, and taking some of their great Cannon. Soon after it happen'd unfortunately for the *Portugueses*, that a Fire arising in the Fort by the carelesness of a Slave, some part of their Magazines of Provisions was consum'd, whereby a great Scarcity being occasion'd in the Fort, many Negroes run over to the Enemy, and gave them a full account of the condition of the Garison, who were now forc'd to feed upon Cats, Rats, Mice, *&c.* At last Heaven was pleas'd to commiserate the miserable State of the *Portugueses*, by sending a prodigious quantity of Locusts from the Sea (a thing not unfrequent in those Parts) which serv'd them both for Food and Refreshment. The Spring beginning to approach, when the *Sammoryn* fearing the Besieged might be shortly reliev'd by their Countrymen, redoubl'd his Fury against the Fort; and having sent them divers considerable Supplys of Men (which had increas'd his Army to 50000 Men) he resolv'd to try his utmost to reduce them by Force (the *Portugueses* being in the mean while supply'd with Provisions by a certain Prince of the Country, an Enemy to the *Sammoryn*) *De Britto* having receiv'd Intelligence that the Enemy were preparing for a general Assault, took care to guard all the Avenues both on the Sea and Landside. The *Moors* assaulted the *Portugueses* with their utmost Fury, promising themselves an assur'd Victory, by reason they continually reliev'd their Men with fresh Troops; but the *Portugueses* receiv'd them so warmly, that after a smart Fight they put them to the Rout, and pursuing them with great Slaughter, the King of *Cananor* thought it his best way to make Peace with the *Portugueses*.

Great Distress in the Fort.

Peace with the King of Cananor.

Thus much of *Cananor* whilst in the Hands of the *Portugueses*; the next thing which falls under our Consideration is, how it came to fall into the Hands of the *Hollanders*. These having made themselves Masters of *Cranganor*, *Cochin*, and *Coulang*, sail'd 1663. from *Cochin* with a considerable Fleet, and a good Number of Land Forces, under the Command of *Jacob Hustar*, *Peter du Pon*, *Henry van Rhede*, and divers other brave Officers, for *Cananor*. Having landed their Men, and soon made themselves Masters of the City (which was without defence) they batter'd the Fort with their great Cannon, but without any great Success: the Bastions and Ditches on the Land side being cut out of the Rocks, and the Fortifications to the Sea side impregnable. However after a Siege of few days the *Portugueses* considering, that by the taking of *Cochin* all hopes of Relief were banish'd, they surrendred upon honourable Terms; and the *Dutch* having put a Garison of 200 Men in the Fort, entr'd into a strict Alliance with the King of *Cananor*, 1664.

How Cananor *was reduced by the* Dutch.

Cananor *surrendred to the* Dutch.

*

CHAP.

Baldæus.

CHAP. XVII.

A Description of Calecut *and* Panane. *The Arrival of* Vasco de Gama. *His Treaty with the* Sammoryn. Panane *fortified, besieg'd, and demolish'd by the* Portugueses. *Alliance betwixt the* Dutch *and the* Sammoryn. *The* Portuguese *Fort in* Calecut *attack'd by the* Sammoryn, *and defended by* John de Lima.

The Kingdom of Calecut.

THE second Kingdom of *Malabar* is that of *Calecut* under the Jurisdiction of the *Sammoryn*; it begins about three or four Leagues to the South of *Bergera*, and ends at the River *Cranganor*; its whole extent being in length 32 Leagues, and 20 in breadth. This King is the most Potent of all the *Malabar* Kings, having a considerable number of *Nairos* under his Jurisdiction, who are very expert both in handling the Bow and Fire-Arms. He has made considerable Encroachments upon his Neighbours of late years; the Revenues of his new Conquests amounting now to 300000 *Fanams* yearly. The *Sammoryn* who reign'd 1662. was when I saw him not above 50 years of Age, and yet much impair'd in his intellectual Parts by the excessive use of *Opium*, a Drug much in request among the *Malabars*.

An. 1502. the Sammoryn brought into the field 50000 Men; and 1529. 100000.

An odd Custom of Succession to the Crown.

In the Kingdom of the *Sammoryn*, and in most others along the Coast of *Malabar*, the Crown is not inherited by the Son of the King, but by him who is next of kin to his Mother or Sister; for they looking upon that as the surer side, they have introduc'd this Custom to prevent the bastardizing of the Crown. Thus the King who reign'd 1642. was succeeded by his Uncle on the Mother's side, and he was to be succeeded by his Sister's Son. The *Sammoryn* monopolizes all the Pepper of the growth of his Country, none of his Subjects being allow'd to sell it to any but his Factors.

Panane.

Betwixt *Cananor* and *Calecut* lies the Town of *Panane*, seated upon the Sea-shoar: Here the *Dutch* came 1607. to treat with the *Sammoryn*, but he being then in the field against the *Portugueses*, the Admiral sent three Deputies to him with a Letter from Prince *Maurice* of *Nassaw*. In this place the *Sammoryn* kept his Residence at that time, when *Don Vasco de Gama* came into these parts. He having cast Anchor before *Calecut*, dispatch'd immediately a Messenger to the *Sammoryn*, to give notice of his arrival, and to let the King know that the Renown of his great Name having reach'd the Ears of the King of *Portugal*, his Majesty had intrusted him with a Letter, which he being desirous to deliver in Person, therefore desir'd leave to wait on his Majesty.

Gama comes to Panane.

The *Sammoryn* being extremely pleas'd with the Complement, sent immediately certain Pilots to conduct the *Portuguese* Fleet into the Harbour of *Capocate*, where there was much better and safer Anchorage, from whence he was conducted with extraordinary Pomp to the *Sammoryn*.

His Reception.

For *Don Gama* being got ashore attended by eight Gentlemen richly attir'd, was receiv'd in the *Sammoryn*'s Name by the *Catual* (or he that manages all Foreign Affairs) accompanied with a vast number of Guards, Hautboys, Drums and Litters, and thence carried through *Calecut* to *Panane* (where the *Sammoryn* then resided) under such a vast concourse of Spectators, that several were crowded to death. At Court *Gama* was welcom'd by the *Caimales* (or chief Courtiers) and afterwards by the High-Priest of the *Brahmans* dress'd in white Callico, who taking *Gama* by the hand conducted him to many spacious Apartments (at the Door of each whereof stood about ten Sentinels) into a spacious Hall, the Walls and Floor whereof were cover'd with rich Tapestry, and Carpets of Silk and Gold, the chief Men of the Kingdom sitting round the Hall upon Wooden Seats, artificially wrought one above another, like the Seats in an Amphitheater.

His Reception at Court.

The *Sammoryn* himself was seated (according to the Custom of the Country) upon an *Alkatyf*, or Carpet, dress'd in white fine Callico, brocado'd with Flowers of Gold, adorn'd with divers rows of Diamonds of great value: In his Ears he had stately Pendants of precious Stones, and on his Head a Cap (after their Country fashion) cover'd with Diamonds, Pearls, and other precious Stones; his bare Feet being likewise adorn'd with Rings set with all sorts of precious Stones.

The Sammoryn's Dress.

Baldæus.

The Reception of Don Vasca de Gama by the Samoryn.

One of the King's Attendants offer'd his Majesty a Golden Vessel with *Arak* and *Betel*, which the *Indians* chaw almost continually to preserve their Teeth and Gums, and treat their Guests with it as we do with Wine, strong Liquors being not much in use here. *Gama* after having paid his Obeysance to the King began thus:

Gama's *Speech to the* Samoryn.

"*Emanuel*, the present King of *Portugal*, " my Master, mov'd by the Renown of " the Greatness of your Majesty among " the Kings of *Malabar*, has sent me " with Credentials, to enter into a strict " League with You, in order to settle a " firm Correspondence and Commerce " betwixt both Nations; which my Ma- " ster would have been willing to have " perform'd in Person, had not the vast " distance of your Majesty's Dominions " prov'd an invincible Obstacle to his " generous Intentions. After which having deliver'd his Presents, the King answer'd by his Interpreter: "That he " had not the least doubt of the good " Intentions of his Brother *Emanuel*, " King of *Portugal*, having such convin- " cing Proofs thereof before his Eyes, " by honouring him with so splendid a " Legation notwithstanding the vast " distance of their Countries; that he " was willing to enter with them into " a strict League and Amity, and that " they should enjoy the benefit of a free " Commerce in his Territories. Then the King having ask'd them several Particulars concerning their Voyage, Shipping and Traffick, order'd *Gama* to be conducted to the Lodgings prepar'd for his Reception.

The King's Answer.

The Moors *endeavour to obstruct the design of the* Portugueses.

The News of this Embassy soon came to the Ears of the *Moorish* Merchants in those parts, who fearing, not without reason, that the *Portugueses* would do them considerable Mischief in their Traffick, join'd with the *Arabians* trading in those parts, to hinder the Consummation of this Treaty; for which purpose having purchased the favour of many of the Courtiers by Mony, they insinuated into the King, that *Gama* was no more than a great Pirate, who endeavour'd to get a footing in the King's Dominions, which in time might prove his ruin; whereas he might rest secure in his Dominions, by incouraging his Subjects in their Traffick with the exclusion of Foreigners. These Insinuations prov'd so effectual, that the *Sammoryn* began to give a favourable Ear to them, and had perhaps prov'd of very ill Consequence to *Gama*, had not a certain *African*, a Native of *Tunis*, who understood *Portuguese*, and had formerly convers'd with them, discover'd the danger to him, who thereupon without further delay got aboard his own Ships with his Attendants, and having weigh'd his Anchors kept at a greater distance from the Shore, whence he writ to the *Sammoryn*.

Gama *gets privately aboard.*

His Letter.

"That the ill Designs of the *Moors* "against his Person being discover'd to "him, he had thought fit to retire a-"board, and to desire his Majesty not to "be diverted from his Promise by their "false Insinuations, assuring him that "he would reap much more benefit by "the Friendship of the King of *Portugal* "than by the *Moors* and *Arabians*. The *Sammoryn* promis'd the Messenger to make a strict Enquiry after and to punish severely these Offenders, who had infringed the Law of Nations; and in his Letter to the King of *Portugal* assures him, "That the arrival of the *Portu-*"*gueses* in his Dominions was very ac-"ceptable to him, provided they might "regulate themselves so, as not to give "any occasion of disturbance there, and "that the League he was entring upon "with his Majesty, might not prove pre-"judicial to the good Correspondence he "had hitherto entertain'd with divers "other Nations. *Gama* having receiv'd this Letter, set sail for the Isle of *Anchediva*, where having furnish'd himself with fresh Provisions, he return'd to *Portugal*, to give an account of his Transactions to King *Emanuel*. The famous *Vasco de Gama* died 1524. being the first who discover'd the Passage into the *East-Indies* by the Cape of *Good Hope*.

The King's Answer to it.

And upon this occasion I can't pass by in silence what is mention'd by *Ferdinand Lopes de Castanheda* *, *viz*. That *Gama* with some of his Retinue being at *Calecut*, and entring into one of the Pagan Temples, paid their Reverence to the Images, as taking them for the same they had left in their own Churches in *Portugal*; a convincing Proof that Superstition and Idolatry very near resemble one another.

* *Hist. Ind.* l. 1. c. 16.

Panane.

Panane being well fortified by the *Sammoryn* with two Forts, erected on both sides of the Entrance of the Harbour, the *Portugueses* notwithstanding this resolve to attempt it. They no sooner appear'd in sight of the Harbour, but a certain number of the *Mahometans* associated themselves in one of the *Pagodes*, and with direful Execrations engag'd to one another to defend the City, or die in the Attempt. *Tristan d' Acunha* the *Portuguese* General detach'd a certain Body of his best Troops under the Command of *Laurence* and *Nonnius* in small Gallies, to lead the Van, being to be follow'd by the great Ships: These enter'd the Harbour with unspeakable Bravery, notwithstanding the Enemies Fire, who sent their great and small Shot very thick upon them from both sides of the Shore, but without any considerable effect, most of their Bullets passing over their Heads, because the Soldiers kept close lying upon their Bellies in the Gallies. The Enemy seeing them enter'd the Harbour, leap'd in whole Troops into the Water, attacking them with incredible Fury in hopes of boarding them: but the *Portugueses* stood to it with so much Resolution, that at last they forced the *Indians* to give way; and pursuing them to the Shore, made themselves Masters of the two Forts, and set fire to all the Ships in the Harbour, which were richly loaden, as also to the City. In this Action a certain *Portuguese* Ensign with his Soldiers did Wonders, and the *Mahometans* fought like Lions; but one of their Commanders, a Fellow of a huge bulk, being slain by *Laurence*, the rest betook themselves to their heels. The *Indians* lost 500 Men in this Engagement, and the *Portugueses* about 22. After which *Almeyda* and *Acunha* sail'd to *Cananor*, from whence the first steered his course to *Cochin*, and the second for *Portugal*. About *Panane* grows besides Cardamom, the best Pepper, and is sold here at a very reasonable rate.

Baldæus.

Attack'd by the Portugueses.

The Forts taken.

500 *slain of the* Indians.

Thus much of *Panane*; we will now proceed to give you an account of *Calecut*, the Capital City of *Malabar*, and the Residence of the *Sammoryn*, where *Steven van der Hagen* the then *Dutch* Admiral, in 1604. enter'd into a strict League with that King, who granted a free Commerce to the *Dutch* throughout all his Dominions. Many years before the *Portugueses* had obtain'd the same liberty of the *Sammoryn*, who had assign'd them certain Habitations in that City; so that they began to flourish in their Commerce, and the *Portuguese* Priests were very successful in the Conversion of many of the Pagans. This exasperated the *Moors* and *Arabians*, who inticed the *Nairos* (always greedy after Prey) to fall

Calecut.

League betwixt the Dutch *and the* Sammoryn.

Baldæus. The Factory of the Provinces of Calicut assaulted by the Indians.

fall to the number of 4000 upon the *Portugueses* (not above 70 strong) in their Factory, who were almost all massacred by them.

Portugueses massacred.

Pedro Alvares Capral the *Portuguese* General in those parts, being inform'd of this barbarous Attempt, and finding that the *Sammoryn* had not been altogether ignorant of the matter, to revenge the Death of his Country-men, burnt ten of their Merchant Ships richly loaden, batter'd the City with his Great Guns, and kill'd them above 600 Men. The same Treatment these *Barbarians* receiv'd afterwards from *Meneses*. We will not in this place pretend to give a particular account of all the Differences and Warlike Exploits of the *Portugueses* here, and of the famous Actions of *Albuquerque*, *Henry Meneses*, *James Sylveria*, *Capral*, &c. we will only mention in this place, that the *Portugueses* having found means to erect a Fort at *Calecut* by the Connivance of *Nanbeadar* the old *Sammoryn*'s Sister's Son (who favour'd the *Portugueses*) the Kings of *Cananor* and *Cochin* were so nettled thereat, that they did not desist till they had engag'd the *Sammoryn* to attack it.

Their Death reveng'd.

The Portuguese Fort besieg'd.

It being then in the Winter-season when the *Portugueses* could scarce expect any Relief, and the Fort provided with a Garison of 300 Men only, they were driven to great Distress; a certain Renegado, a Native of *Sicily*, who had serv'd as an Engineer in the Siege of *Rhodes*, directing the *Moors* in their Attacks. Hereupon *John de Lima* Governor of the Fort did all he could to defend himself, in hopes of the approaching Spring; and having extended his Fortifications (by means of great Casks fill'd with Sand) to the Shore, sent notice of his distressed state to *Henry de Meneses*, who without delay sent 140 Land Soldiers aboard two Ships commanded by *Christopher Jusart* and *Edward Fonseca* to his Relief: but the last being becalm'd near the Shore of *Calecut*, and the other not having above 80 Men aboard, *John Lima* did not think it advisable to land with so small a number, as being not sufficient to break through the Enemies Works into the Fort. However *Jusart* being resolved to venture at all, landed in a Boat with 30 Volunteers, who fought their

Bravery of the Portugueses.

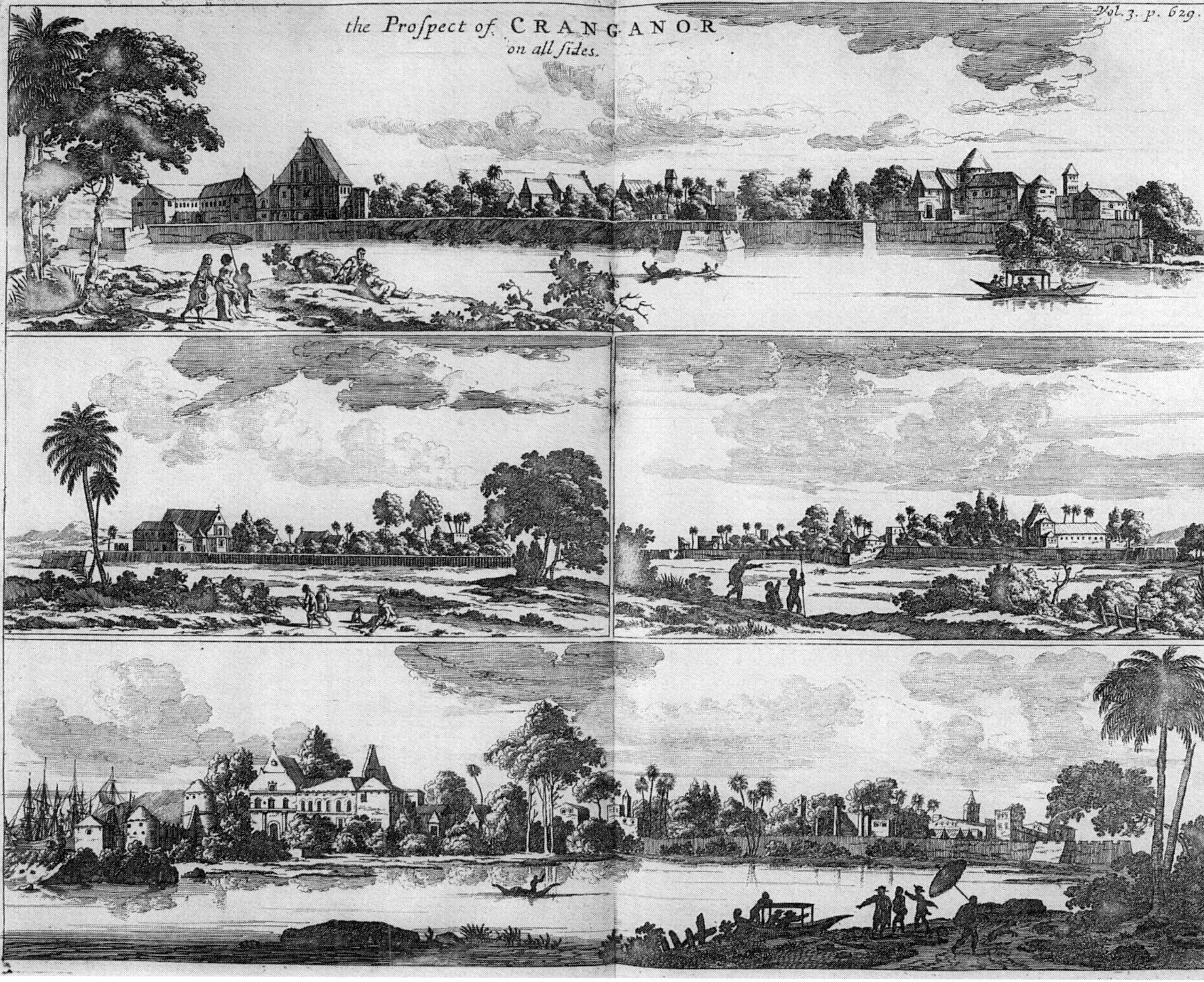
Vol. 3. p. 629.
the Prospect of CRANGANOR
on all sides.

their way through the Enemy, and with the loss of four of their Men reach'd the Fort, which in the mean while was assaulted by the *Barbarians*, who were so warmly receiv'd by the *Portuguese* Granadeers, that they were glad to retire in great Confusion to their Works.

Soon after *Fonseca* arriving with his Ship, convey'd a Letter fastned to an Arrow into the Fort, intimating his arrival, and desiring his Instructions how to serve him. *Lima* sent an Answer, that he thought it not advisable to expose himself and his Men to the same danger as *Jusart* had done, but that he should return with all speed to *Meneses*, and solicit a Succour of 500 Men, with a good quantity of Ammunion, wherewith he did not question but to defend the place. *Fonseca* being return'd to *Cochin*, and having deliver'd his Message to *Meneses*, he dispatch'd immediately *Anthony de Sylva* with some Ships, for the relief of the besieged, whilst he was making all necessary Preparations to follow with a much greater Force in the Spring.

Fonseca *order'd not to land.*

The *Sammoryn* fearing the worst, left no stone unturn'd to oblige the Besieged to a Surrender before that time: and the before-mention'd *Sicilian* having done his utmost Endeavours with Mines, Mortars and Battering Pieces, but in vain, he resolv'd to reduce them by Famine, which he might questionless have effected, had he had only a small Squadron of Ships to block up the Harbour. But the Besieged being from time to time supply'd with Provisions and Refreshments by small Boats which enter'd in the night time, they held it out bravely till Spring, when *Meneses* arriving with 1500 *Portugueses*, landed his Men, and having put the *Malabars* to the rout, with the loss of 3000 Men on their side (among whom was also the *Sicilian*) the *Sammoryn* was so terrified thereat, that to prevent his Country from being ravag'd by the *Portugueses*, he clap'd up a sudden Peace: And the *Portugueses* judging the Fort too chargeable to keep, did afterwards demolish it of their own accord; in the springing up of which many *Malabars* (greedy after Prey) were blown up into the Air.

The Fort reliev'd.

Baldæus.

And demolish'd.

Notwithstanding this Peace, the *Sammoryn* let slip no opportunity of doing mischief to the *Portugueses*; being incourag'd thereunto by the Differences arisen betwixt the *Portuguese* Generals, as betwixt *Meneses* and *Gama*, and *Sampajo* and *Mascarenhas*, about the Viceroyship, which had almost prov'd fatal to the *Portuguese* Affairs in the *Indies*. This is evident from a Letter writ by *Christopher de Sousa* to the said *Sampajo*, in which he represents to him the danger unto which the *Portugueses* (a small number in comparison of their Enemies) were exposed daily in the *Indies*, by his Difference with *Mascarenhas* about the Viceroyalty, exhorting him not to have recourse to Violence, but the Arbitration of such Persons as were competent Judges; telling him, that in case of refusal he must not expect to be obey'd by him. Which coming from a Person noted for his Courage, Liberality and Generosity in these parts, did not a little abate the Haughtiness of *Sampajo*: and *Mascarenhas* returning into *Portugal*, was favourably receiv'd by the King, who having recall'd *Sampajo*, oblig'd him to give full satisfaction to *Mascarenhas* for the Imprisonments, Affronts and Damages he had sustain'd upon that account. For the more ample Relation of which we refer our selves to the *Portuguese* Historians. From *Calecut* we will turn towards *Cranganor*, in order to give you a Description of its Origin and Situation, and by what means it fell into the Hands of the *Hollanders*.

Differences among the Portuguese *Generals.*

CHAP. XVIII.

A Description of Cranganor. *How it was besieged and taken by the* Dutch. *Its Excellencies. The Isle of* Vaypin. Cochin *Fortified. Its Inhabitants, Buildings, plenty of Provisions,* &c. *Is besieged the first time by the* Dutch, *who raised the Siege.*

The River and City of Cranganor.

Cranganor lies five Leagues to the North of *Cochin*, and 20 to the South of *Calicut*, upon a sandy Hill. On the South side of the entrance of the River, is built a small Fort call'd *Paliport*; a mile above which, higher up the River, lies the City and Fortress of *Cranganor*, a Place strongly fortify'd by the *Portugueses* at divers

Baldæus. divers times; for in the beginning they had only a Tower, which they afterwards strengthen'd by a Wall, and at last enclosed the whole by regular Fortifications of Earth. The King of *Cranganor* keeps his Residence not far from *Cranganor:* He that then reigned, was a young, lusty, and tall Person, a declared Enemy of the *Portugueses*, as well as the *Sammoryn*.

In the Year 1661. after the *Dutch* had made themselves masters of *Coulang*, and by strengthening the same with Fortifications, and a good Garison, had secured the South side, they thought it expedient (before they attempted the Conquest of *Cochin*) to get also a firm footing on the North side at *Cranganor*, especially since they fear'd they might be obliged to pass the Winter thereabouts, it being in *December*. According we landed our Men, but found (beyond expectation) the Fortifications in such a state, as not to be attack'd without great Cannon. Above 14 days being spent in raising Batteries, making of Trenches and Breaches, but to no great purpose, and the approaching Season obliging us to carry on the Siege with all possible expedition, it was resolved (upon intelligence given by a certain Person, concerning the Condition of the Place) to attack the Point next to the River, on *Sunday* Jan. 15. 1662. very early in the morning.

Is besieged by the Dutch,

And taken by storm.

The Signal being given accordingly by a Cannon Shot, our Forces advanced, under the favour of the Smoke of our great Artillery, to the Bulwork, which they took with Sword in hand, chasing the *Portugueses* thence to the *Jesuits* Church. In this Action the *Dutch* Captains, *Poolmann*, *Schulenburg*, and *Simon Werding*, as also Lieutenant *Silvester*, acquired immortal Honour, being slain as they were mounting the Breach, with 78 common Soldiers, and many wounded.

Loss on both sides.

On the *Portuguese* side above 200 Christians were killed, besides a great number of the *Nairos*; and among the rest *Urbano Fialho Fereira* the Governour of the Place.

The *Portugueses* then hung out a white Flag, desiring a Parley upon reasonable Conditions; which were granted them, and by virtue thereof the *Portuguese* Soldiers transported into *Europe*. During this Siege we found the Nights very cold, tho the Days were almost insupportable by the excessive Heat. And after the Conquest thereof, being ordered to preach the Thanksgiving Sermon in one of the Parish Churches (of which there were 7) I pitch'd upon a Text in *Deuteronom.* Chap. 23. v. 14.

The *Hollanders* judging it at that time convenient to surrender the Place into the King's hands, the same was done accordingly; but regain'd and refortify'd the same afterwards, when they found themselves engag'd in a War with the *Sammoryn*, who made frequent Excursions as far as *Cochin*; a thing so common among these *Barbarians*, that no settled Peace can be expected with so many Kings.

And upon this Occasion I can't sufficiently commiserate the Condition of the Inhabitants of the Countries about *Cranganor* and *Cochin*, who being guided by ignorant *Romish* Priests, are in great danger of falling by degrees into *Paganism* again; the District of *Cranganor* having formerly been so considerable for the great numbers of Christians of St. *Thomas* (as they are call'd) inhabiting there, that a *Portuguese* Archbishop had his Residence in that City. It is the general Opinion here, that St. *Thomas* the Apostle coming first to *Socotora*, an Isle at the entrance into the *Red Sea*, there preached the Gospel with good success; whence coming to *Cranganor* and *Coulang*, he converted a great number to the Christian Faith. From hence taking his way thro *Coromandel* into *China*, he returned to *Maliapour*, where he suffered Martyrdom. But of these Christians of St. *Thomas*, we shall have occasion to say more hereafter, our present purpose being to say something of the State of Affairs in the *Portuguese* Times.

Cranganor *once an Archbishoprick.*

First then, at our arrival at *Cranganor*, we found there a Noble College of the Jesuits, with a stately Library belonging to it, the Structure it self being not inferior to many in *Europe*. Besides the Church of the *Franciscans*, they had a stately Cathedral, adorn'd with the Tombs of the Archbishops of this Place. Without the Wall of *Cranganor* was the College of *Chanotte*, famous for the resort of the Christians of St. *Thomas* hither, who exercised their Religious Worship here in the *Syriac* Language; and having erected a School for the Education of their Youth, had several Masters and Priests of their own: Of which more in the Description of *Cochin*.

The Jesuits College.

The College of Chanotte.

This Language being in high esteem among the Natives here, and used sometimes also by our Saviour and his Apostles; not only a Printing House, but a Seminary has been erected at *Rome* for the cultivating thereof, and propagating the same among the Youth. Thus

*

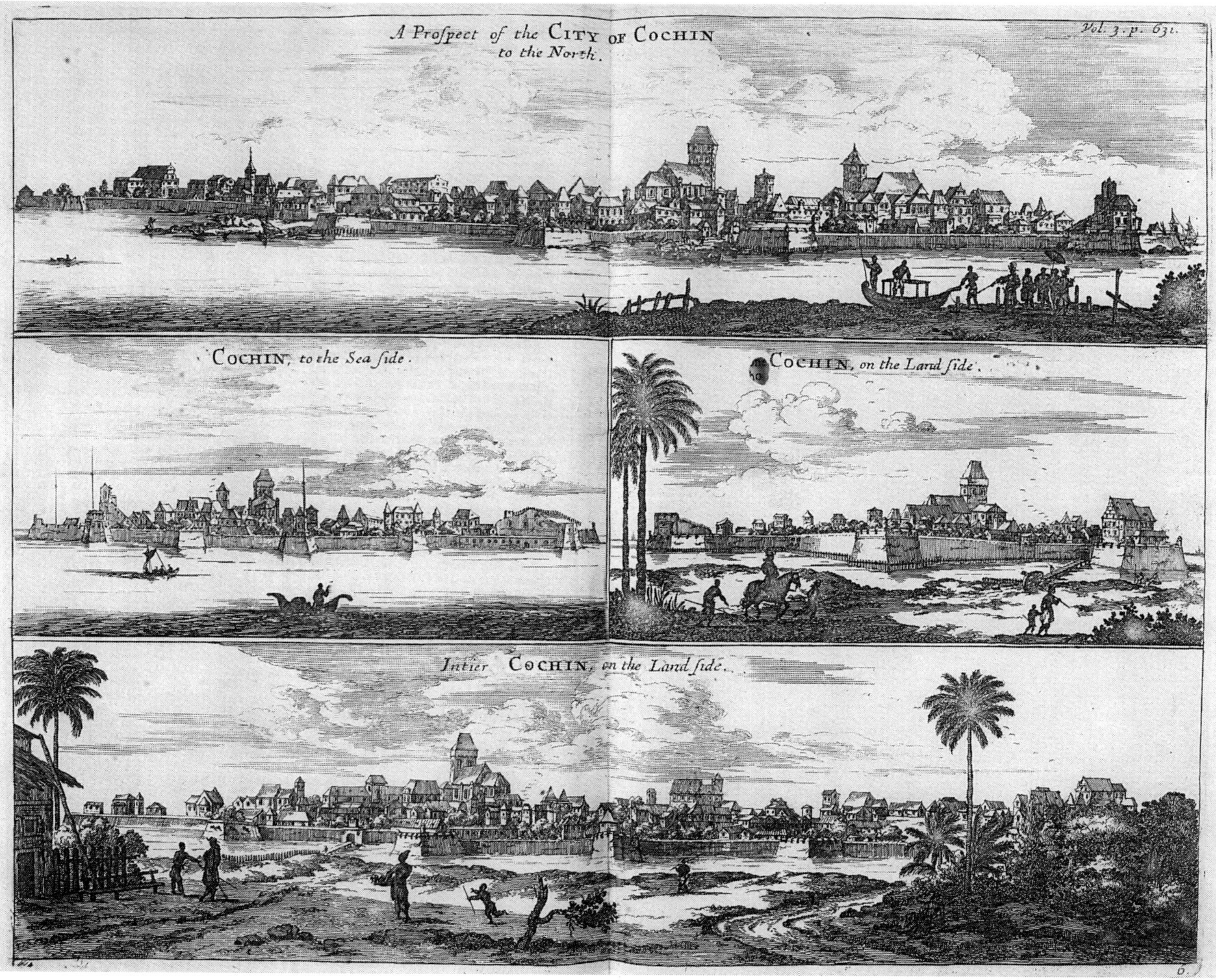

Vol. 3. p. 631.

A Prospect of the CITY OF COCHIN to the North.

COCHIN, to the Sea side.

COCHIN, on the Land side.

Intier COCHIN, on the Land side.

The Syriac *Language propagated at* Rome.

Thus 1622. a *Syriac* Dictionary was published at *Rome*, by *John Baptist Ferrarius*, a Native of *Siena*; and the *Syriac* Grammar of *Georgius Ameira*, a famous Divine and Philosopher of the College of the *Maronites*, born near the Mount *Libanus*. And 1628. *Abrahamus Ecchelensis* obliged the World with his *Introduction to the Fundamentals of the Christian Faith*, in the same Language. Whence it is evident that the *Roman* Clergy exceed ours, in their zeal of propagating the *Roman* Religion; tho on the other hand it must be allow'd that their Plenty furnishes them with sufficient opportunities of performing those things which the *Reformed Ministers* for want of Means are forced to let alone. I have seen divers Books printed with the *Portuguese* Characters, in the *Malabar* Language, for the instruction of the *Paruas*, one whereof I keep by me to this day; tho at the same time I must confess, that in case we should follow the same Method, in printing with our Characters, though in their Language, it would not have the same effect, they being much bigotted both to the *Roman* Clergy and the *Portuguese* Language; so that I have met with some of the *Paruas* who spoke as good *Portuguese* as they do at *Lisbon*. For the rest, the Products of *Cranganor* are the same as in the other Parts of *Malabar*, except that now and then they meet with some Gold Dust, but in no great quantity.

The Isle of Vaypin.

Betwixt the River of *Cranganor* and that of *Cochin*, lies the Isle of *Vaypin*. When the *Dutch*, in *Feb.* 1662. besieged *Cochin* the first time, they erected a Fort upon the Bank of the River, from whence they batter'd the Place, the River being there not above a Musket-shot over: This Fort was call'd the *New Orange*, and here we found a goodly Edifice, formerly belonging to the Bishop of the Place; as also a very large Church, in which I preach'd the 29th of *Jan.* 1662. The Isle it self is tolerably fertile, under the Jurisdiction of the King of *Cochin*, whose Dominions extend from the River of *Cranganor*, six Leagues South of *Cochin*, the whole length being about ten Leagues. The Kings of *Cochin* have always kept firm to the *Portuguese* Interest, ever since *Triumpara*, being conquered by the King of *Calecut*, sought for refuge among the *Portugueses*, who restored him to his Kingdom, tho he afterward prefer'd a private Life before his Crown.

Cochin.

Cochin is a very antient City, but was not fortify'd till 1504. in the time of the two *Albuquerques*, who set sail 1503. from *Belem* in *Portugal*; and after many smart Engagements with the *Sammoryn*, *Alphonsus* return'd into *Portugal*, where he obtain'd the Sirname of *The Great*, his Actions being describ'd in a peculiar Treatise publish'd at *Lisbon* 1576. by *John Batreira*. Soon after the *Portugueses* built a Church there, and entred into a League with the *Sammoryn*, and the Fortifications were considerably augmented by *Edward Patieco*, and a Wall erected by *L. Vasco* towards the Sea side. In some Years after this City began to increase so considerably, that it might compare with some of the best in *Europe*, its length being near two *English* Miles.

Baldæus.

Christians and Mahometans lived first together.

At first the Christians and Mahometans lived promiscuously in the City; which occasioning frequent Disturbances, *Albuquerque* obtain'd from the King *Naubeadora*, that each should have their peculiar Quarters assign'd them to live in. In and about the City of *Cochin*, lived also formerly some *Jews*, who even now have a Synagogue allow'd them without the Fortifications; they are neither White nor Brown, but quite Black. The *Portuguese* Histories mention, that at a certain time, certain blasphemous Papers against our Saviour, with some severe Reflections against the Jesuit *Gonsalvus Pereira* (who afterwards suffer'd Martyrdom at *Monopatapa*) being found in a Box set in the Great Church for the gathering of Alms; and the same being supposed to be laid there by some *European Jews*, who now and then used to resort thither privately, this gave occasion to introduce the Inquisition into *Goa*.

Cochin may for its bigness justly challenge the second Place after *Goa* among the *Indian* Cities formerly in the possession of the *Portugueses*, tho at present it is not near so big as the City of *Batavia*. Its situation lies at 10 Degrees of North Latitude, bordering to the West upon the Sea, and the River has about 17 or 18 fathom Water at high Tide; but its Entrance is very difficult in the Winter-time, being commonly choak'd up by the Sands which are carried thither by the Stream in the Winter Season, which however are again removed by the violence of the Current in the Summer-time.

Cochin *not very wholesom, but plentiful.*

About *Cochin*, as well as all along the Coast of *Malabar*, they have every day two sorts of Winds, *viz.* The Land Wind beginning in the Evening, and the Sea Wind at ten in the Morning. *Cochin* is not accounted so wholesom as most of the other places seated on the Coast of *Malabar*, by reason of its situation in low

and

Baldæus.

and marshy Grounds; but abounds both in Fish and Flesh, and its situation is extremely delightful, by reason of the many Brooks, and adjacent little Islands in the River, wherein many of the *Portugueses* have built themselves very pleasant Summer Seats.

The River runs on the back-side of the best Houses of the City, where they catch Fish with Casting-nets, at which the *Chineses* inhabiting here are very dexterous. Formerly this City could boast of divers stately Churches, since demolished by the *Dutch*. The Jesuits Church and College facing the Sea-shore, had a lofty Steeple and a most excellent set of Bells: The College, which was 3 Stories high, and contained about 20 or 30 Apartments, being surrounded with a strong Wall. The Cathedral was also a noble piece of Architecture, adorn'd with two rows of Pillars, and a lofty Steeple.

Antient Churches and Convents of Cochin.

The Church and Convent of the *Austin* Friers stood upon the Bank of the River; and the Church of the *Dominicans* with their *Convents*, were two rare pieces of Workmanship, beautified with a double row of Pillars of most excellent Stone. The Church and Monastery of the *Franciscans* is the only that remains standing as yet, but has no more than two Brothers left, who are allow'd the free exercise of their Religion.

The best Houses of *Cochin* have their Court-yards and Gardens belonging to them, enclosed with very thin, yet strong and high Walls, so that the Neighbours can't overlook one another. The situation of the City is much more in length than breadth, without any Channels in the Streets; however that end towards the Sea-side is much broader than the other, as may be seen by the annexed Draught, which also representing an exact view of its Fortifications, we will refer the Reader to it.

The Malabar Cochin.

The *Malabar Cochin* is seated somewhat lower, and built after the *Indian* fashion, with very broad Streets: it is very populous, and the Royal Palace is built with Bricks and Mortar after the *European* way, with Apartments very spacious and lofty; near which stands the *Pagode*, with a very large Cistern adjoining to it.

Anno 1662. in *Febr.* at the time of our first landing before *Cochin*, the *Nairos* inhabiting hereabouts (notwithstanding we positively declar'd we were no Enemies of the King, but only of the *Portugueses*) assembled in great Numbers in this Palace and the *Pagode*, and from thence assaulted our Forces, which obliged us to drive them from thence, with the slaughter of 400 on their side, they fighting very desperately, by reason they had beforehand intoxicated their Brains with very large Doses of *Opium*. The old Queen of *Cochin* being taken Prisoner in the Fray, by *Henry van Rhede* an Ensign, was kept in safe custody for some time after.

400 Nairos slain. The Queen of Cochin *taken Prisoner.*

Afterwards we began to form our Attacks against the *Portuguese Cochin* in three several places; that on the Land-side near the Church of St. *Thomas* (which served us for a Chappel and Hospital) being commanded by the General in Person; that along the Sea-side by *Ysbrand Gotsken*; and the third near the River by the Commodore *Roothaus*. After some time spent in making of Trenches, and rasing of Batteries, it was thought expedient to surprize the Enemy on that side near the River. The first *Sunday* in *February* being appointed for that purpose, Capt. *Peter Wash* was ordered to begin the Assault with a certain Detachment at four a Clock in the Morning: but it being after Sun-rising before they could reach the Place, the *Portugueses* took the Alarum; and being timely sustain'd by fresh Troops drawn thither by the ringing of the Bells, gave such a warm Reception to the *Hollanders*, that after a most obstinate Engagement, they were forced to sound the Retreat, with the loss of divers of their best Men, and among them the beforemention'd Captain, who was kill'd by two Musket Bullets. The General *Ryetos van Goens*, and the Commodore *Roothaus*, were also both in great danger, the first receiving several Shots through his Hair, the last being likely to have been cast into a deep Well.

An unsuccessful Assault upon Cochin.

Notwithstanding this Disappointment, the Trenches were carried on with all imaginable speed, tho not without great difficulty, by reason of the marshy Grounds, which cost us a good number of Men, more than we could conveniently spare at that time, when our Forces were not a little weakned before; we having left at least 300 sick and wounded at *Coulang*, and a considerable Garison at *Cranganor*, and in the Fort of *New-Orange* on the Point of the Isle of *Vaypin*. We continued however to batter the Town incessantly with our great Artillery, and to omit nothing we thought might annoy the Enemy; till a whole Month being spent in this Siege, and the Number of our Men reduced to 1400. we began to consider of the approaching Winter, the uncertainty of the Event, and

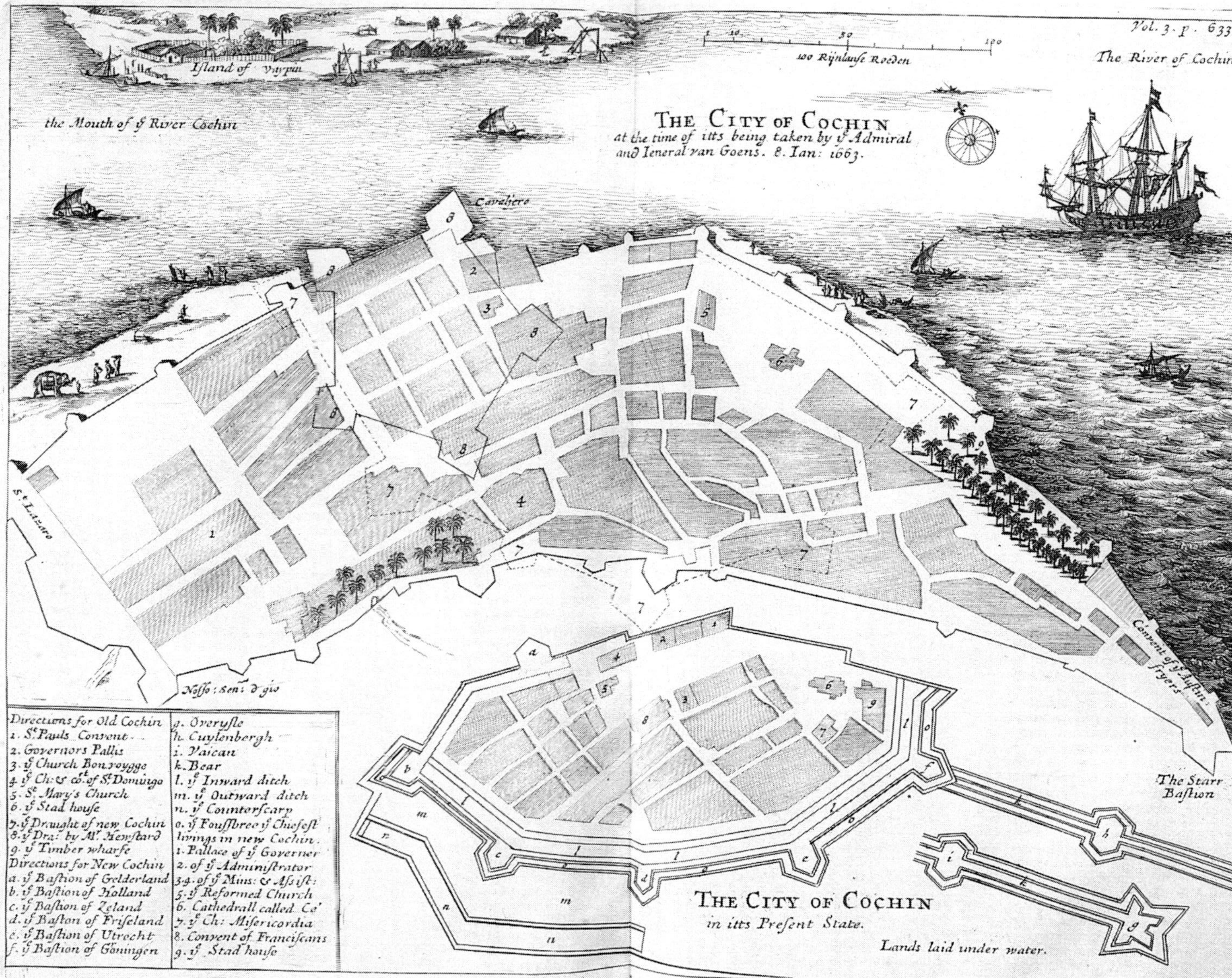
Vol. 3. p. 633.
Island of Vaypin
100 Rijnlanse Roeden
The River of Cochin
the Mouth of ye River Cochin
THE CITY OF COCHIN
at the time of itts being taken by ye Admiral
and Ienerall van Goens. 8. Ian: 1663.
Cavalhero
St Lazaro
Nosso: Sen: d' gio
Convent of ye Austin fryers
The Starr Bastion
Directions for Old Cochin
1. St Pauls Convent
2. Governors Pallis
3. ye Church Bon voygge
4. ye Ch: & cot of St Domingo
5. St Mary's Church
6. ye Stad house
7. ye Draught of new Cochin
8. ye Dra: by Mr Hewstard
9. ye Timber wharfe
Directions for New Cochin
a. ye Bastion of Gelderland
b. ye Bastion of Holland
c. ye Bastion of Zeland
d. ye Baston of Friseland
e. ye Bastion of Utrecht
f. ye Bastion of Gøningen
g. Overysle
h. Cuylenbergh
i. Vaican
k. Bear
l. ye Inward ditch
m. ye Outward ditch
n. ye Counterscarp
o. ye Foussbree ye Chiefest livings in new Cochin.
1. Pallace of ye Governer
2. of ye Administrator
3.4. of ye Mins: & Assist:
5. ye Reformed Church
6. Cathedrall called Co'
7. ye Ch: Misericordia
8. Convent of Franciscans
9. ye Stad house
THE CITY OF COCHIN
in itts Present State.
Lands laid under water.

7.

Baldæus.

and the want of several things necessary to carry on a long Siege; so that after mature deliberation, it was judged necessary to raise the Siege, and delay the Execution thereof to a more convenient time.

The Siege raised.

Accordingly our Cannon, Ammunition and other Moveables being sent aboard upon Floats, the General made a safe Retreat in the Night-time without beat of Drum; and the better to cover his Design, had gain'd a certain *Jew* by Money to make the Clock of S. *Thomas* Church strike as usually: to which also contributed not a little the ingenious Invention of a certain Gunner, named *Henry Boerdorp*, who went the Rounds all Night long, and calling *Who is there? Stand*, and that in a different Tone, deceived the Enemies Centinels, that they had not the least Suspicion of our Retreat; so that all the *Dutch* Forces got safely aboard, without the Loss of as much as one Man, except a *Negro* Slave. When the *Dutch* Soldiers saw the Artillery and Baggage going on board, they were not a little dissatisfyed thereat, but being appeased by Commodore *Roothous*, who told them that it was done only to secure them against the Enemy, who intended to make a general Sally, they were afterwards glad to follow their Officers Directions in the Retreat.

The Retreat of the Dutch.

It was almost noon before the *Portugueses* were convinced of our Retreat, as suspecting the same to be only a Stratagem to draw them into an Ambush; but when they saw us weigh our Anchors, they express'd their Joy with the Discharge of their Cannon round the Walls. The *Dutch* General having left a sufficient Garison for the guard of the Fort of *New-Orange*, another at *Cranganor* under the Command of Captain *Verspreet*, and constituted *Peter du Pon*, a brave Soldier, Commander in Chief of all the Forces in those Parts, sail'd to *Coulang*; which Place being likewise provided with all Necessaries, he took his course towards *Batavia*, with an Intention to give *Cochin* a second Visit in the Spring, which he did accordingly with better Success.

CHAP. XIX.

The Isle of Formosa *surprized by the* Chineses. Cochin *besieged a second time by the* Dutch, *is forced to surrender; the chief Articles of the Capitulation. The City made more compact, and strengthened with regular Fortifications. The* Roman Catholick *Bishop of the* Christians *of* S. Thomas *comes to* Cochin. *His Original Bull of Indulgence.*

BY this time we were sufficiently inform'd of the miserable State of our Countrymen in the Isle of *Formosa* (which the *Portugueses* would often upbraid us with during the Siege) a compleat account whereof would be perhaps too tedious, and look'd upon as beyond our purpose; therefore I will only for the Satisfaction of the Reader, insert a Letter written by the Reverend Mr. *John Kruys*, Minister of the Gospel there in the Fort of *Zealand*, and afterwards at *Negapatan* on the Coast of *Coromandel* (where he died) and directed to me, and Mr. *A. Breyl* my Fellow-Minister in these Parts.

" AFter my Arrival here the *6th Oct.* with my Family, I was seized with so violent a Fever, as disabled me to write to you, yet did not hinder me to remember my hearty Service to you by Mr. *Roos*, Captain of our Ship, and the Factor Mr. *Keuf*. Whether the same was brought to you or not, I am ignorant as yet, having for some time after been so dangerously ill with my Distemper, that my Recovery was almost despaired of; but am now by God's peculiar Mercy so far recovered, that I went first to Church on Thursday last, and preached twice the Sunday following, and intend to visit the Sick to morrow, and to administer the Holy Sacrament on Sunday next. To give you a particular Account of the late miserable State of the Isle of *Formosa*, is both beyond the compass of a Letter, and my present Strength; and tho I tremble at the very Thoughts of it, yet will I mention the chiefest Transactions: The first Assault of the furious *Chineses* was made against the Castle of *Sacam*, whereabouts, after they had cut some of our Soldiers in pieces, they took my eldest Son and my Wife's Brother, who, tho very young,

Miserable Condition of Formosa.

Baldæus. "young, had one of his Arms cut off. "The next day our Ship called the *Hector* being engag'd with a vast Number "of *Chinese Jones*, was blown up, and "in her some of our best Soldiers, among whom was also my Father-in-law *Thomas Pedel.* The Fort of *Sacam* "being, after a defence of a few days, "forc'd to surrender for want of fresh "Water and other Necessaries, the Ministers, Officers, Schoolmasters, Soldiers, and in general all the Inhabitants of the flat Country, were forced to make the best Terms they "could for themselves. The Squadron "of Ships commanded by Mr. *Kauw*, "(after it had for a small time rejoic'd "our drooping Spirits) being dispers'd "by Tempests, and the Ship the *Urk* "forc'd upon the Sands, and taken by "the Enemy, the same was neither seen "nor heard of in five or six Weeks after. To be short, the whole Country "being over-run by the *Chineses*, our "Soldiers every where routed, *Koukerken* laid in Ashes in sight of our Fort: "Such of our Contrymen as had not secur'd themselves by a timely Flight, "fell into the Hands of the merciless Enemies, who sacrific'd the Reverend "Mr. *Hambrock* with his Son, and divers "others in *Tilocen*, to their Fury: As also "Mr. *Peter Mus* Minister of *Favorlang*, "and Mr. *Arnold Winsheim* Minister of "*Sinkan*, who had their Heads cut off, "and their Wives with many others "carried into Slavery. By this there "being great want of Necessaries in the "Fortress, the Soldiers died daily of "the Bloody Flux, Scurvy and Dropsy; "so that in nine Months time, having "lost above 1600 Men, both by Famine "and the Sword, we were forc'd (for "the Preservation of our Lives) to capitulate. Who can without Tears remember the unexpected Destruction "and Ruin of so many Families, and of "near 30 Ministers, partly in their "Lives, partly in their Fortunes (among whom I had my share, having "lost all that I had gather'd in 15 Years "time) the Loss and Dishonour of the "Company, with the unspeakable Miseries, among which I reckon mine none "of the least, as the Loss of three Parts "of my Library? All which we ought to "look upon as the effects of God's just "Indignation, on account of our manifold Sins. I have no more to add, "than that it is none of the least among "my other Afflictions, that Matters are "both so ill represented, and worse taken at *Batavia*.

Several Ministers beheaded by the Chineses.

Subscribed,

Your affectionate Collegue to serve you,

Negapatnam 13. Octob. 1662.

Joannes Kruyf.

But it is time to leave the miserable in the Isle of *Formosa*, and to come to the second Siege of *Cochin*. *Anno* 1662. in *September*, *Jacob Hustart* late Govenour of the *Moluques* and *Amboyna*, and afterwards residing in the same Quality in *Ceylon* and *Malabar*, set sail from *Batavia* with a good Squadron of Ships, *Tsbrand Goske* Commodore, for *Cochin*, leaving Mr. *Ryklof Van Goens* at *Batavia* by reason of his Sickness, but follow'd soon after. In *November* we began to batter the place most furiously, being willing to reduce it before we could receive the News of a Peace concluded betwixt us and the *Portugueses* (which we expected every day) and having the last year receiv'd certain Instructions from the Governours of our Company to allow free Commerce, and Liberty of Religion to all such *Portugueses* as would submit to us, we proposed to the Besieged that they should be left in full possession of their Churches (except one) provided they would receive a *Dutch* Garison. This was not ill relish'd by some, but *Ignatio Sermento* the Governour refusing to comply with it, we resolv'd to lose no time to reduce the place by force.

The second Siege of Cochin.

Proposals made to the Besieged.

Accordingly it was resolv'd in a Council of War to assault it on the River side at low Tide; and to render the Passage the less difficult, a great number of Sacks fill'd with Sand were prepar'd to be thrown into the River. But this Attempt prov'd unsuccessful, our People meeting with so hot a Reception there, that they were glad to think of retreating. But as we had no time to lose, so we soon pitch'd upon another, which was carried on with better success: For that brave Commander *Peter du Pon* being order'd to assault the Bastion on the Bank of the River, he executed his Commission so successfully, that (tho not without great Resistance) he broke through the Enemy, and maintain'd himself in some of the adjacent Houses against the whole Force of the Enemy, till being seconded by fresh Troops of his own, they put out the white Flag, and sent their Deputies

Unsuccessful Attempt of the Dutch.

puties to capitulate upon the following Conditions.

Articles of Surrender of Cochin.

The *Franciscans* to enjoy the free Exercise of their Religion under the Protection of the States: The Clergy to have free liberty to carry away all their Images, Church-Ornaments, Relicks, *&c.* and what else belong'd to them. The Governour *Ignatio Sermento* and his Family, together with all the Officers, to be receiv'd civilly by the *Dutch*. The Garison to march out with Ensigns display'd, Drums beating, with Bag and Baggage, and to be conducted in *Dutch* Vessels to *Goa*, except such of the Soldiers as were in immediate Pay of his Majesty, who were to be transported to *Portugal*. Such of the Inhabitants as were willing to stay behind under the Jurisdiction of the *Dutch* Company, to have free liberty to remain in their full Possessions, and that care should be taken of the sick and wounded. All which was punctually perform'd, and the Keys of the City deliver'd to our General, who soon after enter'd victorious on Horse-back in

great Pomp, and order'd a solemn Thanksgiving to be made in the great Church lately belonging to the Jesuits, for the Conquest of so important a place, which was done accordingly.

Orders given by the Dutch *General.*

Being thus become entirely Masters of *Cochin*, after it had been 150 years in the possession of the *Portugueses*; the *Dutch* General made it his chiefest care to issue his Orders not to molest the *Portugueses*, but to observe punctually the Articles of the Capitulation. The next was to demolish a certain part of the Houses and Churches of the City, in order to draw it into a more narrow compass, and to render the Fortifications the more regular, the former requiring too great a number of Men to defend them. The King of *Cochin* being crown'd, and divers of the neighbouring petty Princes oblig'd to become his Tributaries, several strict Alliances were made with the neighbouring Kings to the South of the River of *Cochin*.

A Roman *Bishop over the Christians here, comes to* Cochin.

About the same time *Joseph de Sancta Maria*, of the Order of the *Discalceated Carmelites*, sent by the Pope in quality as a Bishop among the Christians of St. *Thomas*, came (in his return into *Europe*) to *Cochin* to salute our General, and was

very

Baldæus. very kindly receiv'd by his Excellency: He had two sorts of Enemies to contend with during his stay in these parts; first of all with the *Portugueses*, who could not brook that any other but their Countrymen should be exalted to that Dignity, and that not by the Pope, but by their own King: The other was the *Archidabo* (as the *Portugueses* stile him) or chief Head of the Christians of St. *Thomas* hereabouts, who being a *Negro* would neither submit himself nor his Flock to the *Romish* Jurisdiction.

Concerning the Christians of St. *Thomas* we shall speak more at large anon.

But to return to the Bishop, Brother *Joseph de Sancta Maria*, he was sent from *Rome* with a Bull of Indulgence, granted *Jan.* 16. 1660. in the fifth year of *Alexander* VII. Pope of *Rome*, subscribed by the Cardinal *Barberini*, *Joseph Caetanus*, &c. the true Original whereof being in my Custody, and containing many things tending to the Elucidation of the Affairs of the Christians of St. *Thomas* (of whom we are to treat immediately after) we thought it not beyond our scope to oblige the Reader with the Translation thereof.

Franciscus *Bishop of* Portua, *Cardinal* Barberini, *Vice-Chancellor of the Holy* Roman *Church, and Protector of the Honourable Fraternity of the Church of* S. Jerome.

Josephus Caetanus, *Keeper of both the Seals of his Holiness, Referendary and Prelate;* Carolus Antonius à Puteo, *Knight;* Franciscus Cinus, *Sollicitor-General of the Court of* Rome; Johannes Baptista Valentis, *Abbot;* Petrus Bassanus, Carolus de Comitibus, Pompejus Serinus, Marianus Vecchiarellius, *and* Joh. Bapt. Ciofanus, *Commissioners*:

The Bull of Indulgence. "With to our dearly beloved Brothers and Sisters in Christ of "the most Reverend Fraternity of the "Apostle of St. *Thomas*, of the Church "dedicated to that Saint, without the "Walls of *Cochin*, founded by Legal "Authority, Eternal Salvation in the "Lord.

"The more than ordinary Inclination "you have shewn to Piety, Charitable "Works, and other holy Exercises, have "induc'd us, who according to our Duty "are to take care of the Salvation of "the Faithful, and promoting of Piety "and Religious Exercises, to receive into and unite with our Society your "Fraternity intended for the Exercise "of pious and charitable Works; and "by these Presents receive you as such, "and thereby make you Partakers of all "the Indulgences, Authority and other "Spiritual Gifts granted us by Pope "*Paul* V. of happy Memory. And the "Reverend Father, Brother *Johannes de* "*Sancta Maria*, Frier of the Order of "the Discalceated *Carmelites*, President "of your Fraternity, having in your "Name earnestly sollicited for the said "Reception, and a grant of the Indul-"gences, we the above-mention'd *Prelates* and *Commissioners*, relying upon "the Authority of Pope *Clement* VIII. "of happy Memory, and his Grant of "*Nov.* 7. 1604. and mov'd with a holy "Zeal and Christian Love for the promoting of the true Religious Worship, "we do by virtue of these Letters receive your Fraternity founded according to the Apostolical and Canonical "Institution, with the Approbation of "the most Reverend Bishop, or the Ordinary of that place, into our Communion and Society, pursuant to the Apostolical Authority granted us for that "purpose; and therefore impart to the "said Fraternity and to all its Members "all the Indulgences and other Spiritual "Gifts, specified and granted to our Society by the said Papal Bull of *Paul* V. "to give Encouragement to your Fraternity for the performance of all sorts of "pious Works, and the obtaining of "eternal Salvation (by God's Mercy) "after this Life.

N. B. The Bull of *Paul* V. being very long, fulsome, and not material, was not thought fit to be inserted.

"And

" And it being our full intention that " all the Indulgences, and other Spiritual " Gifts granted us at large, as before- " said, should be enjoy'd by your Fra- " ternity and its Members, pursuant to " the Institution of Pope *Clement* VIII. " of happy memory; we will and com- " mand, that these our Letters shall " have the same Authority (when pro- " duced) as if they contain'd the Origi- " nal it self. For the Confirmation " whereof we have order'd this Letter " to be sign'd by the Secretary of our " Society, and our Seal, together with " that of the Protector thereof, to be " affixed to it. Given in *Rome* at the " usual place of our Assembly, in the " year after the Nativity of our Saviour " Jesus Christ, 1660. of the XIII. In- " diction, the 16*th* of *January*, in the " fifth year of the Reign of our holy " Father *Alexander* VII.

Baldæus.

Subscribed,

Cardinalis Barberinus, Protector.
Joseph Caetanus, Prelate.

Franciscus Cinus,
Carolus Antonius à Puteo,
Marianus Vecchiarellius,
Petrus Bassanus,
John Bapt. Ciofanus,
Philippus de Rubeis,
} Commissioners.

Andreas Leonius, Secretary.

CHAP. XX.

The Voyages, Miracles and Death of St. Thomas *the Apostle. The Doctrine of the Christians of St.* Thomas; *of the* Greek, Syriac, *and* Georgian *Christians*; *of the* Russians, Nestorians, Jacobites, Coptes, Abyssines, Armenians, Maronites. *A good Correspondence betwixt the Eastern and Western Churches very necessary.*

St. Thomas *his arrival in the* Indies.

IT is the general opinion that the Apostle St. *Thomas* did come into the *Indies*, but especially into these parts: His first coming was in the Isle of *Socotora* (at the entrance of the *Red Sea*) where he converted many to the Christian Faith; it being certain that to this day many of the Inhabitants stile themselves *Christians of St. Thomas*, which also induced *Xaverius* to touch at that Island in his Voyage to the *Indies*; and, if we may credit *John de Lucena*, would fain have staid there. From *Socotora* St. *Thomas* sail'd to *Cranganor*, whence, after he had converted many to the Christian Faith, he went to *Coulang*. Upon the Rocks near the Sea-shore of *Coulang* stands a Stone Pillar *, erected there (as the Inhabitants report) by St. *Thomas*. From *Coulang* crossing the high and dangerous Mountains he travell'd into *Coromondel*, where having likewise planted the Seed of the Gospel he sail'd into *China*, where, after he had preach'd the Gospel to the Infidels, he return'd to *Maliapour*, to confirm some of the new converted Christians in their Faith, and there suffer'd Martyrdom.

His several Voyages.

* *I saw this Pillar* 1662.

Maliapour (afterwards call'd St. *Thomas* by the *Portugueses*) was at that time a famous City in *Coromandel*, where this holy Man would fain have built a Church, but was prevented by the *Brahmans*, and their King *Sagam*. They relate a very miraculous thing of St. *Thomas*. The Sea having cast up a Tree of a vast bulk, the King, who was desirous to use it in the building of a House, had imploy'd a great number of Men and Elephants to bring it from thence, but in vain, the Wood being not to be moved from the place: St. *Thomas* standing by told the King, that if he would present him with the piece of Wood, he would carry it alone to the City (then ten Leagues from the Shore). The King looking upon him as a mad Man, told him he should do with it what he pleas'd; whereupon St. *Thomas* tying his Girdle to one of the Branches, and making the sign of the Cross, drew the whole Tree after him with a great deal of ease, follow'd by a vast number of People; and coming to the City erected a *Stone Cross* there, telling the Spectators, that whenever the Sea should rise up to that place, God would send certain Strangers from far distant places to settle the Christian Religion here, which the *Portugueses* would have to be verified at the time of their coming there.

One of St. Thomas *his Miracles.*

St. *Thomas* having by this Miracle, and the

Baldæus. the Conversion of a vast number of Pagans, arriv'd to a great Authority among them; this so incensed the *Brahmans*, that one of them kill'd him with his Launce upon a Hill near the City, where he used to perform his Devotion. They had before that accus'd him falsly of a Murder,
Another Miracle. but St. *Thomas* having resuscitated the Child from Death, he declar'd his own Father to have been his Murderer; which had so powerful an influence upon many of the chief Men of the Country, and the King himself, that they receiv'd Baptism. Some say that St. *Thomas* was kill'd at *Calaminba*, by mistaking this word for *Calurmina*, i. e. *upon a Stone*; *Calur* signifying in the *Malabar* Language a *Stone*, and *mina upon*; St. *Thomas* having been slain upon a Rock: whence it is, that if to this day you ask one of the Christians of St. *Thomas*, where St. *Thomas* suffer'd Martyrdom, they will tell you, *Maliapour Calurmina*, at *Maliapour* upon *the Stone*, where he was ston'd, and at
His Death. last run through with a Launce.

They tell you of a certain Cross made by his Blood, and a vast number of Miracles wrought by it, for which I will refer my self to *Lucena*, *Osorius*, and
* Tom. 1. 1557. *Baronius* *. The Christians of St. *Thomas* teach their Children in their very Infancy these following Heads concerning St. *Thomas*. St. *Thomas* was the Man who first abolish'd Idolatry; it was he who converted the *Chineses* and *Negroes*; it was he that baptiz'd them, and taught them the true Faith, and to profess God the Father, the Son, and Holy Ghost. They also tell you, that he converted the three Kings of the East (one of whom, call'd *Perumal*, they say was King of *Ceylon*) and that St. *Thomas*'s Body was transferr'd from *Maliapour* to *Edessa* in *Mesopotamia*.

But setting aside all these uncertain Relations, the most secure way (founded upon no small Probabilities) is, that St. *Thomas* was actually in these Parts, and converted a great number of People to the Christian Faith; which contradicts that bold Assertion of the *Roman* Catholicks, that all Nations have receiv'd the Christian Faith from *Rome*; it being beyond all question, that at the time of the arrival of the *Portugueses* in those parts under *de Gama*, the Inhabitants declar'd themselves to be Christians from most antient times, desiring the Protection of the King of *Portugal* against the Pagans, and in token of their Obedience presented him with a Silver Scepter gilt. Nay, the Church of *Rome* can't boast of that Honour, even of all parts of *Europe* it self; since the Kings of *England* and *Scotland*, *Lucius* and *Donaldus*, *Vain Boasts of the Church of Rome.*
embrac'd the Christian Faith 124 years after our Saviour's Nativity, without having the least Communication with the Church of *Rome*; whence *Tertullian* rightly says, *Britannorum loca Romanis inaccessa Christo subdita sunt*. And *Cyprianus* says to the same purpose, 240 years after the Birth of Christ, *That the Vine-branches of the Gospel have spread themselves beyond the extent of the* Roman *Empire*. Thus *Dorotheus* Bishop of *Tyrus* under the Reign of *Constantine* the Great, positively asserts, That the Chamberlain of Queen *Candace* did introduce the Gospel into *Ceylon* and the Happy *Arabia*.

The Christians of St. *Thomas* remain'd many years in the Primitive Purity of the Christian Religion, till in time, for want of good Pastors, they began to be infected with some Pagan Superstitions, and were in most imminent danger of losing the Remnants of the Truths of the Gospel, had not *Martome* a Native of *Syria*, taken care of the decay'd state of Christianity in these parts; and being seconded in his Endeavours by divers other Teachers out of *Syria*, *Babylonia*, *Chaldæa* and *Egypt*, the *Syriac* Language *The Christians of St. Thomas decay'd, and afterwards restor'd to their Primitive Purity.*
was introduc'd, and the former Purity of Religion restor'd among them, till in time the *Nestorian* Heresy got footing in *Syria*, and was from thence transplanted hither, as is sufficiently evident from the Records of the *Malabars*.

This *Martome* (signifying in their Language as much as Lord *Thomas*) being much respected by the Kings of *Cranganor* and *Coulang*, and by the Christians of St. *Thomas* in general, was declar'd by them their Head: and the Bishops of *Cochin*, *Coulang* and *Cranganor*, being after- *Had their own Bishops.*
wards sent for out of *Syria*, these introduc'd the *Syriac* Language, and acknowledg'd the Patriarch of *Alexandria* or *Babylon* for their Metropolitan, till at last they submitted to the Pope of *Rome*: For the Supreme Ecclesiastical Head of the *Indians* (at the perswasion of the *Acknowledg the Jurisdiction of Rome.*
Portugueses) did 1562. acknowledg the Supremacy of the Pope of *Rome*, provided they might continue in the former free Exercise of their Religion, which was confirm'd in the Synod of *Goa*, where they would not consent to the least Alteration of any of their Church-Ceremonies. But after the Decease of this Bishop, his Successor 1599, embrac'd with the rest of his Clergy in another Synod, the *Roman* Faith.

Where the Christians of S. Thomas inhabit. The Christians of St. *Thomas* inhabit for the most part on the Coast of *Malabar*, about *Cranganor*, *Cochin*, *Coulang*, *Travancor*, and some in *Coromandel*, amounting in all to a considerable Number. Before they were united with the Church of *Rome*, they were infected with the *Nestorian* Heresy, as some are still to this day; whence it is that they deny the two Natures in the Person of Christ. This *Nestorius* was Bishop of *Constantinople*, and *Eutyches Archimandrit* was Abbot in the same City. His Doctrine was received at first in the Council of *Ephesus*, by the Interest of *Chrysapius* (to please *Eudoxia* the Empress) Lord Chamberlain to *Theodosius* the Emperor; but *Chrysapius* being slain at the Instigation of *Pulcheria*, the Sister of the Emperor, the same was afterwards condemned in another Synod of *Ephesus* held in the Year 431. two Years after the Death of St. *Austin*, wherein *Cyril* Bishop of *Alexandria* presided; as the before-mention'd Council of *Ephesus*, and the Doctrine of *Eutyches* was condemned in the Council of *Chalcedon* 451.

Their Doctrine. For the rest, the antient Christians of St. *Thomas* did administer the Holy Sacrament in both Kinds, using Salt, Bread, and the use of Raisins instead of Wine. It was a very antient Custom among them, not to baptize their Children till they were forty days old, except in case of imminent danger of Life. They used no Unction, neither any Images, except that they had Crosses in their Churches. Their Priests were forbid to marry a second time. They were declared Enemies of *Cyril* of *Alexandria*, a great Antagonist of the *Nestorians*, but reverenced *Nestorius* and *Dioscorus* as Saints. They did not acknowledg the Superiority of the Pope of *Rome*, and used the *Syriac* New Testament in their Churches.

Many Sects in the East. As divers Religions have been broach'd of late Years in *Europe*, so there are many Sects of antient standing in the *East*.

1. The Greeks. The chiefest of these are the *Greeks*, who acknowledg the Patriarch of *Constantinople* for their Head, *viz.* those of *Natolia* (except *Armenia* and *Cilicia*) *Grecia*, *Russia*, *Bulgaria*, *Servia*, *Bosnia*, *Walachia*, *Moldavia*, *Podolia* and *Muscovia*.

2. The Melchites. The next are the *Melchites*, the most numerous of all the Sects in the *East*; they are call'd *Syrians* from *Syria*, and *Melchites* by their Enemies, because they conformed themselves in their Religious Worship, according to the Emperor's Orders. * They acknowledg for their Head the Archbishop of *Damascus*, who antiently had his Residence at *Antioch*.

* *See* Niceph. *Hist. Eccl.* l. 18. c. 58. & l. 28. c. 45.

Baldæus. *3. The Georgians.* The third Sect is that of the *Georgians*, inhabiting the antient *Iberia* between the *Euxine* and *Caspian* Seas. Some would have them to be call'd *Georgians*, because, as they say, they reverence S. *George* as their Patron; but erroneously, the *Georgians* having been mention'd both by *Pliny* and *Mela*, long before S. *George* was known. They are of the same Religion with the *Greeks*, and have eighteen Bishops of their own, besides a Metropolitan.

4. The Russians. The fourth Sect is the *Russians*, who likewise profess the *Greek* Religion, denying with them the Proceeding of the Holy Ghost from Father and Son, the main Point in question betwixt the Eastern and Western Churches.

5. The Nestorians. The fifth Sect of the *Nestorians*, follow the Heretical Doctrine of *Nestorius*, and live for the most part among the Pagans and Mahometans, in *Babylon*, *Assyria*, *Mesopotomia*, *Parthia*, *Media*, &c. Nay, *Paulus Venetus* affirms, that they are found from the North side of *Cataja*, to the most Southerly Parts of the *Indies*; so that on the East side beyond the River *Tigris*, scarce any other Christian Sect is to be met with: The reason whereof they alledg to be, that *Cosroes* King of *Persia*, a declared Enemy of the Emperor *Heraclius*, forced all his Subjects to embrace this Doctrine. The Patriarchal Seat of the *Nestorians* is at *Muzal*, a City of *Mesopotamia* upon the River *Tigris*, now subject to the *Turks*; notwithstanding which it has 40000 Christians and 15 Churches. Some of the *Nestorians* did submit to the *Roman* Jurisdiction under Pope *Julius* III. who was created Pope 1550. and reign'd five Years. And the Patriarch *Abdiesu*, who was invested with the Episcopal Dignity by Pope *Pius* IV. was present at the Council of *Trent*.

6. The Jacobites. The sixth is that of the *Jacobites*, having got their Name from one *Jacob* a Native of *Syria*, and a Follower of the Doctrine of *Eutyches*, 530. according to *Nicephorus* and *Damascenus*. They inhabit for the most part in *Syria*, *Aleppo*, *Cyprus*, *Mesopotamia*, *Babylon*, and *Palestina*, whence the Patriarch of *Jerusalem* is also a *Jacobite*; but the Patriarch of the *Jacobites* resides at *Caranut*, an antient noted City in *Mesopotamia*. They acknowledg but one Nature in Christ, make the Sign of the Cross with one Finger only; they mark their young Children with the sign of the Cross by means of an hot Iron; use both Baptism and Circumcision, and reject the Purgatory, it being their Opinion

Baldæus. nion that the Soul remains with the Body under-ground till the Day of Judgment; and that the Angels are composed of a fiery and lucid Substance.

7. The Coptes. The seventh are the *Coptes*, or *Egyptian* Christians, being rather the Name of a Nation, than belonging to any peculiar Religion: They are the same with the *Jacobites*, the word *Cophti* being the same with *Ægophti*. For notwithstanding the Doctrine of *Eutyches* was condemned in the Council of *Chalcedon*, and *Dioscorus* Patriarch of *Alexandria* deposed upon that score, the same took deep Root in the Eastern Parts, and more especially in *Egypt*. These *Egyptians* (according to *Tecla Maria* an *Abyssine* Priest) agree in Point of Doctrine with the *Abyssines*, and acknowledg the Jurisdiction of the Patriarch of *Alexandria*, whose Residence is now at *Cairo*.

8. The Abyssines. The eighth Sect is that of the *Abyssines*, or *Mediterranean Ethiopians*, being generally *Jacobites*, whence their King (call'd erroneously by some * *Prester John*) is stiled the *Prince of the Jacobites*. They reject absolutely the Council of *Chalcedon*, and will allow it no place in their Writings. To their Patriarch they give the Name of *Albuna*, i. e. *Our Father*, who must be a Native out of the Territories of *Alexandria*, and of S. *Anthony*'s Order; for it is observable that all the Patriarchs and Bishops in the *East*, are either of the Order of S. *Basil* Bishop of *Cesaria* and *Cappadocia*, or else of the Order of S. *Anthony*. The Patriarchs of *Constantinople*, *Antiochia* and *Armenia*, are of the Order of S. *Basil*; those of *Alexandria* and *Ethiopia*, and *Ethiopia*, as also those of the *Jacobites* and *Maronites*, of S. *Anthony*'s Order; but the Patriarchs of the *Nestoreans* are promiscuosly of either of these two Orders. The *Abyssines* have for their Head the Patriarch of *Ethiopia*: They are rebaptized once every Year, on 12*th* day, as indeed are most of the other Eastern Christians. They follow the Rules of the Old Testament in reference to clean and unclean things. It is observable, that contrary to the custom of all the other Eastern Christians (except the *Armenians*) they use unlevened Bread in the Holy Sacrrment; tho some affirm that this is only done on *Thursday* in the Holy Week, and that at other times they use levened Bread. All Persons, both Ecclesiastical and Civil, take and receive the Sacrament standing, and that always in the Church, the King himself not being dispensed with in this Point: The Priest gives the Bread, and the Deacons the Wine; and that day the Sacrament is received (which is generally once a week) they are forbidden to spit. They baptize both with Fire and Water; besides which they circumcise their Children on the 8*th* day, and that both Sexes, not according to the manner of the *Jews*, but after the Mahometan way, whence it seems as if it were rather a Custom than a Point of Religion. And if we deduce their Original from the antient *Ethiopians*, *Herodotus* tells us, that they used to practise the same in very antient Times; if from the *Arabians*, the Matter is sufficiently evident, the *Arabians* being descended from *Ismael*, tho they are generally ambitious to trace their Origin rather from *Sarah* than *Hagar*. For the rest, they reject Purgatory, and Prayers for the Dead; as also all Traditions, looking upon the Word of God as the only Rule of Faith; but with the *Jacobites*, allow no more than one Nature in Christ. Of the Religion of the *Abyssines*, *Damian a Goes*, *Athanas. Kircher*, *Alvarius*, and others, have given a more ample account.

* Prestegan *was the Title of a certain* Asiatick *Prince; some will have it a* Persian *word.*

9. The Armenians. The ninth Sect is that of the *Armenians*, in great esteem among the *Mahometans*, by reason of their Traffick and Riches; tho some alledg another Reason, *viz.* that an *Armenian* did foretel *Mahomet* his future Greatness. In the Year 1656. a certain *Armenian* Merchant, named *Goja Salomon*, a very grave and sober Person, travell'd in our company to *Macassar*, where we were to treat about a Peace with the King, and he to fetch some Mony due to him from the *Danish* Company, who gave us several needful Instructions concerning both the Ecclesiastical and Political Affairs of the *Armenians*. They antiently belonged to the Jurisdiction of the Patriarch of *Constantinople*, pursuant to a Decree of the Council of *Chalcedon*; but afterwards having withdrawn themselves from the *Greek* Church, set up two Patriarchs of their own, *viz.* one in the *Greater*, the other in the *Lesser Armenia*. We were told that they administer the Sacrament to the very Infants, whereas the *Russians* don't allow it to Children under seven Years of Age. They declare positively against the Purgatory and Transubstantiation. They rebaptize such as turn to their Religion from the *Western* Churches; They don't allow any Happiness to the Souls of the deceased till after the Day of Judgment.

10. Maronites. The tenth Sect is that of the *Maronites*, having got their Name, not from the

the famous Heretick *Maron* (as *William Tyrius* and *Prateolus* falsly imagine) but from a certain Holy Man, in certain antient Records, mention being made of the Convent of St. *Maron*, the Friers whereof were call'd *Maronites:* Some of them inhabit in *Aleppo, Damascus, Tripolis, Syria*, and *Cyprus*; but their chief Seat is the Mount *Libanus*, whose whole compass being computed of 700 Leagues, but in most places rocky and barren, is inhabited by about 12000 Families of the *Maronites*, who pay to the Grand Seignior seventeen Crowns *per annum* apiece for every Head that is above twelve years old; and a Crown a year for each piece of Ground of sixteen Spans in the Square. The Mountain is of such a height, that it may be discovered at 40 Leagues distance. The Patriarch of the *Maronites* has eight or nine Suffraganean Bishops, he himself being always a Frier of the Order of S. *Anthony*, and resides sometimes near the Mount *Libanus*, in a Convent of S. *Anthony*, sometimes at *Tripolis*. The *Maronites* are at present under the Jurisdiction of the See of *Rome*; and Pope *Gregory* XIII. (the same who caused the Alteration of the New Stile to be inserted in the Almanack) erected a College of the *Maronites* at *Rome*. The *Maronites* agree with the *Greek* Church in this Opinion, That the Holy Ghost proceeds only from the Father, that every Soul was created in the beginning. They look upon a Female Infant as unclean for eighty days after its Birth, and the Males for forty, which is the reason they don't baptize them before that time; and administer the Sacrament to the Children soon after they are baptized. They don't carry the Sacrament in Procession, and allow not of a fourth Marriage; but don't ordain any Priests or Deacons without they are married before; and allow a Parent the power of annulling the Marriage of his Son or Daughter, if the same be done without his consent. Beatitude they don't believe till after the Day of Judgment. For the rest they follow the Opinion of the *Monothelites*, that there is but one Nature in Christ. The *Maronites* had united themselves 400 Years ago with the See of *Rome*; but when *Saladyn* King of *Egypt* and *Syria* did conquer those Parts, the *Maronites* relinquish'd the *Roman* Communion, till they were reunited to them a second time under *Gregory* XIII. and *Clement* VIII. Of the S. *Thomas* Christians we have spoken before.

The Mount Libanus *inhabited by the* Maronites.

See Will. Tyrius de Bel. Sacr. *l.* 22. *c.* 8.

Among all these *Eastern* Sects, there are few who teach any Points contrary to Salvation, except those of *Nestorius* and *Eutyches*; for they execrate the Adoration of Images, reject Purgatory, allow Marriage to the Clergy, administer the Sacrament to the Laity in both kinds, deny Transubstantiation, and don't acknowledg the Jurisdiction of the See of *Rome*.

Baldæus.

Maffæus relates, that the Patriarch of the *Abyssines* being desired by their King to dispute with the Jesuit *Roterigio*, told the King, That *he would not enter into Dispute with an Heretick*, and charged the King, under pain of Eternal Damnation, not to read their Writings. It is beyond all dispute, that the *Coptes* avoid the *Latin* Church as much as the *Jews*. Cardinal *Baronius* tells us indeed, that *Marcus* Patriarch of *Alexandria*, did send his Deputies to Pope *Clement* VIII. in order to subject himself and all *Egypt* to the Papal Chair; but the same proved abortive, and proved no more than a Complement in the end. See *Thomas* a Jesuit, *l.* 7. *c.* 6. Whence it is evident, that setting aside the Doctrine of the Holy Ghost proceeding from the Father only, they are subject to not near so many Errors as the *Roman* Catholicks.

The Eastern *Churches deny the Supremacy of the* Roman *See.*

The Greeks *used always five days before* Easter *to excommunicate the Pope.*

The *Eastern* Christians exercise their Religious Worship in different Languages: Some are of opinion that all the Primitive Christians, for 120 Years after Christ's Nativity, *viz.* till the Reign of *Hadrianus* the Emperor, used only one Language, *viz.* the *Hebrew*, but without any certainty: Certain it is, that the *Armenians* have a Translation of the Bible into their own Language; which by some is attributed to *Chrysostom* while in exile. *Alvares* affirms that the *Abyssines* have translated the Bible in their own Language, and so have the *Russians*, or *Muscovites*, contrary to what is practised by the *Romans*; for Pope *Pius* IV. put the Bible among the prohibited Books. And *Erasmus* in his Letter to *Charles Utenhofer* tells him, that *Lewis Berquin* was 1529. burnt at *Paris*, for no other reason, but his having asserted, that the *Bible might be translated into the Vulgar Tongue, and read by the common People*; notwithstanding St. *Jerom* and *Chrysostom* had employed themselves in the Work.

In what Language the Christians worship God.

The other *Eastern* Christians perform their Religious Service in the *Greek, Latin*, and *Chaldean* Languages; and use divers Liturgies, as those composed by *Petrus, Jacobus, Sixtus*, &c. Whence it is evident that it would be no very difficult task, to settle a good mutual Correspondence betwixt them and the Protestant Churches of *Europe*, which has

Baldæus.

been too much neglected hitherto, tho we have had several opportunities given us by the *Eastern* Christians to embrace so useful a Design. Thus (as *Camerarius* tells us) the *Greeks* of *Constantinople* did encourage the *Bohemians* and *Hussites* against the *Roman Catholicks*. *Joseph* Patriarch of *Constantinople*, sent one *Demetrius* a Deacon to *Wittembergh*, to confer with the Divines there concerning an Union, who carried a *Greek* Copy of the *Augustan* Confession back with him to *Constantinople*. At the Synod of *Thorn* in *Poland* 1595. certain Deputies sent by the *Greek* Christians appeared to exhort to a Unity, and endeavour a Reconciliation betwixt the *Calvinists* and *Lutherans*. And in the Year 1616. *Cyril* Patriarch of *Alexandria*, sent one of his Priests to *George Abbot* the famous Archbishop of *Canterbury*, in order to have him instructed in the University of *Oxford* in the true Principles of the Protestant Churches. Neither ought we to pass by in silence the Confession of *Cyril* Patriarch of *Constantinople*, of his adhering to the Doctrine of *Calvin*, which drew upon him the hatred of the *Jesuits*, who could not rest satisfy'd till they had underhand procured his Death 1638.

A Correspondence with the Eastern Christians necessary.

His Letter, writ upon that Subject to a certain Friend of his, and preserved by the Learned *Andrew Rivet*, is as follows.

" PErcio ho voluto scriver a V. R. e
" protestarvi che mi siate testimo-
" nio se jo more, que jo more *Catholico*
" *Orthodoxo*, nella fede del N. S. *Jesu*
" *Christo* nella dottrina Evangelica con-
" forme la *Confessione Belgica* la confessio-
" ne mia e le altra delle chiese Evangelice
" che soni tutti conformi. Abhorrisco
" li errori delli *Papisti*, e le superstitio-
" ne delli *Greci*, provo e abraccio la dot-
" trina del dottore meritissimo *Giovanni*
" *Calvino* e de tutti che sentono con lui,
" in questo voglio che mi siate testimo-
" nio, per che con sincera conscienza cosi
" tengo, cosi professo e confesso como
" anco la mia confessione mostra, e re-
" commando a vos questo deposito, caso
" che morssi, di farne partecipi Tutti li
" fratelli Christiani Orthodoxi: e mi re-
" commando alle preghiere di V. R. Al-
" li 15. 25. Marzo.

Cyrillo Patriarcha di Constantinopoli.

*

Which translated into *English* runs thus:

" Therefore I was willing to declare to you, and desire you to be my Witness, that in case I die an *Orthodox Catholick*, and in the Purity of the Faith taught by *Jesus Christ*, agreeable to the *Confession* of Faith of the Church of the *United Provinces*, mine being altogether the same with theirs, and with the other Evangelical Churches. I abhor the Errors of the *Roman* Church, and the Superstitions of the *Greek*, but approve and embrace the Doctrine of the most Worthy *John Calvin*, and of all those that have the same Sentiments with him. I call you to witness, that I believe, confess, and attest the same by these Presents, recommending this my Confession to your care, in order to communicate the same. (in case of my Death) to all truly believing Brethren, and my self to your Prayers.

Letter of the Patriarch of Constantinople.

The 15. 25. *March.*

Cyril Patriarch of *Constantinople*.

As the preceding Letter is a convincing Proof of the stedfastness of *Cyril*, in his adhering to the Doctrine of *Calvin*; so out of what hath been said before, it is evident that most of the *Eastern* Christians have an aversion to the *Roman* Religion. And I remember that *Benjamin* the *Jew* in his Travels, makes the same Observation in particular, in respect of the Patriarch of *Constantinople*. In the Year 1664. being at *Cochin*, I addressed my self to Mr. *Jacob Hustart* our General, to grant leave to the Arch-Deacon, or Chief of the Christians of S. *Thomas* in Ecclesiastical Affairs, to come thither, in order to have a free Conference with him: Which being readily granted, he sent his Letter to the Arch-Deacon for that purpose; but he excused himself, alledging (and not without reason) that we having given so extraordinary a Reception to the *Roman* Bishop, *Joseph de Sancta Maria*, he could not appear in Person among us, without his Prejudice, to my great Dissatisfaction, being extremely sorry it was not in my power to perform my Promise made in my Letters to the States General 1662. And upon this occasion I can't, without praise, mention the generous Zeal of the States General, who at their own Charge did order

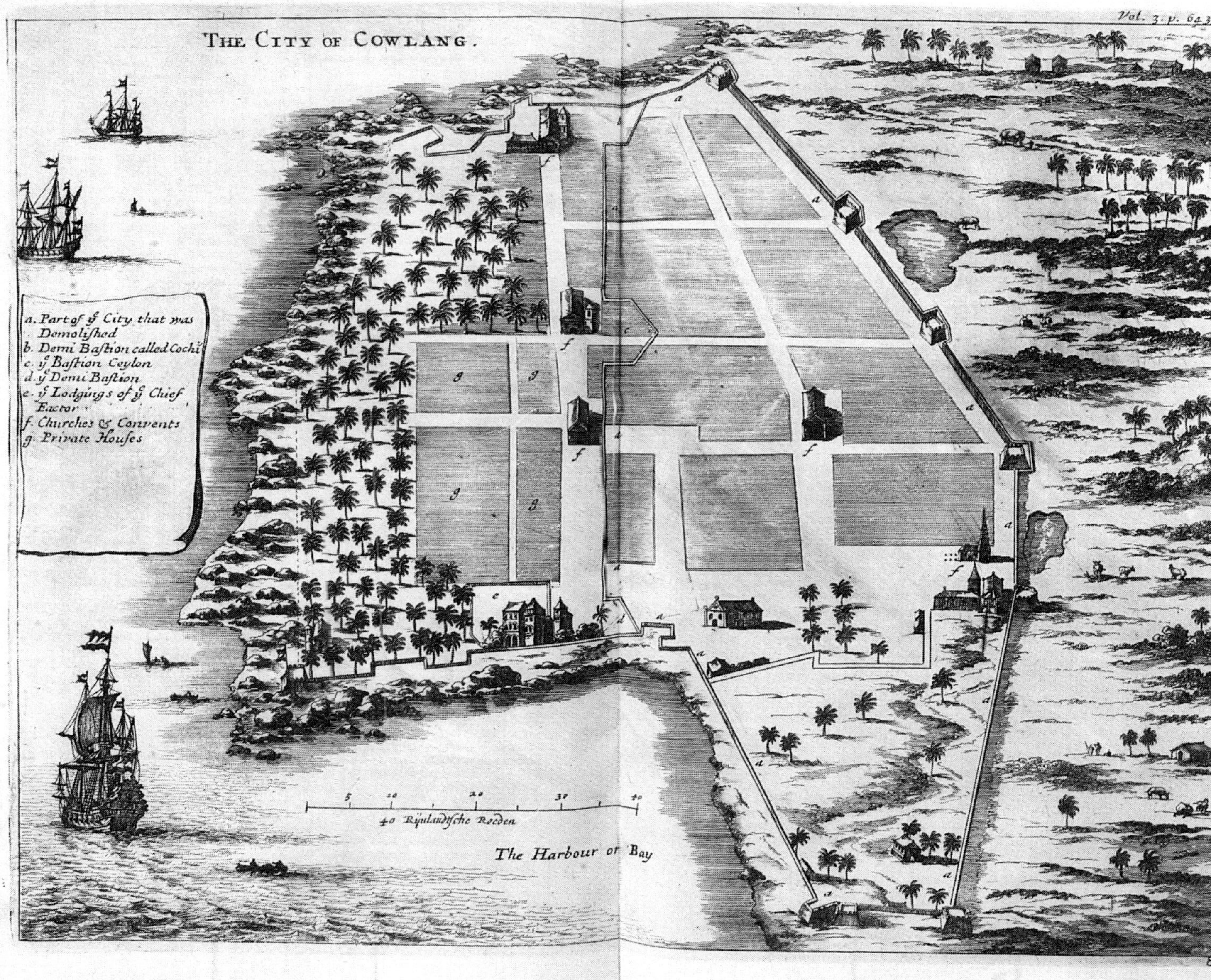
Vol. 3. p. 643.
THE CITY OF COWLANG.
a. Part of ye City that was Demolished
b. Demi Bastion called Cochi
c. ye Bastion Ceylon
d. ye Demi Bastion
e. ye Lodgings of ye Chief Factor
f. Churches & Convents
g. Private Houses
5 10 20 30 40
40 Rijnlandsche Roeden
The Harbour or Bay
8.

order to have the New Testament and our Catechism translated into the Tongue used among the Modern *Greek* Christians, the same being very different from the antient *Greek* Language.

Baldæus.

CHAP. XXI.

A Description of the Kingdom of Percatti, *and* Calecoulang. Coulang *twice taken by the* Hollanders. *The nature and manner of living of the* Nairos. *The* Paruas *made Christians. Extraordinary Zeal of Don* John *King of* Portugal.

The Kingdom of Porca.

THE Kingdom of *Percatti* (call'd by some *Porca*) begins about four or five Leagues to the South of *Cochin*, and extends to *Coulang*, its whole length being about 12 Leagues.

The Dutch *treat with that King.*

In the Year 1642. the *Dutch* appear'd the first time in this Place, and treated with the then King of *Siam*, *Baatchery Vaubaar* (who was not above 23 Years of Age) concerning a free Trade with Pepper. Which the King was very glad to accept of, being three Years past engaged in a War with the *Portugueses*, who had seized upon part of his Dominions, and would have erected some Fortifications there. He delivered to our Deputys a sealed Letter, directed to the General and *Great Council* of the *Indies*, in which he requested, that we would at least once a Year send thither a Ship freighted with such Commodities, as before that time used to be carried to *Cananor* and *Calecut*; whereupon an Interpreter was sent aboard the next day, to desire a Passport from his Majesty for such of our Ships as pass'd that way; which was granted.

The King who reign'd here 1664. of whom Mr. *Jacob Hustart* and I had Audience at that time, was about 24 Years old; a very active and well-limb'd Person; his Hands, Feet, and Ears, adorn'd with Jewels of a great value. Formerly they used to transport their Pepper from hence to *Mocha*; but since that time the *English* have traffick'd there in that Commodity, who had their Factory just upon the Sea-shore. The greatest Strength of this King consists in about 500 small Galleys, wherewith in the rainy Season, when the Rice-fields lie under Water, he used to make his Excursions from the utmost Point of the Cape of *Comoryn* as far as *Panane*, and especially to annoy the King of *Cochin*. He proved a troublesome Neighbour to the *Dutch* Company, till by the Terror of their Arms they brought him to submission, having in the Siege of *Cochin* sided with the *Portugueses* against us.

Factory of the English.

Deeper into the Country live abundance of Christians converted by the *Portugueses*: They get their Livelyhood by managing and gathering the Pepper, which they are obliged to sell to the King's Factor, a *Brabman*.

The Air unwholesom.

The Air of this Country being accounted extremely unwholesom; hence it is, that most of the Inhabitants are troubled with swell'd Legs, the Cause whereof they attribute to the Nitrous Water, which they use for their common Drink; Blindness is also an ordinary Distemper here. For the rest, the Ground is exceeding fertile, and very fit for Tillage, so that most of the Inhabitants live upon Husbandry, especially of Rice.

Calecoulang.

The next adjoining Kingdom is that of *Calecoulang*, of no great extent; here the *Dutch* Company has had their Factory many years ago, which used to buy up a great quantity of Pepper in these parts.

Coulang.

The least among the *Malabar* Kingdoms is that of *Coulang*, extending to the utmost Point of the Cape *Comoryn*, about 15 or 16 Leagues in length. The City of *Coulang* was first built by the *Portugueses*, being much of the same bigness as *Puntegale* in the Isle of *Ceylon*; having no less than seven Churches, some very good Houses, and many thousands of Trees, especially towards the Sea-side. This City is reckon'd one of the wholesomest on the whole Coast of *Malabar* by reason of its pure Air, and most excellent Springs. The *Portugueses* at their first coming erected only a strong House, defend to themselves in case of necessity against the Inhabitants; notwithstanding which, they were at a certain time surpriz'd by them, and cut all to pieces; which Barbarity was afterwards reveng'd by *Laurence Almeyda* Son to *Franciscus Almeyda*, who burnt 20 of their Ships richly loaden.

The Air very wholesom.

Baldæus. In the year 1503. one Brother *Rhoteric* a *Dominican* Frier, coming into these parts to propagate the Gospel, did convert many of the Pagans, and incouraged the Christians of St. *Thomas* inhabiting here to persevere in their Faith.

The Inhabitants treacherous. The Inhabitants are generally very barbarous and treacherous, of which they have given several times sufficient Proofs to the *Dutch*. At a certain time they assaulted the City by night, and had almost carried it by Surprize; and at another time Capt. *Henry Gluwing* taking the fresh Air with some Officers without the Gate, were treacherously murder'd by them.

In the time of the *Portugueses* there stood a certain *Pagode* about four Leagues without the City, famous for its Riches throughout the *Indies*, which induced *Sosa* to plunder it, notwithstanding there was then a Peace betwixt them and the *Portugueses*. The *Nairos* reveng'd the Loss by killing about 30 of the *Portugueses*; and *Sosa* having sent a large Vessel full of *Fanams* (their Coin) to *John* King of *Portugal*, the same was by the advice of the Pope sent back to the King of *Coulang*, by whom it was placed again in the said *Pagode*. *A Pagan Temple plunder'd by the Portugueses in time of Peace.*

The Dutch besiege Coulang a second time, having left it before. In the year 1661. when the *Hollanders* came to these parts to besiege the City of *Coulang*, they were forc'd to have three smart Engagements with the *Nairos*, who to the number of 7000 or 8000 Men, arm'd with Scymeters and Musquets, and being intoxicated with Opium, fell upon them like desperate Men; in which Action Mr. *Dublet* our under-Factor lost his Life.

And upon this occasion we ought not to pass by the *Nairos*. These are the Gentlemen of *Malabar*, descended for the most part either from Royal Families, or *Brahmans*, and are for that reason exceedingly haughty, proud and bold: If they meet any of the common People in the Street, they cry out, *Po, Po*, i. e. *Give way, Give way*. They seldom appear without their Scymeters and Shields, which they leave at the door when (by a peculiar Privilege) they go to give a private Visit to one of their Neighbours Wives, as a sign that no body must enter there in the mean while to disturb them. They are all bred to the War, even from the seventh year of Age, when they begin to anoint their Limbs with certain Ointments to render the Nerves pliable, which makes them very active and nimble, and the best Wrestlers in the World. They are not only well acquainted with the use of Bows and Arrows, but also with Musquets and great Cannon; for I have seen them give a Salvo with the same order and dexterity as our best disciplin'd Troops in *Europe*; and they are of late years arriv'd to that Perfection, that they make their own Gun-barrels, Gun-powder and Matches. They commonly engage naked, having only a piece of Stuff wrapt about the middle: Being very nimble they often turn their Backs, but soon return to the Charge, when they find the least opportunity of having an advantage against their Enemies. On the Hilts of their Swords they wear certain pieces of Metal, which making a noise as they move, serves them for a certain Musick: They are very dexterous in defending their Bodies with their Shields, and consequently are better at handy Blows than at firing, for they commonly fire too high. Among the *Nairos* those who call themselves *Amok* are the worst, being a Company of Desperadoes, who engage themselves and their Families by Oaths to revenge such Injuries as are done them. They are often seen at *Batavia*. The Power of the Kings of *Malabar* is generally esteem'd by the number of the *Nairos* under their Jurisdiction. If any of their Kings should be murder'd, they would sacrifice all to revenge his Death. As they are naturally fierce and addicted to all manner of Lust and Pride, so they are declar'd Enemies of the Christians. *The Nairos.* *The Amok.*

Scarce were the *Dutch* Masters of *Coulang*, but their Fleet consisting of 23 Ships great and small, were surpriz'd by so violent a Tempest (which lasted three days) that they thought to have been all lost, as lying at Anchor under a low Shore, and therefore expos'd to the utmost fury of the Winds. The Ships Names were, the *Vlieland*, *Sea-horse*, *Haddock*, *Bantam*, *Flushing*, *Mary-gold flower*, *Cat*, *Tertolen*, *Red Lion*, *Erasmus*, *Sluyce*, *Achilles*, the *Romer*, *Flower-Valley*, *Walnut-Tree*, the *House of Swieten*, the *Elburgh*, *Stadthouse of Amsterdam*, and the *Exchange of Amsterdam*, the four last being lately come from *Holland* freighted with Provisions, such as Meal, Bacon, Cheese, Wine, Oil and Mum, besides a good number of Land-men, many whereof were ill of the bloody Flux. During this Storm we sent our fervent and constant Prayers up to Heaven for the delivery of our Fleet, on which depended all our Safety; for the *Stadthouse of Amsterdam* was in such distress, that she gave one signal after another for Relief. *The Dutch Fleet in great danger of being lost.*

lief, having above six foot Water; the *Erasmus* had lost all her Anchors, but by good fortune got clear of the Sands; the *Sea-horse* had taken fire, but was soon extinguish'd, so that we came off with the loss of three Sloops only. The fury of the Tempest beginning to allay on the third day, just at the very time when we were coming from Prayers out of the Church, and by midnight the same being quite ceased, a solemn Thanksgiving was order'd to be kept the 23*d* of *Novemb.* 1661. when I preach'd upon the Text of *Psal.* 66. 12. By this time it being judged fit for our Fleet to depart, a convenient Garison was left in the place under Capt. *Kocks* and Mr. *Nyhof*, for the defence of the Fortifications of the City, which were lately made of Earth.

The Fleet sails for Cochin.

The Kingdom of Trevancor.

The Kingdom of *Trevancor* borders upon that of *Coulang:* All along the Sea-shore inhabite the *Paruas*, who being for the most part Christians, you see the Shore all along as far as *Comoryn*, and even beyond it to *Tutecoryn*, full of little Churches, some of Wood, others of Stone. These People owe their Conversion to *Franciscus Xaverius*, he being the first who planted the Principles of Christianity among them; they being so much taken with the reasonableness of the Ten Commandments, that they receiv'd Baptism in great numbers, tho an accidental Quarrel betwixt a *Paruas* and a *Mahometan* prov'd a strong Motive to their Conversion: whence it is that *John de Lucena* says, *As the Differences arisen betwixt the* Jews *and the* Egyptians, *prov'd the means of the delivery of the People of God, and of the recovery of their Spiritual and Temporal Liberty; so by God's Direction a Quarrel which happen'd betwixt a* Paruas *and a* Mahometan, *prov'd the delivery of the first from their Spiritual and Temporal Slavery.*

Conversion of the Paruas.

The *Paruas* being sorely oppress'd by the *Mahometans*, one *John de Crus*, a Native of *Malabar*, but who had been in *Portugal*, and honourably treated by *John* the then King of *Portugal*, advised them to seek for Aid at *Cochin* against the *Moors*, and to receive Baptism. Accordingly some of the chief Men among them (call'd *Patangatys* in their Language) were sent upon that Errand to *Cochin*, where being kindly receiv'd, they (in honour of him who had given this Advice) took upon them the Sirname of *Crus*, a Name still retain'd by most Persons of Note among the *Paruas*. In short, being deliver'd from the *Moorish* Yoke, and the Pearl-fishery (which formerly belong'd to them) restor'd to the right Owners, above 20000 of them receiv'd Baptism.

Baldæus.

But tho they were baptiz'd, most of them being deficient in the knowledg of the true Fundamentals of the Christian Religion for want of Teachers, they had in a little time scarce any marks of Christianity left among them except the Ceremony of Baptism; as *Maffæus*, *John de Lucena*, and *Michael Vas* in his Speech to *Franciscus Xaverius* sufficiently testify. For the *Portugueses* being too eager in baptizing these People, provided they could say by heart the *Creed*, *Our Father*, and *Avemary*, and being unprovided with Teachers to instruct them, they soon return'd to Paganism; so that upon this score the *Romish* Priests need not talk so big as they often do.

Care of the King of Portugal *for their Conversion.*

John the then King of *Portugal* being sensible of this defect, did all that in him lay to remedy this Evil, by sending divers young Scholars to the Universities of *Salamanca*, *Paris* and *Conimbria*, to be educated and fitted for the Missions into the *Indies*. About the same time *Ignatius Loyola*, the Founder of the Jesuits Order, began to be famous at *Rome*, for having with his Society made a Vow to preach the Gospel throughout the World: Whereupon the King of *Portugal* order'd *Peter Mascarenhas* his Ambassador there, to confer upon that Head with *Ignatius*, and to desire six Missionaries for the *East-Indies*; two being only granted, *Simon Roterigius* a *Portuguese* (who had studied at *Paris* at the King's Charge) and *Franciscus Aspilcota Navarrus*, sirnamed *Xaverius*, were selected for that purpose; but the first being seized by a Quartan Ague, and forc'd to stay at *Lisbon*, *Xaverius* (after having receiv'd Pope *Paul*'s Benediction) set out 1540. for the *Indies*.

Xaverius *goes to the* Indies.

He was no sooner come thither, but having understood the deplorable State of the *Paruas* from the mouth of *Michael Vas*, he did not rest satisfied till he might deliver them out of their Darkness: For this purpose having had several Conferences with *John Albuquerque* Bishop of *Goa*, and *Martin Alphonso de Sousa* the Viceroy, he obtain'd leave to go among them; for tho he appear'd there in the quality of the Apostolical Nuncio, yet would he pay his due Respects to the Civil Government.

Comes among the Paruas.

He left *Goa* in the beginning of *November* 1542. in Company of *Franciscus du Mancias*, and two young Interpreters educa-

Baldæus. educated in the College of St. *Paul*; and coming among the *Paruas*, apply'd all his care in having the chief Fundamentals of the Christian Religion translated into the *Malabar* Language, or in instructing the School-masters in the right way of educating their Youth. For the rest, with what Zeal *John* King of *Portugal* prosecuted the Propagation of the Christian Religion in the *Indies*, will best appear out of his Letter written 1546. to *Don John de Castro* his Viceroy of the *Indies*, as follows.

To John de Castro *Viceroy of* India, *all Happiness:*

John *King of* Portugal's *Letter.* "YOU knowing what an abominable "thing Idolatry is in our Eyes, the "same shall for the future not be tolerated in my Dominions. Being inform'd "that in the Country about *Goa* the Pagan Temples are suffer'd and frequented both in publick and private, as "well as divers sorts of Pagan Diversions, we command you once for all "to have the same demolish'd, burnt "and rooted out; and that all imaginable care be taken to prevent the "Importation of Idols, either of Wood, "Metal, Earth, or any other Matter. "The Heathenish Sports shall be abolish'd, and the *Brahmans* not in the "least encouraged, and such as contravene this our Mandat shall be severely punish'd. And, considering that "the Pagans may be brought over to "our Religion, not only by the hopes "of Eternal Salvation, but also by Temporal Interest and Preferments, you "shall for the future not bestow any "Offices, or any other Places in the "Custom-house (as has been practis'd "hitherto) upon the Heathens, but "only upon the Christians. We understand also that you commonly press "the *Indians* for our Sea-service; in "which case we would have you shew "as much Favour as you can to the "Christians, and, if necessity will not "allow you to excuse them from that "Service, to encourage them with good "Pay and Rewards: In which Point "you shall consult with *Michael Vas*, a "Person well known to us for his Piety "and Zeal in propagating the Christian "Religion. Being further inform'd, "that oftentimes Negro Slaves that "might be instructed in the Principles "of our Religion, are for filthy lucres "sake sold to the *Mahometans*, the same "shall be strictly prohibited, and care "taken against all manner of Usury. "In the City of *Bazain* you shall build "a Church, and dedicate it to St. *Joseph*, "and provide for the Subsistence of the "Vicar and his Assistants; to accomplish which you may employ something "out of our Revenues, and the 3000 "*Pardaus* formerly employ'd to the "maintenance of the *Mahometan* Mosque "and their Service, shall for the future "be allotted for the Subsistence of the "Priests, and such other Persons as give a "helping hand towards the Conversion "of the Infidels. Among the new Converts, or all such as have hitherto, or "for the future may be brought over to "the Christian Religion, by the care "of *Michael Vas*, you shall distribute "yearly 900 Quarters of Rice, out of "our Revenue: It being our Will, that "all the Agreements made with the "Christians of S. *Thomas*, concerning "the Weight, Measures, and Price of "their Commodities, shall be inviolably "observed. And understanding nevertheless that the contrary is practised "in and about *Cochin*, in the Pepper-Trade, we command you to assist these "Christians, and to take effectual care "they may not be damnified, but treated with all mildness as becomes Christians. You shall also sollicite the "King of *Cochin*, not to permit any "Sorcery or such like things to be transacted, by the Sale of Pepper; and "being inform'd that the said King bereaves such of his Subjects as embrace "Christianity, of all their means, you "shall earnestly intercede with him "on their behalf, and we will also write "to him for that purpose. We could "wish heartily, that the Business of *Socotora* (which you have recommended "to our care in your Letter) might be "settled so as to deliver those miserable People out of their Slavery, provided the same could be done without "exasperating the *Grand Seignior*, under "whose Jurisdiction they live. You may "upon this Head consult with *Michael Vas*, and act in the matter according "to your discretion. It being also come "to our Ears, that the *Paruas* are sometimes but very indifferently used by "our Officers, who force them to sell "their Pearls (got by fishing or diving) "at what rate they please to take them; "this you shall not allow of, but permit "them to dispose of their Commodities "at the best Price they can get. You "shall make an exact Inquiry, whether "the Inhabitants of the Sea-shoar might

"not

"not be protected, and our Revenues "secured without a Fleet, so that the "Ships employed in that Service might "be made use of upon other occasions. "You shall consult and debate with *Franciscus Xaverius*, whether it were not "practicable for the better increase of "the Christians, that the Pearl-fishery "might be permitted only to the Christians, with exclusion of the *Mahometans* and *Pagans*: and as many among "the *Paruas*, who have embraced Christianity, meet with very ill Treatment "from their *Pagan* Friends and Relations, and are despoil'd of all; these you "shall assist out of our Revenues, according as *Michael Vas* shall judg it "convenient.

Extraordinary Care of the Paruas.

"We have further understood that a "certain Royal Youth has escaped from "his Father or Uncle to *Goa*, in order to "be baptized; as his Conversion is of "great moment, so you shall be very "careful of his Person, and of his Instruction and Education in the College "of S. *Paul*, and provide for his Entertainment in Clothes, Attendance and "other matters, sutable to his Quality. "He having notified to us in his Letter, "that he is the legal Heir of the Crown "of *Ceylon*; you shall make due Enquiry after that matter, and write to us "your Sentiment thereof. The furious "Attempts of the Tyrant of *Ceylon* against such of his Subjects as embrace "Christianity, oblige us to command "you, to take a slow and secure, but a "severe Revenge of him, to let the "World see, that we are ready to give "all imaginable Protection to those poor "Creatures, who have renounced their "Pagan and Diabolical Idolatries. It "being a general Rumour here, that the "Images of our Saviour and the Virgin "*Mary* are made and sold by the *Pagans*, "a thing unseemly and unbecoming the "Christian Name, the same ought not "to be allowed of. The Cathedral "Churches of *Cochin* and *Coulang*, which "have been building for a considerable "time, being (as we hear) going to decay, we command to be finished, and "covered with a good Roof, to keep "out the Rains. It is also our Pleasure, "that a Church dedicated to S. *Thomas* "shall be built in the Street of *Noroa*, "and that the Church of St. *Cruz*, lately begun to be built at *Calapor*, shall be "brought to perfection. In the Isle of "*Cioran*, you shall order a Church and "some Meeting-Houses to be built, for "the conveniency of the new Converts "to be catechized in, and to be instructed in the Word of God. We could "also wish with all our Heart, that Idolatry might be banished out of *Salsete* "and *Bardes*; but in this matter you "must proceed with Caution, for fear of "exasperating the Minds of the People; "which End may be most conveniently "obtained, by shewing them with all "imaginable Mildness, their gross Errors, and how instead of the true God "they pay their Devotion to insensible "Images and Idols. For the same reason you shall not neglect to confer with "their Principal Men upon this Head, "and to encourage such as embrace "Christianity by your Favour, Presents, "and otherwise. It is our Will, that a "peculiar regard shall be had to this our "Letter, and the Contents thereof punctually observed.

Baldæus.

CHAP. XXII.

A Description of Tutecoryn *and the Pearl-fishery. That City taken by the* Hollanders. *The Isle of* Rammanakoyel, Adams-*Bridg*; *the Shape of his Foot imprinted in a Stone.* Tindi. *The taking of* Negapatan, *which is besieged by the* Naike, *reduced to great Extremity by Famine; once more attacked and maintained.*

The Paruas *are now very obstinate in the* Romish *Superstitions.*

THE *Paruas* ever since this Union with the *Romish* Church, are such Zealots in that Religion, that there are scarce any hopes of ever bringing them over to our side; their Ignorance in Religious Concerns being such, that besides the use of their Beads, and making the Sign of the Cross, they know nothing of the true Fundamentals of the Christian Religion they pretend to profess. In the Year 1661. I was ordered to take a Journey from *Tutecoryn* to *Coulang*, to visit the Churches along the Sea-shore, and endeavour to introduce a Reformation there; but my endeavours proved ineffectual by reason of the great number of

Baldæus. of Popish Priests yet remaining in that Country; and supposing a Reformation could have been introduced, there were no Ministers to maintain it in so large a Tract of Land, where the *Paruas* were for the most part great Favourers of the *Portugueses*, and blind Zealots in their Religion, of which I had sufficient Proofs before at *Tutecoryn*. For the *Dutch* being become Masters of that Place, 1658. I was soon after employed in the business of Reformation, but without Success; for when I preach'd in *Portuguese*, scarce any one of the *Paruas* durst enter into the Church, but remained in the Porch, for fear of the *Romish* Priests living among them; for tho these Priests did not then live in the City, nevertheless the Inhabitants would carry their Children a great way into the Country, to be baptized by the Priests.

Blind Zeal of the Paruas. I remember that passing one time thro the Market-place of *Tutecoryn*, a great number of People, at the accidental ringing of a Bell, prostrated themselves upon the Ground, whom I ask'd whether they thought this a fit place for their Devotion, when the Church was so near at hand, desiring them to follow me thither; they answered, that since the Church was despoil'd of the Images and other Ornaments by us, they must look upon us as Enemies to their Religion. I replied, that we were no Enemies of Images, but only of the worshipping of them, as appeared by several Histories of the Baptism of our Saviour, the Conversion of S. *Paul* and others, remaining in the Churches: To be short, I found that the whole knowledg of the *Paruas* (both young and old) consisted in being able to say by Heart the *Creed*, *Our Father*, the *Ten Commandments*, and the *Ave Mary*.

Fereira *employed in reforming the* Paruas. After my Departure the Reverend Mr. *John Fereira Almeyda* a Native of *Lisbon*, was for a whole Year employed in the Reformationof the *Paruas*, but with less Success than my self, they having conceived an *Odium* against him, as one who had quitted that Religion, and whose *Effigies* upon that score was burnt at *Goa*.

Tutecoryn *taken by the* Dutch. In the Year 1658 in *Jan.* we set sail from *Negumbo*, and in the beginning of *Febr.* landed near *Tutecoryn*, after some resistance from the Natives, who set the City and their small Galleys on fire, and so retired deeper into the Country. *Tutecoryn* is properly no more than a large Village without Walls, Ditches, or Gates; it has three spacious Churches, and abundance of goodly Houses built of Stone, which afford a good Prospect at Sea. Hereabouts they make the best Lime in *India*. The *Dutch* Company has been several times endeavouring to erect some Fortifications here; but the *Naike*, or Lord of the Country, not willing to consent to it, they have hitherto been contented with a Factory in one of the three Churches; where always resides a Factor and Under-Factor, with three Assistants, and six or eight Soldiers.

Near this Place is the famous Pearl-Fishery, whereof there are no more than three in the East, *viz.* one near *Ormus*, the second in the Bay of *Ainam* on the *Chinese* Coast, and the third in the Bay betwixt Cape *Comoryn* and the Isle of *Ceylon*, wherein are also comprehended *Manaar* and *Aripou*. The Pearls are found in certain Oyster Shells (which are not good to eat) and are taken by diving 7, 8, 9, or 10 Fathom deep, sometimes not without great danger. The Pearl-Fishery is not allowed every Year, sometimes the Oyster-banks being cover'd with Sand, and sometimes the Oysters not being come to their full Maturity. To make a Trial of the last, they take out a few, and by the quantity and quality of the Pearls taken in them, judg whether it will quit cost to fish or not. If the Fishing be resolved upon, the Inhabitants of the circumjacent Parts come in great Numbers with their Families and Boats, and pitch their Tents near the Seaside, where they remain until the Fishery is over. The *Dutch* Company has a certain share in what is taken for their Protection, the rest being sold publickly in the Markets of *Tutecoryn* and *Calipatnam*. The *Paruas* also dive sometimes for certain hours for a kind of Sea-Snails called *Chancos*, whereof they make Rings, that bear a good Price at *Bengale*. *The Pearl-fishery.* *The* Paruas *tho Christians, never dive before they have made certain Conjurations to prevent their being hurt by the Sharks.*

The Pearls of *Tutecoryn* and *Manaar* are neither in colour nor brightness comparable to those taken near *Ormus* on the *Persian* Coast. The Pearls are questionless nourished both by the Sea and River Water, as being often found at the time of low Tides in the Rivers. Abundance of Pearl Dust is from hence transported into *Europe*, where it is used in the Cordial Medicines. The large Pearls are valued according to their bigness, shape and whiteness. Much Cloth is made at *Tutecoryn*, the Weaving-Trade being very considerable here, which together with the plenty of Eatables, Rice, Sugar, &c. makes this Place to be much regarded by the Company.

This Tract of Land is subject to most furious Winds in *October*, *November* and *December*; and in the Winter Seasons to sudden and heavy Rains. It is very sandy near the Sea-shore, and has nothing but Salt-water, which produces Scabs and other cutaneous Distempers, as I can testify by my own Experience. During the Months of *January*, *February* and *March*, the Nights are extremely cold, by reason of the thick Fogs which fall constantly at that time, the Days being at the same time so excessive hot, that there is no touching of the Ground without their Shoos, called *Seripous* by the Inhabitants.

The Climate of Tutecoryn.

And upon this occasion I can't pass by without making this Observation, that notwithstanding the nearness of *Tutecoryn* and *Comoryn*, they at the same time have very different Seasons: For in *April*, *May*, *June*, *July*, *August* and *September*, those inhabiting on the *South-side* of the said Cape, enjoy all the Blessings of the Summer Season, whilst those living on the *North-side* are at the same time subject to all the inconveniences of the Winter: This side being then constantly pestred with tempestuous Winds, whilst on the other side the Air is serene and calm; the difference of which must needs be look'd for among the Mountains, the receptacles of Winds, Rains and Snow, the same being observed in other Parts of the *Indies*, as well as in *Africa*. For if *Africa* were not mountainous, it would be altogether barren and uninhabitable, no more than the Countries under the *Torrid Zone*, which if they were destitute of Mountains, would also want Rivers (the sources of them being all in the Mountains) nor hard Rains. Thus it is observable, that about *Columbo*, *Gale*, and *Mature*, abundance of Rains fall at different times, because that part of the Isle of *Ceylon* is mountainous; whereas near *Manaar*, *Jafnapatnam* and the other Places, where there is a flat Country, it rains only in *October*, *November*, and a little in *December*, all the rest of the Year being without the least Rains, the defect whereof is however supplied in some measure by the Fogs or Dew; the South Winds, which blow then from the Cape of *Comoryn*, prevent the Rains on that side. The Inhabitants of *Peru* are very sensible of this difference; for whilst the Inhabitants of the Mountains are often rejoiced with sudden Showers of Rain, those of the flat Country, and especially near the Seaside, never feel any Rain, but only a thick Fog or Dew.

Different Seasons on the North and South-side of the Mountains

Whence it is evident, that according as the Mountains send forth the Winds and Rains on one side or the other, they produce the difference of Seasons in these Parts; this is very perspicuous on the Cape of South Point of *Africa*, where such violent gushes of Wind are sometimes sent forth out of the Concavities of the Mountains, that they are able to overturn all that meets in their way. I remember that travelling once that way, I had enough to do to keep my self and my Horse upright; and at another time a Coach belonging to the *Dutch* Company there, was overturn'd by such a gush of Wind. They take it for an infallible Sign of an approaching Tempest on the *Cape of Good Hope*, when they see thick Clouds appear on the top of *Tablemaintainand*. The same is observed in most other Mountains under the *Torrid Zone*; for the Inhabitants near the *Equinoctial Line* have their due rainy Seasons twice a Year, *viz.* in Spring and Autumn, occasioned by the gathering of the Clouds in the Mountains, the Pinacles of which reaching very high, stop the course of the Air (which in those Parts moves constantly from East to West) which thereby being condensed into Clouds, these produce of necessity either sudden Winds or Rains on one side, and blesses the other side at the same time with a serene Air and happy Climate; the tops of these Mountains being in these Parts like a Partition Wall to Summer and Winter. For the further Elucidation whereof, I will refer my self to the most ingenious Lord *Bacon*, and *des Cartes*.

The Mountains occasion the difference of Seasons.

From *Tutecoryn* towards the Isle of *Rammanakoyel*, are to be seen divers Churches of the *Paruas*, as at *Baipaar*, *Manapaar*, &c. where *Xaverius* planted the Christian Doctrine. The Isle of *Rammanakoyel* abounds in Cattel, having got its Name from *Bramma* or *Ramma*, and the *Malabar* Word *Koyel*, i. e. *The Temple of Ramma*; for near the Sea-side is to be seen the *Pagode* of the *Teuver*, or Lord of the Isle, which they say contains an incredible Treasure. The Foundation is strengthened and supported with Stones of a vast bigness towards the Sea-side, to break the Force of the raging Waves, when the South Winds blow. The Isle is however but indifferently fertile, being in some Parts very sandy, which is very troublesome to the Eyes, when the Winds blow very hard. The Lord of the Isle has built a strong Castle opposite to the Coast of *Coromandel*, and the Country under the Juris-

Isle of Rammanakoyel.

Baldæus. Jurisdiction of the *Naik*. In the Year 1662. I and Lieutenant *Herman Egbertsz* travelling that way, were seized upon by the Inhabitants and committed Prisoners, being forced to live without Victuals or Drink for a considerable time; till a certain Inhabitant of *Manaar* coming that way, and knowing me, released us out of our Captivity. The Cannon of the Castle commands a certain strait Passage, which leading to *Manaar*, *Jafnapatnam* and *Negapatnam*, the same may be stopt at pleasure by the Lord of the Isle, by sinking only a few Stones in the Channel, whereby the Navigation that way is at his absolute disposal. *Strait Passage under the Castle of the Isle.*

Adam's Bridg. Not far from hence is that they call *Adams*-Bridg, being a Ridge of Sands and Rocks extending as far as *Manaar*, being sometimes passable in small Boats. In the description of *Ceylon*, we shall have occasion to speak something more of this *Adams*-Bridg, and the *Adams*-Mount. Certain it is, that the *Cingaleses* as well as the *Siameses* have some knowledg of *Adam*; for the last shew you the print of a Foot (said to belong to the first Man) in a rocky Mountain of a yard and a half in length, three quarters broad, and a quarter deep, edged round about with Silver, near which is built a most magnificent Temple, much frequented by the *Siamese* Priests, and other Inhabitants of the circumjacent Country; it being their Opinion, that the least drop of the Water gathered in this Print of the Foot, and dropp'd upon their Heads, cleanses them from their Sins: for which reason they never use it without a great deal of Reverence, no body daring to enter the Temple without 10, 12, or more Wax Candles lighted, according to their respective Abilities; and when they return, they take some of this Holy Water along with them in *Bamboe*-Canes, for the use of their Friends, that have not the Opportunity of coming thither in Person. The King himself goes once every Year on Pilgrimage with all his *Mandarins* (or great Courtiers) to this Temple, where they use this Water at the time of the Full Moon, and conclude the Night with dancing and drinking. Some of the *Siamese* Priests did by special leave from his Majesty, shew to certain *Hollanders*, 1654, in *March*, a Plate of Gold, of the same length and breadth as the before-mentioned *Adam*'s Foot, with 68 Figures engraven upon it, which they said were formerly to be seen in the print of *Adam*'s Foot in the Rock, but vanished as soon as they were engraven in this Plate, and were the following: *A Queen with a Ring on her Finger, divers Roses, a Chain, an Arm, a Bed of Gold, a Chair of the same Metal, an Elephant's Tooth, a Royal Palace, a Golden Sword-belt, an Umbrello, a Royal Hanger or Scimeter, a Fan made of the Leaves of the Terry-tree, a Fan made of a Peacocks Tail, a Royal Crown, a Priest with his mendicant Pot of Iron, a Chain of Precious Stones, a red Cowslip Flower, a double one of the same kind, a white one and a double white one of the same kind, a Cup full of Water, a Pot full of Water, the Sea, the World, a Forest beyond the World, the Purgatory of the* Siamese, *the highest Mountain of the World, the Sun, the Moon, the Evening-Star, the Great God of the Heavens, the God of the four Winds,* 2000 *Servants of the four Winds, a Sea-snail, two Fishes of Gold, the seven chief Rivers, seven Mountains with Precious Stones, seven Royal Ladies, the King of Beasts, the King of the* Caimans *or Crocodiles, an Ensign, another of Paper, a Chair or Litter, a Fan with a long Handle, a Mountain in an Island, the King of Serpents, the King of Tygres, a leaping Horse, a large Elephant, a white one of the same kind, a Water-Serpent, a* Casuarius (a Bird like an Ostrich) *the King of the white Cows, an Elephant with three Heads and as many Tails, a Serpent, a Ship of Gold, an Angel, a Cow with a sucking Calf, a certain Bird half a Man and half a Bird, a Female of the same sort, a singing Bird, the King of the Peacocks, the King of the Cranes, a Bird called* Krapat, *a Bird called* Kuyshit, *six Heavens, sixteen sorts of Heavens.*

Adam's *Foot shewn by the Siameses.*

The Holy Water.

The Figures in Adam's-*Foot.*

Concerning all which the Priests give you their Interpretations. The before-mentioned *Adam*'s-Bridg extends to *Tellemanaar*, the furthermost point of the Isle of *Manaar*, of which more anon in the Description of *Ceylon*.

We will now take our turn in the Southern Parts of *Coromandel*, subject for the most part to the *Naik* of *Madure* and *Tanjouwer*. *Tondy* is the first place next to the Territories of *Jafnapatuam*, and I remember my self, that setting Sail one Morning about 11 a Clock from *Jafnapatnam*, we were within sight of the Shoar by 4 in the Afternoon, and the same Night at 9 a Clock cast Anchor before *Negapatan*. From *Tondy* they transport yearly many hundred Heads of Cattel to *Jafnapatnam*; near the first stands a certain *Pagode*, called *Kailiemeer*, a very high Structure, in the Road to *Negapatan* or *Negapatnam*, i. e. *The City of Serpents*, *Naga* signifying in the *Malabar* Lan- **Tondy upon the Coast of Coromandel.**

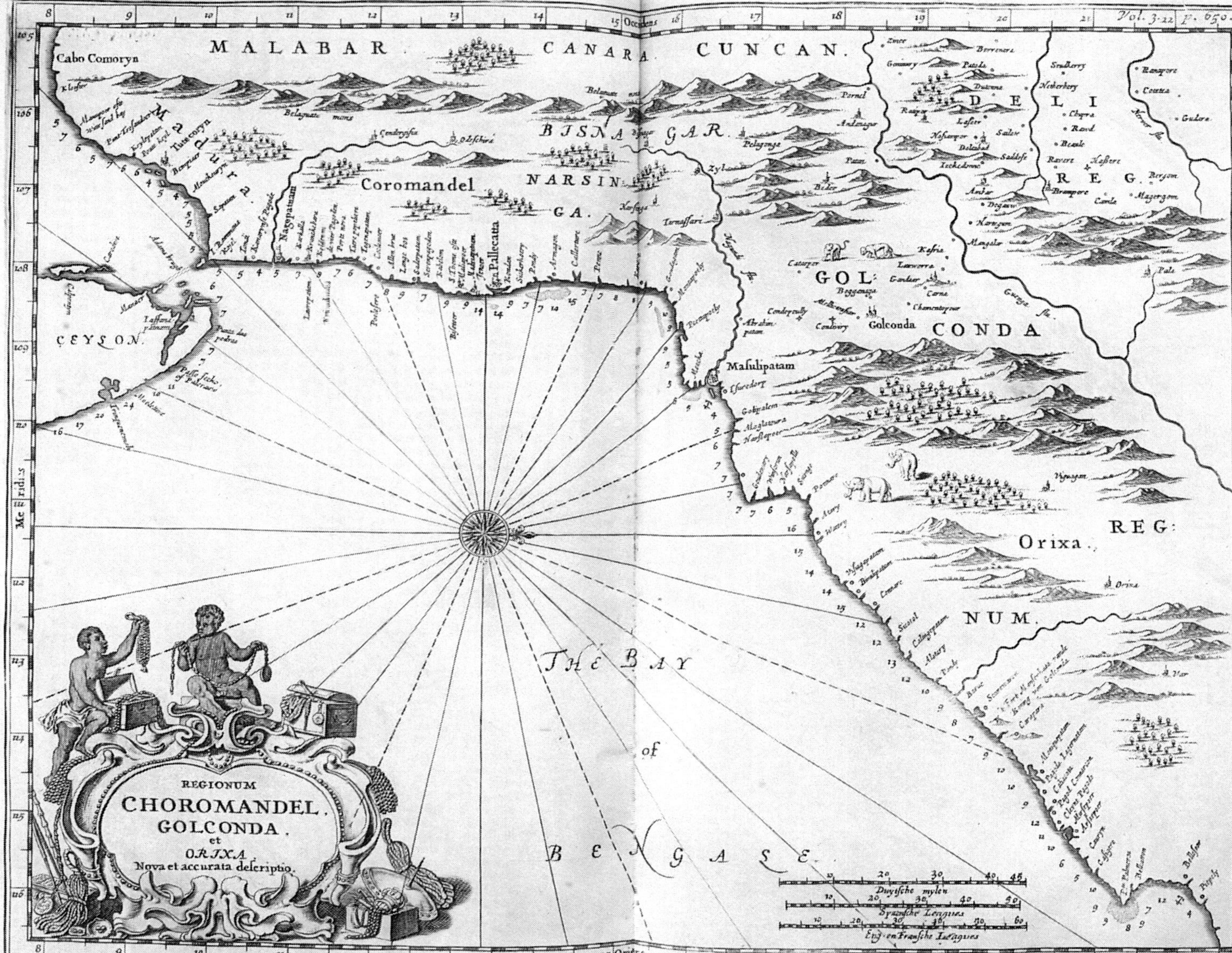
REGIONUM
CHOROMANDEL,
GOLCONDA,
et
ORIXA
Nova et accurata descriptio.
MALABAR
CANARA
CUNCAN
Cabo Comoryn
BISNAGAR
NARSINGA
Coromandel
Nagapatam
Pallecata
Masulipatam
GOL CONDA
Golconda
Orixa
REG:
NUM
DELI REG.
CEYLON
THE BAY of BENGALE
Duytsche mylen
Spaensche Leagues
Eng. en Fransche Leagues
Occidens
Oriens
Septentrio
Meridies

NEGAPATAM.
Rynlandsche Roeden

Language a Serpent, and *Patnam* a City; because the Country hereabouts abounds with a certain sort of venomous Serpents, called by the *Cobres Capellos*, which are in such reverence among the *Pagans*, that if they should happen to kill one of them, they will look upon it as an expiable Crime, and to forebode some great Misfortune.

The City of Negapatnam.

This City was taken by composition without striking a Stroke, by *John van der Laan*, and *Lucas van der Dussen*, Commanders of the *Dutch* Forces, 1658. the last of the two being since made Governor of *Cochin*, and the other Forts on the *Malabar* Coast, subject to the *Hollanders*. The *Portugueses* were permitted to depart with their Goods, Families, Church-Ornaments, *&c.* in certain Ships appointed for that purpose by the *Dutch* Company. The City is seated near the Shoar, has no convenient Harbour, as indeed the whole Coast of *Coromandel* is destitute of them. Its Buildings are very stately, especially the Church, which affords a very goodly Prospect towards the Sea-side: The Land-Winds are excessive hot and stifling here, as on the other hand the Sea-Winds are refreshing both to Men and Beasts. It is observable that whilst the Land-Wind blows, they gather Water in Stone Vessels, which keeps very cool; the worst is, that these Winds prevent People from sweating, which makes the Heat the more insupportable. The same is to be observed at *Masulipatan*, where they are so stifling that many People are killed by them.

Mastered by the Dutch.

In the Year 1660. 14 *July*, I set sail from *Jafnapatnam* to *Negapatnam*, to introduce the Reformed Religion there, and accordingly preached the first time the 18*th*, both in *Dutch* and *Portuguese*, and administred the Holy Sacrament to 20 Persons, and Baptism to several Children. After Mr. *Frederick Fronteuius* and my self had spent sometime there in setling the Protestant Religion, Mr. *John Kruys*, formerly Minister in the Castle, called the *Seelandia* in the Isle of *Tajowan*, was constituted Minister at *Negapatnam*, who after his Death was succeeded by Mr. *Nathaniel de Pape*, a Person of indefatigable care, who in a very small time has made considerable Advancements in the *Portuguese* and *Malabar* Languages, who by the encouragement, and under the Protection of Mr. *Cornelius Speelman* Governour of the Coast of *Coromandel*, and famous for his late Victories obtain'd against the *Macassars*, and the King of the Isle of *Celebes*, has settled and spread the Doctrine of the Gospel in the circumjacent Villages.

The Protestant Religion introduced in Negapatnam.

Baldæus.

Misery about Negapatnam.

At the time of our first Arrival, we found the Affairs of *Negapatnam* in no small Confusion; the City having been just before besieged by the *Naik*, who after a vigorous Sally made by the Besieged, had been forced to retreat with the Loss of 300 or 400 Men. Besides this, the King of *Visiapour* had not long before the Siege made an Inroad into the Country, and by destroying all the Fruits of the Earth, and whatever else he met with, occasion'd such a Famine, that the poor Country Wretches being forc'd to fly to the City for want of Rice and other Eatables, you saw the Streets cover'd with emaciated and half-starv'd Persons, who offer'd themselves to Slavery for a small quantity of Bread, and you might have bought as many as you pleas'd at the rate of 10 Shillings a Head; above 5000 of them were there bought and carried to *Jafnapatnam*, as many to *Columbo*, besides several thousands that were transported to *Batavia*.

In the Year 1669. the *Naik* was again embroil'd with the *Dutch* Company, but being bravely repuls'd was glad to be at quiet. Without the Gates on the Northside of the City stands a very lofty *Pagode*, called *China*, near which is a Summer-Seat, with very pleasant Gardens and Orchards, formerly belonging to *Francisco d' Almeyda*, an antient rich *Portuguese*, now living at *Trangebar*.

Baldæus.

CHAP. XXIII.

A Description of Carcal, Trangebar, Trinilivaas, Colderon, Porto Novo, Tegnatapan, Tirepoplier, Chengier, Sadraspatan, Madraspatan, St. Thomas, Paliacatte, Carnatica, Penna, Caleture, Petapouli, *and* Masulipatan.

Carcal. TWO Leagues from *Negapatan* lies *Carcal*, where, as well as in most other Southern Places, *Adrian van der Meyden* Head Factor of our Company, did erect a Factory some years ago; but since we have been Masters of *Negapatan*, the Factory of *Carcal* is not regarded. The chief Commodities here are certain Stuffs, especially those call'd *Rambotyns*, much in request among the *Japoneses*.

Trangebar. From *Carcal* to the *Danish* Fort call'd *Trangebar* are about three Leagues: It has four Bulworks, and the Garison consists for the most part of *Topasses* and *Negros*, under the Command of one *Eskel Andres*. The Inhabitants consist of *Portugueses*, *Pagans* and *Mahometans*: Their Traffick is very inconsiderable, their chiefest Advantage arising from the Excursions they make upon the neighbouring *Mahometans*, with whom they are in constant Enmity, by reason of the ill usage they have ever received from them. About two Years before our departure thence, one *Simon van Medenblick* had got a Commission from the *Danes*, and took a rich *Moorish* Vessel, and kill'd the whole Ships Crew. I have often wonder'd why the *Danes* should not more encourage their Trade in the *Indies* than they do, since they have the same or rather a better opportunity for so doing than the *English*.

Colderon. From *Trangebar* you go by the way of *Trinilivaas* to *Colderon*, where there is a very dangerous Sand-Bank. From thence you come to the Place call'd the *Four Pagodes*, and so to *Porto Novo* or *Newhaven*, Porto Novo. about 4 or 5 Leagues from *Trangebar*. At *Porto Novo* inhabit some *Portugueses*; their Trade consists chiefly in a certain hard Wood call'd *Hunters-wood*, *Coco-nuts*, *Arek*, *Cair*, &c.

Tegnapatan. About a League from *Porto Novo* stands *Tegnapatan*, where the *Hollanders* have likewise a Factory. Next to this lies *Tirepoplier*, Tirepoplier. upon a River which is navigable, within half a League of the *Dutch* Factory. The Road lies at 11 ¼ Degrees of Northern Latitude, having 77 Fathom Water, with a grey sandy Ground, very fit for Anchorage not above a Mile from the Shore. There is safe riding at Anchor here (as all along the Coast of *Coromandel*) during the South *Mousson*, but very dangerous in the North *Mousson*. The Castle of *Tirepoplier* is tolerably strong, according to the fashion of the *Gentives*. The Factory formerly belonging to the *Dutch* was within the Castle, where is also a stately large *Pagode*, with a high Stone Tower flat at top, which serves the Mariners for a Guide. The Mines of the old Castle, belonging formerly to the *Portugueses*, upon an Ascent near the Sea-Shore on the North side of the River, are also seen a good way at Sea. The Country hereabouts is generally sandy, and sometimes rocky. *Tirepoplier* is under the Jurisdiction of the *Cristappaneyk*, whose Residence is at *Chengier*, about two days Journy to the South of *Tirepoplier*.

The City of *Chengier* is very populous, Chengier. and three times as big as *Rotterdam*, seated in a most pleasant Valley, near a delightful River, to the South of it: It is fortify'd with double Stone Walls, and has four high Rocks without, upon three of which are built as many strong Forts, and upon the fourth a *Pagode*. The first of these Rocks is enclos'd with a very strong Wall, the second with four Walls, and the third with no less than seven, with as many Gates all of Stone, and kept by a considerable Garison; the Ascents to the Forts being cut out of the Rock, and scarce accessible by reason of their Steepness and Straitness. On the top of these Rocks are most delicious Springs, Fresh-water Ponds and Gardens. Besides which there is another Fortress upon an unaccessible Rock without the City, commanding the Avenues towards it on that side. The *Naik*'s Palace stands betwixt two of the before-mention'd Rocks, most pleasantly situate, and well fortify'd. Great Cannon are a kind of rarity here, and those few they have (like those in the Siege of *Negapatan*, 1658.) are made of long and broad Bars of Iron, join'd together with Iron Hoops; their Bullets are of Stone, and cut round.

The *Naik* was at our first arrival in these Parts, very obliging to our Deputys, whom

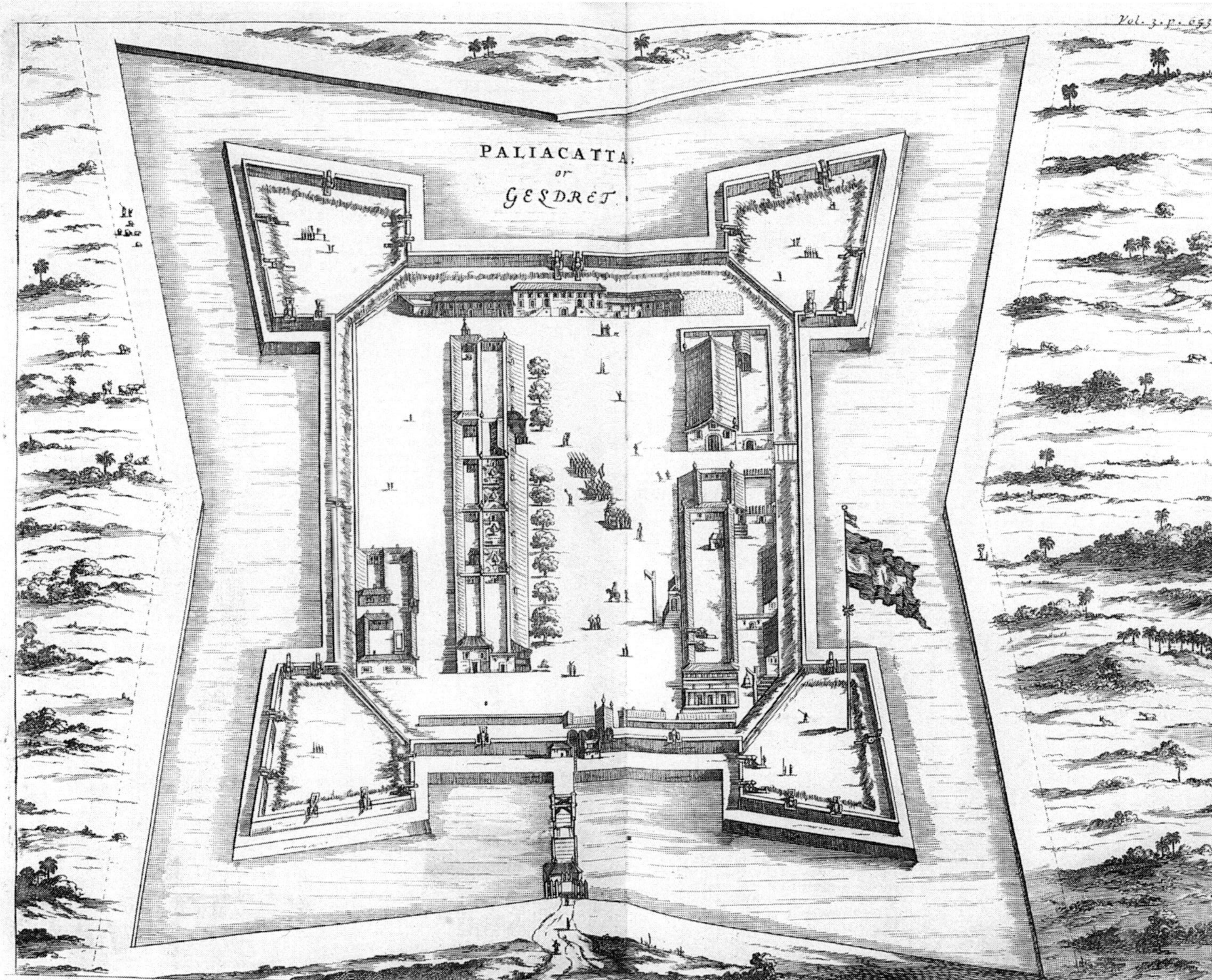
Vol. 3. p. 653.
PALIACATTA
or
GELDRIA
12

whom he treated very splendidly for 14 Days together; and after he had given them a full view of his prodigious Wealth, consisting in most sumptuous Apparel, Silver, Gold, and Jewels, as also of his Wives, Concubines, and Forces, both Horse and Foot, he dismiss'd them very honourably, upon the news of *Iteragio* being on his march against us.

The *Naik* being almost arriv'd to the Age of Dotage, one *Trinvingelaya* (who had emasculated himself) was Administrator of the Kingdom, a cruel and bloody-minded Person, very covetous and implacable in his Hatred, who by his Severity against Criminals had rendred the Country free from Robberies and Pillages. This *Aya* or Administrator General was very urgent with our Deputys to agree with him once for all for the yearly Sum of 1800 Rixdollars in lieu of the Customs, offering to us the Government of *Tegnapatan*, the free Exercise of the Christian Religion, and full Power to rebuild the ruin'd Castle of the *Portugueses*.

The Country hereabouts abounds in Rice, Salt, Fruits, and other Eatables; notwithstanding which, by reason of the vast number of the Inhabitants, they must be supply'd with Provisions from abroad. Their chief Commodities to be exported are Linen and Woollen Stuffs, much in request among those of the *Moluques*, *Amboyna*, *Banda*, and other *Malajan* Places. But great care must be taken these Stuffs agree with their Patterns, especially in the goodness of the Colour, wherein they are very deceitful. The Commodities imported and exchanged here are *Nutmegs*, *Mace*, *Pepper*, *Sandal-wood*, *Chinese Silks*, *Velvets*, *Sattins*, *embroider'd and wrought Carpets* of all sorts of Colours, *raw Silks*, *Patana Girdles*, *Musk*, *Cinnaber*, *Quick-silver*, (but no *Porcellain* or *Chinese Campher*) *Brazain*, *Tin*, *Lead*, *Copper*, &c.

Sadraspatan. From *Tirepopliur* you go over *Poelezere*, *Poelemoer* & *Alembrue* to *Sadraspatan*, where the *Dutch* have a Factory, and from thence Madraspatan. to *Madraspatan*, otherwise *Chinnepatan*, where the *English* have the Fort of *S. George*, garison'd with *Topatzes* and *Mistices*, and from whence they send their Ships every S. Thomas. Year, as well as from *Surat*. *S. Thomas* is a City belonging to the *Portugueses*, situate in *Maliapour*, at 23 ½ Degrees Northern Latitude, about a days Journy from *Paliacatta*; but taken from them about 8 or 9 Years ago by the *Moors*. It is an antient trading City, their chief Traffick consisting in colour'd Stuffs, their Weavers here being famous throughout the *Indies*, as well as their Dyers: They are transported to *Malaga*, *Java*, the *Moluques*, *Siam*, *Pegu*, &c. The Excellency and Lastingness of their Dying are attributed to a peculiar Quality in their Water, the Springs whereof arise out of very white sandy Ground, without the least mixture of Clay. Baldæus.

Paliacatta. *Paliacatta*, *i. e.* the *Old Fort* in the *Malabar* Language, is seated at 13 Degr. 22 Min. of Northern Latitude, 5 long Leagues from *St. Thomas*. About 6 Leagues into the Country, in a direct Line from the Harbour of *Paliacatta*, you see a ridg of high Mountains extending from South to North: On the Southern part you see an Interstice or Valley, where in antient Times stood the Castle of *Rama Geridorgon*; in lieu whereof was afterwards built the Fort *Geldria*, where the *Dutch* Governour keeps his Residence. It is not very large, yet fortified with some Bulworks, sufficient to resist the Power of the neighbouring *Moors*. Mr. *Anthony Pavilion*, Counsellor of the *Indies*, had at that time his Residence there, as Governour, after Mr. *Cornelius Speelman*; and the Garison consisted of about 80 or 90 men. The Road is very good at half a League from the Shore, where you may ride safely at Anchor at 7 or 8 Fathom Depth during the Southern *Mousson*; but not in the Northern *Mousson*, when the Waves breaking forth with great violence out of the Bay of *Bengal* and the *Ganges* against this Shore, render Anchorage very dangerous. *The Dutch Fort Geldria.* *The Road of Paliacatta.*

About 3 ½ Leagues from the Road is a certain Sand-bank, extending from the River into the Sea for a League together, where there is no Anchorage within 4 ½ 5 fathoms Wather. Two Leagues to the North is the Point of *Sicerecourdi*, from whence jets out into the Sea a Sand-Ridg for above two Leagues and half, near which there is no safe Anchorage within 6 ½ or 7 fathoms Water. Near the Bar there is from 6 to 10 fathoms Water in the South *Mousson* at high Tide; but the Boats or Lighters that carry the Merchandizes must keep under the Southern Shoar, there being abundance of Shelves under the Northern Shoar. About a good Cannon-shot within the mouth of the River, within reach of the Castle, is a good Winter-Road for the *Indian* Ships. This River lies at least 5 Leagues to the North-West into the Country, by the City of *Armagon* and the Forest of *Sicerecourdi*, from whence *Paliacatta* is furnished with Wood for Building and Fuel, whereof there is

great

Baldæus. great scarcity in the barren Grounds round that City. A small Brook runs also by the Fort, where we used often to divert our selves in Boats.

The Canal leading to *Paliacatta* is almost dry during the South *Mousson*, but overflows the Country for two Leagues round in the Northern *Mousson*. The Grounds about *Paliacatta* are very nitrous, sandy, and unfit to produce any thing in great quantity; which is the reason that they must be supply'd with most sorts of Provisions (except Fish, whereof they have plenty) from other places. The Fortifications being built upon Fenny Grounds, which reach for four or five Leagues round, have been often in danger of being swallow'd up by the Waters in the rainy season, and were therefore not maintain'd without vast Charges. Under the Cannon of the Fort of *Geldria* lie two Villages, one to the South call'd *Diramamy*, built upon a small Isle, the other on the North-side within reach of a Musquet, call'd *Coupon*, and inhabited by Christian Fishermen, being converted to the Christian Faith in the time of the *Portugueses*.

The Kingdom of Carnatica. We will now proceed to the Kingdom of *Carnatica*, extending 60 *Badagarian* Leagues (one whereof is equivalent to three *Dutch* Miles) from South to North, and 40 from *Paliacatta* to the Coast of *Malabar*. In this Country it was that the three *Naiks*, or chief Lords of the Crown of *Velour*, keep their Residence, who pay a certain yearly Tribute to that Crown, *viz.* the *Vitipanaik* of *Madure*, the King's Bason-Bearer, 200 *Pagodes* (each of which is worth six *Holland* Guilders) *per annum*; the *Christapanaik* of *Chengier* the King's *Betel* Box-bearer, as many; and the *Naik* of *Tanjouwer* his Umbrello-bearer (who is Lord of *Negapatan*) 400 *per annum*. These Dignities being hereditary time out of mind, the Countries of *Madure*, *Chengier* and *Tanjouwer* have been annexed to them, under condition of a yearly Tribute, and are besides this oblig'd to give their personal Attendance at the Coronation of the lawful Successor of the before-mentioned Kingdom.

The three Naiks.

Penna, Caleture. Further to the North (about a days Voyage) from *Paliacatta*, lie *Penna* and *Caleture*, betwixt which places is found the best *Essaye* Roots, which are also to be found in the Isles near *Jafnapatan*: It is a small Root no bigger than a little sprig of about a span in length, used by the Dyers. The way to try its goodness, is to break it to pieces, and to see whether it be very red within, or else to chaw a piece of it, and if you perceive a nitrous taste in it, it is very good. To try the true Dye thereof upon Callico's, you may squeeze some Lemmon Juice upon it, and let it dry in the Sun; if it be not true it will change pale. There is also a five corner'd Fruit call'd *Carunbolle*, the Juice whereof being sharper than that of *Lemmons*, is likewise made use of in trying the true Dye of the *Essaye* Colour. For this Nation being very cunning in their way of dealing, oftentimes make use of a Dye call'd *Sordaco* instead of the *Essaye*, and of the Bark of a certain Tree growing in *Orixa*, but may easily be distinguish'd by the colour, being somewhat darker than the true *Essaye*, and if rub'd with Water, will tinge it. They have a nice way of refining and trying the Gold here, and the *Dutch* Company coin abundance of Golden *Pagodes* here, with the King's Stamp upon them. Abundance of *Nely*, Rice, *Gingely*-seeds, Oil, Butter, coarse Cloths, Iron, Honey and yellow Wax, is brought hither from *Orixa* and *Masulipatan*, the whole Voyage thither and back again being commonly perform'd in four Months. From hence to *Arracan*, *Pegu* and *Tanassery* you pay 8 or 10 *per Cent.* for Freight of Pepper, Sandalwood, Stuffs, Steel and Iron, and make your returns in Gold, Rubies of *Ava*, *Gummi-Lacca*, long white Pepper, Lead, *&c.* Betwixt *Tanassery* and *Occeda* towards *Malacca* are the Harbours of *Tanangar*, *Sencaza*, and *Perach*, opposite to *Achem*, whither they trade with vast Profit, and bring back abundance of Tin, a Commodity much in request with the *Moors*, wherewith they tin their Copper Vessels.

Petapouli is situate at 16 deg. of North-Latitude: As you sail East and East to the North towards this Road, you see an Isle at a League and a half distance made by the North Branch of the River cover'd with Coco-Trees, an infallible Guide to the Road, where at a League's distance from the Shoar, there is good Anchorage at 6 fathoms Water in a Sandy Bottom. This is the securest Harbour on all this Coast, during the North *Mousson*, by reason of a Point of Land jetting out for three Leagues in the Sea to the North of the Isle, and enclosing as it were the Road by a Demi-Circle, whereas in the South *Mousson* the Sea is very boisterous, and the Waves very turbulent here. The Bar of *Petapouli* has some Shallows scarce passable but by small Vessels. The City lies a League within the Petapouli.

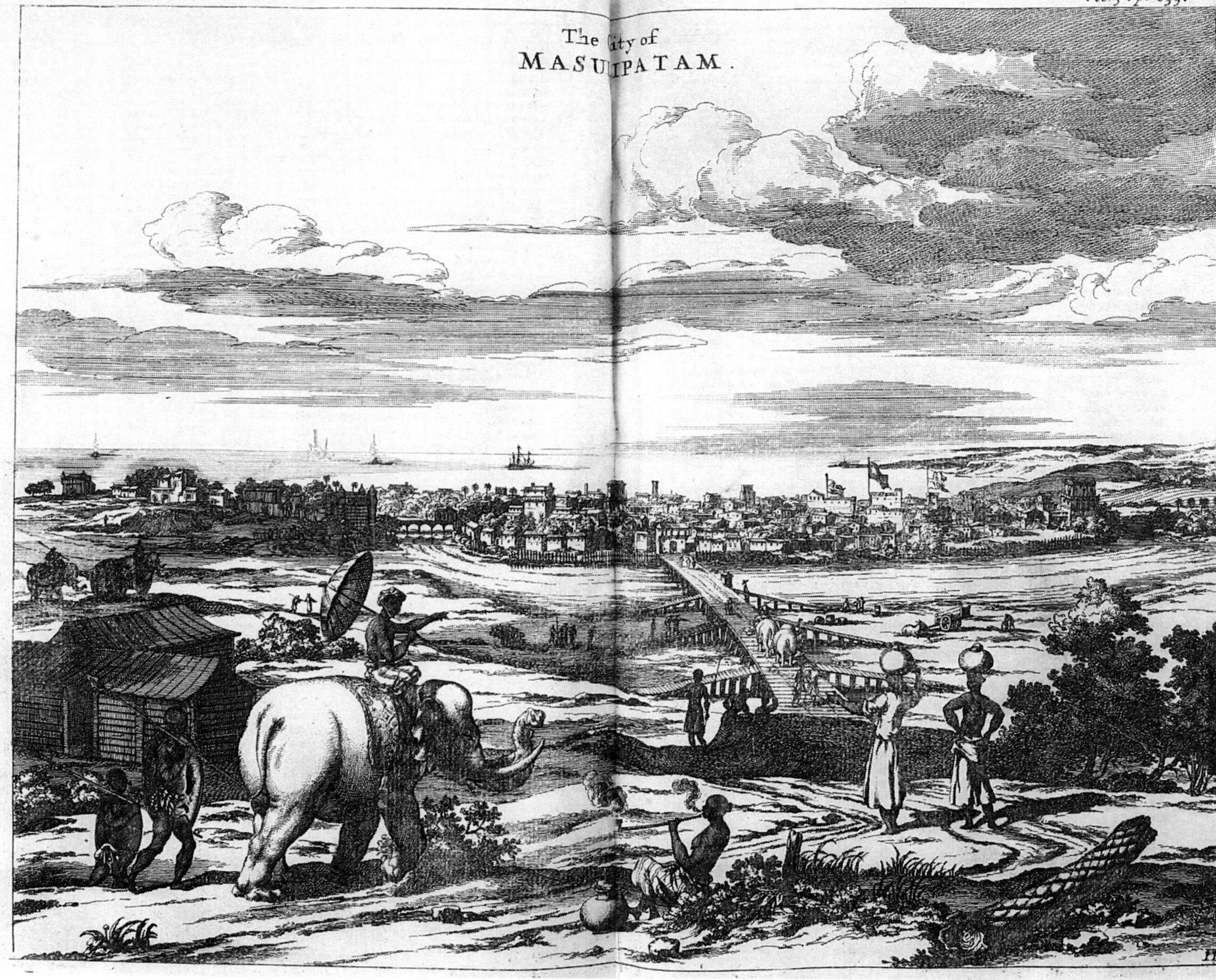
The City of
MASULIPATAM.

the River, which is pretty large, and runs up into the Country till it joins its Waters with the River *Meca*.

Petapouli is of no great extent, inhabited by some *Moors* and *Persians* of Note, but for the most part by *Gentives*, Subjects of the King of *Golgonda*. As hereabouts grows a kind of *Essaye* Colour, exceeding all the rest, call'd *Tambrevelle*, so the painted and dy'd Stuffs of *Petapouli* exceed even those of *Masulipatan*. The Root grows like a small sprig of a foot long, the Colour whereof is so deep that they are oblig'd to mix it with the *Essaye* of *Arrical* and *Ortacour*, to make it the more lively. This *Essaye* Root grows in the Isle made by the River over against the City, whereof the Governour has the Monopoly, and pays a certain yearly Sum for it to the King, which as it is paid most commonly in dy'd Stuffs and Cloths, so he employs the Weavers himself, and for that reason will not easily permit them to be sold to the Merchants (at least not without his Consent) who transport them from thence into *Persia*. Here good Indigo is to be bought, but much dearer than at *Masulipatan*: From hence we also transport Cotton-Yarn, white Stuffs, and several other Commodities to *Holland*.

Masulipatan. *Masulipatan* is a City seated near a large River, where the *English* and *Dutch* have their Factories: It is very populous, and the Residence of a Governour, who pays a certain yearly Tribute to the King of *Golcondar*, which he squeezes out of the Inhabitants, especially the *Gentives*, who are sorely oppress'd by the *Persians* and *Moors* here, who farm all the Weaving Trade from the Great Persons; wherefore there is scarce any trafficking here without Profit, unless you have a Patent from the King, which is not easy to be obtain'd, because the Governours (who pay 140000 *Pagodes* of annual Tribute to the King) constantly oppose it: and it is no difficult matter to approach the King (who keeps his Court at a great distance thence) without purchasing their Favour, or some other Great Mens at Court. For the rest, this City is a Place of great Traffick, where most of our Commodities, as also those transported hither from the *Moluques*, *China*, &c. are sold at a very good rate. Here is also a great Concourse of Merchants from *Cambaja*, *Suratte*, and other Places under the Jurisdiction of the Great *Mogul*, as also from *Goa*, *Orixa*, *Bengale* and *Pegu*. Here is likewise a considerable Traffick in Diamonds and Rubies: The first are digged in the Kingdoms of *Golgonda* and *Decam*, near the City of *Bysilaga* beyond *Suratte*: Each Stone weighing above 25 *Mangely's*, or *Carats*, belonging to the King of *Bysilaga*, the rest to those that have farm'd the Mines. There is a certain Mountain call'd *Cotsa Vuytthia*, in the Country of *Decam*, which affords the choicest Diamonds. *Borneo*, but especially the City of *Succadana*, are likewise very famous for Diamonds. *Baldæus.*

CHAP. XXIV.

An Account of most sorts of precious Stones, as Diamonds, Rubies, Smaragds, Saphirs, Amethists, Jaspirs, Sardonicks, Achats, Granates, &c.

The Diamond. THE most noble of all precious Stones is the Diamond, call'd Ἀδάμας by the *Greeks*, from ἀδάμαστος, *i. e.* impregnable. *Pliny*, and others of the antient Naturalists being of opinion, that it is neither to be broken by the force of the Hammer, nor penetrable by the violence of the Fire; which however has since been sufficiently contradicted by Experience; tho the same is several times used in the same sense in the Scripture*. It is likewise call'd *Adamas* by the *Latins*, *Deamant* by the *Germans*, *Adamanto* by the *Spaniards*, *Almaes* by the *Arabians*, *Jutan* by the *Malajars*, and *Hiera* and *Jua* by the *Indosthans*. The Beauty of a Diamond consists in its Hardness, Transparency and Lustre; tho to speak the truth, there are but few Diamonds without some Defects, which however pass current among those who are no nice Judges of it. Lead is reckon'd to be exactly three times as heavy as a polish'd Diamond.

* Zech. 7. v. 12. Ezek. 3. 9. Isa. 32. 13. Jer. 17. 1.

There is a certain kind of Diamonds call'd *Boschiers*, which are not by a third part so valuable as the rest, tho sometimes they exceed for Brightness all the other sorts; but if they incline to a reddish or yellow Colour, they are not worth half so much, they being only valued according to the weight of the *Carats* without

Baldæus.

out any Multiplication. To try the goodness of a Diamond you must cut one Diamond with another, and if the Powder thereof be of an Ash-colour, it is right, but if white, otherwise; for all other precious Stones except the Diamond afford a white Powder, and the more the Powder of the Diamond approaches to a Grey, the more precious it is. They have another way of trying the Diamonds, by making them red hot, and afterwards quenching them in cold fresh Water, and if they don't crack they are true and good. The true Value of the best Diamonds (provided they are clean and of a just thickness) is computed thus: The just Value of a good Diamond weighing a *Carat* (each whereof is equivalent to four Grains) is 80 *Gilders*, or 32 *Rixdollars*. Now to know the just Value of one or two *Carats*, you must multiply two with two, the Product whereof being four, this must be multiplied with the value of a Diamond of one *Carat*, *viz.* 80 *Gilders*, the Product whereof amounts to 320 *Gilders*; so that according to this Computation, a Diamond of 20 *Carats* is worth 32000 *Gilders*, and according to the same proportion, one of 100 *Carats* no less than 800000 *Gilders*. *The Goodness and Value of the Diamonds.*

The Ruby. The Ruby, call'd *Rubinus* or *Carbunculus* by the *Latins*, *Mamwikam* by the *Malayans*, *Battamora* by the *Siameses*, and *Laal* by the *Indosthans*; it will endure the Fire for a considerable time. There are three several sorts of Rubies, some are of a high red and brillant colour; those of a dark red colour, tho they carry a very fine Lustre, yet are not so much valued as the former. The Oriental Rubies are call'd *Espinelles*, those of *Germany* are very hard, but inclining to a dark brown, and therefore of less Value; notwithstanding which they are true Rubies: they seldom exceed the bigness of a good Pea, and are very thin, and the Stone-Polishers make them thinner, still to increase their Lustre. The *Espinelles* are of much brighter Colour, but not so hard, and consequently of less or more Value in proportion to their Hardness, some being as hard as a Saphir.

Their different kinds, goodness and value. The Carbuncles are adulterated with *Sandaracha*, but these false Colours are soon discovered in the Corners of the polished Stones, which don't receive these Colours. The Oriental Carbuncles are likewise of two different kinds, some are of a dark brown Colour, the others are bright and carry Lustre like Fire, and these are the most precious. The Rubies are apprais'd like the Diamonds by *Carats*, one, two, three, or more, with this difference, that the *Rubies* tho of the same Weight, are somewhat bigger in proportion than the Diamonds, and without the least Clouds or other Defects.

The Emerault. The *Smaradg* or *Emerault*, called *Tamarul* by the *Arabians*, and *Jasche* by the *Indians*, is one of the precious Stones called Σμαράγδος by the *Greeks*, and *Esmaraude* by the *French*. They are of three different kinds. *Of three kinds.* *Scythia* and *Egypt* produce these Stones, as well as the *East-Indies*. They endeavour to imitate them at *Paliacatta* and *Bisnagar* in Glass. Those of *Scythia* are accounted the best, those of *Peru* are the next in Goodness, of a dank green Colour, very hard, and more transparent than those of the *East-Indies*. These last are harder than those of *Peru*, but much less regarded. Those of *Peru* are of a pale Colour and brttle. The general Opinion is, that in case an Emerault should be found excellent in all its Parts, *viz.* in Colour, Shape and Transparency, it would be comparable to a Diamond of the same bigness, nay would even surpass it in value, by reason of its rarity. *Their value.*

The Saphir The *Saphir* is called *Mila* by the *Arabians*, and *Millam* by the *Malayans*. They are of two sorts, those of a dark blue Colour are the best, those of a pale Colour resembling the Diamonds, the worst. They are found in *Malabar*, *Calecut*, *Cananor*, in the Kingdom of *Bisnagar*, in the Isle of *Ceylon*, but *Siam* and *Pegu* produce the best.

The Hyacinth. The Hyacinth called Ὑάκινθος by the *Greeks*, is a red Stone, not unlike the Carbuncle, but does not endure the Fire. It is found in *Spain*: the Jewellers sell sometimes the Stone called *Ethiopis*, for a Hyacinth: they are of two kinds, one red, the other inclining to a yellow.

The Amethist. The *Amethist*, called Ἀμέθυστος by the *Greeks*, is of a purple Colour; those that are found in the *East-Indies* are preferr'd before the rest.

The Jaspir found in China. The *Jaspir* so called by the *Latins*, and Ἴασπις by the *Greeks*, is of two different kinds, some being of a lovely green Colour, like the *Emeraults*, and of such a bigness, as to serve for Materials for Drinking-cups; some have the green mix'd with white; some are of purple, others of a rose Colour with variety of Flowers in them; others are dark brown and blew, with white Veins; some are Marble on one, and *Jasper* on the other side.

The Sardis.

The *Sardis* has got its Name from *Sardinia*, where it is frequently found, as well as in *Epirus*. There are three several kinds, and were by the Antients distinguish'd into the Male and Female. That the *Sardis* is different from the *Sardonic*, is evident out of the Holy Scripture *.

* Apoc. 22. 20. Exod. 28. 17, 20.

The Sardonick.

The *Sardonick*, called Σαρδόνυξ by the *Greeks*, has got its Name from *Sarda* and *Onyx*, or its resemblance to a human Navel.

The Achat.

The *Achat* is found about *Suratte*, but is of no great value, unless it be curiously chequered with Figures.

Amber.

Amber called *Succinum* by the *Latins*, ἤλεκτρον by the *Greeks*, and *Alambre* by the *Portugueses*, is a kind of a Gum or rosinous Substance, found near *Koningsberg*, and some other Places in *Prussia*; in great esteem among the *Japoneses* and the *Indians* in general. It is often chequered with various Figures, and has the virtue of attracting Straw, Paper, and such like light Matters.

Granate.

The *Granate* resembles in Colour to the Coral. There are two sorts, the *Indian* and *Spanish*, the last are very red and bright; those found in *Ethiopia* are scarce to be distinguished from the Hyacinth, except that their Lustre is somewhat less than that of the Hyacinth.

Cats-eyes.

The Stone called *Olbos de Gatos*, i. e. *Cats-eyes*, by the *Portugueses*, is in much greater esteem among the *Indians* than the *Portugueses*; who are of Opinion, that if you rub Linen-Cloth with them, it will be fire-proof: but this I have found contrary to Truth by my own experience.

Blood-stone.

The *Hematites* or Bloodstone (Αἱματίτης by the *Greeks*) has got its Name from its dark red Colour, and its virtue in quenching of Blood. It is found in *New-Spain*, and reputed by them a kind of *Jasper*; the *Indians* make Beads of them, and wear them about their Necks: They also lay them in Water, and afterwards hold them close in their Hands, and look upon this as an excellent Remedy to stop the superfluous Monthly times of the Women, or any other Flux of Blood. This Stone is also found in *Ceylon* and *Cambaja*, where it is called *Silakenea*.

Kidney-stone.

The *Nephritis* or *Kidneystone*, has got its Name from the word Νεφρὸς, *i. e.* a Kidney, because it is worn by the *Indians* against the Pain of the Kidneys, and therefore in great esteem among them. It is found in *New-Spain*, and the greener it is, the better it is.

Hartstone.

The Naturalists tell us, that the Stag, when tormented in his Bowels by certain poisonous Worms, runs up to the Neck in Water, at which time the slimy Tears which adhere to the Corners of his Eyes are coagulated to the bigness of a Wallnut, which thence have got the Name of *Hartstones*; which taken in Wine, are look'd upon as a Sovereign Antidote against all manner of Poisons and Infections.

Baldæus.

The Serpentstone.

The *Serpentstone* is found in the *Indies*, of a dark brown Colour, with a white Spot like an Eye in the middle. Some will have them to grow in the Heads of the Serpents; others are of opinion, that the Water-Serpent hung up by the Tail, with her Head hanging downwards, so near to a Vessel full of Water, that she may lick it, does spew out this Stone, which tied to the Belly, is accounted an excellent Remedy against the Dropsy. The *Spaniards* call this Stone *Piedro della Cobra*, and the *Portugueses Pedra de Cobra*, being commonly of the bigness of a Shilling, less or more. The true *Serpentstone* is found in that kind of Serpents, call'd *Cobra de Cabelo* by the *Portugueses*, and *Serpens Pilosus* by the *Latinists*, being the most virulent of all Serpents. They try the Goodness of this Stone, by putting it into fair Water, which if it bubbles, it is accounted true; another Trial is, when it sticks close to the Lips, or to the Wound, unto which it will adhere till it has drawn out all the Poison, when it falls off like a Leech, and is thrown into Milk: Of this I saw the effect my self with good Success in a Negro Slave stung by a Serpent, belonging to our Head Factor at *Jafnapatnam*, Sir *Jorephas Vosch*. The *Brahmans* make a certain Composition (which they keep very secret) in imitation of the natural *Serpentstone*, the chief Ingredients whereof are suppos'd to be the Head, Heart, Liver and Teeth mix'd with the *Terra sigillata*. Concerning the true Virtues of the Serpent-stones, you may consult *Michael Boimus* *, and *Athanasius Kircher* †.

*A Composition of the Ser*pentstone.

* In Flora Chinensi.
† Lib. 9. Mundi subterran.

Hogs-stone.

The Stone called *Pedra de Porco*, i. e. *Hogs-stone*, by the *Portugueses*, grows in the *Vesica Bilearea* of the Hogs about *Malacca*. It is of a ruddy Colour, and sometimes grey, greezy or oily at the touch like Venice-soap, and of a bitterish Tast. When they will use this Stone, they put it in Water, till it acquires a bitterish Tast, and so give the Water to the Patient, for the cure of Pestilential and other Fevers. They are highly esteemed in the *Indies*.

Baldæus. The *Toad-stone* is found in the Head of a certain kind of *Toads* of the bigness of a good Bean, of various Colours, but most enclining to a green, smooth and shining on the outside, which is bony, but the inside of a stony Substance: They are reputed an excellent Remedy against the Stone in the Kidneys, Poison and Infirmity of the Stomach. To get this Stone, they take a very old Toad, put it in a Vessel full of Holes, and so bury it in a Dunghil near a Pismires Nest, till the Pismires have consumed the whole Substance of the Toad, except the Stone. They try the Goodness of this Stone, by laying it before a Tortoise, which if it is ready to swallow it, it is accounted a true Stone.

Toad-stone.

Bezoar-stone.

Of the *Bezoar-stone* something has been said before in the Description of *Cananor*, being accounted a great Antidote, but esteemed much more in former times than of late Years. The Bezoar-Stone is found in the Stomach of certain Goats in *Persia*, and the Isle of *Borneo* called *Pazan*. It is of a very solid ruddy Substance, growing in different Partitions, like our Onions, which are easily discernable when the Stone is broken: They are of divers Colours, some inclining to an Olive-Colour, others to a dark green, some round, some of an oval Figure; the smoothest and largest are accounted the best. They are also found in the Isle, called *Ilha de Vacas*, i. e. *Cow-Island*, about 6 Leagues from *Jafnapatnam*, but in no great Quantities; for I remember that Mr. *Anthony Pavilion* told me, that out of 70 or 80 Goats, which he ordered to be killed, he had but a few Stones, and these but indifferent ones and very brittle. The *Malayans* try this Stone thus; they rub it five or six times with Mortar, and if it changes the Mortar into a yellow Colour, it is accounted true. Those of *Banda* tell us, that they find the Bezoar-stone in the Heads of certain Apes. The *Indians* and *Chineses* mix it with Rose-water, and use it against Poison, melancholy Humours, and Quartan Agues. They also make use of it as a Preservative; for they purge twice a year, *viz.* in *March* and *September*, and for five days after take from 10 to 30 Grains of Bezoar in Rose-water. They sell this Stone by weight; one of 300, 250, 150, or 140 *Carats*, is accounted equivalent to three times the weight in Gold; each *Carat* reckon'd at 8 *Dutch* Stivers. One of 100, 90 or 80 *Carats*, to 1 ½ the quantity of Gold, or at 6 Stivers the *Carat*. One of 70, 60, 50, or 40 *Carats*, to 1 ½ of Gold, or at 4 Stivers the *Carat*. The lesser ones in proportion of ½ of Gold, or 2 ½ Stivers the *Carat*.

Oriental and Occidental Bezoar.

There are Oriental and Occidental Bezoar-stones; those of the East, especially of *Persia*, much exceed those of the *West-Indies*. *Arabia*, *Malabar*, *Japan*, and *China* produce these Stones, and the Mountains of *Peru* in the *West-Indies*. The *Persians* call this Stone *Belzoar*, i. e. *the Lord of Poison*; and the *Arabians*, *Hagiar Corrabone*. Formerly it us'd to be sold in *Holland* at the rate of 8 Guilders *per* Ounce. If the outward Rind or Skin be taken off, the next appears smoother and brighter than the first. The Bezoar-stone has no Pit, but a Concavity containing a certain mealy Substance, the Virtue whereof is said to excel the Stone it self. Those taken out of the Goats living in the Mountains, are accounted better than of those feeding in the Valleys. These Stones are found in certain Bags of a hairy Substance, growing within the Concavity of the Stomach, of a Span in length, wherein the Stones lie in a row like Buttons on a Wastcoat, as a certain *Portuguese* tells us. They have also another way of trying the goodness of this Stone: They take a Needle with a Thred, and having dip'd the same in the Juice of a venomous Herb call'd *Ballestra*, they draw the Needle and Thred thro the Leg of a Dog or some other living Creature, leaving the Thred in the Wound till the Dog faints away. This done, they give him a certain quantity of *Bezoar* Pouder, which if it recovers him, the Bezoar is good; if not, it is look'd upon as adulterated. Of several other Trials we have spoken in the Description of *Cananor*.

The Indigo.

Among those Commodities which are transported from *Masulipatan*, the *Indigo* being none of the least, it will be requisite we should say something also of this precious Merchandize. The Indigo is of different kinds, and grows in divers Places: The broad Indigo grows about two Leagues from *Amadabath* the Capital City of *Gusuratte*, especially in the Village of *Circhees*, from whence that kind of Indigo has got its Name. The Indigo is a Shrub growing up to a Man's height, with small hard Twigs like the Blackberry-Trees: Its Blossom resembles that of the Briars, and the Seed that of the *Fœnum Græcum*, call'd *Dusenegre* by the *French*. They sow it in *June* and *July*, and cut it in *November* and *December*.

Indigo *of* Chirchees.

The Indigo of *Chirchees* grows three years successively after its first Sowing. The first Year they cut the Leaves about

a

a Foot above the Ground; which being dry'd in the Sun for 24 Hours, they are put into Barrels full of Salt-water, of a Man's height, and kept down to the bottom, by laying great Stones upon them, the better to squeeze out the Tincture. The Water being stir'd often for 4 or 5 days, it is let out into great Casks, where it is stir'd and trod continually by certain Persons, till the Water thickens, and the Indigo settles to the bottom, in the same manner as they manage the Butter in *Holland.* The Sediment being separated from the Water, and strain'd thro thin Cloths, is spread upon the Ground (first cover'd with white Ashes) to dry. The Country People adulterate the Indigo with a certain Earth of the same colour, or with Oil, to make it seem the better upon the Water. The second Year the Indigo grows again on the Stalks that were left in the Fields, which is accounted better than the *Gingy* or wild Indigo. If you intend to preserve the Seed, you must let the Stalks dry the second time, and afterwards gather the Seed. The Indigo of the third Year's growth is of little value, and consumed for the most part by the Inhabitants of *Gusuratte* in dying their Linen and Woollen Cloths.

Its Goodness.

The chief Signs of the goodness of the Indigo are, its Lightness and feeling dry betwixt the Fingers, its swimming upon the Water, and, if thrown upon burning Coals, its emitting a Violet-colour'd Smoke, and leaving but little Ashes behind. The Ground which has born the Indigo must lie fallow the fourth Year, unless you would sow it with some Kitchen Herbs.

Hereabouts also grows the Indigo call'd *Aniel de Biant*, by those of *Gusuratte.* They sow it in *June* in light and sandy Grounds, and it grows chiefly in *June*, *July*, *August* and *September*, the ordinary rainy Months here; which together with the Heat of the Sun-beams brings it to Maturity, it being certain, that too much Rain is pernicious to this Shrub. Great care is to be taken that the Grounds be well cleared from Thorns and Thistles. The Buyers of Indigo ought to be cautious how they buy it; for if it happen to be not very dry, they may lose three Pound weight in ten in 8 days time.

The Indigo Laura.

The *Indigo Laura*, or *Indigo de Bayana*, is of three different sorts: The first Crop is call'd *Vouthy* by those of *Gusuratte*, the second *Gerry*, and the third *Catteel.* The first is cut in *October*, the second about the middle of *November*, and the third in *January.* The first is of a light blue Colour, and held against the Sun, and squeez'd with the Nail of the Thumb, shews a Violet Colour. The second, call'd *Gerry*, the nearer it approaches to a Violet Colour, the more valuable it is. The third, call'd *Catteel*, is the worst of all, of a ruddy colour, and so hard, as scarce to be broken to pieces.

Baldæus.

Trial of the Indigo.

The goodness of the Indigo is try'd in the following manner: About 9 or 10 a Clock in a clear Sun-shiny Morning they take a Piece or two, and after they have broken it in pieces, hold it against the Sun, to see whether they can discover any Sand in it: They also squeeze with their Nails some of the Colour out, which the nearer it comes to a Violet, the better it is. They also try it with Water and Fire: They throw a Piece of Indigo 40 or 50 times successively into a Cask fill'd with Water, and the longer it swims upon the Surface, the better it is deem'd. They also cast a Piece of Indigo upon burning Coals, and if the Smoke or Flame appear of a high Violet Colour, the Indigo is good.

Good Indigo is also made in Coromandel.

It is sowed in several Places: The *Indigo Laura* about *Agra*; in *Fettapour*, 12 *Cos* from *Agra*; near the City of *Byana*, 30 *Cos* from *Agra* (where is the best;) near the City of *Bassaune*, 38 *Cos* from *Agra*; near the City of *Kindowen*, 40 *Cos* from *Agra.* The Country People are obliged to carry their Indigo into the next adjacent City.

Next to *Masulipatan* we must also say something of *Bimilipatan*, where the *Dutch* have had a Factory a considerable time ago, and from thence, as well as most other Parts of *Orixa*, transport abundance of Rice, Pease, and other Provisions, into other Parts. The whole Country hereabouts enjoys a wholesom Air, tho in one Place more than in the other: For tho the Heats are excessive, nay almost intolerable, yet are the same in a great measure qualified by the cool Sea-Winds; so that the reason of the many Distempers and pale Countenances, which often attend the *Europeans* in those Parts, is not so much to be attributed to the Unhappiness of the Climate, as to their own Intemperance and Debaucheries.

Baldæus.

CHAP. XXV.

The Manner of Living of the Hollanders *in the* East-Indies. *Their use of* Tea *and* Chocolate: *Their ordinary Drink; Manner of Sleeping. A Description of the two Rivers, the* Ganges *and the* Nile.

Manner of living of the Dutch. As the manner of Living of the vulgar sort among the *Dutch* in the *East-Indies*, is none of the best, so we will be satisfy'd with giving an account of those of the better sort. They commonly rise with the Sun, Sleep after Sun-rising being accounted very unwholsom here in the Morning. Some have a Custom of washing their Heads, nay the whole Body with cold Water, immediately after their coming out of bed; others do it with luke-warm Water three or four times a week; the last of which I have found the best by experience. They commonly shift their Linen every day. Brandy or any other strong Liquors are not much used by the wiser sort in the Morning, unless it be a Spoonful just before Dinner, and a little at night before they go to bed.

The use of Tea. The *Tea* (always used fasting by the *Chineses*) has got a mighty Ascendant over the *Hollanders* of late Years. The best grows in *China*, being a Shrub rising not very high above-ground, especially in the Province of *Kiangnan*, near the City of *Hocichieu*. The Leaves are dry'd, roll'd up and preserv'd for use. Father *Martinus Martini*, in his *Chinese Atlas*, gives us the following account of the Tea. The Leaves are very like those of the *Rhus Coriaria*, call'd *Sumach* by the *Arabians*, and ῥοῦς by the *Greeks*, of which it seems to be a Species; tho it does not grow wild, but is planted, being a Shrub with small Twigs. In the beginning of the Summer it buds out a light-colour'd Blossom of an agreeable Scent, after which come green Buds that turn black at last. *How prepared.* They take a Leaf, and after they have warm'd it in an Iron Pot with a gentle Heat, they lay it upon a clean Mat, and having well roll'd it, put it again over the Fire, till it be thoroughly dry'd, and twisted together; when they put it up in Tin or Leaden Vessels, to preserve it from the moist Air, which would soon corrupt it. The Tea being of different sorts, consequently bears a lower or higher Price, according to its goodness. Its chief Virtues are to disperse the gross Vapours of the Head and Stomach, and consequently to exhilarate our Spirits. The *Chineses*, as they are never troubled with the Gout, so they attribute the same to the Tea; and *Kircher* ascribes to it a Diuretick Quality. Its Taste is somewhat bitterish, and not very agreeable at first, but well enough afterwards. The *Turks* tell us Wonders of their *Cauwa* or Coffee, and the *Spaniards* of their Chocolate; but it has been found by experience, that the first encreases the Gall, and the last enflames the Blood, and nourishes too fast; whereas the Tea is much more moderate in its Nature, notwithstanding which its immoderate use hinders the Concoction of the Stomach (especially if taken after Dinner) and too much dries up the Moistures of the Body, which is the reason the *Chineses* never take it after Meals. The *Chinese* Tea is both in Goodness and Price much superior to the *Japonese*. I have found by experience that four or five Cups of the Extraction of the fresh Leaves of the Tea makes one light-headed; and I remember, when the best Tea was sold at the rate of 24 Gilders *per* Pound in *Holland*.

The ordinary Drink of the *Hollanders* is a Mixture of Water and Sugar boil'd together. Some fill certain Earthen Vessels over night with Water, and add to it 3 or 4 Glasses of *Spanish* Wine, which exposed together all night in the Dew, turns white, and affords a pleasant Liquor; but is a little too cool, for which reason some put a certain quantity of Mum in the Vessel. The *Brunswick* Mum is both more pleasant and wholsom here than in *Europe*; the worst is, that it is excessive dear, a Cask being sometimes sold from 40 to 100 Rixdollars. *What sort of Drink is most proper for the* Indies. Among the Wines, those of *Spain* are most in request: It's true they sometimes inflame the Gall; but against that they make use of *Rhubarb* and *Cremor* of *Tartar*. The *French* and *Rhenish* Wines are not strong enough in these hot Countrys, where the Stomach requires more lively Cordials, as a little Brandy, or a moderate share of Canary. Their ordinary Food is Goats, Sheep, Fowl, Hares, Peacocks, and such like.

The *Hollanders* most generally take their Afternoons Sleep here, as the *Italians* and some other *Europeans* do in hot Countries; a thing sufficiently commendable in in the *Indies*, where the Heat of the Sun Beams invites the Inhabitants to pass away the middle of the Day (when they are unfit for Business) at their ease. They have also a constant Custom of washing their Mouths after Dinner. About three or four a Clock in the Afternoon they take their Tea, and after that a Walk; the Evenings and Nights being pretty cool and very pleasant here, especially when the Moon shines. They sup commonly about 7 or 8 a Clock, but very moderately, and go to sleep about 10 or 11 upon Quilts, Feather-beds being not us'd in the *Indies*: But care must be taken to cover well your Belly, Hips and Legs, for fear of the Cramp, especially if you lie expos'd to the open Air in Moon-shiny Nights, the neglect of which often proves fatal to the Soldiers and Seamen, after they have heated themselves with *Arak*, or other strong Liquors.

Feather-beds not used in the Indies.

Thus much of the manner of Living of the *Hollanders* in the *East-Indies*. Concerning the different Clans or Families of the *Indians*, the manner of Living, Austerity and Prerogatives of the *Brahmans*, their *Vedam* Fasts, Marriages, Feasts, Burials, Mr. *Abraham Rogerius* has given so exact an account, that it would be needless to repeat them here. The Foundation, Strength and Magnificence of their *Pagodes*, especially of those dedicated to *Wisnou* and *Eswara*, with their Revenues and Idols, are likewise most exactly describ'd by the same Author; and among other things, that their *Pagodes* have no other Light but what they receive thro a Hole on the top; that they are divided into three several Vaults, supported by Stone Pillars: The first whereof stands open to all Goers and Comers: The second has two strong Doors, which are kept open in the day time, and guarded by a certain number of *Brahmans*: The third part is always kept close, being the Residence of the Idol, before which hang Lamps, which never cease to burn. But of the religious Worship of the Inhabitants of *Coromandel*, *Malabar* and *Ceylon*, we shall treat more at large in the third Part of this Treatise.

And since we have had occasion to speak so much of the Places between the Rivers *Indus* and *Ganges*, commonly known by the Name of *India* on this side the *Ganges*, we must also say something concerning these two Rivers. The *Ganges* exonerates it self into the Sea of *Bengale*, call'd otherwise *Sinus Gangeticus* and *Sinus Argaricus* by *Ptolomey*, dividing the most Easterly Part of the *Indies* from the Western Parts; the first whereof comprehend *Bengal*, *Aracan*, *Pegu*, *Malacca*, *Sumatra*, &c. According to the opinion of St. *Austin*, St. *Jerom*, *Ambrose*, and many others of the antient Fathers, the *Ganges* is the same which is in the Holy Scripture call'd *Pison*; but *Cornelius a Lapide* has sufficiently demonstrated that *Pison* cannot be the River *Ganges*, no more than *Gihon* the *Nilus*. The general Opinion is that the Source of the *Ganges* is in the Mount *Caucasus*, as those of the *Euphrates* and *Tigris* are in the *Armenian* Mountains, and that of the *Nile* among the *Mountains of the Moon*, near the *Cape of Good Hope* on the *African* Coast; tho Father *Kircher* puts the original Rise of the *Nile* in the Country of *Agaos* near *Sagela* bordering upon the Kingdom of *Gojam*. The Source arises in a Plain on the very top of the Mountain, surrounded with delightful Trees; but does not gather into a Rivulet till at the Foot of the said Mountain; and being augmented by the accession of divers other Brooks, gathers into a Lake of 30 Leagues in length, and 14 in breadth. From hence it pursues its Course, and by various Turnings and Windings returns near the Place of its Source, whence passing thro the Rocks and Precipices, it continues its Course into the middle of *Ethiopia*. * *Isaac Vossius* derives the Rise of the *Nile* out of *Goyome*, a Province of the *Abyssines*, and says, that among other Titles that King makes use of this: *King of* Goyome, *where the* Nile *has its Rise*. The antient *Egyptians* had so great a Veneration for the *Nile*, that they bestow'd the Title of the Arm of *Osiris* upon it: For as the Pagans numbred the rest of the Elements among the Gods, so they had no less opinion of the Waters, especially in the Great Rivers. Hence it is that the Inhabitants near the *Ganges* call it the Heavenly River, and are of opinion, that the Waters of that River cleanse them from their Sins; nay those of *Bengale* are so superstitious in this Point, as to carry their sick and dying Friends to this River, where they lay them up to the middle in Water: And for such as have no Opportunity or Strength to be carry'd thither, they are perswaded, that if they wash themselves with any other Water, and at the same time think upon the said River, saying, *Ganges, purify me*, they shall be cleansed from their Sins. † *Servius* observes, that it was the general Opinion of the Heathens, that the Water would cleanse them from their Sins: Which seems to agree with what is related of *Pilate*,

The River Ganges.

Baldæus.

The Source of the Nile.

*L.2.c.71. Ægypti habent Ostia Nili, Æthiopes autem ejus Fontes.

† Annot. in lib. 6. Æneid.

Baldæus. *Pilate* *, and of the *Pharisees* and *Jews* in general. The *Mahometans* are to this day not free from that Superstition, the Water of the *Ganges* being sold among them in Bottles at a very good Price, as we do our Spaw-Waters; and they pay a considerable Custom for it.

* Mat. 27. 24. ch. 25. 26. Mark 7. 3.

Hence it is, that the *Persians* look upon it as a Crime to do ones need into the River, or to throw Carrion into it, nay even to spit into it; and that they have attributed such surprizing Qualities to the Waters of many Rivers. When the Water of the *Nile* is carried in order to be sacrific'd upon the Altar, the People pay their Reverence to the Vessel that contains it, by prostrating themselves upon the Ground in the same manner as the *Malabars* do to the Water of *Rameswara*, near the *Pagode* call'd *Ramanakoil*, to which they attribute likewise a peculiar Virtue of purging them from their Sins.

Kircher puts the Source of the River *Ganges* in the Mount *Thebeth*, where he says is a large Sea, whence arise the four Capital Rivers of *India*, *viz.* the *Indus*, *Ganges*, *Ravi*, and *Athec*. The *Indian* Pagans deduce its Origin from *Dewendre*, or the Heavens, from whence it descends into the *Dewendre Locon*, or sublunary World; and thence into the Earth, as may be seen in the beforesaid *Abraham Rogerius*. They farther believe, that if they cast the Bones of their deceas'd Friends into the *Ganges*, their Souls will enjoy the Bliss of *Dewendre* for as many thousand Years as the Bones remain single Years in that River; it being their Opinion, that tho this Water has not the Power to introduce them to future Bliss, yet it is a Guide to Heaven thro the seven sublunary Worlds, which they believe every one must pass thro before he can enter the Heavens. They have each its proper Name, but are comprehended under one general Name, viz. *Dewendre Locon*; and among them that of *Bramma Locon*, or the Place where *Bramma* governs, is next to Heaven; and none are suffer'd to enter there, except such as are pass'd from Heaven to the Earth, and thence again thro the before-mention'd sublunary Worlds. It is beyond all doubt that many both among the *Jews* and *Gentiles* have assign'd certain Places for the Souls to dwell in, besides Heaven and Hell; in which they are imitated by the Purgatory-mongers, and such as believe a separate Place for the Antient Fathers and Innocent Children.

Before the River *Ganges* puts a stop to our Voyage, and the Description of the Places mention'd in this Treatise, we must add something concerning the *Malabar* Language.

A

Baldaus.

A short Introduction to the Malabar Language.

THE *Malabars* write upon the Leaves of the wild Palm-Trees with Iron Pencils; their Letters are very antient, and distinguish'd into (1.) *Short or running* Letters, (2.) *Long ones*, (3.) *Vowels*, (4.) *Consonants*, (5.) *Dipthongs*, (6.) Letters us'd only in the beginning of a Word, (7.) Such as are us'd only in the Middle, and (8.) Such as are us'd only in the End, as will more clearly appear out of the annexed Cuts. And seeing that the *Malabar* Letters have hitherto not appeared in publick Print, either in *Holland* or *Germany*, it will not be amiss to alledg the Reasons thereof, and to shew that this Language is no less worth our care now-a-days, than the *Hebrew*, *Chaldean*, *Arabian*, *Persian*, *Samaritan* and other Languages.

The main reason why the *Malabar* Language has remained so long unknown to us, is, because that Country was not conquered by the *Dutch* Company till in the Years 1661, 1662, 1663. from the *Portugueses*; and it is not their Custom to send any Ministers into those Places, where they are not Sovereign Masters. 'Tis true, I assisted at the Sieges of *Coulang*, *Cranganor*, *Cochin*, &c. and 1658. at the Sieges of *Tutecoryn*, *Manaar*, *Jafnapatnam* and *Negapatan*; but was immediately after order'd to *Pscephina* in the Kingdom of *Jafnapatnam*, where I had the oversight over 24 Churches. During the space of near four Years that I staid here alone, I was sensible what Obstacle the Ignorance of the Native Language was to my good Intentions: For tho many of the Christians here were well enough versed in the *Dutch* and *Portuguese* Languages, yet some belonging to the more remote Churches, who had been but slenderly instructed in the Principles of the Christian Religion by the *Roman* Missionaries, were strangely at a loss till I got a good Interpreter, who being well skill'd both in his Mother Tongue the *Malabar*, and the *Portuguese* Languages, did me great Services for eight Years together. His Name was *Francis*, and it was chiefly with his Assistance, that the fundamental Points of our Religion, being comprehended in a small Treatise, were translated out of the *Portuguese* into the *Malabar* Language, which has been since printed, 1671. at *Roterdam*, by *John Borstius*. The multiplicity of Business in so weighty a concern as the Salvation of Souls, having been no small hindrance in encompassing so difficult a Language as the *Malabar*; I was forced to be contented with what part thereof I could attain, and those few Intervals of time I had left, whereof I have given some Specimen in the following Pages and Cuts. I can't upon this Occasion pass by in Silence the Considerations which might induce us to propagate the *Malabar* Language with more care, than has been done hitherto; it being certain, that if our Religious Worship could be firmly established in those Parts (whereof the Knowledg of the Language is one of the chief means) it would be very instrumental to reconcile not only many of the Inhabitants, but also even of the *Indian* Princes themselves to our Interest; a piece of Policy well understood by *Emanuel* King of *Portugal*, when he introduced the *Roman* Catholick Religion by the help of the *Jesuits* in the *Indies*.

I rest your Servant and Friend in Jesus Christ,

Geervliet, 21 *Jul.* 1671.

Philip Baldaus.

Some

Some Rules for the attaining the knowledg of the Malabar *Language.*

THE first Declension among the *Malabars* comprehends the Nouns only of the *Masculine Gender*, which terminate in the Singular Number in *n*, and in the Plural in *r*. They have their Singular and Plural Numbers like us, and name their Cases as follows.

The Nominative	*Pradamei,*
Genitive	*Dutiei,*
Dative	*Tritei,*
Accusative	*Chadurti,*
Vocative	*Panchami,*
Ablative	*Xasti.*

An Example of the first Declension.

Sing.	Nom.	*Vanan* Fullo,	the Fuller (of Cloth)
	Gen.	*Vananureja*	the Fuller,
	Dat.	*Vananucu*	to the Fuller,
	Accus.	*Vananer*	the Fuller,
	Vocat.	*Vanano*	O you Fuller,
	Ablat.	*Vananiratil*	of the Fuller.

It is to be observ'd that they have four sorts of Ablative Cases.

(1.) The *Localis*, as the last mention'd.
(2.) *Causalis*, *Vananale*, because of the Fuller.
(3.) *Socialis*, *Vananore*, with the Fuller.
(4.) *Comparationis*, *Vananil*, in comparison with the Fuller.

Plur.	Nom.	*Vanar* Fullones,	the Fullers,
	Gen.	*Vananareja*,	the Fullers,
	Dat.	*Vanarcul*, *Vanaruccu*,	to the F.
	Accu.	*Vanarei*,	the Fullers,
	Voc.	*Vanare*,	O you Fullers,
	Abl.	(1.) *Vanar iratil*, *vanar iratile*,	of the Fullers,
		(2.) *Vanaral*, *vanarale*,	because of the Fullers,
		(3.) *Vanarore*, *vanarorum*,	with the Fullers,
		(4.) *Vanaril*, *Vanarilum*,	in comparison of the Fullers.

An Example of Conjugation in the Affirmative.

The Present Singular Tense.

I *nan*	*Vichuvadigirren*,	I believe,
you *ni*	*Vichuvadiguirray*,	you believe,
he } *avan*	*Vichuvadiguirran*,	he believes,
she } *avan*	*Vichuvadiguirral*,	she believes,
it } *avan*	*Vichuvadiguirradu*, or *Vichuvadiguidu*.	it believes.

The Plural.

We *nangal* *Vichuvadiguirron*, we believe,
you *ningal* *Vichuvadivirgal*, you believe,
they *adugal* { M.F. *Vichuvadicrargal*, you (Men or Women) believe, N. *Vichuvadicradu*, or *Vichuvadiguidu*, the things believe.

In the Negative.

The Present Singular Tense.

I *nan*, &c. as before. *Vichuvadichren illei*, I don't believe it,
Vichuvadicrei illei, you don't believe it,
Vichuvadiezan illei, he does not believe it,
Vichuvadiezal illei, they don't believe it,
Vichuvadicrad' illei, it don't believe it.

The Plural.

We *nangal*, &c. *Vichuvadicrem illei*, we don't believe it,
Vichuvadicrirgal illei, you don't believe it,
Vichuvadicrargal illei, they (*Masc.& Fem.*) don't believe it.
Vichuvadicrad' illei, they (*Neut.*) *Vichuvadiguid illei*, don't believe it.

The Present Tense of Honour, *i.e.* when you speak to Persons of Quality, in the Affirmative.

Vichu-

A Short Orthography of the MALABAR LANGUAGE.

The Malabars Commonly write upon the Leaves of Palm trees with Iron Pencels, Their Letters are distinguished thus (1) some are accounted short (2) others long (3) some are Vowells which they call Letters of life, because they give life to the Consonants. (4) some Consonants which they call Bodily letters, because the vowels are their sound and life. (5) others they call Mixed letters, the same with our Dipthongs, composed of two Vowells, (6) some are called Initiall letters, used in the beginning of a word (7) some only in the middle, (8) and some in the end of a word.

The following are the Vowels

அ	ana	a short a	a
ஆ	avana	a long à	à
இ	ina	a short i	i
ஈ	yana	a long í	í
உ	una	a short u	u
ஊ	urana	a long ú	ú
எ	ena	a short e	e
ஏ	eana	a long é	é
ஐ	ayana	ay diphthong	ay
ஒ	ona	a short o	o
ஓ	órana	a long ó	ó
ஔ	aurana	au diphtong	au
ஃ	aquana	ac	ac
ை	ei	ei, l, ei diphthong	ei

These are Initial Letters called by them Taleyelutu.

These are Consonants.

க	cana	c, l, k	ம	mana	m
ங	nagana	ng	ய	yana	y
ச	chána	ch	ர	rana	r r
ஞ	nhana	nh	ல	lana	l
ட	ïana	ï	வ	vána	u
ண	hnana	hn	ழ	lana	l
த	tana	t	ள	lana	l
ந	nana	n	ற	rana	r
ப	pana	p, l, b	ன	nana	n

Consonants united with the Vowels, make a Syllable short.

க	cana	ca, l, ka short	ca, l, ka
கா	cavana	ca, l, ka, lang	ca, l, ka
கி	quina	qui short	qui
கீ	quiyana	qui lang	quí
கு	cuna	cu short	cu
கூ	curana	cu lang	cú
கெ	quena	ke short	que
கே	queana	ke, lang	que, l, ke
கை	caeyana	caey dipthong	caey
கொ	cona	co short	co
கோ	corana	có, lang	có
கௌ	caurana	cau, dipthong	cau
க்	iquana	q	
ங	ngnana	ngna short	ngna
ஙா	ngnarana	ngná lang	ngná
ஙி	ngina	ngni short	ngni
ஙீ	ngniana	ngní lang	ngní
ஙு	ngnuna	ngnu short	ngnu
ஙூ	ngnurana	ngnu lang	ngnu
ஙெ	ngnena	ngne short	ngne
ஙே	ngnéana	ngné lang	ngné
ஙை	ngnayana	ngnay dipthong	ngnay
ஙொ	ngnona	ngno short	ngno
ஙோ	ngnorana	ngnó lang	ngnó
ஙௌ	ngnaurana	ngnau dipthong	ngnau
ங்	ingnana	ngn	

ச	chana	cha short	cha
சா	charana	chá lang	chá
சி	china	chi short	chi
சீ	chiyana	chí long	chí
சு	chuna	chu short	chu
சூ	churana	chú long	chú
செ	chena	che short	che
சே	cheana	ché long	ché
சை	chaeyana	chaey diphtong	chaey
சொ	chona	cho short	cho
சோ	chórana	chó long	chó
சௌ	chaurana	chau diphtong	chau
ச்	ichana	ch.	
ஞ	nhana	nha short	nha
ஞா	nharana	nhá lang	nhá
ஞி	nhina	nhi short	nhi
ஞீ	nhiyana	nhí lang	nhí
ஞு	nhuna	nhu short	nhu
ஞூ	nhurana	nhú lang	nhú
ஞெ	nhena	nhe short	nhe
ஞே	nhéana	nhé lang	nhé
ஞை	nhaeyana	nhaey dipthong	nhaey
ஞொ	nhona	nho short	nho
ஞோ	nhorana	nhó lang	nhó
ஞௌ	nhaurana	nhau diptong	nhau
ஞ்	inhana	nh.	
ட	ïana	ïa short	ïa
டா	ïarana	ïá lang	ïá
டி	ïina	ïi short	ïi
டீ	ïiyana	ïí lang	ïí
டு	ïuna	ïu short	ïu
டூ	ïurana	ïú lang	ïú
டெ	ïena	ïe short	ïe
டே	ïéana	ïé long	ïé

டை	ïayana	ïay diphtong	ïay
டொ	ïona	ïo short	ïo
டோ	ïorana	ïó lang	ïó
டௌ	ïaurana	ïau diphtong	ïau
ட்	ïïana	ïï	
ண	hnana	hna short	hna
ணா	hnarana	hná lang	hná
ணி	hnina	hni short	hni
ணீ	hniana	hní lang	hní
ணு	hnuna	hnu short	hnu
ணூ	hnurana	hnú lang	hnú
ணெ	hnena	hne short	hne
ணே	hnéana	hné lang	hné
ணை	hnaeyana	hnaey diptongh	hnaey
ணொ	hnona	hno short	hno
ணோ	hnorana	hnó lang	hnó
ணௌ	hnaurana	hnau dipthong	hnau
ண்	hnana	hn	
த	tana	ta short	ta
தா	tarana	tá lang	tá
தி	tina	ti short	ti
தீ	tiyana	tí lang	tí
து	tuna	tu short	tu
தூ	turana	tú lang	tú
தெ	tena	te short	te
தே	téana	té lang	té
தை	taeyana	taey diphtongh	taey
தொ	tona	to short	to
தோ	torana	tó lang	tó
தௌ	taurana	tau diphtoagh	tau
த்	itana	t.	

ந	nana	na short	na
நா	nárana	ná long	ná
நி	nina	ni short	ni
நீ	niyana	ní long	ní
நு	nuna	nu short	nu
நூ	núvana	nú long	nú
நெ	nena	ne short	ne
நே	néana	né long	né
நை	næyana	næy dipht:	næy
நொ	nona	no short	no
நோ	nórana	nó long	nó
நௌ	nauvana	nau dipht:	nau
ந்	inana	n.	

ப	pana	pa short	pa
பா	párana	pá long	pá
பி	pina	pi short	pi
பீ	píyana	pí long	pí
பு	puna	pu short	pu
பூ	púvana	pú long	pú
பெ	pena	pe short	pe
பே	péana	pé long	pé
பை	pæyana	pæy dipht:	pæy
பொ	pona	po short	po
போ	pórana	pó long	pó
பௌ	pauvana	pau dipht:	pau
ப்	ipana	p.	

ய	yana	ya short	ya
யா	yárana	yá long	yá
யி	yina	yi short	yi
யீ	yíana	yí long	yí
யு	yuna	yu short	yu
யூ	yúvana	yú long	yú
யெ	yena	ye short	ye
யே	yéana	yé long	yé
யை	yæyana	yæy dipht:	yæy
யொ	yona	yo short	yo
யோ	yórana	yó long	yó
யௌ	yauvana	yau dipht:	yau
ய்	yana	y.	

ர	rana	ra short	ra
ரா	rárana	rá long	rá
ரி	rina	ri short	ri
ரீ	ríyana	rí long	rí
ரு	runa	ru short	ru
ரூ	rúvana	rú long	rú
ரெ	rena	re short	re
ரே	réana	ré long	ré
ரை	ræyana	ræy dipht:	ræy
ரொ	rona	ro short	ro
ரோ	rórana	ró long	ró
ரௌ	rauvana	rau dipht:	rau
ர்	irana	r.	

ல	lana	la short	la
லா	lárana	lá long	lá
லி	lina	li short	li
லீ	líyana	lí long	lí
லு	luna	lu short	lu
லூ	lúvana	lú long	lú
லெ	lena	le short	le
லே	léana	lé long	lé
லை	læyana	læy dipht:	læy
லொ	lona	lo short	lo
லோ	lórana	ló long	ló
லௌ	lauvana	lau dipht:	lau
ல்	ilana	l.	

வ	vana	va short	va
வா	várana	vá long	vá
வி	vina	vi short	vi
வீ	víyana	ví long	ví
வு	vuna	vu short	vu
வூ	vúvana	vú long	vú
வெ	vena	ve short	ve
வே	véana	vé long	vé
வை	væyana	væy dipht:	væy
வொ	vona	vo short	vo
வோ	vórana	vó long	vó
வௌ	vauvana	vau dipht:	vau
வ்	ivana	v.	

ழ	lana	la short	la
ழா	lárana	lá long	lá
ழி	lina	li short	li
ழீ	líyana	lí long	lí
ழு	luna	lu short	lu
ழூ	lúvana	lú long	lú
ழெ	lena	le short	le
ழே	léana	lé long	lé
ழை	læyana	læy dipht:	læy
ழொ	lona	lo short	lo
ழோ	lórana	ló long	ló
ழௌ	lauvana	lau dipht:	lau
ழ்	ilana	l.	

ள	lana	la short	la
ளா	lárana	lá long	lá
ளி	lina	li short	li
ளீ	líyana	lí long	lí
ளு	luna	lu short	lu
ளூ	lúvana	lú long	lú
ளெ	lena	le short	le
ளே	léana	lé long	lé
ளை	læyana	læy dipht:	læy
ளொ	lona	lo short	lo
ளோ	lórana	lo long	lo
ளௌ	lauvana	lau dipht:	lau
ள்	ilana	l.	

ற	rrana	rra short	rra
றா	rrárana	rrá long	rrá
றி	rrina	rri short	rri
றீ	rríyana	rrí long	rrí
று	rruna	rru short	rru
றூ	rrúvana	rru long	rrú
றெ	rrena	rre short	rre
றே	rréana	rré long	rré
றை	rræyana	rræy dipht:	rræy
றொ	rrona	rro short	rro
றோ	rróvana	rró long	rró
றௌ	rrouvana	rrou dipht:	rrou
ற்	irrana	rr.	

ண	nana	na short	na
ணா	nárana	ná long	ná
ணி	nina	ni short	ni
ணீ	niyana	ní long	ní
ணு	nuna	nu short	nu
ணூ	núvana	nú long	nú
ணெ	nena	ne short	ne
ணே	néana	né long	né
ணை	næyana	næy dipht:	næy
ணொ	nona	no short	no
ணோ	nórana	nó long	nó
ணௌ	naurana	nau dipht:	nau
ண்	inana	n.	

ம	mana	ma short	ma
மா	márana	má long	má
மி	mina	mi short	mi
மீ	míyana	mí long	mí
மு	muna	mu short	mu
மூ	múrana	mú long	mú
மெ	mena	me short	me
மே	méana	mé long	mé
மை	mæyana	mæy dipht:	mæy
மொ	mona	mo short	mo
மோ	mórana	mó long	mó
மௌ	maurana	mau dipht:	mau
ம்	umana	m.	

Our Father in ye Malabar language & Characters

வாணநுகளிலஒருக
Pater noster
கிரணுகளபிதாவெ
qui es in cælis
உணணுடையநாமம
Sanctificetur nomen
எலலாரகுளுகததம
tuum Veniat
ாகஉணணுடையஒ
tuum regnum tua
ாாசசியம்வா.உணம
Fiat in terra
ணதிணபடவாணவ
voluntas ut
ாகளவாணததரசெ
in cælis
யயுமாபபொலெபூ
hodie Panem
மியிவுமளலலாரு
da nostrum
ளுசெயய.வுணரண
nobis quotidianum
வளளஎநுகளப
et debita nostra
பமஎநுகளுககுஒ
nobis remitte
ணவதாஎநுகளபி
ut et nos
ழைகடணகாரருக
remittimus nostris
குநாநுகளபொாவ
debitoribus et non
ககுமாபபொாலெந
inducas nos
ப்மெநுகளபாாவக
in tentationem
கடணகள்படொா
verum tu
வளநுகள்ததொா
libera nos
விதநுககுளதுவாக
a malo
ஒடடாகெளநுகளு
nam est
ககுபபொாலலாநுத
tibi
வாாாமலவிலகு
et tuum
.வதெணணுமழண
regnum
பயஒாாசசழமவ
et quoque
லலழமமொாககிபிழமபெ
potentia et
யயபொாதுழண
gloria in sæcula
பாவதாச.ஆமெண
sæculorum Amen.

the Creed in the Malabar

வாணழமபுமியும
in Deum
பைததசவவதது
Patrem omnipotentem
ககுமவலலபிதாவ
cæli et terræ
ாணகமபிராாணயெ
creatorem Credo ego
விசகவதிககிரெணவு
et in Jesum
வளைடயமகணெ
Christum Filium
ருவணநமழணடைய
ejus unigenitum
நாயணஒசெசுககிரி
Dominum nostrum
சததைமெயவிசசுவி
qui est
ததகிரெணஒவணக
conceptus ex
ததமாணஒசிபபிரி
Spiritu Sancto
ததுவிளுலசசணத
natus ex
துககணணிமரிபநள
Maria virgine
வபிரரிலநிணவபிரநத
Passus est
ாணபொாளுசிபொாப
sub Pontio
பிலாததிணகிளப
Pilato crucifixus
பாடுபடடுககுருசி
est et mortuus
லெவுறையணடுெ
et sepultus est
சரவுபகபபப
ad inferna
பாணபாதாளநுக
descendit die
ளிலஒரநுகிழணரு
tertia resurrexit
நாளசசெரரவாகள
a mortuis ad cælos
ஒடையிலநிணவஉ
ascendit ad dextram
யிததாணவாணநு
sedet Dei
களிலஎரிசசவவதது
Patris omnipotentis
ககுமவலலபிகாவா
unde ille
கியதமபிராணவலப
judicatum veniet
பாகததலஒருககிரு
et vivos et
ணவுபிடததலநிணவ
mortuos in
ஒருககிரவாகளுக
Spiritum Sanctum
குளுசெததவாகளு
Credo ego
ககுமநடுததரகவரு
Sanctam et
வாணசுததமாணஒ
Catholicam
சிபபிரிததுணைவெ
ego et Credo
யவிசசுவதிகரெணக
Ecclesiam et
ததொலிககவாகிய
Sanctorum quique
சுததமாணஒகரொண
ego Credo
சயுளுசுததமாணவ
communionem
ாகளகூடடமழமஉ
peccatorum
ணடெணவவிசசுவதி
et remissionem
கக்ரெணபிறைகளெ
carnis hujus
பாவததவுளுசெத
et quoque
தவாகளஉயிாதத
resurrectionem
வுமளணரெணணைக
et vitam
குமஉளளஆயிரவ
in secula
மஉணடெணவபிக
seculorum
சுவதிககிரெண.ஆமெண
æternam Amen.

Vichuvadicrora, We (our Majesty, Highness, *&c.*) don't believe it.
Vichuvadicrir, You (your Majesty, *&c.*) don't believe it.
Vichuvadicrare, They (their Majestys) don't believe it.

In the Negative.

Vichuvidcron illei, We (our Majesty) don't believe it.
Vichuvadicrir illei, We ——— don't believe it.
Vichuvadicrar illei, They ——— don't believe it.

Whence it is evident that the *Malabar* Language is very difficult to be learn'd; especially by reason of the vast number of words whereof it consists, one and the same thing being frequently express'd by divers Words or Names. Thus not only every Day in the Week, but also throughout the Year, has its peculiar Name. It is further manifest from hence, that the *Indians* are not so unpolish'd as some *Europeans* represent them, and that they treat one another (especially Persons of Quality) with singular Civility and Respect.

The Imperfect Tense.

Vichuvadicrane apo Vichuvadieren, I believed.
Vichuvadicreye apo Vichuvadierom, we did believe it.

The Perfect Tense.

Vichuvaditen, I have believed.
Vichuvaditom, we have believed.

The Preterperfect Tense.

A ductu mune vichuvaditay, I had believed.
A ducu mune vichuvaditon, we had believed.

The Future Tense.

Vichuvadipen, I will believe.
Vichuvadipon, we will believe.

Our Father in the *Malabar* Language.

Baldæus.

Vanan galil yrucrà engal pidàve,
In Heaven who art our Father,
unureya namam ellatcum chutamga; unu-
thy Name be sanctified; thy
reya irakjam vara; un manadin paryel
Kingdom come; thy Will be done
à navargal vanatil; cheyuma pelepumy-
in Earth as in Heaven; give our Bread
lum elarum cheya; andandulla engàl piley-
to us daily; pardon us our
caran, carracucu nàngal pava caran-
Trespasses, as our Trespassers for-
galey perru; engaley tolxatricù è duvagù,
give we; lead not into Temptation us,
ottàde engaluck polàngn varàmal. Vilagù.
but of the Evil deliver thou us. So it be.

The Creed.

Vananum pumium pareyta
Of the Heavens and the Earth Crea-
charvatucum vala pidavagmia, tamby-
tor, Omnipotent Father,
raneye vichuvadicren: Avanureyà maguan
God, I believe. And in Son
oruven namureyà nayen Xeju Christeye
his only Jesus Christ
vichuvadicren. Tven chetamana espirity
I believe. Who was conceiv'd from
màl, chanitù kanni
the Holy Ghost, born from the Virgin
Marial: vaitil nindù pirranda Ponxio
Mary, &c.
Pilatin kil parulattu cruxile arraiandù chetù aracapata padalangalil errí charruvatucum valla pidaguia tambiram balagapatil irucran avaratil nindu irucra vagalacum chetavargalucum narutytbà varnvan. Chutamana espiritù veye vichuvadicren. Chutamana vargal custanum undanu vichuvadicren. Pileygal porrutalu chetavàrgàl buirtalum endendeycum ulla aytum vindanum vichuvadicren.

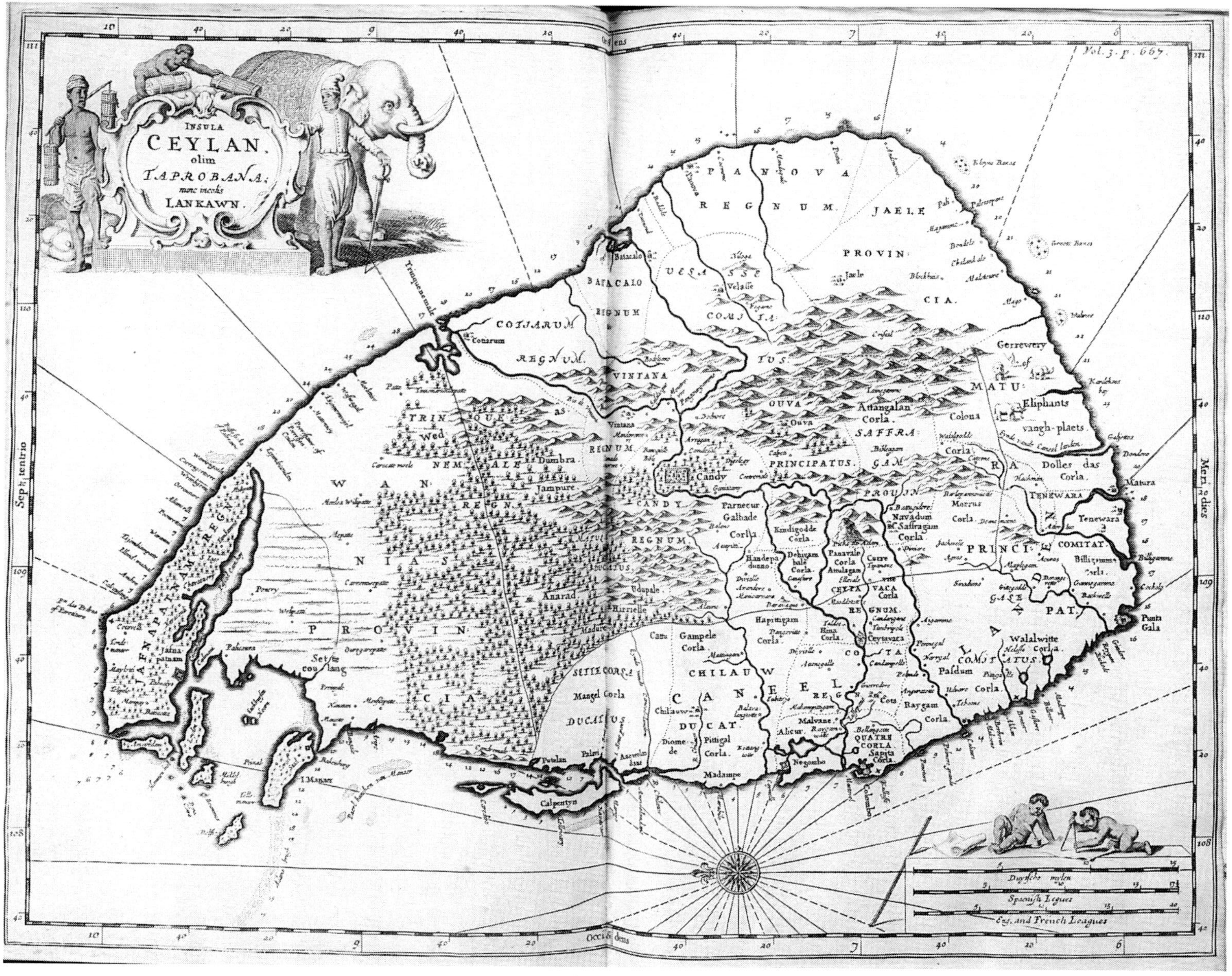
Vol. 3. p. 667.
INSULA
CEYLAN,
olim
TAPROBANA;
nunc incolis
LANKAWN.
Septentrio
Meridies
Occidens
Trinquenemale
Cotiarum
COTIARUM REGNUM
Batacalo
BATACALO REGNUM
PANOVA REGNUM
JAELE PROVINCIA
VELASSE COMITATUS
VINTANA
Candy
CANDY REGNUM
OUVA
Ouva
Attangalan Corla
SAFFRAGAM PRINCIPATUS
Gerrewery
MATURA
Eliphants vangh-plaets
Colona
Dolles das Corla
Matura
Tenewara
TENEWARA
Billigamme
Billigamme Corla
Punta Gala
GALE
Walalwitte Corla
Pasdum Corla
Raygam Corla
Colombo
Negombo
QUATRE CORLA
Madampe
Chilauw
CANEEL
Pittigal Corla
SETTE CORLA
Mangel Corla
Calpentyn
Putalan
Anaradgburro
Udupale
Dumbra
Jampure
WANNIAS PROVINCIA
Setecoulang
Jafnapatnam
I. Manaer
Duytsche mylen
Spanish Leagues
Eng. and French Leagues

A DESCRIPTION Of the Great and most Famous Isle of CEYLON.

CHAP. I.

The Situation, Extent and Discovery of Ceylon.

Ceylon. THE Isle of *Ceylon* (the *Taprobana* of the Antients according to *John de Barros*) has got its Name among the *Portugueses*, as well as the other *Europeans*, from its Capital City call'd *Ceylon*, known among the Natives by the Name of *Laukauwn*.

This Isle extends from the *6th* to the *10th* degree of Northern Latitude. Formerly its Circumference was reckon'd to be about 400 Leagues, tho since that time the Sea has wash'd away about 40 Leagues on the North-side of it. In antient times it was questionless (as we shall see anon in the Description of *Manaar*) annexed to the Continent. The Figure of this Isle represents (according to *Maffæus*) an Egg, but in my opinion resembles rather a *Westphalia* Ham, whence without doubt the *Dutch* Fort near *Jafnapatnam* has got the Name of *Hams-beel*.

Its Extent. The beforementioned *Maffæus* affirms, that its Circumference is at this time not above 240 Leagues, its Length 78, and the Breadth 44. But the *Dutch*, since they have been Masters of it, after the taking of *Columbo* 1656. and of *Manaar* and *Jafnapatnam* 1658. have more exactly computed its Compass to be 360 Leagues. It has many excellent Harbours, Cities and Fortresses, and is divided into several Provinces, as may be seen by the Title of the King of that Island, who *Title of the King of Ceylon.* stiles himself, *Raja Singa*, Emperor of *Ceylon*, King of *Candea*, *Cota*, *Ceytavaca*, *Dambadan*, *Amorayapore*, *Jafnapatnam*; Prince of *Ouva*, *Mature*, *Dinavaca*, and the four *Corles*; Great Duke of the seven *Corles*, *Matale*, Earl of *Cotiar*, *Trinquenemale*, *Batecalo*, *Velase*, *Vintana*, *Drembra*, *Panciapato*, *Veta*, *Putelaon*, *Vallure*, *Gale*, *Belligaon*; Marquess of *Duranura*, *Ratienura*, *Tripane*, *Acciapato*; Lord of the Sea-ports of *Alican*, *Columbo*, *Negombo*, *Chilau*, *Madampe*, *Calpentyn*, *Aripiture*, *Manaar*, and of the Fishery of precious Stones and Pearls; Lord of the Golden Sun. All which Places, Cities, and Fortresses we shall have occasion to treat of hereafter. *The Titles of Duke and Earl have been introduced by the Portugueses.*

The Isle of *Ceylon* abounds also in excellent Rivers, such as *Chilau*, *Matual*, *Alican*, *Mature*, *Batecalo*, *Trinquenemale*, and others. It produces various sorts of precious Stones, and is extremely fertile, especially in Cinnamon: Here are also found the best Elephants of the whole *Indies*.

Its Discovery. This Isle was first discover'd by the *Chineses* in the following manner: Certain *Chineses* having suffer'd Shipwrack, were forc'd ashore on that Island, where they professed their King to be the *Son of the Sun*. The Inhabitants of *Ceylon* adoring at that time the *Sun*, as the *Malabars* do to this day their *Eswara*, i. e. the *Sun*, they were so well pleased with their new Guests, that they elected the Captain of the *Chinese Jonke*, or Vessel, their King; whence the present Kings of *Ceylon* trace their Origin, and have taken upon them the Title of Lord of the *Golden Sun*, this first *Chinese* King having *By the Chineses.*

Baldæus. *Pedegree of the Kings of Ceylon.*

having stil'd himself, *The much beloved Son of the always moving Sun.* From this King *Lankauw Pati Mahadascyn* deduced his Origin, who took upon him the Name of *Well-beloved Lord of the whole Isle.* His Son was *Lankauw Singe Madahascyn*, i. e. *The well-beloved Lion of the Isle*, and after him his Son, *Marasinge Mahadascyn*, i. e. *The well-beloved Conqueror of the Lion.* This King left behind him two Sons, the first named *Lankauw Patti Mahastane*, or, *The Eye-apple of the Country*; the second *Radgora Adascyn*, or, *The well-beloved King.* These two quarrelling about the Succession, at last divided Kingdoms, that of *Candy* falling to the share of *Radgora Adascyn*, and all the rest to the eldest. The Posterity of these two Kings rul'd for a considerable time after, the eldest Son always succeeding before the others. Among these *Lankauw Patti Mahastane* dying in the 70*th* year of his Age, left a Son named *Marandonna Madgora*, i. e. *The Conqueror of the Eye-apple*, who came no sooner to the Crown, but he engag'd in a heavy War against his Uncle by the Father's side, which was ended at last by a Marriage betwixt *Marandonna Mahastane*, the Son of *Madgora*, and *Malabande Wandige.* They left a numerous Issue of Sons and Daughters, and among the rest one named *Fimala Darma Soria Adascyn*, i. e. *The Conqueror of the whole Kingdom*, (born after his Father's Death) who no sooner came to Age of maturity, but he attack'd all the Neighbouring Princes that refused to submit to his Jurisdiction; and having by degrees subdu'd them all, and establish'd himself in the Throne, by the Death of all such as had opposed him, he married at last *Rokech Wandige*, i. e. The *Beautiful Queen*, his Sister's Daughter, by whom he had a numerous Issue of Sons and Daughters, from whom the present Kings are descended.

CHAP. II.

The first Arrival of the Portugueses *in the Isle of* Ceylon, *under the Command of* Laurence d' Almeyda.

Arrival of the Portugueses in Ceylon.

WHilst these Intestine Wars were carrying on in *Ceylon*, *Laurence d' Almeyda* by the Command of his Father was imploy'd in cruising upon the *Mahometans*, who were then transporting their Effects from *Malacca* and *Sumatra* over the *Maldive* Islands into *Arabia.* The *Portugueses* being inform'd of the Condition of the Island, and knowing that it was best fishing in troubled Waters, did turn their Arms against it, and after many bloody Engagements, made themselves Masters of all the Places which produce the best Cinnamon, which they used to transport in vast quantities into *Europe.*

Raja Singa Adascyn an Enemy of the Portugueses.

At that time *Raja Singa Adascyn* reign'd in *Ceylon.* The general opinion is, that he was a King's Son, and Nephew to the King of *Cora*, tho I have often heard the *Portugueses* and some of the *Hollanders* say that he was no more than a Barber, who being well skill'd in divers Languages, and of a Warlike Inclination, aim'd at the Crown, and at last was so fortunate as to reduce the whole Island (after he had kill'd all the Great Men) to his Obedience. This King being a declar'd Enemy of the *Portugueses*, he besieg'd *Columbo* with a powerful Army, and reduc'd them in a short time to such extremity for want of Provisions, that the Garison knowing the Governour to be averse to come to a Capitulation, they at first broke out into injurious words, and at last resolv'd (unless they receiv'd Relief from *Goa* in a week's time) to kill their Officers, and to surrender at Discetion. But the Governour being advertis'd of their Design by one of his Pages, did all that lay in his power to keep the Soldiers in Obedience with fair Promises, till the arrival of the so long wish'd for Succours from *Goa*, which having defeated the *Indian* Fleet, they forced them to raise the Siege.

Columbo reliev'd.

This *Raja Singa Adascyn* having made himself Master of the whole Kingdom, except *Gale* and *Columbo*, forced the Emperor *Mahadascyn* to fly the Country, who in his pursuit scattered his Treasure of Gold and Jewels upon the Road, thereby to stop the pursuit of his Enemies. *Raja Singa* being thus become Master of the Empire, constituted *Vinne Lamantia* one of the late Emperor's Favourites, Governor over the Highland Countries, whose Son, named *Don Jon*, afterwards obtain'd the Sovereignty. This *Vinne Lamantia* finding himself in a condition to cope with his new pretended Master, took up Arms against him, and having

Vinne Lamantia rebels against Raja Singa.

having brought over the greatest part of the Country (grown weary of the Tyrant) to his side, was proclaimed Emperor, under the Title of *Vinne Ladarma Soria*, i. e. *The Deliverer of the Empire.*

This War being carried on with various Success for a considerable time, the *Portugueses* got time to breath, and induced *Raja Singa* to come to a Composition with *Vinne Ladarma Soria*, offering him the whole Treasure he had taken of *Mahadascyn* the late Emperor, provided he would resign the whole Sovereignty into his Hands.

Comes to a Composition with Raja Singa.

Whilst they were treating of the Peace, *Vinne Ladarma* had a Son born him (who bearing his Father's Name, succeeded him in the Empire) but he was scarce a Year old, when *Raja Singa*, not thinking himself secure in the late Treaty concluded with *Vinne Ladarma*, he at last found means to cajole him to his Court (notwithstanding those of *Candy* strongly opposed it) where he was no sooner arrived, but being seized upon with all his Attendance, *Raja Singa* order'd him to be buried in the Ground up to his Breast, and so to be kill'd by the means of certain Wooden Balls, which were thrown at his Head, till his Brains were dash'd out, the chiefest of his Attendants being likewise put to death by the Tyrant's Orders.

Baldæus.

Is betray'd to Court.

And murder'd.

An Usurper Stoned to Death

Candy *conquer'd by* Raja.

This done, he bent all his Force against *Candy*, and having made himself Master of the whole Country, sold many of the Inhabitants for Slaves, and disarm'd the rest, making the Empress his Prisoner. The *Zingaleses* being much oppress'd by the Tyrant, who forc'd them to carry Earth and other Materials upon their Heads for the building of Fortifications all the way betwixt *Candy* and *Settavaca*, sought for Relief by the *Portugueses*, who glad of so favourable an opportunity of strengthning their Interest in that Island, sent *Andrew Furtado* a great Warrior with a considerable Force to *Jafnapatnam*, which he surprized, and having got the King of that Place in his power, requir'd his Consent and Assistance to pass through his Country for the Relief of *Candy*. The Inhabitants of that Kingdom being not as yet enter'd into any settled Treaty with the *Portugueses*, were not a

The Portugueses *side with the* Zingaleses.

Baldæus.

a little surpriz'd at the sudden arrival of the *Parangys* (so they call Foreigners) fearing (which prov'd true afterwards) that instead of their pretended Delivery they should only change their Slavery; which the cunning *Portuguese* Generals having well foreseen, had brought *Don John* and *Don Philip*, the last Uncle of *Donna Catharina*, and both educated in the *Romish* Religion, to *Candy*, the last of which he constituted King, and *Don John* Generalissimo; leaving *Donna Catharina* the Daughter of the late Emperor *Mahadascyn*, and the sole Heiress of the Empire, at *Manaar*. He also took care to give notice of his coming to those of *Candy*, with full Assurances that he was come for no other end than to deliver them from the Usurper's Yoke, which had so good an effect upon them, that they enter'd with him into an Offensive and Defensive Alliance against *Raja Singa Adascyn*.

Enter into an Alliance with them.

The Usurper got soon scent of this Treaty, which made him advance with a Potent Army towards *Jafnapatnam*, to prevent the *Portugueses* from marching to *Candy*; but these were too nimble for him, and coming to *Candy* before he was arriv'd in that Kingdom, immediately crown'd *Don Philip* King, and declar'd *Don John* Generalissimo, under condition that both should marry *Portuguese* Ladies, and the Inhabitants take an Oath of Allegiance to the King of *Portugal*.

Make Don Philip *King.*

Don John in the mean time seeing *Don Philip* prefer'd before him by the *Portugueses*, conceiv'd a mortal hatred against them, but thought fit to dissemble it, till he should meet with a favourable opportunity of shewing his Resentment. With this intention he took care to have *Candy* fortified so, as not to fear any thing from *Raja Singa*, and the Royal Palace (lately demolish'd by that Usurper) to be rebuilt with more Splendor than before, for the Reception of the new King, tho at the same time he consulted with a certain famous Sorcerer how to remove the said King by Poison, which he effected afterwards.

Don John *exasperated at the* Portugueses.

CHAP. III.

Don Philip *poison'd.* Don John *succeeds him. He routs* Raja Singa, *who dies soon after. His Secretary* Janiere *takes up Arms against* Don John.

THE *Portugueses* fearing not without reason the approach of *Raja Singa*, had fortified *Gonnoor*, and sent *John de Melo* in Company of certain Religious Men to *Manaar*, to bring them fresh supplies of Men, Arms, and Ammunition to *Candy*, the Inhabitants whereof were all disarm'd by the Usurper, having first introduc'd *Don Philip* in great Pomp, and plac'd him in the Royal Palace with the general Applause of the Inhabitants.

Don Philip *settled at* Candy.

But he scarce tasted the first Fruits of his Greatness, when *Don John* (taking the opportunity of the absence of the chief of the *Portugueses*) got some Poison administred to him, which not having the desir'd effect, he gave him another Dose, which put an end to his Life; and by promises of great Rewards and other Enticements, brought most of the Inhabitants of *Candy* over to his side, who declar'd him their Emperor, and gave him the Title of *Vinne Ladarma Soria*, after his Father, mention'd before to have been murder'd by the Command of *Raja Singa*.

Is poison'd by Don John.

Who is made Emperor.

The *Portugueses* fore-boding themselves no good from *Don John*, whom they knew to be their Enemy, sent Messengers after Messengers to *John de Melo* at *Manaar*, to represent to him their dangerous State, wherein they found themselves not mistaken: For no sooner was *Don John* seated in the Throne, but he sent a Herald to the *Portugueses* in Garison at *Gannoor*, who upbraiding them with Perjury and perfidious Designs, order'd them in the Emperor's Name to quit their Posts within five or six days, which if they refused, they must expect no Quarter. The *Portugueses* finding themselves unable to resist his Power, and despairing of the desir'd Relief, thought it their safest way to come to a Capitulation with *Dohn John*, who granted them a free Passage with their Swords only, being forc'd not only to leave all their Booty, but also their Bag and Baggage behind them.

And forces the Portugueses *out of* Gannoor.

The very next day *John de Melo* arriv'd with the Succours from *Manaar*, but too late, whilst *Raja Singa* was advancing towards *Candy*, threatning a most severe Revenge to the Inhabitants of that Country. *Don John* finding himself now destitute

tute of the assistance of the *Portugueses*, and understanding that his Enemy had pitched his Tents near *Walane*, was sorely put to it how to cope with so great a Force; but being oblig'd either to fight or quit his Advantage, he resolv'd to engage the Enemy, cost what it would: for which reason having afresh taken the Oath of Allegiance from the Inhabitants, and furnish'd them with Arms (such as they could get in haste) he advanced towards them in order of Battel. *Raja Singa* being not a little surprized at his Boldness, sent him word, that *He had best take warning by his Father* Vinne Ladarma Soria's *Death, and that in case he refused to submit to his Mercy before it was too late, he must expect no other Treatment than to be cut in pieces.* Unto whom *Don John* smiling, sent for answer, *That he would take care to put it out of his Power, and if his Father had been as cautious of him as he was resolved to be, he need not have come to so lamentable an end, to revenge which he was come to this Place*; exhorting him at the same time to implore his Mercy before it was too late. *Raja Singa* was so exasperated at this Message, and the Aversion he found in the Inhabitants of the Country, that he declar'd, *He would punish with Death all that should oppose him*; and so order'd his whole Army to march to *Donlan*, with an Intention to surprize that Place, before *Don John* could come to its Relief. *Don John*, tho he knew himself much inferiour in number, yet resolv'd to follow him close at the Heels; and to put the better Countenance on the matter, march'd in great Pomp, with most splendid Umbrellos born before him, and such other Royal Ensigns, as the Kings in those Countries use in their Wars. *Raja Singa* seeing *Don John* thus bravely advancing towards him, resolv'd either to vanquish or to die gloriously in the Enterprize, could not forbear to break out into these Words, *Verily* Don John *is a courageous Warrior, and I presage that one day or other he will ascend the Throne.* O Raja Singa! *Where is thy noble Boldness, where are all thy great and ambitious Designs, where thy Fortune which no body could resist! I am afraid of a sudden Change; O changeable Fortune, why hast thou turn'd thy Back towards* Raja Singa, *who was once thy Favourite!*

Message of Raja *to* D. John.

His resolute Answer.

Raja's *Surprize.*

Is defeated.

Thus the Signal being given, the Battel begun, wherein *Don John* and his Forces gave way at first, the better to bear the first Assault of the Enemy; but afterwards *Don John* at the Head of his Guards, charg'd them so furiously, that (notwithstanding *Raja Singa* did all that could be expected from a Great Captain) they were forc'd to give way, and at last to seek for their Safety in their Heels: And so he return'd victorious to *Candy*, having lost no more than 700 Men in the whole Engagement; whereas the loss of *Raja Singa* amounted to above 3000, who was so dejected at this Defeat, that he struck voluntarily a Thorn into his Foot, and refusing to have his Wound dress'd, it gangren'd, and put an end to his days at *Settevaca*.

Baldæus.

Dies.

He shew'd not the least remorse upon his death-bed for his Cruelties, except those committed against the Priests of *Daldowanse*, whom he caused to be burnt alive; for being ask'd by the Tyrant, whether the Murder he had committed upon his Uncle, Mother-in-law and Brothers, could not be forgiven, they answered, No; *Well then* (said the Usurper) *I am now at Liberty to do what I please*, and so committed them all to the Fury of the Flames, except the High Priest, called *Tireanco*, i. e. *God's Vicegerent*, by the *Cingaleses*. The Priests of *Paraneydeyo*, being ask'd the same question, forewarn'd by the Disaster of the others, gave for Answer, *That a Person guilty of such a Sin could not enter into Heaven, but if truly repenting, he might by their Intercession be brought to remain betwixt Heaven and Earth, without being sensible of the Torments of Hell.* This Answer was so pleasing to *Raja*, that he dismissed them unmolested, telling them, *That he had ordered the Priests of* Daldowanse *to be burnt, because they would make God delight in Evil; but you who make him a merciful God, I will always look upon as my Friends.* Just before his Death, he sent for the beforementioned *Tireanco* or High Priest, desiring him to forgive the Death of his Brethren, offering him considerable Presents at the same time; he refused the last, but pardon'd the Crime, and so return'd to *Candy*, where he died in the 120*th* Year of his Age.

The Priests of Daldowanse *burnt.*

Raja's *remorse for that Action.*

Don John had no sooner received Intelligence of *Raja*'s Death, but he put himself at the Head of his Army, to take possession of the whole Kingdom. But the Chief Secretary of *Raja Singa* having got all his Master's Treasure into his Hands, and thinking himself in a capacity to cope with *Don John*, got himself proclaimed King, under the Name of *Janiere Wandaar*, and at the same time sollicited for Succours by the *Portugueses*. Neither was it long before *Pedro Lopes de Sousa* arriv'd from *Goa*, at the Head

Janiere *usurps the Crown.*

Baldæus. Seeks for Assistance by the Portugueses.

Head of 12500 *Portugueses*, besides a good number of *Mistices* and *Indians*, which occasion'd no small Consternation in *Don John*'s Army, who had been lately Spectators of the Ravages committed by those of *Gale* and *Columbo* (with the assistance of the new King) in the *Low-Lands*, and therefore had all the reason to fear so strong a Force of the *Portugueses* ready to join with his Enemies. However *Pedro Lopes* finding the *Low-Lands* laid desolate (the best of the Country) and consequently promising himself but small Advantages by his Stay, was for returning to *Goa*, had he not been opposed by the rest of the Officers, who alledged, that the best part of the late King's Treasure remain'd as yet entire at *Candy*; and that in order to make themselves Masters of the whole Isle, they must take this Opportunity of conquering the Petty Princes one after another, which they put in execution accordingly. For having partly by Force, partly by Promises, brought the Kings of the *Low-Lands* over to their Party, it was agreed to assemble a strong Army against *Don John*. The *Quota*'s of the several Princes to be furnish'd for this Expedition was regulated in the following manner.

A great Army raised against Don John.

The King of *Cota* 6800 Men, four War-Elephants, 50 other Elephants, 1800 Oxen for Carriage, and 1000 *Colys* or Pioneers. King *Janiere Wandaar Ragora* 28980 Men, 24 War-Elephants, 200 others, 5000 Oxen for Carriage, 3000 Pioneers. The Kingdom of *Jafnapatnam* 19900 Men, 10 War-Elephants, 40 of the common sort, 3000 Oxen, and 2000 Pioneers. The King of *Cotiar* 7980 Men, 600 Pioneers, 1000 Oxen, 30 War-Elephants, 25 others. The K. of *Palugan*, 5890 Men, 1000 Pioneers, 3 War-Elephants, and 25 others. The King of *Batecalo* 9800 Men, 2000 Pioneers, 2500 Oxen, 4 War-Elephants, and 30 others. The King of *Panua* in conjunction with some other Princes, 59896 Men, 2140 Pioneers, 630 Elephants, and 16000 Oxen. So that the whole Number of these Forces amounted to 151086 Heads, among whom were 139246 fighting Men, and 11740 Pioneers, 75 War-Elephants, 1000 other Elephants, and 29500 Oxen for Carriage. The Quota of the *Portugueses* under *Pedro Lopes* amounted to 1474 *Portugueses*, 1200 *Mistices*, and 1224 *Indians*, 47 War-Elephants, 945 others, and 19900 Oxen.

The first thing they took care of was to secure their Retreat, by erecting 3 Forts, call'd *Manikeroweri*, *Mapati* and *Gannatari*; which done, they directed their March with their joint Forces towards *Candy*.

CHAP. IV.

Don John *draws out his Forces against* Janiere *and the* Portugueses, *attacks them with Success, but is routed at last.* Donna Catherina *declared Empress,* Janiere *murdered.*

DON *John* having received Intelligence of their March, was put to a great Nonplus what course to take in this Exigency of his Affairs, his whole Army consisting of no more than betwixt 30 and 40000 Men: but knowing them to be resolute and entirely devoted to his Interest, he kept as close to the Enemy as possibly he could, and in several Engagements got the better of them, till at last being attack'd with incredible Fury by the *Portugueses*, they put him to the rout, and took the City of *Walane*, with the Loss of 49 Men only on their side, killing above 1500 of the Inhabitants, which struck such a Terror into the rest, that the whole Country submitted without the least Opposition, except *Dolleswagge*, which they were not able to take.

Don John *routed.*

Retreats into the Deserts.

Don John not being able to rally his scattered Forces, retired with his Empress into the Woods and Deserts, where they were forced to feed upon Herbage for some time; and the *Portugueses* being now Masters of the Country, required the *Cingaleses* to own the King of *Portugal* for their Sovereign Lord. These on the other hand desired that *Donna Catherina*, the Daughter of *Mahadascyn* their Legal Emperor, might be brought from *Manaar*, and declar'd their Empress: *Don Pedro Lopes* being well enough pleas'd with this Proposition, yet willing to consult with *Janiere* about the matter, he found him not averse to it, his Intention being to marry her with the consent of the *Portugueses*, who had underhand promised the same as a Reward of his Services done to them.

Ac-

Donna Catharina brought from Manaar.

Accordingly a numerous Train and splendid Equipage was sent to bring the new Empress to *Candy*; but one of the Ships foundring at Sea in a Storm, 150 Soldiers, a great Number of Slaves, and two Chests with Money were lost with her: one *Portuguese* and two Negroes only had the good Fortune to escape of the whole Ships Crew, who heard the Captain of the Ship, whose Name was *Perere*, take his last Farewel in these Words, *O brave* Perere, *Is it thus thy Fate to be swallow'd up by the Sea! but since it is God's Will, Patience; Christ receive my Soul.*

A Portuguese Ship lost.

In the mean while all imaginable Preparations being made for the Reception of *Donna Catherina*, she was preparing for her Departure from *Manaar:* As she was carry'd along in her Litter or Chair, one of the Poles of Cane happen'd to break, which the new Empress looking upon as an ill Omen, she cry'd out aloud, *Stop, stop, don't carry me any further, for this portends some great Misfortune.* Unto which the Governor of *Manaar*, who attended her Person, reply'd, *May it please your Majesty, we ought to consider that we are no Heathens but Christians, and must therefore despise such Superstitions; God will be the Supporter of you and your Cause.* Then the Empress bid them take another Pole, and soon after embark'd with a fair Wind, which carry'd her in 8 days to *Candy*.

Superstition of D. Catherina.

Baldæus.

Leaves Manaar.

Here she was met by *Pedro Lopes* the *Portuguese* General, and several of the *Cingalese* Kings and Princes, attended by a great Number of Nobles, who paid their Reverence (according to the Custom of the Country) by lying their Faces flat upon the Ground, this they call *Sambaja*. The Empress arising out of her Litter, return'd them hearty Thanks, and returning to her Litter was accompanied into the City by *Lopes* and the before-mentioned Princes with incredible Pomp, and under the general Acclamations of the People, who were infinitely pleas'd with the Gold and Silver that was thrown among them, as the Cavalcade marched along, which was so splendid, that the whole Charge thereof amounted to 1900000 Livres, the Remnants of the Treasure of the late deceased Usurper, *Raja Singa Adascyn*. *Donna Cathe-*

Her Reception at Candy.

Baldæus. *rina* after having rested herself from the Fatigues of the Voyage for three days, was crown'd with the usual Solemnities, and put into possession of the Empire.

Is crowned there.

Don John disguised as a Beggar.

About that time *Don John* came in the disguise of a Beggar into *Candy*, where he set several Houses on fire, in hopes of firing the whole City, but was frustrated in his Design, the Fire being always quenched in good time, tho it often broke out in divers Places at once.

The Portugueses offer a good Sum for his Head.

The *Portugueses* suspecting the Matter, offer'd a Reward of 10000 *Pagodes* (20000 Crowns) to any that could take him dead or alive, which made *Don John* desist from his Enterprize, and to return to his Desert.

The *Portugueses* finding themselves now in the quiet possession of the Country, were no longer able to disguise their natural Vices, their Pride, Avarice and Insolence, which occasion'd frequent Complaints to the Empress, but without Redress; which obliged the Inhabitants to enter into an Association to deprive them of all Subsistence, by cutting off their Supplies of Provisions: This obliged the *Portuguese* General to send in conjunction with King *Janiere Wandaar*, 2000 *Cingaleses* and 1000 *Portugueses*, to the Dukedom of *Ouve*, and 2000 *Indians*, and 200 *Portugueses* to *Halalmia* beyond *Candy*, to fetch in Rice and other Provisions.

They commit great Insolences.

The *Portuguese* Soldiers, tho they were very well received by the Inhabitants, yet did they commit all manner of Insolences in their Quarters, even to the ravishing of their Wives, killing their Children, and setting their Houses on fire; so that the *Cingaleses* finding themselves in a worse condition now than they were under their tyrannical Emperors, entred into a Conjuration to kill the *Portugueses* at a certain appointed time.

In the mean while *Janiere* sollicited the *Portuguese* General *Lopes*, for leave to marry the Empress *Catharina*; which he handsomely deny'd, alledging, that he could not consent to it, without special Order from the King of *Portugal*, but that he would write to the King about it. *Janiere* looking upon this only as an Excuse, desir'd to let him marry his Sister's Daughter; which being likewise refused by the General, *Janiere* conceived from that Moment a mortal Hatred against the *Portugueses*, and could not forbear to tell the General, that *He did not expect to have met with such a Reward for the Services he had done them, swearing that they should have occasion to repent it.* The *Portuguese* being somewhat exasperated at this unexpected Reply, told him that he ought not to take it amiss, if he denied him what was not in his Power to give, *viz. Donna Catherina* the legal Heiress of the Empire, to him who had usurped the Title of a King, merely by being got into the possession of the Treasure of *Raja Singa Adascyn*, but that he should be very ready to serve him upon any other occasion. *Janiere* being put out of all Patience by these insulting Words, replied smartly, *I am sensible of your Design; you that came here as Strangers, now you have got your Ends thro my means, are the first who would tyrannize over me.* Then recollecting himself, he began to turn the Discourse, dissembling his Resentment; but the same Night dispatched a Letter to *Don John* in the Desert, wherein he advertis'd him of what had passed betwixt him and the *Portuguese* General, offering him the Empire, provided he would receive him as King of the *Low-Lands*; which *Don John* approving of, they entred into a Confederacy to rid their Hands of the *Portugueses*.

Difference betwixt the Portugueses and Janiere.

Janiere enters into a League with Don John.

Things being thus settled, *Don John* began to appear among the *Cingaleses* (already much exasperated against the *Portugueses*) representing to them the Danger they were in, and how he was resolved in conjunction with *Janiere* to drive them out of the Island; which they readily accepted of, promising all the assistance they were able to give. But as *Janiere* sent frequent Letters to *Don John*, it happened that some of them fell into the hands of the *Portugueses*, who being thereby fully convinc'd of the Design carried on against them, begun, not without great reason, to fear, that unless they consented to the Marriage of *Janiere* with *Donna Catherina*, they would scarce be able to maintain themselves in the Isle.

The Portugueses consult about Janiere.

A Council being called for this purpose, they were much divided in their Opinions, some being for consenting to the Marriage to prevent farther Mischief, and to have *Don John* murdered; whilst others were for hazarding all, rather than to consent to the Match, and to have *Janiere* murdered, under pretence that he had laid a Design to murder the Empress and the General; for which purpose some forged Letters were to be produced, to justify their Conduct.

Resolve his Death.

To encompass this Design, they took the Opportunity, when *Janiere* was one day in conference with the *Portuguese* General and some other Officers: The General seeing him have a Scymeter on his side

side beset with Precious Stones, he desired to let him see it, feigning that he liked it so well, that he would take it for a Pattern to have such another made after it. *Janiere* not suspecting their Design, unadvisedly parted with his Scymeter, which was no sooner done, but a certain *Portuguese* Captain (upon the Signal given by the General) did run him thro the Body with his Sword, his Attendants undergoing soon after the same Fate. His Guards being advertised thereof, cryed out, *Haddy, Haddy, Treason, Treason, Radgore Janiere Marupue, King Janiere is murdered*; which being a Signal to the rest, all the *Indians* left the *Portuguese* Camp, except the King of *Cota* with his Forces, who had not immediate notice of this most detestable Murder.

Is murdered.

Baldæus.

The *Portugueses* did all they could to justify their Proceedings upon this account to the Empress, who (tho but young) being highly displeased thereat, told them, *That supposing he was a Traytor, he ought not to have been thus barbarously murdered, but either kept a Prisoner, or at least had the Benefit of a Legal Tryal. Rest assured*, added she, *that this treacherous Fact will turn to your Ruin; for who is it that hears of it, but will curse you, and never trust you in whatever you pretend to? And alas*, said she, *how ill have you served your King and me, who am likely to be involved in your Ruin? Be therefore upon your Guard, for you will pay dearly for having rewarded thus a Man who had done you such Signal Services.* These Words, tho coming from a young Woman, and scarce well initiated in the fundamentals of Christianity, were actually fulfilled afterwards, when the *Portugueses* were driven by our Forces out of *Batecalo, Gale, Columbo, Negumbo*, and last of all out of *Jafnapatnam*.

Donna Catherina's *Reflections upon it.*

Baldæus.

CHAP. V.

The Portugueses *leave* Candy, *are routed by the* Cingaleses. *The Empress taken Prisoner.* Don John *becomes Master of the Empire*; *Marries* Donna Catherina. Jeronimo Oriedo *defeated.*

Don John *improves the Fact to his advantage.* DON *John* was not wanting to turn the Hatred of the People (which must needs ensue upon so barbarous a Fact) to his advantage, and to represent the perfidious Designs of the *Portugueses* in the worst colours, offering them his Assistance against these Foreigners, as he had done before against *Raja Singa*; which succeeded so well, that they resolv'd unanimously to side with him, in order to drive them out of the Country.

The *Portugueses* having receiv'd intelligence of the great Preparations made against them, and that *Don John* was advancing with his Army towards *Candy*, began now, but too late, to repent of the Murder of *Janiere*; and seeing their Ruin at hand, unless they took timely care of their Safety, they retreated from *Candy* to the Fort of *Gannoor*, whence they sent to *Columbo* for Relief. *The* Portugueses *leave* Candy. The *Cingaleses* having got notice of their Flight, pursu'd them so closely, that many of them fell into their hands, especially of those Detachments sent to *Goa* and *Halalmia* for Provisions, 50 whereof they sent back with their Ears, Noses and Privy Parts cut off, in revenge of the Ravishments committed upon their Wives and Daughters.

Are miserably treated by the Cingaleses. 1590. The *Portugueses* were so terrify'd thereat, that finding themselves destitute of all hopes of Relief, they resolved likewise to leave *Gannoor*, and to retire to *Walane*, which they put in execution 1590. on a Sunday; and the better to cover their Flight, or at least to divert the *Cingaleses* from pursuing them, set the circumjacent Country on fire. But these preferring their Revenge before all other Considerations, follow'd them at the heels, and attack'd them most furiously in four several Parts at once. *And routed.* The *Portugueses* defended themselves most courageously; but being over-power'd in Number, were forc'd to give way with the loss of many of their best Soldiers, either kill'd or taken Prisoners, among whom was the *Portuguese* General *Lopes* and *Donna Catherina*. Pedro Lopes *and* D. Catherina *taken Prisoners.* The General dy'd within three days after of his Wounds, after he had recommended his Son to *Don John*'s care, who was afterwards by him (pursuant to his Promise) sent to *Columbo*.

The *Indians* got a considerable Booty, besides a vast Quantity of Arms, Cannon and Ammunition, in this Engagement; and *Don John* pursuing his Victory with the utmost vigour, made himself Master of all the Forts belonging to the *Portugueses*; some by Assault, the Garisons whereof he put to the Sword; some by Composition, which was punctually observ'd. All which struck such an Amazement into the circumjacent Kings and Princes, that they appear'd in Person before him, and asking Pardon for their having been engag'd with the *Portugueses*, brought him considerable Presents, and did him Homage with the usual Solemnity of prostrating themselves with their Faces to the Ground. Don John *restor'd to the Kingdom.*

Being thus settled a second time in the Throne, he thought it the safest way to secure himself of the Fidelity of his Subjects by marrying *Donna Catherina* (she being then but 12 years old) which was celebrated with great Solemnity for 110 days successively; *Marries* D. Catherina. notwithstanding which the Charges thereof did not amount to above 5000 *Pagodes*: But the Presents bestow'd upon many of the Nobility (to reconcile them to his Interest) to no less than 968754 *Pagodes*, or 4859538 *Dutch* Guilders, making the Sum of 1943815 Rixdollars. His next Care was to strengthen his Frontiers by three strong Forts; and he built himself a Palace, surrounded with several Bulworks, wherein he imploy'd the captive *Portugueses*, who, to their great grief, were forc'd to see their Ensigns display'd upon the Towers of their Enemies.

Don John having for some time enjoy'd the quiet Possession of the Throne, *Don Jeronimo d' Oriedo* was sent in the quality of *Portuguese* General to *Ceylon*, with a considerable number of Land Forces, compos'd of *Spaniards* and *Portugueses*, brought thither from *Goa* and other Places on the *Indian* Coast. Oriedo *a* Portuguese *General in* Ceylon. Having by great Presents brought over to his side most of the Princes of the *Low-Lands*, he order'd several Forts to be erected to serve him for a Retreat upon occasion. *Don John* was so far from annoying his men in perfecting these Fortifications, that he seem'd to despise it, saying, *Let them go on, I will*

find

find a way to pull down as fast as they can build: But understanding that the *Portugueses* were advancing towards *Walane*, in order to surprize *Candy* (where they intended to erect a strong Fort betwixt *Triquenam* and *Palugan*, to bridle the Country) he attack'd them in their March; so that a most furious Battel ensu'd, which remain'd dubious for some time, the *Portugueses* fighting like Lions; but at last were forc'd to yield to the number of their Enemies, who pursu'd them for five days as far as *Columbo*; they keeping their Ranks close, and making good their Retreat with unspeakable Bravery, tho not without considerable Loss on their side. Among their Wounded was *Oriedo* the General, who was oblig'd to King *Cota* for his Liberty, he having conceal'd him in some retir'd Place, without which he had infallibly fallen into the hands of the *Indians*. These, tho not a little tir'd with so long and troublesom a Pursuit, yet in their return made themselves Masters of the new *Portuguese* Forts, and cutting the Garisons in pieces, laid them level with the Ground. This Victory prov'd so considerable to *Don John*, that during his Life *Oriedo* either durst or could not attempt any thing further against him.

Is routed by D. John.

Baldæus.

CHAP. VI.

Dominico Corré *goes over to* Don John: *Besieges* Gale, *but is repuls'd.* Simon Corré *returns to* Columbo. *The* Portugueses *miserably massacred.* Joris van Spilbergen *comes to* Ceylon.

Dominico Corré *deserts.*

About that time *Dominico Corré*, a renown'd Soldier (known by the name of *Goliah*) being disoblig'd by the *Portugueses*, came over to *Don John*, having first cut off the Noses and Ears of several Monks who had offended him. He also entic'd *Corke Bandaar*, a revolted Prince, into *Don John's* Camp, who caus'd him to be tormented to death, and bestow'd his Principality upon *Dominico Corré*, to whom they gave the Name of *Idel Soria Bandaar*. Whilst he was doing Homage to the Emperor, a very large Tree that stood hard by, split in two pieces, without being touch'd; which the Inhabitants (a superstitious Generation) interpreted as an ill Omen.

Is made General.

Not long after the Emperor sent a considerable Army under the Command of *Dominico Corré*, and his Brother *Simon Corré*, to besiege *Gale*: But the *Portugueses* defended themselves so well, that the greatest part of this Army was ruin'd, and *Dominico* himself taken Prisoner, whom the *Portugueses* (contrary to their Promise) carry'd to *Columbo*, where he was privately murder'd. This barbarous Action so highly exasperated *Don John*, that he order'd some *Portugueses* to be kill'd by the Elephants, others he cut off their Noses and Ears, and sent them to *Columbo* to tell the General, that in case they did not set all the Prisoners at liberty, the *Portugueses* in his hands should receive the same Treatment.

Is murder'd.

His Death revenged by Don John.

The Soldiers in Garison at *Columbo* seeing this miserable Spectacle in their Companions, broke out into a Mutiny against the General, who by murdering *Corré* against his Parole, had given occasion to this Disaster. There was nothing to be heard among them but, *Kill the Dog, kill him*; whilst *Jeronimo d' Oriedo* cry'd for Mercy. Notwithstanding which, a whole Troop of them were advancing with their drawn Swords against him, and had certainly kill'd him upon the spot, had not some Monks thrown themselves (to their no small danger) betwixt him and them, and speaking to the Soldiers, calling them Gentlemen, and begging them for the Love of Christ, not to act against the Crown of *Portugal* in the Person of their General, appeas'd their Wrath; tho even then the General was forc'd to hide himself in a Convent, till the Tumult could be entirely appeas'd, which was not till 16 days after.

Simon Corrè *goes over to the* Portugueses.

Notwithstanding the barbarous Usage *Dominico Corré* had met with from the *Portugueses*, his Brother *Simon Corré* went over to them, pretending to the Emperor that he intended to advance towards *Columbo* to revenge his Brother's Death. He was very honourably receiv'd by the *Portugueses*, who not only bestow'd the Government of a Province upon him, but also marry'd him to a *Portuguese* Lady, whom together with his Son (begotten in this Marriage) they kept as Pledges of his Fidelity, whilst he was imploy'd in carrying on the War against *Don John*. How-

Baldæus.

However having got intelligence that the *Portugueses* had form'd a Design against the Life of the said *Don John*, he gave notice thereof to him, desiring him to be upon his guard.

Emanuel Dias *pretends to come over to the* Portugueses.

The Emperor being willing to be fully satisfy'd in a Matter of such moment, apply'd himself to one *Emanuel Dias*, who being formerly a Foot-boy to the *Portuguese* General *Lopes*, was advanc'd by the said *Don John* to the Dignity of one of his Gentlemen of the first rank, and had received many other Favours at his hands. *Emanuel Dias* willing to contribute what lay in his power to his Master's satisfaction, propos'd to go to *Columbo*, under pretence of having deserted his Service, but in truth to dive into the real Design of the *Portugueses*. Accordingly he arriv'd
1602. at *Columbo* on Easter-day 1602. where he propos'd to *Don Jeronimo Oriedo* several ways of murdering *Don John*, and that with so much assurance and seeming probability, that he was highly caress'd by that General, who agreed with him concerning the Method how the Design should be put in execution. For this purpose five *Portugueses* were pitch'd upon to share the Danger and Glory of so brave an Action (as they stil'd it) among whom were three Captains, viz. *Christian Jacobo*, *Alberto Primero*, and *Caspar Perere*. *Emanuel Dias* being promis'd no less a Reward than the Crown of *Candy*, play'd the Hypocrite so artificially, that he took a solemn Oath upon the Crucifix to be true to his Trust, and so he was dismiss'd to *Walane* with a good Sum of Money, from whence he return'd to *Candy*.

He deceives the Portugueses.

There he gave an account to the Emperor how Measures had been concerted betwixt *Don Jeronimo* and him, that a certain Body of Troops should be posted near the Fort of *Walane*, to be ready at hand to surprize that Place as soon as they should receive the Signal of the Murder of the Emperor being put in execution; for which purpose those who had undertaken that Task were within a limited time to appear near *Candy*. Hereupon the Emperor advanc'd secretly in the night time at the head of a good Body of Troops to *Walane*, where the before-mention'd Accomplices appearing according

Betrays them.

ing to agreement, well arm'd with *Japonese* Scymeters, call'd *Traſſados*, they were kindly receiv'd by *Emanuel Dias*, and introduc'd into the Emperor's Preſence; but ſoon after were ſeiz'd by his Guard, and the Signal given at the ſame time from the Fort of *Walane*. So that the *Portugueſes* believing every thing to have ſucceeded according to expectation, advanced with all poſſible ſpeed towards the Fort, where they queſtionleſs would have met with ſo warm a reception, that few of them would have return'd home, had not a certain Servant, who had deſerted from the Enemy, diſcover'd the whole matter to them, which made them retreat with all ſpeed towards *Columbo*, leaving all their Baggage and ſome Arms a Prey to the Enemy. *Emanuel Dias* got a vaſt Reputation by this bold Enterprize, and was rewarded with vaſt Preſents by the Emperor; but the five *Portugueſes* were after a long Captivity put to a moſt painful Death.

Baldæus.

About this time the *Dutch* General *Joris Spilbergen* coming with two Ships on the Coaſt of *Ceylon*, went to *Candy* on purpoſe to ſalute the Emperor in the Name of the States of the *United Provinces*, and his Excellency Prince *Maurice* of *Naſſau*; and was favourably receiv'd by *Don John*, and diſmiſs'd with conſiderable Preſents. Having left *Eraſmus Martens* and Mr. *Hans Pempel*, two very good Muſicians, there, he return'd highly ſatisfy'd, 3 *Sept.* 1603. by the way of *Metecola*, to *Achen*. But the *Portugueſes* were not a little diſſatisfy'd at his arrival there, as fearing that in caſe the *Dutch* ſhould enter into a Confederacy with the Emperor, their Stay would not be long in that Iſland, which proved true afterwards, they being quite chaſed thence in the Year 1658.

Joris Spilbergen *comes to* Ceylon.

1603.

CHAP. VII.

Sebald de Weert *comes to* Ceylon. *Great Diſſatisfaction betwixt the Emperor and him. Is murdered.* Don John *falls ſick, and dies. His Qualifications.*

Sebald de Weert *comes to* Ceylon.

SEbald de Weert and *Vibraads van Warwick* came ſoon after into *Ceylon*, where they entred into agreement with the Emperor. Afterwards they ſail'd to *Achen* to aſſemble more Forces, and landing at *Matecola* with 7 Ships, 26 *April*, 1603. *De Weert* gave notice thereof to the Emperor, who deſired him to come and put an end to the Conferences begun before, for the conſummation of the Treaty. *De Weert* coming into the Emperor's Preſence, was ask'd by him why he had ſet the *Portugueſe* Priſoners at liberty; which, as it had been done unadviſedly, ſo he made the beſt Excuſe he could upon that ſcore, which being not ſatisfactory to the Emperor, caus'd in him no ſmall ſuſpicion; the ſame was much augmented by what his Ambaſſador (who had been with the Vice Admiral *De Weert* at *Achen*) related to him, that during his ſtay with the *Dutch* he could not obſerve but that they were Friends of the *Portugueſes*, whereof they had given ſufficient Proofs, when they ſet the *Portugueſe* Officers that were their Priſoners, above him at the Table. He further added, that he had received information from credible hands, that the Vice-Admiral intended to invite the Emperor and the chiefeſt men of his Court, aboard his Veſſel to a Banquet; but in effect, to detain them Priſoners, and make themſelves Maſters of the Country: That he had thought it his Duty to give this Caution to his Majeſty, that he might not truſt the *Dutch*, and thereby with the reſt of his Princes be drawn into the Snare, to the irreparable ruin of the whole Country.

Difference betwixt the Emperor and him.

Is augmented by the Emperor's Ambaſſador.

Don John finding the Ambaſſador's Reaſons not to be ill grounded, and having conceiv'd no ſmall jealouſy at the Vice-Admiral's diſcharging the *Portugueſe* Priſoners contrary to his Promiſe, it was debated in Council, whether they ought to treat with him any further, or break off the Treaty already begun. After various Deliberations, it was agreed to endeavour to perſwade the Vice-Admiral to ſail with his Fleet to *Gale*, in order (according to mutual Agreement) to beſiege that Place, whereby they would not want opportunity to judg of his Conduct in reference to the *Portugueſes*.

Sebald de Weert ſoon after invited the Emperor aboard his Veſſel, which he refuſed, alledging that the chief Men of the Empire did not approve of a thing never known before. *De Weert* ſeeing the Emperor reſolute in his refuſal, deſir'd

De Weert *invites the Emperor on board.*

Baldæus.

sir'd him to do him the honour of coming only to the Sea-shore to view his Ships, and that he had order'd a Tent to be pitch'd there for his Reception. The Emperor not only refused also this Offer, but his Suspicion was increased, the before-mentioned Ambassador whispering him in the Ear, *Are you now sensible, my most gracious Lord, that I was in the right, and that they intend to catch you in the Snare?* And the *Dutch* Vice-Admiral *De Weert* being not a little disturb'd at so flat a Denial, told him frankly, that since *His Majesty did not think fit to come either aboard him, or at least to the Shore, he was resolv'd not to fight for him against the* Portugueses. *Don John*, tho not a little exasperated at so bold a Reply, yet dissembl'd his Anger, telling him only, that he should pursuant to his Promise, sail to *Gale* with his Fleet, whilst he would take a turn to *Candy* to visit the Empress, who was alone there, his Brother-in-law having taken a journy to the Frontiers; and that from thence they would hasten with all their Forces to the Siege. *Sebald de Weert* being somewhat heated with strong Liquor, reply'd undiscreetly, *That certainly the Empress could not be in distress for a Man, and that he was resolv'd not to sail to* Gale, *or to fight against the* Portugueses, *before the Emperor had done him the honour of viewing his Ships.* *Don John*, who was naturally a cholerick Person, was so incens'd at this Answer, that he left the Room, and in going out said, *Bind the Dog*; whereupon four of his Gentlemen advanced to lay hold of him, but he endeavouring to draw his Sword, and making a noise to call his Attendants to his Assistance (who were left near the Sea side by the Emperor's order) they laid hold of him from behind, and one of them splitting his Head with a Scymeter laid him dead upon the ground.

Which is refused.

De Weert *speaks with too much boldness.*

Which proves the occasion of his Death.

The Prince of *Ouve* being the only Person who durst give an account to the Emperor of what had happen'd, he appear'd somewhat disturb'd thereat, asking him, *why they did not make him a Prisoner, according to his order:* whereupon the Prince telling him, that it was impossible to be done, because he stood upon his Defence; *Don John* reply'd, *Nay, since he sought for his Death let him have it,* and

And of his Attendants.

and let his Attendants follow their Master; which was put in Execution immediately, scarce any one of those that came ashore with him escaping the fury of these Barbarians, except a Boy named *Isaac Plevier*, a Native of *Flissingen*, who was still alive, and in the then Emperor's Service, 22 *Nov.* 1614. Some few also had the good fortune of escaping by swimming to the Ships.

The Emperor soon after went to *Candy*, from whence he writ these few Lines in *Portuguese* to the Commanders of the *Dutch* Vessels; *Que bebem vinho, noa he bon. Deos fes justitia; se quisieres pas, pas; sequires guerra, guerra:* i. e. *Who drinks Wine is not good; God shews his Justice; If you desire Peace, you shall have Peace; if War, War.*

Don John falls sick of a burning Fever.

However *Don John* did not survive long this barbarous Action, being seiz'd with so violent a burning Fever, that to cool himself he was kept in cold Water without any Relief: He also drunk frequently of the Water of the Brook call'd *Hal gradoje*, betwixt *Ouve* and *Matarette*; which being so cold, as not to be held in the Mouth without shivering, yet could not in the least quench his Thirst. He often bewail'd the barbarous Murder of the *Dutch*, but said that *De Weert* had no more than what he deserv'd. Thus languishing for some time in continual Agonies, he was in no condition to dispose of his Affairs, but ended his Life in Misery 1604. He left behind him one Son, named *Mahastanne Adascyn*, and two Daughters, one named *Soria Mahadascyn*, i. e. *Beloved Sunlight*, the other *Cathan Adascyn*, i. e. *Beloved Peace*; all three born from *Donna Catherina*, call'd by the *Cingaleses Mahabandige Adascyn*, i. e. *Beloved Empress*.

Dies. His Issue.

Baldæus. His Character.

Don John was a valiant and great Captain, as his whole Life sufficiently testifies; he was tall of Stature, and well limb'd, black, and rustical in his Speech: He had gather'd a vast Treasure of Gold and Jewels, and had founded many Forts, Palaces, and publick Inns, call'd by the *Cingaleses Ambolan*, i. e. *Resting Places.* He kept a strict Hand in the Government; and as he never pardon'd Crimes, so he was very liberal to all such as behav'd themselves well in their Civil or Military Stations, on whom he confer'd Honours and Riches. He was a compleat Statesman, and stood firm to his Engagements with all Foreign Princes except the *Portugueses*, upon whom looking with a jealous Eye, he had conceiv'd a mortal hatred. As he despised all Religions, so he allow'd the free exercise thereof to all without distinction.

Divisions among the Great Men.

The Corps of the deceased Emperor was no sooner interr'd with extraordinary Magnificence, but the Great Men of the Kingdom began to divide into several Factions, every one aiming at the Crown: The most potent among them was the Prince of *Ouve*, who publickly set up for the Empire, but was opposed by *Cenuwieraat*, Brother-in-law to the late Emperor, who pretended to be Regent for his Nephew (his Brother's Son) till he should come to Age of Maturity. *Donna Catherina* well foreseeing the ill Consequences that might ensue upon those Pretensions, declar'd her self Regent of her young Son, and by taking off the Heads of some of the most suspected Lords, remov'd the present Danger, and appeased the Troubles that threatned her Ruin for some time.

Appeased by D. Catherina.

CHAP. VIII.

Divisions among the Great Men in Ceylon. *The Prince of* Ouve *murder'd by* Cenuwieraat, *who marries* Donna Catherina *the Empress.*

The Portugueses offer a Confederacy, which is deny'd.

THE *Portugueses* rejoic'd at the Death of *Don John*, sent Messengers after Messengers to *Goa*, to advertise the Viceroy of this welcome News, and to desire his Advice in this juncture. The said Viceroy being of opinion, that they ought to engage in an Alliance with *Donna Catherina* (as a means to make themselves masters by degrees of the whole Isle) the same was proposed accordingly, but rejected by *Donna Catherina*, who told them, that she would remain Sovereign Mistriss in her Territories. However the Princes of the *Lowlands* being sorely oppress'd by the Incursions and Ravages committed in their Territories both by the Prince of *Ouve* and the Emperor's Brother-in-law, hearkened to the Enticements of the *Portugueses*, and enter'd into a Confederacy with them.

Baldæus.

Ouve *and* Cenuwieraat *don't appear at Court.*

The Empress being not a little disturb'd at these Intestine Commotions, fearing she should be sacrificed to the prevailing Party, call'd a General Assembly of all the Lords of the Empire, who all appear'd accordingly in Person, except the Prince of *Ouve* and *Cenuwieraat Adascyn*, who thereupon were by Proclamation declar'd Rebels by the Empress, and their Estates confiscated. However *Cenuwieraat* having given sufficient Reasons for his Absence, and the Prince of *Ouve* having at the Intercession of his Friends obtain'd his Pardon, they afterwards appear'd at Court, but well guarded, neither Party trusting one another.

Prince Ouve *resolves to kill* Cenuwieraat.

Things thus passing on for some time, the Prince of *Ouve* resolv'd, after the Conclusion of the Assembly of the States, to rid his hands of *Cenuwieraat*, and afterwards to secure to himself the Crown by marrying *Donna Catherina*: but *Cenuwieraat* having got scent of this Design, resolv'd to be before-hand with him; to accomplish which, he disturb'd his thoughts, shewing to the Prince of *Ouve* upon all occasions most singular marks of his Respect and Friendship. But having in the mean while strengthned his Interest by ingaging most of the Great Men to his side, he took his opportunity when they were both going to take their leave of the Empress: For coming at the outward Gate, the Prince of *Ouve* would have given the Precedency to Prince *Cenuwieraat*, as descended from the Imperial Blood; which he refusing to accept of, told him that it was his due by reason of his Age: so that, after some time spent in Compliments, Prince *Ouve* went in first, and was instantly run through the Back, and laid dead upon the ground by *Cenuwieraat*, who said no more than, *Traitor, thou hast thy Reward*; and so retiring to his People, left the City immediately.

Is murdered by Cenuwieraat.

Those belonging to the Prince of *Ouve* hearing of the Murder of their Master, run thro the Streets, crying out, *Treason, Treason*, which put the City into such an Alarm, that the People (believing the Empress was kill'd) cut all to pieces they met with, so that the Streets were every where fill'd with Horror and Slaughter, which would have continued longer, had not *Donna Catherina* by shewing her self to the People, somewhat appeas'd their Fury. However, they not ceasing to exclaim, and uttering most horrid Threats against the Prince of *Cenuwieraat*, for the Murder of Prince *Ouve*, the Empress, to prevent further Mischief, thought it her safest way to prohibit under pain of Death, that any Injury should be done to Prince *Cenuwieraat*, declaring that what had been done was done by her own Orders; which somewhat settled the Minds of the People.

A Commotion in Candy.

Is appeased by the Empress.

But her thoughts were very different from what she shewed to the People, having conceived such a Horror at the Fact, that she resolved not to let it go unrevenged upon the Prince *Cenuwieraat*. He being advertised hereof by his Friends, kept constantly upon his guard, not neglecting in the mean while to have it represented to the Empress (not without good reasons) that he had been forced to undertake this Fact for his Self-preservation and the Welfare of the Kingdom, her Majesty and his Brother's Children: which had so good an effect upon the Empress, that by the Mediation of certain Great Men a Match was concluded betwixt the Empress and him, as the most proper means to restore Tranquillity to the Empire. At his Coronation he took upon him the Name *Camapati Mahadascyn*.

Cenuwieraat *clears himself.*

Marries the Empress.

He no sooner saw himself establish'd in the Throne, but he apply'd himself to the *Hollanders*, in order to enter into an Alliance with them against the *Portugueses*, as will appear out of the Sequel of this History.

Truce betwixt the Spaniards *and* Dutch.

For their High and Mightinesses the States-General of the *United Provinces* having 1609. made a Truce for twelve years with Arch-Duke *Albert* and *Isabella Clara Eugenia* Infanta of *Spain*, by virtue whereof it was among other matters agreed, that the same should take place also in the *East-Indies*: The then Directors of that Company being willing to improve this Interval for the better setling their Commerce in these parts, did petition their High and Mightinesses, and his Highness the Prince, to send their Letters to all the *Indian* Kings and Princes to enter into a Confederacy with them; which being granted accordingly, the said Letters, with certain Articles and Instructions, were by the Directors of the said *Dutch East-India* Company dispatch'd immediately to the *Indies* aboard the *Greyhound* Yacht, Capt. *Wemmer van Berchem* Commander: which done, they equipp'd a Squadron of Ships, which set sail out of *Holland* the 30*th* of *January* under the Command of *Peter Both*, Governor-General of the *Indies*, and arriv'd safely the 18*th* of *November* following at *Bantam*, with full power from their High and Mightinesses, and his Highness the Prince, to enter into such Alliances

Alliances with all the *Indian* Kings and Princes, as they thought most expedient for the settling of their Commerce, and ruining that of the *Portugueses* in those parts.

Baldæus.

CHAP. IX.

Letters from the States-General of the United Provinces, *and Prince* Maurice, *sent by* Marcellus de Boschhouwer *to the Emperor of* Ceylon.

THE Letters from their High and Mightinesses, and his Highness the Prince of *Orange*, to the Emperor of *Ceylon*, were as followeth.

Most Potent King!

The Letter of the States-General to the Emperor of Ceylon.

" IT has pleased the Almighty God " through his Mercy so to bless our " Arms, taken up for the maintaining " of the Rights and Privileges of our " Native Country against the King of " *Spain* and *Portugal*, that after a bloody " War carried on 42 years successively " both by Sea and Land, the said King " being convinc'd of our Unanimity, " Power and Constancy, supported by " the Strength of our Friends and Neigh- " bouring Allies, has thought fit to make " us the same Offers, for which we " had been oblig'd to commence a War, " *viz.* to declare us a free People, in- " dependent from his Power; and that " he was inclin'd to enter upon a Treaty " of Peace or Truce with us for a con- " siderable number of years. Which " Offers (after mature deliberation) " having been accepted by us, a Treaty " was set on foot accordingly with the " said King of *Spain* and *Portugal*, which " being brought to a Conclusion the 9th " of *April* last past, a Truce was agreed " upon for 12 years next ensuing, by " virtue whereof all the Subjects of this " State are not only at liberty to carry " on their Traffick, Commerce or Na- " vigation in all the Kingdoms and " Countries where they used to enjoy " the same before the War, but also " in all other Countries, Kingdoms or " Princes, and with all other Nations " or Provinces without exception; and " with this Proviso, that neither the " King of *Spain* and *Portugal*, nor his Offi- " cers and Subjects, shall in respect of " this Traffick hitherto carried on, or " to be carried on for the future, molest " or be troublesome (either directly or " indirectly) to our Subjects, or those " belonging to any King, Prince, or " other Superior Power, with whom we " have any Commerce; and that your " Majesty, as well as all other Kings, Prin- " ces, States and Nations, as well in the " *Indies* as in other parts, shall be compre- " hended in the said twelve years Truce, " and not be molested or attack'd on ac- " count of their Friendship and Com- " merce with us. But if (contrary to " our Expectation, and the solemn Pro- " mise made by the King of *Spain* and *Por-* " *tugal*, confirm'd by his Hand and Seal) " it should happen that your Majesty's " Subjects and Countries should be in- " volved in any Troubles with the said " King, either by Sea or Land, by rea- " son of their Friendship, Alliance or " Commerce with us, your Majesty may " rest assur'd, that we shall want neither " Will nor Power, neither Ships, Am- " munition nor Forces, as well of our " own, as of such other Kings and Prin- " ces our Allies, as are Guarantees of " the said Treaty, and have engag'd to " see the same executed in all its parti- " culars, and consequently in respect of " your Majesty's Dominions, as well as " of all other Countries and Dominions " both in the *Indies*, and elsewhere, to " protect and defend your Majesty's Do- " minions and Subjects against all Ag- " gressors, who upon that account shall " molest them. We don't doubt but " that some of the King of *Spain* and " *Portugal* his Creatures and Officers " will be apt to insinuate into your Ma- " jesty, his Subjects, and other Kings, " Princes, Nations and Republicks, a " quite different Sentiment of the said " Treaty. But we assure your Majesty " by these Presents upon our Faith, with- " out any tergiversation, unto which your " Majesty and Subjects, and all other " Kings, Princes, Nations and States " may give entire Credit, and desire " that your Majesty will be pleased " to rely upon it accordingly, to the " firm Settlement of a mutual and good " Correspondency, Navigation and Traf- " fick betwixt our Subjects; we on our

Baldæus. " side will not be wanting to entertain " the same with the utmost Sincerity, " confiding in the Omnipotent God, the " King of Kings, who knows the depth " of the Hearts of Men, that he will be " pleas'd to take both your and our Sub- " jects into his Protection, and increase " their well-being thro his Power and " Mercy. Dated in the *Hague*, *Sept.* 15. " 1609.

Subscribed,

A. Coenders.

And somewhat lower,

Your Highnesses most hearty Friends the States-General of the *United Provinces*, by their Order and Command,

C. Aertzen.

" *Maurice* Prince of *Orange*, Earl of " *Nassau*, *Catzenellebogen*, *Diest*, *Vi-* " *anden*, *Meurs*, Marquess of *Vere* and " *Ulissingen*, Governour, Captain and " Admiral General of *Guelders*, *Hol-* " *land*, *Zealand*, *West-Friesland*, *Zut-* " *phen*, *Utrecht*, *Over-Yssell*, &c.

Most Potent King,

Pr. Maurice's Letter to the Emperor. " GOD protect your Majesty, and " give you all the Blessings upon " Earth. We have for a considerable " time been engaged in a War against " the King of *Portugal*, in order to op- " pose his ambitious Designs, the same " Motive having induced your Majesty to " defend your Dominions against his At- " tempts; the Almighty God has been " pleas'd to bless our Arms with such " Success, as to oblige our Enemy to a " twelve Years Truce, which by the " Mediation of several neighbouring " Kings has been brought at last to a hap- " py Conclusion: But, finding that the " said King did continue his Warlike " Preparations, and imagining that the " same was intended chiefly, in order to " attack your Majesty and some other " Princes in the *Indies*, our Allies (after " being bereaved of our Assistance) we " thought it absolutely requisite, not to " agree to the said Truce, unless your " Majesty were included therein, toge- " ther with the rest of our Friends and " Allies. Whereupon the same was con- " cluded at last, under condition, that " we and all our Friends and Allies " should enjoy full Liberty, to send our " Ships into what Countries we pleas'd " without any Molestation from the *Por-* " *tugueses*; and that in case your Ma- " jesty, or any other of our Confede- " rates, should be attack'd by him, we " should deem the same as done to our " selves: to accomplish which we shall " be ready upon all Occasions to be " assistant in revenging any Damages done " upon that Score to your Majesty, or a- " ny other of our Allies. We have " some reason to suppose, that the In- " tention of the said King is, to sepa- " rate by this Artifice your Majesty from " our Interest, which ought to be a mu- " tual caution to us, to be upon our Guard " for the future; for since the occasion " of dividing us by Force of Arms is re- " moved, they will not be sparing to at- " tain to their end by Fraud and other " Sinister Means. It is therefore, that " we have order'd our Governour-Gene- " ral, to treat with your Majesty, and " to find out such means, as may be most " proper to prevent their Intrigues, and " to unite us against those, whose Word " and Faith we dare not altogether rely " upon. We did not think fit to stipu- " late in the said Treaty, that his Sub- " jects should be excluded from the " Traffick of *Ceylon*, but left the same " to your Majesty's Discretion, not " questioning, but that according to " your Wisdom and Understanding, you " will act in that respect, so as that no- " thing may be transacted that may tend " towards the Dissolution of our Alli- " ance, which we hope the Almighty " will maintain by his Blessing, to the " Honour of his Holy Name, and the " Welfare of your Majesty, and our Be- " loved Subjects.

Dated in the Hague *Octob.* 5. 1609. *Maurice de Nassau.*

The Superscription was as follows.

" To the most Illustrious and most Noble " Emperour of *Ceylon*, King of *Can-* " *dy*, *Trinquenemale*, *Jafnapatnam*, *Set-* " *te-Corles*, *Manaar*, *Chilaw*, *Cota*, " *Batecalo*, *Punte-Gale*, our Beloved " Brother in the Wars.

These Letters were no sooner brought in the *Greyhound* Yacht to *Coromandel*, but the Director of our *East-India* Company there, named *John van Wesick*, ordered immediately *Marcellus de Boschhouwer* our Under-Factor, aboard the Ship called the *Black Lyon*, to *Ceylon* along with *Peter Both*, a Native of *Amensfort*, Commodore, bound likewise for that Island. Marcellus Boschhouwer *sent to* Ceylon.

CHAP.

Baldæus.

CHAP. X.

Marcellus de Boschhouwer *comes to* Candy. *His Treaty and Agreement with the Emperor of that Isle.*

M*Arcellus de Boschhouwer* coming accordingly, *March* 8. 1612. to *Candy*, had Audience of his Imperial Majesty *Cenuwieraat Adascyn*, unto whom having delivered the before-mentioned Letters, the Emperor received him with all imaginable Demonstrations of Joy, placing him on his side on a Chair of Gold, clad in a White Garment: Whereupon the Treaty being begun, immediately the same was concluded *May* 11. following, upon the following Conditions.

I. This Confederacy shall be kept inviolably, and stand firm for the future.

II. All Hostilities shall cease, and a general Amnesty be granted.

III. In case the *Portugueses* should attack his Majesty, the States-General shall be obliged to assist his Majesty with all their Forces.

IV. His Majesty grants leave to the *Dutch*, to erect a Fortress at *Cotiarum*, provided the King of *Cotiarum* may enjoy his Customs and other Revenues.

V. The Emperor obliges himself to furnish Bricks, Lime and other Materials for the building of the said Fortress, as also Labourers to be paid by the Company.

VI. His Imperial Majesty shall take care to have Ware-houses of Stone or Brick erected at *Candy*, for the Security of our Company against Fire.

VII. His Majesty shall take our Ships and Seamen under his Protection, and defend them to the utmost of his Power against the *Portugueses*, as the *Hollanders* shall be obliged to do the same, in respect of his Majesty's Subjects.

VIII. His Majesty obliges himself to transact nothing in all Military Affairs, that have any relation to our Company, without the Knowledg of their Officers; for which purpose two *Hollanders* shall sit constantly in his Council of War, to be present at all Debates, and other Matters to be transacted there.

IX. He engages himself to have all the Merchandizes of the *Dutch* carried upon Beasts fit for Carriage to *Candy*, and such Commodities as are bought there, to be carried back to the Sea-shoar at *Cotiarum*, at his own Charge.

X. In case any Vessels, Sloops or Boats, should happen to be cast away on these Coasts, his Majesty's Subjects shall be obliged to save as much of the Goods as they can, without any Reward, for the use of our Company.

XI. The *Dutch* shall be permitted to export their Merchandizes, without exception, Custom free.

XII. All and every one of his Majesty's Subjects shall be at Liberty to traffick with our Company.

XIII. His Imperial Majesty obliges himself to purchase any Rarities, or other uncommon Commodities at such a rate, as may bear a proportion, in respect of other Commodities agreed upon with our Company in their Exchanges.

XIV. His Majesty engages to deliver yearly all the Cinamon that is to be got to our Company, to be paid either in Money or in Merchandizes, according to the usual Exchange.

XV. It is agreed, that not any sorts of Merchandizes shall be delivered to such Persons, as are entred into Contracts of Commerce with the *Hollanders*, before the Natives of *Holland* are satisfyed in this Point; and in case the contrary be prov'd, their Persons and Goods shall be detain'd, till they have made good the said Contract.

XVI. His Majesty shall not allow free Commerce to any of the *European* Nations, without peculiar Consent from their High and Mightinesses, and his Highness the Prince of *Orange*.

XVII. His Majesty obliges himself to furnish Timber and other Materials, for the building of Vessels, Yachts and Boats, to be delivered upon the Shoar.

XVIII. All Prisoners taken on both sides shall be released.

XIX. All the Officers of the *Dutch* Company shall be exempted from his Majesty's Jurisdiction; and if any of them happen to commit any Trespass, they are to be punished by the Heads of the *Dutch* Company, as his Majesty's Subjects shall enjoy the same Benefit.

XX. His Majesty obliges himself to dispose of all his Precious Stones and Pearls to the *Hollanders*, as they on their side engage to sell all their extraordinary Jewels, Precious Things and other Rarities,

Baldæus. ties, at a reasonable Rate; but in case any difference should arise upon that account, the same shall not be alledged as a Reason for the dissolving of this Confederacy.

XXI. For the same Reason his Majesty and the States-General, shall maintain this Alliance inviolably, and assist one another upon all Occasions.

XXII. All Acts of Hostility committed on both sides, shall be buried by a general Oblivion.

XXIII. No body, except his Majesty, shall have Power given him to coin Mony, or to enhaunce the Value of the Coin, beyond what has been agreed betwixt his Majesty and the *Hollanders*, in proportion to the Mony transported hither from *Holland*; and if any of his Majesty's, or our Subjects are found to have coin'd false Money, they are to be punished with Death.

XXIV. His Majesty and the *Hollanders* shall agree upon the most proper Methods for settling both the larger and lesser Coin, for the promoting of Traffick.

XXV. Such Coin as shall be adjudged current by both Parties, shall be changed every three Years by turns, once at *Candy*, and the next three Years in one of our Places.

XXVI. The Coin shall be either enhaunced or lowered, according to the present exigency of Affairs in time of War.

XXVII. All the *Indian* Nations shall be free to come and traffick in their own Vessels, in his Majesty's Dominions, without paying any Customs, for the space of three Years next ensuing.

XXVIII. After the Expiration of the Term of these three Years, his Majesty shall be at Liberty to enter into a Treaty with the Plenipotentiaries of their High and Mightinesses, concerning the Rate of Customs of all Commodities.

XXIX. His Majesty agrees, that their High and Mightinesses, and his Highness the Pr. of *Orange*, shall enjoy one Moiety of all the Customs, for which purpose certain Commissioners and Clerks shall be appointed by the Consent of both Parties.

XXX. All the Prizes taken on the Coast of *Ceylon*, shall be divided share and share alike, betwixt your Majesty on the one side, and their High and Mightinesses, and his Highness the Prince of *Orange* on the other side; provided that what Prisoners are taken, shall be ransom'd, but never put to Death.

XXXI. All Factors or other Officers belonging to their High and Mightinesses, and his Highness the Prince of *Orange*, shall give Passes to such of your Majesty's Subjects as intend to traffick in those Parts; as his Majesty shall do the same, without which they shall be liable to be seized, and their Goods confiscated.

XXXII. His Majesty, their High and Mightinesses, and his Highness the Prince of *Orange*, shall be obliged to take effectual Care, to have the Roads and Passages both by Sea and Land, in the Isle of *Ceylon*, to be kept well and clear from Highwaymen and Pirates; for which purpose his Majesty obliges himself to furnish Timber, for the building of Galleys and other Vessels, for the clearing of the Seas; and in case any Highwaymen or Pirates are taken, they shall be punished with Death.

XXXIII. His Imperial Majesty, their High and Mightinesses, and his Highness the Prince of *Orange*, do promise to keep this Confederacy inviolably, to the utmost of their Power, nor to suffer the same to be violated by their Subjects; to inflict severe Punishments upon such as shall go about to violate it, and give full Satisfaction for all Damages sustained upon that account.

CHAP. XI.

Marcellus de Boschhouwer *desires leave to depart, which the Emperor will not consent to. Has considerable Dignities bestowed upon him. The* Portugueses *rob and murder the* Dutch *at* Cotiarum. *The Emperor convenes the Estates of the Empire. The* Portugueses *routed near* Jafnapatnam.

Boschhouwer *desires to be dismiss'd.*

THE Articles of this Confederacy being thus concluded, Mr. *Boschhouwer* desir'd leave from his Imperial Majesty to depart, with the Elephants that were ready to carry certain Commodities to *Tegnapatan*, for the use of the *Dutch* Factory there; from whence he might go to *Paliacatta*, to give the *Dutch* Governor of that Place an account of his Negotiation. But the Emperor and his Coun-

Which is denied. Council were not willing to consent to his Dismission, alledging, that since according to one of the before-mention'd Articles, they were obliged not to transact any thing in Warlike Affairs, without the Knowledg and Consent of the *Dutch*, it was requisite he should stay with them for that purpose. These Reasons prevailed so far with Mr. *Boschhouwer*, that he resolv'd to stay; and the Emperor heaped Favours after Favours upon him, having created him Prince of *Migonne*, *Kockelecorle*, *Ananagepora*, and *Miwitigael*, Knight of the Order of the Golden Sun, President of the Council of War, the second Person in his Privy Council, and Lord High Admiral: and he knew so well how to improve the Emperor's good Opinion of his Person, that scarce any thing of Moment was undertaken without his Advice.

Has great Dignities bestowed upon him.

Portugueses murder and plunder the Dutch. In the Year 1611. *Jun.* 20. the *Portugueses* took the Field, with a Body of 1000 *Portugueses*, and 3000 *Indians* their Allies, under the Command of *Simon Corre*; and having got a certain *Candinese* for their Guide, they march'd thro unknown ways to *Cotiarum*, where they surpriz'd the *Dutch* belonging to Mr. *Boschhouwer*, put them all to the Sword, and plunder'd the Place, and then retir'd with all Speed to *Sette Corle*, for fear of being overtaken by the Emperor's Forces.

For the Emperor had no sooner notice of their March, but he sent a Body of 5000 men, commanded by *Marasinge Atsile*, an old experienc'd Captain, and under him *Mayndappo* and *Vire Segre*, two brave Noblemen, to *Cotiarum*; but coming too late, they pursu'd the *Portugueses* Day and Night, till they overtook them near *Sette Corle*, kill'd 23 *Portugueses*, 600 *Indians*, set several Villages on fire, and return'd with many Prisoners and a good Booty to *Candy*.

About the same time an Envoy of the King of *Palugam* came to Court, representing that *John Sangati* his Master's Brother, and King of *Podere*, was entred into an Alliance with the *Portugueses*, in order to deliver all his Harbours into their Hands, and afterwards to carry on a War against his Imperial Majesty with their Assistance. Hereupon the King of *Podere* being summon'd to appear at Court at a prefix'd time, he sent an Envoy to clear his Innocence with the Emperour, unto whom he represented the Perfidiousness of the King of *Palugam*, who had kill'd his own Brother at Table, for no other reason, but that he might be sole Master of the whole Kingdom, offering besides to remain there as a Hostage for his Master's Fidelity. The Emperor, tho not very well satisfy'd with the King of *Podere*, by reason of his not appearing in Person; yet considering, that what had been alledged by his Envoy, concerning the Murder of his Elder Brother, was no more than Truth, and that certain Differences were arisen lately betwixt them about the Customs of the River of *Palugam*, one half whereof was allotted by the Estates to the King of *Podere*, he dismissed the Envoy well satisfied, resolving to suspend his Judgment, till time should unfold the matter.

Difference betwixt 2 Brothers.

Baldæus.

The Emperor convenes the Estates. The Emperor having bent his Thoughts upon a War, he convened the Estates of the Empire, *viz. Idele* King of *Cotiarum*, *Celle Wandaar* King of *Palugam*, *Comaro Wandaar* King of *Batecalo*, *Corre Witty Raelhamy* Prince of *Ouve*, *Marcellus de Boschhouwer* Prince of *Migonne*, *Meter Raelhamy* Prince of *Vellene*, *Jallago de Rale* Prince of *Cotomale*, *Mewater Rale* Prince of *Mewater*, *Wik Venesinge* Earl of *Quatre Corle*, *John Sangati* Prince and Lord of *Podere*, *Cole Rale* Duke of *Ode*, *Jattenore* Brother of the Prince *Jalagode*, *Gael Heberad* Governour of the County of *Harcipate*, *Corope* Governour of the County of *Odogo d' Askeri*, *Wanategere* Governour of the Province of *Matere*. In the same Assembly appear'd also the Governours and Commanders in chief of the lesser Provinces, and the Ambassador of the King of *Jafnapatnam*, the King of *Patania* being the only one, who tho summoned by a peculiar Letter, dated *July* 16. 1611. made several frivolous Excuses for his not appearing there.

What was concluded there. Among other matters of the greatest Moment, it was resolved in this Assembly to raise an Army of 50000 Men, one half whereof was to be employed in the Siege of *Puntegale*, under the Conduct of the Prince of *Ouve*; the other against *Walane*, under the Command of the Prince of *Migonne*: And in case they met with good Success, both Armies were to join and attack *Columbo*. For the carrying on of this Enterprize, 4 Millions and 500000 Livers were to be raised. Concerning the Differences betwixt the King of *Palugam*, and his Brother *John Sangati*, they were both enjoin'd under pain of Death, not to hurt one another, till the matter could be further enquired into.

A High Court of Judicature was also settled, to examine and decide all such Matters, as before that time used to be de-

Baldæus. determined by the Emperor and his Privy Council. The Judges of this Court were, the Prince of *Migonne* President, the Prince of *Ouve*, the Prince of *Velaren*, and the Prince of *Cottomale*. None of the inferiour Courts were to take cognizance of criminal Matters, without the approbation of this High Court, from whence no Appeal was to be allowed. The Prince of *Ouve*, the Prince of *Migonne*, the Prince of *Velaren*, the Prince of *Cottomale*, and the Earl of *Quatre Corle*, were appointed Members of his Majesty's Privy Council.

It was also further decreed, that not only Liberty should be granted, but also Houses and Lands allotted to such Seamen as would settle in his Majesty's Dominions; by which means they proposed to get in time a sufficient number of able Seamen to man their Gallies, of which three were order'd to be built immediately, with some other Vessels, to cruize upon the *Portugueses* on the Coast of *Orixa* and *Bengale*, &c. It was also agreed, that no Quarter should be given to the *Portugueses* and their Confederates, unless they were Women or Children; and that a Pardon should be published for all Deserters that would return within 60 Days into his Majesty's Service, which was done accordingly at *Candy*, 23 *July*, 1612.

Portugueses *march to* Jafnapatnam. Whilst these things were transacting, Advice was brought that the *Portugueses* were on their march towards *Jafnapatnam*; whereupon the Emperor having sent part of his Forces design'd for the Expedition against *Walane* and *Gale*, to observe their Motions, they attack'd the Reer of the *Portugueses*, who imagining no otherwise than that the whole Force of the Emperor was on their back, were soon brought into confusion; but finding their Mistake, rallied again, and retreated towards *Columbo*, making themselves Masters in their March thither of the Dukedom of *Migonne*, where they committed all manner of Cruelties. *Are beaten.* The *Modeliar* or Governor being accus'd of having betray'd his Trust, sent a Letter to the Prince of *Migonne*, wherein he declared, that after having sustained three Assaults, he was forced to surrender; adding, that they were ready to shake off the *Portuguese* Yoke with the first opportunity that offered, tho the *Portugueses* had taken most of their Wives and Children, (and among the rest the Governour's Wife) along with them, as Hostages and Pledges of their Fidelity, to *Columbo*. They sent also a Present to their Prince, as a Token of their Obedience. The Letter was dated 30 *Aug.* 1612. by the Command of the chief *Visego Modeliar*.

The Prince, after having consulted about this Letter with the Emperor, sent answer, that he was extremely concerned at the loss of his Country and Subjects, exhorting them to persist in their Fidelity, and that as soon as possible he would appear among them at the Head of the Imperial Army.

CHAP. XII.

The Death of the Hereditary Imperial Prince. His Funeral. The King of Panua *rebels, is taken Prisoner, and kill'd, with all his Adherents.*

Death of the Imperial Prince. About the same time the Hereditary Imperial Prince *Mahastanne*, Son of the late Emperor *Don John*, died after a Sickness of six days. The occasion of his Death was variously reported; but the general Opinion was that he had been poisoned by *Cenuwieraat* his Father-in-law, to make way for his eldest Son *Comara Singastanne* to succeed him in the Empire. Certain it is that his Death was generally lamented, the Guards were doubled all round the Imperial Palace, and great Preparations made for his Funeral, which was perform'd the 23*d* of *August* in the Afternoon. The Empress especially gave most evident Marks of her Grief, calling him at parting, *Her own precious Flesh and Blood, her only Hopes, Life and Satisfaction*, vowing to revenge his Death, and not to take any Nourishment, that she might follow her Son. She did afterwards fall into a Swoon, and was fain to be remov'd out of the Room by her two Daughters, who also were melted in Tears.

The Corps of the deceased Prince being expos'd to the view of the People, they broke out into most lamentable Exclamations, crying, *Where is the Traitor that murder'd our Prince? We will tear him to pieces.* So that the Emperor fearing a general Insurrection, got the Prince of *Migonne* and the Prince of *Ouve* to tell them,

The Funeral Pomp of ye Royal Prince.

Baldæus. them, that the Prince was not poison'd, but died of a Fever, which somewhat appeas'd the Tumult. The Corps being put into a Mourning Herse adorn'd with Gold and precious Stones, was carried to the place of Burial in the following manner:

His Funeral. First of all went the Prince's Musicians, clad in black *Gingam* or Linen; then the Musqueteers and Pikemen, three in a Rank: These were follow'd by the Shield-bearers and Halberdiers with their Halberds downwards: After these came 40 War-Elephants guided by as many Gentlemen, and 8 *Persian* Horses led by eight Knights of the *Golden Sun*; and after these the Grooms of the Bed-chamber all richly attir'd. Then came the Scepter and Crown, carried each upon a black Velvet Cushion, and the Prince's Arms. These were followed by the Corps attended by eight of the greatest Lords of the Country; then the Empress's *Palankin* or Litter attended by 16 with Fans, four Umbrello's, and eight *Betel* Boxes, as also a Nosegay of Gold to be worn by the Emperor only. After these came the Emperor supported by the Princes of *Migonne* and *Mewater*, follow'd by the chief Lords of the Empire and the Governours of the Provinces. They pass'd along the Streets under several Arches made of fine Stuffs and Plaister-work. The Corps being deposited on the Place of Burial with a deal of Solemnity, the Priests mutter'd out certain Prayers, and the common People express'd their Sorrow by frequent mournful Outcries.

The Place of Burial. The Place of Burial (called *Hona* by the *Cingaleses*) was a four-Square raised from the Ground seven Steps high; it was level on the top, and adorned with several Rows of Trees. In the midst of it was the Grave, into which the Lords who had carried the Corps threw a great quantity of Sandal-wood, and sweet-scented Spices; and having put the Corps upon it cover'd with the same Spices, as high as a Man could reach, they also poured in among it three large Vessels full of Oil of Cinnamon, and another with Butter. Over the Grave was erected a large Canopy rising up like a Pyramid of seven Foot high, under which stood the Lords whilst the Ceremony lasted: which being over, the Prince of *Migonne* took a Bundle of Straw, which was given him by the Prince of *Amme*, and a golden Chafindish with Fire, and two lighted Torches, and being attended by the said Prince of *Amme* and two Gentlemen of the Bedchamber, set fire to the Spices and Corps in the Grave, under the most dreadful Ejaculations and Outcries of the People, which lasted till the Corps was quite burnt to Ashes; which done, the whole Train return'd to Court to condole the Empress and her Daughters. *His Corps burnt.*

The King of Panua joins with the Portugueses. In *September* Advice being brought to Court that the King of *Panua* had join'd the *Portugueses* against the Emperor, and that the King of *Cotiarum* intended to follow his Footsteps, the Emperor with the Advice of his Privy Council sent his Letters dated the 23 *Sept.* to both these Kings, to make their personal Appearance at Court within 16 days, under the forfeiture of all their Estates, and Banishment. The King of *Cotiarum* happening to be ill at that time, he sent his Uncle to know the reason of his being summoned to Court, and thereupon appeared in Person on the 9th *Oct.* following, giving such Proofs of his Innocence, that he was soon clear'd by the Emperor. But the King of *Panua* knowing himself guilty, did not think fit to appear; so that it was resolved to reduce him by Force, his Defection having put a stop to the Expedition against *Walane* and *Gale*. Accordingly the Princes of *Migonne* and *Ouve*, at the head of an Army of 35000 men, march'd 1 *Jan.* 1613. directly towards *Panua*, with a resolution to destroy all with Fire and Sword: But the Inhabitants finding themselves not in a condition to oppose so formidable a Force, sent Deputys with Presents to the Princes, desiring they might be spared, as having no hand in this Defection; which being granted, they were amerced in 457000 *Larynen* (besides their yearly Tribute) amounting just to two Months Pay of the whole Army, and to give Hostages for the King's Appearance at Court in 5 or 6 days after.

Appears at Court, and is accus'd of Treason. Accordingly he was no sooner come there, but being brought before the Privy Council, his Accusation was read to him in Writing, *viz.* "That he had entred into an Engagement with the *Portugueses* against the Emperor, and was to have marry'd the young Princess *Hantan Adascyn*, and with her as a Dowry the Kingdoms of *Batecalo* and *Palugam*: That he had despised the Emperor's Order in not coming to Court; and hired a certain Ruffian for 5000 *Larynes* to murder the Emperor, with a Promise of 20000 more, and certain Possessions, after the same was accomplished, as appeared both by his own Hand-writing, and the Confession of the Ruffian. Which being so evident against

against him, that he had scarce any thing to reply, he acknowledg'd himself guilty, craving the Emperor's Mercy, in regard of his being descended from the Imperial Blood, and of the many Services done to the Crown by his Ancestors.

Is committed to Prison. He was by Order from the Council ordered to be committed Prisoner in the Castle of *Meddema Honore*, from whence he sent a most submissive Letter to the Emperor, imploring his Mercy to save his Life, and to condemn him to a perpetual Imprisonment. About 62 Persons found to have been his Accomplices in this Conspiracy were sent to other Prisons, and afterwards punish'd with Death.

His Trial. The 20th of *March* being the Day appointed for the Trial of the King and his Accomplices, 50 Lords of the Empire appointed for that purpose, after a full Hearing found them all guilty of High Treason, and accordingly pronounc'd the *Sentence.* following Sentence: That the King of *Panua* should be beheaded, and the rest be thrown before the Elephants, and all their Goods and Estates be confiscated. This Sentence being signed by his Imperial Majesty, was put in execution accordingly the 24th of *March* following in the Forenoon.

Execution. Accordingly a Scaffold cover'd with White (the Royal Colour here) being erected in the Castle of *Meddema Honore*, the King was brought thither, and seated *Behaviour.* himself upon a gilt Chair. He at first appear'd undaunted; but being depriv'd of all his Dignities, in the view of the People, and the Sentence read to him, he began to bewail his unfortunate Condition, asking frequently whether there were no hopes of a Pardon? Being told no, he suffer'd himself to be undress'd by some of his Gentlemen of the Bedchamber (who were all in Tears) unto whom he made rich Presents of Jewels, and order'd his Chancellor (who had not had the least Knowledg of this Design) to bind up his Eyes. In the mean while the the King took some *Betel* and *Arek*, and then said, *Why do we stay? Unfortunate I, what am I reduc'd to!* *Speech.* Then taking three turns round the Scaffold, he sat down, and taking a little *Betel* told the Spectators, *I am a King descended from the Imperial Blood; but since I must die, this is my only Request, that my dead Corps may not be left to the management of vile Persons, but be honoured with a Royal Sepulture.* Which being promis'd by some of the Lords there present, he seem'd to be well satisfy'd, and having ask'd their Pardon for what had pass'd, he had his Eyes ty'd up, and laying his Head upon a Block, it was sever'd from the Body, which (at the Intercession of the said Lords) had a Royal Sepulture allowed it by the Emperor.

Baldæus.

His Successor. After his Death *Samatway* the King's Uncle being with a general approbation declared his Successor, marched at the head of an Army of 50000 men, the 8th of *April*, to *Panua*, to take possession of that Kingdom, which he found involved in no small Troubles, there being a strong Party who opposed his Succession: But 125 of the Ringleaders being cut to pieces by the new King's Forces, the rest rest thought fit to submit. So soon as he found himself in the quiet Possession of the Kingdom, he sent back the Forces, as also the Arrears of the annual Tribute, besides considerable Presents. The *Portugueses* not long after sent their Deputys to entice those of *Panua* with vast Promises to engage with them afresh; but these were sent back without being heard.

CHAP. XIII.

The Emperor sits down before Walane. *The Prince of* Migonne *equips a Squadron of Ships. The Empress falls sick, disposes of her Affairs, and dies.*

The Emperor besieges Walane. IT was not long after that the Emperor with a good Army form'd the Siege of *Walane*, and took the Castle by Assault; but his Souldiers being too intent upon the Plunder, the *Portugueses* recovered themselves, and beat them from thence. The Emperor being highly exasperated at this Miscarriage, caused 105 *Cingaleses* to be hang'd, which proved of the worse consequence, because the *Portugueses* receiving fresh Succours soon after, he was forc'd to raise the Siege. *Raises the Siege.*

A Squadron of Ships sent a cruising. In the mean time the Prince of *Migonne* had not been idle to equip some Gallies and *Fustes* (small Vessels) to cruize upon the *Portugueses* between the Cape of *Comoryn* and the Isle of *Ceylon*. The same set sail the 16th of *May* out of the Harbour of *Cotiarum*, under the Command of a Nephew of the Prince of *Ouve*, as Admiral,

Baldæus.

ral, and *Wandige Nay Hanni* Vice-Admiral. The first Gally was called the *Candy*, one *Sanderappo* Captain. The 2*d* call'd the *Holland*, *Kistena* Captain. The 3*d* the *Migonne*, one *Dingappe* Captain. The 4*th* called the *Fortune*, one *Ordia* Captain. 5*th* the *Good Luck*, one *Marasinge* Captain. 6*th*, The *Faithful*, commanded by Captain *Sanderappo*. These Ships returned the 6*th* of *March*, 1613. with a great Booty amounting to near 600000 Livers. For they had taken two *Portuguese* Vessels near *Chilau* to the North of *Negumbo* and *Manaar*, called *Patasios*; and three *Fustes*, besides 20 Barks which they set on fire. Not far from *Calecut* and the Cape of *Comoryn* they took another Ship, whereof they threw (according to Order) the *Portugueses* over-board, forced another ashoar, and took a *Moorish* Vessel richly laden coming from *Ormus*, and bound for *Cochin*, and another *Portuguese* Ship coming from *Bengal*. The *Portugueses* and *Mistices* of all which they threw into the Seas, keeping only the *Portuguese* Women and *Negros*. In the Road of *Panaca* they met with another *Portuguese* Ship riding at anchor, deserted by the Ship's Crew, which they brought into the Harbour of *Cotiarum*. His Majesty order'd the Booty to be distributed among the Officers and Seamen.

1613. *The Empress falls sick.*

In *July* 1613. the Empress *Donna Catherina* being with child, fell dangerously ill of a Fever: She sent for the Prince of *Migonne* and the Prince of *Ouve*, unto whom (after having taken an Oath of Secrecy from them) she discovered the whole Sentiments of her Heart, and (with the Emperor's Consent) constituted them Governours of her Children. She had conceived such an immoderate Grief at the Death of her eldest Son, the Prince of *Mahastanne*, that she would scarce take any Sustenance. She declared, that nothing troubled her more, than that before her Death she should not see the Downfal of the *Portugueses* in *Ceylon*; and would often, with a great deal of eagerness enquire, whether the expected Succours were not arrived out of *Holland*. Such was her Grief, as I told you before, about the loss of her Son, that she would scarce rest day or night; which had questionless prov'd the occasion of this Distemper: and she was no less troubled how to dispose of her Children after her Death; she bequeathed to them all her Jewels and Treasure she had been gathering for a considerable time; as also certain Legacies to all her Servants, and restored all her Slaves of both Sexes to their Liberty.

Takes care of her Children and Servants.

Her Sickness increasing daily, she was carried from *Welmantotte* (her ordinary Residence) to *Modeni*, where in the Presence of the Emperor, she charged her eldest Son to revenge the late deceased Prince's Death upon the Physician, who she said was the Author thereof: But as she was sometimes not well in her Senses, so this was not much regarded. In the mean while the Emperor took care to prevent all Disorders which might be occasioned by the Empress's Death, by reinforcing the Frontier Garisons, and doubling the Guards in other Places. The Empress having pretty well recover'd her Senses, sent for her five Children, *Comara Singastanne* Hereditary Prince of the Crown, and his two Brothers *Janiere Astanne* and *Lamait*, and the two Princesses *Mahadascyn* and *Hantan Adascyn*: She clasp'd them one after another with Tears in her Eyes, in her Arms, and kissing them, said, *See here, you dearest part of my own Flesh and Blood, your Mother that has brought you into the World, but must leave you in a little time.* Then she call'd to her the two before-mentioned Princes, unto whom she deliver'd her Children in these Words: *I now deliver to you the dearest Pledges I have; take care of them as of your own Eyes, and retaliate upon them the many Obligations you have received at our hands.* Then turning towards the Emperor, she told him, *You are the occasion of my Death.* Which so sensibly touch'd him (he loving the Empress extremely) that soon after it threw him into a violent Distemper. After that she scarce spoke to any body, except to the Prince of *Ouve*, unto whom she declared her Sorrow for having adored and sacrificed to the Pagan Idols, contrary to her better Knowledg, having been educated a Christian, telling him, that she saw the Devils ready to strangle her. The Prince of *Migonne* (upon whom she fix'd her Eyes all the while) answered her, *That the infernal Spirits had no Power over a Christian, provided they heartily repented of their Sins; that therefore she ought to rest satisfy'd, and to implore God's Mercy for her Soul, for Jesus Christ's sake.* She returned for answer, *I am a Christian, and would willingly pray, I desire you to pray with me.* The Prince of *Migonne* pray'd aloud, *Our Father*, and the 12 Articles of the Christian Creed: Unto which the Empress reply'd in *Portuguese*, *O Christi Ajuda mi! O Christ help me!* Soon after being carried back to *Welmantotte*, she spoke her last Words: *O my dear Princes and Princesses*, said she, *where must I leave you? My Lords*, (pointing to the Prince of *Mi-*

gonne

gonne and Prince of *Ouve*) *perform your Promises, farewel, I am departing; O God, take care of my Soul:* and so she expir'd the 20th of *July* 1613. in the 35th year of her Age, and was buried the 21st with the same Pomp, and in the same place as the Prince her Son was before.

Baldæus.

CHAP. XIV.

The Emperor falls very ill: Assembles the Estates. The Transactions of that Assembly.

The Emperor falls sick.

THE Emperor finding himself worse and worse, would needs be carried to a small City call'd *Dilege*, where he appointed the States of the Empire to meet *Aug.* 18. in order to settle the Succession of the Crown. The Members of this Great Assembly (according to the Schedule read to the King) were, *Idele*, King of *Cotiarum*; *Celle Wandaar*, King of *Palugam*; *Comaro Wandaar*, King of *Batecalo*; *Samarway*, King of *Panua*; *Namacar* the King of *Jafnapatnam's* Ambassador; *Coriwitte* Prince of *Ouve*; *Marcellus* Prince of *Migonne*; *Materael Hani*, Prince of *Velaren*; *Jalagode Rale*, Prince of *Catemale*; *Mewater Rale* Prince of *Mewater*; *Jane Sengati*, Prince and Lord of *Podere*; *Wiek Venesinge*, Earl of *Quatrecorle*; *Gael Heneraed*, Governour of the Earldom of *Harsipate*; *Corope*, Governour of the Earldom of *Odogodas*; *Kery Wanasegre*, Governour of the Province of *Matele*; *Attapatte* Governour of *Wluat Gamme*, and *Pasgrame Halvenrale* Governour of *Atapeli* and *Wilwele*; besides a great number of other Noblemen, unto whom his Imperial Majesty made the following Speech.

Assembles the Estates.

His Speech.

"My Lords; This present Assembly "being occasion'd by my Sickness (perhaps the fore-runner of my approaching End) I first of all desire you to "forgive me all Miscarriages I may have "committed, the same having been done "without my knowledg; and feeling "my self very feeble, and decaying in "Strength, I thought fit to take effectual "care about the Succession, to avoid "all Contests that might likely arise "after my Decease. You can't be forgetful what Disturbance arose in the "Empire after the Death of my Brother "*Vinne Ladarma Soria*, which ought to "serve us as a Caution to prevent the "same at this juncture, by committing the "Tuition of *Comara Singastdnne*, the eldest Hereditary Prince of the Crown, "to such as you shall judg best qualified "for so high a Trust, with a full Authority to manage the Administration of all publick Affairs during the "Prince's Minority, the Choice whereof "I recommend to your present Care. The Lords being not a little surpriz'd at this Proposition, gave in their Opinions in writing, wherein they pitch'd upon the Prince of *Migonne* and the Prince of *Ouve*, who both excused themselves, pleading their Inability, and desiring his Majesty to chuse some more able Persons in their steads. The Emperor reply'd sighing, *And are you then so backward in doing me this piece of Service? Can you be so forgetful of all the Obligations I have heap'd upon you?* They answer'd, that they were ready to sacrifice their Lives and Estates for his Majesty, but that they were afraid their Shoulders were too weak for so great a Burden. *Well then*, reply'd the Emperor, *we will leave the Choice to my Son the Prince*, wherewith the whole Assembly was satisfy'd. The Emperor then order'd the King of *Cotiarum* to bring in the Prince, which being done accordingly, he told him, *Son, make your Choice from among all these Kings and Princes of two Persons, such as you love best, who shall be Administrators of the Empire after my Death.* The Prince answer'd all in Tears, *Good Father! and will you die dear Father, pray don't leave me!* Which words drew Tears both from the Emperor and the whole Assembly. The Emperor answer'd, *I don't know how soon my time may come to leave you; wherefore I would have you pitch upon two Persons, such as you love best next to my self. Well then*, reply'd the Prince, *I love the Prince of* Migonne, *and likewise the Prince of* Ouve, *and next to him the Prince of* Velaren. *I am satisfied*, said the Emperor, *bring them to me, that I may surrender you to their Care.* Accordingly the Prince having led the two before-mentioned Princes to the Emperor, he told him, *These shall be my Governors now, and when come to Maturity my chief Counsellors.* The Emperor return'd for Answer, not without

Baldæus. without some Emotion, *My dear Son, see here your Father, whose Life perhaps will not be long; you are but young, therefore be always advis'd by these two Princes.* A Torrent of Tears which trickled down his Cheeks having stopt his Voice, he order'd himself to be carried out of the Assembly, enjoyning only in a few words all the Lords there present, to persist in their Fidelity, which they unanimously promised to do, and in token of their entire Submission, saluted the Emperor with the usual *Sambaje*, or Reverence, according to the Custom of that Country.

The next day the Royal Patent to invest the before-mentioned two Princes with the Administration of the Empire was read in the Assembly. *Cenuwieraat* by the Grace of God Emperor of *Ceylon*, King of *Candy*, *Settevaca*, *Trinquenemale*, *Jafnapatnam*, *Settecorles*, *Manaar*, *Chilaon*, *Panua*, *Batccalo*, *Palugam* and *Jaele*; Prince of *Ouva*, *Dennevaque*, *Passadon-Corle*, *Velaren*, *Coromale*, *Mewatre* and *Ventane*; Duke of *Willegamme*, *Cale*, *Ody* and *Jattenore*; Earl of *Quatre Corle*, *Harkepatte*, *Odegodascary*, *Craiwitty* and *Batagedre*. Peace to all those that read these Presents.

The Administrators of the Empire declar'd.

" Being much indisposed, and consequently in no small danger of Life, we " thought fit to convene all the Great " Men of the Empire to consult the " Welfare of the Publick, and of our " dearly beloved Son *Comara Singastan* " (whom God preserve) It is for this " reason that we have appointed two " Princes Administrators (after our decease) not only of the Empire, but " also of our Hereditary Prince during " his Minority, with full Authority to " govern the Realm; the two Princes " chosen for so great a Trust, being the " Prince of *Migonne* and the Prince of " *Ouve*, declar'd such by the unanimous " Consent of the Assembly. We do by " these Presents surrender to the said " Princes all our Kingdoms, Provinces " and Dominions, to be govern'd by " them, during the Minority of our " dearly beloved Sons; and as we are " very glad to have been able (in our " life-time) to prevent all Intestine " Commotions by this Settlement, so " we require and desire the two before-mentioned Princes to take upon them " the Government of all our Dominions till our Recovery, or, in case of " my Decease, till the Hereditary Prince " comes to an Age of Maturity, or his " Brothers, in case he should happen to " die before that time: We therefore " command by these Presents expresly, " that no body else shall presume to take " upon him the Administration and Tuition of the before-mentioned Princes " and Princesses, but shall obey the said " two Princes without the least opposition, under forfeiture of their Lives. " These two Princes shall take effectual " care of the Education of the young " Princes and Princesses under proper " Tutors, and to see the eldest Prince, " when come to Age, quietly settled in " the Throne; and in case of his Decease *Janiere Astan* to succeed, as after " him *Lamostanne*, the third is to be the " next Heir to the Crown; but in case " all the said Princes should die without Issue, our dearly beloved Daughter, the Princess *Mahadascyn*, and " after her her Sister, the Princess *Hanta* " *Madascyn*, shall succeed them in their " due turns. But in case these also should " leave no Children behind them, the " Empire shall devolve into your hands, " and you shall be at full liberty to chuse " with the unanimous Consent of the " Great Men of the Empire, such a Person of the Imperial Blood as you " think the best qualified for the Welfare of the Empire, which I leave to " the Wisdom of this Assembly. In " the mean while, every one (after my " Decease) shall be oblig'd to be accountable to the two Administrators for " all the Revenues of their respective " Lands without failure, upon pain of " Death and loss of their Estates. The " two Administrators shall have a due " regard for all such Counsellors as were " in our life-time, and not turn them " out, unless they should not behave " themselves as they ought to do, when " they shall have power to put others in " their places.

Settlement of the Empire.

" All Mandats shall be issued by the " two Administrators in the Name of " the whole Empire, and the Hereditary Prince; according to which all the " Great Men and Nobility, without exception, shall appear at Court when " requir'd, and obey them in all other " respects: They shall also be oblig'd " to take the usual Oath of Allegiance " to the Hereditary Prince, and his " two Administrators, and to promise " to persist in their Fidelity, and not to " suffer any Alliance or Engagement to " be made with our Enemies the *Portugueses*, or any Rebels, under what pretence soever. They shall be oblig'd " to assist in the reducing of all such

" (tho of the next Kindred) as pretend to disturb the publick Peace: " And lastly, all the Kings and Lords " shall take an Oath, that after our " Decease they will raise no Disturbance " in the Empire, but will submit quietly to the present Disposition, under " forfeiture of their Lives. For which " reason our Grant written in Golden " Letters, is to be deliver'd to the Princes " of *Migonne* and *Ouve*, pursuant to " which they shall have full Authority to " govern and protect in our and the " Hereditary Prince's Name our Dominions, and to administer Justice both " in Civil and Criminal Causes. We " therefore order and command all " Kings, Princes, Dukes, Earls, Clergymen, Nobles, Governours, and Heads " of Provinces and Cities, Captains, Presidents, Counsellors, Admirals, Chancellors, and all other Persons in our " Service, as Deputies, Administrators, " Farmers, Inhabitants, Souldiers, Citizens, and others inhabiting the Cities, " Villages, or any places whatever, all " and every one in particular, to receive " and acknowledg the before-mentioned " two Princes, Administrators and Governours of the Realm, till the Hereditary Prince came of Age, and to take " the Oath of Fidelity to them, and shew " them the same respect as to our own " Person, and, as becomes faithful and " true Subjects, to behave themselves in " all respects according to the true intent " of this Patent. We also annul by " these Presents all Laws or Constitutions which may seem contrary to the " true meaning thereof; and to give it " all the Authority and Weight that " can be, have in Conjunction with the " Hereditary Prince, and the Princes, " Dukes and Lords of this Assembly, " sign'd it with our own Hand, and order'd the Great Seal to be affix'd to " it. For the same reason we have also " commanded the same to be register'd " in all the Courts, Councils and Treasuries of our Empire, that no body " may plead Ignorance of this our last " Will. Dated at the Imperial Court " at *Digelege*, 19 Aug. 1613.

Baldæus.

CHAP. XV.

The Hereditary Princes are carried to Cockelecorle. Gale Heneraed *is routed, and being summoned to Court, is made Prisoner, and executed.*

The Emperor surrenders his Children to the Administrators.

THE said Patent being publish'd by his Imperial Majesty's order, the Administrators as well as the rest of the Estates took the Oath of Allegiance to the Hereditary Prince; which done, the Administrators upon their Knees return'd his Majesty thanks for the Honour he had bestow'd upon them, wishing him a long and happy Life. His Majesty lifting them up, order'd them to sit down by him, and disclosed to them some of his Treasures which were buried under ground, besides several other matters relating to the Administration of the State.

Then the three Princes and two Princesses being call'd in, he exhorted them to follow the Directions of their Governors; and taking the eldest Prince in his Arms, *My dearest Son*, said he, *I wish you and your Brothers and Sisters all imaginable Prosperity*: and then turning to the Princes of *Migonne* and *Ouve*; *Receive*, says he, *from my hands these my dearest Treasures, which I commit to your care*; and thus deliver'd them up to the two Administrators, who took care to have them convey'd in the night-time to the Dukedom of *Cockelecorle* for their better security, charging those who conducted them, upon their Lives not to divulge whither they were carried: which done, the Assembly was dissolv'd the 20th.

They are carried to Cockelecorle.

The *Portugueses* had no sooner notice of the Death of the Empress, and the Sickness of the Emperor, but they left no Stone unturn'd (notwithstanding the miscarriage of their Design upon *Panua*) to raise new Troubles. For this purpose they had found means to bring over to their side the Son of *Gael Heneraed* Governor of *Harcipate*, President in the Dukedom of *Cockelecorle*, who all along had supply'd them with Provisions at *Walane*, and had engag'd several of the Nobility to raise Divisions, thereby to give opportunity to the *Portugueses* to make themselves Masters of the Kingdom. The two Princes Administrators having got some notice of the matter, they resolv'd to find out the bottom of this Design. For this purpose the Prince of

Baldæus. of *Migonne* march'd the 15*th* of *September* at the head of a good Body, under pretence of changing the Garisons on the Frontiers, but near *Ode* and *Jatteno* met *Heneraed*'s Forces, who being not a little surpriz'd at the sight of the Prince, pretended they were order'd for *Cottamale* upon some particular business. The Prince being now more than ever confirm'd in the matter, order'd their chief Commander to be brought before him immediately, who being search'd, a Letter of *Gael Heneraed* was found about him, *viz. That all things look'd with a good face towards the accomplishment of the Design concerted betwixt them. That he had consulted with his Son* Abecque, *President of* Cockelecorle, *and that they had agreed with many of the Nobility to murder the Princes and Princesses, and likewise the Princes of* Migonne *and* Ouve, *the Issue whereof they should know as soon as it was put in Execution. He sent them in the mean time a certain quantity of Powder, Ball and Provisions, advising them to be upon their Guard, because the Garison of* Candy *had been reinforc'd considerably of late, which seem'd as if some Design were in hand against them.*

A Letter intercepted of Heneraed's.

The Prince gave immediate Orders to seize the Commander, who standing upon his Defence, was cut to pieces: his Soldiers and Pioneers attempted to save themselves by flight, but being pursued were most slain, except a few that sav'd themselves in the Woods. The Prince dispatch'd a Messenger immediately to the Governour with orders to come immediately to Court, having particular occasion to concert some Matters of moment with him.

Heneraed's Forces routed.

He is summon'd to Court.

He who knew nothing of what was passed, appear'd accordingly the 17*th* of *September* at the Court in *Candy*, where being well receiv'd by the Prince, they talk'd of several matters relating to the Government; upon which occasion he gave him repeated assurances of his Fidelity, telling him, that he was ready to venture his Life for the Welfare of the Empire. The Prince of *Migonne* had much ado to dissemble his Anger, only told him, *We have nevertheless received certain Advice that you hatch Treason against the Crown, and are enter'd into a Confederacy with the* Portugueses *our Enemies, contrary to the Oath you have so lately taken.* He declar'd his Innocence with many Asseverations, desiring that he might be confronted with his Accusers: Whereupon the Prince of *Ouve* told him, *We could wish you innocent, but are too well inform'd of your Treachery,* and so order'd him to withdraw (after some further Excuse) to be disarm'd, and his Person to be secur'd.

Is seiz'd.

The Captain of the Guard coming to seize him, he said, *Friend, you are wrong,* and so made the best of his way towards the Gate, in hopes of making his escape; but the Captain asking him, *Are you not the Governour* Gael Heneraed? he answer'd, *Yes.* The Captain reply'd, *Then I am not wrong, I beg your Pardon, being oblig'd to execute his Majesty's Orders:* So that seeing there was no hopes of escaping, he desir'd to be brought before his Majesty, or before the Princes Administrators. The Captain told him, that he had no such Orders; whereupon some of the Governour's Soldiers put themselves in a posture of Defence, but were all made Prisoners, and put to death the next day, being 32 in number. Another Party attempted to escape by night, but 50 of them were taken and committed to Prison, which made his case worse.

His Soldiers taken.

In the mean time the two Administrators took care to have the Emperor's Children transported to another Castle, and sent Orders to all the Governours to stop all the Soldiers of *Heneraed*, unless they were provided with a Pasport from his Majesty.

The Emperor's Children carried to another place.

The 22*d* *Heneraed* was examin'd in the Council, where at first he boldly deny'd every thing alledg'd against him, but soon after confess'd the whole, and beg'd Mercy, alledging, that what he had done was out of Discontent, because he had not been promoted to a higher Station. He did not deny that 26 Noblemen had been concern'd in this Conspiracy, yet refus'd to name them; but seeing the *Brahman*, who had made the first discovery, appear, he said, *No question but you will soon know their Names now, however I will not discover them.* The *Brahmans* declar'd, that *Gael Heneraed* had caused two Gentlemen to be murder'd, because they refused to have a hand in this Conspiracy. The 26 Noblemen being apprehended confess'd the Fact, and the 25*th* being appointed for their Trial, they were all condemn'd to Death. The 27*th* they were executed in the following manner: The 50 Soldiers who had endeavour'd to make their escape, had their Heads cut off. The 26 Noblemen, who had sign'd the Confederacy, had the Heads cut off first, and then their Bodies thrown before the Dogs. Four of his chief Counsellours were drawn with hot Pinchers, had afterwards their Hands cut off, and their Bodies

He is examined.

Tried and condemn'd, with 26 Gentlemen.

Their Execution.

Bodies quartered, which were hung up about the Castle. The unfortunate Governour, who had been a Spectator of the miserable Exits of his Accomplices, being likewise burnt with red hot Pinchers at each Corner of the Streets, was broken alive upon the Wheel, and afterwards thrown before the Elephants, one of which threw him up to a considerable height, and afterwards catching him again, crush'd him to pieces with his Teeth. The rest had the good Fortune to escape to *Columbo*. *Baldæus.*

CHAP. XVI.

A Battel betwixt the Emperor and the Rebels. The Portugueses *propose a Treaty of Peace, which is refused. They march towards* Candy, *but are routed.*

SOON after the Princes of *Migonne* and *Ouve*, together with the Earl of *Quatrecorle*, took a Progress to *Cockelecorle*, being followed by 2000 Men, and honourably received by the Inhabitants; they settled Matters upon the old Foot, and made some Alteration in the Coin, giving strict Orders not to raise the Mony above the prefix'd Value.

An Engagement betwixt the Emperor and Rebels. In the Year 1614. there happened a bloody Engagement betwixt the Imperial Forces and the Rebels, wherein 4000 Men being kill'd on both sides, and the last finding themselves too weak, retreated in the Night time, and sollicited the *Portugueses* for Help. The Emperor remaining thus Master of the Field, order'd his Camp to be strongly fortify'd; and keeping only 2000 Men, and 1000 Pioneers for his Guard, he sent his General with the whole Army to cut off the Retreat of the Enemy. The *Portugueses* having got notice thereof, gathered secretly a Body of 100 *Portugueses*, and 5000 Natives; and marching thro unpassable ways, surpriz'd the Outguards, and entred the Camp without much Opposition, every one seeking how to save themselves by a timely flight. *The* Portugueses *surprize the Emperor's Camp.* In this Action the Prince of *Migonne* was wounded with a Lance in his Right Leg, and the Prince of *Ouve* in the Right Arm, and 500 were slain upon the Spot on the Emperor's side.

Anno 1614. *March* 14. *Don Munno de Feriera*, Brother of the Earl of *Fere*, arriv'd at *Columbo*, in the Quality of Viceroy of *Goa*, to relieve *Don Jeronimo d' Oviedo*. He brought along with him about 132 *Portugueses*, besides a good number of *Mistices*, to reinforce the Garisons, with positive Orders to endeavour, if possible, to procure a Peace with the Emperor of *Ceylon*.

Pursuant to these Orders he sent the 3d of *June*, *Don Francisco de Menezes* his Envoy to *Candy*, with full Power to treat with the said Emperor upon the best Terms he could. *Proposes a Peace.* Accordingly the said Envoy delivered to the Emperor a Letter from the General, and another from the Viceroy of *Goa*, written in the King of *Spain*'s Name, the chief Contents whereof (besides some Compliments) were, "That his Catholick Majesty being averse to the Effusion of human "Blood, was inclined to enter into a "Treaty with his Majesty, in order to "settle a firm and lasting Peace; for "which purpose he had granted full "Power to certain Persons of Note to "treat upon that Head, desiring that "his Majesty would be pleased to accept "of them as such, and give them a favourable Reception. *Goa*, *Feb.* 22. 1614. *The King of Spain's Letter.* The General's Letter was much to the same purpose.

The Emperor having proposed the matter the 13*th* following in Council, it was resolved they should bring in their Propositions in Writing, which being done the 18*th* of the same Month, were as follows.

Articles proposed by him.

1. The King of *Spain* is willing to enter into an amicable Treaty with the Emperor.

2. The Peace to be concluded either for ever, or for a certain space of Years, to be kept inviolably, and all Hostilities to cease both by Water and Land immediately.

3. Each Party to keep what they are in possession of at present.

4. His Imperial Majesty shall renounce his Alliance with the *Dutch*, and engage himself never to enter into any other with them for the future, or any other State at Enmity with *Spain* and *Portugal*, and to permit no other *European* Nation to traffick there.

Baldæus.

5. Both Parties to be at Liberty to traffick in what Commodities they please, without entring into any Articles upon that Head.

6. His Majesty shall grant Liberty for the free Exercise of the *Roman* Catholick Religion in *Candy*, and the building a Church and Convent, with convenient Habitations for two or three hundred Persons, both of the Clergy and Laity.

7. His Majesty shall send one of his Hereditary Princes to keep his Court at *Columbo*, in lieu whereof they will send a Person of Quality to stay always near his Majesty.

8. His Imperial Majesty shall restore all the Jewels, Mony, Prisoners, Slaves of both Sexes, Cannon, *&c.* taken in the last War.

Are rejected. These Propositions being read and debated in the Council, it was resolved not to enter into any further Treaty with the *Portugueses*, as fearing not without reason, that some treacherous Design (as often had happened before) lay concealed under this pretended Treaty. An Answer was therefore return'd to the *Portuguese* Envoy, *Jun.* 20. That his Imperial Majesty was not inclined to treat with the King of *Spain*, before all the Lands and Lordships taken from him were restor'd: That however the *Spaniards* should remain in possession of *Gale* and *Columbo*, with the Territories thereunto belonging; but that his Imperial Majesty would by no means renounce his Alliance made with the *Dutch*, but keep the same inviolably. Furthermore his Majesty requir'd a full Compensation of all the Damages he had sustain'd in this War, and was resolved to have Custom paid him of all Goods exported or imported.

The Portugueses propose a Truce. The *Portugueses* finding them so resolute, would fain have made a considerable Abatement in their Pretensions; for which purpose they propos'd a Cessation of Arms, which being likewise rejected, the Envoy return'd the 8*th* of *June* without effecting any thing, with a Letter from the Emperour, directed to the *Porguese* General, containing in Substance, *That he was resolved not to violate his Oath with the* Dutch, *and that being sensible no Faith ought to be given to the* Portugueses, *he intended to pursue them by Force of Arms, and that they might make their account accordingly.*

The Portugueses march towards Candy. The *Portugueses* not a little exasperated at so resolute an Answer, march'd with an Army of 25000 Men towards *Candy*. The Emperor's Army consisted of 29000 Men, and meeting just near *Walane*, *Aug.* 6. a smart Engagement ensu'd, in which the *Portugueses* were worsted, 2100 *Indians* and 40 *Portugueses* being slain on their side, with the Loss of 700 Men on the Emperor's side. The *Portugueses* saved themselves from a total Defeat, by the favour of the adjacent Woods. *Are beaten.*

This Victory occasion'd no small Joy at *Candy*, where the Prince of *Migonne* and the Prince of *Ouve* who had led the Van, were receiv'd with more than ordinary respect. Soon after a Deserter came to *Candy*, who gave them an account of the whole condition of the *Portuguese* Camp, which might have been entirely ruin'd, had the *Cingaleses* pursu'd their Victory: He told them that before the Battel, they had not left above 300 Men at *Columbo*, which had occasion'd such Fears and Tumults in that City, that the same might have been easily surpriz'd with a moderate Force; and that upon the return of the General from the Army, he had order'd several to be hang'd upon that account.

The 29*th* of *Aug.* The Emperor declar'd, that he would marry the Daughter of the late Empress by her first Husband, alledging, that he had debauch'd her before, which made most of the Great Men consent to the Match; but the Prince of *Migonne* oppos'd the same, telling the Emperor with a great deal of Freedom, *That to commit Incest was directly contrary to the Word of God; and that for that reason he could never approve of it, but was obliged to put his Imperial Majesty in mind of his Salvation.* These Words having drawn Tears from the Emperor's Eyes, he promised to lay aside all Thoughts of that nature for the future, and to converse with her no otherwise than a Father might do with his Daughter. *The Emperor would have married his Daughter-in-law.*

The 5*th* of *Octob.* those of *Candy* defeated a Convoy of 900 *Portugueses*, that were marching with Provisions and Ammunition to *Candy*, but had not the same Success in another Enterprize; for having laid an Ambush of 500 Men, to intercept the *Portuguese* General, as he was coming from *Columbo* to *Walane*, the *Portugueses* having got Intelligence thereof, sent a stronger Body, which surrounded them, and cut them all to pieces, except two *Cingaleses*, who hid themselves among the Dead, till the Night gave them an Opportunity to make their Escape. *The Portugueses surprize 500 Candineses.*

Towards the end of the Year 1614. the Inhabitants of *Batecalo* having murder'd

Vol. 3. p. 698.

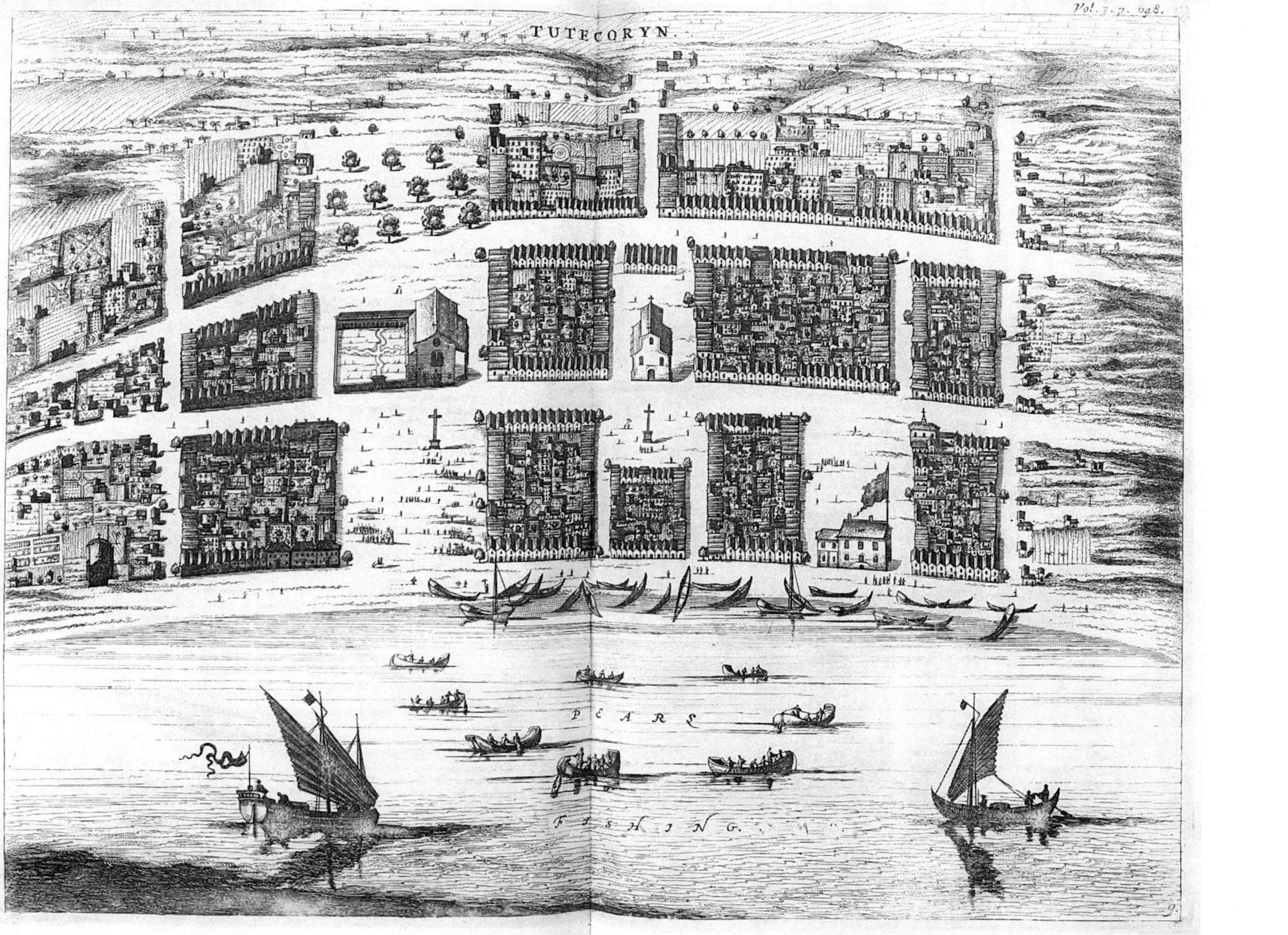

der'd the Ambassadors of the King of *Palugam* upon the Road, a furious War ensu'd betwixt them, in which the last worsted (with the assistance of the Prince of *Ouve*) the King of *Batecalo*, who was himself treacherously murdered, and his Kingdom bestowed upon the King of *Palugam*.

Baldæus.

CHAP. XVII.

Mr. Boschhouwer *sent as an Ambassador to the* United Provinces, *enters into an Engagement with the Crown of* Denmark, *dies in his Return to the* Indies. Gule Gedde *the* Danish *Commodore arrives in* Ceylon, *returns without effecting any thing. The* Portugueses *erect divers Fortifications by Fraud. The Emperor's Enterprize upon* Columbo. *The* Portugueses *beaten.*

MArcellus de Boschhouwer, who had (as we have understood) attained to the highest Dignities in the Empire of *Ceylon*, being desirous to make himself known by some great Enterprize, obtained leave from the Emperor 1615. to go to *Masulipatam*, to sollicite the so long promis'd Succours against the *Portugueses*, with full Power to enter into Alliances with all such Kings, Princes and States as he thought might contribute any thing towards clearing his Majesty's Dominions from the *Portugueses*.

Having for this purpose obtain'd divers Letters and Credentials, wherein his Majesty promis'd to ratify every thing the said Mr. *Boschhouwer* should treat of, with any Prince upon that Subject; he set out in Quality of Ambassador and Plenipotentiary from *Ceylon*, the 9th of *May* 1615. and arrived *Jun.* 2. at *Masulipatam*, where at that time one *Hans van Hase*, Director and Visitor General of the *Indies*, commanded in chief, who went along with *Marcellus de Boschhouwer* to *Bantam*, in order to concert measures with *Gerard Reynst*, the *Dutch* General there, concerning the intended Succours against the *Portugueses*.

Boschhouwer sent Ambassador.

But the said General being dead sometime before, and the War carried on at that time by the *Dutch* Company in the *Molucque* Islands and those of *Banda*, as also against *Poulo Ay*, hindring the *Dutch* at that Juncture from sending the promis'd Succours to the Emperor of *Ceylon* (it being absolutely requisite to secure the *Moluques*, before they cou'd think of any New Conquests) it was resolved by the Council of *Bantam* to permit Mr. *Boschhouwer* (at his earnest request) to go to *Holland*, in order to represent the true State of matters in the Empire of *Ceylon* to their High and Mightinesses the States-General, his Highness the Prince of *Orange*, and the Directors of the *East-India* Company.

Comes to Bantam.

But upon his Arrival in *Holland*, he found things not in any wise to answer his Expectation: for in regard of his Quality and high Station in *Ceylon*, pretending to much more Respect and Honour than the Company was willing to grant him; this occasion'd such Contests among them, that he resolved (notwithstanding his Allegiance due to the States) to go into *Denmark*, where he arriv'd *June* 16. O. S. 1617. and not long after entr'd into an Engagement with the *Danes* at *Copenhagen*, which was ratify'd by their King *Christian* IV. 1618. *March* 30. Accordingly he set sail from *Denmark* with his Lady (who challenged the Title of Princess of *Migonne*) and a Retinue of some Servants and Soldiers, but died before he came to the end of his Voyage, after which most of the Soldiers deserted on the Coast of *Coromandel* (where his Lady died also afterwards) whereby tho all his Designs vanished into Smoke, yet will it perhaps not be beyond our purpose, to give a more circumstantial account of this unfortunate Voyage.

And thence into Holland.

Engages with the Danes.

Sets Sail for Ceylon.

Dies.

Mr. *Boschhouwer* having (as we told you) obtain'd a Man of War and a Yacht from the King of *Denmark*, on account of the Emperour of *Ceylon*, and the *Danish East-India* Company (lately erected) having join'd five Ships with them, under *Gule Gedde* a *Danish* Nobleman, they set Sail out of the Sound, and after many Tempests and other Difficulties, having pass'd the *English* Channel, they did not arrive in *Ceylon* till twenty two Months after, *viz.* 1620. not without the Loss of a considerable Number of their Men (among whom was Mr. *Boschhouwer* himself) that perished for want of Provisions, and the Fatigues of so tedious a Voyage.

A particular account of his Voyage.

Some of these Ships arriving in the Harbour of *Batecalo*, others at *Coutjare*, *Gule Gedde* gave notice of his Arrival, and

The Danes arrive in Ceylon.

Baldæus. and of the Occasion thereof, as also of the Death of *Boschbouwer*, to the Emperor, who no sooner understood his Death, and that the *Danes* pretended to put the Equipment of this Squadron to his account, but he appeared much surpriz'd thereat, declaring that he had given no Authority to *Boschbouwer* to enter into such an Engagement; so that the *Danes* had nothing but bare Words, in recompence of the vast Charge they had been at upon this account.

The Emperor rejects their Offer.

The *Danish* Commodore *Gule Gedde*, finding himself thus disappointed in all his hopes, apply'd all his Thoughts, how to reimburse the King his Master part of the Charge he had been at in the Equipment of this Squadron; for which reason he seiz'd upon all *Boschbouwer*'s Effects aboard his Vessels, after having taken care of his Burial, which was perform'd with little Pomp; but that of his Son of three Years of Age (who being born at *Copenhagen*, was Godson of K. *Christian* IV. and died likewise in this Voyage) was done with more Solemnity. The seizing of *Boschbouwer*'s Effects being perform'd in the Harbour of *Trinquenemale* by *Gule Gedde*, he sent his Widow at her request to *Candy*, stript of every thing, except what she had saved privately by the assistance of some Friends, from whence after a stay of seven Years, she was by the Emperor *Zenerat* (at the request of General *Roland Crape*) sent with some Servants to *Tranquebare*.

The Danish *Commodore seizes* Boschhouwer's *Effects.*

After the Departure of *Boschbouwer*'s Widow for *Candy*, the Commodore *Gule Gedde* set Sail with part of his Squadron from *Coutjare*, in order to join the rest of his Ships at *Batecalo*, and to sollicite once more Satisfaction from the Emperor; but in the mean while, one of his Ships that was left at *Trinquenemale* being seized upon by the Ships Crew, and afterwards split upon the Rocks, the Seamen and Soldiers got with their Boats to the Coast of *Coromandel*, where some of them took Service among the *Portugueses* at St. *Thomas*, the rest among the *Dutch* at *Paliacatte*. *Gule Gedde* having but small hopes of Success, and fearing that some of the other Ships might follow their Example, thought fit to weigh Anchor, and take his next course for *Denmark*.

Returns to Denmark.

The *Portugueses* being infinitely glad at the Departure of these unwelcome Guests out of *Ceylon*, now bent all their Thoughts how to exclude all other Nations from the Traffick of that Country: To encompass which, they judged it the most proper means to erect a Fort near that Harbour, the Place whereof (after a narrow View taken of the Ground, and various Debates) was pitch'd upon at the North-West Point of the Bay, upon a Neck of Land jetting out into the Sea, on the back-side of the *Pagode* of *Trinquenemale*, the Walls whereof would be of considerable Advantage to them.

Accordingly the said Fort being begun 1622. was carried on with all imaginable Vigour, to bring it to perfection, before the Emperor of *Candy* (with whom they were at Peace then) could have any notice of it. For no sooner was that Prince advertis'd of this treacherous Design, but he protested against it, and sent a considerable Force to demolish it; but being repuls'd by the *Portugueses*, these continu'd the Fortifications, being an irregular Triangular Fortress, which they furnish'd with great Cannon taken out of the Sea, belonging formerly to the *Danish* Ship that was cast away near that Place.

The Portugueses erect a new Fort.

Whilst the *Portugueses* were embroil'd with the *Cingaleses* upon that account, a certain *Radye* of the *Malabars* entred the Kingdom of *Jafnapatnam* with a considerable Force, in hopes to recover the same from the *Portugueses*, who had lately conquer'd the same: But *Philippo d' Olivere* their General, an old experienc'd Captain, receiv'd them so bravely, that few of them return'd into their Native Country.

Rout the Malabars.

The *Portugueses* having thus once more rid their Hands of their Enemies, yet not thinking themselves secure, unless they strengthen'd their Conquests by some additional Fortifications, order'd certain new Works to be made, which afterwards were chang'd into a Royal Fortress with four Bastions. The Foundation whereof was laid 1624, but not brought to perfection till the Year 1632, being lin'd with white Stone.

Build two more Forts.

But to establish themselves the better in this Island, they concluded a Peace (by the Mediation of certain Clergymen) with the Emperor, who was willing to embrace it, till he could find a more convenient Opportunity of revenging himself for the many Affronts they had put upon him; one of the main Conditions of this Peace was, that the *Portugueses* should not build any other Forts or Fortifications in any Place of the Empire, but might remain in possession of what they had at present.

Make Peace with the Emperor.

Notwithstanding this Agreement, which was so advantageous to the *Portugueses*, *guefes*, finding that the *European* Nations had ftill a free accefs into the Kingdom of *Candy* by the River *Palliagamme* (otherwife call'd *Batecalo*) they were contriving all poffible means to fecure that Paffage to themfelves.

Contrivance of the Portugueses.

To accomplifh their end with all imaginable Secrecy, they pitch'd upon a *Miftice*, an experienc'd Engineer, who being of a dark Colour, was fent in the difguife of a *Gufuratte Jogy*, or *Mendicant Frier*, from *Columbo* to *Batecalo*, who fettled himfelf in the Village of *Samanture*; from whence having taken a full view of all the circumjacent Country for two years together, he pitch'd upon a fandy Place about 2 ½ Leagues from the Village, for the erecting of the defigned Fort; but finding upon ftrict enquiry, that the Channel leading that way from the Mouth of the River, was the greateft part of the Year chok'd up with Sand, and that confequently there would be no conveniency of getting frefh Water there, he was forc'd to go about 6 Leagues lower down the River, where meeting with a fmall Ifle of a League in circuit, and not above a Mile diftant from the main Channel, convey'd thither directly from the Mouth of the River, he returned to *Columbo*; and having given a full account to the Government there of the advantageous Situation of this Ifle for their intended Project, the *Portuguefes* fent him back in 1627. with 13 Companies of Soldiers, in order to put it in execution. Thefe, at their arrival, having fecured themfelves by throwing up fome Intrenchments inclos'd with Palifadoes, to work they went with all expedition to perfect the intended Fortrefs, which was of a Quinquangular Figure, with three Baftions.

The Cingaleses are repuls'd.

The King of *Candy* had no fooner intelligence thereof, but he fent a good Body of Troops thither to prevent their Defign: They made fhift to land in the Ifland, but were forc'd to retreat without effecting any thing, and leave the *Portuguefes* to perfect their Fortifications, which they did foon after, being well provided with all forts of Materials for fuch a Purpofe.

The Emperor engages with the Cingaleses at Columbo.

The Emperor finding himfelf thus by no lefs than feven Capital Forts, built on all the beft Avenues of the Ifle, reduc'd to fuch Straits by the *Portuguefes*, that without their Confent he was not in a condition to keep the leaft Correfpondence with any foreign Nation, refolved to try his utmoft to draw thefe Thorns out of his Flefh. For this purpofe he thought fit to try the Inclinations of the *Cingalefes* inhabiting at *Columbo*; and finding them ready to revolt by reafon of the many Indignities received from the *Portuguefes*, he engaged them to his Party. Things being thus fettled, the only thing remaining was how to entice their General *Conftantine de Saa* to take the Field, by which means they might find an opportunity of going over to the Emperor. Knowing therefore that *Don Michael de Noronha*, *Conde de Linharos*, the then Viceroy of *Goa*, had lately wrote an affronting Letter to the faid General, wherein he told him, that he was more fit for a Merchant than a Soldier, and that he regarded more his own Profit than the King's Glory, and his Conqueft; they infinuated into him, that fince both his Expeditions againft *Candy* had prov'd unfuccefsful, it would not be amifs (to retrieve his Honour) to try his Fortune againft *Ouve*, promifing to appear in the Field with all their Power, which they did accordingly.

Baldæus.

Conftantin de Saa the *Portuguefe* General was fo highly pleas'd at this Propofition, that he not only gladly embraced it, but alfo fent a Challenge to *Comarre Singe Haftanne*, Prince of *Ouve*, eldeft Son of the Emperor *Zenerat Adafcyn*, who fent him word, that he would expect his coming like a Man of Honour. Accordingly the *Portuguefe* General took the Field the 30th of *Auguft*, with 1300 of his own Countrymen, 1700 *Miftices*, and 8000 *Cingalefes*; and the Prince of *Ouve* being join'd by his two Brothers, *Vyfiapalla* and *Raja Singa*, made up an Army of 23000 men, who (according to the Advice of the Emperor their Father) kept at a diftance, feeming to avoid an Engagement. The *Portuguefes* being much furprized at their being fuffer'd to pafs the Mountains of *Ouve* without the leaft Oppofition, march'd directly to *Badule* the Capital City of that Dukedom, which they took and plunder'd with all the circumjacent Country, and fo retired again towards the Mountains, the Princes being all the while Spectators of their Ravages, with a refolution to watch their opportunity of taking a fevere Revenge, fo foon as the *Cingalefes* (according to their Promife) fhould defert the *Portuguefes*.

The Portugueses take the Field.

Plunder Badule.

Thefe things were not fo fecretly carried on, but that *Conftantin de Saa* got fome fcent of the matter. This made him fummon before him all their chief Officers, unto whom he reprefented the Reafons of his Sufpicion, but in very obliging Terms, thinking it his beft way to

Baldæus. to dissemble, yet to use all imaginable Precautions against them. They positively denying what was alledged against them, he continu'd his March till Night, when finding the Enemy to keep closer to him than they us'd to do, and being confirmed in his former Suspicion by fresh Intelligence, he order'd the *Cingaleses* (contrary to what they us'd to do) to pitch their Tents in the Center of the Camp, and the next morning with break of day for the whole Army to set fire to all their Baggage (except wearing Apparel) the better to further their March. They had scarce marched a few hours, when the Princes coming up pretty close with the *Portuguese* Army, the 8000 *Cingaleses* joined with their Countrymen, and with their joint Forces attack'd them in the Flank at the Descent of a Mountain, firing upon them very furiously thro an adjacent Wood, whereabouts a great number of the *Portugueses* were slain, the *Cingaleses* falling in Pell mell among them with their Scymeters and Pikes, especially after a sudden Storm had rendred the *Portugueses* Firelocks almost useless, without which they might probably have made a tolerable good Retreat. *Constantin de Saa* their General had his Head cut off by one of the rebellious *Cingaleses*, which he presented to *Raja Singa* upon a Drum, whilst he was washing himself in a neighbouring Brook. To confess the Truth, *de Saa* deserv'd a much better Treatment, both in respect of his Valour, and the many good Offices he had done to the same *Cingaleses* at *Columbo*, who now so basely betray'd him and his whole Army.

Are attacked in their March.

And routed.

It is not easy to be imagin'd what a consternation this general Defeat occasion'd among the *Portugueses* in the Isle of *Ceylon*, and especially at *Columbo*, for the defence whereof there were scarce any Troops left behind, except a few of the most antient among the Inhabitants. This encouraged the Emperor to send his youngest Son *Mahastanne* (afterwards named *Raja Singa*) to form the Siege of that Place, which he did accordingly; but was so bravely received by *Lancerotte de Sesies* their Governour, that after a whole Month's Siege, he was forced to retreat without effecting any thing. The Besieged being afterwards reinforced from *Goa* with 400 men (among whom were 300 *Caffers*) with a considerable quantity of Provisions, Ammunition, and other Necessaries, began to hold up their heads again, and bid defiance to the *Cingaleses*.

Columbo *besieged by the* Cingaleses.

CHAP. XVIII.

The Emperor dies. Intestine Divisions betwixt his two Sons. The Portugueses *at War with the new Emperor; make Peace with him. The* Hollanders *invited by his Majesty's Letter to the Governour of* Paliacatta, *to come into the Isle of* Ceylon.

The old Emperor dies.

SOON after, *viz.* 1632. the old Emperor happening to die, left the Empire betwixt his three Sons, viz. *Ouve* to *Commarra Singa Hastanne* his eldest Son, *Matele* to *Visia Palla Hastanne* his second, and *Candy* to *Mahastanne* the youngest, who besides this assum'd the Imperial Title under the Name of *Raja Singa Adascyn*, to the no small dissatisfaction of his eldest Brother *Commarra Singa Hastanne*, whom he knew so well how to amuse under different Pretensions, that the matter remained undecided as long as he lived; and immediately after his Death seized upon the Province of *Ouve*, which *Visia Palla* the second Brother (who claimed one half for his Share) took so heinously, that Matters came betwixt them to an open Rupture.

The youngest Son seizes upon the Imperial Title.

The *Portugueses* having by this time received divers Supplies from *Goa*, and pretty well recover'd of their late Disgrace, resolved to improve this Opportunity to their advantage. For which purpose entring the *Low-Lands*, they forced most of the Princes there to side with them, but durst not venture to attempt the Passage of the Mountains. They pitch'd their Tents therefore near *Allago*, as the most proper Place to keep the adjacent Country in awe: But *Raja Singa* the new Emperor surpriz'd them in their Camp, and forc'd them to retreat with all haste to *Columbo*.

The Portugueses begin a War against the Emperor.

Are beaten.

The *Portugueses* now finding themselves unable to cope with the Emperor, thought it requisite to come to an agreement; for which purpose having sent their Envoys to *Candy*, a Peace was concluded accordingly, but soon broken again on the

Make Peace.

the *Portuguese* side, who let slip no opportunity to improve their advantage, notwithstanding the said Peace.

Raja Singa being thus fully convinc'd, that no firm Peace was likely to be settl'd with the *Portugueses* in *Ceylon*, dissembled his Resentment, but in the mean time resolved to invite the *Hollanders* to force them out of the Isle; and accordingly sent the following Letter dated *Sept.* 9. 1636. to the Governour of *Paliacatta*.

The Dutch *invited into* Ceylon *by the Emperor's Letter.*

" I *Raja Singa*, Emperor of the Isle of " *Ceylon*; King of *Candy*, *Settevaca*, " *Danbadany*, *Anorayapore*, *Jasnapatnam*; Prince of *Ouve*, *Mature*, *Dinavaca*, *Quatrecorle*; Great Duke of " *Settecorle*, *Matalte*; Earl of *Catajar*, *Trinquenemale*, *Batecalo*, *Valefebuitena*, *Dumbra*, *Panoa*, *Patoveta*, " *Putelaon*, *Vassare*, *Gale*, *Billigaon*; " Marquess of *Duramira*, *Ratenura*, " *Tinipane*, *Axcepaon*; Lord of the " Ports of *Alicaon*, *Caleture*, *Columbo*, *Negombo*, *Chilao*, *Madampe*, " *Calpentyn*, *Ariputure*, *Manaar*, and " of the Pearl-Fishery.

" THO I don't question but that " Fame has already made known to " you the good Success of our Arms against the *Portugueses*, yet did judg it " absolutely requisite to give a more particular account thereof to the Governour of the Fortress of *Paliacatta*. " First of all the Emperor did regain " from the *Portugueses* the two Fortresses " of *Walane* and *Forago*, as likewise the " City of *Marua Goma*, with 500 *Portuguese* Inhabitants, and a good number " of Monks of divers Orders. *Don Nuno* " *Alvares Perere* being then their General, thought thereupon fit to make " Peace in order to recover the Prisoners taken by the Emperor's Forces. About eleven Years after the Conclusion " of the said Peace *Constantine de Saa* " being made their General, did treacherously surprize *Jasnapatnam*, and " built the Forts of *Batecalo* and *Trinquenemale*, giving no other reason for their " so doing to the Emperor, than that " having certain Intelligence, that some " of their *European* Enemies were coming to settle there, they were forc'd " to erect these Fortifications for their " own defence. About a year after the " Frier they had left their Hostage at " *Candy*, being releas'd by the Emperor " (according to his Parole) they made a " powerful Irruption into the Empire: " and after their Retreat the Emperor " happening to die, I had scarce ascended " the Throne, but within eleven Months " after they made another Incursion; but " encountring them near *Ambatana*, we " forced them to retreat with considerable Loss. Seven Months after they " invaded the Dukedom of *Ouve*, where " we routed them in a smart Engagement; and the rebellious Natives having deserted them, and joined with us " (according to their Duty) compleated " our Victory: Their General, a Major " General, and the Governour of *Dinavaca*, being slain upon the spot, with " 400 Soldiers; and their Colonel of the " Artillery, their Governour of the seven *Corles*, and *Matura*, with 300 Soldiers, many Captains and Ensigns, taken " Prisoners. Since that time we took " the Fort of *Mantea Ravane* with 100 " *Portuguese* Soldiers with their Captains, " and another Fort in *Sofragaen*, with " three Companies, besides that two other Fortifications of theirs were demolished. It was much about the same " time that I kept the City of *Columbo* " invested for 30 days; but finding my " self ill, I returned to *Candy*, leaving the " Command of my Forces to *Mara Tana* " *Wandaar*, who within 15 days after " my departure retreating thence, thereby gave an opportunity to the Enemy " to protract the War for a Year and " half, and afterwards deserted in Person to the Enemy. I did also fall into " the Enemies Dominions, and having " entrench'd my self near *Ganetena* in the " four *Corles*, I did considerable Mischief, " so that the new Governour of *Columbo* " *Diego de Melo de Castro* (formerly Governour of St. *Thomas*) sent thither " from *Goa*, was forc'd to sue for Peace, " which I granted to prevent the Miseries and Calamities of a long War; " the said General having sworn by the " Name of his God, and in his King's " stead, to deliver up the Forts of *Trinquenemale* and *Batecalo*, and to release " all Prisoners on both sides. Thirteen " Months after the conclusion of this " Peace, the Governour of *Batecalo* did " side with certain Rebels, in order to " assassinate one of my Governours, aiding and assisting them also in robbing a " Bark belonging to me, and committing divers treacherous Acts in many " Parts, as well of our own Kingdoms, " as those of other *Indian* Princes; therefore I have taken a resolution to rid my " hands of these Enemies, and to declare " my self a Brother in War with the " King of the *Hollanders*, as long as the

Baldæus.

" Sun

Baldæus.

"Sun and Moon shall rejoice us with their "Light, and the Viceroy of *Jacatra*, "and the Governor of *Paliacatta* shall "be willing to assist me, in hopes that "this Confederacy with the *Dutch* Na-"tion will answer my good Intentions "and Sentiments of them. I the King "let the Governour of *Paliacatta* know, "that, during the seven years since my "Accession to the Throne, I have made "the best enquiry I could, who was the "most Potent King in *Europe*, in order "to oppose the Designs of the *Portu-"gueses:* And being at last inform'd that "the King of the *Hollanders* was not "only a Scourge to their King, but also "supported by the Strength and Power "of several other Kings his Confede-"rates, I took a firm Resolution (re-"lying upon the Fidelity of the Gover-"nor of *Paliacatta*) to declare my self "a Brother in War to the King of the "*Hollanders* as long as Sun and Moon "shall continue in the Firmament. 'Tis "true, some Treaties of this kind have "been made formerly betwixt my Pre-"decessors and the Viceroy of *Jacatra*, "and the Governor of *Paliacatta*; but "these having prov'd ineffectual, it "seems as if it had pleased God to bring "the same Perfection under my Reign, "in hopes that the Governor of *Palia-"catta* will with all possible care second "our Endeavours, whereof we give "him Assurances upon our Royal Word, "that they shall be at liberty to erect a "Fortress either at *Cotiar* or *Batecalo*, "for which purpose they may employ a "Squadron of five Ships (a Force suf-"ficient to ballance the present Strength "of the Enemy) who may be secure of our "Assistance, either by my self in Person, "or by my Brother. All the Cannon or "Booty taken by them shall be at their "own disposal, and they shall be provi-"ded with all sorts of Materials requi-"site for the building of a Fort either "at *Batecalo* or *Cotiar*. I further engage "my self by my Royal Word, to repay "the Governor all the Charges he shall "be at in equipping the said Squadron "to be sent to my Assistance, to which "of the before-mentioned Harbors you "please. If the Governor approves of "these Propositions, let him send a Vessel "to *Trinquenemale* or *Cotiar*, in order to "transport my Ambassadors with safety "to him, whom I would have rest se-"cure, that in case he can bring this "business to Perfection, he shall be well "rewarded for his Service according to "his Dignity and Merits: But if it be "beyond his power, let him dispatch "this Messenger with all speed to the "Viceroy of *Jacatra*.

Dated the 9th of *Sept.* 1636. *Raja Singa*, Imperador.

A certain *Brahman* being dispatch'd with this Letter, the same liv'd for six months undiscover'd among the *Portugueses* at *Jafnapatnam*, before he could meet with a conveniency to be transported to the Coast of *Coromandel*, from whence he pursued his Journy by Land to *Paliacatta*, where he delivered *Raja Singa's* Letter to the then Governor *Charles Reyniers*.

CHAP. XIX.

A Treaty, and Letter in return of that of the Emperor's. The Dutch *Deputies in* Ceylon *are honourably receiv'd. Their Transactions, and Return with the the Emperor's Ambassadors. The* Portugueses *endeavour to render the* Dutch *suspected. The Emperor's Answer to the* Dutch *Admiral.*

CHarles Reyniers the Governor of *Paliacatta* (afterwards General of the *Indies*) had no sooner receiv'd this Letter, but he sent the same to *Batavia* to the General and Great Council of the *Indies*, who after mature deliberation resolv'd to send a Person fitly qualified for such a Trust aboard the *Falcon* Yacht in order to enter into a strict Amity and Commerce with the Emperor, and to procure a considerable Cargo of Cinnamon; whereof immediate notice was also to be given to the *Dutch* Fleet before *Goa*.

Resolution of the Council of the Indies.

It is to be observ'd, that sometime before this Letter was brought to *Batavia*, the General *Anthony van Diemen*, and the Council of the *Indies*, had already taken the Affairs of *Ceylon* into their Consideration, having order'd the beforesaid Mr. *Reyniers* to make all possible Enquiry, whether it were not feasible to get some share as well as the *Portugueses* in in the Cinnamon Trade. One *John Thijssen* a Master of a Vessel (afterwards Governour of *Malacca*, and now a Member of the Council of the *Indies*) who had bin a Prisoner in *Ceylon*, having also lately given the said Council an exact account of the Condition of the Isle, it was resolv'd 1637. to send him forthwith with three Yachts, the *Falcon*, the *Voorburgh*, and the *Lesser Hollandia*, and the *Ruttem* Frigot, to the Coast of *Coromandel*; where coming to an Anchor before *Paliacatta* the last day of *August*, and their Commissions being open'd, he was, in conjunction with the Factor *Andrew Helmont*, constituted Envoy to the Emperor of *Ceylon*.

Dutch Envoys sent to Ceylon.

Accordingly the 21*st* of *October* they took their way towards *Tegnapatnam*, where having furnish'd themselves with two Negroes (acquainted with that Country) they set sail for *Ceylon*, where they arriv'd within five or six days after, and cast Anchor near the Village of *Calmony* or *Calarme*, about seven Leagues from the *Cabo de Fradres*, i. e. the *Monks Cape*. They sent immediately one of the two before-mentioned Negroes ashore, to get intelligence what part of the Country they were in; which being done by a certain Signal (a Fire made upon an adjacent Hill) they sent him after his return, in Company of the other Negro, with a Letter of Recommendation from the Factor *Chrimma* to the Emperor of *Ceylon*, under promise that they were to return in 16 days, which they did accordingly, bringing along with them not only certain Hostages, and among them a certain *Hollander*, who living at the Emperor's Court, was willing to accompany them, and gave them very good Intelligence, but also the Lord High-Treasurer of his Majesty, and *John Alberts* another *Dutch*-man, a Native of *Embden* (who having deserted from Mr. *Anthony Caens* Ship, had since serv'd the Emperor in the quality of a Court-Martial) in order to conduct our Envoys to the Imperial Court.

Accordingly they set out on their Journy from the Village of *Samanture*, and in four days arriv'd at *Pangergame* in the Country of *Vintane*, where they were introduc'd the same night by the Light of Torches into the Emperor's Presence, who then kept his Residence at one of his Pleasure-houses on the other side of the River *Mavilgange*. Their Reception was very magnificent, as will appear anon by the Entertainment given to Mr. *Gerard Hulft*, whereof we shall have occasion to give a move ample Description. The Credential Letters written by the Governour of *Paliacatta*, and deliver'd by the Envoys to his Imperial Majesty, were as follows.

Have Audience of the Emperor.

Baldæus.

To the most Potent Emperor *Raja Singa*, &c.

Most Potent Emperor!

Letter from the Governour of Paliacatta to the Emperor of Ceylon.

"GOD protect your Imperial Majesty! Your Majesty is not ignorant of the long and tedious Wars we have for so many years last past carried on (by the Blessing of God) with good success both in *Europe* and the *Indies* against the King of *Spain* and *Portugal*, and how at this time we keep *Goa*, their chief City in the *Indies*, block'd up with so numerous a Squadron of Men of War, that they are not in a Condition to relieve any of their Subjects from thence. We have understood by your Majesty's Letter the many Outrages, Insolencies, Treasons and Wars carried on by the *Portugueses* against your Majesty since their Settlement in your Territories, contrary to the Engagements, Treaties and Confederacies made betwixt you and them; all which they have treacherously broken, in order to make themselves Masters of your Empire, and to impose the most miserable Slavery upon your Subjects. Our General of *Jacatra* being inform'd of these Designs, and your Majesty's most commendable Intentions to free your Country from such unwelcome Guests, and to secure your Subjects against all Violences, by sweeping out the very Remnants of the *Portugueses*: The General, I say, being extremely rejoic'd at this Resolution, and more especially that your Majesty desired our Assistance, did give immediate Orders for the dispatching of these Envoys, to treat with your Majesty, and to declare to you the sincerity of our Intentions towards your Majesty and your Subjects, in the same manner as the Effects thereof have been sufficiently approv'd by many of your Neighbouring Princes and Nations. If your Majesty will be pleased to allow us the Exportation of some Cinnamon, we oblige our selves to assist your Majesty with Musquets, Powder, Ammunition, and other Arms; so that in case you will order two or more Ships Cargo's of Cinnamon to be got ready for our use against *May*

Baldæus.

" next, we either will pay ready Mony " for it, or exchange the same for Ammunition or other Merchandizes, as " your Majesty shall think fit. So soon " as our Envoys are assur'd of your Majesty's Resolutions upon this Head, and " of your Intentions to enter into a further Treaty with us, they shall (according to orders) set sail immediately to our Fleet before *Goa*, to confer " with the Admiral how soon and how " many Ships may be detach'd out of his " Fleet, either for the Transportation " of the Cinnamon, or your Majesty's " Aid, according to the present Exigency " of Affairs. We desire therefore your " Majesty to give these Envoys, sent with " a most sincere Intention to your Majesty, a sutable Reception, and a favourable Audience; and afterwards " to dispatch them with all convenient " speed, to further their arrival at our " Fleet before *Goa*, before the *Mousson* " be passed, which otherwise might " prove no small Obstacle to our Design. " We acknowledg we ought to have presented your Majesty with some Foreign " Rarities (according to Custom) but " being ignorant of the Condition of " your Country, and in no small fear " that these Envoys might perhaps be detain'd by the *Portugueses*, we hope your " Majesty will excuse the same for this " time. We pray, most Potent Emperor, that God may grant your Majesty " Health, Prosperity, and Victory over " your Enemies.

Dated in the Fort *Geldria*, the 20*th* of *Octob.* 1637.

Subscribed,

Your Majesty's most devoted Servant,

Charles Reyniers.

Transactions of the Envoys.

The Emperor, whilst the Envoys were making their Propositions, stood with the Crown on his Head, and a Scymeter in his Hand, his Head, Arms and Legs adorn'd with Jewels, Rings and Chains of Gold. He enquired after the State of Affairs in *Holland*, the Health of the Prince of *Orange*, and whether the Envoys had a full Power to treat with him; unto which they answer'd, No, but that the Admiral of the *Dutch* Squadron before *Goa* had: So they were conducted to the Apartments prepar'd for their Reception, to rest themselves after so fatiguing a Journy.

The next day being again admitted into the Emperor's Presence, he ask'd them several Matters concerning the present state of Affairs in *Europe*: The *Portugueses* having made it their business to represent the *Dutch* as an inconsiderable *Mob*, and the Emperor nevertheless having by the great Naval Strength that appear'd of late years in the *East-Indies* conceived a quite different opinion of their Strength than what had been whisper'd about by the *Portugueses*, was very glad to find the Truth to prove agreeable to his former Sentiments concerning the Power of a Nation, with whom he was going to enter into a strict Confederacy against the *Portugueses*. The next following day they began to enter upon a Treaty about the Cinnamon, and the Fort of *Batecalo*. Whilst his Majesty held frequent Conferences (twice a day for a whole Week) with our Deputies, a Letter was sent to the King or Prince of *Mateli* (the Emperor's Brother) by *Diego de Melo de Castro*, Governour of *Columbo*; wherein he complained *of the intended Breach of the Peace, stiling the* Hollanders *rebellious Subjects of the King of* Portugal, *who had incur'd the Hatred of all the other* Indian *Princes.* He added, *That the Emperor was guilty of this Rupture whereof he had given notice in a Letter to the Viceroy of* Goa. His Majesty desir'd that the said Letter should be translated into the *Dutch*, and be deliver'd by the Envoys to the Admiral before *Goa*; and told them for the rest, that he was too well acquainted with their ways, to give Ear to these Calumnies: That he would endeavour to amuse them with Compliments, till he could find an opportunity of surprizing the Fort of *Mankewarc* in the *Low-Countries* near the South Shore of the Isle. He writ also a Letter to the Admiral *Westerwold*, and order'd three Deputies to go along with our Envoys to take a view of the Fleet before *Goa*, and to give an account thereof to him.

The Portugueses *endeavour to render the* Dutch *suspected.*

The Emperor's Courtesy to the Dutch.

The 27*th* of the same Month his Majesty thought fit to dispatch the Envoys: *Palankyns* or Litters were order'd for their Journy, with some Elephants for their Baggage, and a Convoy of 20 *Lascaryns*, under the Command of a Colonel to conduct them, with orders to defray their Charges in all places through which they passed. It was further remarkable, that whilst the Governour of *Paliacatta*'s Letter was deliver'd to his Majesty, and the Envoys made their Propositions, he arose from his Chair, and remain'd standing all the while, an Honour never done to the *Portugueses*. The *Dutch* Envoys set sail the 4*th* of the next following

Their honourable Dispatch.

* Month

Month of *December*, with the three before-mention'd Deputies aboard the *Falcon* Yacht, and coming up the 19*th* following with the *Dutch* Squadron before *Goa*, they deliver'd to *Adam Westerwold* their Admiral, the following Letter from his Imperial Majesty.

Letter of the Emperor to the Dutch *Admiral.*

"HAving sent a Letter in *September* "to the Governour of *Paliacatta*, I "receiv'd an Answer thereupon the 19*th* "of *Novemb.* 1637. but the Envoys not "being instructed sufficiently to treat "with me, but the same being referr'd "by the General of *Jacatra* to the Admi-"ral of the Fleet, I thought fit to send "certain Deputies to treat with your "Excellency. The before-mentioned "Governour having made mention also "of the Transportation of a certain quan-"tity of Cinnamon, your Excellency if "you please may send five Men of War "to attack the Fort of *Batecalo*, and some "other Vessels to other Harbours, in or-"der to take in all the Cinnamon that "is to be had there. I am inform'd that "you intend to stay before *Goa* till *April* "next, and then are to return to *Jacatra*, "in order to return afterwards with all "possible speed to the Harbour of *Co-*"*lumbo*, and from thence to detach three "Ships to the Harbour of *Batecalo*, in "order to make themselves Masters of "that place. I will at the same time ad-"vance with my Forces to *Columbo*; and "in case God be pleased to bless our "Arms with Victory against our Ene-"mies, I dare assure you upon my Royal "Word, that the City shall be preserv'd "for our mutual use, and that we will "enter into a Contract with you con-"cerning all the Pepper and Cinnamon "in the Isle. It is therefore that I judg "it advisable to come with your whole "Strength, in order to accelerate our "Confederacy, which may be as dura-"ble as the Sun and Moon: But if this "should not be convenient, pray send "a trusty Person whom we may treat "with, there being little time to be lost, "since things being already come to a "Rupture with the *Portugueses*, we shall "stand in present need of your Assistance. "I expect the return of the three De-"puties with the arrival of your Fleet.

From *Vintane* 28 *Nov.* 1637. Signed,

Imperador, *Raja Singa.*

Sealed with the Pummel of his Majesty's Scymeter, printed in Red Wax.

It was directed,

To the Lord Admiral of the *Dutch* Fleet before *Goa*.

CHAP. XX.

Sea Engagement before Goa, *betwixt the* Dutch *and* Portuguese *Fleets.*

Sea Engagement before Goa.

WHilst the Envoys were honourably entertain'd aboard the Fleet by *Adam van Westerwold* the *Dutch* Admiral, a Sea Engagement happen'd the 4*th* of *January* 1638. betwixt us and the *Portugueses*. The *Dutch* Squadron was composed of the following Ships.

A List of the Dutch *Squadron.*

The *Utrecht*, aboard whereof was the Admiral *Adam van Westerwold*, Capt. *Reynier Wybrandz*, Head Factor *James Nolpe*, carrying 42 Brass and Iron Cannon mounted, and 150 Men, among whom were 35 Soldiers, commanded by Lieutenant *Hans Maagdelyn*.

The *Flissingen*, aboard of which was the Vice-Admiral, Head Factor, Fiscal, and Commissary *John van Twist*; *Hubert Hubertson* Captain, carrying 38 pieces of Cannon, and 140 Men, among whom were 20 Soldiers, commanded by a Serjeant named *Cornelius Bloem*.

The Arms of *Rotterdam* Reer-Admiral, commanded by *Herman Wolters*, *Baak*, and *John David Wolfswinkel* Clark, carrying 38 pieces of Cannon, and 130 Men, among whom were 20 Soldiers.

The *Hague*, aboard of which were *Floris van Castel* Head Factor, *Minne Williams Keert de Koe* Captain, and *James van Capel* under Factor, carrying 34 pieces of Cannon, and 110 Men, among them 20 Soldiers.

The *Harderwyk*, commanded by *Paul Clasen*, *Peter Bruchart* under Factor, carrying 36 pieces of Cannon, 115 Men, among them 20 Soldiers.

The *Vere*, commanded by *Isaac Dickson Kien*, *Laurence de Marshal* under Factor, carying 30 pieces of Cannon, and 105 Men, among them 20 Soldiers.

Baldæus. The *Texel*, commanded by Captain *Cornelius Leendard Valk*, *Joost van Wielyk* under Factor, carrying 24 pieces of Cannon, and 77 Men, among them 12 Soldiers.

The *Breda*, commanded by *Francis Thyse*, *John Fox* under Factor, carrying 24 Cannon, 77 Men, and among them 12 Soldiers.

The Yacht the Little *Amsterdam*, *Jacob Jacobson Struck* Commander, carrying 8 Guns, and 25 Men.

The little *Enchuysen* Yacht commanded by Captain *Reynier*, carrying 2 Brass and 6 Iron Guns, and 20 Men.

The *Falcon* Yacht, *John Thysen* Captain, *Adrian Helmont* Factor, carrying 16 Iron Guns, 40 Men, and among them six Soldiers.

The *Dolphin* Frigat, commanded by *Peter van der Kamer*, carrying 6 Iron Guns, and 20 Men.

A List of the Portuguese Ships. The *Portuguese* Squadron consisted of these following Ships.

The *Bon Jesus*, *Don Anthonio Telles de Meneses* Admiral, carrying 76 Brass Guns, and 400 Men, among whom were 300 *Portugueses*, the rest Negroes.

The *S. Sebastian* Vice-Admiral, commanded by Capt. *Anthonio Menezes Bourette*, carrying 50 Brass Guns, 150 *Portugueses*, and 200 Negroes.

Madre de Deos Reer-Admiral, commanded by *Lewis Gonsalves*, carrying 35 Iron and Brass Guns, 130 *Portugueses* and 120 Negroes.

The S. *Bartholomew*, *Lewis de Castelbranco* Commander, carrying 26 Iron and Brass Guns, 140 *Portugueses*, and 160 Negroes.

The S. *Francis*, Captain *Domingo Fereira* Commander, carrying 26 Guns, 100 *Portugueses*, and as many Negroes.

The S. *Philip*, commanded by *Don Diego de Vaes*, carrying 24 Guns, 100 *Portugueses*, and 100 Negroes.

With these 6 Galeons, and 20 small Frigats, the *Portugueses* set sail out of the Road of *Goa*, *Jan.* 4. 1638. in sight of the *Dutch*, who no sooner got sight of them, but they weighed their Anchors, and in form of a Crescent sail'd with a Land-wind and low Water out into the Main. The *Portugueses* divided into two Squadrons follow'd them with all the Sails they could make, their

The Sea Ingagment betwixt the Portuges and Dutch near Goa.

Admiral

Admiral making up towards the *Dutch* Admiral, as their Vice-Admiral (tho not so good a Sailor as the rest) did to the Ships the *Rotterdam*, the *Vere*, and the *Falcon* Yacht. In the Morning about Nine a Clock both Fleets began to come within Cannon-shot, about three Leagues from the Road of *Goa*, where the Engagement began betwixt the two Admirals, who plentifully exchang'd their Broad-sides for three hours successively, as did three others of the *Portuguese* Ships with the *Dutch* Fleet, the rest of their Galleons not being able to come up immediately for want of a Wind. The *Portuguese* Vice-Admiral coming at last up with the rest, was briskly saluted by our Ships the *Rotterdam* and the *Vere*, whilst the rest of the *Dutch* Vessels did what they could to advance closer to the Enemy; and at last having got the advantage of the Sea-wind, they were for boarding the *Portuguese* Ships, having sent the *Texel* and *Dolphin* Frigats, two Fire-ships, to get in among them; but these setting it before the Wind, avoided that danger. The *Dutch* Admiral *Westerwold* did his utmost in his Ship the *Utrecht* to board the *Portuguese* Admiral; which he perceiving, retreated towards his Squadron, which made the *Dutch* Admiral set it with all the sail he could make upon their Vice-Admiral, which he did with such success, that the *Portuguese* was forced to cut his Sails and Cables to get rid of his Enemy, whilst the whole *Portuguese* Squadron ply'd the *Dutch* Admiral with their Cannon, who thereby receiv'd considerable damage, especially in his Rigging. Our Ship the *Vere* would have boarded the S. *Bartholomew*, but they got clear of one another, yet not without receiving a good Broad-side from the Ship the *Hague*; and the *Flissingen* finding the *Portuguese* Admiral engag'd with these two Ships, she laid the *Bartholomew* aboard, and with the assistance of the *Hague* ply'd her so warmly, that she was set on fire, the rest of the *Portuguese* Ships retreating in the mean while towards the Shore. Such was the violence of the Flames, that notwithstanding all the Endeavours that were used, the *Hague* was also set on fire, and soon after the *Flissingen*, and were all three consum'd by the Flames.

Sea Engagement betwixt the Portugueses *and* Dutch.

A Portuguese *Ship with two* Dutch *Vessels set on fire.*

The *Portugueses* in the mean while taking the advantage of the Confusion, made the best of their way towards the Road of *Goa*, being pursued for one League and a half by the *Rotterdam*, *Vere*, and *Texel*, close under their Forts; the rest of our Ships being busied in saving the Men from the danger of the Fire, and in repairing their Masts and Rigging, so that the Victory remain'd on our side, which would have been very considerable had the same been not allay'd by the burning of the two before-mentioned Ships.

Baldæus.

The Loss of the *Dutch* amounted to 35 Men, among whom were Capt. *Herman Wouters Baak*, besides 50 wounded, among whom was the Factor *James Nolpe*: The loss on the *Portuguese* side amounted to 78 *Portugueses*, and 150 *Mistices* and Negroes. *Don Lewis de Castelbranco*, and Father *Laurence de Merinda* a Jesuit, were taken Prisoners, with 90 *Portugueses*, and 49 *Mistices* and Negroes, being sav'd by the same Boats that came to save their own Men, and exchang'd afterwards for a Captain, a Factor, and eight other *Dutch*-men belonging to the *Wieringen* Yacht (burnt near *Malacca*) besides a Sum of 2000 Crowns paid to *Don Pedro de Silva* Viceroy of the *Indies*. The first of *March* a *Portuguese Caraque*, half loaden with Pepper and Cinnamon, and bound for *Portugal*, immediately after the departure of the *Dutch* Fleet was burnt by accident; and the Galeon the *Madre de Deos* underwent the same fate in *April* following, to the great detriment of the *Portugueses*, whose Naval Force in the *Indies* was not a little impair'd by the loss of these three great Ships.

Loss on both sides.

The Emperor of *Ceylon*'s Deputies who were present in the Engagement, were surpriz'd at the Bravery of the *Hollanders*, who with their small Ships durst board the *Portugueses* so much stronger both in Men and Cannon. After the Engagement the *Dutch* Fleet came to an Anchor near the Islands on the South-side of *Goa*, to refit their Ships, and to venture a second Engagement. Soon after the *Hertogenbosch* a brave Vessel commanded by *William Jacob Koster*, join'd our Fleet, coming lately from *Suratte* with a rich Cargo of the best *Indian* Stuffs, Indigo, Saltpeter, and other *Indian* Commodities, valued at 412000 Gilders at the first hand, which for meer safety sake were dispersed among the other Vessels. The 12th of *January* arriv'd likewise the Ship *Henrietta Louisa* from *Batavia*, having on board 76000 Crowns, besides other Merchandizes for our Factory of *Suratte*, and was sent thither in company of the *Breda* and *Enchuysen* Yachts.

The Dutch *refit near the South Isles of* Goa.

Are reinforc'd with two Ships.

CHAP.

Baldæus.

CHAP. XXI.

William Jacob Koster *sent to* Ceylon *by Admiral* Westerwold. *The* Portugueses *march to* Candy, *are totally routed by the Emperor. The* Dutch *besiege* Batecalo.

A Dutch *Squadron sent to* Ceylon.

THE 23*d* of *Jan.* 1638. the *Falcon* Yacht being likewise dispatch'd to *Batavia*, with Advice of the late Engagement, and some Merchandizes, as also the Sick and Wounded to be dispos'd in the Hospital there, our Squadron consisted only of 7 Capital Ships and 2 Yachts. But the *Dutch* Admiral perceiving the *Portugueses* to make not the least Preparations of attacking them a second time, it was resolv'd in a Council of War to send Mr. *William Jacob Koster* Commodore, with the *Texel*, the *Amsterdam*, and *Dolphin*, mann'd with 180 Men and 70 Souldiers, to the Isle of *Ceylon*, to give notice to the Emperor of the intended Succours against *May*, and in the mean while to offer his Assistance in the Siege of some Fort or other belonging to the *Portugueses*; for which purpose the Admiral writ the following Letter to his Imperial Majesty.

The Dutch *Admiral's Letter to the Emperor of* Ceylon.

" *Adam van Westerwold*, Counsellor Extraordinary of the *Indies*, and Admiral of the *Dutch* Fleet, wishes the most Potent Emperor of *Ceylon*, King of *Candy*, &c. all Happiness and Prosperity, with the utmost Offer of his Service, for the throwing off the intolerable Yoke of the *Portugueses*.

Most Potent Emperor,

" WHilst the Illustrious General and Council of the *Indies*, under the Jurisdiction of the *United Provinces*, were employ'd in equipping a Squadron of 16 Ships, to be sent from *Batavia* before *Goa*, in order to annoy our common Enemies the *Portugueses*, and to prevent their sending any *Caracques* or Galeons during the late Northern *Mousson* to *Portugal*, the Ship the *Husduynen* arriv'd at *Batavia* from the Coast of *Coromandel*, with Letters from the Governour of that Coast, wherein was enclos'd your Majesty's Letter, dated at *Candy*, *Sept.* 9. 1636. The said General and Council of the *Indies*, having understood by these Letters, the many Treacheries and Outrages committed by the *Portugueses* in your Majesty's Dominions, and that you were pleas'd to crave their Assistance for the defence of your Country, and rooting out our common Enemies, offering for that purpose to have either *Batecalo* or *Cotiar* (which of the two we should pitch upon) fortify'd at your own Charge for our use, as likewise to give Satisfaction for all the Charge we should be at in the Equipment of such Ships as should be sent to your assistance: These Propositions having been well weigh'd by the General and Council of the *Indies*, it was resolv'd by them, pursuant to the good Inclinations they have to your Majesty, to comply with your Desires. And it appearing by your Majesty's Letter, dated *Novemb.* 21. 1637. and sent to me by the *Faulcon* Yacht, that you still persist in the same laudable Sentiments, I took immediate care to send a Vessel and two Yachts, to advertise your Majesty of our Coming, under the Commodore *William Jacob Koster*, the second Member of my Council, who is to treat with your Majesty concerning our intended Design, and to concert measures which of the *Portuguese* Forts may be most conveniently attack'd at our Arrival, and where your Majesty's Forces are to rendevouz, in order to assist in the taking of the said Forts; for which purpose a certain quantity of Ladders of Bamboes, besides some other Materials, must be got ready. Your Majesty's Deputies who come with these Ships, will be able to give you a more compleat account by word of Mouth, concerning out Intentions. If the Blockade of *Goa* be rais'd by the end of *April*, I intend (pursuant to the Orders receiv'd from the General and Council of the *Indies*) to set sail in Person with three of my biggest Ships, well provided with Men and Ammunition, for *Ceylon*, to confer and treat more amply with your Majesty concerning our projected Design. I hope your Majesty will according to your Promise, order two Ships Cargos of Cinnamon to be got ready against our Arrival. I wish your Majesty a long

* Life

"Life, and Victory against your Enemies.

Commodore Koster *arrives in* Ceylon. The before-mentioned Commodore *Koster*, having set Sail accordingly, *March* 17. from *Goa*, with the 3 Ships the *Texel*, little *Amsterdam* and *Dolphin*, came to an Anchor the 2d of *April* following near *Trinquenemale*, a Harbour on the Northside of the Isle of *Ceylon*; where the Emperor's Deputys being set ashore, in order to deliver the Admiral's Letter at *Candy*, and give notice of the Arrival of the *Dutch* Ships, they understood, that the Emperor immediately after the Departure of the *Falcon* Yacht, had caused a good Quantity of Cinnamon, Wax and Pepper, to be laid up for our use. The *Portugueses* had no sooner notice thereof, but they sent a Letter to his Majesty, asking *the Reason why he had ordered such a Quantity of Merchandizes to be laid up, which, pursuant to the Contract stipulated betwixt them, belonged only to them.* The Emperor return'd them no other Answer than that, *He having promised the same to his Friends the* Hollanders, *he would try who should dare to oppose it.*

This resolute Answer so nettled the *Portugueses* at *Columbo*, that being now fully convinc'd of the Confederacy betwixt the Emperor and the *Dutch*, and that they must soon expect to be attack'd at *Batecalo*, they were put to the greatest Nonplus, what Resolution to take in this present Exigency of Affairs. *The* Portugueses *put to a great Nonplus.* Some considering that having scarce been able to cope with the Emperor alone, they would not be able to resist his Efforts, when sustain'd by the *Dutch*, were of Opinion to embark all their Treasure, Men and Artillery, to demolish the Fort, and set Sail for *Goa*.

But the braver sort rejecting this Proposition as base, and inconsistent with their King's Honour, resolv'd, rather than thus to quit an Isle, which they had fix'd themselves in with the Loss of so much Blood and Treasure, to venture the utmost and die in the Attempt. *Damijao Bottado*, who had laid the first Foundation of the Fortress of *Batecalo*, propos'd among the rest, that they ought to gather all their Forces, and march up to *Candy*, before *Raja Singa* could be join'd by the *Dutch*.

This Advice being approved of, they *They march towards* Candy. marched in *March* 1638. under the Command of their General *Diego de Melo*, the before-mention'd *Damijao Bottado*, and the Major-General *Sorde*, towards *Candy*.

Baldæus. The Emperor having got notice of their March, retir'd from thence with all his People, leaving the City to their Mercy, which they took without any Opposition; and having plunder'd and burnt the same, *Take and burn it.* directed their March to the Mountains of *Gannör* or *Gannero*, where they pitch'd their Tents, their whole Force consisting of 2300 *Portugueses* and *Mistices*, and 6000 Negroes.

This it was that the Emperor had so long look'd for, who immediately order'd the Road to *Walane*, and all other Places thro which they were to pass, to be stopp'd, by laying great Trees cross the Roads. The Enemies finding themselves reduc'd to these Straits, the *Cingaleses* unanimously revolted to the Emperor; so *Are defeated by the* Cingaleses. that the *Portugueses* seeing not the least hopes of escaping by Force of Arms, had recourse to two Friers, one a *Franciscan*, and the other an *Austin* Monk, who were sent to endeavour to obtain them a free Passage from the Emperor to *Columbo*: But the Emperor gave them such an Answer, that the Friers thought it their safest way not to return to their Camp; so that the *Portugueses* finding themselves past all Reprieve, the General *de Melo* ask'd *Bottado* what was to be done, and which way they should escape the Danger into which they were drawn by his rash Advice, who gave him no other Answer, than that they must die together. The Emperor *Raja Singa* in the mean while kept close in his Camp, watching all the Opportunities of attacking them, with the utmost Advantage, which soon happen'd; for a violent Storm of Rain (which he knew would render the *Portuguese* Firelocks in some manner useless) made him draw out his Troops against the Enemy; and putting the Musqueteers in Front, *And put to the Rout.* he order'd them after the first Discharge to retire, and give way to 5000 Bowmen of *Mangelcorle*, who being sustain'd by as many Pikes, did break in with such Fury among the *Portugueses*, that they soon put them into Disorder, and immediately after to the Rout, with the Slaughter of all the *Portugueses*, except a very few who obtain'd Mercy at their Conqueror's Hands, amounting in all not to above 70 Persons.

The Emperor was a Spectator of this Engagement from a Tree near the Bank of a River, which ran betwixt him and the Mountain of *Gannor*, whither they brought the Heads of the *Portugueses* slain in the Battel, which were heap'd up in *A Pyramid of Heads.* form of a Pyramid before him. All the Great Officers of the *Portugueses* lost their

Baldæus. their Lives near the Mountain of *Gannor*, and among them their General *de Melo*, whose Sword was afterwards presented by the Emperor to the Admiral *Wester-wold*.

Siege of Batecalo. In the mean while matters having been concerted with the *Modeliar*, or Governour of *Mattaclape*, concerning the *Portuguese* Fortress of *Batecalo*, they set sail thither; and having landed 100 Soldiers, and as many Seamen in two Troops, they soon rais'd two Batteries, with the assistance of the Natives, one on the East, the other on the South-side of the Fort, upon each of which were mounted four brass Demi-Culverins; and the Emperor having left the Gross of his Army under the Command of his Brother the Prince of *Mateli* to invest *Columbo*, join'd our Forces before *Batecalo*, *April* 14. in Person, with a Detachment of 2000 Men. Commodore *Koster* being receiv'd by his Imperial Majesty with all possible Marks of Honour, they immediately enter'd upon a Debate, how to attack the Fortress with the utmost Vigour upon the Arrival of the rest of our Ships.

CHAP. XXII.

Adam Westerwold's *Arrival in* Ceylon. Batecalo *taken*. *A Treaty betwixt the Emperor and Mr.* Westerwold.

Wester-wold *comes before* Batecalo. THE Admiral *Westerwold* having set Sail *April* 22. from before *Goa*, arriv'd at *Batecalo*, *May* 10. with the Ships the *Maestricht*, *Harderwick*, *Rotterdam*, *Vere*, and the *Enchuysen* Yacht, having on board 840 Men, Officers, Soldiers and Mariners. The next following Day having landed his Men, with 6 great Pieces for Battery, the same were mounted immediately, in order to facilitate the Passage of their Forces into the Isle upon which the Fort was built: This being executed

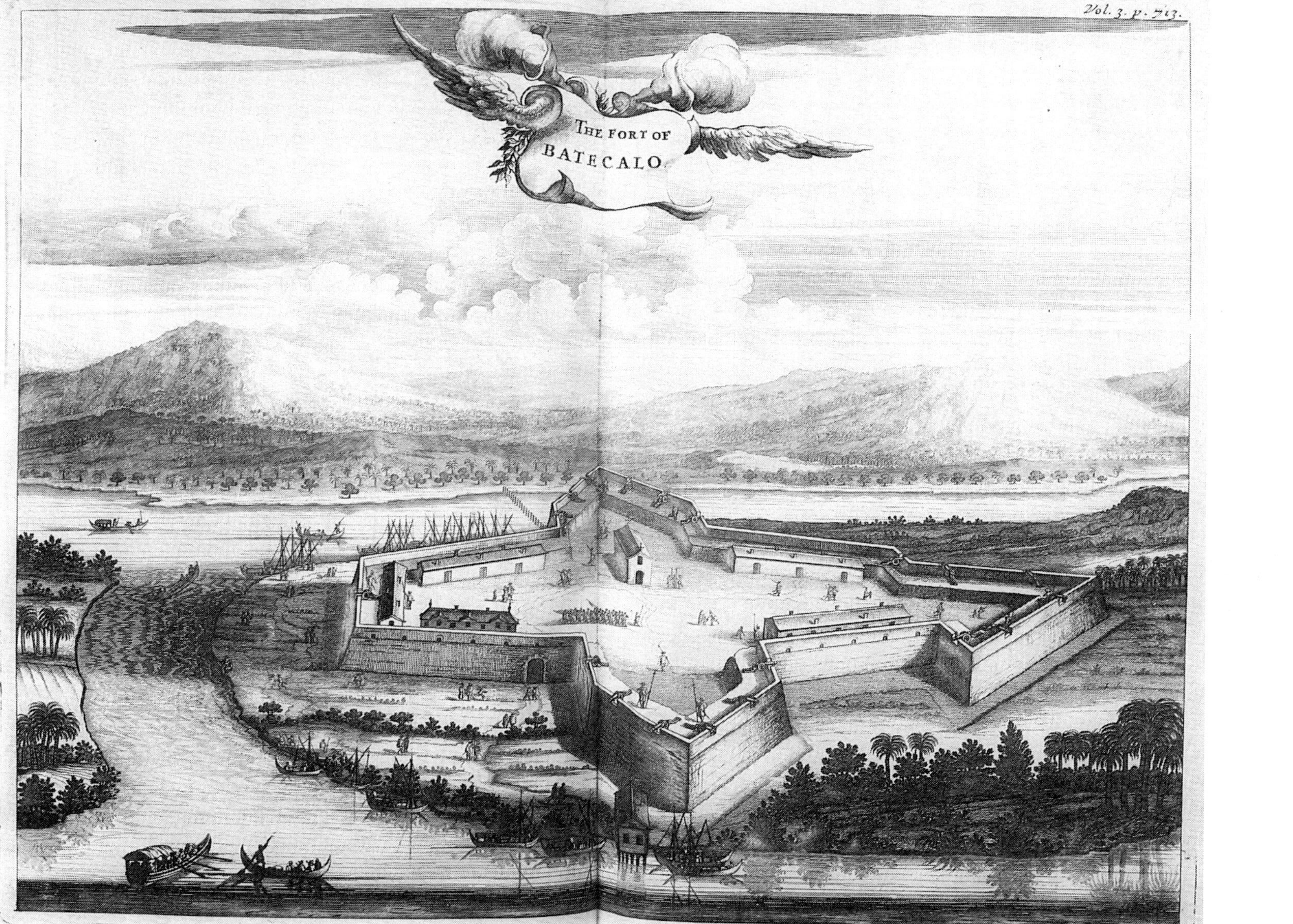
THE FORT OF
BATECALO.

Batecalo surrendred upon Articles. accordingly the 18*th*, and 500 Men brought over under favour of the Cannon, which play'd incessantly for four Hours upon the *Portugueses*, they put out the white Flag immediately, and sent two Deputies to capitulate with the *Dutch* Admiral, which was soon done upon the following Conditions: That they should surrender the Fort immediately, and be permitted to march out without Arms or Baggage. The *Portugueses* and *Mistices* to the Number of 108, with their Wives and Children, to be transported in a *Dutch* Vessel to *Negapatan*, but the Natives to be delivered up to the Emperor, which was executed accordingly, fifty of them (who had murder'd one of his Majesty's Gentlemen) being empal'd alive, and the rest sold for Slaves with their Wives and Children.

Severe Punishment of the Cingaleses.

A Description of Batecalo.

The Fort of *Batecalo* is seated in an Isle of about two *Dutch* Leagues in compass, three Leagues within the Mouth of the River of *Batecalo*, which has given it its Name. It was fortified with high Stone Walls and three passable Bastions, upon which were mounted 11 Iron and Brass Cannons, besides some lesser Ones, with a sutable Proportion of Ammunition. We found in it Rice sufficient for two Months, but their Fresh-Water being about a Musquet-shot without the Fortress, the *Dutch* had made themselves Masters of that Spring. Commodore *Koster* was made Governor of the Fort, with a Garison of one hundred *Dutch* Soldiers.

After the taking of this Fortress, the Admiral *Westerwold* made an Alliance with the Emperor of *Ceylon*, in the Name of their High and Mightinesses the States-General of the *United-Provinces*, his Highness *Frederick* Prince of *Orange*, and of the Honourable *East-India* Company, with the Approbation of the General and Council of the *Indies*, upon the following Conditions:

Alliance betwixt the Emperor of Ceylon *and the* Dutch.

I. A Firm and stedfast Amity shall be maintain'd betwixt his Majesty and his Subjects, and the *Dutch* Nation, and their *East-India* Company, who shall assist his Majesty upon all Occasions against the *Portugueses*.

II. As often as any Place or Fort is taken by the *Dutch*, with the Assistance of his Majesty, from the common Enemy, the Booty to be divided share and share alike.

III. After the taking of any Forts, the *Dutch* shall provide the same with necessary Garisons and Ammunition; and if any thing be wanting to compleat the Fortifications, the same shall be done at the Charge of his Majesty, as it shall be thought requisite by the *Dutch*. *Baldæus.*

IV. His Majesty obliges himself to pay punctually every Month their Soldiers and Officers.

V. As also to build in the conquered Places or Forts (where no Houses are before) a House of Stone (as the *Dutch* shall think fit) to be us'd for a Warehouse, as also a Magazine for their Arms and Naval Stores.

VI. In case his Majesty designs any thing against the common Enemy, the same is to be consulted with our Chief Officers.

VII. For the Security of the Rivers, his Majesty is to furnish a certain Number of Gallies and Gally-Slaves, which are to be provided with Soldiers and Ammunition by the *Dutch*.

VIII. His Majesty and his Subjects oblige themselves to make full Reparation of the Charges the *Dutch* have been at in equipping the present Fleet, Yachts, Vessels, *&c.* and furnishing them with Men, Soldiers, Officers, Ammunition, Provisions, *&c.* or of such other Ships as the General and Council shall for the future send to his Majesty's Assistance into *Ceylon*, with their necessary Men, Ammunition, Provisions, *&c.* the Charges whereof shall be reimbursed in Cinnamon, Pepper, Cardamom, Indigo, Wax, Rice, and such other Commodities as are of the Product of his Majesty's Dominions, except the *Mato* or *Wild Cinnamon*.

IX. His Majesty in respect of his Friendship and good Inclinations to the *Dutch* Nation, allows them free Passage and Traffick in all his Dominions, in the Isle of *Ceylon*, in all his Cities, Towns, Villages, Seaports, Roads, Bays, Rivers, *&c.* with their Vessels, Yachts, Boats, *&c.* to buy, sell or exchange, import or export without the least Molestation, or paying any Customs under any pretence whatever. His Majesty's Subjects shall not be permitted to sell the *Dutch* any Cinnamon, Pepper, Wax and Elephants Teeth, except what is sold by the Emperor's Order; who engages himself, that in case he should have occasion to sell 4, 10, 20, or more Elephants, he will procure them the like Number at the same rate as they were sold.

X. His Majesty, and all the Great Men of the Empire promise, not to allow their Subjects to traffick, either with any *European* or *Eastern* Nation, either by Sale or Exchange, in such Commodities as are of the Product of *Ceylon*; much

Baldæus.

less to permit the Ships of these Nations to tarry in the Harbours of *Ceylon*, but to oblige them to depart forthwith. However the Neighbouring Nations of *Daucy* and *Tanjouwer* may pass and repass freely with their Vessels, to and from *Ceylon*.

XI. His Majesty obliges himself to send yearly to *Batavia*, one or two Shiploads of Cinnamon, Pepper, Cardamom, Indigo, Wax, *&c.* as a Reimbursement of the Charge bestowed in the Equipment of the Vessels sent to his Assistance; and in case the said Cargo should amount to more than the Charges, the Surplus to be paid to his Majesty, either in ready Mony or such Commodities, as his Majesty shall think fit.

XII. His Majesty having granted full Liberty for the *Dutch* Merchants, to travel, traffick, buy and sell, the Inhabitants shall be obliged to furnish them with Beasts fit for Carriage, for the carrying of such Goods as they have bought, either to their Warehouses, or aboard their Vessels. Furthermore, the said Merchants or other *Hollanders* shall remain under the Jurisdiction of the respective Commanders or Heads of their own Nation, as the Natives of *Ceylon* stand under the Subjection of the Emperor.

XIII. No body, without exception, that trades with the *Dutch* here, shall have Freedom to sell any such Commodities bought from them to others, before the *Dutch* have fully received their Quota; and in case of Contravention, the *Dutch* shall have a Power to seize his Person, and to compel him to produce the said Goods. Furthermore, in case any of the Natives stand indebted to the *Dutch* for a considerable Sum, they shall be subject to the same Treatment, with this Proviso nevertheless, that in case any of his Majesty's Subjects be taken into Custody by the *Dutch*, notice shall be given thereof to the Emperor or his Governor.

XIV. No body of what Quality whatever shall pretend to raise or diminish the Coin, otherwise than has been agreed betwixt his Majesty and the *Dutch*; and such as contravene this Article on either side, shall without Mercy be punish'd with Death, and Confiscation of their Estates to his Majesty's use.

XV. In case a *Hollander* should fly into his Majesty's Dominions, the same shall be deliver'd up; as on the other hand the same shall be done on our side, in case any of his Majesty's Subjects shelter themselves in our Dominions.

XVI. After the Conclusion of this Treaty, neither his Majesty nor any of his Subjects shall maintain any secret or publick Commerce or Correspondence with the *Portugueses*, our common Enemies, much less to traffick with them under any pretence whatever, but look upon them as their constant declar'd Enemies: And in case any of his Majesty's Subjects shall be discover'd to have sold them any Commodities, the Transgressors shall be punish'd with Death.

XVII. His Majesty shall not suffer any Priests, Friers or Clergymen to dwell in his Dominions, but oblige them to depart as the Authors of all Rebellions, and the Ruin of Governments.

XVIII. In case any *Dutch* Ships employed in his Majesty's Service, shall take any Prizes from the Enemies, the same shall belong to the *East-India* Company, with this Proviso however, that the said Company shall alone bear all the Damages sustained by the said Ships, in any of these Engagements.

XIX. In case the *Dutch* furnish any great Cannon for the Fortresses, or otherwise for his Majesty's Service, the same may freely be taken back, if Occasion requires, without any Hindrance, and be brought aboard of Ship or otherwise, where it shall be thought most convenient.

XX. Transacted and concluded thus, in the Presence of his Imperial Majesty of *Ceylon*, and of *Adam Westerwold* Member of the Council of the *Indies*, and Commodore of the Squadron of Ships on the Coast of *Ceylon*; as also of *William Jacob Koster*, Vice-Commodore of the said Squadron, at the Royal Palace, in the Country of *Batecalo*, *May* 23. 1638.

Additional Article,

The *Dutch* oblige themselves to shew all possible Favour and Assistance to such Vessels, as shall go from hence with his Majesty's, or any of his Governors Passports to other Harbours.

Signed,

Raja Singa Imperador,
Adam Westerwold,
William Jacob Koster.

Sealed with his Majesty's and Mr. *Westerwold*'s Seals.

Pursuant to this Agreement, his Majesty order'd 400 Balls of Cinnamon, 87 Quintals of Wax, and 3059 Pounds of Pepper to be deliver'd to Mr. *Wester-*

* wold

wold, in part of the Reimbursement of Charges they had been at, promising to deliver the rest, as soon as it could be brought together at the Seaport of *Sammature*, and to hasten the Ratification of the said Alliance; his Majesty sent two Ambassadors to *Batavia*, in Company of Mr. *Westerwold*, with some Presents to the General and Council of the *Indies*, who being honourably received and treated there, were afterwards sent back with Letters and Presents for his Majesty, with the Yachts the *Grijpskerk*, *Faulcon* and *Venlo*, bound for the Coast of *Coromandel*.

Ratification of the said Alliance.

Baldæus.

The Emperor's Army in the mean while being about 20000 strong, continued before *Columbo*; and the *Portugueses* having been very unsuccessful in divers Sallies, it was more than probable that this Place (tho the Capital City of the *Portugueses* in this Isle) would be forc'd to surrender upon the Arrival of the expected *Dutch* Fleet, under the Admiral *Anthony de Caan*.

Columbo *besieged.*

CHAP. XXIII.

Puntegale *taken by Storm by* William Jacob Koster. Caleture *besieged.*

Puntegale *besieged.*

THE 8*th* of *March*, Commodore *Koster* being come to an Anchor about noon in the Bay of *Puntegale*, under the Enemies Cannon, he landed his Men before Night on the North-side without any Resistance. Intelligence was brought by some Negroes, that they expected a Reinforcement in the City of 250 *Portugueses* from *Columbo*; notwithstanding which the *Dutch* divided their Forces into three Bodies, and advanced close under the Fort: The 9*th* early in the Morning, they were attack'd by the said *Portugueses*, whom they repuls'd, tho not without some loss. Neverthelesss they kept our Forces in constant Alarm, those of *Can*-

Baldæus.

dy being by the 11*th* of *March* advanced no further than *Billigamme*, 6 Leagues from *Gale*; but (thro God's singular Mercy) three of our Ships, *viz.* the *Harlem*, *Middleburgh* and *Breda*, coming on the same day to anchor in the Bay, and landing 400 men, as well Soldiers as Seamen, we were soon exempted from all Fear.

The 12*th* finding they had made a sufficient Breach in the Bastion of St. *Jago*, they began to make all necessary Preparations for the storming of the Place, which was done accordingly the 13*th* with such undaunted Bravery, that after an hour and half's stout resistance it was taken by Assault. This City was afterwards, *viz.* 1663, and 64. render'd almost impregnable by the *Dutch* by several additional Fortifications; and this Day is ever since celebrated yearly by a solemn Thanksgiving.

Is taken by Storm.

Mr. *Koster* (who was treacherously murder'd by the *Cingaleses*, as *Sebald de Weert* was by his own Imprudence) was succeeded by *John Thyssen*, who is yet living, and has render'd himself famous for his many Services done the Company in those Parts. In his stead came *John Maatzuyker*, since Governour of the *Indies*, who has served in that Station 15 Years. He was succeeded by *Jacob van Kittenstein* in the Presidentship of *Gale* (the Affairs of the Company hitherto not admitting of the Quality of a Governour here) who died afterwards at *Batavia*, and was succeeded by *Adrian van der Meyden*, in whose time *Caleture*, *Columbo*, *Manaar* and *Jafnapatnam* were taken. He was succeeded by *Ryklof van Goens* and *Jacob Hustart*; by which time the Company having considerably enlarged their Limits in this Isle, a Governour was constituted at *Columbo*, the City of *Gale* being left to the management of a Commander in chief, the first in that Station being one *Ysbrand Gotsken*, a Native of the *Hague*, a brave Soldier, sufficiently known for his signal Services done at the Sieges of *Columbo*, *Manaar*, *Jafnapatnam* and *Cochin*, whereof he was Governour afterwards, and since chief Director in *Persia*. *Adrian Rootbaas* his Successor is a Person who has render'd his Name famous by Sea, especially in the *Levant* and before *Goa*, as the former had done by Land.

Gale

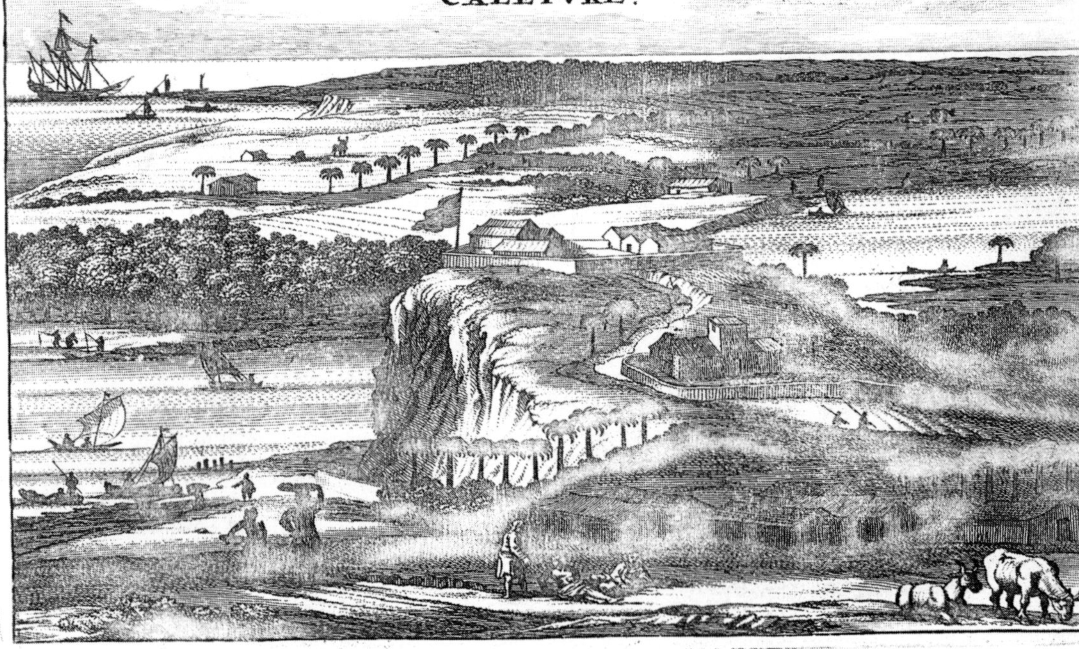

CALETVRE.

THE CITY OF GALE
19.

A Description of Gale.

Gale has a commodious Bay, fit for Anchorage, except that with a South-West Wind the Sea runs very hollow there. At the very Entrance of the Harbour lies a dangerous Rock, near to which all Ships must pass, and against which the *Hercules*, one of our Ships, was stav'd to pieces. There is no coming into the Bay, unless you pass by the Water-Fort, which is well provided with Cannon for the Security of the Harbour. The Fortifications of the City it self consist only in three Bastions, the rest being so inclos'd with the Sea and Rocks, that there is no approaching to it even with the smallest Boats. On the top of a Rock which jets out into the Sea is a Lanthorn, and an Iron Cannon, wherewith they give warning to the Ships, and near it you see the Company's Flag display'd. The City is well built of Stone, very high, with goodly Houses, a stately Church, pleasant Gardens, and most delicious Springs; the Mountains which surround it affording a pleasant Prospect, over which you pass thro Roads cut out of the Rocks, call'd by them *Gravettes*.

Caleture.

About a days Journy from *Gale* stands the Fort of *Caleture*, in a most delightful Country, near the Entrance of a large and broad River, on the Sea-shore, surrounded by a double strong Wall of Earth. It was reduced by the Director General *Gerard Hulst*, 15 *Oct*. 1655. in the following manner.

Is invested by the Dutch.

Having rendevouzed his Forces, consisting of 593 men, near *Bentotte*, and being join'd the 28*th* of *September* by some more Troops under *Christopher Egger*, *Leonard Wiltschut*, and *Melchior van Schoonbeek*, they directed their March towards *Caleture*. But being informed that the Enemy were resolved to make a vigorous Defence, and our Artillery being not yet come up, it was thought advisable to detach Capt. *Abraham Cous* and *Jurian Gevels* with five Companys, to secure the Pass of *Oucatte* over the River, thereby to prevent the Enemy from receiving any Supplies, till the arrival of our Ships, that were expected every day with more Forces.

The 29*th* we took a view of all the Avenues leading to the Place; and Guards being plac'd in all convenient Posts, the Factor *Renier Serooskerken* and Mr. *Ysbrand Godsken* were dispatch'd to our Ships, to send us the necessary Artillery and Ammunition.

The 5*th* of *October* Advice was brought by two of the Natives, that the Garison, consisting of 300 men, was but slenderly provided with Provisions, their whole Store consisting only in 50 * *Parras*, and two small Packs of dry'd Fish, and that they were forc'd to live upon *Cansies*, or Water and Rice.

Baldæus.

* *Each* Parras *is* 40 *Pound*.

The 6*th* of *October* after we had mounted some Great Guns upon our Batteries, a certain † *Topas*, who had been Secretary to Captain *Marcello Fialho*, came over to us, who discovered to the General *Hulst* the whole Strength of the Enemy, and the Names of their Officers; adding, that 4 or 5 days before his departure there were about 210 *Parras* of Rice in the Store-house, whereof they distributed a certain quantity to each Soldier every day, and to the King's Negroes call'd || *Caffers*, a Quart a piece: That they had no *Lascaryns* in the Place, and as he believ'd could not hold it above 10 days, tho they seem'd resolved to defend it to the last extremity, in hopes of being relieved the next week by *Caspar Figeiro*.

† *A Topas is the Son of a* Portuguese *and an Indian Woman*.

|| Caffers *are Negros like those of* Angola.

The same day Major *John van der Laan* brought word that all was well secured on his Attack; and Captain *James Swart*, and the Factor *Abraham Hartman* brought up with 60 Seamen the two great Cannon that were left behind. Capt. *Dianteiro* was also detach'd with 40 *Dutch* Soldiers, and a good number of *Lascaryns*, to the Pass of *Wellikande*; and the General *Gerard Hulst* with Mr. *Adrian van der Meyden* having taken a view of our Batteries, did go to take a view of the Pass near *Palletotte*, where, as well as on the other side, they found every thing to their satisfaction, 756 men being imployed on that side.

The 7*th* of *October* they went up the River as far as *Wellikande*, to see whether the Enemy could receive any Supplies of Provisions by the Brook, or from above by the way of *Anguratotte* and *Tiboene*; but found it not feasible by reason of the shallowness of the Water. However five Ferry-boats were shew'd them in the narrowest Places of the River, where having placed some *Lascaryns*, they committed the management thereof to Mr. *John van der Laan*. The 11*th* of *October* a Mortar of a large size and a 12 Pounder were mounted on the Battery, and Mr. *John van der Laan* came to tell the General that the second Battery would be ready to play on his side the same night.

The 14*th* in the Morning we saw a *Portuguese* Lieutenant and Drummer with a white Flag, coming out of the Fort, sent by *Anthonio Mendes d' Aranha* their Commander in chief, with the following Letter.

" Having

Baldæus. *They offer to capitulate.* "Having for several days past discharged our Trust as a Captain ought "to do, and finding you not so furiously "imployed to day, I thought fit to take "this opportunity to try whether you "would treat with me according to the "Custom of War; for which purpose I "have sent you a trusty Person. In the "mean while all Hostilities shall cease "on our side, hoping the same from you. "We recommend you to God's Protection. *Caleture*, Oct. 14. 1655.

Anthonio Mendes d' Aranba.

A Cessation of Arms being agreed upon, *Martin Sholtes* an Ensign was sent back with the *Portuguese* Officer to treat about the Conditions, whilst a Messenger was dispatch'd with a Letter to the *Dissave* (or Deputy-Governour) of *Saffra Gamme*, to desire him to have it rumor'd abroad, that the *Portugueses* in *Caleture* had lately been supply'd with Provisions; in hopes thereby to amuse *Caspar Figeiro* (who stood with his Forces near *Moutapelle*) not to hasten to their Relief.

The Capitulation was soon after concluded upon the following Terms:

Articles of the Capitulation. "The Soldiers to march out with their "Matches not lighted, Balls in the "Mouth, and Ensigns display'd; the "Officers with their Scarfs, which they "shall lay down roll'd up before the Standard of the Company. All the Great "Officers, to the Captains inclusive, to "be transported during this *Mousson* to "*Goa*; the rest of the Officers and Soldiers to *Batavia*, and from thence to "*Portugal* at the charge of the Company. "All the Officers and Soldiers shall be "allowed to carry their Baggage along "with them; but their Servants shall "be left to the Discretion of the *Dutch* "General. All Church Ornaments shall "be removed. All such as have married "*Portuguese* Women, and the *Mistices*, "shall be conducted to *Columbo*, or whereever else they think fit. But the *Lascaryns* and *Negros*, whether married or "unmarried, shall remain Prisoners of "War. The Fathers and Clergymen "shall enjoy the same Liberty as the "highest Officers, and shall be transported from *Caleture* on the same day. "These Articles are to be ratify'd to "morrow morning by Sun-rising. All "the Superior Officers, including the "Captains, shall have liberty to take "their Swords along with them. It "was signed,

Anthonio Mendes d' Aranba.
John Alonzo.

"After the ratification it was thus "subscribed by both Parties.

Gerard Hulst.
Adrian van der Meyden.
John van der Laan.
Anthonio Mendes d' Aranba.
John Alonzo.

The 15*th* early in the Morning the *Portuguese* Officer returned with the Articles; towards Noon the Garison, consisting in nine Companys making in all 255 men, marched out of the Fort, and having paid their Reverence with their Ensigns as usual, the Soldiers were disarmed. *They march out.* The Companys were the following: The Royal Company commanded by the Captain Major *Marcello Fialbo*, consisted of 31 *Portugueses*: That of *John Anthonio Felbaon* of 27. That of *Pedro de Barbos* of 28. That of *Manuel Rodrigos* of 28. That of *Diego Freir* of 36. That of *Jacomo Padraon* of 28. That of *Manuel Mendes* of 27. That of *Lewis Alvres Periero* of 24. And that of *Leonardo de Silva* of 26. In all 255.

Besides the Persons of Note living in the Place, with their Families, that were conducted to *Callamoende*, and 50 more that were with the Governour *Anthonio Mendes d' Aranba* (afterwards our Prisoners at *Jafnapatnam*) that were carry'd to *Gale*, the other Superior Officers were sent to *Macoene*, and the rest kept under a good Guard in the Fort.

Immediately notice of this Victory having been given to the Emperor *Raja Singa*, General *Hulst* and Mr. *Adrian van der Meyden* took a view of the Fortifications of the Place, whereat they were not a little surprized, and found therein 10 Ensigns, 5 great Guns, 4 Brass ones, 10 8 and 5 Pounders, and one Iron 8 Pounder, 40 Barrels of Gun-powder, 204 Bamboe Canes fill'd, 710 Bullets, 180 Musquets, 62 Pikes, 7 Chests with Musquet Balls, another Barrel with larger Bullets fit for Musquetoons, 116 Ammunition Pouches, 5 Musquetoons, some firy Bullets, 60 Spades and 8 Hatchets.

CHAP.

CHAP. XXIV.

Engagements near Paneture *and near* Montual, *both to the disadvantage of the* Portugueses.

Ysbrand Godskens *made Governour of* Caleture.

YSbrand Godskens being constituted Governour of *Caleture*, with a Company to keep Garison there, Major *John Vander Laan* march'd the 16*th* from the other side of the River towards *Paneture*, being followed by the General and Mr. *van der Meyden* with the rest of the Forces. In the dusk of the Evening we came up with the *Portugueses*, whom we saluted so briskly with our Firelocks, that they thought fit to retreat, leaving 17 dead, and all their Ammunition, with their Standard, behind them. On our side we had 15 wounded, besides *Arent Jansz van Norden* an Ensign. According to the report of one of their Captains, who was taken Prisoner, they consisted of six Companys commanded by *Dominges Sermento* Captain Major of *Montual*, detached towards *Caleture* to secure this Pass till to morrow, for *Caspar Figeiro*, who was on his march at the head of 600 men, to attempt the Relief of that Place. Whereupon it was thought convenient to make a Halt betwixt *Paneture* and *Galkisse*, near a good Spring, and there to expect the coming up of the rest of their Forces.

The same night, the Moon shining very bright, a Prisoner was brought into our Camp, who being a Native of *Antorf*, and well vers'd in the *Dutch* Tongue, told the General, that he had served the King of *Portugal* 11 Years, and that *Figeiro* would doubtless be with them by day-light.

An Engagement betwixt the Dutch *and* Portugueses.

The 17*th*, being Sunday, word being brought that the *Portugueses* were at hand, Major *John van der Laan* and Capt. *Kous* were posted with five Companies and two Field-Pieces, on a convenient Place, to receive the first Shock of the Enemy, whom, after a general Discharge of their Fire-Arms and Cannon, they received so warmly with Sword in hand, that they were soon brought into confusion, and pursu'd as far as to the Church call'd *Nossa Senhora de Milagres*, i. e. *That of our Lady of Miracles*, with a Slaughter of 150 on the Enemies side. Among our Troops Major *van der Laan* was wounded in the Cheek, and a Gunner, two common Soldiers and a Serjeant, kill'd.

The 18*th* of *October* happen'd another Engagement betwixt us and the *Portugueses* near *Montual*. Our Forces attack'd them in ther Entrenchments, from whence they fired furiously upon them; but no sooner had they broke thro their Works, but they threw down their Arms, and made the best of their way to *Columbo*, leaving all their Ammunition behind them, and 22 kill'd upon the Spot; whereas we had not so much as one wounded on our side. We left two Companys as a Guard of the Church of St. *Sebastian*; and advancing nearer towards *Columbo*, a Body of *Portugueses* retreated in Boats from *Montual* to *Columbo*, leaving the Pass open to us, where we found 3 Iron Guns and some Cinnamon, and put a Guard of 16 Soldiers in it under a Serjeant.

A second Engagement.

Here we received intelligence, that of the whole Body commanded by *Caspar Figeiro*, consisting of 600 *Portugueses*, and sent from *Columbo* to the Relief of *Caleture*, not above 160 were returned to that City.

The 19*th* before Noon some *Portugueses* being got into a Coco-Garden, some of our Soldiers forced them to retire; but those of the City firing upon them, kill'd one of our Serjeants, and wounded *Hans Christophers* a Lieutenant, and two common Soldiers. The same day the General was certify'd by Letters from Capt. *Kous* and Lieut. *Wilstchut*, that they had already told above 300 slain of the *Portugueses* upon the Roads, and that daily more Heads and Prisoners were brought in. They sent at the same time a Wastcoat of *Caspar Figeiro*, wherein was the following Letter.

Instructions to Caspar Figeiro.

"YOU are not ignorant of the Resolution taken the 12*th* of *October* "concerning your Endeavours to relieve "the Fort of *Caleture*. All the Forces "we have been able to gather for this "Expedition consist in 420 men, which "we hope will prove sufficient thro the "Blessing of God and your good Fortune and Conduct, to make you return "victorious. We leave the Management "of that Affair to your approved Experience, it being impossible for us "to foresee all the Circumstances and "Accidents that may attend a Business "of this nature. It must be your care "to

Baldæus. "to get frequent intelligence of the Posture of the Enemy, and how to bring the Provisions laid up for the Relief of the Place at *Belantotte*, into the Fort; the Success whereof you shall notify to us with the first opportunity, that we may send fresh Supplies of Rice both for your use, and of the Garison in the Fort. If you can meet with any Provisions in the Country, you will not fail to seize them for your Conveniency.

"In case you should prove successful in the relief of *Caleture*, you must join your Forces, and the Captain Major of the Place must submit to your Command. We don't question but you will not be wanting in your Duty in a Business of such vast moment, whereon depends the Preservation and Welfare, not only of this City, but also of the whole Isle.

"If after the Relief of *Caleture* you find, that for want of Provisions, or for other weighty reasons, the Fort is not to be maintain'd, you shall agree among your selves what is fittest to be done for his Majesty's Interest, whether it be not the best way to bring the Fortifications into a narrower Compass, and leaving only 150 Men for the defence thereof, to join the rest with your Body.

"If you find it impracticable to bring any Supplies into the Fort, you shall entrench your self at a convenient distance, and from thence give notice to *Anthonio Mendes d' Aranha*, the Governour, that he shall nail up all the Cannon, destroy all the Ammunition, and make the best of his way to your Camp, thereby to preserve such brave Troops, on whom in some measure depends the Defence of this City.

At Columbo, *Oct.* 13. 1655. Signed, *Antonio de Souza Coutinho.*

And lower,

"Just upon the Conclusion of these Presents we have received the expected Succours from the *Indian* Coast, which consisting of 200 men, is to be joined with your Troops. We recommend you to God's Protection.

Columbo, 15 *Oct.* 1655.

CHAP. XXV.

A famous Highway-man taken. The Beginning of the Siege of Columbo. *The Emperor offers the* Dutch *his Assistance. His Letter to the* Dutch *General.*

* Apahamie is an Officer of Note.
† Haratie is a Serjeant.
|| Lascaryn a common Soldier.
* Dissave a Governour.

ABout the same time arrived three * *Apahamies*, and as many † *Haraties* with some || *Lascaryns*, from the Imperial Court; and the * *Dissave* of *Saffragamme* with Letters from Mr. *Joris Hervendonck* our Resident at *Candy*, intimating that he had been commanded by his Majesty to notify his being ill of an Ague, and that he hop'd before long to be with all his Nobility at *Columbo*. In return of which another Letter was sent to his Majesty, to notify our Victory over the Enemy.

A famous Robber taken. The same day Advice was brought that the famous Highway-man *Francisco Anthunes* was fallen into the hands of some of our *Lascaryns*, wherefore a Detachment was order'd to bring him into the Camp; but either thro the Cold and Inconveniences of the Journy, or rather out of fear, he dy'd by the way, and was bury'd.

A Thanksgiving-day. About the same day a Thanksgiving-day was also appointed to be held the 28*th* of *October*, to return thanks to God for having blessed our Arms with Success, and begging his Mercy for the future.

The 21*st* the General with some other Officers of Note having taken a view of the Situation of the City of *Columbo* at *Quia de Lobo*, order'd all sorts of Materials to be brought thither from *Montual*, for the raising of a Battery, and hired 50 Pioneers for that purpose.

The 22*d* the *Dissave* of *Saffragamme* appear'd in Person in a House formerly belonging to *Diego Melo de Castro* Governour of *Columbo*, offering certain Supplies of Men from his Majesty, which was thankfully received by the General.

The 23*d* another Battery was erected near the Church of St. *Sebastian*.

Two days after came into the Camp the Emperor's *Dissave* of the *Four Corles* at the head of 700 men; and the same Evening the General received a Letter writ with his Majesty's own Hand, and brought by one of his own Post-men: It was curiously perfumed with all sorts of Spices, and on each side you saw the

Figure of a Woman, with her Hands folded, lifting her Eyes up to Heaven, being an Answer to Mr. *Adrian van der Meyden*'s Letter writ to his Majesty from *Batecalo*. The King seem'd not well satisfied, that the said Letter had not been wrapp'd in white Linen as usual, and that some of his Titles had not been inserted; yet he testify'd his Satisfaction about the arrival of the *Dutch* Fleet, alledging for the rest, that pursuant to the Promise made him by Mr. *Jacob Kittenstein*, and the Agreement with him and *Adrian van der Meyden*, the City was to be delivered into his Hands: But that as he made no great account thereof, he was satisfy'd, provided they would allow him the Honour of the Conquest, which he would acknowledg upon all Occasions. In the Conclusion of the Letter he told them, that he had ordered Lodgings to be prepar'd for them in all the Places thro which they were to pass.

The 26*th* we were busy in mounting the Cannon upon a Battery, and had four Men wounded and one kill'd. The same Day we receiv'd a Supply of Ammunition and Provision, brought aboard the *Lyon* Yacht to *Puntegale*. Sunday the 28*th* after Sermon, a Deserter with a Negro came into the Camp from the City, who having made his Escape thro the Fens, told the General, that *Caspar Figeiro* was by the Governor of *Columbo*, welcom'd with these Words, *You deserve to be hanged*, and that he had alledged many Falshoods in his Defence, and among the rest that he could not attack us, because we were so deeply entrench'd near the Sea-shoar.

Welcome of Figeiro *at* Columbo.

The same day the Emperor's *Dissave* of the seven *Corles* arriv'd in the Camp with 500 Men, who together with the other *Lascarins* were employed in carrying Ammunition. The 29*th* a Deserter came over to us from the City, his Name was *Herman Lucas*, a Native of *Hertogenbush*; who having formerly deserted our Service at *Gale*, in company of one named *Walraven*, had obtain'd the Name of *John de Rosa* among the *Portugueses*; but having had the Misfortune of killing another at *Columbo*, was fled to *Candy*, where he pretended to have been sent by the Governor, to view the Outworks of the Place: He gave the General an account of divers remarkable Passages, and among the rest, that he had been present in the Engagement, which happen'd the 17*th*, and that of that whole Body, not above 150 *Portugueses* return'd to *Columbo*, where there were as yet nine Companies, amounting in all with the Citizens able to bear Arms to 800 Men: That the Governor was highly concerned at the loss of these Troops, and the ensuing Siege, especially since some of the Citizens shew'd no great Inclination to fight. We play'd the same day very furiously upon the City, and the Battery rais'd against S. *Sebastian* was likewise brought to perfection.

A noted Deserter gives an account of the Condition at Columbo.

Baldæus.

Columbo *furiously ply'd with great Cannon.*

The next following Day a certain *Portuguese* Prisoner was brought into the Camp; he was sent from *Milagre*, and had lived 14 days upon Grass and Herbs in the Woods. The 3*d* of *Novemb.* a Carpenter and Cannoneer were kill'd by a Cannon-shot upon the Battery raised at *Quia de Lobo*, and the same Afternoon the Sloop call'd the *Delft* arriv'd from *Caleture* with Pouder. About the same time a Deserter came to us out of the City, but being lately come from *Goa*, he could tell no great matter. The same Evening the Ship call'd the *Brown-fish* arriv'd with Letters from *Laurence Pit*, Governor of the Coast of *Coromandel*, having on board 44544 Pounds of Gun-powder; she brought also Advice, that the Yacht the *Fopkensburg* was safely arriv'd at *Gale*, but that they had no News of the Ship called the *Haddock*. The same Night we were busy in raising a Battery near the Sea-shoar.

The 4*th* of *Novemb.* early in the Morning, News was brought to the General from *Negumbo*, that according to the Report of certain Inhabitants of *Annarolundane*, 12 Sail of Ships were discover'd off of *Chilaon*; whereupon immediate Orders were given to the Commodore *Edward Hauw*, to use all possible Endeavours to get Intelligence thereof: the same was also recommended to the Head Factor of *Gale*, *John Kroon*, and to be upon his Guard. The same Afternoon, a Cannon-Bullet from the Bastion of St. *Stephen*, passing thro a Gallery of the Church of *Quia de Lobo*, whilst the Surgeons were dressing some wounded Soldiers, a Soldier was kill'd, two others had their Arms shot off, and three more were dangerously wounded.

News of 12 Sail being discovered.

About the same time *Tenecon Apuhamy*, came in the Quality of the Emperor's Messenger, with a Breast-shield of Gold, beset with precious Stones, and fasten'd to a Gold Chain, and brought the following Letter from his Majesty to the General.

"RAJA Singa the greatest Monarch
" and most Potent Emperor of the
" Empire of *Ceylon*, wishes Health to
" *Gerard*

The Emperor's Letter to General Hulst.

Baldæus.

"*Gerard Hulst* Admiral of the Fleet, "belonging to the most faithful Nation "of the *Dutch*.

"By the Letters sent to me from the "Governor of our Fortress of *Gale*, I "have understood, that immediately af- "ter your Arrival with the *Dutch* Fleet "there, you have made your self Master "of the Fort of *Calcture*; and that one "half of the *Portuguese* Prisoners were "sent aboard a Ship, the rest being re- "served for our Service. The News of "your Success in the Engagement be- "twixt *Calcture* and *Columbo*, without "any considerable Loss on the side of "our faithful *Hollanders*, being likewise "receiv'd by me with singular Satisfacti- "on, I sent immediate Orders to all my "*Dissaves* (Governors) and chief Com- "manders, to bring into the Field all "the Forces of our Empire. In the "mean while I receiv'd an *Ola* (Letter) "from the *Dissave* of *Saffragam*, dated "*Octob.* 23. wherein he informs me, that "having been sent for by your Excellen- "cy, you enquired after my Health, "telling him at the same time, that you "were come to no other end, than to "deliver the Cities of *Columbo*, *Manaar* "and *Jafnapatnam* into our Hands; "which done, you would in Person ap- "pear in our Imperial Majesty's Pre- "sence. I have been very ill for many "Days past, which however has not pre- "vented my taking the necessary mea- "sures for the raising of the Forces of "the Empire. No sooner had I recei- "ved the welcome News of your Excel- "lency, but I was in a manner immedi- "ately restor'd to my former Health, "being now twice as strong as before, "and able (thro God's Mercy) to assist "in Person in the intended Expedition, "which I intend to begin the 2*d* of *Nov.* "I have sent with this Letter one of the "Officers of our Court, to enquire after "your Excellency's Health, and to bring "you a Present from me, which I hope "your Excellency will value, not so "much in regard of its Value, as in re- "spect of the Love and good Inclination "of the Giver.

Dated at our Imperial Court in the City of *Candy*, *Oct.* 29. 1655. *Raja Singa Raju*, most Potent Emperor of *Ceylon*.

CHAP. XXVI.

Resolutions and Instructions concerning the intended General Assault upon the City of Columbo.

THE 9*th* of *Nov.* a new Battery with four great brass Cannon, having be- gan to play against St. *Stephen*'s Bastion; a General Council of War was call'd of all the Chief Officers, in order to con- sult (after having implor'd the Divine Assistance) whether it were convenient to venture a General Assault upon *Columbo*: The General having openly declar'd, that every one there present should be at his full Liberty to discover his real Senti- ments concerning this great Undertak- ing; it was agreed by unanimous Con- sent, that seeing the Alacrity of the Sol- diers, it was convenient to attempt a Ge- neral Assault.

A general Assault is agreed upon by general Consent.

Soon after the General dispatch'd a Trumpeter, bearing a Flag of Truce in his Hand, to the *Portuguese* Governor, *Anthony de Souza Continho*, with the fol- lowing Letter.

The Dutch *General's Letter to the Governor of* Columbo.

"The Success that has attended our "Arms in the taking of *Calcture*, and the "Defeat of the Troops under *Caspar* "*Figeiro*, near the Shoar of *Panature*, "together with the Advantages obtain- "ed already in the Siege of *Columbo*, "may as I suppose sufficiently entitle "me to demand, without Vanity, the "delivering up of the City, in the Name "of his Imperial Majesty *Raja Singa*, "and the most Noble *Dutch-East-India* "Company. I hope your Excellency "will not put a wrong Interpretation "upon this Demand, when you consider "that, pursuant to the Tenor of your own "Letters sent to *Don Anthonio Mendes* "*d' Aranha*, and *Caspar Figeiro*, the first "dated *Septemb.* 30. and the second the "13*th* and 15*th* of *Octob.* (both which are "fallen into our Hands) you were then "sufficiently sensible, that the Defence "of *Columbo* depended on the Preserva- "tion of the Forces in *Calcture*, and "those under the Command of *Caspar* "*Figeiro*. It is upon this score that I "am of Opinion, I don't put the least

"Ble-

Baldæus.

“ Blemish upon your Courage, since being bereav'd of these means, you have nevertheless given such ample Proofs of your Zeal and Bravery in the Defence of this Place. My Request is only founded upon this, to avoid the Effusion of Innocent Blood, the almost necessary Consequence and unavoidable Fate of all Places taken by Assault, it being sufficiently known, that the Fury of the conquering Soldiers is not easily stopp'd upon those Occasions.

Nov. 9. *Gerard Hulst.*

The Trumpeter returning a little while after, told, that coming near to S. *John*'s Bastion, the Letter was taken from him by a *Portuguese* Officer, who assur'd him, that the Governor should return an Answer the next Day: Hereupon the Cannon being ordered to play as before, three Companies under the Lieutenants *William de Wit*, *Henry Gerritsz*, and *Christopher Egger*, were sent to *Montual*, in order to be put on board the two Yachts, the *Ter Goes* and the *Erasmus*.

The 10*th* of *Novemb.* an Answer was sent to the General upon his Letter.

The Governor's Answer. “ As God Almighty disposes the Chances of War according to his Pleasure, so he may as well declare now for our side, as he has done for you before: The Place you require, belongs to the King of *Portugal* my Master, who having entrusted me with the same, I must be accountable to him for it. The Reasons alledged by your Excellency, are not sufficient to move me to lay aside the Defence of this City; not questioning, but that Time and Experience will convince you, that our Condition at present is much beyond what you imagine. I recommend you to God's Protection.

Nov. 9. *Antonio de Souza Coutinho.*

After the Receit of this resolute Answer, the General thought fit to give the following Instructions for the intended General Assault.

Instructions for the General Assault. “ The Yachts, *viz.* the *Maid of Enchuysen*, commanded by *Volkert Adrian Shram* (who afterwards rendred himself so famous in the North, during the *English* War) and the *Workum*, *Arent Groenfield* Commander, shall approach into the Bay, as near to the Water-Fort as possibly they can; for which purpose they shall be provided with 110 chosen Seamen, 5000 Pounds of Gunpowder, and with Shot in proportion.

“ The Yachts shall anchor in any part of the Bay, where they can best annoy the Water-Fort, and under favour of their Cannon land their Men. For this purpose the Yachts the *Ter Goes* and *Erasmus*, shall keep within Cannon-shot of the other two Yachts, and have aboard, besides their Ships Crew, 100 Landmen each, *viz.* the Companies of *William de Wit*, *Henry Gerritsz*, and *Christopher Egger*, in order to land, in conjunction with the Men of the other Yachts. The Boats, Tenders and other small Vessels shall keep near the before-mention'd Ships, *viz.* the Tender the *Amsterdam* with her Sloop, near the *Ter Goes*, and the Sloop the *Wesel*, the Boat of the *Marygoldflower*, with her Sloop the *Delft*, and the Tender the *Naarden* with the rest. The Tenders the *Hair* and *Brownfish* shall keep near the Shoar, to be ready upon all Occasions to carry Advice where it shall be thought necessary. In short, all the Boats shall attend the Vessels that are engag'd against the Fort, in order to save their Men, in case any of them should be sunk or disabled. When the Companies Standard is fix'd above the red Flag, this shall be the Signal of landing: If the said Standard is set up on the Mainmast yards Arm, it shall be the Signal for the Boats to come to succour the Ship, she being in danger of sinking.

“ When the Prince's Standard is set up on the Ramparts, it is a Sign that we are Masters of that part of the Fortifications, when the Attack either upon the Castle or Fort may cease, till the said Standard be set up in Captain *Kuylenburg*'s Quarters, near the Seashoar; this being intended for a Signal, that we are also Masters of the Town on the Landside, when the Officers in their respective Attacks may either stop or go forward, according as it shall be thought convenient by the Majority of Voices.

“ Whilst the Ships the *Maid of Enchuysen* and *Workum*, are under Sail to enter the Bay, all the rest of the Ships shall weigh their Anchors, and put up the red Flag, as if they would enter the Bay, but keep without Cannon-shot. So soon as the Forces are landed, all the Officers, Soldiers and Seamen, shall obey Mr. *Adrian Roothaus*, as their supreme Commander.

Baldæus. "Whilst the Ships and Men are engaged against the Water-Fort, the City "is to be assaulted at the same time, "near the Sea-shoar, at the Bastion of "St. *John*, and on the Land-side near "the Gate of *Rajuba*: The Attack upon the Bastion of S. *John* shall be commanded by Captain *Kous*, and the other by Captain *Kuylenburgh*, either of "them to be seconded, as Occasion requires, by Mr. *John van der Laan*, the "Companies of *Kuylenburgh*, *Govert* "*Quartel*, *Jurian Gevel*, *Andrew Steckens*, *Lambert Steenhagen*, *Hans Christopher*, *Joachim Block*, *Melchior van Schonenbeck* and *John Moll*, with 36 *Javaneses*, and half a Company of *Bandaneses*, to be employ'd in the Assault of "the first Bastion: The scaling Ladders "shall be carried and fixed by the *Bandaneses*, *Javaneses* and *Mardykers*, mix'd "with some *Dutch* Seamen, arm'd with "Hand-Granadoes, Pikes and Hangers. "The Bastions of *Clergos* and S. *Philippo*, "near that of Saint *Sebastian* (at the "Gate of *Rajuba*) shall be attack'd "by the Companies of Captain *Westrenen*, Lieutenant *Wildtschut*, *John* "*Hartman*, *John Cooper*, *Hardenbergh*, "*Roggenkamp*, *James Alenbier*, *Diedelof* "*van der Beek*, *Henry Broekhuysen*, *John* "*Coertsen*, with the *Javaneses*, half a "Company of *Bandaneses*, and the Company commanded by Captain *Ruysch*.

"Captain *Westrenen* shall command "the Attack against the Bastion of *Clergos*, and Captain *Ruysch* that of S. *Philippo*, to be seconded by fresh Forces as "Occasion requires. The *Bandaneses*, "*Javaneses* and *Mardykers*, in conjunction with the *Dutch* Seamen, shall fix the "scaling Ladders, and the *Lascaryns* of "*Ceylon* be employ'd in carrying off "the Slain.

About the same time we received Intelligence, that the *Portuguese* Succours were arriv'd at *Goa*, and that they intended to come to the Relief of *Columbo*: Word whereof was sent immediately to *Gale* to be upon their Guard, for fear of a Surprize. The 11*th* of *Novemb.* (the Day appointed for the General Assault) it being calm, so that the Ships could not enter the Bay, the same was defer'd till the next Day, tho we did not cease in the mean time to play more furiously with our Cannon than ever before, and we observ'd that the Enemy had taken in their red Flag upon the Bastion of S. *Crus*.

CHAP. XXVII.

A General Assault both by Sea and Land made upon Columbo, *but without Success. Letters from* Raja Singa *to the General.* Dutch *Prisoners come out of* Columbo.

The Water-Fort battered by the Ships. THE 12*th* by break of Day, the *Maid of Enchuysen*, and soon after the *Workum*, being followed by the *Ter Goes* and the *Erasmus*, thunder'd most furiously against the Water-Fort, from whence they answer'd them very briskly. Immediately after the Assault was begun on the Landside in three several Places: The General in Person with ten Compadies attack'd the Gate of *Rajuba*, and the Bastions of S. *Philippo* and *Clergos*; and Major *John van der Laan* with nine Companies, those of St. *John* and *Couras*; whilst *James Lippens* with two Companies of Soldiers and some Seamen, pass'd the Fens in seven *Chinese Champans* or Boats, in order to attack the City where it was least fortify'd.

Columbo assaulted by Sea and Land. But the Besieg'd fir'd so furiously upon our Men, especially with their Firelocks, that the Seamen could not be brought forward to fix the scaling Ladders; which the General perceiving, he advanc'd in Person with some of the bravest Officers, and fix'd the scaling Ladders to the Cortin: but having receiv'd a Wound in his Left Thigh, he was forc'd to be carried off. In the mean while News being brought that they had enter'd the Breach on Major *van der Laan*'s Attack, he return'd to his Station (before his Wound was dressed) but found things in such a Confusion, that he was forc'd to retreat, the Major and his Forces not being able to maintain themselves in the Breach, retreating at the same time, after they had in vain attempted three times to recover it. Lieutenant *Melchior van Schoonbeek*, a *High-German* by Birth, and of a Noble Family, was the only Person who got upon the Bastion of S. *John*, but for want of being seconded, lost his Life there like a brave Soldier, his Head being afterwards stuck upon a Pike by the *Portugueses*, upon the same Bastion. *With ill Success.*

The Forces under Captain *Lippens*, having not without some Resistance from four *Manchous* or Boats, passed the Fens, got into the City; but the Captain being sorely wounded, made shift to retreat with some few, the rest for want of timely Succours being all made Prisoners of War. The Yacht the *Maid of Enchuysen*, was so sorely batter'd from the Fort, that being ready to sink, her Crew was carried off by the Sloop the *Langerack*; but the *Workum* cut her Cables, and got out of the Bay without any considerable Loss. The Number of the Slain on our side amounted to 200, and 350 wounded, not including the two Companies of *John van Hardenburg* and *Roggencamp*, and the Seamen commanded by *John Lippens*, that were made Prisoners in the City. The Ships the *Ter Goes* and *Erasmus*, who had aboard the Soldiers that were to assault the Water-Fort, not being able to get near enough by reason of the Wind, soon got out of the Bay.

Number of the slain and wounded.

Letter from the Emperor to the General.

" ON this unfortunate Day the General received a Letter from his " Imperial Majesty, testifying his good " Opinion of his Excellency, not questioning but that after the taking of *Columbo* he would deliver the said City " into his Hands, pursuant to the Agreement made with Mr. *Westerwold*. That " he desir'd to have such of his Rebellious Subjects, as should fall into our " Hands, deliver'd up to his *Dissaves*, either alive or dead, in order " to punish them with the same Severity, " as he had done those at *Baticalo*; and " that he had order'd his Governors to " ravage and destroy all the Villages in the " *Low-Lands*. He sent at the same time enclos'd a Letter from the *Portuguese* Governor, *Antonio de Souza Continho*, dated *Octob.* 27. at *Columbo*, to the Emperor, the chief Contents whereof were, " That " he could not forbear to put his Majesty " in mind of the antient Friendship betwixt him and the *Portugueses*, which " he was sorry to have been interrupted, " by the *Dutch* making themselves Masters of *Calcture*, and having routed " their Forces near *Paneture*, by laying " so close and vigorous a Siege to the City of *Columbo*, that they were in great " Danger of being forc'd to surrender. " Wherefore they craved his Majesty's " Assistance against the *Hollanders*, who " after they were Masters of the City, " would certainly not deliver up the " same to his Majesty, but lord it over " his Subjects; which his Majesty, according to his Wisdom, might easily see, " how much it would tend to his Dishonour; whereas if he join'd with the " *Portugueses* against them, he might " promise himself all the Advantages " due to so great a Monarch.

Baldæus.

The 13th of *Novemb.* was spent in carrying the wounded Soldiers to *Negumbo*, *Gale*, and *Montual*: The same Day the Enemy in a Bravado, put two of our Ensigns upon the Bastions of S. *John* and S. *Philippo*. At the same time Advice was brought, that the Ships the *Avenhorn* and *Campen* richly laden from *Persia*, were arrived at *Gale* in their Voyage to *Batavia*. For which Reason the Yacht the *Brownfish* was dispatch'd to *Gale*, to carry some Letters thither, to be sent further to *Batavia*, as likewise a Letter to be sent by Land to the Emperor *Raja Singa*. The Yacht the *Popkensburg* arriv'd also with Gunpowder and other Necessaries for our Camp.

The wounded sent away.

The 19th, a Letter from the Emperor *Raja Singa* was deliver'd by his *Dissaves* to the General, wherein he condol'd him about his Wound, and the ill Success of the late Assault, telling him, that he was employ'd Day and Night in making Preparations to join him with his Forces, and desiring not to venture a second Assault before his Arrival. A Letter of Thanks being order'd to be written to his Majesty, the Yachts the *Workum* and *Popkensburg*, with a Frigate, were dispatch'd to *Negumbo*, to cruise to the North of that Harbour, to get timely Intelligence of the Enemies Approach.

Some Ships sent a cruising.

The 26th some Cannon-shot being heard at a good distance, it was generally believed to be the Signal from the Fortress of *Negumbo*, to advertise the Arrival of the *Portuguese* Fleet. Whereupon Mr. *Adrian van der Meyden* took two Companies of Soldiers and as many Seamen, out of the Church of *Quia de Lobo* (where they had their Post) and marched directly to *Montual*, in order to embark them there, to prevent the Enemies Landing. The General, notwithstanding his Wound, follow'd thither in Person, and found them ready to embark, which was however defer'd for that time, till they should receive more certain Intelligence. Only the Yachts the *Mars* and the *Flissingen*, with some Officers aboard them, were commanded to cruise off the Northern Point of *Montual*.

Much about the same time arriv'd the *Roman* Yacht from *Suratte* with 16 Loads of Wheat. The Officers reported that

a

Baldæus. A whole Fleet of Portugueses lost. a *Portuguese* Fleet consisting of 30 Frigates, was entirely destroy'd by a Tempest near *Wingurla*, but that no body knew from whence they came, or whither they were bound; and that the Cannon we heard some Days before, was discharg'd by them as a Signal of their Distress, to the *Workum* and *Popkensburg*.

The 29*th* Captain *Kuylenburgh*, who died of the Wounds he received in the late Assault, being honourably interr'd; the 1*st* of *Decemb.* two Serjeants came into our Camp, who being formerly taken Prisoners at *Anguratotte* by the *Portugueses*, had taken the Opportunity, as these were flying from *Manaar* to *Tutecoryn*, to desert and hide themselves among the *Moors* of *Kilicare*, from whence they were brought in one of our Vessels hither. On the other hand a certain Seaman, named *Claas Claasz*, did swim cross part of the Bay into the City.

The same Night a new Trench was open'd against the Bastion of S. *John*, and carried on with all imaginable Diligence. The Yacht the *Roman* was sent a cruising to get Intelligence, whether any of the Enemies Ships could be discover'd at Sea, as the *Flushing* Yacht was dispatch'd to the Coast of *Malabar*, and the *Erasmus* sent out in her stead a cruising.

CHAP. XXVIII.

Want in Columbo. Anthony Amiral de Menezes *taken Prisoner. The Continuation of the Siege.*

Want in Columbo. THE 7*th* of *Decemb.* we got Intelligence, that most of the Inhabitants of *Columbo*, for want of Rice and other Provisions, had been forc'd to list themselves among the regular Forces; that in the late Assault they had taken 70 or 80 of ours Prisoners, whereas their whole Loss did not amount to above 20 or 25 *Portugueses*, among whom were however two Persons of Note, *viz. Anthonio Barboso*, and *Felicio Leesio*, Lord of *Macoene*. That they had mounted the Cannon taken out of the *Maid of Enchuysen* upon their Bastions, and were busy in making divers Retrenchments, in hopes of being soon succour'd from *Goa*, and that their whole Force consisted in 700 *Portugueses*.

Anthonio Menezes *taken with Letters.* The 10*th* of *Decemb. Antonio Amiral de Menezes* (then Governor of *Jafnapatnam*, and afterwards 1658. kill'd at the taking of *Manaar*) was taken Prisoner at *Montual*, as he was going from *Manaar* to *Columbo* with some Letters one whereof being written in Characters, was unciphered by the General's Order, and was as follows.

To the General Antonio de Souza Coutinho.

"BEfore I had the least Intelligence "of the Approach of the Enemies "Ships, I writ to your Excellency by "Land, tho I have not heard since what "is become of the Messenger. The "three *Pados* are well arriv'd at *Goa*, and "the five Messengers sent thither; the "sixth sent by *Anthony d' Abreu*, did not "stay in the least in this Fort, but tarried two Days at *Negapatan*, and brings "along with him full Instructions concerning the Relief of *Columbo*. I have "not been idle in my Station, both in "advising how to raise Men for our Service in the *Indies*, and in contributing "all that lay in my Power of my own "accord, which by some others has not "been done without reluctancy, especially in giving my Assistance in equipping "some Vessels of Bulk, and Galleys "well mann'd for the Relief of the City. "I have hitherto heard no News from "the Fleet at Cape *Comoryn*, sent for "that purpose. I wish they may reach "the Isle of *Manaar*, when we shall have "Opportunity to debate the whole matter with the Commander in Chief, how "to contrive matters for the Defence of "the Place: You may rest assur'd, that "nothing shall be wanting on my part, "that may tend towards the Accomplishment of its Relief, which I heartily "wish may take effect; it being my Opinion, that a good Fleet is the very "means now to preserve that Place, till "we receive our Supplies from *Goa*. "Perhaps it may please God to destroy "the Hereticks in this Siege, and to abate their Haughtiness, occasion'd by "their late Success, caus'd by our "Neglect; it being certain, that the "same might have been foreseen a considerable time ago. Orders are given "to have a good quantity of Matches "made,

"made, which shall be brought by the "first *Pado* that goes from hence; the "other two shall follow soon after, one "of them being to be armed for the "Defence of the other: Their approach "you will know by the Signals agreed "upon. Perhaps the Governor of *Manaar* may have got Intelligence of our "Fleet, and has given you intelligence "thereof. God preserve and deliver "your Excellency from all danger.

Jafnapatnam 11. Nov. 1655. *Anthonio Amiral de Menezes.*

The Contents of another Letter were as follows.

"I Writ to your Excellency under Co-"vert of *Sebastian Martino* with the "Galliots of *September*, when I little "dream'd of what we heard afterwards "at *Cochin*, and on the Cape *Comoryn*, "concerning the present danger of the "City, and of the loss of so brave a "Captain as *Anthonio Mendes d' Aranha*, "with a good number of our choicest "Men. I have since understood several "other things of this nature, which "have cost me many Tears; we did all "we could to make the Cape *Comoryn*, "but the contrary Wind prevented us: "However, tho we have fail'd in this, "you may assure you self, that the Vice-"roy will not fail to succour the City of "*Columbo* with all his Forces in the *In-*"*dies*. It is rumour'd here, that *Don* "*Manoel Mascarenhas* intends to leave "this place, there being very bad News "brought lately from *Jafnapatnam*; but "we hope and pray to God that he will "be pleased to preserve the City till *Fe-*"*bruary*.

11 Novemb. 1655. *Nicolao d' Olivera.*

The rest of the Letters were very near the same, with this addition only, that the *Portugueses* set sail in *October* with 15 Frigots, but were forc'd back near the Cape *Comoryn*, so near that they had landed some Soldiers, who were marched by Land to *Jafnapatnam*, with an intention to come to *Columbo*, to give notice there of the Equipment of six Galeons at *Goa* intended for the Succours of the City; and that in case the *Dutch* should block up that Habour, they would fight their way through them. All these Letters were sent to his Imperial Majesty.

200 Negroes make a Sally. The 12 *Decemb.* 200 Negroes being seen to sally out of the Gate of *Mapane*, keeping along the Sea-shore, three Companies were order'd to attack them; but they no sooner espied our People advancing towards them, than they retreated in haste to the City: However three of them deserted to us, and gave an account that the reason of their coming out was only to fetch and cut some Faggot-Wood for the repairing of the Bastions of S. *John*, S. *Stephen* and S. *Philippo*; and that they had made betwixt the two former a Retrenchment, in case they should be forced to quit the Bastions. *Baldæus.*

Report of some Deserters. The same day we finish'd our second Redoubt, and the next two *Portuguese* Deserters confirm'd the Report of the Negroes, adding that they much dreaded our Mines, that the Bastion of S. *John* was guarded by two Companies (of 25 or 30 Men each) under *Caspar Figeiro*, the Gate of *Magapane* with three, and the rest in proportion. At the same time we saw a whole Troop of half-starv'd Wretches forc'd out of the Town, but were made to return from whence they came, except a few *Portugueses*, who could give good intelligence about the Condition of the Place.

The 14*th* in the morning 10 or 12 Boats came out of the Town to fetch Faggot-wood; but finding us prepare to attack them, they retir'd with Precipitation, after they had wounded three of our Men.

The 15*th* the General agreed with 20 Pioneers to work continually (six at a time) in the Trenches, at the rate of 20 Pence *per diem*, besides a good Reward after they had finish'd the Work. In the Afternoon a Battery of 6 Guns was order'd to be erected.

An unfortunate Accident. The 18*th* a Gunner having out of carelesness double charg'd a Gun upon a Battery, kill'd three of our own Pioneers, and wounded 7 Negroes; and in the Evening four great Cannon were not without some loss planted upon the before-mentioned Battery.

The 19*th* we play'd thence most furiously upon the Bastions of S. *John* and *Stephen*, and two more Cannons were mounted upon it the same Evening.

The 20*th* a new Redoubt was begun, the Trenches being then carried on within two Rods of the Counterscarp. In the Evening we missed *Simon Lopes*, who was again gone over to the Enemy.

The 26*th* three Negro Carpenters coming over to us, reported that the *Portugueses* had undermin'd the Bastion of S. *John*, and laid 5 large Barrels with Gunpowder in five divers places underneath it,

Baldæus. it, having laid the Train by the means of certain Bambocanes, which were to be lighted on the top whilst we were assaulting the said Bastion, which was the reason that they had not discharg'd their Cannon from thence these two days past. They added, that the Son of *Anthonio de Souza Coutinho* the Governor of *Columbo*, being busy in incouraging the Workmen by his own Example, receiv'd a Wound by a Musquet-shot in the Head, of which he died soon after. A Council of War was also call'd, in which it was resolv'd to carry on the Trenches with all imaginable vigor, to prevent the Enemy in perfecting his Retrenchments before the Breach of the Bastion of S. *John*, and to fix our Miners there.

Resolution taken in a Council of War.

The 27*th* the General gave notice to the Dissaves of *Saffragam* and the four *Corles*, that he intended to send an Envoy to his Majesty, to know his Inclinations, whether he intended to appear in Person in our Camp or not: he desir'd them to write to him upon the same Subject, the time for attempting a second general Assault drawing near; and that in case his Majesty had the least doubt left of our sincere Intentions, he would give him full Satisfaction upon that Head.

CHAP. XXIX.

The Portugueses *throw Stones out of a Mortar. We make a third Redoubt: Endeavour to lay the Gallery over the Ditch. A Spy hang'd. Letters from* Coromandel.

THE 28*th* of *December* in the Evening the *Portugueses* began to throw several Stones out of a Mortar into our Works, which something surpriz'd us at first, but afterwards we guess'd that it was *Simon Lopes* who lately deserted our Service that had put them in the way of it. The next day Capt. *John Hartman* was sent with Letters to the Emperor at *Candy*, and we were hard at work to bring the third Redoubt near the Sea-shore to perfection, where we planted a Mortar, and continued our approaches to the Counterscarp.

Another Redoubt erected.

A *Chinese* Deserter, a Native of *Macao*, reported that they were indifferently well provided with Provisions in the City, and that it was true that the Governor's Son was dead. Letters were at the same dispatch'd to Mr. *Laurence Pit*, Governor of *Coromandel*, to send us some Ammunition, and to order the Ships which upon the arrival of the Vessels from *Tajouan* sail from thence to *Batavia*, to touch at *Gale*, to be employ'd in thwarting the intended Succours of the *Portugueses*, or to take aboard part of the *Portuguese* Prisoners among us.

The 8*th* of *January*, finding the Enemy busy in planting Palisado's in the Ditch, some Seamen arm'd with Hand-granado's made them soon quit that Enterprize. But the next following day finding the Enemy to have made some Entrenchments there, a Hole was order'd to be made in the Wall; and Captain *Henry Gerard*, the head Gunner and Ingineer, and Carpenter, being order'd to view the Work, they reported that the Enemy had planted a row of Palisado's close to one another, extending to the Sea-shore, which made them imagine that they expected the most fierce Assault on that side.

Portugueses fortify themselves in the Ditch.

Six expert Carpenters having offer'd their Service for perfecting the Gallery, 100 Crowns were promised them as a Reward; and it being resolv'd to fix the said Gallery the next day under favour of our great Cannon and Fire-locks, a certain number of Musqueteers were order'd to the extremities of the Trenches: but the Wall being thicker at the bottom than at the top, it was almost Evening before they could make a Breach in it, when attacking the Enemy with their Hand-granado's, they forced them from the Ditch, where they posted 12 Fire-locks; but these receiv'd so warm a Salute from the Enemy's Cannon and Fire-locks both of the Bastions of S. *John* and S. *Stephen*, and the Palisado-work, that they were forced to retreat, and the fixing of the Gallery was thought fit to be delay'd till a more convenient time, having lost only one Carpenter and two Negroes in this Enterprize. *John Roothaus* the *Dutch* Reer-Admiral sent 12 *Jan.* three Negro Prisoners from the Fleet into the Camp, who were taken coming with Letters from *Manaar*, in order to carry them into *Columbo*; but they were of little moment, except what was contain'd

The Dutch *endeavour in vain to fix their Gallery.*

tain'd in the following Passage taken out of *Lorenso Barboza*'s Letter directed to *Don Francisco de Souza*.

Some Letters intercepted. "Your Fleet could not make the Cape "*Comoryn*, because they came too late, and "were overtaken by a violent Tempest; "the Soldiers aboard were sent by Land "to *Tutecoryn*, and from thence by Sea "to *Manaar*. That they understood "that great Endeavours were used to "equip a Squadron of great Ships and "Frigots, to be joyn'd by 8 Galeons "for the relief of *Columbo*, and that they "had certain Advice that the Galeons "were getting ready for that purpose: "That the rest they would be inform'd "of by the Captain-Major's Letter to the "Governor, *&c.*

The said Prisoners reported that *Anthonio Amiral* had brought a Reinforcement of six Companies from *Jafnapatnam* to *Manaar*; and that it was reported there, that 5 Galeons and 28 Frigots were to come from *Goa*, and being joyn'd with some other Vessels and Forces at *Manaar* were to sail to the relief of *Columbo*: whereupon the General sent his Instructions to our Squadron to watch the coming of the Enemy, but especially to our Cruisers, the *Workum*, *Popkensburgh*, *Mars* and *Erasmus* Yachts; 30 *Bandanese* Soldiers, and as many *Mardykers* were also order'd aboard these Vessels, and a Negro Deserter reported that those come from *Manaar* to *Columbo* were half naked, and had brought no Letters, one of them being wounded, but knew nothing further.

New Instructions sent to the Dutch Fleet.

The 15*th* of *January* some of our *Lascaryns* brought in a Spy, whom they had taken under pretence of going into the City to sell Tobacco; but upon the Evidence of two *Cingalese* Carpenters that he was a Spy, he was hang'd on a Gibbet near the place where he intended to have got into the place.

Letters from Coromandel. The 19*th* Letters were brought to the Camp, sent by *Laurence Pit*, then Governor of *Coromandel*, intimating that we might expect a Supply of 35000 Pounds weight of Gunpowder with the Yachts the *Codfish*, *Rabbit*, and *Patience*; that for the rest the Company had lost 50 loads of Rice, and 250 *Ammenams* * of *Areek* † by an accidental Fire. That several private Merchants having lately sent certain Ships loaden with all sorts of Provisions, we need not fear any thing upon that account. The *Rabbit* alone had a Cargo of 26822 Pounds weight of Gunpowder, 50 Packs of *Guinea* Linen Cloth, and 10 Loads of Rice, valued altogether at 23860 Gilders.

* *A certain Measure.*
† Areek *is a certain* Indian *Fruit of which they make strong Liquors.*

It was further advised, that in all probability the King of *Golconda* was likely to be embroil'd in a War with *Mirza Mula* his General, who had put strong Garisons in the Fortresses of *Gendecalte*, *Gronconde* and *Goeti*. That the General *Chan Channe* was lately retir'd with the Forces of *Visiapour*, consisting of 8000 Horse, and 40000 Foot, from *Velour* to *Visiapour*, but for what reason was not known. A Copy was also sent of a Letter written by *Leonard Johnson* Factor, *Decemb.* 8. from *Wingurla* to *Batavia*, whence it appear'd that they were making great Preparations at *Goa* for the relief of *Columbo*. "But, added he, the *Portuguese* Viceroy having sufficient Intel"ligence of our Strength before *Co"lumbo*, it seems to me to be rather a "Bravado than a real Design, unless it "were (as some affirm) that the Re"lief of that City was so positively com"manded by the King of *Portugal*, that "the Viceroy would be forced to attempt "it, unless he were prevented by the "*Dutch* blocking up the Harbour of *Goa* "before that time. That it was ru"mour'd there that the *Portuguese* Sol"diers should be oblig'd by Oath, con"firm'd by the Blessed Sacrament, that "in case they were not able to worst the "*Dutch* Fleet, they should set fire to "their own Ships; but he hoped that "the City would fall into our hands "before they could put their Design in "Execution. But, as it were not safe to "despise ones Enemy, so he would take "care to give from time to time Intelli"gence of what he could learn to the "Director-General *Gerard Hulst* with all "imaginable speed, for which purpose "he hoped to purchase the Diligence of "some of the Natives by Mony. The following List was annex'd of such Ships as were to be employ'd in the said Expedition, 2 *Caraques*, 2 large Galeons, one lesser one, 2 *Caravals*, 6 *Patacho's* or Yachts, 20 light Frigots, 24 more from the Coast of *Sipaveneick*, with some Galeons, and other Boats call'd *Singazeeles*. His further opinion was, that the said Squadron might be ready towards the end of *January*, and that the same was to be reinforc'd by some Yachts from *Chaul*; that besides the Garison to be left at *Goa*, 2000 *Europeans*, not reckoning the *Mistices* and Negroes, were to be embark'd aboard the said Fleet. He advised further, that two *English* Ships being some days before come to an Anchor before *Goa*, the Viceroy had offer'd the Captains a considerable Sum of Mony, pro-

Baldæus.

List of the Portuguese Ships for the relief of Columbo.

Baldæus. provided they would sail along with the Fleet to *Ceylon*; but that they refused to accept of the same, and were sail'd to the Northward.

The 21*st* of *January*, two hours before break of day, the General being got aboard the *Ter Goes*, call'd a Council of War there, wherein it was resolv'd to send forthwith the Ship the *Cod-fish* to *Negombo*, in order to unlade her Cargo (intended for *Gale*) there in company of the *Amsterdam* and *Marygold-flower*; and the *Hare* Yacht was order'd to keep as close to the Bay as possibly she could, to observe the small Vessels that might pass and repass in and out of the City.

The 24*th* of *January* the *Flushing* Yacht coming from *Wingurla*, brought Letters from our Factor *Leonard Johnson*, dated the 6*th* of *January*, intimating, that the Viceroy of *Goa*, instead of sending the pretended Succours to *Ceylon*, had now resolved to send two *Caracks* to *Portugal*, and three Yachts to *Mosambique*; and that the Design of the Relief of *Columbo* seem'd to be laid aside: in confirmation whereof he sent the following Translation of a Letter written by one of our Spies there.

To the Commodore of the Dutch *Squadron near* Wingurla.

Letter of a Spy from Goa. " TWO Ships (both arrived this " Year) viz. *Bon Jesus* carrying 65 " Guns, and the *Nossa Senhora da Grazia* " of 60 Guns, are intended to be sent to " *Portugal*, being now busy in unloading, " and expecting only the return of our " Fleet from *Cochin* and the Cape. It is " supposed they will be ready to sail by " the end of the first Month of the Year. " Three Yachts more are order'd from " *Mosambique*, being now taking in their " Cargo, besides another Yacht, design'd " for *Macassar*. The *Caravel* intended " for *China* is not ready to sail, and it " remains uncertain whether she will go " thither. But, if she does, it will not " be till next Spring. Hitherto we see " no Preparations either of Men or Ships " for *Ceylon*; and they seem unresolved, " whether they had best send any Relief " thither, for fear they should fall into " the hands of the *Dutch*. But if any be " sent, it will certainly not be till after " the departure of the Ships for *Portugal*, for which the Viceroy shews a " great concern, being afraid they will " be intercepted by the *Dutch* before " they can reach *Portugal*.

Dated January 6. 1656.

Your Excellency's constant Slave,

Uragami Sinay.

Hereupon it was agreed in a Council of War, to order the Ships the *Ter Goes*, *Mars*, the *Arms of Holland*, *Amsterdam*, *Flushing*, *Erasmus*, *Naarden*, *Zierik-see*, *Marygold-flower*, and the *Hare*, forthwith towards *Goa*, there to expect the coming of the Ships from *Trajouan*, in company of those from *Persia* and *Suratte*. And that the Yachts the *Workum*, *Popkensburgh*, *Codfish* and *Rabbit*, with some light Frigats and Sloops, should be kept for the Blockade of the Harbour of *Columbo*. *Dutch Ships sent to Goa.*

CHAP. XXX.

Mr. Hartman *presented by the Emperor. Some Spies hang'd. The Arrival of several Ships. Letters from the Emperor and* Dutch *General.*

ABout that time the Emperor sent his Letter to the *Dutch* General Mr. *Hulst*, in answer to his sent by Mr. *Hartman*, the chief Contents of which were, " That he intended to come into our " Camp in the night-time, having been " detained hitherto by the Advice of the " Great Men of his Court (these *Pagans* " being very superstitious in chusing their " time) but that now he was resolved to " speak with the General in spite of all " the pretended Obstacles. That he was " glad to understand, that notwithstanding our Loss in the last general Assault " we kept our Posts, and that he intended to dispatch Mr. *Hartman* the next " Thursday. It was dated at *Balane*, *January* 20, 1656. and subscribed,

Raja Singa Rajou, most potent Emperor of *Ceylon*.

Mr. *Hartman* returned, being presented with a Golden Chain and a Ring, and reported, that some of the Emperor's *Dissaves* having brought him the news, *Mr. Hartman's Return.*

that

that we had lost a considerable number of men by the springing of a Mine, he was very glad to hear the contrary afterwards. The 26*th* of *January* early in the Morning a Letter was delivered from our Head Factor at *Gale*, *John Kroon*, that the Ships the *Patience*, the *Bengale*, the *Black Bull* and the *Grey-hound* from *Tajouan* by the way of *Masulipatan*, loaden with Merchandizes from *Persia*, and the *Vlieland* belonging to those of *Suratte*, were arrived there, and that he had ordered them to sail for *Columbo*. Two Spies come lately out of the City, to view the Condition of our Attacks and Batteries, were hang'd two days after.

Some Dutch Ships arrived.

Two Spies hang'd.

At the same time Letters were brought into the Camp, dated the last of *Novemb.* at *Malacca*, intimating, that the 14*th*, 15*th* and 19*th* of *November* 1655. the Ships the *Vlieland*, *Black Bull*, *Arnemuyden* and the *Sweet-briar*, were arrived there from *Tajouan*, their Loading being valued at 1349436 Gilders at the first hand: and that the *Sweet-briar*, the *Domburg* and *Lion* were with a good quantity of Tin of *Malacca* sent to *Bengale*. The Cargo of these Ships consists commonly of *Japonese* Silver, Bars of Copper, Alum, Gold, *China* Tea, and Sugar of *Formosa*, besides a considerable quantity of Tin of *Malacca*. Upon the Coast of *Malabar*, and in *Ceylon* (where they commonly arrive at the same time) they load with Cinnamon, Pepper and Cardamom. They generally make a long Voyage: For they set sail from *Batavia* to *Japan* and *Tajouan* in *May*, and come to *Malacca* in *December*: From thence they steer their Course by the *Nicebares* to *Ceylon*, or *Bengale*, or *Coromandel* (but never from these Places to *Ceylon*, but sometimes return from *Bengale* or *Ceylon* to *Malacca* or *Batavia*) and from thence by *Malabar* to *Suratte* and *Persia*, and return in *May* to *Ceylon* (and sometimes straitways to *Batavia*) and so further with their Cargo (they have taken in at *Suratte* or in *Persia*) to the Coast of *Coromandel*, where being loaden with Linen Cloth, painted Callicoes and other Merchandizes, they return to *Batavia* in *June* or *July*. By Letters from *John Thyssen* Governour of *Malacca*, advice was given that the Tin Trade (the chiefest of that Country) had been but very indifferent that Year.

Advices from Malacca.

Two Deserters give an account of the Condition of the City.

But it is time to return to the Siege of *Columbo*. The last day of *January* two *Portuguese* Deserters, who had made shift to let themselves down by Ropes from St. *Stephens* Bastion, reported, that many of their Comrades were willing to desert for want of Pay, but that they were strictly guarded; that the Garison consisted still of 650 *Europeans*, and they had Rice for two Months longer; that they still rely'd upon the promised Succours of 6 Galeons. Soon after we saw a whole Troop of half-starv'd Wretches coming out of the Town; but 120 were forced to return without Relief. The 12*th* of *February* about 500 of them, Men, Women and Children, being forced by extremity of Hunger, came to the General's Quarter imploring his Mercy; but they were forced back into the Town along the Sea-shore near the Bastion of St. *John*. In the mean while the Emperor sent the following Letter to the General.

Raja Singa Rajou.

The Emperor's Letter to the General.

" OUR Imperial Majesty has formerly (thro God's Mercy) been victorious over our Enemies in *Malvane*, where I routed their whole Army commanded by *Don Constantino*; after which laying Siege to *Columbo*, I had my Head Quarters in the Garden of *Lewis Gomes Pinto*. It then pleased God to afflict me with a Distemper, which the Viceroy having got notice of, he desired me to return to *Candy*; which I did accordingly, leaving my Brother *Carnana Singa* King of *Ouve*, with the Prince of *Visiapalla*, to command the Siege, who put no small Blemish upon our Imperial Family. Whilst they were imployed in that Siege, the treacherous *Portugueses* having at that time forced a Multitude of starved Wretches out of the City, they had mix'd with them certain Villains, who set all our Works on fire. Wherefore I hope your Excellency will keep a strict Guard; for I can't forbear, for the Love and good Inclinations I bear to your Excellency, to put you in mind, that the *Portugueses* are a most perfidious Nation, and that even my Forces are composed of divers sorts of People: So that your Excellency ought to have a particular regard for your own Person, which will be a singular Satisfaction to me. For you must know, that there being variety of People in the Isle of *Ceylon*, who have served divers Princes, and are us'd to Ravages and Rapines, these are generally treacherous, and not to be trusted by your Excellency, tho perhaps they will endeavour to obtain your Favour by

Baldæus. "Flatteries and Pretences of Friendship, "they being such profligate Wretches, "as to be induced by the hopes of a small "Gain to undertake any base and treacherous Act. The Letters sent from this "Court to your Excellency being generally "written in an unknown Tongue, I desire "you, if you find any Defect or Inconveniency in them, to give notice thereof "immediately, to remove all Obstacles "and Misunderstandings on our side; "it being our resolution, that the Peace "made with you shall continue as long as "the Sun and Moon furnish us with Light, "as you on your behalf have engaged it "shall last as long as the World stands. "I once intended to have sent you an "Answer to your Letter dated *Jan.* 8. "but understanding that your Excellency "had dispatched to this Court a Captain of the Guards, I thought fit to "defer it for some time. In former "times whilst I was very young, I was "encamped with my Army in *Malvane*; "but that being many years ago, I did "send thither certain Persons to view "the Place, who assur'd me, that the "Place pitch'd upon by the *Dissave* of "the four *Corles*, was unfit for our Reception, which was the reason I order'd "my Head Quarters to be settled in the "Fortress of *Reygamwatte.* In consideration of which and other Miscarriages "of the said *Dissave*, I have put another "in his Place, with whom you may consult in relation to such matters as tend "to our Service. I further issued my "Orders to the *Dissaves*, and sent certain Persons to prepare my Quarters "with the utmost Expedition, which "done I intend to be there immediately "after.

Dated in the Camp and Court of Giiramibula, *Feb.* 14. 1656.

Subscribed,

Raja Singa Rajou, most potent Emperor of *Ceylon.*

The General being extremely pleased with the Emperor's Approbation concerning the sending back of the poor starv'd Wretches forc'd out of *Columbo*, thought fit to send the following Letter to the Governour of *Columbo.*

The Dutch *General's Letter to the Governour of* Columbo.

"Finding that you suffer the poor *Negro* Citizens, after that you have "received all the Services you possibly "could from them, to perish for want of "Sustenance; and whereas you prevented their Desertion formerly by strict "Watches, you now permit them to go "where they please in order to be rid of "them: I thought it my Duty (for the "discharge of my Conscience) to desire "you to let the said *Negro* Citizens know, "that such as for the future come out of "the City, shall be punish'd with Death. "This I thought fit to let your Excellency know, in hopes of moving you to "compassion. I remain for the rest "your Excellency's Servant,

Dated in the Dutch *Camp before* Columbo, *Feb.* 15. 1656.

Gerard Hulst.

The 17*th* of *February* the Yacht the *Saphir* came into the Road from *Coromandel*, and brought a Letter from the Governor *Laurence Pit*, dated *January* 29. at *Paliacatta*: Her Cargo consisted in Rice and Gun-powder, tho not so much as was expected, the full quantity of Brimstone not being brought from *Tajouvan.*

But notwithstanding the beforesaid Warning given to the *Negro* Citizens, many of them coming every day into our Camp, one of them was ordered to be hanged to deter others from doing the like; so that afterwards 15 and more died every day in the City of Famine, and a Scorbutick Dropsy began also to reign among the *Europeans* there. The 19*th* a *Mistice* Deserter brought advice, that they had equip'd a Boat, which lay ready to sail against the next Night for *Manaar*; whereupon Orders were sent to Commodore *Roothaus* to intercept her, if possibly he could. The 20*th* Mr. *John Hartman* came with the following Letter from the Emperor to the General. *Famine in* Columbo.

Raja Singa Rajou.

The Emperor's Letter to the General.

"YOUR Letter dated the 8*th* of *February*, I received the next following Day, wherein you testify your "desire of being admitted into our Royal Presence, in order to assure me in "Person of the sincere Intentions of the "*Dutch* Company to continue in their "Confederacy with our Imperial Majesty, made from the time of your Arrival with your Fleet in our Empire. "It has always been my hearty Wish to "see you in my Presence, which I hope "will be fulfill'd with the arrival of your "Excellency in our Camp near *Raygamwatte.* You further mention the Misbehaviour of some of our *Lascaryns* "under the *Dissaves*; so soon as our Imperial Majesty arrives in the above-

"said

"said Camp, these Forces and Officers "shall be relieved by others, and such "as have not done their duty to the "Crown be punished, as is practised in "the Camps of other Great Kings and "Monarchs. Your Excellency did also "give notice that you had sent away 9 "Ships the 5*th* of this Month. God Al-"mighty I hope will bless your Excellen-"cy's Designs with Success, according to "the utmost of my Wishes, there being "nothing that can more rejoice our Im-"perial Majesty than the Welfare and "Prosperity of the *Hollanders*: And I "hope, that after my arrival in the "Camp, such Measures may be taken "betwixt us, as may soon reduce the "City. The refractory Party among "my Troops you have mentioned, shall "be branded with Infamy, not only for "themselves, but also their Generation; "so that their Names shall be despised "hereafter for ever. Whenever I shall "see your Person, I shall imagine to have "the whole State of *Holland* before me; "and since according to our Constitu-"tions Matters of this nature are not to "transacted but on fortunate Days and "Hours, your Excellency shall be adver-"tised thereof by some Person of note. "Just as I was leaving *Candy*, the Prince "my Son, given me by God for the "Welfare of my faithful *Hollanders*, "took leave of me, desiring to be re-"membred to your Excellency.

Baldæus.

In the Camp of Guiramibula, *Feb.* 18. 1656. *Raja Singa Rajou.*

Hartman presented with an Elephant.

The said Mr. *Hartman* was presented by the Emperor with a tame Elephant, and told the General, that the Emperor had given him some private hints, that the Prince his Son would take it as a peculiar Obligation, if the General would honour him with a small Present. The Emperor's *Dissaves* coming the 21*st* of *February* to the General, in order to fetch the Answer to the Emperor's Letter, they were told, that the Letter was not finished, by reason of many things of moment to be inserted therein: But the General took this opportunity to advise with them what Present might be most acceptable to the Prince. They answered, they could not tell, but would consider of the matter. In the Afternoon they received the desired Letter sealed up under the Discharge of the Cannon, as is usual upon such occasions, when each of the Captains is presented with a piece of Sattin, and two of the *Dissaves* with a red *Roan* Cap, a thing highly valued by them (called *Toppy Honday* in their Language) with a *Japonese* Buckler for one of the Prince's Attendants.

CHAP. XXXI.

The Besieged fire furiously upon the Besiegers. The Emperor's Envoys. Negro *Deserters forced back. Letters intercepted. The Emperor presents the General with an* Elk. *A new Battery erected.*

The Besieged fire briskly upon the Besiegers.

THE 22*d* of *February* the Enemy play'd most furiously with their Cannon from the Bastions of St. *Stephen* and St. *John*, and kill'd us several Men. His Majesty being that day come to his Camp at *Reygamwatte*, to take a view of the Quarters prepared for his reception, perceiving a more than ordinary Smoke, sent a Messenger to know the truth of the matter. In the Evening about Supper-time, word was brought that certain Deputys from his Majesty were arrived at a Farm about two Miles from the Camp, and that they had sent a Messenger to signify, that they were desirous to speak with the General that Evening; which being readily granted, an Ensign was sent thither with some Soldiers to conduct them to the Camp, and to make an Excuse, that the time of the Night had hindred their Reception to be sutable to their Quality. They told the General, that his Majesty had received his Letter with a great deal of Satisfaction, and that they were sent to tell his Excellency, that his Majesty was at present at *Walewitty*, and that as soon as his Quarters were fitted up, he should be sent for; for which reason they were commanded by his Majesty to order the *Dissave* of *Saffragamme* to have the Roads leading to *Reygamwatte* repaired. They would willingly have returned the same night; but it being excessive dark, their Quarters were assigned them in the Camp till next morning.

Deputys sent into the Camp from the Emperor.

The same day *Edmund Ruysch* sent word, that a great number of poor Wretches were coming out of the City: The Men, to the number of 50, were secured at

Milagre;

Baldæus. *Milagre*; but the Women and Children being brought before the General, he order'd them (pursuant to their former Resolution) to be whip'd back into the Town near the Bastion of St. *John*, this being look'd upon as the most proper means to straiten the Enemy, and to bring them to our Terms. Towards the Evening the Men, with 20 more, who since had join'd them, being also brought into the Camp, the General took two of them aside, and told them, that they must look upon it as a particular Favour, to be sent back once more; but if they return'd they must expect nothing but the Gallows, unless they would engage with some of the *Aratches* that had deserted our Camp, to surprize some Bastion or other for our Service. They were likewise forced back with a good Whipping, and the 24*th* 150 more had the same Entertainment.

Deserters whip'd back into the City.

The 26*th* of *February* the *Dissave* of the four *Corles* came to tell the General, that those of *Saffragamme* were still busy in repairing the Roads and Bridges, and produced a Letter from certain Great Men of the Court, enjoining him to demand 10 certain Persons, that had made shift to get out of the City with the Enemies Troops, and sheltred themselves in the adjacent Villages, having deserted the King's Service before. The General was not unwilling to grant his Request; but withal told him, that if these Persons of Quality had been as forward in furthering their King's Service as we, there would not have been so many Deserters. The same day a Letter was deliver'd to the General written by one of our *Aratches* to the *Vidane* of *Pasdun-Corle*, as follows:

An intercepted Letter.

"HAngedera Lionayde, Son-in-law to *Ranatonge Arachie*, wishes Health "to *Vidane*, and the three Chieftains of "the three *Pattos* of *Pasdun-Corle*. Im"mediately upon the receipt of these, "you shall without fail or delay gather, "in the time of 8 days, out of all the "circumjacent Villages, 50 *Pingues* of "Pullets, Butter, Pepper, *Atchiar*, and "Earthen Vessels; and with them, in "company of all the Heads or *Majo"rals* of the Villages of *Anguratotte*, "come towards *Horne*, and from thence "into the Imperial Camp, there to pay "your Obeysance to his Majesty. Such "as fail in their Duty must expect to "receive condign Punishment. You "must not publish my Name, what I do "in this respect not being by my own "Authority; but when you come to "Court, you may then declare, that it "was *Hangedera Lionayde*, *Ranatonge* "*Rale*'s Son-in-law, who gave you this "Invitation.

The *Aratche* who had been the Author of this Letter, being seized and examin'd the same Evening by Mr. *Adrian van der Meyden* and Major *van der Laan*, did not disown his Hand, but refused to discover (tho he was threaten'd with present Death) by whose Command he had writ it. The General being of opinion that there was some Mystery hid under this pretence, especially since this *Cingalese* liv'd under the Company's Jurisdiction, and had receiv'd signal Obligations from them, commanded his Head to be cut off, and deliver'd him up for that purpose to the Provost, in hopes of extorting a Confession from him by this means; but under-hand order'd him to be secur'd only aboard the Ship the Arms of *Amsterdam*, for fear, that, in case he should be executed on a sudden, they might be bereaved of the Opportunity of discovering the Truth.

February 27*th* being Sunday, the General sent a Letter to *Raja Singa*, to advertise his Majesty what had pass'd with the *Aratche*, and at the same time enclosed the Original of the intercepted Letter. The same day the *Dissave* of *Saffragamme* coming to the General to tell him, that the Roads and Bridges were now repaired according to his Majesty's Orders; he was commanded by him to imploy the same People in perfecting the Pallisadoes intended for the new Redoubt near the Gate of *Rajuba*, which he promised to do. The General also told him what had happen'd with the *Aratche*; which he approving of, the General further desired him to provide some *Bufflers* for the use of the Seamen, who were sorely afflicted with the Scurvy, which he likewise agreed to.

Letter sent to the Emperor.

Word being brought that four Fishermen were coming over to us in a *Tony* or Fisher-boat, they were forewarn'd not to come into the Camp, under the pain of being hang'd, unless they could engage all the Fishermen to come at once. About the same time a certain *Moorish* Vessel came into the Road from *Puntegale* with a Passport from *John Kroon* our Head Factor there. They brought advice that the Lands and Villages under the Jurisdiction of *Gale* were farm'd out at 15849 Rixdollars, for the next Year, to be paid by four quarterly Payments, and that the *Areck*, which the Company had taken at the

A Moorish Vessel brings Advice concerning the Condition of Gale.

A Moorish Vessel brings Advice concerning the Condition of Gale.

the rate of 24 *Laryns* the *Ammenam* the last year, was now to be deliver'd at the rate of 16 *Laryns*. Five more Ships arrived at the same time laden with Rice.

The last day of this month, finding that the Enemy work'd against us near the Gate of *Rajuba*, Lieutenant *Alenbier* was sent with 6 Firelocks to secure their Workmen; but these saved themselves by an early Flight, and our People return'd without receiving any Damage. About the same time Letters were brought by the Yacht the *Arnemuyden*, dated the 17*th* of *February*, on the Coast of *Coromandel*, others being also expected, dated the 11*th*, with the Yacht the *Codfish*, not arriv'd as yet, having aboard 100 Loads of Rice of *Bengale*, a good Quantity of Gunpowder and 60 Soldiers: The other Vessels Cargo consisted in 18877 Pound-weight of Gunpowder, 2781 Bullets of divers Sizes, *viz.* 231 of 24 Pounds, 750 of 18, 1800 of 12, 1500 Stone-Bullets, and 10000 Pound Weight of Lead, besides some other Merchandizes, and 16 Loads of Rice, amounting to the Value of 6098 Guilders, on account of those of *Ceylon* only. At the same time the *Rabbit* sail'd out of the Road, being order'd to cruise on the South Point of *Negumbo*, and to be relieved every eight Days by another Ship.

Ships from Coromandel.

The General presented with an Elk by the Emperor.

Pretty late in the Evening, three Deputies from the Emperor presented the General with an Elk, which his Majesty himself had hunted the same Morning in an adjacent Wood, which was received with great Reverence by his Excellency.

Baldæus.

The General and Mr. *van der Meyden*, hearing the Beat of Drum in the new Redoubt, near the Gate of *Rajuba*, they went thither in Person; and in their way met with 17 *Lascaryns*, and 2 *Aratches*, who being posted in an Outwork near the said Gate, had quitted the same; they being order'd to be secured in the Head Quarter, they went forward, and found that the Alarm had been occasion'd by the coming over of the *Lascaryns*, whom they mistook for Enemies. They reported that the City was provided with Provisions till *May*, their Allowance, *viz.* 25 *Mididos* to a Head, being given them for the Month of *April*: They added, that it was whisper'd about, that the Governor had embark'd all his Moveables, Mony and Jewels in a Boat, and sent them in the Night-time to *Manaar*; which News was very unpleasing to us, because they had escaped the Sight of our Ships.

Deserters give an account of the Condition of Columbo.

The 6*th*, 7*th*, 8*th* and 9*th* of *March*, we advanced bravely towards the Gate of *Rajuba*: two *Portuguese* Deserters, with some *Lascaryns* well armed, being examined apart, deposed, that the City could not hold out longer than towards the end of *May*, the Remnants of the Rice being very stony and unclean, nay wet and corrupted. Hereupon the General ordered that a Battery of two Guns should be erected opposite to the utmost Point of the Bastion of St. *John*, the better to batter and lay level the Flank of that of St. *Stephens*, and under favour thereof to open again the Trench leading to our Mine, and so working along the Wall, to take Post upon the Counterscarp.

CHAP. XXXII.

Many Deserters give account of the Condition of Columbo. Ysbrand Gotskens *sent Envoy to the Emperor. His Letter to the General, and that of the Besieged to the Emperor.*

About that time divers *Lascaryn* Deserters, and among them a *Portuguese*, made heavy Complaints that they were forced to feed upon corrupted Rice: The last told us, that there were no more than 40 left of our Prisoners, and that such of our Officers as were not slain in the Assault, died afterwards of their Wounds, except a Serjeant. He also discover'd to us, that the Besieged had carried all their Guns from the Bastions of S. *Stephen*, S. *Philip* and *Clergos* into their Outwork, before the Gate of *Rajuba*, in order to discharge the same the next following Night upon our Pioneers. *Paul Meno*, who was then upon the Guard there, was thereupon order'd to let the Labourers cease, till they had spent their Powder and Ball in vain, and then to let them return to their Work. In effect, they shot very furiously the next Night both with their Cannon and Firelocks upon our Works; and by break of Day the General went on Horseback to *Milagre*, to view the Works of the *Dissaves* on that side, which he found

to

Baldæus. to be well secured by a strong Set of Palisadoes, reaching from the Sea-shoar to the Fens; and being guarded by four Companies, these were thought sufficient to oppose any Sally of the Enemy on that side.

One of our Soldiers being some days before missing, we understood that he had sought for shelter with his Majesty for a Crime he had committed, which at his Majesty's Request was remitted him, yet not without being discharg'd from our Service. The *Dissave* who made this Request, told the General, that the Grapes sent to the Emperor had been very well accepted.

A Boy Deserter brings certain Advice. The 13*th* of *March* a Boy, who had deserted the *Portugueses*, came to the General, and told him in private, that having been let down from the Bastion *Clergos* with a Rope, by some *Lascaryns* who kept Guard there, they intended the next Night with the rising of the Moon, to come all over to us, or else to deliver up the Bastion. The Boy according to his own Desire being soundly whipp'd, was sent back into the City, to take away all suspicion of a private Correspondence with us.

To second his Endeavours a Company of the Guards was posted in a convenient Place; but the Besieged fir'd so briskly from the Bastions of St. *Stephen* and St. *Philip* that Night, that there was no Opportunity of putting it in execution at that time. A *Toupas* Deserter reported the next Day, that the Bastion of St. *Stephen* was guarded only by 16 Men, having questionless disposed the rest in other Places, as being sensible that the gaining of that Bastion would stand us in no great stead. Six *Lascaryn* Deserters confirmed the same soon after, and two among them assured the General, that the Governor of *Columbo* had sent a Letter to the Emperor *Raja Singa*.

2 Dutch Soldiers go over to the Enemy. The 14*th Edmund Ruysch*, whose Quarters were at *Milagre*, sent word, that *Henry William Boogare* a Corporal, and *Peter van Bruysingen* a common Soldier, were gone over to the Enemy. The same day ten *Lascaryns* well arm'd came over to us, and the same Evening with the rising of the Moon, two Cannon for Battery were planted upon the Battery against St. *John*'s Bastion. His Majesty having desir'd, that some Person of Note might be sent to him, to confer with him in private, our Factor *Ysbrand Gotskens*, a Native of the *Hague*, a Person equally dextrous with his Pen as the Sword, was sent with all Expedition thither. About the same time some *Lascaryns* with their Wives and Children coming out of the City, were turn'd back again; a Letter being at the same time deliver'd to a certain Boy for *Simon Lopes*, lately gone over to the Enemy, intimating, that, *If he would endeavour to make the Negroes in the City rise, he should not only deserve his Pardon, but also a good Reward.* *A Letter to the Deserter* Simon Lopes.

At Midnight we made a false Attack, which put the whole City into such an Alarum, that there was nothing to be heard but ringing of Bells, and the noise of Drums, but in half an Hour all was quiet again. The next Day his Majesty sent three Deputies, to know the reason of such fierce firing; which being told them, they inform'd the General that *Ysbrand Gotskens* had not as yet had Audience of the Emperor, but would questionless be admitted the next Day. A Letter was also sent to the General from the Emperor *Raja Singa*, wherein were enclos'd 20 others, one from *Antonio de Souza Coutinho* Governour of *Columbo*, the other from the chief Citizens of that City, both dated the 10*th* of *March*, in which they implore his Majesty's Assistance. *A false Attack upon Columbo.*

RAJA SINGA RAJOU.

The Emperor's Letter to the General.

"THE present Opportunity has invited our Imperial Majesty, to dispatch these few Lines to your Excellency: Two Days ago, being Wednesday the 15*th* of *March*, I broke up from *Guiramibula*, and marching along the other side of the River by the way of *Walewitty*, have fix'd my Tents in this Place, from whence I have dispatch'd immediately some of my Great Courtiers, to notify my Arrival in the Camp at *Reygamwatte*, and to enquire after your Excellency's Health. I commanded them at the same time (having not as yet an Answer to some of your Excellency's Letters directed to me) to desire you to send a Person of Note, unto whom I might by word of mouth give an Answer to the said Letters. It being Night when I arriv'd in the Camp at *Reygamwatte*, I could not order the Disposition of my Forces till next Morning, when the two enclosed Letters were delivered to me, one from the Governor, the other from the Citizens of *Columbo*, the Contents whereof

Baldæus.

"of you will underſtand from the Ori-
"ginals.

Subſcribed,

At our Court and Camp of *Reygamwatte*, Mar. 17. 1656.

Raja Singa Rajou, moſt Potent Emperor of *Ceylon*.

Moſt Potent Emperor Raja Singa, *&c.*

The Governor's Letter to the Emperor.

"IMmediately after our Enemies did "engage into this unjuſt War, which "continues to this Day, I let your Ma"jeſty know the Reaſons which induced "me to ſollicite ſome Supplys from "your Majeſty; not queſtioning, but "that you would not leave me in ſuch "an Extremity, it being always the "Ambition of great Monarchs, to take "the leſs powerful under their Protecti"on; tho thro God's Mercy, we have "hitherto not only defended this City, "but alſo at ſeveral times given the Ene"my ſufficient Proofs of our Bravery, "in deſtroying and diſperſing his Forces, "of which we have ſent an accouut to "your Majeſty. But perhaps theſe Let"ters never came to your Majeſty's "Hands, being intercepted by the Ene"my; which ſeems the leſs ſurprizing to "me, ſince they have treated the Natives "of this Iſland (without any juſt Cauſe) "that went out of this City like Slaves, "forcing many of them to retire back "without the leaſt Mercy. The City "of *Columbo* is an antient Inheritance "of the *Portugueſes*, beſtowed upon 'em "by the Kings and Emperors, your Pre"deceſſors, who always were ready to "honour them with their Protection; "neither do we want Opportunity to "make your Majeſty (if you pleaſe) "ſenſible of the manifold Services done "by the *Portugueſes* in this Iſle, in caſe "we did not believe the ſame to be ſtill "in the Memory of your Majeſty, and "many of your Great Ones. We don't "know to have given the leaſt reaſon of "Diſpleaſure to your Majeſty, which "makes us imagine, that you will be "pleaſed not to leave us in this Extremi"ty, in regard it ſeems much more rea"ſonable, to aſſiſt the *Portugueſes* your "antient Friends, than the *Hollanders* "your new Gueſts. Time has already "diſcovered the Intentions of the *Dutch*, "and Experience will ſoon convince you, "that all their Aim is founded upon Lu"cre and Intereſt, which they diſſemble "for the preſent; but ſo ſoon as they "are Maſters of this Place, your Majeſty "will too late be convinc'd of the Truth "of what I ſay. I will not pretend to "urge that matter any further for the "preſent, leaving the Determination of "the whole to your Majeſty's Wiſdom, "and the Conduct of your Counſellors. "God preſerve your Imperial Majeſty.

Columbo, Mar. 10. 1656.

Antonio de Souza Coutinho.

Moſt High and moſt Potent Emperor and Lord, Raja Singa, *&c.*

The Citizens Letter to the Emperor.

"IMmediately after the *Hollanders* had "laid Siege to this Place, our Magi"ſtrates and Governors did give notice "thereof to your Majeſty, as likewiſe "of the enſuing General Aſſault made "by the Enemy both by Sea and Land; "which being done in the Day-time, we "let them advance into the City, but "afterwards made them glad to ask for "Quarter, which was granted them. "According to the Confeſſion of the "*Dutch* themſelves, they were 240 ſtrong "when they paſſed the Fens, the great"eſt part whereof with their Boats fell "into our Hands, beſides a Ship of 30 "Guns taken by us, and another much "damaged, which they had enough to "do to carry off, not to mention thoſe "that were ſlain in the Ships, and in the "Aſſault. Being afterwards advanc'd "to the Ditch, they fix'd their Miners, "and were buſy in bringing over their "Gallery; but we forc'd them to retire "with conſiderable Loſs, and took the "Gallery with the Loſs of one Man on"ly. There remains nothing now but "for your Majeſty to vouchſafe us your "Favour, which we heartily wiſh for "and deſire. From what has been ſaid, "we hope your Majeſty is ſufficiently "convinc'd of our good Will and Zeal, "in defending a Place, beſtow'd upon "us by your Imperial Majeſty's Ance"ſtors, and that, if ſupported by your "Favour, we ſhall never ceaſe to perſiſt "in the ſame Reſolution, in hopes that "your Majeſty will rather aſſiſt the *Portu"gueſes* your antient Friends, than the "*Hollanders*. God protect your Majeſty, "and your Dominions.

Columbo, Mar. 11. 1656.

By Order from

Diego Leitaon de Souza, Chief Secretary.
Manoel de Fonſeca.
Diego de Souza de Cunba.
Ruy Lopes Coutinho.
John Coelbo de Caſtro.
Bento Fereiro d' Abreu.

Baldæus.

The 20*th* of *March* a Negro Pioneer came over to us, who having worked in the Ditch, discover'd the Place to us, and that four *Portugueses* being taken as they were coming to our Camp, had been hanged. That our new Battery had killed two *Canaryns* and a Gunner, and wounded several others upon the Bastion of St. *Stephen*. Concerning their Provisions, they confirmed what had been told us before. The General went with the said Negro in Person to the Ditch, to see the Place where the Negro had been at work, and perceiving three *Portugueses* close together in the Ditch, he got upon the Wall, and discharged his Fusee twice at them; but soon got down again, without which he had been in great Danger, three Bullets passing immediately after that way.

The General in danger of being killed.

CHAP. XXXIII.

Ysbrand Gotskens *returns from the Emperor's Court, gives an account of his Transactions. Letters sent to* Columbo. *A Battery raised. A circumstantial account from* Goa, *and its Condition.*

A Boy taken as a Spy.

ABout noon a Boy was taken in our Works, where *Paul Meno* then kept guard, inquiring after our Strength; and being ask'd why, he answer'd that the Governor of *Columbo* had sent him to enquire after it: In considtration of his Youth and Simplicity, he came off with a good whipping, and so was sent back into the City. Major *van der Laan* sent word, that the Enemy having made a Hole thro the Wall, played from thence directly upon his Works, and had kill'd a Negro; and the same Night they play'd with a Cannon upon the same Works, but without hurting any Body.

The 23*d* of *March* towards Evening, the Factor *Ysbrand Gotskens* having taken his Leave the same day of the Emperor, return'd to our Camp, where he gave the following account in Writing of his Negotiation: "That in answer to "five several Letters written by General "*Hulst* to his Majesty, he had commanded him to tell the General, that having received a Letter dated the 16*th* "at *Columbo*, he would let him know "the Contents thereof. That his Majesty was well satisfied with the Proceedings against such as were fled out "of the City; which tho it might seem "somewhat cruel, yet was he contented "to have the Blame thereof himself, "as tending to his Service, and the speedy reducing of the City. That because his Majesty was sensible that whatever Presents he could make to the General of rich Apparel, and such like "Ornaments, he was sufficiently provided with before, he had thought fit "to bestow upon him the Title and Dignity of his *Director-General*, and that "for the future he should be acknowledged as such throughout his Dominions. That he further desired the General not to take it amiss, that after "the *Dissaves* had notified his Arrival "in the Camp of *Reygamwatte*, a Guide "had been denied to the Captain of the "Guard, it being contrary to the Custom "of his Country for any one to be introduced at Court, without notice "being given of his Arrival to the Emperor.

Ysbrand Gotskens gives an account of his Negotiation.

"What the General had alledged "concerning the *Mousson*, and the Soldiers being fatigued by so tedious a "Siege, his Majesty was very sensible "thereof, and that when the General "should come into his Presence (which "he hoped would be within three or "four days) they would confer upon "that Point, and settle the matter to "his Satisfaction: But his Majesty being "inform'd that his Excellency frequently expos'd his Person, and regarding "him with the same tenderness as his "own Eyes, had desir'd his Excellency "for the future to take more care of "his Person, commanding all his Officers "of what Quality soever, to be careful "of him to the last degree.

"What his Excellency had alledged, "concerning his Majesty's being constantly employed in Weighty Affairs, and "that therefore he was unwilling to disturb him with frequent Letters, his "Majesty replied, that the Subject of his "Excellency's Letters being such, as "most nearly concerned his Service, nothing could be more acceptable to him, "than to bestow his time in perusing the "Letters of the most trusty Servant

"that

Baldæus.

"that ever he had in his Life, desiring "therefore, that his Excellency might "supersede these Excuses. That what "his Excellency had alledged in his be-"half, concerning the mistake in com-"manding his Forces at *Reigamcorle*, as it "was intended for his Majesty's Service, "so it was very acceptable to him, and "needed no farther Excuse; as was like-"wise the Punishment inflicted upon the "Author of the Letter writ from *Pas-dun-Corle*, to deter others from the like "Undertakings. Concerning the Trea-"ty made with Mr. *Westerwold*, his Ma-"jesty declar'd, he would keep the same "inviolably, notwithstanding that seve-"ral Generals of the *Indies*, and *Dutch* "Governours of the Isle in *Ceylon*, had "done many things which had given oc-"casion to no small Disturbances: but "that as he call'd God to witness of his "Innocence, so he was extremely glad "to have met with a Person of Honour "in his Excellency's Person, who having "done already considerable Services to "his Crown, he intended to enter with "him into a strict Confederacy, which "should stand firm as long as the Sun "and Moon should furnish the World "with Light.

"It was therefore that his Majesty was "very desirous to know his Excellency's "Intentions, whether, after the taking "of *Columbo*, they should attack the King-"dom of *Jafnapatnam* or the Isle of "*Manaar*, and whether it were not con-"venient to send some of his Forces "under certain *Dissaves* thither imme-"diately: That he had received two "Letters from the before-mentioned "Places, which should be communicated "to his Excellency. His Majesty also de-"clared, that either next Sunday or "Thursday (which of these two his "Excellency should pitch upon) he would "expect him at Court, and that he would "send some of his Courtiers to conduct "him thither.

At the same time certain Deputies from his Majesty brought along with them two Letters pen'd by Mr. *Hulst* our General, in answer to those sent from *Columbo* to the Emperor, and dispatch'd to his Majesty; which being well approv'd of by him, and signed by his Excellency in his Majesty's Name, were carried the next day into the City.

Two Letters sent into Columbo.

Soon after news was brought from *Montual*, that 400 *Portugueses*, commanded by four Officers, had been seen near the Sea-shore on the other side of the River, but hitherto had not made the least attempt of passing the same. Abundance of the Inhabitants of the Inland Countries, who perhaps had never had a sight of a Man of War, or any well disciplin'd Forces, flock'd thither (with his Majesty's Permission) to see them. About the same time we received a Reinforcement of 50 men from *Puntegale*, being all they could spare.

A Supply of 50 men comes to the Dutch Camp.

The before-mentioned Letters sent in his Majesty's Name, and carried by some of his *Aratches* and *Lascaryns* into *Columbo*, were at first received with a general Salute of the Cannon and Small Arms; but being open'd, the Inhabitants sufficiently testify'd their Resentment, telling the Messengers, that in case their Condition was not so desperate, they would play them another Game before they return'd; of which usage the Messengers desired the General to make his Complaint to the Emperor.

How these Letters were receiv'd there.

The same day arose a violent Tempest, with Rain, Thunder and Lightning, which kill'd one of our Sentinels, and struck three Musquets, in the Church of *Quia de Lobo*, all to pieces. The Emperor was so complaisant, as to enquire the next day by one of his Messengers, whether we had suffer'd any damage in our Tents or Works, and was answer'd, that God had preserv'd us from all the Danger. The same day, being the 25*th* of *March*, two *Europeans* came over to us; one of them, a Native of *Marseilles*, was over-taken by the way, and received 9 Wounds, so that he narrowly escap'd to our Works, but died the next Morning.

A violent Tempest.

The 26*th* a Serjeant, a *Mistice*, came over to us, and reported, that two more of the same Company watched only an Opportunity to desert: That they had already distributed to each Soldier his Quota of Provisions, *viz.* a *Parra* of Rice *per diem*, for the Month of *April*: That they were much afflicted with the Dropsy and the *Beribery*, a Swelling in the Knees, which takes away the use of their Legs.

Soon after Commodore *Roothaus* sent in three Fishermen taken by our Boats within Musquet-shot of the Water-Fort. The Seamen had 50 Crowns given them (the usual Reward for every *Tony* or Fisher-boat) and 25 more as an Encouragement, these Fishermen being the chief Persons who supply'd the City with Provisions. Orders were also sent to the Commodore, not to expose his Seamen without an absolute necessity.

Some Fishermen taken.

Some of our best Workmen were also consulted about the erecting another Battery

Baldæus. tery against the Bastion of St. *John*, in order to destroy their Pallisado Work in the Ditch, and to facilitate the bringing over of the Gallery. The General told the Emperor's *Dissave*, that he stood in need of 4 or 500 Pioneers and Workmen; but he declined the matter, telling him, that when he came to the Emperor, he would doubtless not deny his Request.

A Portuguese Merchant comes into the Camp. About the same time a *Portuguese* Merchant came in a Boat cross the Bay into our Camp, in company of a *Negro* Trumpeter: They reported, that they were reduced to great extremity in the Place; that no less than 130 had been buried yesterday; and that if most of the *Portugueses* had not their Legs swell'd by the Dropsy, they had deserted long before this.

The 29*th* of *March* the Enemy were preparing to attack the Redoubt of *Paul Meno* two hours before day; but the *Negro* Pioneers with the Sentinel retreating in time, and giving the Alarm, they retired, after having exchanged some Musquet-balls without doing any harm. Four Deputys arriving soon after to enquire the occasion of such smart Firing, they were shewn the Works, and told, that we wanted 4 or 500 *Colys* or Labourers. Three other Fishermen were also brought up by the Seamen, who had the usual Reward given them.

News from Goa advised by Leonard Williams. At the same time the *Popkensburgh* Yacht arriving from *Wingurla*, brought the following Advice:

That *Don Rodrigo de Lobo, Conde de Secredo*, Viceroy of *Goa*, and his Secretary, with three of his Domesticks, having been poisoned, died within 4 or 5 days after. His Death being concealed for some time, *Manuel Mascarenhas Homem*, formerly Governour of *Ceylon*, was (pursuant to the King's Orders) constituted two days after Viceroy in his stead: But the *Fidalgos* or Gentlemen not being satisfy'd with his Person, they expected daily a Revolt (just as it happen'd against him at *Columbo*, 1652.) However, not long after the Viceroy's Death, the Merchants of *Goa* began to load all the Yachts that were there, as also one Galeon and a *Carack*; whilst the Governour was busy in equipping of Men of War and other Vessels, intended for *Ceylon*, offering 20 *Seraphyns* (or *Dutch* Guilders) to every Soldier that would list himself. Our Resident of *Wingurla* further advis'd, that they had sent from *Goa* 160 Ships, and among them 16 Men of War, the 8*th* of *February*, to the North, to fetch Provisions and some other necessary Commodities; and that the said Fleet had tarried four or five days in sight of *Wingurla* by reason of the contrary Winds. That three *Patachos* or Yachts were sailed for *Mosambique*; but one being leaky, was forc'd to return to *Bombassa*: Two more to *Macassar*, two more to *China*; and one *Carack* and a Galeon, *viz.* the *Bon Jesus* and *Nossa Senhora de Gratia*, set sail the 19*th* of *February* for *Portugal*; aboard of which were carried the following Gentlemen, being accused of certain Crimes against the Government, *viz. Don Bras de Castro*, late Governour General; *Don Lewis de Souza*; *Don Pedro de Castro*; *Manuel de Souzo Cabraer*, Master of the Artillery; *Diego de Salvaar*, Captain Major; *Estevaon de Melo*, late Governour of *Bassyn*; *Charles Hudsart*, a rich Merchant; Dr. *Caldero*; and *Jeronimo Lobo de Falbetta*. In the *Bassyn* (under the Jurisdiction of *Goa*) remained Prisoners, on account of being concern'd in the declaring *Don Bras de Castro* Viceroy, *Don Rodrigo Monsanto*, a Captain in the *Bassyn*; the *Veador de Fazendas*, or Sur-Intendant of the Merchants; and *Leon Corre*.

He advised, that the before-mention'd *Carack* and Galeon had aboard a very large Cargo of Stuffs and Callico's, of Cinnamon, Indigo, Pepper, Bezoar-stones, Cloves, *&c.* And that several of the richest Merchants of *Goa* having embark'd all their Effects aboard the said two Vessels, were gone privately along with them to *Portugal*.

Two days before the Yachts the *Zierick-see* and *Naerden* arrived before *Goa*, 4 *Patamars* *, with a *Portuguese*, came to that Place to bring advice of the desperate Condition of *Columbo*, and that they stood in great need of the so long expected Succours. But the Government of *Goa* finding a great aversion in the *Portuguese* Soldiers, as well as the *Negro* Seamen, to go to *Ceylon*, especially in this dangerous Season; they pretended to have receiv'd Letters from *Don Anthonio de Souza Coutinho*, Governour of *Columbo*, with advice, that the *Dutch* had bin forc'd, with the assistance of *Raja Singa*, to raise the Siege; and to make this News pass for current, the new Viceroy *Manuel Mascarenhas Homem* got the Governour of *Columbo* his Hand counterfeited, and order'd for three days successively Ringing of Bells, Illuminations, Bonfires, and

* Patamars *are Indian Advice-boats cover'd all over for the Carriage of Letters, which they tie round in Wax Cloths to the Masts.* Patamars *are also flying Foot-Posts.*

other

other Demonstrations of Joy to be made for its Relief.

By the same Letters from *Wingurla* Advice was brought, that our Ships design'd for *Persia* and *Suratte*, were sailed from thence; and that according to the Intelligence received from *Ditsely* (a *Mahometan* City not far from *Goa*) the so long expected Squadron, consisting of between 20 and 30 Ships, was to sail within three days with Men and Provisions for *Ceylon*; tho this proved afterwards only a Rhodomontade.

He further added, that after the departure of the before-mentioned Vessels bound to *Persia* and *Suratte*, frequently Yachts had been sent to the River of *Goa*, to get intelligence of the motion of the said Squadron. That as far as they could learn, they stay'd only for the return of the before-mentioned Fleet sent out to fetch Provisions from the North; when they intended to force all the Seamen, before they could set foot ashore, aboard the Men of War, in order to carry them, together with 7 or 800 *European* Soldiers, and good store of Provisions, to the Isle of *Ceylon*, for the Relief of *Columbo*. According to the Governour of *Wingurla*'s Opinion, the said Suceours could not be ready before *April*; and that, if by that time they had no certain news at *Goa* of the Surrender of *Columbo*, they would besides the before-mentioned Squadron gather all their Naval and Land-Forces, and endeavour to penetrate, with the strong North Wind, which commonly blows in that Season, into the Harbour of *Columbo*, for its relief. *Baldæus.*

He further added, that there lay two Galeons and a *Carack* at anchor in the River of *Goa*, one whereof, which lay near *Marmagon*, would scarce be fit to go out this Season. Lastly, that the Yacht the *Roman* lay ready to sail upon the first News he should receive of the going out of the said Squadron for the relief of *Columbo*, to give us timely notice of their Coming.

CHAP. XXXIV.

Letters betwixt the Emperor and General. Several Deserters come over to us. The General invited to the Emperor's Camp.

THE 30th of *March* a good number of *Portugueses* passing the Fens in two Boats, call'd *Manchous*, attack'd our Forces in their Works near the Gate of *Mapane*, but after some firing on both sides, were forced to retire in confusion. Soon after a certain Captain of a Village was taken by our People, who was sent out to fetch in some Fascines, intended to be made use of in strengthening the Cortyn betwixt the Bastions of St. *John* and St. *Stephen*. Two *Tonys* or Fisher-boats were likewise brought in with 5 Fishermen, and the Seamen rewarded according to Custom.

Letter from the General to the Emperor. At the same time the General writ a Letter to the Emperor, wherein he imparted to his Majesty the News he had received concerning the intended Relief of *Columbo*. In the Evening two *Portuguese* Deserters that came from the Bastion of St. *Stephen* (having sent the Sentinel upon an Errand) gave us a tolerable account of the Condition of the City; and the next day another *Portuguese* Deserter bore the Marks of their Extremity in his Countenance, which was very meager. The Seamen also brought in 4 Fishermen more, who making up the number of 15 in all, they were sold for Slaves by the Sound of Trumpet, to reimburse us the Mony that was given to the Seamen for the taking of them. *Fifteen Fishermen sold for Slaves.*

The 1st of *April* the *Dissaves* of *Ouve* and the four *Corles* came at the head of a Troop of 100 *Lascaryns*, divided into certain Companies, into the Camp; and bringing along with them a Letter from his Majesty to the General, neatly laid together, they were received with all possible Marks of Honour. The Letter ran thus:

The Emperor's Letter to the General. "YOUR Excellency's Letter, dated "the 24th of *March*, I received the "same day, wherein you declare your "readiness to serve our Imperial Majesty "upon all occasions; which, together "with the Proofs we have received thereof "ever since your Landing in this Island, "could not but be highly acceptable to "our Imperial Majesty. Your Excellency "declares, that you will reserve what "you have further to propose till the "time you shall be admitted into our "Presence. Our dearly beloved *Director General* being so near our Camp, has "never-

Baldæus. "nevertheless not as yet appear'd in our "Presence, which we easily pass by in "regard of the Affection our Imperial "Majesty bears to your Person. We "have sent the *Dissaves* of *Ouve* and of "the *Four Corles* to conduct you hither. "When they are arrived, your Excellen-"cy may order the *Dissaves* of the *Four* "*Corles*, and of the *Seven Corles*, and of "*Saffragamme*, to take care in the mean "while of the Forces, and what else "you shall find most requisite for our "Service, and to chuse one of them "(whom you please) for your Con-"ductor, not questioning, but that (ac-"cording to your Wisdom and Expe-"rience) you will provide for the Secu-"rity of our Forces, and our dear *Hol-*"*landers*. God conduct your Excellen-"cy with his Blessing, that our Imperial "Eyes may see your Person, which hap-"py Hour and Day I expect with joyful "Eyes; assuring your Excellency, that "whatever you shall propose to us will "be as acceptable to our Ears as the most "harmonious Musick in the World.

At Reygamwatte, *April* 1. 1656.

Consultations about the General's going to Raja Singa. It was then consulted what Method was most convenient to be taken, and what Preparations were necessary in order to attend the Emperor with the utmost Splendour; his *Dissave* having (by his Majesty's Orders) appointed the next following Wednesday for the General's reception. But before his Departure he order'd two twelve Pounders to be planted upon the Battery against St. *John*'s Bastion, where the next day a Seaman was kill'd, and a Souldier shot by the same Ball thro the Hat, without touching his Head, or any other part. The same day 16 Lascaryns well arm'd coming over to us from the Bastion of St. *Stephen*, were overtaken by some *Portuguese* Forces, with whom there happen'd a smart Skirmish before they could get clear, two of them being wounded. They were employed in our Works near the Gate of *Rajuba*.

Two more Cannon planted on a Battery.

Sixteen Deserters.

In the Afternoon the *Dissaves* of *Ouve* and the *Four Corles* came with a numerous Retinue to attend the General, leaving it to his choice whom of the two he would pitch upon to conduct him to his Majesty. After some Discourse the *Dissave* of *Saffragamme* was named by his Excellency for that purpose, and order'd to get every thing in readiness for their departure against the next Morning. News was brought at the same time that seven *Canaryns* were taken by some of the Emperor's Forces above *Negombo*, coming in a Fisher-boat from *Columbo*.

The 4*th* of *April* in the Afternoon, Advice being given that his Majesty was come on Horseback to the Pass of *Welecande*, the General was preparing to meet him there; but as they were just ready to take Horse, certain *Dissaves* came Post with a Message from the Emperor, desiring the General not to come till to morrow, because his Majesty was return'd immediately.

Accordingly the 5*th* of *April* the General set out on his Journy, in order to wait on his Majesty, attended by the two Factors *Edward Ooms* and *Ysbrand Gotskens*; the Fiscal *Lucas van der Dussen*, *Cornelius Valkenburgh* Secretary, *James van der Rhee*, the Interpreter *George Bloom*, and *Don John de Costa*; accompany'd by the Imperial *Dissaves* of *Ouve* and *Saffragamme*, and a Company of Firelocks under Capt. *John Hartman*; Mr. *Adrian van der Meyden*, Major *van der Laan*, the *Dissave* of the *Four Corles*, besides several Officers of Note; conducting them as far as to the Pass of *Nacolegamme*, his Majesty being then encamp'd upon the River of *Reygamwatte*. *The General sets out on his Journy to the Emperor.*

The first Testimony of Respect shew'd to the Director General of his Majesty, was the offer of three fine and well-accoutred Horses, for the Courtiers to make use of them at pleasure. These were follow'd by five tame Elephants, with their Guides, who were order'd to keep in the Van. Then came a considerable number of Noblemen and Officers, at the head of their respective Troops, paying their Respects to his Excellency, and asking after his Health. As they approached the Imperial Head Quarters, they were met by some of the chief Men of his Majesty's Court, accompany'd by a vast number of Soldiers, Umbrello-Carriers, Trumpets, Musicians, 11 Elephants, and two fine Horses, with Saddles, Bridles, and other Ornaments beset with Gold and precious Stones, to complement his Excellency in his Majesty's behalf. Thus they marched on thro a Guard of Fusileers and Bowmen ranged on both sides, for a quarter of an hour together, till they came to a House prepared for the General's Reception, neatly furnish'd, the outward Rooms being hung with Hanging of a white Linen Cloth, and the Bed-Chambers with Gold Stuffs. Here the General entred with his Retinue under a Salvo of Fire-locks, placed on the other side of the River near the Imperial Palace. They had scarce arrived here *Honourable Reception of the General.*

two hours, but his Majesty's *Dissaves* came to enquire after the General's Health, being inform'd that his Excellency was seiz'd with an Ague, which had made him resolve to come to him in Person, had he not received nearer Advice, that his dearly beloved Director was on the mending hand, of which he expected the confirmation with the utmost impatience. These Compliments were return'd by the General with the utmost demonstrations of Respect and Duty, telling the *Dissaves*, that he was highly desirous to appear in the Presence of so famous and potent a Monarch so soon as possible could be, his Presence being absolutely necessary in the Camp.

The General prepares for his Return. Next day being the *6th*, great store of Provisions of the best kind were brought in Boats for the General and his whole Retinue. In the Afternoon some Courtiers brought word to the General in private, that his Majesty being seiz'd that Morning with a sudden Illness, could (to his great Affliction) not speak with his Excellency that day. His Excellency reply'd, that he was heartily sorry, his Presence was so absolutely necessary in the Camp, that he could not without great hazard stay, since it was uncertain how soon his Majesty mighty recover; for which reason he desired leave to depart for this time, till a better opportunity, desiring, that four Horses might be laid by the way, which, as soon as his Majesty thought convenient, might carry him with all speed to Court. Whereupon Orders were given to *John Hartman* to prepare for the March, which was done accordingly the same Night.

Soon after we understood, that his Majesty had been forc'd to have been let blood in the Arm, and that he had show'd a great deal of Sorrow for the intended departure of the General; telling his Courtiers, that being sensible how necessary his Presence was in the Camp, he would either the next morning, or at furthest in the Evening, admit him into his Presence, in case he found the least abatement of his Illness. In the mean while the General sent the following Letter to his Majesty:

Most Serene Emperor,

General's Letter to the Emperor. "THREE days being already pass'd "since I came hither by your Ma"jesty's Command and Desire; but "not being able hitherto to appear "in your Majesty's Presence, I most "humbly beg leave to return to the "Camp, the whole Burden whereof "rests upon my Shoulders; promi"sing to be ready to attend your Ma"jesty whenever you shall think fit to "send for me, and living in constant "hopes, that in case some Miscarriage "or other should happen in my Absence, "the same will not be alledged against "me, and put upon me as a Blemish to "blot out the remembrance of my for"mer Service. God protect the Empe"ror.

April 7. 1656. Your Majesty's most humble Servant,

Gerard Hulst.

This done, the General order'd *Ysbrand Gotskens* and *Don John de Costa*, with some of his trusty *Lascaryns*, to take a view of the King's Guards upon the Road, with an intention, that in case he saw no certain Prospect of going to Court to day (as indeed there was but little appearance he should, considering the Emperor's Indisposition) he would privately go Post to the Camp. The 8*th* of *April* the following Letter was delivered to the General from the Emperor.

The Emperor's Letter to the General. "THE Persons sent to enquire after "your Excellency's Health, deli"ver'd to me with a great deal of "satisfaction your Excellency's Letter "wrote on Friday last at 4 a Clock. "I was extremely pleas'd to hear you "were in health, and retain'd the same "Inclinations for our Service. It was "on the other hand no small Affliction "to me that you had stay'd so long "in my Court, without being able to "see you. I assure you, that the same "has happen'd far beyond my Wishes "or Intention; but it seems to have been "so ordain'd by God, that your Excel"lency should be a Witness of my Illness, "and at the same time have an op"portunity of receiving the Present "sent to you by the Prince (born by "God's Providence for the Welfare of "my Subjects) and deliver'd into my "hands before my Departure from *Can*"*dy*. Your Excellency may prepare your "self against to morrow, when I will "send word for your Appearance in my "Presence; which done, you shall have "liberty to return into the Camp, when I "will also issue my Orders for the fur"nishing

Baldæus.

" nishing you with all things requisite " for the accomplishment of such Mea-" sures as shall be taken betwixt us. Af-" ter my Recovery I intend to come in " Person into your Camp, for which " reason I have commanded the *Dissave* " of *Ouve* to prepare my Quarters there. " No more, but that our Imperial Ma-" jesty does not cease to pray to God for " your Excellency's Welfare.

April 7. *before break of Day.* *Raja Singa*, most potent Emperor of *Ceylon*.

CHAP. XXXV.

The General's most magnificent Entry. He is admitted into his Majesty's Presence. What pass'd at their Interview. The General's Return. His unfortunate End.

The General's Entry.

ABout Noon, just as the General was at dinner, we heard a Noise of Drums, Trumpets and other Musick on the other side of the River, and soon after saw some of the chief Courtiers of the Emperor, with three of the choicest Horses of his Stable, adorn'd with most magnificent Saddles, Bridles and other Accoutrements, to advance in very good order towards us; some Persons of the first Quality marching before to invite his Excellency to Court. The General order'd immediately his Guards to pass the River with the Presents, with an intention to follow them in Person with his whole Train, where his Excellency was complimented by the *Dissaves* of *Ouve* and *Matule*, the Captain of his Majesty's *Guard du Corps*, and a great number of other Courtiers. The whole Cavalcade was order'd in the following manner: His Excellency's Guards led the Van, 15 Ensigns and Standards being by the first Ranks carried trailing upon the Ground,

to

A Draught of the most Splendid Audience given by yͤ Emperor of Ceylon, King of Candy &c. to Gerard Hulst yͤ Dutch General. Vol. 3. p. 745.

20.

to shew the Spoils of their Enemies. These were follow'd by his Majesty's Horses and Musicians, and then by five tame Elephants; without the Gate of the Palace were ranged a vast number of Musqueteers, and passing over the Bridg they found the Guard in the outward Court ranged on both sides, through which they marched into the Imperial Palace.

His Audience. The Doors being shut after them, all the *Hollanders* there present were conducted through a large Square into a spacious Hall (call'd by them *Mandonoe*) on the West-side whereof they found his Majesty seated in great Pomp upon a Chair of State, mounted some steps from the ground. No sooner had they enter'd the Hall, but all the great Courtiers paid their Reverence by falling flat with their Faces upon the ground, and the *Dutch* upon their Knees, till his Majesty was pleased to order them to rise by a Nod. Then they began to approach the Imperial Throne, adorn'd with most precious Tapestrys of Gold (call'd by them *Alcatives*;) coming to the middle of the Hall, they fell upon their Knees a second time, according to the Custom of the Eastern Nations, till his Majesty was pleased to arise from his Seat, and commanded the General to come nearer, who made the following Speech to his Majesty.

His Speech to the Emperor. "Most Potent Monarch! Your most "humble Servant approaches your Imperial Throne with a most violent Passion, "in confidence of your generous Inclinations, and wonted Clemency, which "has encourag'd me to address my self "to your Majesty (whose Name is Renown'd throughout the World) with "a most sincere wish that God Almighty "will be pleased to bless your most Illustrious Imperial Majesty, and the "Prince, with a long and happy Life for "the Welfare and Protection of your "Subjects.

"I am come hither to renew and confirm the most sincere Confederacy establish'd betwixt your most Potent Majesty and the *Dutch* Nation; and to "desire that whatever Differences or "Disturbances may have happen'd hitherto betwixt your Imperial Majesty "and our Nation, may be buried in "eternal Oblivion, in order to establish an eternal Peace and Confederacy, which may be as durable as the "Bodies of the Sun and Moon. It can't "be deny'd but that several Misunderstandings have happen'd betwixt your "Majesty's Officers and those of our "Company; but these ought now to be "remov'd even out of our Memory, "at a time when we are so profuse of "the Blood of our Countrymen, to force "our common Enemies out of this Isle, "and ready to give your Majesty every "day new Proofs of our Sincerity and "hearty Inclinations towards you.

Baldæus.

His Majesty appear'd highly satisfied with what his Excellency had said, ordering him at the same time to rise, which he seem'd not to understand, and at the same time offer'd certain Presents, being, as he said, of little Value in themselves, but nevertherless much regarded by the most Potent Emperors and Monarchs, to wit, some Standards taken from those very Enemies who had for many years together so cruelly and barbarously oppress'd his Majesty's Subjects, especially in the *Low-Lands*. His Majesty then, speaking of the Presents sent to his Excellency by the Prince his Son, his Excellency acknowledg'd the same with extraordinary Reverence, pointing at the same time at a Jewel he wore upon his Breast, presented him before by his Majesty; and so approaching the Throne, he kneel'd upon a Cushion laid upon the Step of the Throne, and touching his Majesty's Hand, told him, that he thought it the greatest Honour he ever was capable of receiving, to be admitted to kiss his Majesty's Hands. *What passed betwixt him and the Emperor.*

The Emperor took a *Gargantinbo*, or Collar of Gold, which he threw about his Excellency's Neck, and drawing his own Ring from the first Finger of his Left-hand, he desir'd he should extend his Finger, and wear it in remembrance of his Majesty, who put it upon his Finger. His Excellency was so surpriz'd at this extraordinary favour, that he had scarce power to put out his middle Finger of his left-hand, telling his Majesty, that this Finger having had the misfortune to be disfigur'd by his Enemies, was now abundantly recompensed for his pains by the Honour his Majesty had been pleased to bestow upon him. Then retiring somewhat backwards, and standing upon a Tapestry, he declar'd to his Majesty, *Extraordinary Honour done to the General.*

"That he was sent into this Isle with full "Power by the General and Council of "the *Indies* to propose to his Majesty, "whether he would be pleased to continue the antient Alliance (made with "Mr. *Westerwold*) or have the same renew'd, and some other Articles added, "assuring his Majesty, that whatever "should be agreed upon should be kept "inviolably on their side. Unto which *Certain Propositions made by the General.*

Baldæus. his Majesty reply'd, that he was highly satisfied with his Proposal.

Then the General giving a short account of their Success against the Enemy, his Majesty said, that he had heard of the same to his signal Satisfaction, and that he had a Present from the Prince his Son for his Excellency: Whereupon approaching the Throne a second time, his Majesty presented him with a Garter of Gold, which he said had been worn by the Prince himself.

Is presented with a Garter.

This done, our Presents being order'd to be brought in, Capt. *Hartman* enter'd with 15 of his stoutest Soldiers, each of them trailing one of the Enemies Colours upon the ground; which being thrown carelesly down in the Hall of Audience, a white Buckler formerly belonging to the *Portuguese* Governor *Anthonio Mendes d'Arenha*, was laid upon them, as also an *Indian* Scymeter, the Hilt whereof was of Achet and Gold curiously wrought, which his Excellency declar'd to be intended for the Prince, wherewith to defend his Subjects (when come to riper years) against all the Enemies of the Crown, not excepting the *Hollanders* themselves, if they deserv'd it. Wherewith his Majesty seem'd so highly satisfied, that he put the Scymeter next to his Throne.

The Presents sent by the Company to his Majesty were as follows.

Two very fine *Persian* Horses, one *Turky* Gun, two *Persian* Bows, with their Arrows and Quivers richly embroider'd; one *Japonese* Gown, very rich; two Greyhounds, two *Persian* Sheep, two Rock-goats of *Visiapour*, one piece of Sandelwood.

Those for the young Prince were:

One very fine *Persian* Horse, two Fusees with very curious Barrels, one Silver Bason, wherein were laid two pieces of *Persian* Stuffs wrought with Gold, two Silver Boxes of *China*, one Hog Stone call'd *Pedra de Porco*, one piece of Sandelwood, *&c.*

Whilst the Presents were deliver'd, his Excellency begg'd his Majesty's Pardon for having detain'd him so long; and as the time of his stay could be but short, he told him that he had three things more to propose to his Majesty (whereof the want of the Pioneers was one) desiring that he would be pleased to hear the same from the mouth of *Ysbrand Gotskens* in private, he being the only Person whom he had entrusted with the Secret. The Emperor then commanded all his Courtiers to withdraw, desiring that our Officers might be order'd to do the same; which being done accordingly, his Excellency again approach'd the Throne, and having by his Interpreters *George Bloem* and *Cottemaley*, discours'd with his Majesty a quarter of an hour, he desir'd leave to depart to the Camp, which being granted, he was reconducted with the same Pomp to his Lodgings.

The General takes leave of the Emperor.

The same Evening the General sent to the Emperor by *George Bloem* two noted Partisans, who had done a great deal of mischief in the Country under *Gaspar Figeiro*, to dispose of them at pleasure. Mr. *Bloem* was receiv'd by the Emperor in a private Room, and presented with a Golden Chain and Ring.

The 9th of *April* early in the Morning the General took Horse, and came pretty early with his whole Retinue to *Naccle-gamme*, from whence he was conducted by Mr. *Adrian van der Meyden* and Mr. *John van der Laan* with two Companies to the Camp. At his arrival there he found the Gallery fix'd in the Ditch (without any considerable loss) and every thing else in a good Condition.

The General returns to the Camp.

The 10th in the Afternoon the General took a view of all the Works, and among the rest commanded Capt. *Henry Gerard* to set up a Ladder, and take a view of the Condition of the Enemy on the other side of the Ditch; he found the Enemy had made an Entrenchment extending towards the Sea-shore, with a Ditch before it, 8 foot deep, upon which having planted two pieces of Cannon, they were likely to prevent our fixing the Miners on that side, our Trenches being carried on directly against that place; wherenpon it was agreed to make a Breach in the Wall on this side of the Ditch, and to plant a Cannon there in order to ruin the said Entrenchment.

Takes a view of the Works.

About Sun-set his Excellency returning to the same place to encourage the Workmen both by his Words and Example, the *Portugueses* began to use their utmost endeavours to set fire to the Gallery, throwing all sorts of combustible Matter upon it, which the General perceiving, he advanc'd with the rest to assist in extinguishing the Fire; but whilst he was busy in the midst of the Gallery in performing his Duty with his Breast open, he was heard on a sudden to cry out, *Good God help me! O help me!* which Capt. *Joachim Block* who stood hard by hearing, and finding him all over bloody, he carried him with the assistance of Major *Van der Laan* from thence to a Bed, where without speaking one word more he expir'd.

The Portugueses set fire to our Gallery.

He is wounded.

His Excellency GERARD HULST, *first Counseller, and Director Generall of ye* INDIES, *Comander in Chief of all the Sea & Land Forces sent to* CEYLON, *and the Coast of the* INDIES.

Baldæus. pir'd. His Wound being searched, they found it to be done by a Musquet-Bullet, which passed in under the right Shoulder, quite through under the right Arm.

Dies.

His Character.

This was the unfortunate End of this most excellent Person, in the Vigor of his Age, descended of a good Family, and of great Experience both in Civil and Military Affairs; being for the rest of a very affable Conversation, eloquent and well-vers'd in divers Languages: He was besides this of a very good Aspect, tall, and well-made, brisk and indefatigable in what he undertook; and to be short, *Nature and Industry had fram'd so exact an Harmony betwixt his Soul and Body, that few Men can pretend to the same degree of Perfection.*

CHAP. XXXVI.

The General's Death notified to the Emperor, who sends his Envoys into the Camp. Mr. Adrian van der Meyden *succeeds him. A* Portuguese *Captain comes over to us.*

The General's Death notified to the Emperor.

THE same night *George Bloem* Interpreter being dispatch'd with a Letter to the Emperor, to carry the doleful News of the General's Death, his Majesty sent the 11*th* of *April* the *Dissaves* of the *five* and *seven Corles* to take a view of his Corps. It being also agreed in a Council of War, that the same should be conducted by the Factor *Ysbrand Gotskens* and Capt. *John Hartman*, under a Guard of 20 Fire-locks, to *Puntegale* (9 *German* Leagues thence) the same was done accordingly with a great deal of Splendor. The same night his Majesty sent the *Dissaves* of *Matule* and *Adigar*, attended by divers other Courtiers, to condole the Death of his dearly beloved Director-General. They were very inquisitive, whether he was slain by some of his own People, or by the Enemy, or by some unexpected Accident: Being shewn the place where he receiv'd his Wound, they crawl'd thither trembling for fear upon the ground, from whence they took a handful of Earth, and desir'd that no body should set a foot in that place.

His Corps carried to Gale.

Envoys sent from the Emperor.

Take a view of the place where he was wounded.

His Corps was deposited in a Vault under ground at *Gale* till 1657. when by order from Mr. *Van der Meyden* it was inter'd with great Solemnity in the Church there near the Pulpit; his Arms, Buckler, Sword and Spurs being hung against the Wall. In the year 1658. the said Corps being transported from thence to *Columbo*, was put into a stately Monument there, with an Inscription upon it, containing in substance, *That he had purchased the Conquest of* Columbo *by his Death, for the bonour of his Native Country.*

After the Decease of the General, the Burden of the supreme Command of the Siege was laid by unanimous Consent upon the Shoulders of Mr. *Adrian van der Meyden* Governor of *Gale*, who had the good fortune to see the City reduc'd in the next following Month of *May*.

Mr. Van der Meyden *succeeds the General in that Dignity.*

The 13*th* of *April* a Letter was brought to the Camp from *Leonard Johnson*, dated the 2*d* at *Wingurla*, intimating that 22 Frigats under the Command of *Francisco de Seixa Cabreira*, with all sorts of Provisions, and 800 *Portuguese* Landmen aboard, were sail'd from *Goa*. Whereupon the Commodore *Roothaus* and *Peter de Bitter* being sent for, to consult what was best to be done, it was resolved (in order to prevent their bringing into the City the intended Succours) to attempt a vigorous Assault upon the Bastion of St. *Stephen*, for which purpose four brave Officers were chosen, who with 80 Volunteers (who had offer'd themselves for a Reward of 50 Crowns a piece) were to make the Attack.

A Letter from Wingurla *concerning the* Portuguese *Succours.*

The same Evening the *Flussing* Yacht coming to an Anchor in the Road, soon after *Adrian van der Maart* her Captain came ashore, and told the General, that about three days before meeting with the *Portuguese* Squadron near *Coulang* and the Cape *Comoryn*, he had attack'd one of their Frigots so successfully, that he saw her sink before his Eyes, 16 *Portugueses* only with Capt. *Simon Souza* being sav'd of all that were aboard her. That soon after he had lost sight of them all, supposing they were return'd to the Cape *Comoryn*, it being his opinion that as the Wind stood, they must before this have been near *Columbo*. In the night time a certain *Portuguese* Captain, one of the *Fidalgos*, or Gentlemen, who had been concern'd in declaring *Don Bras de Castro* Viceroy of *Goa*, came over to us, having been

The Flussing *Yacht meets the* Portuguese *Fleet.*

A Portuguese *Gentleman comes over to us.*

been detain'd Prisoner in the Bastion of S. *Stephen*, and made his escape with four of his Servants through *Don Francisco de Rolyn*'s House by means of a Boat. He entertain'd the new General for a considerable time. It was in the mean time resolv'd to delay the Assault upon the Bastion of S. *Stephen*'s for two or three days. Our Interpreter *George Bloem* return'd also with the following Letter of Condoleance from his Majesty.

Raja Singa Rajou, most potent Emperor of *Ceylon*, wishes Health to Mr. *Adrian van der Meyden*, Governor of the Imperial Fortress of *Gale*.

Letter of Condoleance from the Emperor.

" YOUR Letter dated in the Evening " at seven a Clock on Monday the " 10th of *April*, did arrive in the Imperial Camp about Midnight, and was " deliver'd to our Imperial Majesty on " Tuesday about Noon. The Death of " our Director-General has caused an excessive Affliction in our Imperial Heart. " Whilst our beloved Director was at " our Court, I was unwilling (according to the singular Love I bore to his " Person) to let him know my Illness; " but being now on the mending hand, " I am forced to hear of his Death, " which now we must commit to Providence, and submit to his Will. Our " Imperial Majesty has likewise understood by your Excellency's Letter that " you are invested with the same Power " as our beloved Director-General was. " It is a general receiv'd Custom in the " Courts of all the great Monarchs, that " in case a Person of note, and in good " esteem with them dies, his Successor " appears before the said Monarch, and " receives his Confirmation and Blessing " at his hands. As you have always " been serviceable to us, it is our Pleasure that you come to Court (in the " same manner as the Director-General " did) in order to receive the Honours " due to your Merits; being sensible that " you have render'd us considerable Services, without having receiv'd any Reward hitherto; wherefore it is my " Pleasure, that when you resolve to " come, you give notice thereof beforehand what day you have pitch'd upon, " in order to receive you with the same " Respect as the Director-General your " Predecessor. I doubt not in the mean " while but you will be very careful in " your high Station. At the closing of " this Letter Advice is brought that " the *Portugueses* expect every day " Succours, which has made me give " strict Orders to keep a strict Guard " both by Sea and Land.

Baldæus.

In the Camp and Court of *Reygamwatte*, 15 *April* 1656.

Raja Singa Rajou, Most Potent Emperor of *Ceylon*.

11 Lascaryn, 3 Topasses, 2 Portuguese Deserters.

In the night 2 *Portugueses*, 3 *Topasses*, and 11 *Lascaryn* Deserters gave a doleful account of the miserable condition of the City, and of the Sickness and Mortality that reign'd there. The 16*th* we play'd most furiously against the Gate of *Rajuba*, and the General having sent Advice of the expected Succours in the City to the Emperor, gave Orders to Commodore *Roothaus* to keep the *Flussing*, *Popkensburgh* and *Lion* Yachts in readiness to pursue the Enemy's Squadron. About the same time a *Portuguese* Captain came over to us with 18 *Lascaryns* and three *Topasses*; his pretence was, that having receiv'd an Affront from the Governor, he had taken this method to revenge himself. *Diedelof van der Beek* writ from *Mapane*, that the poor starv'd Wretches in the Plain betwixt our Works and the City butchered one another, two Women having lately devour'd their new-born Babes. The 19*th* of *April* a Letter was deliver'd to the General from the Emperor.

More Deserters.

The Emperor's Letter to the new General.

" YOUR Excellency was deliver'd " to me after Midnight, by which " you declaring your readiness to serve " me, the same was receiv'd with singular satisfaction, knowing that your " Excellency ever since your landing in " this Isle has shewn a more than ordinary Inclination for our Service. Your " Excellency being now through God's " Mercy put into this high Station, it is " expected you should give more signal " Proofs thereof than before. You also " mention the expected *Portuguese* Succours, and the Success of our faithful " *Hollanders* against them. I hope in " God that this Victory will prove the " forerunner of others. What I writ " in my last concerning your care in " the Camp, was not intended as if I " question'd your Conduct, but because " it belong'd to me to mention it. You " further advise, that the Enemy's Squadron has orders to sail directly for " *Columbo*, but considering the ill Treatment *Manoel Mascarenhas Homem* the " present Viceroy of *Goa* met with at " *Columbo* (whilst Governor there) it " seems to me most probable, that he " has sent this Fleet rather to be worsted

" by

Baldæus. "by the *Hollanders*, than with a real intention to relieve *Columbo*.

"Your Excellency says that one *Nicolao de Moura* Captain-Major of the City is come over to us: I desire you would give a good Entertainment to all such as come to us with a sincere Intention. The other News has been very acceptable to me, God I hope will crown our Endeavours with Success. Your mentioning the late deceased Director-General's Name has renew'd my Grief; and as I lov'd him entirely, so I must recommend to you the Jewels which were presented to him (whilst living) from our Imperial Majesty, that the same may be sent into *Holland* to his next Kindred; it being our Will and Pleasure to give upon this occasion a convincing Proof to our *Hollanders* of the most sincere Affection we bear them. For, tho the unfortunate Death of the said Director has rob'd him of the opportunity to execute those Designs he had projected for our Services, yet his Counsels, Care and Watchfulness will remain for ever in our Memories. I am very sollicitous to know what method you intend to take in reducing the City, whether by Force or Famine: If you intend to take it by Assault, let me know of it two or three days before-hand secretly. My Illness has hitherto prevented me from prosecuting my Resolution of coming into the Camp, to take a view of all the Works of the *Hollanders*; however I am resolv'd to come nearer to the Camp, which as soon as it is done I will give you notice thereof, and desire your Presence there, in order to concert Measures with you before you return to the Camp. No more, &c.

He orders the late General's Jewels to be sent into Holland.

Reygamwatte 28 *April* 1656.

Raja Singa Rajou, Most Potent Emperor of *Ceylon*.

P. S. "It is desir'd that the Captain who sunk one of the Enemy's Frigats, and forced the rest to return back, may come along with the General to the Emperor, in order to make himself known to his Majesty.

The Superscription was,

Raja Singa Rajou, Most Potent Emperor of *Ceylon*, wishes Health to *Adrian van der Meyden*, Governor of our Imperial Fortress of *Gale*.

In the Afternoon a Cessation of Arms being order'd for some time, the following Summons were sent into the City.

"HAving by the present Siege reduc'd the Citizens of *Columbo* to the last Extremity, and bereaved them of all hopes of the so long expected Succours from *Goa*, we thought fit to summon the City a second time in the Name of his Imperial Majesty *Raja Singa*, and of the Honourable the *Dutch East-India*. For the Squadron sent the 11*th* of this Month from *Goa* by the new Viceroy *Manoel Mascarenhas Homem* (*Conde de Secredo* his Predecessor dying the 13*th* of *January*) to the relief of *Columbo*, being pretty well provided with Provisions, but very indifferently man'd, was engag'd so briskly by our People, that some of their Frigots were lost, others much damag'd, and the rest forc'd to retire in Confusion to *Tutecoryn* and *Manaar*. According to the Opinion of your own Captain *Simon de Souza*, and some others, that are our Prisoners, most of the Men aboard them are likely to desert, for fear of falling into the hands of our Ships that are cruising thereabouts; and the rest will scarce be able by reason of the *Mousson* to reach this place. Perhaps you may flatter your self, that the same *Mousson* will oblige our Ships to leave before long, as well those Parts as this Bay; but if you rely upon this Point, we declare our selves innocent of all the Grievances and Sufferings put upon the poor Citizens, who will besides this be thereby put in danger of losing all they have, whereas at present they may expect honourable Conditions, which they can't hope for hereafter. We recommend this to your Excellency's Consideration, and your Person to God's Protection.

Summons sent into Columbo.

In the Imperial Camp before *Columbo*, 18 *April* 1656.

Adrian van der Meyden.

The following Letter was sent in Answer to the former.

"THE Letter sent to me by the most noble General *Gerard Hulst*, dated the 9*th* of *Novemb.* last, I answer'd at that time; which, as it can't be unknown to your Excellency, so the same Answer may serve to your Letter; neither the Change of War, nor want of

The Answer.

" of Provisions having given me sufficient " Occasion hitherto to alter my Resolution, which is, to take care of and defend the City to the utmost of my Power, for the Service of the King my " Master. God protect your Excellency.

Columbo, Apr. 19. 1656. *Antonio de Souza Coutinho.*

Baldæus.

Being convinced by this Letter, that nothing but Force could reduce them to reason, the Cannon were order'd to play again as before.

CHAP. XXXVII.

Many Deserters. Letters from the Emperor. Ysbrand Gotskens *sent to his Majesty. Resolution taken to assault the City. Succours arrived from* Batavia.

THE 21*st* of *April*, 7 *Lascaryn* Deserters reported, that the Citizens and Soldiers beginning to murmur for want of Rice, it was resolv'd to give to each Citizen and Soldier ½, and to each *Topas* and *Lascaryn* ¼ *Medide per diem*, besides their former Allowance. Soon after a *Portuguese* Deserter related, that they had barricadoed up most of the Streets, and planted Cannon in them. About the same time the new General received the following Letter from the Emperor.

RAJA SINGA RAJOU, &c.

The Emperor's Letter to the General.

" OUT of your Letter dated the " 19*th* of *April*, I have (with a " great deal of Satisfaction) understood " your good Health, and good Inclinations for my Service, as well as of Major *John van der Laan*, and the rest of " the Chief Officers. Before the Arrival of the late Director-General (of " Blessed Memory) I had taken a Resolution within my self, to come and take " a View of your Camp; but being then " prevented by my Illness, I still continue " in the same Resolution, not only to " view the Works there, but also to be " a Spectator of the brave Actions perform'd there for my Service. My faithful *Hollanders*, who are come hither " from far distant Countries, have for " several Months last past endured many " Miseries, not without much effusion of " Blood; and as I am stedfastly persuaded that both I and our Imperial Family may promise our selves the same " and more for the future, so shall I think " it no Trouble to come so far into the " Camp, to be an Eye-witness (to my " great Satisfaction) of the brave Actions performed there for our Imperial " Majesty's Service. That no notice has " been taken hitherto by this Court of " the Captain-Major, is to be attributed " to his being employed Day and Night " in the Company's Service. Some foolish Peope are much deceived, if they " judg that there can be the least Separation of Interest betwixt our Majesty " and the Company, the wiser sort being convinced that our Interest is the " same. The said Major *John van der Laan* has done me considerable Service " ever since his coming into this Isle; " and therefore I declare, that since the " late Director-General appear'd at this " Court, I did lay aside all Animosity, " in consideration of his great Qualities " and Services; so that now the said " Major who has spill'd his Blood more " than once, and been wounded with Bullets in my Service, shall be made sensible of the Love and Affection I bear " him, whenever he comes into my Presence. What you mention about *Mascarenhas*, is no less than the Truth, " and an undeniable one, to convince the " World, that God will take Revenge " of such as offend their Sovereigns, " which induces me to believe, that this " War we jointly carry on against our " Enemy, will be blessed by God with " Success. I was very glad to understand " by your Excellencies Letter, that the " Jewels presented by me to the Director-General have been sent to *Batavia*, " in order to be transported from thence " by trusty Persons into *Holland*. The " said Director-General having done me " such Signal Services, ever since his " Coming into this Country, I intend so " soon as the War is brought to a Conclusion, to send a Letter with the first " Ship to the States-General of *Holland*, " to give them an ample Testimony " thereof. The Resolution taken in " the

Baldæus.

"the Council of War is very acceptable to me: But as your Excellency in his High Station has the chief Management of such Matters, as tend to our Majesty's Service, in your Hands, so I am most inclined to follow your Advice. The Method proposed for the reducing of the City has been debated in our Imperial Council; but as the same must be expressed in a different Language (which carries along with it a considerable Alteration) I will pass it by in silence, earnestly requiring you, that whenever the said Resolution is to be put in execution, to send me Advice of it, that I may assist you there in Person. You are of Opinion that it would be more convenient for me not to come into the Camp, till after the taking of the City; but what Business have I in the Camp then, unless it be to see the Conditions perform'd? whereas the late Director-General had given me his Word, that the City should be delivered into my Hands. In the Letter I sent to your Excellency, I desir'd that the Captain who had sunk the *Portuguese* Ship should come along with you to our Court; and you having made no mention of him in your Answer, I am at a stand to guess the Reason thereof. The aukward Answer of the *Portugueses* in *Columbo* to your Summons, shews them to be void of Sense; and I, who am well acquainted with their Bravadoes, look upon it as an infallible Sign of their Distress; being convinc'd by my own Experience in divers Engagements, that when they were most at a pinch, they would brag most. I have for a considerable time consider'd with my self, whether I should write a Letter to those in the City, but for fear of a haughty Answer, I resolve to let it alone. No more, &c.

The 22d *of* April, 1656. *Raja Singa Rajou*, Most Potent Emperor of *Ceylon.*

The following Letter was enclosed, and directed to the *Sabandaar* of *Gale*, *Don John de Costa.*

"HAving been inform'd by several of our Messengers sent from hence with Letters, that since the Arrival of the late Director-General of Blessed Memory, you have given all imaginable Satisfaction in reference to his Person, I intended to have sent you a Present at that time, but that the said Director's Departure (which was so sudden, that my Servants did not overtake him before he came to *Krabenhof*) prevented it. But when the new General shall appear at Court, you as well as the rest of the Officers shall not be forgot. You have been an Eye-Witness of the Respect paid by me here to the Director-General; and whenever the new General makes his Appearance before us, the same shall (not without great Reason) be increased, our Imperial Majesty having receiv'd more Signal Services from his Excellency, whereof I would have you give notice to him at the first Opportunity. If you should happen to discover any Error in such Letters as are sent from this Court, you shall excuse them to the General. You shall also put him in mind, that we stand in need here of an Anvil, and a pair of Smiths Bellows; and as there is frequent Occasion for Writing, don't forget to let us be furnish'd with some white Paper; you may send also some *China* Ware. Farewel.

At the Court of Reygamwatte, April 23. 1656.

The 24*th* of the same Month, a *Topas* Deserter, named *Lazaro Henrico*, who came over to us during the Siege of *Caleture*, but afterwards run over again to the Enemy (notwithstanding he was well entertained by the late Director-General) brought a Letter from *Manoel Fonseque de Moniis*, a Merchant of *Columbo*, directed to Major *van der Laan.*

A Topas Deserter brings a Letter from a Merchant in Columbo.

Mr. *van der Laan.*

"I Beg of you to believe what I am going to tell you, concerning the present Condition of the City. Be careful not to venture a Storm, they having provided Retrenchments in all Posts, well provided with Cannon, besides four Mines, to be discovered to you by my Servant. The Rice is sold still at three *Seraphyns*, and is very scarce. If you intend to hasten the Surrender of this City, send some body from *Caleture* hither, to convince them that they are still living there; this being the Reason why they would not hitherto hearken to any Conditions. I send my Servant with this Letter to you, to shew the same to the General, tho it is rumoured abroad here that General *Hulst* is dead, but I don't believe it.

" The

"The next thing I have to request for "God's sake, and as you tender our "Friendship, is to preserve and secure "the Bearer hereof, being resolv'd like-"wise to come over to you, which I "can't do at present, being so narrowly "watch'd, but hope to be with you in a "few Days. God grant you a long "Life.

Your Servant and Slave,

Manoel Fonseque de Moniis.

Whereupon it was resolv'd to secure the said *Topas* aboard a Ship till further Order.

Gotskens sent to the Emperor. Soon after *Ysbrand Gotskens* was dispatch'd to his Majesty, to represent to him some matters of the greatest Consequence, and to know his Sentiments. It was not long before he return'd in Company of the *Dissaves* of *Saffragam*, and the *Four Corles*, and the *Curupele Apobami*, and gave an account of his Negotiation to the General *van der Meyden*; and among other things, that his Majesty was well satisfied with the Resolution taken *April* 21. but seem'd to be inclin'd to have the Assault delay'd till Sunday the last Day of the Month, when he intended to be an Eye-Witness of it. *An account of his Negotiation.*

The 23*d* of *April*, it being resolved to give the General Assault the next following Night, especially upon the Bastions of S. *Stephen* and *Clergos*, and (in case they succeeded) afterwards upon that of S. *Philippo*, every thing was preparing for the execution thereof, and every one order'd to his Post. The following Instructions in Writing were given to each commanding Officer in Chief, which they were strictly to obey.

Instructions for the intended Assault. "Those that are order'd to give the "Assault upon the Bastions, shall be ob-"lig'd to fix the scaling Ladders them-"selves, and use their utmost Endea-"vours to make themselves Masters "thereof, and to maintain themselves "there: In case the Bastion of S. *Stephen* "be taken, the commanding Officer shall "let the Trumpeter sound the Tune *Wil-"liam of Nassau* as a Signal, that God "has blessed us with Victory on that side. "So soon as the Assault begins from the "Redoubt, betwixt St. *Stephen* and St. "*John*'s Bastion, the Companies of *John* "*Hartman*, *George Gebel*, *Henry Gerard*, "and *James Baker* shall be in a readiness "to second them, as Occasion requires.

"During the Assault, the *Javanses*, "*Bandaneses*, *Lascaryns*, *Topasses*, with "some *Europeans*, shall endeavour to "pass the Ditch, in order to force the "Enemy from their Works at the Foot "of the Bastion of St. *John*, and shall "be commanded by Captain *N. Scherf*, "*Arent Johnson*, *N de Wit*, *N. Chample*, "and *James van Driel*. Whilst the As-"sault continues upon the Bastion of St. "*Stephen*, Major *van der Laan* shall with "his Forces attack the Gate of *Rajuba*; "and in case God bless us with Success, "no Officer of what degree soever shall "presume to grant leave or suffer any of "his Soldiers to leave their Colours or "enter the City, being forewarn'd that "the Enemy have planted their Cannon "there, charged with small Shot. *Baldæus.*

Dated Apr. 27. Subscribed by Command from the General,

Adrian van der Meyden,
James van Rhee Secretary.

Immediate notice of this Resolution was given to the Emperor, but there happening no small Differencrs and Heats in the Council of War that was held that Evening about the Execution of this Design, the same was thought fit to be deferd to another time. Scarce was the Council broken up, but a *Lascaryn* Deserter coming from St. *John*'s Bastion, reported, that this Evening they had reinforced the ordinary Guard of the Bastion of St. *Stephen* with 30 of their choicest Men, called *Valiantons* or Bravoes by them, besides 10 other Soldiers, which made us imagine that a *Javanese* Deserter, who had got perhaps some scent of the matter, had discover'd our Design to them. *Is delayed till another time.*

At the same time News was brought of the Arrival of the Yachts the *Red Lion*, *Avenhorn* and *Pelican*, who left *Batavia* in *March*. The 28*th* of *April*, the Lieutenant *Christopher Egger*, *James Viry*, *Martin Sholtes*, and Ensign *Brewer* were sent in the Night-time to view the Ascent to the Bastion of St. *Stephen*; they gave an account that they had found them well upon their Guard there, and the Ground being sandy would afford no firm footing. The 29*th* of *April* a Letter was brought into the Camp from *Abraham van der Mart*, sent by the *Lion* Yacht from the Isles of *Tutecoryn*, with the joyful News that the *Portuguese* Squadron being met by the *Dutch* the 19*th*, off of *Tritchianadour* and *Caylpatnam*, they were forced to retreat betwixt the Isles of *Tutecoryn*, where *3 Ships arrive from Batavia.* *The Condition of St. Stephen's Bastion viewed.*

Baldæus. *Great News from the Dutch Fleet.* where they were block'd up by our Ships, and *van der Mart* gave no small hopes of preventing their coming out again, provided he were reinforced in time with two or three nimble Yachts. Letters were at the same time deliver'd from the Head Factor *Reynier Serooskerke*, concerning the Preparations of the *Portugueses*, and that they intended to pass the *Mousson* on the Coast of *Malabar*. That the Traffick of the Company at *Calicoulang* was in a good Condition, and that he intended to buy up a good Quantity of Pepper and other Commodities against the Year 1657. *A Succour of 225 Men from* Batavia. News was also brought from *Batavia*, that a Succour of 225 Men was sent from thence to *Ceylon*, who within a few Days were to come by Land hither from *Gale*. At the same time we received a Letter written in *Latin* by the Serjeant *Severin Dolander*, which being thrown over the Ditch, required a speedy Answer.

A Letter of a Dutch Serjeant from Columbo. "SEverin wishes his Ensign Health: "The Message brought me by the "Father was very acceptable to me. I "and my Comrades are above half dead, "of 74 there being no more than 10 "left, and these in a most miserable "Condition, for want of Bread, Wine and "Meat, being not used to feed upon Rice, "therefore we desire to be supply'd with "the same (if possible) for the Preser-"vation of our Lives, and the Recove-"ry of our Strength; in return where-"of I will acknowledg you the Preser-"ver of my Life, as long as I live. Mr. "*Cornicularius* is also very near Death's "Door, but perhaps a little Bread and "Wine might recover him. I beg you "once more for God's sake not to for-"get us, and to deliver it to the before-"mention'd Father, who is our trusty "Friend. God protect you.

Severin Dolander.

CHAP. XXXVIII.

Ships sent to Tutecoryn. Raja Singa *dissatisfied. Prisoners exchanged. Letters from* Raja Singa. *The Bastions of* St. John *and St.* Stephen *taken by Storm, not without a considerable Loss.*

A Reinforcement sent to the Dutch *Fleet near* Tutecoryn THE Council having taken into Deliberation, the Condition of the Enemies Fleet near *Tutecoryn*, it was resolv'd to dispatch thither forthwith the Yachts the *Mars*, *Rabbit*, the *Roman* and *Lyon*, besides two other Vessels under Commodore *Roothaus*. At the same time an Answer was order'd to be sent to the *Dutch* Prisoners in *Columbo*.

"YOURS we have receiv'd by the "Father, and understood your "miserable Condition; these are the "chances of War, the best Comfort "you can have in this Extremity with "your Fellow-Prisoners. At your ear-"nest Request we send you a Bottle of "*Spanish* Wine, ten new-bak'd Loaves, "and a piece of Meat and Bacon; the "Effects and Mony design'd for Captain "*Simon de Souza*, who is kept among "the Prisoners at *Calcture*, are put aboard "the Ship: and because one of the "*Portuguese* Soldiers did this Forenoon "call from the Bastion of St. *John* to one "of our Sentinels, that the Governor "was willing to exchange 10 of his Men, "that are our Prisoners, for your ten; "we have sent Word to the Governor "*Anthonio de Souza Coutinho*, that as soon "as he will discharge you, we will send "back 10 *Portuguese* Prisoners from *Ca-"leture*.

May 1. 1656. *Adrian van der Meyden.*

An Offer for the Exchange of Prisoners. Accordingly the 2*d* of *May* in the Forenoon, a *Portuguese* Captain, named *Domingo Coelho*, deliver'd a Letter to Ensign *Peregrin* in our Service, offering, that in case we would exchange eight *Portuguese* Prisoners at *Caleture* for the Serjeant and seven Soldiers, they would send them to us, which was denied, and in lieu thereof offer'd seven common Soldiers and one Officer in exchange for them. About the same time his Majesty sent back a Letter, which he seem'd highly displeas'd at, with another as follows.

"YOUR Letter writ to some of my "Courtiers last Monday, was deli-"vered to them before Sunset; what "you relate of Major *van der Laan*'s go-"ing to *Mapane*, to observe what past "there, and that finding those that were "come

" come out of *Columbo*, to be supplied underhand with Provisions, he commanded " to fire among them, and to secure the " *Modeliar Jazondere*, who had been ac- " cessory to the matter; has been very ac- " ceptable to me, as tending to my Service. " The Letter deliver'd to me by *Curupule* " *Meynde*, written upon half a Sheet, I " did not think fit to read, much less to " answer, being fill'd with nothing but in- " sipid Stuff: If perhaps a sudden Muti- " ny or Accident, or any other Misfor- " tune had happen'd in the Camp, I " could have excused such a Letter, in " respect of the Love and Inclination I " bear to the *Hollanders*, my most trusty " Servants; but every thing being in a " very good Condition, I can't sufficient- " ly admire what could induce *George* to " write such a Letter. Truly the Gene- " ral (who has the supreme Command " there) ought not to have been so care- " less in this matter, such a Neglect be- " ing not very sutable to the Conduct " that may be expected from a Person " entertain'd in the Service of a Great " Monarch; wherefore I send you this " Letter, together with the *Ola* (Letter) " in order to have it read in the Presence " of the General, and to let him know " word by word the true Contents there- " of.

An angry Letter from the Emperor.

Thursday, May 2. 1656.

Considering the nicety of the *Cingaleses* and *Malabars* in this Point, it must be confessed, that more caution ought to have been used in this respect.

8 Dutch Prisoners sent out of Columbo.

Towards Evening the *Portugueses* sent our eight Prisoners out of the City, half dead for want of Food, three of them being so weak, that they could neither go nor stand; they unanimously deposed, that there had been a great Disorder among the Officers, which had prevented their marching to the Bastion of *Clergos*, after they had enter'd the City, as they ought to have done, the same being guarded only by 15 Men. But whilst they staid in expectation for Orders from the Sea-Captain *Lippens* (of whom they spoke very indifferently) they were attack'd both in Front and Rear by a great Number of *Portugueses*, and charg'd so furiously, that scarce 26 of them escaped, without being either kill'd or wounded, after they had spent all their Powder and Ball. They added, that what had been related of their having fell to plundering was not true, that they were secur'd in a Warehouse belonging to *Lewis Tavera*, where they had the same daily Allowance of Rice with the King's Soldiers, and that they had fed as well as the rest of the Inhabitants upon the Flesh of Elephants, Bufflers Hides, nay upon Dogs, Cats and Rats. That most of the 74 Prisoners died for Want of good Food, and according to all Appearance these 8 would not live long. They further said, that as they were going out of the City, they saw a Body of 400 or 500 Men, some *Europeans*, some Negroes, near St. *John*'s Gate.

Their Account.

Baldæus.

The 4th of *May* the Emperor *Raja Singa* sent the following Letter.

A Letter from the Emperor.

" About three Years ago Captain *Joris Hervendonk*, with some other " Officers and Soldiers entring into our " Service; and their time being expir'd " since, for which they had agreed with " the Company, I resolv'd with my self " (since I had no great Occasion for them " here) to send them to the Camp. An " Account of what Services the said " Captain had done me, may be seen in " a Letter written by him (according to " my Command) to the late Director- " General, immediately after his Land- " ing near *Columbo*. He had neither be- " fore nor since the same Sense he had " when he writ that Letter, which then " induc'd me to a Resolution to bestow " certain Favours upon him before his " Departure. But his insolent Behavi- " our having drawn upon him several " Chastisements, without any hopes of " Amendment, I thought fit to remove " him from his Station, and to put *Fran-* " *cis Has* (who happen'd then to come " as a Messenger with Letters to our " Court) in his Place. This Man having " lived for some time among the *Portu-* " *gueses* our Enemies, seem'd to have " laid aside all the Modesty of the *Portu-* " *gueses*, and addicted himself to all " sorts of Villanies, which made me dis- " charge him from my Service, and to " restore the before-mention'd *Joris Her-* " *vendonk* to his former Place. I would " not have my *Hollanders* entertain such " an Opinion of me, that I would let a- " ny one who has serv'd so long in our " Imperial Court, be dismiss'd without " a Reward; for whoever gains our Im- " perial Favour, shall never depart un- " rewarded: But such as are not willing, " or can't apply themselves to that Study, " may be sure that they will be sent a- " way like this Person. The reason why " the said *Francis Has* stayed in *Candy*, " is not unknown to your Excellency;

Baldæus. "but as he is a *Hollander*, it is but just "he should be dismissed at his due time. "I won't say all concerning him, what I "could; my *Dissaves* will give your Ex- "cellency a more ample account of him, "or when your Excellency appears at "this Court, you will be further satisfi- "ed in this matter. No more; God pro- "tect your Excellency.

At Reygamwatte, May 4. 1656. *Raja Singa Rajou*, Most Potent Emperor of *Ceylon*.

It is beyond all question, that the Differences arisen betwixt this *Joris Hervendonk* and *Francis Has* gave occasion to many Disturbances; *Hervendonk* being accus'd, of having by his Insinuations been the Occasion of *Francis Has* his detention in *Candy*, even to the Year 1656, from whence perhaps he may not be discharged whilst he lives. These and some other Accidents had put the Emperor's Mind into such a ferment, that for three Days together he show'd all the Marks of a severe Displeasure, even to the best of his Courtiers, so as to turn even his Face from them. But his Majesty's Letter deliver'd to the new General, *May 6.* seemed to leave him in a much better Humour.

RAJA SINGA RAJOU, &c.

Another Letter from the Emperor. "YOUR Excellency's Letter dated "the 3*d*, was deliver'd to me on "Thursday the 4*th*, wherein you express "your Sorrow for the Mistake in the Let- "ter I sent back with my last Letter: "As among all other Foreign Nations, "our Imperial Majesty has chosen the "*Hollanders*, as the fittest to be employ- "ed for the increase of our Glory, Fame "and Empire, by reason of their Fide- "lity (which renders them very dear to "me, beyond my own Subjects) so when "they commit any Mistake, it touches "me so sensibly, in regard of the other "Nations that frequent our Court, that "I can't forbear to make them sensible "of their Error, even upon the least "Occasion, in order to their Amend- "ment for the future. If therefore "your Excellency will apply yourself to "such things as tend to our Imperial "Service, the same will be highly ac- "ceptable to us. Our Beloved Direc- "tor-General of Happy Memory did, "during that small time he continued in "our Empire, follow this Rule with the "greatest exactness imaginable: But "being snatch'd away on a sudden by "Death, we were depriv'd of the Op- "portunity of rewarding his Services, "according to our Wish. And as the "said Director-General has not been "wanting, in leaving certain Marks of "the Methods and Customs to be made "use of in our Service, so it will be no "difficult Task for your Excellency to "follow his Footsteps. Your Excellen- "cy mentions the Resolution you have "taken of attempting a second Assault "upon the City, by reason of the ap- "proaching Season, which does not per- "mit our Ships to tarry longer with "Safety in that Road; and that the Ene- "my is much lessened in his Strength "since the last Assault: all which as it is "altogether reasonable, so I approve of "it with much Satisfaction. On the o- "ther hand, our present Illness is no small "Affliction to us, which bereaves us of "the Opportunity of appearing there in "Person, and being an Eye-Witness of "this Engagement, and to be nearer at "hand to second you with our Troops, "in case there should be Occasion; but "let come of it what will, we are resol- "ved to be in the Camp by next Sunday. "If your Excellency thinks fit to stay "for our Coming, it is well; but if "not, and that an Opportunity presents "of gaining the Place, without impai- "ring our Honour and Reputation, I "am satisfy'd, living in hopes, that God "Almighty will crown our Endeavours "with Victory. Your Excellency men- "tions at the end of your Letter, that "you have exchanged eight of your Peo- "ple that were Prisoners in the City "(the Remnants of 74) for as many "*Portugueses* your Prisoners. I am very "glad you sent word of it, that it may "not be alledged against the *Hollanders*, "that they treat with the Enemy with- "out our Knowledg. In the mean time "I am desirous to know how the rest "died, whether for want of Food, or "being well look'd to in their Sickness; "and further, what Instructions you "have sent to the *Portugueses* by those "that were sent into the City; if it "be a Secret worth knowing, your "Excellency will be pleased to re- "veal it to us. Ever since the Death "of our Director-General, no sound "of the Drum has been heard in our "Camp; but in our March nearer to "the Enemy and your Camp, it will "be requisite to make use of our Drums "and other Warlike Musick; where- "of we thought fit to give notice to

"your

" your Excellency. No more for the " present; God protect your Excellency's Person.

Raja Singa Rajou, most potent Emperor of *Ceylon*.

This Letter being read in Council, it was resolv'd to give the Assault the 7th of *May* about 7 or 8 a Clock in the Morning, and to make the fiercest Attack upon the Bastion of St. *John*; which was put in execution accordingly, *Martin Sholtes* Lieutenant of the Fusileers of *Gale* (now Captain in *Gale*) being the first who with undaunted Courage mounted the Breach, and being bravely seconded by his Men, they entred even into the City; but being surrounded on all sides by a great number of *Portugueses*, were forc'd to retreat to the Bastion of St. *John*, where at last they maintain'd their Post, after having three several times repuls'd the Enemy, who endeavoured with all the Force they could bring together to dislodg them from thence, (our Men being constantly reliev'd with fresh Troops) till the Evening, when the Firing somewhat ceasing, they took that opportunity of entrenching themselves with Fascines and Earth towards the side of the City, being nevertheless still exposed to the Enemies Shot from the Water-Fort and the Bastions of St. *Stephen* and *Couras*, which cost us many a brave Soldier.

The Dutch *enter the City.*

Are forc'd to retreat to the Bastion of St. John.

In the beginning of the Assault the *Dissaves* of *Saffragamme* and of the *Four Corles* came into the Trenches with the *Cingalese* Forces; and soon after his Majesty sent likewise the *Dissaves* of *Ouve* and *Matule*, the *Adigar Amracon*, and *Curupele Apohamy*, at the head of a great number of *Lascaryns*: but these brought along with them more Confusion than real Assistance, the *Cingaleses* being always better at making a noise and plundering, than fighting.

Baldæus.

We had no sooner fix'd our Guards upon the Bastion, but a *Negro* Slave (call'd *Caffers*) brought us advice, that in the last Assault the Enemy had the Captain Major, the City Major, and a good number of their best Men wounded, and betwixt 40 and 50 kill'd. We imployed the greatest part of the Night in fortifying our selves with Pallisadoes and Earth-works on the Bastion, in discovering the Mines, and planting some Cannon; to facilitate which, it was order'd that a false Attack be made at two a Clock in the Morning, and with break of day we saw the Prince's Standard display'd there in token of our Victory; which however we had purchased at a dear rate, being even then much expos'd to the Enemies Shot from three Bastions. Upon a general Muster we found 290 Wounded, 80 Sick, and 86 Kill'd; so that we had in all not above 1287 *Europeans* left fit for Service. However *John Maatzuyker* a Lieutenant brought a Supply of 75 Men into our Camp, and 30 more from *Candy*; besides these Lieutenant *Didelof* was posted with 66 men at *Milagre*, and at *Montual* 68.

Among the Slain were the following Officers, whose Names well deserve to be transmitted to Posterity: *Christopher Egger*, *Jurian Gebel*, *James Viry*, *James Scherf*, *Jurian Smith*, *Paul Meno*, *Warnaer vander Heyde*. Among the Wounded, Major *van der Laan* wounded by a Splinter on his Shoulder, and near the Ear; Capt. *Henry Gerard Gluwingh* mortally wounded in four Places; *James de With* wounded with a ten Pounder in the Thigh, of which he died afterwards; *Martin Sholtes* in the Arm; *John Cowper* in both hands; *James Alenbier* in the Leg; *Paul Ketelaer* in the Hand; *John Bartels* in the Belly; *Herman Wynantz*, &c.

Slain and wounded in the Assault.

CHAP. XXXIX.

Our Cannon upon the Bastion of St. John *turn'd against the City. The* Portugueses *offer to capitulate. Articles for the Surrender of the Place. The Ratification. The* Portugueses *march out of the City.*

Our Cannon ready to play from the Bastion of St. John.

THE 10th of *May* having planted our Cannon upon the Bastion of St. *John* against the City, the General and Major *van der Laan* came in the Afernoon to take a view of them. Soon after we saw the Enemy put out a white Flag, and Capt. *Manuel Cabreira de Pontes* deliver'd the following Lines to Major *van der Laan*:

" CApt. *Manuel Cabreira de Pontes*, the " Bearer hereof, comes to desire a " Passport for three Persons of Note to " come

Baldæus. "come into your Camp to treat with you "concerning some Matters of moment. "God protect your Excellency.

Columbo, May 10. 1656. *Anthonio de Souza Coutinho.*

Major *van der Laan* having told him, that he would deliver it to the General, ask'd him, whether he desired a formal Passport in Writing, or would be satisfy'd with his Parole. The *Portuguese* Officer reply'd, that his Parole was sufficient; so they parted, and all Hostilities ceased.

Within two hours after our People were order'd to call to those in the City, and to ask them why they did not send their Deputys; but they answering, that they would not come without a Passport, the same was sent with all possible speed; but it being then pretty late, they excused themselves, that it was not customary to stay a Night out of a Fortress at such a Conjuncture. Whereupon we began to fire again till next Morning about 8 a Clock, being the 11*th*, when the Deputys came into the Camp, *viz. Laurenzo Feriera de Britto* late Captain Major of *Puntegale*, *Hieronimo de Luzena Tavares*, late *Viador das Fazendas*, *i. e.* Sur-intendant of the Merchants in *Columbo*, and *Diego Leitaon de Souza* Secretary of the City, who delivered to the Council the following Articles:

Articles propos'd by those of Columbo.

I. THat a Cessation of Arms shall be agreed on till the 20*th* of *May* next, in order to see the Issue of the expected Succours, which if it arrives before that time, and is strong enough to raise the Siege, this Treaty shall be of no effect. In the mean time no Correspondence or Commerce is to be allowed on either side, except what is done by Messengers, for the Performance whereof Hostages are to be given on both sides.

II. In case of a Surrender of the City, the Churches and Images shall not be defiled, and the Priests and Friers shall have full liberty to take along with them, without any molestation, all the Images, Relicks, sacred Vessels, Silver Lamps, and other Church Ornaments belonging to the Performance of Divine Service, not excepting the Moveables belonging to each Clergy-man in particular.

III. The Governour and Deputy-Governour, *Anthonio de Souza Coutinho* and *Francisco de Melo de Castro*, as likewise the Son of *Anthonio de Souza Coutinho*, shall be treated with all due Respect and Civility, and have full liberty to leave the City with all their Moveables, Gold, Silver, Rings, Jewels, Servants, *Portuguese* Pages, and Slaves of both Sexes; and to remain in their Houses till they embark, under the special Protection of the General, who shall be obliged to provide them (for their Mony) with Provisions during their stay here, and with Necessaries for their Voyage, as likewise with convenient Shipping for themselves and their Families, with able Seamen, Arms, Ammunition, and what else may be requisite for that purpose, whenever the same shall be required.

IV. The Major of the City, Captain Major of the Garison, and Serjeant Major, and the late deceased Captain's Family, shall receive the same Treatment.

V. The Captains of Foot, Reformado's, and other Officers of what degree soever, shall march out with all the Marks of Honour, Ensigns display'd, Matches lighted, Balls in the Mouth, and with their Baggage, and shall be provided with Shipping to transport them beyond Sea to the *Indian* Shore. They are in the mean while to be maintain'd by the *Dutch* General, out of the Superplus of the Mony belonging to the King of *Portugal*, or for want of such, at his own Charge, or of the Company, till the time of their Transportation, and they shall not be molested either by Sea or Land.

VI. The *Ovidor*, Judg, and other Officers of the Exchequer, the Head Factor, *Alcade* Major or Chief Magistrate, and the Farmers of the King's Demesns, shall enjoy the same Favour granted to the Major of the City.

VII. All Gentlemen, Cavaliers, and the chiefest Citizens and Inhabitants, shall have liberty to challenge the same Conditions granted to the City *Major*; and, if any of them are inclin'd to remain under the Jurisdiction of the *Hollanders*, they shall be left undisturb'd in the full Possession of their Houses, Estates, Villages, and every thing belonging to them, and be treated in all other respects like the Natives of *Holland*. For the free exercise of their Religion they shall have a Church, with a convenient number of Clergymen allow'd them; and if hereafter any of them shall think fit to go to some other part of the *Indies*, they shall be at liberty to sell both their real and personal Estates, or otherwise dispose of them without molestation. They shall also be provided with Shipping at the publick Charge, except such as have Ships of their own, who shall be free to traffick where they please, paying the usual Customs.

All

VIII. All Foreign Merchants, both *Europeans* and Negroes, that were come to *Columbo* to traffick, ſhall be free to depart with their Veſſels, Goods, Gold, Silver, and other Merchandizes bought up here, eſpecially the Cinnamon bought for the King or the City's uſe, whether aboard a Ship or not: Proviſions ſhall be likewiſe provided them for their Mony, and a ſafe retreat; and in caſe they ſtand in need of Seamen, they ſhall be ſupply'd with them.

IX. The Negro Inhabitants both married and unmarried, and even the Foreigners of what Condition ſoever, ſhall enjoy the ſame freedom granted to the *Portugueſe* Citizens.

X. All the *Modeliars*, *Aratches* and *Laſcaryns* that have hitherto been in the King of *Portugal*'s Service (notwithſtanding they have left the Service of the Company, or of his Majeſty) ſhall be at liberty to depart with their Moveables whither they pleaſe.

XI, XII. *Simon Lopes de Baſto*, a *Portugueſe* by Birth, but ſince in the Service of the *Dutch*, ſhall be pardon'd for his Offence in coming over to us, and be free to depart in Company of the Governor: Likewiſe all *Dutch* Deſerters that have taken Service in the City ſhall not be moleſted, but have liberty to march out along with our Forces.

XIII. All ſick and wounded Soldiers or Inhabitants, ſhall be entertain'd there at the Charge of the Company (if the Superplus of the King's Mony proves inſufficient) till they recover their Health, and afterwards provided with Conveniences for their Tranſportion.

XIV. Upon the Surrender of the City after the *Dutch* are put in Poſſeſſion thereof, their General ſhall take effectual care that no Affront or Miſchief be done to the Governors, other Perſons of Note, Soldiers, and Inhabitants, and their Families, but the ſame ſhall be protected by the ſaid General, as well within as without the City, againſt all Violences from the King of *Candy*'s Forces. Sign'd,

Anthonio de Souza Coutinho.

After mature deliberation in the Council, the following Articles were in Anſwer to the former, deliver'd the 12*th* to the three Deputies in the Name of his Imperial Majeſty of *Ceylon*, their High and Mightineſſes the States-General of the *United Provinces*, the Governors of the *Eaſt-India* Company, and of *John Maatzuyker* Governor-General, and the Council of the *Indies*.

Baldæus. Articles granted to the Portugueſes.

THE City ſhall be ſurrender'd this day before Noon, without any further delay, upon the following Conditions.

What was deſir'd in the ſecond Article in relation to the Clergy is granted, and two Places ſhall be appointed for them to be in till their departure.

To the third Article it is anſwer'd, That it is not in the Power of the General to have the Governors, *&c.* tranſported at this time to *Tutecoryn* or *Manaar*; but that it ſhall be done with the firſt conveniency; or elſe to *Cochin* or *Wingula*: But in caſe they have a mind to be tranſported to the other Shore, the ſame ſhall be perform'd by ſome of the Company's Ships within 15 days after the date hereof. They are allow'd to carry along with them all their Slaves of both Sexes, and thoſe belonging to the Governor's Son *Chriſtovaon de Souza*, in hopes that they will not take any but their own, as likewiſe all their Moveables, Gold, Silver, Rings and Jewels; and they ſhall be protected in their Houſes till the time of their departure.

The Officers mention'd in the 4*th* Article ſhall be treated according to their reſpective Dignities, and be protected againſt all harm. They may take along with them their Gold, Silver, Clothing, and what elſe they carry about them: But as to their Slaves of both Sexes, they ſhall be conſider'd according to their reſpective Qualities. In *what they carry about them* ſhall be comprehended Beds and Bed-clothes, Hangings, Tapeſtry, Bolſters, Quilts, *&c.* The Officers and Reformades ſhall march out with the uſual marks of Honour, and be tranſported to the Coaſt of *Coromandel* with as much of their Moveables as their Slaves or other Servants (allotted them by the General's favour) ſhall be able to carry.

The Soldiers ſhall march out with their Baggage, Colours diſplay'd, Matches lighted, Ball in their Mouth, and Drums beating to the General's Quarters, where they ſhall ſurrender their Arms under the great Standard, and from thence with the firſt conveniency be tranſported into *Europe*. Such as are married or born in the *Indies* ſhall be tranſported to the Coaſt of *Coromandel*, and be maintain'd till the time of their departure at the Charge of the Company.

The Officers mention'd in the 6*th* Article ſhall partake of the ſame Favour granted to other Perſons of Note; the City Major and Head Factor to be comprehended in the ſame.

All

Baldæus.

All such as intend to submit to the Jurisdiction of the *Dutch* shall be civilly and favourably treated, and remain in the quiet Possession of their Estates; but in case they have a mind to depart, their Goods are left to the Discretion of the General.

The chiefest of the Citizens and married *Portugueses*, with their Children, who are not inclinable to stay in this Isle, shall at the time of their departure receive the same Treatment as the Officers; but the Natives of the Isle shall be left to the Disposition of the General.

The *Modeliars*, *Aratches* and *Lascaryns*, shall receive the same Treatment as the *Dutch* Deserters.

All sick and wounded Persons, whether Inhabitants or Soldiers, now in the Hospital, or any other place of the City, shall stay there till the recovery of their Healths, and be furnish'd with what they desire.

All the Officers, Inhabitants, Soldiers and unmarried Women, shall be protected by the General against all Violences and Oppressions.

The General does also agree, that if any Ships approach the City for its relief betwixt this and the *30th* of *May*, notice shall be given them of its Surrender, with orders to depart, and shall be protected at least till they are out of sight of *Columbo*. The *11th* of *May* 1656.

Signed,

Adrian van der Meyden, *John van der Laan*,
Peter de Bitter, *Edward Ooms*,
Ysbrand Gotskens.

I *Adrian van der Meyden*, Governor-General for the *Dutch East-India* Company in the Isle of *Ceylon*, with the rest of the Members of the Council, promise and engage by these Presents, That, in case the Deputies bring back this Capitulation, approv'd as such by the Governor *Anthonio de Souza Coutinho*, and his Council, we will punctually observe all the Articles contain'd therein without the least limitation or exception; and further grant such Favours as are in our power to allow of. In Confirmation whereof we have in Conjunction with the said Deputys signed the same, in the *Dutch* Camp before *Columbo*, the *12th* of *May* 1656.

Sign'd on our side by

Adrian van der Meyden, *John van der Laan*,
Peter de Bitter, *Edward Ooms*,
Ysbrand Gotskens, *John Hartman*.

On the Enemy's side by

Anthonio de Souza Coutinho,
Francisco de Melo de Castro,
Anthonio de Silva,
Gaspar de Ronga Pereira,
Laurenzo Fereira de Britto,
Hieronymo de Luzena Tavares,
Diego Leitaon de Souza.

Ratification of the Capitulation.

In the Morning about Nine a Clock the Deputies return'd with the Capitulation approv'd and sign'd as before, with a Letter of Intercession from the Governor and Deputy-Governor for *Simon Lopes*, who had deserted our Service. The Capitulation being sign'd once more, and the Council dismiss'd, *Ysbrand Gotskens* and *James van der Rhee* our Secretary of War, were immediately after Dinner sent into the City, to demand the Keys from the two *Portuguese* Governors, and to take account of all the Arms, Ammunition and Provisions, as also to settle certain matters concerning the marching out of the Troops pursuant to the Capitulation.

The Portugueses march out of Columbo.

Accordingly there marched out of the place *Anthonio de Melo de Castro* Captain-Major at the head of the King's Troops, consisting in 14 Companies, and 36 Captains (call'd *Reformados* by the *Portugueses*) with their Ensigns display'd, Drums beating, Matches lighted, and Ball in the mouth, marching through our Forces rang'd on both sides, to the General's Quarters, where having surrender'd their Arms, they were conducted to the place prepar'd for their Lodging that night. These were follow'd by the Citizens, Sick, Wounded, and Criples. In the mean while their chief Engineer discover'd to two of our Deputies four Mines on the side of the Bastion of *Rajuba*, betwixt the Bastions S. *Stephen* and *Clergos*, each whereof being fill'd with four Barrels of Gunpowder, the Trains were remov'd, and Sentinels plac'd near them.

The Dutch march into the City.

This done, our Forces march'd into the City, follow'd by the General, Major *Van der Laan*, and the rest of the Head Officers. Near the Sea-shore not far from the Bastion of *Couras*, the Governor and Deputy-Governor (both venerable aged *Portugueses*) came with their Retinue to salute the General. After some Complements on both sides, Orders were given to our Forces where to take their Posts, and to disarm all the *Lascaryns* in the City. Towards Evening the Prince's Standard was planted in the Water-

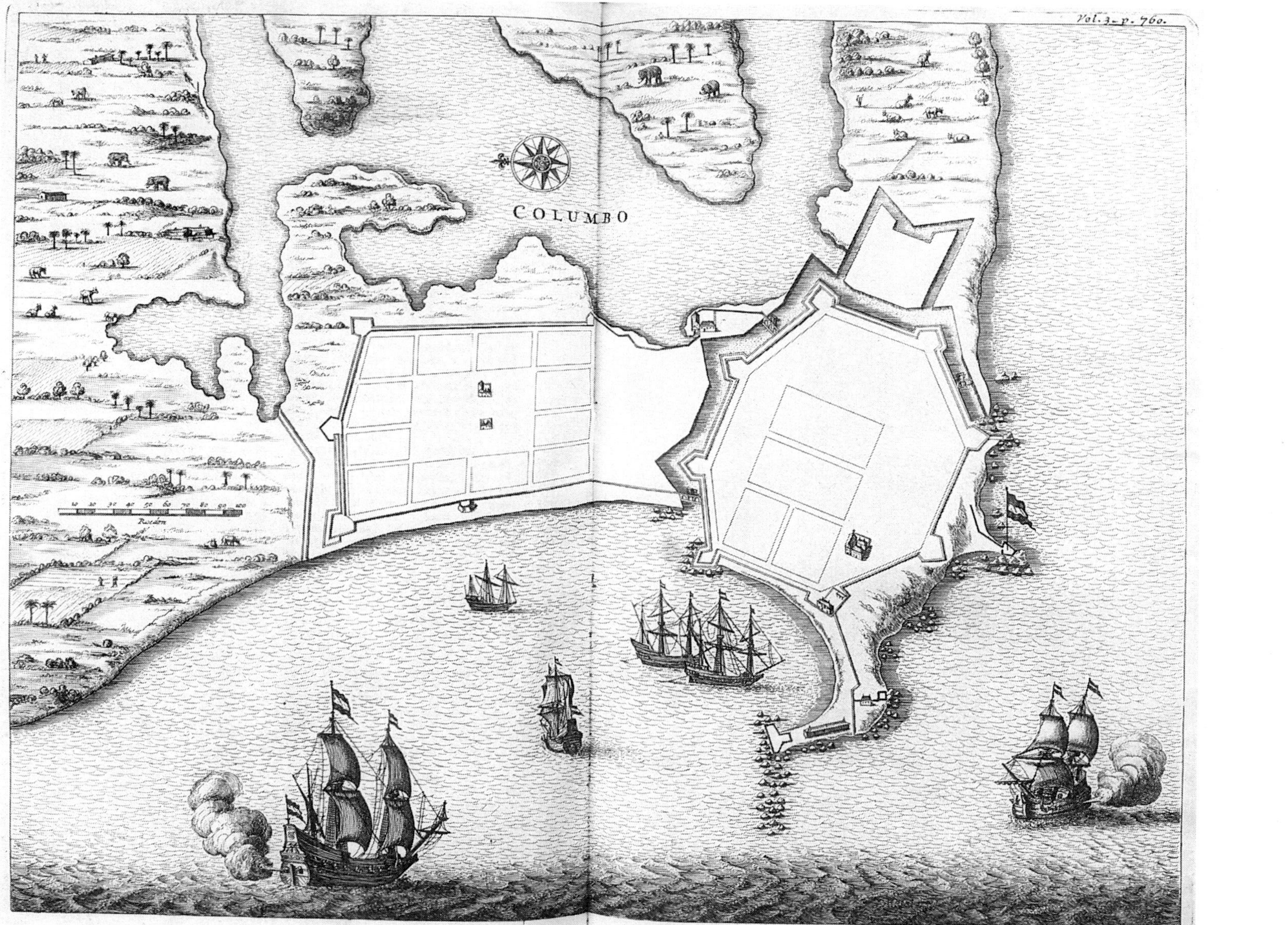
COLUMBO
10 20 30 40 50 60 70 80 90 100
Roeden

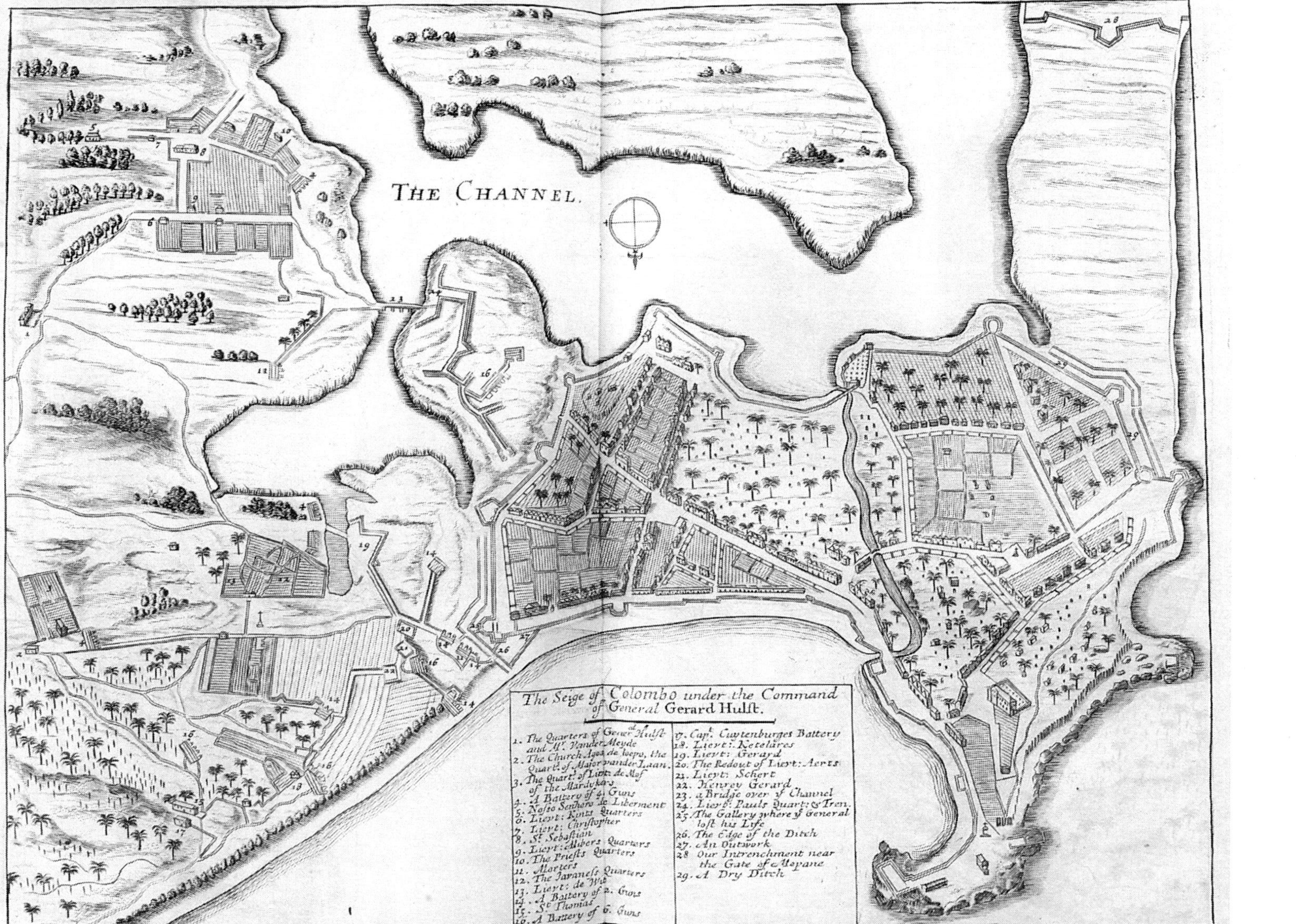
THE CHANNEL.
The Seige of Colombo under the Command of General Gerard Hulst.
1. The Quarters of Gener.al Hulst and Mr. Vander Meyde
2. The Church Agoa de Iuepo, the Quart.s of Major vander Laan.
3. The Quart.s of Lieut: de Mos of the Mardykars
4. A Battery of 4. Guns
5. Nosso Senhoro de Liberment
6. Lieut: Kints Quarters
7. Lieut: Christopher
8. St. Sebastian
9. Lieut: Albers Quarters
10. The Priests Quarters
11. Marters
12. The Javanese Quarters
13. Lieut: de Wit
14. A Battery of 2. Guns
15. St. Thomas
16. A Battery of 6. Guns
17. Capt. Cuytenburges Battery
18. Lieut: Ketelares
19. Lieut: Gerard
20. The Redout of Lieut: Aerts
21. Lieut: Schert
22. Henrey Gerard
23. a Bridge over ye Channel
24. Lieut: Pauls Quart: & Tren.
25. The Gallery where ye General lost his Life
26. The Edge of the Ditch
27. An Outwork
28 Our Intrenchment near the Gate of Mapane
29. A Dry Ditch

Water-Fort, and the great Cannon discharg'd round the place as a Signal of our Victory. Thus the City of *Columbo*, not inferior in Strength to most of *Europe*, fell into the hands of our Nation, after she had been 150 years in the Possession of the *Portugueses*. In acknowledgment of which a Thanksgiving Day was appointed the Sunday following, being the 14*th* of *May*, which was celebrated accordingly, and the Thanksgiving-Sermon was preach'd by the Reverend *Francis Wyngarten* in the Church of S. *Francis*, since call'd the *Town Church*.

Baldæus.

A Thanksgiving Sermon.

An Account of the Siege of *Columbo* taken from their own Journals, and (for the publick Good) communicated to the Author by *Matthæus van den Broek*, formerly a Member of the Council of the *Indies*, now Governor of the *East-India* Company. Faithfully translated from the *Portuguese*.

A true Account of the Siege of Columbo *carried on by* Raja Singa *King of* Candy *and the* Hollanders, *till the Surrender of that Fortress under* Anthonio de Souza Coutinho, *Captain General in the Isle of* Ceylon.

IN the Month of *September* 1655. 10 *Dutch* Ships came to an Anchor near *Negumbo*, two more being out at some distance at Sea, having landed 11 Companies of *Europeans* of 80 Men each; and being join'd by a good number of Negroes, they march'd to the Pass of *Betal*, but by reason of the violent Rains were forced to return to *Negumbo*. Mr. *Gerard Hulst* the *Dutch* General having reimbark'd his Forces with some others taken out of *Negumbo*, sail'd with the before-mentioned 12 Ships to *Columbo*, where much about the same time we had receiv'd a supply of Provisions in three Galliots sent from *Cochin* by the brave and faithful *Simon Gomes de Silva*, Governor of that place. Our Governor *Coutinho* took part of the Rice, in order to carry it to *Caleture*, where they stood in great need of it, but was prevented in his Design by the shallowness of the River. The 22*d* of *Septemb.* we receiv'd another Supply from *Tutecoryn*, consisting in 28 Sail; under the Command of *Nicolas de Moura*, the Fleet being chiefly laden on the account of private Merchants.

The Enemy having left six of their best Ships before *Columbo*, sail'd with the rest to *Caleture*; whereupon our Governor gave Orders to Capt. *Caspar Figueira de Serpe*, then encamp'd upon the Frontiers of the King of *Candy*, to come to *Columbo*, which he did accordingly *October* 7.

Without the City were at that time encamp'd the famous *Dissave Francisco Antunes* towards *Mature*, and *Alvares Rodrigo Boralho* sent out with three Companies to get Intelligence of the Enemy, who from the 23*d* of *September* to the 15*th* of *October* laid before *Caleture*, and had raised three Batteries against it.

Our Governor being sensible of the Condition of the Place, sent thither a Convoy of Provisions commanded by *Nicolas de Moura*, under a good Guard of *Europeans* and *Negroes*, landed by *Manoel de Gil*, Dissave of *Negumbo*, who has so often signalized himself in our King's Service in the Isle of *Ceylon*. This brave Man attempting to pass the River with 12 of his choicest Men (the Boat holding no more) was so warmly receiv'd by some of the Enemies Forces, that, after they had kill'd several of his Men with their Fire-Arms, he was forc'd to retire; the Commander in chief follow'd his Footsteps contrary to the Opinion of Capt. *Domingo Coelho de Alla*, who would fain have perswaded him to advance as near as he could to *Caleture*, to incommode the Enemy in the Siege. Upon this occasion *Alvares Rodrigo Boralho* did considerable Service, in sending Intelligence from time to time of what pass'd, till at last this whole Body came back to the City.

It being then resolv'd to succour *Caleture* to the utmost of our Power, and four Galliots being at the same time arriv'd from the Viceroy of *Goa*, we made up a Body of 600 *Portugueses*, the Command whereof was committed to *Caspar Figueira* to attempt the Relief of the Place in conjunction with some *Cingaleses*, notwith-

notwithstanding the Enemy's Force consisted of 3000 *Europeans*, besides a good number of *Bandaneses* and *Cingaleses* sent to their Assistance by the King of *Candy*.

Accordingly *Caspar Figueira* encamp'd with his Troops the 16*th* of *October* two Leagues from *Caleture*, having receiv'd Advice before, that the Enemy were already possess'd of the Pass on this side, and had posted three Companies there. Pursuant to this Intelligence he order'd six Companies under the Command of *Domingo Sarmento* and *Francisco Antunes* to attack the Enemy in the Night, which they did accordingly with incredible Bravery for a considerable time, but very indifferent Success; for instead of being engag'd with three Companies of 80 Men each (as they supposed) they found the Enemy much superior in Number, to charge them so furiously both in Front and Flank, that they were put into Confusion with great Slaughter, before they could recollect themselves. *Figueira* being by this time come up with the rest of his Forces, unadvisedly attack'd the Enemy a second time; but these opening their Ranks on both sides, discharg'd two Cannon among our Forces, which occasion'd such a Confusion, that the Enemy improving their advantage, once more put us to flight. *Figueira* and his Lieut. *Manoel Cabreira* were for trying their Fortune once more; but finding the Flower of their Forces either slain or dispersed, and no means left to make them return to the Charge, they thought fit to retreat and bring off their wounded Men, among whom were *Sebastian Pereira* and *Joseph Antunes*, the only two that escaped alive of eleven Captains. Of the Reformades, *John Cordeiro*, *Manoel Fernandes de Miranda*, *Manoel de Santjago Garcia*, with 200 common Soldiers, came off alive.

Figueira *routed.*

This ill Success caus'd an unspeakable Consternation in the City of *Columbo*, where there was nothing to be heard but Outcries and Lamentations in the Streets; the Shops were shut up, and the Gates kept close, with strict Orders that nobody should appear arm'd without doors. The next thing to be done, was to give an account of their present ill Condition to the Viceroy of *Goa*; and the same being (at their earnest request) committed to the care of *Damian Vieira* a Jesuit, and *Manoel Saraiva*, an Inhabitant of *Manaar*, the last of these two went no further than from *Columbo* to *Manaar*, from whence he dispatch'd the Letters to *Antonio Amiral de Meneses* at *Jafnapatnam*, a Neglect that deserv'd a very severe Punishment.

Consternation occasion'd by this Defeat at Columbo.

By this time the Hospital was fill'd with the sick and wounded Soldiers, where Brother *Golsal* an *Austin* Frier did both the Duty of a devout, religious, and charitable Lay-man: The number of those that died here for want of good looking after, being scarce inferior to what was lost in the Engagement.

On the other hand, the *Dutch* had purchas'd this Victory with very little loss on their side; notwithstanding which Major *Van der Laan* (a mortal Enemy of the *Portugueses*, and a zealous Heretick) having receiv'd a Wound in the Cheek, took a most barbarous Revenge from all the *Portugueses* he met with, who were all massacred in the Woods (sometimes 20 and 30 together) by his Orders in cool Blood, he having often been heard to say, *That if the* Portugueses *were at his disposal, he would cut them all off at one stroke.* Their General Mr. *Hulst* being of a more compassionate Temper, order'd Quarter to be given to the new listed Forces, but this Heretick told him that they ought to be cut to pieces, in retaliation of what they did to the *Dutch*, whom they never gave any Quarter: However through the General's Mercy about 60 of the new listed Men had their Lives given them. In this Engagement the brave *Francisco Antunes*, who had render'd his Name so famous in *Ceylon* by his many Victories, also lost his Life in a Wood, who deserv'd to have had a *Mausolæum* erected to his Memory.

This must be look'd upon as a Calumny.

Thus the Enemy by this Victory becoming Master of the Field, afterwards soon made himself Master of the whole Island of *Ceylon*, the City of *Columbo* (after the loss of *Caleture*) expecting no less than to be reduc'd to the utmost extremity. For after they had endur'd for some days all the Inconveniences of Hunger in *Caleture*, *Anthonio Mendes d'Aranha* represented to his Soldiers, that they had rather try the utmost, than to perish for want of Food, exhorting them to fight their way with Sword in hand through the Enemy. He prevail'd at last so far with them, as to agree with them in his Resolutions; but the appointed time approaching, they found themselves so enfeebled for want of good Food, that not being able to put their Design in Execution, they were forced to surrender, upon Condition that they should march out with their Arms, *&c.* Thus the King of *Portugal* lost at once a strong Fortress, one of his most experienc'd

Surrender of Caleture.

The Garison was kept in Prison at Gale.

rienc'd Officers in the whole Isle, and 250 choice Men, through the mismanagement of some who prefer'd their own Interest before that of his Majesty.

The Dutch *come before* Columbo.

The 17*th* of *October* the Enemy marching directly to *Columbo*, posted themselves in sight of the City near S. *Sebastian*, where *Anthonio de Souza Coutinho* the then Governor, together with *Francisco de Melo de Castro*, order'd immediately some Works to be cast up to hinder their approach: But the 18*th* they were so vigorously attack'd in these Intrenchments, that they had enough to do to escape to the City, and to cut down the Bridges behind them.

We then apply'd our selves to the strengthening of our Batteries, whilst the Enemy kill'd all they met with without the City, and immediately fell to the raising of their Batteries, which was no difficult task for them to do, being back'd by an Army of 20 or 30000 Men under *Raja Singa* King of *Candy*, and furnish'd by him with Pioneers and other Necessaries in abundance.

The several Posts assign'd upon the Bastions.

Our Governor and *Francisco de Melo de Castro* did leave no Stone unturn'd for the defence of the City; they visited the Magazines and Armories, and furnish'd with Arms all such as were capable of bearing them, not excepting even the old Men and School-boys. The Posts on the Bastions were assign'd to the following Commanders; on the Bastion of S. *John*, *Manoel Correa de Barros*; on that of S. *Sebastian*, *Francisco Gorian de Fialho*; on that of *Madre de Deos*, *John de Pavia de Quintal*; on that of S. *Conception*, *Domingos Peixoto*; on that of S. *Hieronymo*, *Alphonso Carvalho de Souza*; on that of S. *Anthonio*, *Manoel Carvalho da Maya*; on that of S. *Jacob*, *Manoel Nunes*; on that of S. *Austin*, *Luys de Paiva Quintal*; on that of S. *Laurence*, *Anthonio de Silva*; on that of S. *Crus*, *Caspar d'Aranja Pereira*; on that of S. *Francisco Xaverio*, *Manoel Caldeira de Brito*; and on that of *Galvoca*, *Dominges Pires*; who all gave sufficient Proofs of their Bravery in their respective Posts during the Siege, as did likewise Father *Damian Vicira* a Jesuit, especially in the Attack upon the Garden of *Antonio de Mota*, and some Houses standing upon an Eminency at S. *Thomas*, in which tho they were repulsed the first time, yet the next day our Forces commanded by *Alvaro Rodrigo* and *Manoel Caldeira*, being seconded by some Companies posted on the other side of the Ditch, made themselves Masters of it, being of no small Conveniency to us, to hinder the approach of the Enemy.

Baldæus.

Notwithstanding this the Enemy advanced apace under favour of their Artillery, of which they brought great store daily from their Ships. And on our side we found the Bastion of S. *John* most expos'd, we strengthned the same with Masts, Earth and Fascines; we made also a cover'd way from the Wall to the brink of the Ditch, the same was done near the Bastions of S. *Sebastian* and *Rajuba*; both Clergy-men and Lay-men without distinction of Persons imploying themselves in this Work, and furnishing Materials for so useful a Work, especially *Caspar Figueira de Serpe*, who having great store of Baskets, Spades, and other such like Instruments, sacrificed them all for the publick Service.

The Enemy play from their Batteries.

The 20*th* of *October* the Enemy began to salute us with 12 great pieces of Cannon from three Batteries, *viz.* 3 from that of S. *Thomas*, 5 from that at *Agua de Luphe*, and 4 from that of S. *Sebastian*, from whence they sent 800 Bullets, 18, 20, 24 and 28 Pounders, in one day into the City. But tho the Enemies Bullets did considerable Execution, some of the King's unfaithful Servants did more mischief by introducing adulterated Coin, and engrossing the Provisions under pretence of the King's Service for their own lucres sake.

Number of People in the City.

There were at that time not above 1300 Souls, young and old, *Europeans* and *Indians*, *viz.* 500 that receiv'd Pay, and among them, some married, some unmarried, some Children and *Topasses*; 300 married People who serv'd without Pay, 400 *Lascaryns*, and about 60 Labourers; the whole number of the *Europeans* not amounting to above 500 Men. The Governor with the Consent of the whole City, pitch'd upon *Anthonio d'Abreu* an Inhabitant of *Negapatnam*, to be sent to *Goa*, to give an account to the Viceroy of the City. He was favourably receiv'd by the Viceroy, who told him that he had already sent a Squadron under *Manoel de Magalhais Coutinho*, to carry a Supply of Provisions and Men thither, brought together for that purpose by *Anthonio Amiral de Meneses* at *Manaar*. But this Convoy came no further than the Cape *Comoryn*, and could not make the Cape, tho some were of opinion it was rather for want of Will; so he return'd to *Columbo*, where the Viceroy being dead in the mean while, the whole face of Affairs was changed, and *Columbo* lost for want of timely Supply.

Anth. d'Abreu *sent to* Goa, *to give an account of the Condition of* Columbo.

Baldæus.

The before-mention'd three Batteries being raised above 200 Paces from our Walls, they erected another against the Bastion of St. *John*, within 400 Paces of it, from whence they batter'd us most furiously with three Demi-Cannon. Immediately after, one of our Engineers, a *Hollander* by Birth, named *John de Rosa*, deserted to the Enemy; 'tis true, he was no great Conjurer in his Art, yet did us considerable Mischief. For the Enemies Batteries play'd so furiously upon our Outworks, that in two days time they were all laid level with the Ground, and our Bastions and Walls were so sorely battered, that with much ado we could stop the Breaches, which was done by continual and indefatigable Labour; each Soldier and Officer employing the Intervals they had, when they were not upon Duty, in working like the meanest Labourer.

One of our Engineers deserts.

The Governor *Anthonio Coutinho* spent Day and Night in visiting the Works, animating his Soldiers both in Words and his Example, leaving his Habitation, and contenting himself with a small Tent near the Bastion of St. *John*, where the Enemies made their greatest Effort. Afterwards he took up his Quarters in a Warehouse, scarce undressing himself all the time the Siege lasted, and employ'd much of his time in keeping an exact account of the Stores, and distributing Provisions with his own Hands, without which Precaution the City could not have held out half so long. *Francisco de Melo de Castro* followed his Footsteps, having not been seen without his Clothes and Arms for seven Months together. The City-Major *Manoel Marques Gorjaon* did assist them in his Station, as did likewise *Caspar Figueira de Serpe*, the *Dissaves* of the *Corles* of *Negumbo* and of *Mature*, *John Coelho de Castro*, *Manoel Gil*, *Manoel Seixas*, and *John Banha*, who were present in all Places, where there was the most danger to encounter. The Clergy, but especially the Capucins, were very assiduous in confessing the Soldiers, in praying and doing all manner of good Offices without Intermission; and some of them would not be backward in being upon the Guard with the Soldiery, and give the Enemies ample Proofs of their Valour.

Care and Conduct of the Governor.

The Enemy thunder'd so furiously against the Bastion of St. *John*, that it appear'd like a heap of Rubbish; then they turn'd their Fury against the H.rn-work of St. *Stephen* and the adjacent Point; but *Manoel da Veiga* the Commanding Officer on the Bastion of St. *Stephen*, *Francisco Gorian Fialho*, *John Ferraon d' Abreu*, *Gonzal Martinho Piementel*, *Manoel Carvalho*, and others employ'd in the Defence of the Works towards St. *Sebastian*, were indefatigable in repairing the Breaches, and rendring the Bastions tolerably defensible.

Bravery of the Besieged.

Hieronymo Lucena shew'd the same care in the Bastion of *Madre de Deos*, till he was reliev'd by *Lewis Tavera de Cunha*; and the Wall which extended towards St. *Sebastian* being found very weak, the General recommended the Defence thereof to the four Captains of the *Galliots*, lately come from *Goa*. These order'd an Entrenchment to be made there of 150 Yards long, one broad, and six Foot high. Father *Damian Vieira* the Jesuit being employ'd in furthering this Work, a Bullet taking away a great piece of the Wall, struck him on the Head, so that he fell dead upon the Ground; but soon recovering himself, he fell to his Work again, his Servant constantly attending him with a Sword and Fusee, wherewith he did considerable Execution, being commonly one of the foremost in charging the Enemy. Finding that the Bastion of *Xaverius* (otherwise call'd *Couras*) began also to be sorely batter'd by the Enemy, the care thereof was committed to an old famous Soldier, *Manoel Rodrigos Franco*, who soon put it out of all Danger.

The 29th of *Novemb.* the *Dutch* General *Gerard Hulst* sent a Drummer with a white Flag with a Messenger into the City, to summon our Governor to a Surrender, who delaying his Answer till next day, the Enemy fir'd most furiously with his Cannon all that Night; but the next Morning we sent *Diego de Souza de Castro* and *Thomas Fereire Leite* with an Answer, the last personating a Drummer, in order to get some Intelligence of the Condition of the Enemy; but they were upon their Guard, and therefore sent a Captain and a Lieutenant, attended by two Soldiers to receive our Governor's Letter, wherein he told the General, that he wanted neither Will nor Power to defend the Place to the utmost for his King's Service, being still sufficiently provided with Powder and Ball, and other Necessaries; and to add the more weight to his Words, we fir'd most furiously all that Night.

The City summoned to surrender.

The *Dutch* repay'd us in the same Coin, sending us commonly a Present of 800 Cannon-ball and 900 Granadoes every Day. The 12th of *Novemb.* they celebrated the Feast of St. *Martin* the Pope by a new Invention of Fireballs, whereof they sent a good Number into the City, and

General Assault given upon Columbo. and seconded the Game by a general Assault. For early in the Morning three of their stoutest Ships appearing in sight of the City, one of them called the *Maid of Enchuysen* enter'd the Harbour, carrying the red Flag in her Stern; and coming to an Anchor within Musquet-shot of the Bastion of St. *Crus*, gave us several warm Salutes, under the sound of Drums and Trumpets; but *Manoel d' Abreu Godinho* and *Anthonio de Silva*, the Commanding Officers on the Bastion of St. *Laurence*, did ply them thick with their Cannon, that having first brought by the Board all her Masts, they made soon after so many Holes in her sides, that she was ready to sink, and a few of her Crew made hard shift to escape in the long Boat. The other two Ships seeing the other so ill treated, did not think fit to follow her Footsteps, but made the best of their way to the Road, alledging in their behalf, that they were not able to come up with the other.

At the same time they attempted the Assault on the Land side. Mr. *John van der Laan* assaulted with 7 Companies the Gate of *Acouras*, advancing boldly with Sword in hand to the very Faces of our People, the foremost of which began to give way, and in all likelihood the rest would have follow'd their Example, had not Father *Antonio Nunes* a Jesuit, with his drawn Sword threatn'd such as were ready to fly with present Death; nay his Comrade *John Cordeiro* wounded one of the Soldiers as he was flying with his long Rapier. Soon after *Caspar Figueira de Serpe* coming with fresh Supplies, this so animated our Soldiers, that they not only stopp'd the Enemies Fury, but also made them give way in a little while after. In this Action an Ensign and Serjeant acquired Immortal Honour, and *Manoel d' Almeyda*, tho a very old Soldier, yet did not leave his Post till he had received 11 Wounds. *Felicio de Seixas* and *Contrero de Seixas* lost their Lives with their Swords in their Hands; *Manoel Guerreiro*, i. e. the *Warrior*, did great Service with his Cannon from his Redoubt, he being an expert Cannoneer.

The Dutch repulsed. Major *van der Laan* seeing there was no likelihood of succeeding, sounded a Retreat, leaving the Ground covered with the dead Carcases of the *Hollanders*. The Enemy receiv'd also considerable Damage from the Tower, where *Diego de Souza de Castro* commanded, and no question much more might have been expected had we been provided with good Gunners: for it must be confessed, that we wanted not Officers of Courage and Experience, but only such as understood the Mathematicks and the Art of Gunnery; an Instance of which might be given in one of our Gunners, who having double charged a Cannon, did wound one of our Captains and two others, *viz. Thomas Fereira Leite*, and *Pedro Gonsalves Salgado*, tho for the rest their Fidelity ought not to be pass'd by in silence; it having been observ'd, that not one of our Cannoneers deserted to the Enemy, but most of them lost their Lives in the Service. *Baldæus.* *Not one Portuguese Cannoneer deserted.*

The Gate of *Rajuba* was attack'd with 800 choice Men by General *Hulst* in Person, who endeavoured to mount the Walls with scaling Ladders: As they passed the Bridg, they were sorely gall'd from the Bastions of St. *Stephen*, St. *Sebastian*, and that of *Madre de Deos*, the Defence whereof being committed to *Rodrigo Boralho*, *Antonio de Mota d' Oliveira*, and *Manoel Cabreira de Ponte*, they gave such a hot salute with their Firelocks from behind their Pallisado Works to the *Hollanders*, that many of them were laid dead upon the Ground. A certain Cannon of Stone did them considerable Damage, and would have done more, had it not burst in pieces. Three times they renewed the Assault with incredible Fury, and as often were they repulsed with an unspeakable Bravery. At last General *Hulst*, to encourage his Men, cried out aloud, *Soldiers, the Princes Standard is set upon the Bastion of St.* John (which in effect was not so) and so with a Curse (*Sante Diabo*, i. e. Holy Devil) he snatch'd a Ladder out of a Fellow's Hand; but finding no body ready to follow him, whilst he was encouraging his Men, and fixing his Ladder to the very Gate, he was wounded in the Thigh, and so forc'd to retreat. On the side of the Lake or Fens (called *Lagoa* by the *Portuguese*) 240 Men were embark'd in 8 *Chinese* Boats brought from *Batavia* for that purpose. They were met by *Domingos Coelho d' Alla* in 5 *Manchous* or Barges, who fought with them courageously for some time, but was forced at last to suffer them to land, but retir'd into a Pallisado-Work near *Maria Telles*, from whence he with *Sebastian Caldeira*, and 5 or 6 more (the rest being run away) fir'd briskly upon the *Hollanders*; who at last finding a Hole or Gate near the House of *Sebastian Caldeira*, they forc'd their way, notwithstanding the brave Resistance made by *Manoel Rodrigues Franco*, *Guardian de Varo*, and *Francisco Rebello de Palsares*, who sent a good quantity of Hand-granadoes and Fire-balls among them

Baldæus. them, the said *Guardian* having receiv'd two Wounds by Musquet-Balls. The *Dutch* forcing their way into a narrow Street, were there met by *Manoel Fernandes de Miranda*, who tho sorely wounded yet continued fighting with his Sword and Buckler, till exhausted of his Strength by the Loss of Blood, he was ready to drop, and would infallibly have died upon the Spot, had not *Francisco de Lemos* carried him off. In his Place succeeded *Diego Leitaon de Souza*, who discharging a Musquetoon on the Corner of a Street among the *Dutch*, made them halt; the same was done by Father *Damian Vieira* the Jesuit, who with another Musquetoon made such a Havock among the Enemy, that these two stopped their farther Progress, till *Antonio de Leaon* appear'd at the Head of a good Troop of Souldiers; he being provided with another Musquetoon, charged the Enemy so briskly (as they were endeavouring to break into the backside of some Gardens) that they were forc'd to retreat back into the narrow Street, where he maintain'd the Fight (tho his Musquetoon, by reason of its being too frequently charged, struck him down to the Ground) till *Anthonio de Melo de Castro* came with his whole Company to his Relief, when after some firing Quarter being offered to the Remnants of the *Dutch*, they accepted of the same; so that 74, tho most of them wounded, were made Prisoners of War, whereof 8 only return'd into the *Dutch* Camp afterwards, the rest dying in the City, many whereof were converted to the Catholick Faith, by the indefatigable care of the Jesuits, and especially of *Damian Vieira*.

This was the Success of the general Assault begun early in the Morning, and not ended till two in the Afternoon, during which the Governor *Anthonio de Souza Coutinho*, and *Francisco de Melo de Castro*, kept in Person the Guard with some other Officers of Note in the Market-place, from whence they dispatch'd their Orders, as Occasion requir'd. The City-Major *Manoel Marques Gorian*, did likewise appear in all Places where the Danger was most pressing; and *Caspar Figueira* was very careful in sending what Succours he could spare from the Bastion of St. *John*. In short, the Streets, Breaches, the Lane and Ditch were all tainted with the Blood of the *Hollanders*, and the Ground cover'd with Colours, Arms, Drums, Scaling-Ladders and dead Carcases, their Loss being computed at no less than 1000 Men, and among them many brave Officers. On our side we had not above 30 Men killed, tho the Enemy to dissemble their Loss, gave us a general Salvo of at least 1000 Musquets. *Loss on both sides.* The next day Father *Damian Vieira* going without the Walls in order to bury the Dead, was saluted by three Firelocks from the Enemy, which made him retire, and defer his charitable Resolution till the next following Night. We observ'd a black Flag in one of their Works, as a Signal, that they would give Quarter to no body without exception, the same Order having been given them likewise before the Assault begun. We got no less than 30 pieces of Cannon out of the Ship that lay under the Water-Fort, which were planted on our Works. Some Refreshments were also distributed among the Soldiers, tho to confess the Truth, the Publick Stores being very low, every one provided for himself, as well as he could, without any regard to the poor Soldiers. However about 18 days after, Father *Damian* (by Order from the General) went with some *Dutch* Prisoners aboard the Vessel, where they found some Casks of Wine, and some Meat and Bacon. *Some Provision taken out of the Dutch Vessel.*

In the mean time the Enemies were not idle, but daily encreased their Works; they made a Covered Way within 40 Paces of St. *John*'s Bastion from West to the East, in form of a Redoubt, upon which they planted six great Guns, *viz.* three against the Bastion of St. *John*, and the other three against that of St. *Stephen*. From thence they carried on their Trenches to the Sea-side from South to North, closed with another Redoubt, which being provided with two pieces of Cannon, much annoyed the Wall betwixt the Bastion of *Couras* and St. *John*. This made the Governor *Coutinho* order some of the Citizens to raise a kind of an Entrenchment of about two Foot thick and three high behind it. From the second Redoubt the Enemy carried on their Trenches into the open Field, and at last added a third Redoubt, from whence they could batter the Wall betwixt the Bastions of St. *John* and St. *Stephen*, which being likewise forc'd to be strengthened by some Works of Earth and Fascines, no body, not even the Governor himself, were sparing in laying hand to so useful a Work, which being 400 Ells in length, each Division had its share allotted, in order to bring it the sooner to perfection.

Domingo Coelho d' Alla, assisted by *Caspar d' Aranja Pereira*, *John d' Andrade Machado*,

* *chado*,

chado, and *Don Francisco Rolim*, all Inhabitants of the City, did great Service with their Slaves, in the *Manchous* or Boats, in protecting our Workmen on that side, as well as the *Dissaves*; and to be short, there was no body so young, no body so old, that was exempted from continual Labour or Watching.

The *Dutch* on the other hand carried on the Trenches from the Redoubt with six Guns, to the Hill of *Aqua de Lupe*, and made another Trench from the Redoubt in the Plain, which was to meet another Redoubt thrown up on the Front of the Bastion of St. *Stephen*, beyond the Lake or Fens. They also raised another Battery in the Garden of *Antonio de Mota*, against the Bastion of St. *Stephen*, and another near the before-mention'd Redoubt of six Guus, in a parallel with that in the Plain, and another just at the Foot of the Bastion of St. *Crus*, which being so near the Ditch, was likely to be a Thorn in our Eye, there being nothing but the Ditch betwixt us and the Enemy, so that we could throw Stones at them, and often talk'd with one another.

Figueira *lays down his Commission.*

About the same time *Caspar Figueira de Serpe* desir'd leave to lay down his Commission, not to shun the Danger or Trouble of his Station, but because many of the Gentlemen and Subaltern Officers refused to obey his Command; so he was discharg'd, and *Antonio de Melo de Castro*, Nephew to the late Governor *Francisco de Melo de Castro*, who had behav'd himself with more than ordinary Bravery in his Post during the Siege, put in his place.

As we shrewdly suspected the Enemy to have a Design of undermining the Bastion of St. *Stephen*, a Cavalier was order'd to be rais'd near it, in case the same should succeed. This was done by the contrivance of a certain *Indian* Merchant of the Coast of *Coromandel*, who also order'd the Redoubt, demolish'd since the last general Assault, to be repaired: By the direction also of another certain Merchant (who was Surveyor of our Magazine) a Countermine was contriv'd, which did us great Service. It was a most deplorable thing to have in such a Fortress as this, not so much as one *Portuguese* Engineer, nay not so much as a good Carpenter of our Nation, the Defect whereof can be attributed to nothing else but to the Covetousness of some of the King's Officers, who put the Mony design'd for that use into their Pockets, and at the same time put it to the King's Account. Neither were our Fortifications in such a Condition as they

Covetousness of some of the Officers.

ought to have been; for whereas we had had sufficient time to enclose that part of the City near the Sea-side, call'd *Galvoca* (comprehending a third part of the whole) with strong Walls, and to render it impregnable, by reason of the natural Situation thereof, being accessible only in certain Places in small Boats, they had planted only some Coco and Palm-Trees there, which perish and are wash'd away by the Waves in a short time. Thus the Bastions, which ought to have been fac'd with Stone, were only made of Earth, which are not durable, and easily spoil'd by the Water-Floods; the effects whereof were then obvious enough, from the Hospital to the Gate of the Jesuits College, which comprehends a very large Tract of Ground. Besides this, the Carriages of our great Guns were so rotten, that most of them after the first Discharge broke to pieces; so that we were forc'd to take the Wood from the Houses, nay even out of the Churches (as we did in that of St. *Domingo*) to make new Ones.

Baldæus.

My Pen wants Words to express the Affronts put upon the Holy Images by the Hereticks, whereof I will give you only one Instance. They took the Image of the Holy Apostle St. *Thomas*, and after they had cut off the Nose, Ears and Arms, set it up for a Mark to shoot at; afterwards they knock'd it full of great Nails, and so shot it out of a Mortar *Nov.* 16. into our Ditch, whence it was taken up and carried to the Jesuits College, by Father *Damian Vieira*, and two Reform'd Officers, *Manoel de Seixas*, and *Manoel de S. Jago Garcia*. But the *Franciscans* laying Claim to it, they carried it in Publick Procession to their Church, and placed it upon the High Altar. Father *Francisco S. Mattheus* solemniz'd the Day with a learned Speech.

The 20th of *Novemb.* the holy *Thomas* blessed us with the Arrival of a certain *Portuguese*, a Native of *Aveiros*, named *Simon Lopes de Basto*, who for certain Reasons being retir'd from *Goa* to *Wingurla*, had served among the *Dutch* in a very good Station in the Camp; but finding his Countrymen in Distress, left all and came over to us, and did us most signal Service in the Siege.

The Enemy carried on their Trenches from the Foot of the Bastion of St. *Crus*, to the Edg of the Ditch, with an Intention to fix their Miners under the Bastion of St. *John*; but we made a Countermine, and defended the Ditch on the other side with a good Breast-work, to secure our Peo-

Baldæus. People against the Granadoes, which the Enemy threw in without Intermission. This Post being recommended to the care of *Domingos Coelho*, he strengthen'd the same by Pallisadoes, from whence he commanded the Passage over the Ditch with his Fire-arms; and *Manoel Rodrigos Franco*, and *Manoel de S. Jago Garcia*, would often skirmish with the Enemy on their own Bridges; two whole Companies under the said *Coelho*, and *Diego de Souza de Castro*, being appointed to second them as Necessity requir'd.

The 10th and 11th of *Jan.* the Enemy advanc'd to the Ditch in two Places, *viz.* thro the before-mention'd Breast-work, and somewhat lower: From the first Place they played with a great Cannon, and on the other side having made a great Breach thro the Wall, they threw Fascines, Logs of Wood, Baskets with Earth, and such like Materials into the Ditch; and the better to cover their Workmen, and afford an easy Passage to their Souldiers, they fix'd their Gallery: but *Emanuel Guerreiro* at the Head of his Company, *Domingos Coelho d' Alla*, *Emanuel de S. Jago Garcia*, and *Diego de Souza Castro*, did receive them so courageously, that from 10 at Night till break of Day, there was nothing to be heard or seen but firing, both at the entrance of the Mine, and from the Bastion of St. *John*, from whence Don *Diego Vasconcelhos* did considerable Mischief to the *Dutch* with his great Cannon, who meeting with so unexpected a Reception, thought fit to retire with considerable Loss, leaving most of their Materials behind them, which were brought into the City. We lost only two Men in this Action, and the *Dutch* for ever after were not so forward to come so near us, but ply'd us chiefly with their Cannon-balls, Stones and Bombs; whereas we had but one Mortar, which was useless to us (for want of expert Cannoneers) till *Simon Lopes de Basto* came over to us, who now and then saluted the Enemy with Stones out of that Mortar, who answer'd us briskly, tho most of them broke in the Air, and did no other Mischief but to some Houses, that were miserably shatter'd. One of the Enemies Bombs happening to fall entire upon the Ground, *Matthias d' Albuquerque*, a Native of *Goa*, standing hard by, took it up, and threw it into the next *Dutch* Mine, with an unparallel'd Courage, with such Success, that it blew up into the Air immediately. *Bravery of Matthias Albuquerque.*

The 28th of *Jan.* four Ships arriv'd from *Gale*, and soon after two more, which with the 14 that were in the Bay before, made up 20 in all. The same day the *Dutch* planted a Cross upon the Redoubt call'd *Conception*, under the tripple Discharge of their Cannon and Small Arms. This Redoubt had been made by the Direction and Assistance of the Governor, the Master of the Ordnance, and several of our best Officers, and the *Dissaves*. That day two new listed Men, belonging to Don *Rodrigo de Castro* his Company, deserted to the Enemy; and *Fernaon Martinho de Souza* the Governor's Son, a Gentleman who had given several Proofs of his Courage, was unfortunately shot with a Musquet-ball in the Head on the Bastion of S. *John*, of which Wound he died soon after. *The Governor's Son killed.* About the same time died also *Anthonio Barboza Pinheiro*, one of our Captains of the Artillery, a Person of indefatigable Care, and who had signaliz'd himself upon many Occasions, both in the Field and the City.

The 1st of *Feb.* two other new listed Soldiers of *Manoel de Veigas* his Company deserted to the Enemy, and the 6th nine Ships return'd from the Bay to *Gale*. By this time we began to be reduc'd to great Extremity for want of Provisions, a little Measure of Rice being then sold at half a *Seraphyn*; so that we saw the poor Wretches (as well *Europeans* as *Negroes*) drop down dead in the Streets: The *Berbery*, Bloody-Flux and spotted Fevers being grown so common, that few were free from them. To be short, we were in a constant Conflict with three most dreadful Enemies, the Plague, Hunger and Sword. To add to our Affliction, the Heat was so excessive for want of Rain (which usually falls in *Ceylon*) that many were stifled for want of Air, which made us drive about 300 of these miserable Creatures (unfit for Service) out of the City on the 8th, who were forc'd to return by the *Dutch* the 9th. *Negroes forced out of the City.* The 12th, 500 *Negroes* were forc'd out of the City, but were sent back by the *Hollanders* the same day. The 17th, we saw divers Gibbets erected without our Walls, on which they did hang divers of the miserable Creatures that were forc'd out of the Town. We had so many dead in the City, that we wanted room to bury them. The 19th two of our Soldiers deserted, one whereof being taken, was hang'd up immediately. The 23d, 50 Negroes (the Remnants of the last 500) return'd to the City. The 27th, the Bridg made by the Enemy on this side of their Trenches, was set on fire from the Bastion of St. *John*, but the Fire was soon quench'd.

quench'd. The 29*th* the Besieged made a kind of a Cover'd Way, near the Gate of *Rajuba*, from the Bastion of *Madre de Deos*, to that of St. *Sebastian*.

The 2*d* of *March*, our City-Major was sent in a small Vessel to *Manaar*, to sollicite for Succours there, in case any should have been lately arrived from *Portugal*; for at *Goa* they thought of nothing less than *Ceylon*, for they did not want either Men or Ships to send to *Macassar* or *Mosambique*, but could find none for *Columbo*; for tho the Cinnamon was upon the King's Account, the rest of their Cargo belonged to private Persons, who would not venture their Ships for the Publick, without extraordinary Rewards.

Columbo *neglected by those of* Goa.

The same day an Advice-Boat arriv'd from *Gale*, and we made the beginning of a *Cavallier* on the Bastion of *Madre de Deos*; but finding that the Enemy were raising a Battery against it, it was not brought to Perfection. Two *Portugueses* and nine *Lascaryns* deserted. The 3*d*, the Enemy began to open their Trenches on the side of the *Mapanese* Fields. The 6*th* one *Dyke* deserted, and the 7*th* another did the same, leaving the Boat, where were some *Canaryns*, who returned. The 11*th* another Soldier belonging to *Alvaro Rodrigo Boralho*'s Company, went over to the Enemy, who receiv'd that day a Reinforcement of 10 Ships.

The 12*th* early in the Morning we found that the Enemy had posted himself upon an Eminency at the Foot of the Bastion of St. *Crus*, just over against our Redoubt, and that they had carried on their Trenches a good way into the Field. A Soldier of *Manoel Cabreira* deserted to the Enemy. The 13*th* we sent away four *Pachas*, or Advice-boats. The 14*th* we discovered three Sails with some Sloops, which occasion'd great Joy in the City, thinking that it had been the so long look'd for Succours, but soon found our Mistake; the same day two *Dutch* Deserters and a Boy came into the Town. The Enemy having strengthen'd their Battery against the Outworks of the Bastion of St. *Stephen* and St. *John*, they laid the 16*th* one side of St. *Stephen*'s Bastion level with the Ground.

Famine encreases.

The Famine encreased every day, a Fig-Tree or a Papey-Tree was now sold for 50 *Pardaus*: Herbage we had none, some Roots there were, but miserably dry, by reason of the Heat of the Season, which caused a great Mortality.

The 17*th* an *Aratche* and two *Lascaryns* went over to the Enemy, and perceiving that they had raised an Eminency, in order to erect a Redoubt and Battery near the Gate of *Rajuba*, we demolished the same by planting a 28 Pounder against it. We had an Advice-Boat sent us from the Northern-Quarter, and about Midnight the Enemy alarm'd us by a false Attack. The 20*th*, five Soldiers being taken that were going over to the Enemy, four of them were hang'd immediately, the fifth who had discover'd the rest, escaping with his Life.

Baldæus.

4 Deserters hanged.

The 21*st* we made a Countermine, about ten Foot from the Enemies, which was carried to the Palm-Trees planted on the Fortifications; whilst *Simon Lopes de Basto* Master of our Ordnance, *Manoel Fernandes da Miranda*, *Manoel de S. Jago Garcia*, Father *Damian Vieira*, and several other *Portuguese* Officers, were employed in encouraging the Workmen; one of our Cannon-balls fell among some Granadoes and other Fire-works, which caused a great Alarm in the whole City, and the brave *John Pereira Corte Real*, a Native of *Negapatnam*, who had signalized himself upon a thousand Occasions in the Service of our Artillery, here lost his Life, being generally regretted by all who new his Merit. The 22*d* and 23*d*, the Enemy continued to perfect their Works near the Gate of *Rajuba*, against which we play'd with a Demi-Cannon from behind the Wall of St. *Stephen*'s Bastion.

Two Messengers with Letters from Raja Singa *come to* Columbo.

The 24*th* two Messengers from the K. of *Candy* brought a Letter to the Governor, and another to the Inhabitants of *Columbo*, in answer to a Letter sent to that King, at the beginning of the Siege. They appear'd in Mourning-Apparel, to intimate (according to the Custom of that Court) how much concern'd his Majesty was at the many Injuries and Affronts put upon him during the late War. They contain'd in Substance, that the King summon'd them to a Surrender, promising all the Inhabitants the free possession of all their Estates, Villages, *&c.* for their Sustenance, as the only means to deliver them from the Miseries and Oppressions they now groan'd under, alledging that the same were the effects of God's just Vengeance for their Ingratitude, shewn upon so many Occasions to his Imperial Majesty, in return of the many Benefits they had receiv'd at his Hands, and not admitting his Ambassadors sent to them with Proposals of an Alliance. These Letters were likewise subscribed by the *Dutch* General *Hulst*, which being read publickly, the Messengers were dismissed

Baldæus.

miss'd with much Respect, but were scarce got out of the City, when they were overtaken by a most dreadful Storm of Rain, Thunder and Lightning.

The 25th *Alvaro Rodrigo Boralbo* kill'd a Soldier as he was going over to the Enemy.

They send an Advice-Boat for News.

The 26th an Advice-Boat was dispatch'd to get Intelligence whether there were any hopes of Succours for *Columbo*; but all the News we could learn, was that the Viceroy of *Goa* (the only Person we put our Confidence in next to God) was lately dead; which tho it was doleful News for us, yet was it resolv'd to hold out to the last Extremity, which was perform'd to the greatest nicety, the *Dutch* never being able to become Masters of the Place, till most of us were consumed either by the Sword or Famine. Advice was also brought us, that Bonfires had been made at *Goa*, upon certain Advice brought by some Negroes (under Protection of the *Dutch*) taken at *Putelaon* in *Ceylon*, that *Columbo* was not in so desperate a Condition as had been represented, which they had reported upon the Credit of a certain *Dutch* Master of a Vessel.

The 27th of *March* one of our Serjeants was devour'd by a Crocodile in the Fens, his Clothes and Arms being found afterwards. At this time a *Parra* of Rice was sold at 25 *Seraphyns*, or Gilders; and all our Church-yards being fill'd with dead Corps, we were forc'd to have another consecrated for that purpose.

The 28th in the Morning the Enemy had thrown up another Redoubt near the Wall of the Gate of *Rajuba*. One of the Inhabitants, a Native of *Cranganor*, went over to the Enemy from the Bastion of S. *John*, being forced thereunto by Hunger, which was grown so excessive, that Dogs, Cats and Rats, and other such like things were sold at a very high rate.

Cats and Dogs sold at a great Price.

The 31st two Soldiers and a *Lascaryn* went over to the Enemy. The next Morning we saw some small Batteries raised against the Redoubt of S. *John*'s Bastion, where our People had made some Entrenchments raised like steps of 10 Paces high, cover'd with a Breastwork like a cover'd way, call'd *Aleapaon* by the *Portugueses*. At the same time we began to work on a Countermine, within 20 Paces of the Enemy's Mine at S. *John*'s Bastion. The same day above 50 of our sick died in the Hospital, besides what were daily found dead in the Houses and Streets, the Ammunition-Bread being by this time become a most precious Commodity.

The first of *April* one of the Enemy's Advice-Boats came into the Road. The second 7 *Lascaryns* deserted, and ever after 20 or 30 a day went over to the Enemy. The third two *Dutch* Yachts came into the Road, aboard one of which was a Chirurgeon. At the same time a *Parra* of Rice was sold for 59 *Seraphyns*, or *Gilders*; but the worst was, that there was not enough of it, and could not be purchas'd but with ready Mony. The Governor's Steward (tho without his knowledg) * refusing to part with any without ready Gold, to the great Disreputation of his Master, who tho a Gentleman of great Honour, yet was highly blam'd for committing a thing of such moment to the management of so avaritious a Person.

* Semper inveniuntur mercatores humanarum calamitatum. *Basil.*

The 4th of *April* the Enemy had raised a new Redoubt and Battery provided with two pieces of Cannon, near the Gate of *Rajuba*, wherewith they had so batter'd our Palisado's, and other wooden Fences, that there was no safe passing betwixt the Fortifications and the Wall on the other side of the Ditch. The Enemy receiv'd a Succour of two Ships, and the next day four more. The Enemy made their Approaches with so much Circumspection, that they advanc'd to the Ditch (where it was dry) with the loss of a few of their Men, who improvidently exposed themselves to our Fire-Arms.

The 6th we begun another Countermine, and the 7th the Enemy threw abundance of Fascines and Faggots into the dry Ditch, and set fire to our Palisado's, which was soon quenched by the industry of our Men; whilst the *Dutch* were employ'd on the other side to cut a Breach with Pickaxes in the Wall, but were soon chased from thence by our Firelocks, not without considerable loss.

The 8th of *April* we began another Countermine, which being fenced with a kind of Palisado Beams cover'd with Earth to resist the Enemies Fire-works, was carried on under the Conduct of the Master of the Ordnance *Antonio de Melo de Castro*, the Serjeant-Major *Antonio de Leaon*, *Diego de Souza*, and *Manoel de S. Jago Garcia*. The same day at least 70 sick Persons (most *Europeans*) died in the Hospital; many of the Negroes lay dead in the Street for want of room to be buried in, which produced a most nauseous scent. The Hunger was encreased by this time to such a degree, that they began to feed upon Mens Flesh;

several

Utmoſt extremity for want of Proviſions. ſeveral Mothers murder'd their own Children to feed upon, two whereof were executed. It was a moſt doleful Spectacle to hear the poor miſerable Wretches cry out in the Streets for Bread, ſome imploring Heaven for Aſſiſtance, others curſing thoſe who were the occaſion of their Miſery, others expiring and breathing their laſt in the Houſes and Streets.

The *9th Domingo de Ramos* forced a multitude of poor Wretches out of the Town; but theſe being driven back by the Enemy, and expos'd to our ſmall ſhot, periſh'd either by them or by Famine upon the ſhore.

The Enemy advanc'd this day briskly with their Trenches, as we did on our ſide in our Retrenchments.

The 10*th* we ſet fire to the Enemy's Gallery, which however did not ſucceed according to expectation for want of ſufficient Fuel; but Father *Damian Vieira, Manoel Guerreiro,* and *Simon Lopes de Baſto* did kill many of the Enemy upon this occaſion.

The 11*th* we planted a Cannon betwixt our Paliſado's againſt their Gallery, but they had ſtrengthned it ſo well that we could effect nothing of moment. One of our Soldiers run over to them.

The 12*th* we began two other Mines with incredible labour, but indifferent ſucceſs, for want of skilful Engineers. Four ſelected Men were poſted in the Redoubt of S. *John*'s Baſtion, who defended that Poſt, which was within a few Rods from the Enemy's Works, with a great deal of Bravery, as they did in moſt other places, notwithſtanding we were reduced to a very inconſiderable number, there being not above five or ſix Men left in ſome Companies, as thoſe of *Diego de Souza de Caſtro, Manoel de S. Jago Garcia,* and *Don Diego de Vaſconcelbos,* who perform'd Wonders in the defence of the Baſtion of S. *John.*

The 13*th* the Enemy having receiv'd a Reinforcement out of two Yachts, they bour'd very hard in their Mine on the Baſtion of S. *John* under favour of their Cannon, which play'd inceſſantly: At that time Father *Damian Vieira* kill'd a ſtout *Hollander* who had the Direction of the Work, which advanced apace, tho we ply'd them very warmly with our Fireworks. Two of our Soldiers deſerted to the Enemy.

The 18*th* we began to work on our Countermine from the foot of the Baſtion of S. *John* towards that of S. *Stephen,* under the Direction of Father *Damian Vieira, Simon Lopes de Baſto* and *John Fereira d' Abreu,* whilſt the Serjeant-Major *Antonio de Leaon, Diego de Souza de Caſtro,* and *Ruy Lopes Coutinho* ply'd the Enemy with their Fireworks, and other combuſtible Matter. *Baldæus.*

The ſame day we got intelligence by an Advice-Boat that the ſo long expected Succours under the Command of *Franciſco de Seixas Cabreira* was come upon our Coaſt; it conſiſted of 21 Ships, and two Galliots with Proviſions, one whereof was upon the King's account, the other of *Simon Souza,* a Gentleman of Honour, who took Compaſſion of our preſent Condition. They ſet ſail from *Goa* the 29*th* of *March*; but as they were endeavouring to make the Cape *Comoryn,* one of the Galliots, in which was *Simon de Souza,* was attack'd ſo furiouſly by a *Dutch* Veſſel coming from *Calecoulang* with Pepper, that after having loſt her Maſt ſhe ſunk, *Simon de Souza* being narrowly ſav'd with a few Soldiers, and carried to *Columbo.* The *Dutch* Ship then falling in among the reſt fought ſo manly, that ſhe forced our Ships to retreat into the Harbour of *Tutecoryn,* from whence they could not come to *Columbo* till *Auguſt*; tho if the ſaid Fleet had arriv'd ſafely, they had brought ſcarce Rice enough to ſerve only for a little time. *News of the defeat of the Succours deſign'd for* Columbo.

About the ſame the ſame time Father *Damian Vieira, John Fereira d'Abreu,* and *Simon Lopes de Baſto,* went with ſome other Officers (call'd *Reformado's* by the *Portugueſes*) into one of our Mines. Father *Damian* and Lieut. *Nunes* going about 6 paces before the reſt, to diſcover whether any of the Enemys were at hand, and being miſtaken by their Comrades for *Hollanders,* theſe diſcharged their Muſquetoons upon them, notwithſtanding which the Jeſuit eſcaped miraculouſly the danger, without receiving the leaſt hurt. This happy eſcape was attributed to the Prayers of Father *Frey Luys* a Capucin, to whom ſuch as were going upon ſome deſperate Enterprize us'd to recommend themſelves. *A ſtrange Eſcape.*

The 15*th Nicholas de Moura* eſcap'd out of Priſon (where he was detain'd ever ſince the buſineſs of the Count *d'Obidas*) and with five *Miſtices* went over to the Enemy, as did much at the ſame time a Serjeant and a Soldier. About 80 Paces from the Gate of *Rajuba* the Enemy batter'd part of our Wall betwixt the Baſtions of *Madre de Deos* and S. *Sebaſtian,* from a Battery of 5 pieces of Cannon, from whence they ſhot 350 Cannon-Balls againſt it in one day.

Baldæus.

The 16*th* we made a falſe Alarm to try whether every one would repair readily to his Poſt: two new-liſted Soldiers took this opportunity to deſert, and being now deſtitute of Men to work in our Mines, nobody was excuſed from that Service, from the Governor to the private Centinel.

The 17*th* the Enemy having fix'd another Cannon upon the Battery before the Gate of *Rajuba*, they laid the Wall level with the ground; our People being ſo weakned by Famine, that they were not in a condition to carry thither any Faſcines or Earth to repair it. At the ſame time *Manoel Fragoſa* a Reform'd Captain who had done ſignal Services in the *Indies*, and eſpecially in *Ceylon*, went over to the Enemy, becauſe his Pay (which was given to others who much leſs deſerv'd it) was refuſed him, nay he could not even get Suſtenance for his Mony, which put him upon this deſperate Reſolution; two common Soldiers Natives of *India* deſerted at the ſame time. There died ſuch a vaſt number every day in the Hoſpital for want of Neceſſaries, that many of the Soldiery choſe rather to abide with their Companies, where they expir'd in ſight of their Comrades.

Great Mortality at Columbo.

The Enemy receiv'd a Succour of two Ships, a Yacht and a Galliot, whereas the poor Beſieged had not the leaſt Relief in ſeven Months.

The 18*th* Mr. *Adrian van der Meyden* Governor of *Gale*, ſent us a Letter (their General being lately dead) and to terrify us the more, preſented all his Forces in order of Battel betwixt his Trenches; but our Men commanded by *Alfonſo Correa*, *John Ferraon d' Abreu*, *Manoel Pereira Matoſo*, *Ignatio Fernandes*, *Simon Lopes de Baſto*, and Father *Damian Vieira*, made a vigorous Sally the next following Night out of the Gate *Rajuba*, when *Franciſco Aſca* a Reform'd Captain took the opportunity to deſert us.

The 19*th Diego de Souza de Caſtro* was ſent with an Anſwer to the Governor's Letter; and the Son of *Manoel de Souza* went over to the Enemy.

The 20*th* a Soldier deſerted from the Baſtion of S.*Crus*, on which ſide the Enemy had attack'd us with the greateſt fury ever ſince their loſs ſuſtain'd there under the Command *Caſpar d' Aranja Pereira*, who ſucceeded *Manoel d' Abreu Godinho*, after his Poſt was aſſign'd him, behind the Wall betwixt St. *John*'s and S. *Stephen*'s Baſtion. The City Major having four Bufflers left which had drawn a Waggon for a conſiderable time, had them kill'd for the uſe of the Gariſon, who, after the Meat was conſumed, feaſted alſo upon the Hides, which they cut into ſmall pieces.

The four laſt Bufflers.

The 21*ſt* the Enemy had drawn a Line of Communication from the Battery near the Gate of *Rajuba* to the Lake: At the ſame time five Perſons were wounded by one of their Bombs, and Capt. *Manoel Guerreiro* mortally, who had kill'd many a brave *Dutch-man* with his Fuſee during this Siege.

A Bomb kills five Perſons.

The 22*d* the Enemy having ſet fire to our Countermine, the brave *Joan Ferraon d' Abreu* and *Simon Lopes de Baſto*, were the chiefeſt that gave their Aſſiſtance in quenching of it amongſt a ſhower of Bullets and Hand-granadoes. At the ſame time a *Topas* went over to the Enemy, the only one that deſerted of that kind, tho we had a good number of them among us, who for the moſt part died with the *Portugueſes* in the Defence of the City.

The 23*d* Father *Damian Vieira*, *John d' Abreu*, *John Pereira* (Inhabitants of S. *Thomas*) *Simon Lopes de Baſto*, *Manoel Pereira Matoſo*, *Sebaſtian Rodrigues*, *Ignatio Fernandes*, *Joſeph Coelho* and *Manoel Fereira Gomes*, got early in the morning croſs the Fens, in order to ſurprize one of the Enemy's Works, but were ſo warmly received, that they were glad to retreat, and fight their way through the *Dutch*, who had encloſed them on all ſides.

The 24*th* a *Tony* was ſent to get Intelligence, the Enemy fir'd moſt furiouſly from their Battery againſt S. *Stephen*'s Baſtion and the Gate of *Rajuba*, where the Wall being laid level with the ground, the Houſes ſuffer'd much by their Cannon.

The 25*th* the Enemy planted two pieces of Cannon at the extremity of their Trenches againſt S. *Stephen*'s Baſtion, and *Raphael de Torres* a Priſoner for Debt, eſcaped out of Priſon.

The 26*th* the *Dutch* continued to play without intermiſſion upon the Baſtions of S. *John*, S. *Stephen* and *Madre de Deos*. The ſame day 9 *Portugueſes* were buried in one Pit or Grave, there being no place left to bury them in. A *Candil* of Rice was ſold at that time for 2500 *Seraphyns*, or Gilders, and a Candil of Wheat for 3400 Gilders, and happy was he who could purchaſe it; for you would ſee Women throw their Babes into the Streets for want of Suck and other Suſtenance, and others to part with their Jewels for

Great Extremity in Columbo.

a slender Measure of Rice, a Commodity more precious at that time than all the precious Stones. During this general Calamity the City-Major *Manoel Marques Gorian* shew'd himself a true Patriot in all his Actions, but especially in distributing what Rice he had left among the Soldiers, which if he had sold must have amounted to a considerable Sum of Mony at that juncture; but he was willing to part with all, in hopes to preserve the Place for his King. At the same time a false Attack was made near the Gate of *Rajuba*.

The 27*th* one of our Serjeants belonging to Capt. *Santjago*'s Company deserted to the Enemy. At the same time we saw them carry on their Trenches from the Battery raised against the Gate of *Rajuba*, towards the Bastion of S. *Sebastian*. Their Batteries continued to play without intermission day and night. The same night Father *Damian Vieira* with seven more made a Sally upon the said Trenches, and carried off most of the Tools of their Workmen. *Simon Lopes de Basto* took this opportunity of sending two Spies into the Enemy's Camp, who being discover'd had much ado to save themselves, being forc'd to pass through a shower of the Enemy's Bullets. They return'd the 29*th*, and brought Advice of the Death of General *Hulst*, and the Commodore * of the *Dutch* Fleet. At the same time an Advice-Boat † carrying three Guns came into our Harbour, aboard whereof was the Fiscal. An Alarm was order'd to be given at four in the Morning with the sound of Drums, Trumpets, and other Warlike Instruments, and a general discharge of our Cannon and small Arms.

* *He means* Dirk Ogel *the Vice-Commodore.*

† *Call'd the* Lion, *which brought the News of the defeat of the* Portuguese *Succours.*

The 30*th* Father *Damian Vieira, Simon Lopes de Basto, John Pereira, Alphonso Correa, Sebastian Rodrigos,* and *Joseph Coelho*, went out to take a view of the Enemy's Works, and advanced within 10 paces of them, which they found defended by a kind of Breast-work made up with Hurdles; notwithstanding which they attack'd them with Sword in hand.

The 1*st* of *May* the Enemy desir'd to have their Prisoners exchang'd for some of ours, which being agreed to, the second we deliver'd up eight of their Prisoners, the only Remnants of those taken in the last general Assault, in lieu of which we had as many of ours restor'd to us. They then began a fresh to play most furiously from their Mortars and Cannon.

The 3*d* at seven in the Morning, Father *Damian, John d' Abreu,* and *Simon Lopes de Basto* went without the Fortifications, to gather up the Bullets near the Bastion of S. *Stephen*, which used to be taken up by the Enemy in the night time. Father *Damian Vieira, Simon Lopes,* and two more made another Sally, to level some of the Enemy's Works, but without Success. The same day two Soldiers went over to the Enemy.

Baldæus.

The 4*th* Father *Vieira, Simon Lopes, Francisco Valente dos Compos, Antonio Madeiro, John Pereira, Manoel Pereira Matoso, Alfonso Correa, Manoel Fereira Gomes, Manoel Nuguera Freire,* and *Thomas Fereira Lete*, made a vigorous Sally, and with Sword in hand attack'd the Enemy's Batteries raised against the Outworks of S. *Stephen*, S. *Sebastian*, and the Bastion of *Madre de Deos*, with such Success, that they ruin'd them entirely, and set fire to the Fascines, Hurdles and other Woodwork that sustain'd them, notwithstanding the *Dutch* came with a considerable Body to the relief of their Countrymen, but were repulsed not without a considerable loss, and among the rest one of their bravest Officers, who was buried under a triple Salvo of their Firelocks; so that our People remain'd Masters of the Posts, and return'd victorious into the City.

A successful Sally.

The 5*th* *Ignatio Fernandes, Manoel de Santjago Garcia, Sebastian Rodrigues, John Pereira de Lago,* and Father *Damian Vieira* (who never staid behind upon such like occasions) made another Sally, but not meeting with any Enemy where they expected him, return'd without effecting any thing.

The 7*th* about six in the Morning (it having been rainy before, which is a rarity here at this season) the Enemy made an Assault upon the Bastion of S. *John*, defended by *Don Diego Vasconcelhos*, and two Youths, *Don Constantino de Meneses*, and *Diego Jaques*, both under 14 years of Age, all the Soldiers being swept away by Famine; for within these two months above 400 Men died in our Hospital, and our so long expected Succours being block'd up at *Tutecoryn*, we were past all hopes of Succours, whereas at *Goa* there was nothing to be heard of but Divertisements. To be short, the Enemy made themselves Masters * of the Bastion, after having kill'd the Captain and the two Youths, who defended themselves like Lions set upon by a multitude of *Dutch* Dogs. This done, they turn'd the Cannon against the City, whereby many of the *Portugueses* that were

* Martin Scholtes *first enter'd the Breach.*

Baldæus.

were hastening to its relief, were slain in the Streets. The second Bastion, assaulted at the same time by the *Dutch*, was bravely defended by *Manoel Figeiros*, who with two pieces of Cannon kill'd abundance of them; but being constantly seconded by fresh Troops, especially of the *Cingaleses*, they sent such showers of Arrows and Bullets among our People, that they were forced to quit that Bastion also.

From thence marching into the City, they were met at the entrance of a Street by the Commander in chief *Antonio de Melo de Castro*, *Diego de Souza de Castro*, Father *Anthony Nunes* the Jesuit, *Sebastian Rodrigues*, *John Pereira*, *Vincente de Silva*, *Francisco Valente dos Campos*, *Alfonso Correa*, *Sebastian Periera*, *John Ferraon d' Aureu*, *Anthonio de Magalhanes*, and an Ensign under Capt. *Alla*. These, tho few in number, but many in Valour, charg'd the *Dutch* with incomparable Bravery. The *Portuguese Alexander Manoel Marques Gorjaon*, making the best of his way over the dead Carcases that cover'd the ground, singl'd out a *Dutch* Captain of a Gigantick Bulk, who shot him with a Pistol through the Body, notwithstanding which he run him through with his Sword, and sent him immediately to the other World; then pushing on his Fortune, made the *Dutch* give ground, and having rallied his Men secur'd the Post for that time. The *Dutch* renew'd the Charge five times successively, but were as often courageously repulsed by *Anthonio de Melo de Castro*, and those few that follow'd him; and being resolv'd either to conquer or to die, they broke in with Sword in hand amongst the Enemy, and again possess'd themselves of the first Bastion, and soon after also of the second: the first who enter'd the last was *Anthonio de Magelhanes*, who fought with an uncommon Zeal against the Enemy; for before they became Masters of our Cannon, he ply'd them very warmly from behind the Wall (the only defence he had left) so that it cost them many a brave Fellow before they could make themselves Masters of it; and being now posted again upon the same Bastion, he was bravely seconded by two Demi-Cannons from the new Bastion, and a smart shower of Fire-works, which set the circumambient Air into such a flame and smoak, that at a distance it appear'd like the Mouth of Hell.

A sharp Engagement in the City of Columbo.

At the same time the Governor *Anthonio de Souza Coutinho* and *Francisco de Melo de Castro* did all that could be expected from brave Men on the *Couras*, or the Bastion of *Xaverius*, both by way of Command, and by charging the Cannon in Person, and performing the Duty of common Soldiers. The Fathers *Philippo* and *Pedro de Castelbranco*, both *Austin* Friers, were not behind-hand with the rest in giving their utmost Assistance for the defence of the Place, being appointed to keep a watchful Eye upon the Enemy whenever they were going to alarum or amuse us with false Attacks.

It must certainly be confess'd, that this Engagement was one of the most remarkable that ever happen'd in the East, considering that a few, and these most wounded, sick, or weakened by Famine, did engage a much greater number, continually sustain'd by fresh Troops, from six a Clock in the Morning till eight in the Evening, during which time the Enemy was repulsed not only once but five several times, by a much inferior number, who having not the least relief or time to breath, were forced all that time to endure the danger and fatigues of the Action, which cost the Enemy above 400 Men kill'd, besides those wounded and burnt by our Fire-works: On our side we lost also the flower of our Forces, some whereof were slain, others wounded and burnt to that degree, that they were disabled from bearing of Arms for a considerable time after. Among the slain were, *Diego de Vasconcelhos*, who had given a thousand Proofs of his Bravery in this Siege; Father *Antonio Nunes* the Jesuit, a Pattern of Virtue, who signaliz'd himself not only all along on the Bastion of *S. John*, as well as in other parts of the City, by incouraging the Soldiers, comforting the Sick, and burying the Dead: He was shot at the Gate of the Bastion with a Musquet-Ball, receiv'd afterwards a deep Cut, and at last slain by a hand-granado after he had kill'd several of the Enemy with his Musquetoon. At the same time died in the Bed of Honour (after they had given a thousand Proofs of their Bravery) *Alfonso Correa*, *Vincente da Silva*, *Francisco Valente de Campos*, *Sebastian Pereira*, and that brave Sea-Commander *Sebastian d' Abreu Godinho*, besides an Ensign, a Native of *Bazain*, belonging to Capt. *Alla*'s Company; *Manoel de Seixas* an Inhabitant of *Columbo*, and *Anthonio Caminha d' Alzevedo*, were sorely burnt; *Diego de Souza de Castro* was mortally wounded with two Bullets, notwithstanding which he would not retire from the Engagement till he receiv'd a deep Cut. *Manoel Caldeira de Britto*

Incredible Bravery of the Portugueses.

Their Loss.

* *Vidave*

Vidave was wounded by a Musquet-ball, as were likewise *John Ferraon d' Abreu*, *Andreas de Seixas*, *Manoel Nugueira Freire*, *Manoel de Souza*, and *Manoel Segaldo*. *Laurence Days* a Native of *Columbo*, was wounded with no less than 3 Musquet-balls; *Ruy Lopes Coutinho*, *Domingos Pires*, Inhabitants of *Negapatan*, Lieut. *Arrais*, Captain *S. Jago*, *Manoel Correa*, Commander in Chief upon the Bastion of S *John*, *Francisco Pereira*, *Simon Lopes de Basto*, and many more were miserably burnt. Most of these received their Wounds by the accidental setting on fire of a Vessel fill'd with Gunpowder, thro the carelesness of our own People. The Reverend Father *Paulo* was wounded, as he was furnishing the Combatants with Fireworks, as was likewise Father *Manoel Velles*, who was touch'd by two Bullets, without receiving the least harm by 'em; a Granado did also fall just before his Feet, without doing him the least harm, as he was busy in defending his Post with *Alvaro Rodriges Boralho* at the Gate of *Rajuha*.

Father *Damian Vieira* with his Company did considerable Mischief to the *Dutch* from the Church of St. *Domingo*, being bravely seconded by *Caspar Aranja Pereira*, Knight of the Cross, and an old Servant of the King (who succeeded the City-Major in his Place) with 9 or 10 of his Followers; this being the Place most exposed to the Enemy: The Commander in chief *Antonio de Melo de Castro*, no less annoy'd them from the new Bastion, and with their Shot so scoured the Streets, that there was no safe Passage for the *Dutch* and *Cingaleses*.

The *Dutch* without the Town, did on the other hand exert their utmost Efforts against the old Bastion, which being almost laid level with the Ground, the Wall without serv'd for a Breastwork; and being continually supply'd with fresh Troops of the *Candineses* and others, put our Men, but few in Number, most of them sick, wounded or half-starved, and besides that but ill provided with Ammunition, very hard to it on that side. For by this time we had not only but few Men, but also not above 15 days Provisions left, and scarce so much Gunpowder as would suffice for two Charges of our Artillery.

Consultation about a Surrender. Things being come to this Pass, it was debated in the Council (consisting of 34 Persons) whether it were not best to think of a Surrender; 13 were of Opinion rather to die upon the Spot, than to treat with the Enemy: but the most being of a contrary Opinion, and nine of them positively insisting upon it, that it would be most conducing for the King's Interest, that seeing the Place was no longer tenable, to preserve the Remnants of these brave Fellows, who had behaved themselves so courageously, it was agreed to enter upon a Treaty. *Baldæus.*

Accordingly the 10*th*, *Manoel Cabreira* was sent with a Letter to Mr. *John van der Laan*, concerning the Conditions of the intended Treaty; an Answer to which being sent the 11*th*, *Laurence Fereira de Britto*, *Diego Leitaon de Souza*, and *Hieronymo de Lucena* were dispatch'd as Plenipotentiaries, to demand a Cessation of Arms till the 25*th* of *May*, against which time we expected the so long desir'd Succours. But the Enemy, who were not ignorant of our present Circumstances, would hearken to no other Conditions, than to surrender the City the next day by 12 a Clock at Noon, which if we refused, they threatn'd to give us no Quarter; so that we were forc'd to obtain the best Terms we could, without any longer Hesitation, the Articles whereof being drawn up in hast (for want of time) I had not the Opportunity to peruse them, and therefore can only tell you upon this Head, that *Columbo* was forc'd to surrender, tho I can't precisely tell upon what Terms. *Is surrendred.*

No sooner was the News of the Treaty divulged among the People, but nothing was heard but dreadful Outcries and Lamentations: The Ecclesiasticks (or at least the most cautious among them) hid the Images and Relicts, and unfurnish'd the Altars, for fear they should be defiled by the Hereticks, as had frequently been done before upon such like Occasions. The *Dutch* having taken possession of the Bastions, our Garison consisting of 90 Soldiers and 100 arm'd Inhabitants, including Officers, nay even the lame and maim'd, marched out, some with their Swords and Musquets in one Hand, and a Stick or a Crutch in the other. *The Garison consisting of 190 Men march out.*

The *Hollanders* seeing these poor Remnants, most of which appear'd more like Skeletons than living Men, were astonished at their Bravery, in the defence of a Place they had been forced to purchase with so much Blood. Ten *Dutch* Companies march'd into the City, at the Head of which appear'd the General, *Adrian van der Meyden*, and Mr. *John van der Laan* on Horseback, not to reckon the *Cingaleses* sent to guard the Governor of *Columbo*'s House; which was no sooner done, but a Messenger was sent to him to demand *Simon*

Baldæus. *mon Lopes de Basto*; being not in a condition to refuse him, he order'd immediately the said *Simon Lopes*, with a certain *Aratche* of *Negumbo*, and some *Dutch* Deserters, to be deliver'd to him, who were all hang'd on a Gibbet soon after in sight of the *Portugueses*, who were forc'd to be Eye-witnesses of the miserable Exit of this *Simon Lopes*, who for the signal Services he had done them in the Siege, deserv'd to have a Monument of Brass erected to his Memory. To the Shame of those be it spoken, who ought to have endeavour'd to afford him a much better Recompence for his past Services, and rather exposed him in a Boat to the chance of the Seas, than to a certain shameful Death.

The *Hollanders* were sufficiently sensible of the Bravery of the *Portugueses* during this Siege, which lasted 7 Months (without receiving the least Succours or Supplies) by the Loss they sustain'd of their bravest Soldiers and best Officers, which amounted to 3000 Men, besides the wounded and maimed; besides that the Charges of the Siege amounted to more than would have built such another *Columbo*.

The General and Mr. *John van der Laan* were no sooner settled in their Habitations, but they gave Liberty to the Soldiers to plunder the Place (contrary to their Parole) for one day, which was extended to five by Mr. *van der Laan*, *viz.* from the time of their coming into the City, till the time we march'd out, which was perform'd by the Hereticks with the utmost Rigour; nay whilst our Soldiers were embarking, and the Inhabitants within three days after, they continued their Robberies even upon the Seashoar. Almost all our People went aboard along with them, except a few who staid behind with the Governor and Deputy-Governor; and some, that (by great Promises) were engag'd in the King of *Candy*'s Service, which perhaps has happen'd by a singular Providence of God, as a means to influence that King's Counsels, in order to expel the *Dutch* one time or other out of the Isle of *Ceylon*.

This is a gross Falsehood, a Soldier having been whipp'd at that time for stealing

Our People were transported to *Negapatan*, where they were most kindly received and provided with Medicines, Clothing and other Necessaries by the Inhabitants, till they received their Pay, after the Arrival of *Antonio Amiral de Menezes* Governor of *Jafnapatnam*, who at the same time intreated *Anthonio Mendes d' Aranha* (who after having been detain'd a Prisoner at *Gale*, was now come to *Negapatan*) to go along with him to *Jafnapatnam*, in the Quality of his Deputy-Governor, as not questioning but that he should be the next against whom the Enemy would exert their utmost Efforts, which he accepted of; tho considering the Fatigues and Miseries he had endur'd of late, he might very well have excused the same, as well as the rest of the Soldiers; who notwithstanding this, half sick and half starv'd as they were, did embark for one of the most dangerous Places in *Ceylon*, to give fresh Proofs of their Bravery.

This was the end of this Siege, one of the most remarkable in all its Circumstances that ever was heard of, considering that a Place of that bigness was defended by so slender a Number for the space of seven Months (without the least Supplies) against a powerful Force of the *Dutch* and *Cingaleses*, who first defeated the *Portuguese* Forces (composed of the Flower of their Men) in two smart Engagements; so that the whole Number of the *Portugueses* was at last reduc'd to 200 Souls. The Account of this Siege being spread among the Eastern Moors and Pagans by several Persons, who had been Eye-Witnesses of the great Actions perform'd there, did beget an incredible Reputation of the Bravery of the *Portugueses* among those Nations, tho the same proved unfortunate in the end.

Thus his Majesty of *Portugal* lost a Place, and with it a whole Kingdom, three times bigger than *Portugal* it self, and much richer and more plentiful, the very Center of the World, the richest Tract of Land under the Sun, and with it (probably) all that is in the possession of the *Portugueses*, to the South of Cape *Comoryn*. His Majesty lost a considerable Squadron of Ships sent to the Relief of *Columbo*. The first Squadron intended for this Expedition, did come no higher than the Cape *Comoryn*, the pretended Succours from *Manaar* came to nothing: And the second Squadron promised by the Viceroy of *Goa* in *January*, did not set sail till the 29*th* of *March*, and was forced to retreat without effecting any thing.

Some Pretences for the not relieving of Columbo.

The want of Money was alledged as the main Reason of this delay, when it is sufficiently known that the King had both Ships and Mony enough at *Goa*, which could not have been better employed than for the Relief of a Place of such vast Importance: We know what vast Sums *Nuns Alvares Botalho* consumed at *Mosambique*, which was nevertheless not disapproved by

Baldæus.

by the King of *Castile*, and why might not the same be expected from the King of *Portugal*? To conclude, *Columbo*, and with it the whole Isle of *Ceylon*, being lost for want of Succours, all such as have deserved well in the Defence of that Place, ought to be rewarded for their Services, as those who have been neglectful in their Duty for the Preservation thereof, deserve condign Punishment at his Majesty's Hands. And as nothing is more common, than that Courtiers employ their Favourites in Places of Trust (without any regard to Merit) and afterwards endeavour to conceal their Miscarriages from the King; it is for this reason that we lay this account at your Majesty's Feet, taken from the Journal kept at *Columbo* and other authentick Records, confirm'd by the Testimony of many Persons of Credit, both Ecclesiasticks and Laymen, that were present from the beginning to the end of this Siege.

Address to his Portuguese Maj.

CHAP. XL.

The Origin of Columbo. *Arrival of the* Portugueses. *Their Engagements with and Conquest of the* Moors. *They fortify* Columbo. Raja Singa *dissatisfied.*

Origin of the City of Columbo.

THE City of *Columbo* is an antient City, seated at 6 ½ Degrees of North Latitude, in a pleasant Country, near a delightful River; which questionless induc'd the *Portugueses* to fix upon this Place for their chief Residence in this Island. For *Emanuel* King of *Portugal*, having been fully inform'd concerning the Condition of *Ceylon*, order'd a Fort to be erected there, for the better Establishment of his Affairs there, and to curb the Emperor. *Lup. de Britto* being sent thither with a good Number of Soldiers and Workmen, *John Silva* deliver'd the said Fort up to him. For *Zoares* who was lately sail'd with 20 Ships and 700 Landmen to *Ceylon* (after *Laurence d' Almeyda*, who some Years before entred into a Confederacy with the King of *Ceylon*) had just before made an Agreement with the Governor of *Columbo* about a Settlement in that Place, which he look'd upon as the most proper for a Fortification, both in respect of its Situation, and the Plenty of the best Cinnamon that grows in the whole Isle, being seated in the Form of a Crescent, and affording safe Anchorage for Ships, provided they are not too bulky.

Accordingly it was agreed to erect a Fortification there, under pretence of securing the Commerce of the *Portugueses*, but in effect to curb the King and the Natives. He who reign'd at that time in the Isle being a *Brabman*, was not a little jealous of the *Europeans*; but being sensible to what pitch of Greatness the King of *Cochin* was lately arriv'd by the Assistance of the *Portugueses*, he gave his Consent, tho not without some Reluctancy, and consequently was of no long Continuance. For the *Saracens* who were chased thither from the Continent, and had settled their Traffick in this Isle, found means by the Promises of great Sums of Mony, and of their Assistance, to entice the King and Court to oppose the Designs of the *Portugueses*, who intended to enslave them, under pretence of settling their Commerce; for which purpose they raised some Works, and having mounted some Iron Cannon upon them, seiz'd some *Portugueses* that came ashore, without suspecting any harm.

Treaty betwixt the Portugueses and the Cingaleses

Is soon broken.

Zoares coming ashore with his Workmen, in order to rase the intended Fortifications, was surpriz'd to find some Forts erected by the *Cingaleses*; and having receiv'd certain Intelligence, that the same had been done at the Instigation of the *Moors*, he easily guessed that nothing but Force was likely to establish the *Portugueses* in *Ceylon*. Accordingly having landed his Men, he attack'd the Enemy, who at a distance somewhat gall'd his Forces with their Arrows; but after they came to a close Engagement, the *Cingaleses* were quickly put to the Rout, and pursued by the *Portugueses* with considerable Loss: The *Portugueses* had many wounded but few killed, among the last was the brave *Patieco*, lately come from *Malacca*.

The Portugueses rout the Cingaleses

Zoares having allow'd one day only to his People to refresh themselves, began the next Morning an Entrenchment, reaching from the Harbour to the Seaside, without the least Opposition: within this he order'd a Fort to be erected, whereupon having mounted his Cannon, and streng-

Baldæus.

strengthen'd it by a Wall that surrounded it, he soon made the King repent of his Inconstancy, who sent his Envoys to *Zoares*, asking Pardon for what was pass'd, and desiring that the former Alliance might be renew'd: But *Zoares* refused to hearken to these Propositions, demanding Satisfaction for the Affront, and a yearly Tribute to be paid to K. *Emanuel*; which the King of *Ceylon* (who dreaded the *Portugueses*) not daring to refuse, it was agreed that he should pay to *Portugal* an annual Tribute of 124000 Pound Weight of Cinnamon, 12 Rings set with the most precious Rubies and Saphirs, and 6 Elephants, under Condition that K. *Emanuel* should assist the King of *Ceylon* and his Successors both by Sea and Land, against all his Enemies.

Force the King to pay a yearly Tribute.

The Treaty being thus concluded, *Zoares* continu'd his Fortifications, which being brought to perfection with the assistance of the *Cingaleses*, he left *John de Silva* with a good Garison there, and *Anthonio Miranda Azevedo* with four Ships to guard the Coast; which done, he return'd in *December* to *Cochin*, where he was received with all imaginable Demonstrations of Joy. *Lup. de Britto* (before mentioned) succeeding *John de Silva*, brought along with him abundance of Workmen and Bricklayers, who made a kind of Mortar of the Sea-cockles, and lin'd the Fortifications with a strong Wall, deepned the Ditches, and added what Works they thought necessary for the Accomplishment thereof.

Is ill digested by the Cingaleses.

This created no small Jealousy (not without reason) in the *Cingaleses*, which was encreased by the Insinuations of the *Moorish* Merchants, who told the King that their Prophecies were like to prove too true, since he was now made sensible, that these Foreigners had not only excluded all other Strangers from the Traffick of this Isle, but also had made him a Tributary of *Portugal*, and shortly would make him their Vassal, if he did not in time hearken to the Counsel of his Friends.

These Insinuations had the desired effect, for the King not only cut off all Supplies of Provisions and other Necessaries from the Fort; but the common People being also incensed by these Discourses, murdered several *Portugueses*, who ventur'd a little too far without the Fort. *De Britto* at first dissembled the matter, but finding he could no longer contain his Soldiers (burning with Revenge) he chose 150 of his best Men, and with them assaulted the City of *Columbo* (which lay near the Fort) just about noon, when most of the Inhabitants were asleep to avoid the Heat of the Day, and at the first Alarum betook themselves to their Heels, leaving the City to the Enemies Mercy.

Britto *surprizes* Columbo.

De Britto seeing himself Master of the Place without the least Opposition, forbid his Soldiers to plunder, or commit any other Outrages; but order'd the Women and Children to be tied to the Posts of the Doors, with an Intention to convince the *Cingaleses*, that he was not come like an Enemy to destroy, but like a Friend to preserve them. But as he had but little reason to rely upon their Generosity, he thought fit to make a Trial of their Inclinations; so he ordered some Houses that lay next to the *Portuguese* Fort to be set on fire: this had the desir'd Success; for the *Cingaleses* out of the Affection they bore to their Wives and Children, had gather'd all their Force in order to relieve them at any rate; but finding their Houses on fire, run first with all Speed to quench the Flame, whereby *Britto* got leisure to retreat in good Order into the Fort, and to provide himself against the intended Assault, which however could not be done without some Loss, above 30 of his Men having been wounded in the Retreat.

However *Britto* reaped no other Benefit by this Enterprize, than that the *Cingaleses* (exasperated to the highest Degree) besieged the Fort with 20000 Men; and tho they were often bravely repuls'd, yet did they persist in their Resolution, in hopes of reducing the Place by Famine, because the approaching Month of *May* (the first of the Winter-Season) did bereave them of all hopes of Succours. In the mean while the *Cingaleses* did not cease to carry on their Works to the very Ditch, from whence they annoy'd the *Portugueses* with their Arrows, their Number making up the Defect of their Force, which was not comparable to the *Portuguese* Artillery and Fire-arms. They also gather'd up 600 Bullets that were shot at them from the Fort, of which they made the best use they could.

Portugueses *besieged in the Fort.*

But what most troubled the *Portugueses* was, that they were to fetch all their fresh Water without the Fort, and that they were extremely harassed with continual watching: However they hoped to defend the Place till the next Summer, in hopes of Succours, in which they at last found themselves frustrated; *Anthonio de Lemos* coming only with one Galley and

and 50 Landmen to their Relief, *Seguera* with the rest of the Forces having staid behind.

The *Cingaleses* in the mean time had found means to erect two Wooden Towers fill'd with Earth, which being plac'd near the Ditch, they intended to make use of to cover their Pioneers, whilst they were busy in filling it up. *Britto* was not a little startled at this Device, and finding himself now reduc'd to such Straits, as to be obliged to venture at all, he order'd *Anthonio de Lemos* to draw as near to the Shore as possibly he could, and to endeavour to ruin these Towers with his great Cannon, whilst he would make a Sally with 350 Men, and attack the Enemy with the utmost Vigour; this was put in execution accordingly with such Success, that the Towers were entirely ruin'd, and the *Cingaleses* beaten out of their Works.

Make a vigorous Sally.

Notwithstanding this Defeat, the *Cingaleses*, encourag'd by the *Moors* who came to their Assistance with 150 Horse, and 25 Elephants, resolved to try their utmost against the *Portugueses*. These Elephants having Turrets fill'd with Men arm'd with Cutlashes on both sides, did strike no small Terror at first into the *Portugueses*, but afterwards turn'd to the disadvantage of the *Cingaleses*; for these Beasts not able to bear the Wounds that were given them by the *Portuguese* Artillery, soon turn'd their Backs, and put their own Troops into Disorder, with a great Slaughter among the *Cingaleses* and *Moors*, who now beginning to despair of Success, raised the Siege immediately, and the King sent his Ambassadors to *Britto*, to ask Pardon for what was past, and to desire a Reconciliation.

The Siege raised.

Thus we see how the *Portugueses* have been forced to settle, or at least to maintain themselves in *Ceylon* by the Sword; and the better to attain their end, it was their constant Practice in the *Indies* to sow the Seeds of Division among those Princes; an Instance whereof is given us by *Maffæus* himself, in his History of the *Indies*.

The King of *Cota* had three Sisters Sons, who (according to the Custom of the Country) being his Legal Heirs, began to be very uneasy at the long Life of their Uncle, found means to remove him out of the way, and to divide the Country betwixt them: But *Parea Pandar* the eldest of the three, having murder'd the second, *Maduyn* the youngest began also soon after to conceive a Jealousy at his Brother's Proceeding, complaining that he was not rewarded according to his Deserts, as having been the Adviser and Executer of the Murder of their Uncle. *Parea Pandar* finding his Brother dissatisfied, thought it his securest way to fore-arm himself against him, and therefore enter'd into a Treaty with the King of *Portugal*, to settle the Succession of the Crown upon his Daughter's Son (with the Exclusion of *Maduyn*) directly contrary to the Custom of that Country. *Maduyn* exasperated to the highest degree at this Proceeding, denounc'd open War against his Brother, and after having ravag'd the Country thro which he passed, laid Siege to *Cota*.

Baldæus.

Differences betwixt 2 Brothers fomented by the Portugueses.

The elder Brother disdaining to be attack'd in his City, march'd out against *Maduyn*, and pitch'd his Tent in an advantageous Post. He had a Troop of *Portugueses* in his Camp, one whereof (whether hir'd thereunto by *Maduyn*, or by chance, is uncertain) shot him thro the Head. After his Death the *Portugueses* set his Daughter's Son upon the Throne with the usual Solemnities: but in consideration of his Youth, and the Weakness of his Title, introduced contrary to the Custom of the Country, they much feared the Hatred of the People, back'd by the Interest of *Maduyn*; they sent therefore for Succours to *Noronha*, who soon after arriv'd with a good Squadron of Ships and 3000 Men, under pretence of assisting the young King (as *Maffæus* expresly tells us) but in effect to make himself Master of the Treasure buried at *Columbo*, 100000 Crowns of which he carried off along with him.

In the mean while *Maduyn* fortified himself with all possible Diligence in the City of *Ceta-Vaca*, nine Leagues from *Columbo* (according to *Maffæus*) but *Noronha* having with little Opposition taken and burnt the said Place, return'd victorious to *Goa*. What further became of *Maduyn*, is not mention'd by *Maffæus*, or any other Historian.

Thus we have seen the beginning of *Columbo* under the *Portugueses*, and its Surrender to the *Dutch* 1656. They found about 6 or 7 Loads of musty Rice in the Place, some Packs of Cinnamon, good Store of *Areek*, some good, some not, 24 Light Frigates, 9 whereof were sunk, 1500 Guilders ready Money coin'd in the City, 33 Packs of Clothes, 25 Bells of Metal, 60 Brass, and 68 Iron pieces of Cannon, one Mortar, and six lesser Pieces, 10000 Cannon-Bullets of different Sizes and Weight, 6500 Pound Weight of good Gunpowder, and 1150 bad,

What was found in Columbo.

Baldæus. bad, a good Quantity of Brimstone and Saltpeter. No sooner were we in possession of *Columbo*, but *Raja Singa* shew'd his Dissatisfaction by the following Letter.

Raja Singa's Letter. "YEsterday and the Day before yesterday it was reported at our "Court, that there was a Treaty on "foot with the *Portugueses* about the "Surrender of the City, since which I "have receiv'd Intelligence, that the "same is brought to effect. If it be true, "you ought to have given notice there- "of to our Imperial Majesty, which is "the reason, I can't as yet give entire "Credit to it: But in case it should be "so, I desire to know with all possible "speed the Articles of the said Treaty. "Whilst our Beloved Director-General "was alive, I writ to him concerning "certain matters he promised should be "perform'd, which I desire you to re- "member.

From our Imperial Court at *Reygamwatte*, May 11. 1656.

Signed,

Raja Singa Rajou, Most Potent Emperor of *Ceylon*.

CHAP. XLI.

Deserters severely punished. Raja Singa *forbids all Commerce with the* Hollanders. *His Letter of Complaint. Divers* Portuguese *Ships taken.* Raja Singa *ravages and plunders the Lands and Subjects belonging to the Company.*

Deserters punish'd with Death. IT was now thought high time to punish such as had deserted our Service during the Siege. Among these *Simon Lopes*, a *Portuguese* by Birth, who had 50 Guilders *per* Month Pay in our Service, and after we were repulsed in the general Assault was gone over to the Enemy, did lead the Van, and was, notwithstanding all the Intercessions of the *Portugueses*, hang'd on a Gibbet. Two other *Europeans* (whose Names we will pass by in silence) underwent the same Fate; and another was severely whipp'd, and forc'd to stand with a Rope about his Neck for 12 Hours under the Gallows.

The next thing to be done was to take care of the Transportation of the *Portugueses*, among whom the Ecclesiasticks and Inhabitants of *Columbo* were sent beyond Sea to Mr. *Laurence Pit* our Governor, who was to dispatch them further to the Isle of S. *Thomas*. About that time we receiv'd a Letter from *Raja Singa*, wherein he sufficiently testify'd his Dissatisfaction. *Walraven Thomas* our Book-keeper sent word from *Montual*, that he had sent the Corporal *Hans Jacob Lambert*, 10 *Mardykers*, and a Serjeant to the Pass of *Nacclegamme*, with Orders to oppose the Forces gather'd thereabouts by the *Dissaves* of *Ouva*, of the four and of the seven *Corles*; which not agreeing with the Sentiments of the General and his Council, they order'd the said Corporal to send back the *Mardykers* to *Montual*, and not to stop the Passage of any of the Royal Forces, for fear of giving any occasion of Offence to the Emperor.

Raja Singa shews his Dislike. Notwithstanding this, we soon found the effects of the Dissatisfaction of *Raja Singa*, who having cut off all means of receiving Supplies by Land from the *Sabandar*, *Don John de Costa* was dispatch'd to the *Dissaves* of *Saffragam*, and those of the four and seven *Corles*, who told him, that their People were at their full Liberty (tho we knew to the contrary) to bring their Provisions to our Market, but that they durst not give a Visit to the General, without express Orders from Court.

2 Yachts come before Columbo. The 22d of *March*, the Yachts the *Mars* and *Lyon* came to an anchor in the Road of *Columbo*, aboard one whereof was the Vice-Commodore *Roothaus*, who (upon the Receipt of a Letter from our Head Factor Mr. *Reinier Serooskerke*, intimating that a small Yacht laden with Provisions upon the King of *Cochin*'s Account, was gone from thence to *Columbo*) had left the Yachts *Flissingen*, *Popkensburg*, *Sea-Coney*, the *Haddock* and the *Roman*, with two other Vessels on that Coast, who were supplied with fresh Provisions by the Inhabitants of *Caylpatnam*. The Inhabitants thereof being very desirous to renew their Commerce with our Company, they were then equipping two Frigats there.

Cingaleses *go over to the Emperor.* About the same time notice was given us, that *Cannangere Aratchie*, a faithful Servant of the Company, had (to our great Dissatisfaction) submitted to the King of *Candy*,

Candy, and that 90 of the *Lascaryn* Deserters had taken the way of *Angretotte*. These proved the Forerunners of many ensuing Misfortunes. In the mean while *Raja Singa* urg'd stifly the Surrender of *Negumbo* and *Columbo* into his Hands, under pretence that these Places belong'd to him, by virtue of an Agreement made betwixt him, and the late Director-General Mr. *Gerard Hulst*; upon which account he writ the following Letter.

Letter of Complaint from the Emperor.

" OUR Imperial Majesty being very " desirous to introduce the *Dutch* " Nation into our Dominions, *Adam* " *Westerwold* came on this Coast with a " Squadron of Ships, just as we had " made our selves Masters of *Batecalo*, " when we thought fit to conclude a " Peace with him; which being confirmed by Oath, was but slenderly observ'd by some Officers afterwards: " As for instance by Captain *Burchart* " *Kocks*, alias *Coque* (who was afterwards kill'd by a Soldier at *Puntegale*) " and Commissary *Peter Kiest*, who being sent as Plenipotentiaries to our " Court, did confirm the before-mentioned Peace by Oath; pursuant to which " at their Departure for *Gale*, they " took along with them one of our *Dissaves*, in order to deliver into his " Hands the Country of *Mature*. But " at his coming there, they found means " to render the same ineffectual, by finding out certain Difficulties, which " made the said *Dissave* return to our " Court, to our great Dissatisfaction. " It was about that time that our Beloved Director-General did come into " our Kingdom from *Holland*, with full " Power to act as he should find it most " sutable to our Service, and to the " Establishment of a firm Peace and " Friendship; pursuant to which, he desir'd us by way of Mouth to bury all " pass'd Miscarriages in Oblivion, promising at the same time in the Name " of the Prince of *Orange* and the *East-India* Company, full Satisfaction for the " same; as also, that the Fortresses of " *Negumbo* and *Columbo* (when taken) " should be deliver'd into the Hands of " our Imperial Majesty, and certain *Hollanders* to be allotted in the said Places for our Service. It is upon this account that we sent our Auxiliaries to " assist our dearly Beloved *Hollanders* in " the taking of *Columbo*; which being " taken since, they are become forgetful of their Promise, and do continue " to do so to this Day. Your Excellency " is left at your own Liberty to do what " you think fit, till notice of this Proceeding can be given to the Prince of " *Orange*, and the Honourable Company. " But I would have you remember, that " such as don't know God and keep their " Word, will one time or other be sensible of the ill consequences thereof; " I am sensible I have God on my side.

Baldæus.

By way of Postscript was writ.

" TWo Letters have been dispatch'd " from our Imperial Court. Your " Excellency has writ in *Dutch* to *George* " *Bloem*, but without mentioning any " thing relating to our Service. Your " Excellency may write such frivolous " Pretences to whom you please, but " ought not to impose them upon our " Imperial Majesty; it being in vain to " alledg, that the Director-General had " receiv'd his Instructions from *Batavia*, " whereas he brought his full Power along with him out of *Holland*. Such " sinister dealings, as they create no " small Jealousy, so I can't see with what " Face you can expect any further Credit from us. I have taken care to have " this translated into *Dutch*, that you " may have no reason to plead Ignorance. *George Bloem* shall stay here, " till I receive your Answer, when I intend to send him back with a Letter. " No more, *&c.*

From our Imperial Court at *Reygamwatte*, *May* 11. 1656.

Unto which was annex'd the following Account, not thought fit to be inserted in the Imperial Letter.

" THIS Day, being the 22d of *March*, " his Imperial Majesty having sent " for me, order'd the Letter writ in " *Portuguese* to be translated into " *Dutch*, to be sent among others to your " Excellency. When I shew'd the Translation to his Majesty, he told me, that " after the Arrival of the Director-General in *Ceylon*, he had sent word to " him, that several Rebels shelter'd themselves in and about *Columbo*, especially " one *Caspar Figeiro*, who had done considerable Damage to his Majesty's " Lands; as also concerning certain Presents sent to his Court by the Viceroy " of *Goa*, some whereof were sent only " by the said Director-General. His " Majesty further desir'd me to give you

" to

Baldæus.

"to understand, that it had been agreed, "not to recede in the least from the "literal Sense of the Treaty, especial"ly in what related to that Article "concerning any City or Place taken "with the Assistance of his Majesty's "Forces; whereas your Excellency had "not as much as taken the least care "(since the taking of *Columbo*) to send "to his Majesty his rebellious Subjects, "nor any of the Presents, except two "*Persian* Cats, a Ship, *&c.* deliver'd by "me to his Majesty. The not sending "of the Rebels has been very ill re"lish'd here.

Raja Singa *is angry with the* Dutch.

Our General took care to send a most obliging Answer to the Emperor's Letter, which however was so far from giving any real Satisfaction to *Raja Singa*, that on the contrary he conceiv'd such a Hatred against the *Dutch*, as made him engage with the *Portugueses* against them. For notice having been sent to our Council by *Anthonio de Motte*, and *Manoel Fonseque de Moniis*, two *Portugueses*, that they had been sollicited by *Raja Singa* to enter into his Service, with Promises of vast Rewards, and the full Enjoyment of the same Revenues they had been possess'd of before, in their most flourishing Estate; it was order'd that none of the Imperial Soldiers should be for the future admitted into the City, except such as should be sent in the Quality of Messengers from the King, or any of his *Dissaves*, to the General and Council: 32 Men were also commanded to guard the Passes near *Caleture*. Most of the *Portugueses* at *Columbo*, were sent under a Convoy of a whole Company to *Gale*; and upon a scrutiny of the Muster-roll, it was found that there were 300 Men missing from among the *Lascaryns* of *Matule*, and many more follow'd their Footsteps soon after.

3 Portu*guese Frigates taken.*

The 30*th* of *May* early in the Morning, four Frigates being discover'd near the Shore, towards the side of *Galkisse*, we took in our Princes Flag, in order to entice them into the Road: the Commodore, who led the Van, perhaps began to suspect the matter, and therefore steer'd his course to the North; but the other three were no sooner come within the reach of our Cannon, but we sent out our small Vessels to fetch their Officers ashore. These told us, that they left the Bar of *Goa* the 22*d* with six Frigates, and that two of them being separated from the rest by a most violent Tempest near *Coulang*, were either lost, or perhaps had saved themselves in some Port or other; one of them having been seen without Masts. They added, that a *Portuguese* Caravan was come to an Anchor in the River of *Goa*. These six Frigates had aboard 68 Soldiers, besides good Store of Provisions, Ammunition and all other Necessaries, intended for the Relief of *Columbo*, in case the Squadron under *Francisco de Seixa* should miscarry. Their Cargo stood us in great stead, considering the Scarcity that was among us at that time.

Another Yacht and Frigate taken.

The 1*st* of *June* we took another Frigate and a Yacht, the Officers whereof being likewise brought ashore, told us, that the City of *Cochin* had contributed a good Sum of Money towards the relief of *Columbo*. Their Letters being open'd, contain'd nothing material; except that they were embroil'd with the King of *Cochin*.

Certain Advice was brought to the Governor, that the Day before, as the before-mention'd Ships of *Cochin* were passing along the Shore of *Galkisse*, the Imperial *Dissaves* of *Matule* and *Ouva*, had been seen to give them a Signal with a white Cloth, and had taken abundance of Pains to get aboard them, offering 400 *Larynes* to the Fishermen, if they would carry them aboard of one or the other; and that they had got ready two Boats, but durst not venture thro the Waves. Considering the Pains the Emperor had lately taken to entice away some of the best Officers belonging to the Company, and divers Outrages committed by the King's *Lascaryns* in the Park of the Company: These together, I say, seem'd to us the infallible Forerunners of the ensuing Broils.

For it was not long before *Cornelius van der Dûyn*, Deputy-Governor of *Mature*, sent word from thence, that the King's Officers and Soldiers had forbid all the Inhabitants thereabouts to furnish the *Hollanders* with Provisions, or to obey their Orders, but to retire into the King's Dominions, where they should have full Liberty to make their Excursions into our Dominions, as they had done already at *Billigam*, *Mallimande*, and *Baigam*.

To prevent such like Outrages for the future, three Companies of 40 Men each were sent out of *Gale*, two of which were order'd towards *Accuras*, to protect the Inhabitants against the Inroads made by the King's Soldiers, in the quiet possession of such Lands as were granted to the Company by the Emperor; for by this time we began shrewdly to suspect, that most of the Great Ones were enter'd into a Confederacy with the King against us; this appeas'd by the Tergiversations of the *Adigar*, who passing by the way of *Angretotte* to *Mature*, pretended he was come by Orders from our General, which was a manifest Falshood: some of their Proceedings may be seen out of the following Letter.

" Cattepitty *Apubamy* is come to *Mallimanda*, from whence he has sent " an *Ola* or Letter, intimating that he " was come by the King's special Order, " to take possession of the Country of " *Mature* in his Majesty's Name, and to " enjoin all the Inhabitants, not to sup- " ply the *Dutch* with any Provisions or " otherwise. *He further said*, that he " had intended to have been with them " before this; but being now come with " full Authority, he exhorts them to " obey the Emperor's Orders, for the " Honour of his Court, and of the *Dissave* of *Mature*, which if they do, " they may assure themselves of all ima- " ginable Favour from the Court. The " *Dissave* of *Saffragam* has sent the *Dissave* of *Mature*, to assist you upon all " Occasions.

In *Pasdumcorle* and *Caleture* things went at the same rate, where they had taken *Cotteneynde*, his Mother, and Brother (besides many others) Prisoners, and carried them to the Pass of *Caleture*: their Intentions appear by the following *Ola*.

" T*Udoculle Mandonna Apobami* makes " known to all the *Aratches*, *Lascaryns*, and the chief *Majorals* and Colo- " nels of *Caleture*, *Macoene*, and *Barbaryn*, " that as soon as this *Ola* comes to their " Hands, they shall not keep the least " Correspondence with the *Dutch*, nor " pay any Duties to them, from the " Villages (formerly granted to them) " or furnish them with Labourers to work " on their Fortifications. Those that " shall act contrary to the Tenor of this, " must expect to be severely punish'd; " wherefore come and join with me.

Manoel Andrado (who signaliz'd himself before *Jafnapatnam*, of which anon) was likewise advertis'd by a Letter from his Brother-in-law, that the King's Forces had wounded a Woman and a Slave near the Pass of *Caleture*, and that therefore he should keep a watchful Eye over his *Lascaryns*. About *Negumbo* they play'd the same Game, and *Raja Singa* had made his Addresses to *Patangatti*, the Colonel of *Coquielle*, in hopes by great Promises to bring him over to his Party. On a certain Tree near the Church of *Guia de Lobo*, was affixed the following Paper.

Baldæus.

A Paper affix'd to a Tree.

" THE City of *Columbo* is now taken, " and was according to Agreement " to be surrendred to his Majesty, but " has not been perform'd; if any fatal " Consequences attend this Breach of " Promise, we declare our selves inno- " cent thereof: But as we are well assu- " red of his Majesty's good Inclinations " towards the *Dutch* Nation, so if you " intend to send any Deputies to treat " with him, you shall have Liberty so to " do, and a Passport for them.

Contents of the Letter sent to Raja Singa.

Our General and Council finding themselves under an absolute Necessity of representing to *Raja Singa* the Injustice of his Proceedings in a Letter, they told him, that these Proceedings being directly contrary to their mutual Intentions of annoying the *Portugueses*, and consequently tending both to his Majesty and the Company's Prejudice, they desir'd that all Hostilities might be laid aside, and instead thereof their former good Correspondence be renew'd. They desir'd *Raja Singa* to send his Answer, and with it an Envoy, or one of his *Dissaves*, unto whom they would deliver the Fortress of *Negumbo*, after the Fortifications were demolish'd. And to leave no room for any further Pretences, the General acquainted the Emperor, that in case his Majesty would let him know what further Satisfaction he requir'd at his Hands, he would be ready to comply with his Majesty's Demands, provided the same could be done without great Prejudice to the Company's Service. But that in case his Majesty thought fit to persist in his unjust Oppressions of the *Dutch* and others under our Jurisdiction, he protested and declar'd in the Presence of God, and to all the World, that he was innocent of all the Calamities and Effusion of Blood, that needs must be the Consequences of such Proceedings, which must oblige us (tho much against our Will) to have recourse to such means as God had put into our Hands for the Defence of our Subjects. With this Letter they sent a Faulcon and a Sparrow-hawk, with a *Persian* Faulconer, as a Present to the Emperor.

Advice was brought at the same time from *Caleture*, that the King's *Lascaryns* were

Baldæus. were very troublesome to our Subjects, who were forc'd to leave their Habitations for fear of being carried away, and that they had wounded some and pursued them to the River side. That the two *Aratches Cannangere* and *Pittikeri*, lay encamp'd near *Alican*, and had summoned the Country thereabouts to join with them within three days; that 10 of our *Lascaryns*, and 42 Labourers sent from *Calcture* to *Columbo*, were carried away by a Party of Vagabonds. To prevent the like for the future, and especially to protect our Workmen imploy'd in the peeling of the Cinnamon (call'd *Chalias*) 200 Soldiers were order'd to *Bentot*, under the Command of *Martin Scholtes*, *Peter Chample* and *Joris Hervendonck*, who for their better Security were to be join'd by the *Lascaryns* under the Captain of *Gale-Corle*.

Outrages committed by the Lascaryns.

200 Men sent against them.

CHAP. XLII.

A Feast appointed. Two Caffers *come over to us.* George Bloem *escapes from* Candy. *A Skirmish betwixt the* Dutch *and* Cingaleses. *Robbers punish'd. News of the* Portuguese *Squadron. The arrival of some* Dutch *Ships, their mistake. A strange Notion among the* Indians *concerning* Columbo*'s being impregnable.* Negumbo *taken and retaken.*

IT being now a Month since the Surrender of *Columbo*, a Thanksgiving Day was appointed to give Thanks to God Almighty for this great Success, and to implore his Mercy to bless our Arms for the future. The said Day is kept ever since on the 12*th* of *May*.

Raja Singa's Answer to no purpose.

Raja Singa did send an Answer to the General's Letter, but said scarce any thing in relation to the matter in hand, declaring only his satisfaction about the present, and desiring that the *Persian* Faulkoner might stay with him, which the General (to gratify the Emperor) did consent to, at least till such time that the Ships should be ready to return to *Gamron*. However these Civilities did not answer the end for which they were intended; *Raja Singa* ordering soon after his *Lascaryns* to take all the *Dutch* they could light on Prisoners, and to cut off the Noses and Ears of all the Negroes, *Cingaleses*, *Moors* and *Slaves* that serv'd the *Hollanders*; but the 200 before-mention'd Soldiers struck such a Terror into the King's Forces, that they retreated back, and gave liberty at least to 1000 of the Inhabitants to return to their Houses.

Raja Singa in the mean time continued now as before his Hostilities, one of his Parties having lately carried away a *Duria* and two Labourers within half a League of *Columbo*, which oblig'd us to be continually upon our Guard. The *Dutch* still residing at *Candy*, being afraid they should be detain'd there against their will, writ to the General to hasten the departure of the *Persian* Faulkoner with the Hawks, in hopes that thereby the King might be brought into a good humour to let them depart.

About the same time a certain Messenger named *Chitty Maley* came to *Columbo* with some Hawks and other Presents for the Emperor; six Hawks more with their Faulkoners were also brought from the Coast of *Coromandel* for the same purpose.

Two Caffers come over to us.

The 20*th* of *July* two *Caffers* came over to us, one whereof having been the King's Trumpeter, the other a Drummer, they reported that his Majesty continued still in his Camp at *Reygamwatte*, but intended shortly to break up for *Ruanelle*, the *Dissave* of *Matule* having been sent before already to take care of the High-ways through which they were to pass. They further told us, that the Emperor having granted to divers *Portugueses* certain goodly Villages, this had created ill Blood among the Courtiers.

Our Interpreter escapes from the Camp of the Emperor.

Our Interpreter *George Bloem* was forced to continue there till he found means to make his escape in the night-time from the Camp of *Reygamwatte*, by means of a *Tony* or Boat, wherewith he got to *Montual*, having deceiv'd his Guards by giving them a good dose of strong Liquors. Five other *Dutch* Men who had deserted our Service continued with the King at Court.

News was brought at the same time, that some of the King's Forces having got Intelligence that Mr. *Rabel* a brave *Cingalese*, a Native of *Mature* in our Service,

Baldæus.

Service, was absent from *Hakman* with a Serjeant and most of the Soldiers, having left only a Guard of 10 *Europeans* and 15 *Lascaryns* in the place, they to the number of 100 Men attack'd them on a sudden, in hopes to carry the Place by surprize, but were notwithstanding so hotly receiv'd, that they were glad to retire.

The Cingaleses in vain attack'd.

Things began thus to grow worse and worse, without hopes of Amendment, because we were frequently bit by our own Dogs, I mean the perfidious *Cingaleses* under our Jurisdiction, who gave constant Intelligence of all our Designs, so that we could not send abroad the smallest Party but the Enemy had beforehand notice thereof; whereas we could never discover the least of their Intentions, of which we were sufficiently convinc'd by divers intercepted Letters.

The King's Forces having surpriz'd a Serjeant named *Peter Johnson*, a Native of *Dantzick*, with some Inhabitants of the Country, and four Soldiers Wives, they carried them before the *Dissave* of the seven *Corles*, who told them, that they had been long enough in the *Dutch* Service, and must resolve now to be his Majesty's Slaves.

Two Robbers punish'd.

The 2*d* of *August* we receiv'd a Letter from *Laurence Haurwyk* our Under-Factor at *Caleture*, that several Robbers had been seen about *Boemboele*, who had cut down the Fruits of the Earth; that *Andrado* being sent after them with some *Lascaryns*, had met only with two of them, who refusing obstinately to confess by whom they were sent out to cut down the Rice, they had cut off their Heads, and set them upon Poles near the place where they had spoiled the Rice.

The 13*th* of *August* being Sunday, the Yacht call'd the *Columbo* came into our Road, having left *Tutecoryn* the 11*th*: she brought Letters from the Commodore to the General, intimating that the Enemy's Squadron compos'd of 15 Frigats had escap'd his hands the 7*th* of *July*, taking the opportunity of the Night, and the advantage of the Flats betwixt the Isles; that they were pursued by our Ships as far as *Pambanaar*, which could not come up with them by reason of the Sands. He further told him, that suspecting the *Teuver* or Governor of the Country to have been corrupted with Mony, and to have given them a free Passage betwixt *Manaar* and *Jafnapatnam* (which he commands by either laying in or removing certain Stones from the entrance thereof) he had been oblig'd to return to *Tutecoryn*.

The Portuguese Squadron gets clear of the Dutch.

We had at the same time advice of the arrival of our Ships, the *Amsterdam*, the *Avenborn*, *Saphir*, *Haddock*, *Workum*, *Pelican*, *Patience*, and *Black Bull*, upon the Coast of *Coromandel*: But it was no small Mortification unto us, that the *Saphir* (contrary to the General of *Ceylon*'s Orders) had left the Prisoners and *Portuguese* Soldiers (who according to the Articles of Surrender were to have been carried to *Batavia*) ashore near *Negapatnam*, and that she had not touch'd in the Southern Harbours, where there was a considerable Cargo of Clothes and other Commodities ready, which could not be dispos'd of otherwise; and by the first oversight the Enemy had been reinforc'd with 80 brave Soldiers contrary to the intention of the Agreement.

Oversight of the Ship the Saphir.

We had at the same time Letters from the Factor *Adrian van Newland*, dated in the *Danish* Fort call'd *Tranguebare*, whereby we understood that the before-mentioned *Portuguese* Frigats were pass'd through the Straits (by the assistance of the Governor) to *Jafnapatnam*, from whence *Anthony Amiral de Meneses* (afterwards kill'd by one of our Cannon-balls near *Manaar*) had sent his Forces in Boats to *Negapatnam*, in order to gather a Body (at the request of *Raja Singa*) in those parts, which, as the case then stood, might have prov'd very dangerous to us, had not God through his Mercy prevented their Designs.

During all these Troubles, our General kept a watchful Eye upon the Enemy's Motions, and order'd Mr. *John van der Laan* with 300 Men to scour the Country. These Differences continued for a considerable time, *viz.* to the year 1665. and tho some glimpses of Peace appear'd at certain Intervals, yet is it certain that *Raja Singa* is not reconcil'd to us to this day, and perhaps never will whilst he lives.

We have hitherto treated of *Columbo*; we now will pass the River at *Montual*, and take our course higher up to *Negumbo*. But before we come thither, I can't forbear to say a word or two concerning the general Opinion of the *Indians*, *viz.* That *Columbo* was impregnable. Hence it was that the *Portugueses* boasted in all places, that the King of *Portugal* and Viceroy of *Goa* would never suffer so strong a Fortress to fall into the hands of the Hereticks, especially after we were repulsed in the first general Assault. I happen'd to be then at *Macassar*, where the *Portuguese* Father and some Missionaries lately come from *China* used

Opinion concerning the strength of Columbo.

Baldæus. used to make this Siege their Sport; and one *Francisco Viero*, one of the richest Merchants in the *Indies*, offer'd to lay vast Wagers that it was not taken by the *Hollanders*.

The King of *Celebes* and *Macassar* (the Capital City of that Isle) had the same opinion concerning the Strength of *Columbo*, he and most of his Courtiers being much inclin'd to the *Portuguese* side. But within three Months, just at my return to *Batavia* (after the Conclusion of the Peace betwixt us and the King of *Macassar*) we had the News of the Surrender of *Columbo*, brought to *Batavia* by *Peter Bitter*, to the general satisfaction of the People.

But after this Digression it is time to come to *Negumbo*, which lies about two Leagues and a half, or five good hours walking along the Banks of the River to the North. I am not able to tell you the exact time of its beginning, the *Portuguese* Historians being silent as to this Point, being no more than a Fort built for the conveniency of protecting the Country, which abounds in Cinnamon.

I told you before, how *Adam Westerwold* made himself Master of *Batecalo*: After which *Anthony Caan* took 1639. the Fort of *Trinquenemale*, the most spacious Harbour on the East-side of *Ceylon*. *Philip Lucas* the *Dutch* Director-General in the *Indies* took *Negumbo* the first time *Feb.* 9. 1640. and soon after (as has been told before, *viz.* 13 *March* following) our Commodore *William Jacob Koster* took *Gale* by Storm, but was afterwards treacherously murder'd by some of *Raja*'s People with four of his Guards.

Mr. Koster *treacherously murder'd.*

For the said Mr. *Koster* coming to *Candy* in Person, was detain'd there with vain Promises, without the least probability of success, till growing impatient he began to utter Threats and very harsh Words (a great piece of Imprudence) against some of the Great Ones at Court; which coming to *Raja*'s Ears, he was dismiss'd without the usual marks of Honour, and conducted towards *Batecalo*, but murder'd by the way by the *Cingaleses* his Conducters. This was the Reward bestow'd by *Raja* upon *Koster*, who had reduc'd *Trinquenemale*, *Gale* and *Mature*, with all the Countries thereunto belonging, to his Jurisdiction.

Certain

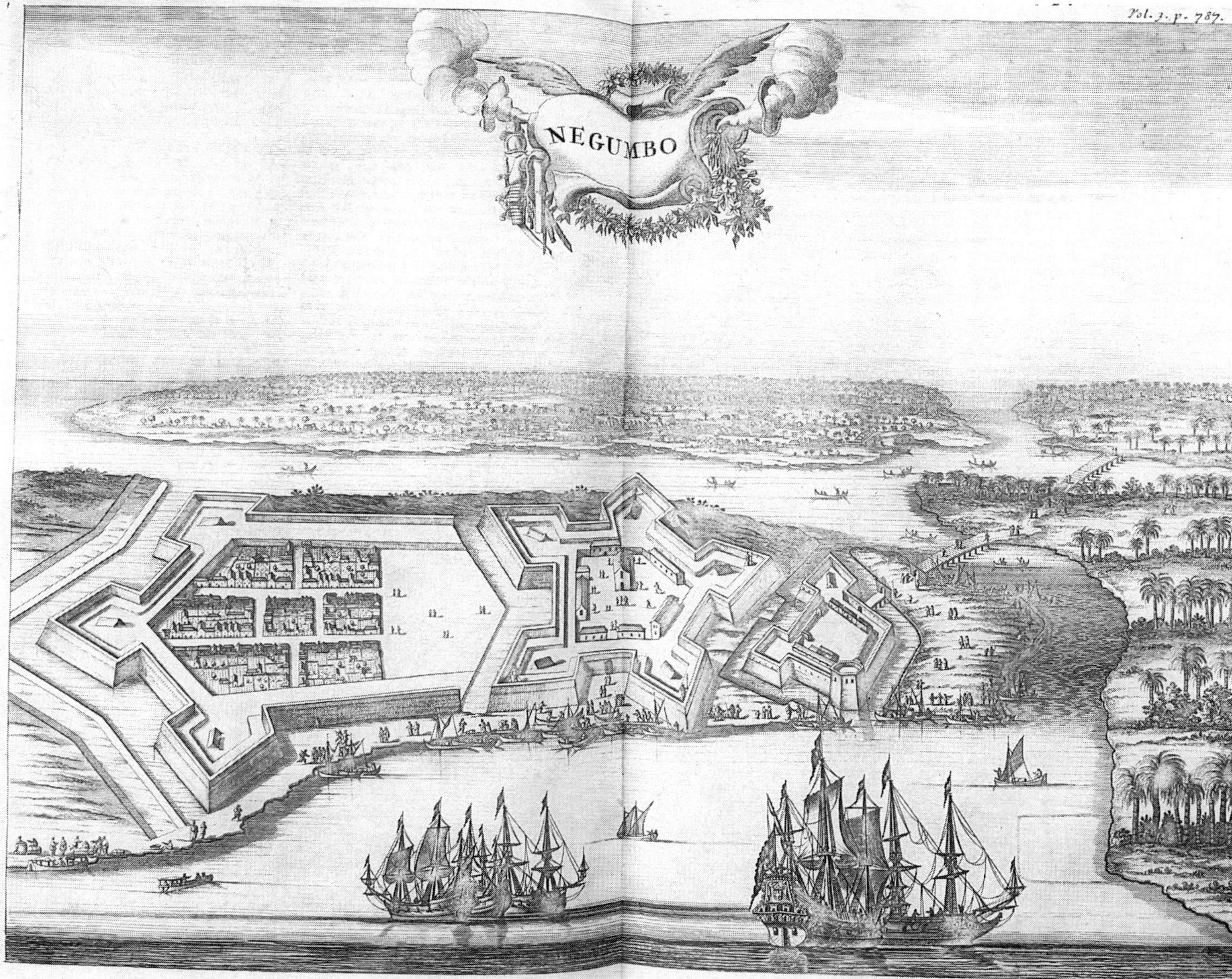
NEGUMBO

Certain it is, had *Raja* been sincere, we might with his Assistance easily have made our selves Masters at that Juncture of *Columbo*, when all their regular Forces being sent to the Relief of *Gale*, there were but a few old Soldiers, Priests and Citizens left for the defence of the Place. But *Raja* thought it better to play the Trimmer betwixt two *European* Nations, than to be in danger of being conquer'd by one, and so thought it his best way to give Opportunity to the *Portugueses* to recover a little Breath.

For the *Portugueses* having received a strong Reinforcement from *Goa*, found means to regain the Fort of *Negumbo*; which done, they sat down before *Gale*, but were bravely entertain'd by *John Thyssen*, who gave them many a Brush; *Raja Singa* sitting all this while by like a Spectator, tho the *Portugueses* remain'd Masters of all the *Low-Lands*, tho we deliver'd *Batecalo* into his Hands, and made much greater Offers by *Peter Borrel* our Ambassador. Things continued in the same State till the Year 1644, at the beginning whereof *Francis Caron* took *Negumbo* from the *Portugueses* a second time, and having strengthen'd it with four new Bastions of Earth, surrounded with strong Pallisadoes, left a Garison of 500 Men there for its Guard. After the Departure of our Fleet, and some Detachments sent to *Gale*, and other Places, *Don Philippo Mascarenhas* made an Attempt upon the Place, but being bravely repuls'd, was glad to retire in confusion to *Columbo*. It was about this time that Mr. *John Maatzuyker* (now Governor-General of the *Dutch East-Indies*) coming to *Goa*, enter'd into a Treaty with the *Portuguese* Viceroy, *John de Silva Telles de Menezes*, Earl of *Aveiras*, concerning the Limits betwixt both Nations in the Isle of *Ceylon*; which being brought to a Conclusion 1645, the said Mr. *Maatzuyker* remain'd in those Parts, in the Quality of Governor of *Puntegale*.

Baldæus.

Negumbo *taken a second time by the* Dutch.

The Portugueses *attempt in vain to recover it.*

CHAP. XLIII.

Raja Singa *treats underhand with the* Portugueses, *his tame Elephants detained.* Raja *declares against the* Portugueses. *The* Dutch *lose* Angretotte. *Both the* Portugueses *and* Dutch *are reinforced. Engagement near* Tiboene. Caleture *deserted.* Portugueses *worsted both by Sea and Land.* Manaar *taken.*

RAJA *Singa* at the Instigation of the *Portugueses* being grown very jealous of the *Dutch* being in possession of the 7 *Corles*, conniv'd at the Robberies that were committed in those Parts by his People, which at last obliged Mr. *John Thyssen* to proclaim open War against them; and accordingly *Nicholas Jacobson Overschie*, Governor of *Negumbo*, and Overseer of the *Dutch* Limits (who died afterwards at *Voorburgh*) caused all the King's tame Elephants to be seiz'd, which so exasperated his Majesty, that he drew all his Forces together and entered the seven *Corles*, where our People had the worst of it, because they surrendred without being reduc'd to the utmost Extremity. However after the return of Mr. *Maatzuyker*, *Negumbo*, *Gale-Corle*, and *Mature*, with the Countries thereunto belonging, were soon secur'd against all further Attempts; the Cinnamon was gather'd and peel'd as before, the wild Elephants tam'd, and every thing else settled for the Advantage of our Company: nay *Raja Singa* himself was appeas'd, who retreated with his Forces, tho without doing any harm to the *Portugueses*, an infallible Sign that there was no ill Understanding betwixt them.

Raja *sides with the* Portugueses.

His Elephants seized.

Matters thus continu'd till 1649, when Mr. *Maatzuyker* redeem'd all our Prisoners, and by a Messenger sent with some Presents, brought matters to an honourable Composition. In the beginning of the Year 1650, Mr. *Rampot* left *Gale* and *Mature*, to the great Dissatisfaction of *Raja Singa*, who however was so far from breaking with us upon that account, that when we entred into a War with the *Portugueses*, 1652. *Raja* declar'd against them, laying hold of the Opportunity that presented it self, by a late Mutiny among the *Portuguese* Soldiers and chief Inhabitants of *Columbo*, rais'd against *Manoel Mascarenhas Homem* their Governor, whom they had taken into Custody.

Mutiny at Columbo *against their Governor.*

These Mutineers having gather'd what Forces they were able near *Columbo*, march'd

Baldæus. Angretotte lost by the Dutch. march'd on a sudden with 800 *European* Soldiers and as many Negroes towards our Fort of *Angretotte*, which they oblig'd to a Surrender the 8*th* of *Jan.* 1653. after a Siege of 11 Days, in which they lost a considerable Number of Men; 98 *Germans*, 24 *Javaneses*, and a greater Number of *Lascaryns* were made Prisoners of War, under condition that they should be dismiss'd for a reasonable Ransom. The same Afternoon a Body of 300 Men were sent to their Relief, who happen'd to come too late; tho as the case stood, their Endeavours would have prov'd in vain, considering the Enemy was twice as strong and advantageously posted; and we had not come off at so cheap a rate, had not *Raja Singa* given the Enemy a strong Diversion near *Cottegore*, whereabouts they attack'd the Pass near *Columbo* with such Vigour, that the Governor and Deputy-Governor were glad to send for their Forces from *Reygam* and *Pasdum-Corle* to oppose the Imperialists. These were no sooner retreated, but the *Portugueses* attack'd our Outguards near *Negumbo*, and possess'd themselves of the 4 and 7 *Corles*: But *Raja Singa* rallying his Forces, march'd from *Ouva* to *Saffragam* (the Capital City of the five *Corles*) the *Portuguese Dissave* was glad to retreat with his Forces to *Gurbeville*, and thereby gave us Opportunity to join our Forces, and secure the Countries of *Gale* and *Mature*.

Raja makes a Diversion in favour of the Dutch.

The Portugueses *are reinforced.*

In the mean while, *viz.* the 10*th* of *May*, the *Portugueses* in *Columbo* receiv'd a Reinforcement of 12 Frigates, with a good number of Officers and Soldiers from *Goa*, under the Command of *Francisco de Melo de Castro*; our Cruizers being scarce two days before (to our great Misfortune) forc'd to retreat from their Stations by stress of Weather into the Harbour of *Gale*. Notwithstanding which, they made no considerable Attempt against us, being contented to secure only their Workmen employ'd in peeling of the Cinnamon, and other Inhabitants of the Country against our Parties.

Raja Singa finding that in 1653 in *September*, the *Portugueses* had receiv'd a fresh Supply from *Tutecoryn*, whereas our four Ships did not bring one single Soldier to relieve the rest; that our Governor *Jacob van Kittenstein* had obtain'd leave to depart; and that when Commissary *Rijklof van Goens* touch'd with his four Ships towards the latter end of *October* in *Ceylon*, in his way to *Persia* and *Suratte*, without bringing us the least Succours, he retreated with his half starved tatter'd Troops from *Caravanella*, thro the 7 and 4 *Corles* to *Candy*, to refresh themselves.

The *Portugueses* finding themselves secure on that side, did appear with all the Forces they could bring into the Field before *Columbo*, in hopes of drawing our Forces out of the Fort; but finding themselves frustrated in their hopes, they retreated in the beginning of 1654, towards *Reygam* and *Pasdum-Corle*, whence they sent frequent Parties to take away our Cattel, and to spoil the Fruits of the Earth. But Major *John van der Laan* was always at hand with a good Body to observe them.

The 20*th* of *March* our Governor *Adrian van der Meyden*, marched from *Gale* to *Caleture*; and being join'd there the 23*d* by all his Forces, he follow'd the *Portugueses* thro *Berberin*, *Dodangodde*, and *Tiboen*, where he attack'd them the 26*th* in the Morning, in their advantageous Post: the Engagement was very fierce for a whole Hour, when our Forces feign'd a Retreat, in hopes to draw the Enemy from his Post, but they were too wise to follow us; they had more Men slain on their side than we. After our Forces had refresh'd themselves a little while at *Tiboen*, we march'd to *Caleture*, and the Enemy retreated out of our Dominions cross the River to *Columbo*.

An Engagement betwixt the Portugueses *and* Dutch.

Soon after 5 Galeons with 1000 *Portuguese* Landmen aboard them, arriving upon our Coast, engag'd three of our Yachts call'd the *Greyhound*, the *Rhinoceros*, and *Dromedary*, and pursu'd them to the Flats of *Negumbo*, but took none of them, our Vessels retiring under the Cannon there, and the *Portugueses* to *Columbo*, having lost their Captain-Major, and many others in this Engagement.

5 Portuguese *Gallies engage* 3 Dutch *Vessels.*

A Council being call'd to consult what to do in this Emergency, it was resolv'd to leave *Caleture*, and to employ our whole Force in the defence of *Negumbo*, without which we were not in a condition to maintain that Fortress, which was of the greatest consequence to us. Accordingly *Negumbo* being well provided with what Forces we were able to gather, the Enemy (whose Forces were considerably encreas'd by the late Reinforcements) march'd from *Galkisse* to *Caleture*, and thence to *Alicaon*, where they pitch'd their Tents; to oppose which we brought into the Field about 200 *Europeans*, 80 *Javaneses*, and a good Number of *Lascaryns*, wherewith we made a shift to defend our Country as well as we could.

About

Van Goens beats the Galeons.

About this time Commissary *van Goens* in his return from *Persia* and *Suratte* to *Ceylon*, had the good Fortune to beat the Galeons near the Cape *du Ramos*, and thereby to release 20 of our People made Prisoners at *Angretotte*, who were set ashore at *Puntegale*. This was the reason that the *Portugueses* could not spare many Men for the use of their Frigates, having sustain'd a considerable Loss of them in the late Engagement with Mr. *van Goens*, near *Achiera*; neither were they so active in the Field till the ensuing *July*, when we having receiv'd some Reinforcements, appointed our Rendevouz at *Bentotte*, in sight of the Enemy, having only a River betwixt us and them. We kill'd the *Portugueses* about 30 *Europeans* in divers Skirmishes, and took from them divers Boats, which made them not so eager afterwards to attack our Countries, in order to spoil our Cinnamon and *Areck* Harvest, and the taking of Elephants, wherein consists the chief Revenue of this Isle, belonging to our Company.

Some Supplies brought to the Dutch.

The 13th of *Septemb.* the Yachts the *Turtle-Dove*, the *Red-Lyon* and the *Haddock*, arriv'd with fresh Supplies and 50 Soldiers. The 4th of *Decemb.* the Yacht the *Kanien* brought us a Supply of 54 Soldiers more; besides which, 159 Seamen were taken out of four Ships (come with the Director *Henry van Gent* into *Gale*, to provide themselves with fresh Water) all which being join'd with our Forces encamp'd at *Bentotte*, we embarked the 16th of *Decemb.* all our Forces, 690 strong (including Officers) composed of Seamen, Land-Soldiers, *Javaneses* and *Cingaleses*, in 20 *Catapaneels* or Land-Boats, and thus passed the River *Alicaon*.

The Dutch pass the River Alicaon.

But scarce had we reach'd the opposite Bank of the River, but we met with so warm a Reception from 300 chosen *Portugueses*, and some *Topasses* and *Cingaleses*, that most of our *Indian* Forces betook themselves to their Heels; but being rallied again upon the Bank of the River, return'd to the Charge; and being bravely seconded by the rest, forced the Enemy to retreat, leaving one of their Cannon of 1000 Pounds Weight behind them, 60 slain, and many more wounded. They behaved themselves bravely, but were forc'd after this Defeat to retire by the way of *Malvane* to *Columbo*.

Beat the Portugueses.

The *Portugueses* finding us not ready to attack *Caleture* (after they had given the usual Pay to the Soldiers) they broke up in the beginning of 1655, and surpriz'd *Raja*'s Forces, under the Command of the *Dissave* of the four *Corles*; and being reinforced by some other Forces from *Jafnapatnam* and *Manaar*, besides a good Number of *Lascaryns*, they pursued the *Dissave* of the seven *Corles*, as far as to the Straits of *Candy*, plundring all the Country thro which they passed: which so exasperated the King, that he order'd all his Forces to appear in the Field; but his Van being routed in *April* near *Attapitin* by *Caspar Figeiro*, the King quitted the Field full of Dissatisfaction.

Baldæus.

Raja's Troops routed.

It happen'd to our good Fortune, that the new Governor and *Portuguese* Admiral, *Anthonio de Souza Coutinho* (under whose Government *Columbo* was lost) coming with 8 Frigates and 500 Landmen into these Parts, was the 18th of *May* forc'd towards the Coast of *Gale*: We sent out two Yachts, *viz.* the *Lyon* and *Kanien*, who coming up with them, took two with all the Men and Provisions, and forc'd two more ashore; so that no more than two or three of them got safe to *Columbo*, and *Coutinho* himself was forc'd to take his Course round the Point *das Pedras* to *Jafnapatnam* and *Manaar*, from whence he came with a good Troop by the way of *Putelaon*, *Calpentyn*, and the seven *Corles*; in *August* to *Columbo*, where he was no sooner establish'd in his Dignity, but he visited with *Anthonio Mendes d' Arangie* the Fort of *Caleture*, where he left a Garison of 300 *Europeans*, and a good Number of Negroes, but resolv'd to keep *Caspar Figeiro* near his Person.

The Portugueses routed at Sea.

By that time the Director-General *Gerard Hulst* came in Company of Mr. *John van der Laan* (a Person well versed in the Affairs of *Ceylon*) into those parts. About the middle of *Septemb.* three Yachts were dispatch'd from Cape *Comoryn*, in order to observe the Frigates sent from *Columbo* to *Tutecoryn* for Provisions, and either to take them or to block them up betwixt the Islands. It was also resolved to force the *Portugueses* to quit *Caleture*, whilst the Enemy were yet under apprehension of the Strength of the Forces come along with the Director-General, and lately landed at *Negumbo*, from whence he intended to give the Enemy a Visit on the other side of the River at *Montual*.

However the *Portuguese* Squadnon, consisting of 20 Frigates and some Barks, loaden with all sorts of Necessaries at *Jafnapatnam*, and some other Places on the *Indian* Coast, made shift to pass by with full Sails within sight of *Negumbo* (where our Ships lay at anchor) and to our

Baldæus. our signal Regret got into *Columbo*. Mr. *Hulst* receiv'd at the same time Advice by a small Advice-boat, that a new Viceroy was arriv'd at *Goa* with three Galeons, one Yacht, and a good Number of Landmen. A Council being call'd, it was thought convenient to try whether these Galeons might not be surpriz'd near *Marmagon* or *Agoada* (two Castles in the Bay of *Goa*) At the same time Mr. *Hulst* came with four Ships and a good Number of Soldiers before *Berberyn*, where having landed and join'd his Forces with the rest the 28*th* of *Septemb.* he soon after made himself Master of *Caleture*, an account whereof has been given before.

A new Viceroy comes to Goa *with some Galeons.*

But it is time to leave *Negumbo*, provided with a good Garison (first by Major *John van der Laan*, and afterwards by the Head Factor *Edward Hauw*) and to go towards *Manaar*. In the Year 1661. I undertook a Journy over Land from *Jafnapatnam* to *Columbo*, 49 or 50 Leagues distant from one another, which I accomplish'd in seven Days.

Distance betwixt Jafnapatnam *and* Columbo.

From *Negumbo* you travel by the way of *Cajuel*, to the River *Chilauw*, and so thro the Countries of *Madampe* and *Putelaon*, leaving the Isle of *Calpentyn* to the left; then thro *Aripou* (where the Christians have a Church) to *Manaar*, thence to *Wannias*, the Church of *Mantotte*, and so to *Jafnapatnam*, of which more hereafter. We made this Observation in this Journy, that no Cinnamon grows, except on the other side of the River *Chilauw*, and beyond *Jafnapatnam*. For the rest, all these before-mention'd Countries have a very fruitful Soil (except *Calpentyn*, which is somewhat barren) especially about *Madampe*, but are destitute of Inhabitants: The Bufflers feeding here in vast Herds, which makes me believe that it would afford plenty of every thing were it well cultivated.

Goodness of these Countries.

We will now proceed to give you some account of the Isle of *Manaar*, which formerly adhered to the Continent, as sufficiently appears by the Sand Bank, called *Adams-Bridg*. Next unto this lies the Isle of *Rammanakoyel*, where is to be seen a rich and famous *Pagode*, belonging to the *Teuver* or Governor, who has a Fort on the Continent. At certain Seasons there is a Passage with small Boats, thro some Depths of this *Adams-Bridg*, one whereof I had once occasion to pass my self.

The said Isle was reduced by the *Hollanders*, 1658. in the following manner, by Mr. *Rjiklof van Goens*. The *Portugueses* had made Entrenchments all along the Shore, which were defended by 1000 chosen Men and 12 Frigates, to hinder the Approach of our Boats. Our great Ships were order'd to advance as near as they could, under favour of which our Boats landed the Men. Serjeant *Henry van Wel* (since a Lieutenant) was the first who set foot on shore; and being bravely follow'd by the rest, were as courageously receiv'd by the *Portugueses*, who did all that Men could do to second their Comrades; but our Cannon from the Ships, together with our small Arms, made such a Havock among them, that they were forc'd to quit their Entrenchments. Here it was that *Antonio Amiral de Menezes*, the *Portuguese* General, lost his Life by a Cannon-Bullet, and *Anthonio Mendes d' Arangie*, a famous Soldier, was mortally wounded, with many other brave Officers.

The Isle of Manaar *taken by the* Dutch.

On our side we lost an Ensign, and before our Landing (when the Long-boat of the Ship *Naarden* was taken) the brave Lieutenant *Block*, which we return'd 'em with full measure; all their Frigates, as they passed by our Squadron, being either sunk or taken, with a great Slaughter of their Men. Major *John van der Laan* (tho he had a heavy Fall before our Landing, being a very large and fat Person) did nevertheless behave himself upon this Occasion with incredible Bravery, breaking thro the thickest of the Ranks of the Enemy, whereby he made good the Title bestow'd upon him long before, of being *the Terror of the* Portugueses.

After this defeat, the *Portugueses* not thinking themselves secure in the Fort *Manaar*, retir'd over the Water to *Jafnapatnam*, leaving only *Andrew Villosa* with a very moderate Force in the Castle of S. *George*. They would not have escaped our Hands at so cheap a rate, had we not been stop'd by the great Rains and Tempests.

Portugueses *leave the Fort* Manaar.

The 22*d* *Andrew Villosa* being deserted by most of his Men, was oblig'd to surrender the Castle of St. *George* upon reasonable Terms. We took about 200 Prisoners, both *Europeans* and Negroes, and among them a *Caffer* (or *African* Negro) who pretending to be a Captain, was so stubborn, that he would not take up his Arms or arise from the Ground (as he was commanded to do) without a good Bastinado.

S. George *surrendred.*

The 24*th* of *Febr.* I preach'd the Thanksgiving-Sermon in the great Church upon the Text of 1 *Sam.* 7. 7. for the most fortunate Reduction of this Isle, whereof our General might say with *Cæsar*,

sar,

sar, *Veni, vidi, vici*, being beyond all question one of the greatest Actions that ever happen'd betwixt us and the *Portugueses* in the *Indies*, considering we were forc'd to attack the Enemies Forces, composed of Veteran *European* Soldiers, and to chase them from their advantageous Posts, and that only with 800 Men, and consequently with the utmost hazard; being resolv'd either to overcome or die in the Attempt, because we had quite drain'd the Garison of *Columbo*, leaving only a few, and those infirm Persons to guard that Place, because we expected hourly the Arrival of the Ship the *Salamandar* with some 100 Soldiers, and good Store of Ammunition and Provision, having aboard the Commodore *Peter de Bitter*, the Factor *Edward Ooms*, and Captain *Peter Wasch*. The same having been detained by Calms and Tempests for near six Months, and endur'd great Hardships about the *Maldive* Islauds, arriv'd at last safely at *Columbo*, but was soon after order'd by the Governor *Adrian van der Meyden*, to sail to *Manaar*, where she came to an Anchor immediately after we had made our selves Masters of that Isle, and were just then preparing to march towards *Jafnapatnam*. But before we leave *Manaar*, we must add something concerning the true Condition of this Island.

The Salamandar brings a Supply of Men and Provisions.

CHAP.

Baldæus.

CHAP. XLIV.

A Description of Manaar. *How the Christian Religion was planted, and might be further promoted there. A Description of the Country of the* Wannias. *Our March towards* Jafnapatnam. *We pass the River; rout the* Portugueses, *and take the Water-Fort.*

Manaar *whence it got its Name.*

MANAAR derives its Name from the *Malabar* Language, from the word *Man*, i. e. *Sand*, and *Aar* a *River*, signifying as much as a *Sand-River*; it being observable, that both the *Cingalese* and *Malabar* Languages are spoken in the Isle of *Ceylon*. The first is used beyond *Negumbo*, viz. at *Columbo*, *Caleture*, *Berberyn*, *Alican*, *Gale*, *Belligamme*, *Mature*, *Dondere*, &c. But in all the other parts of this Isle opposite to the Coast of *Coromandel*, and all along the Bay, they speak the *Malabar* Tongue; whence it seems very probable, that that Tract of Land (as the Inhabitants of *Jafnapatnam* themselves believe) was first of all peopled by those of *Coromandel*, who brought their Language along with them; it being certain that in the Inland Countries about *Candy*, *Vintane*, *Ballaney*, &c. they speak only *Cingalese*.

The Cingalese *and* Malabar *Tongues both used in* Ceylon.

Situation of Manaar.

The Isle of *Manaar* is situate at 9 deg. of Northern Latitude, its length being about two and a half *German* Leagues, and one broad, including the Salt-water River (as you will see in the Map) which reaches as far as the great Church call'd *Carcel*. The Castle is seated upon a Canal able to bear small Yachts, which draw 3, 4, or 5 foot Water, and can go from thence to *Jafnapatnam*. This Castle was strengthened with some additional Fortifications, and surrounded with a deep Ditch, after we had taken it from the *Portugueses*. The whole Isle has no more than seven Churches, unto each whereof belong divers considerable Villages: The first is the *City Church*, next that call'd *Tottavaly*, then *Carcel*, *Erkelampatti*, S. *Peter*'s Church belonging to the Fishermen; *Peixale*, and the last *Tellemanaar*, lying at the furthermost, and near the Sea-side.

Its Churches.

Pearl fishery at Manaar.

This Island was formerly celebrated for the *Pearl Fishery*, as well as the City of *Tutecoryn*; but no Pearls having been taken there for these 10 years last past, the Inhabitants are reduc'd to great Poverty; whereas the sumptuous Edifices, Churches and Monasteries, with their Ornaments, are sufficient Demonstrations of its former Grandure.

In the year 1666. (after my departure) our Company order'd the first time the Pearl-fishery to be renew'd again, with no ill success; and according to several Letters I have receiv'd from thence, they took a considerable quantity of Pearls, the second time, in the year 1669.

The Inhabitants of Manaar *speak also* Portuguese.

The Inhabitants of *Manaar* speak (besides the *Malabar*) most generally *Portuguese*, being long ago converted to the Christian Faith, for which reason they have suffer'd most cruel Persecutions from the Kings of *Jafnapatnam*, who baptiz'd many of the new converted Christians with Blood, after they had receiv'd the Baptism with Water. Many of them fled for this reason to *Goa* by Land, being above 100 Leagues, and among them a young Gentleman of Royal Extraction, who embrac'd Christianity there.

Persecution of the Christians in Manaar.

It was *Franciscus Xaverius* who converted the Inhabitants here, as well as those on the Cape *Comoryn* and the *Paruas*, as we have told you before in the Description of the *Indian* Coast, and in the account of his Life. The said *Xaverius* establish'd among them certain Teachers call'd *Canacappels*, who were to instruct the Inhabitants in the first Rudiments of the Christian Religion, as the Ten Commandments, the Creed, Our Father, *&c.* which they did with indefatigable Care and Industry: These were succeeded by the Jesuits (call'd *Paulites* here, because they were sent into the *Indies* by Pope *Paul* III.) who in their way of teaching both the old and young ones, did far exceed the *Franciscans*, and all other Orders among the *Romanists*. And I am very free to confess, that I have frequently follow'd their Footsteps in reforming the Churches and Schools in *Manaar* and *Jafnapatnam*, as far as they were consistent with our Religion, and consonant to the Genius of these Nations. It being absolutely necessary, that he who undertakes this task should be well acquainted with the method to be used among these People in the Infancy of their Conversion, intricate Questions and Mysteries being more apt to confound than to instruct them: For which reason it is most proper to teach them the naked Truth of the Gospel in as few Points as possibly can be done (the Youth

What Method is most proper for the Conversion of these Nations.

Vol. 3. p. 752.

THE ISLAND of MANAER.

24.

Youth being very apt to retain here what they have been told) to catechise frequently the young ones in the presence of their Parents, thereby to excite in them a laudable Emulation to follow their Footsteps. St. *Paul* himself leads us the way, when he says, that you must first lay the Foundation of the Doctrine of Christ, before you can raise the Edifice of the Church.

It is also absolutely requisite, that the same Catechism that has been at first introduc'd among the Native Christians should be retain'd without any alteration, which, as it would over-charge their Memory, so it would breed nothing but Confusion instead of Profit. It was for this reason, that when by order from the supreme Magistrates, the Reformation of these Churches was committed to my care, I reduc'd the chief Points of the Christian Doctrine into Questions and Answers, which were afterwards introduc'd into the Churches of *Jafnapatnam*, *Manaar*, *Gale*, *Columbo*, *Negumbo* and *Mature*, and receiv'd by the succeeding Ministers, by special Command from the General and Council of the *Indies*, and the Governor of these places; and were afterwards confirm'd by the General Assembly of the Clergy of *Ceylon* held at *Columbo* 1659. from the 24*th* of *February* till the 3*d* of *March*.

The Catechism once introduc'd among the Natives, must not be alter'd.

They had had enough of the Mischiefs that ensued upon these Alterations, introduced by new Ministers into the Isle of *Formosa*, who instead of following the footsteps of *Robert Junius* and *George Candius* (Ministers of the Gospel there) would introduce certain Novelties. I found it also absolutely necessary to have these Questions and Answers put, not only in the *Portuguese* but also in the *Malabar* Tongue, several Copies whereof were sent to our Brethren at *Columbo*, *Gale* and *Negapatnam*.

It is beyond all dispute that the *Low-Dutch* Tongue is not so proper to propagate our Religion here as the *Malabar* and *Portuguese*; and consequently, that the Ministers of the Gospel sent into those parts should rather apply themselves to these Languages, than to impose their own upon the new Converts, which always meets with great difficulty, and can't be introduc'd without vast Trouble and Charges: besides, that it is much more reasonable one Man should accommodate himself to many, than these to one Man. It is furthermore requisite, that as the Ministers ought to pay all due Respect to the Magistrates, so these should treat them with all imaginaale Civility and Honour, to acquire them the more Authority among the Natives.

Baldæus.

The Isle of *Manaar* abounds in Fish to such a degree, that the Inhabitants here (as well as at *Negumbo*) dry and send them into other parts in vast quantities. They have here a peculiar Fish (properly a Sea-Calf) of an amphibious nature; the Females have Breasts and give Suck, and the Flesh when well boil'd tastes not unlike our Sturgeon, and might easily be mistaken for Veal.

Manaar has plenty of Fish.

A peculiar kind of Fish.

But it is time we pass the River of *Manaar* towards *Mantotte*. This River is not very deep; nay on that side where you come to it over the Canal near the Castle, it is so shallow, that you may wade through it with ease, the Water scarce coming up to your Knees, tho it is so broad that it will take up half an hour before you can pass it. The Country on the other side is call'd the Country of the *Wannias*, under the Jurisdiction of our Company; their Churches make up together with those of *Manaar* no less than 14, and are under the Inspection of the Minister who resides in the Isle of *Manaar*, and duly visits them once a month. This Country, tho it acknowledges the Jurisdiction of our Company, pays the usual Taxes, furnishes them with Elephants, &c. yet must they be mildly treated, it being their general Maxims to disoblige neither *Raja Singa* nor the Company.

The Country of the Wannias.

In the year 1658. in the beginning of *March* (after the taking of *Manaar*, and providing it with a good Garison) we march'd into that Country towards *Jafnapatnam*. *Mantotte* begins to the North of the *Salt River* near the Village of *Peringaly*, extending to the South along the Sea-shore, as far as the River *Aripouture*, where *Moussilipatte* begins, near the Village of *Aripou*, extending further Southward to the Mountains of *Condremale*, which face the Bay opposite to the Isle of *Calpentyn*, and cross the Country *Mantotte*, stretching to *Setecoulang*, 6 Villages whereof belong to *Manaar*, 6 to *Jafnapatnam*, and 5 to *Mantotte*.

The rest of *Mantotte* and *Moussilipatte* extends to the East to the great Forest (the Boundary of the Country on that side) *Mantotte* it self has 64 Villages, *Moussilipatte* 24, and that part of *Setecoulang* 6, amounting in all to 84. All these Countries are very fertile, especially-

Baldæus. ly in Rice, which produces a hundred-fold Crop; but the worst is, the Elephants do great Mischief in those parts that are not very populous.

It is very remarkable what *John de Lucena* observes in the Life of *Xaverius*, *viz.* That on the Cape *Comoryn*, and all along that Tract of the *East-Indies*, whilst it is Summer and dry Season on the West-side of the Cape, the Winter and rainy Season appears on the opposite side: the same is to be observ'd in the Isle of *Ceylon*. For whilst the Winter continues about *Jafnapatnam*, the *Wannias* and *Manaar*, during the Months of *October*, *November* and *December*, it is Summer in all the other parts: On the contrary, in the Months of *April* and *May*, whilst it is Summer about *Jafnapatnam*, which continues six or seven Months, it is Winter and rainy Weather at *Columbo*, *Gale*, and the Countries thereabouts. In the Low-Lands remote from the mountainous part of *Ceylon*, there blow only two Winds; but about *Columbo*, *Gale*, and some other places, you have duly a Day and Night-Wind, as upon the Coast of *Coromandel*. From *April* till *October* the Wind blows constantly a brisk Gale from the South with a clear Air and bright Sun-shine, as does the North-wind from *November* till *April*. In *January*, *February* and *March* it is generally very calm, with intolerable Heat; but a Dew falls in the Night, which being very unwholesom, the Inhabitants return with Sun-set into their Houses: and were it not for these Dews and the strong Winds which cool the Air, the Heat would be unsupportable here.

Winter and Summer at once in divers parts of Ceylon.

Our March from Manaar *to* Jafnapatnam.

As we march'd through the Country of *Wannias*, we kept a most exact Discipline; and as we had no great plenty of Provisions, we allow'd only a small measure Rice every day to each Soldier, rather than incommode the Inhabitants: and finding our Forces to be extremely tir'd by long Marches, and consequently uncapable of engaging with the same advantage with the Enemy in case they should be attack'd, it was resolv'd instead of marching up to the head of the River through the sandy ground, to pass the River in Boats, tho it would require near an hour and a half for every Boat to pass it.

Passage over the River.

The worst was, that upon our arrival on the other side of the River we expected the Enemy ready to give us a warm Reception, because we could not transport above 200 or at most 300 Men at once over the River, and that the Bank was very muddy; for I remember that some years after two Elephants passing over to the *Jafnapatnam* side, one of them stuck in the Mud, and was kill'd by the Inhabitants, nothing being more common than for the Elephants to come cross the River to feed upon the Fruits of the Palm-trees, to come at which they trample the Roots of the Trees so long with their Feet till they loosen, and afterwards throw them down with their Bodies, and so eat the Fruit.

However the first Troop of our Forces got over without any opposition, and no sooner had put themselves in order of Battel, but receiv'd Intelligence that the Enemy were retreated from thence the day before, in order to expect us at the head Spring of the River.

We march towards Jafnapatnam.

After we had transported all our Forces over the River, the Inhabitants treated us very civilly, and furnish'd us with plenty of Provisions and Fruits. The first place we came to was the chief Church of the Province of *Tenmaracbe*, call'd *Chavagatzari*, where after we had refresh'd our selves with a good Dinner, we march'd forward the same day with two Field-pieces to *Navacouli* (two hours from *Jafnapatnam*) where we encamp'd that night.

A Skirmish with the Portugueses.

The next day (after Morning-Prayer) we march'd on to the River, where we expected to meet with a vigorous Opposition; but finding no Resistance, we advanced by degrees towards the Castle near the Church of *Sundecouli*, where in the Evening we had a smart Skirmish with the *Portugueses*, of whom we kill'd many upon the spot, and posted our selves that night round about the before-mentioned Church.

The City of Jafnapatnam *taken.*

The next following day we advanc'd to the City, which being without any Fortifications, we broke through the Wall and Houses; and pursuing the Enemy from Street to Street, under the favour of our Cannon, which opened us the way, we advanc'd towards the Castle. The 9*th* of *March* we made our selves Masters of the Jesuits Church and College at the West-End of the City, and the 18*th* following of the Church and Monastery of the *Dominicans* on the East-side: which made us give publick Thanks to God Almighty for his Blessings, the Text being the 7*th* Verse of the 20*th* Psalm.

The Enemy being thus forced to quit their Houses, had no other way left than

to

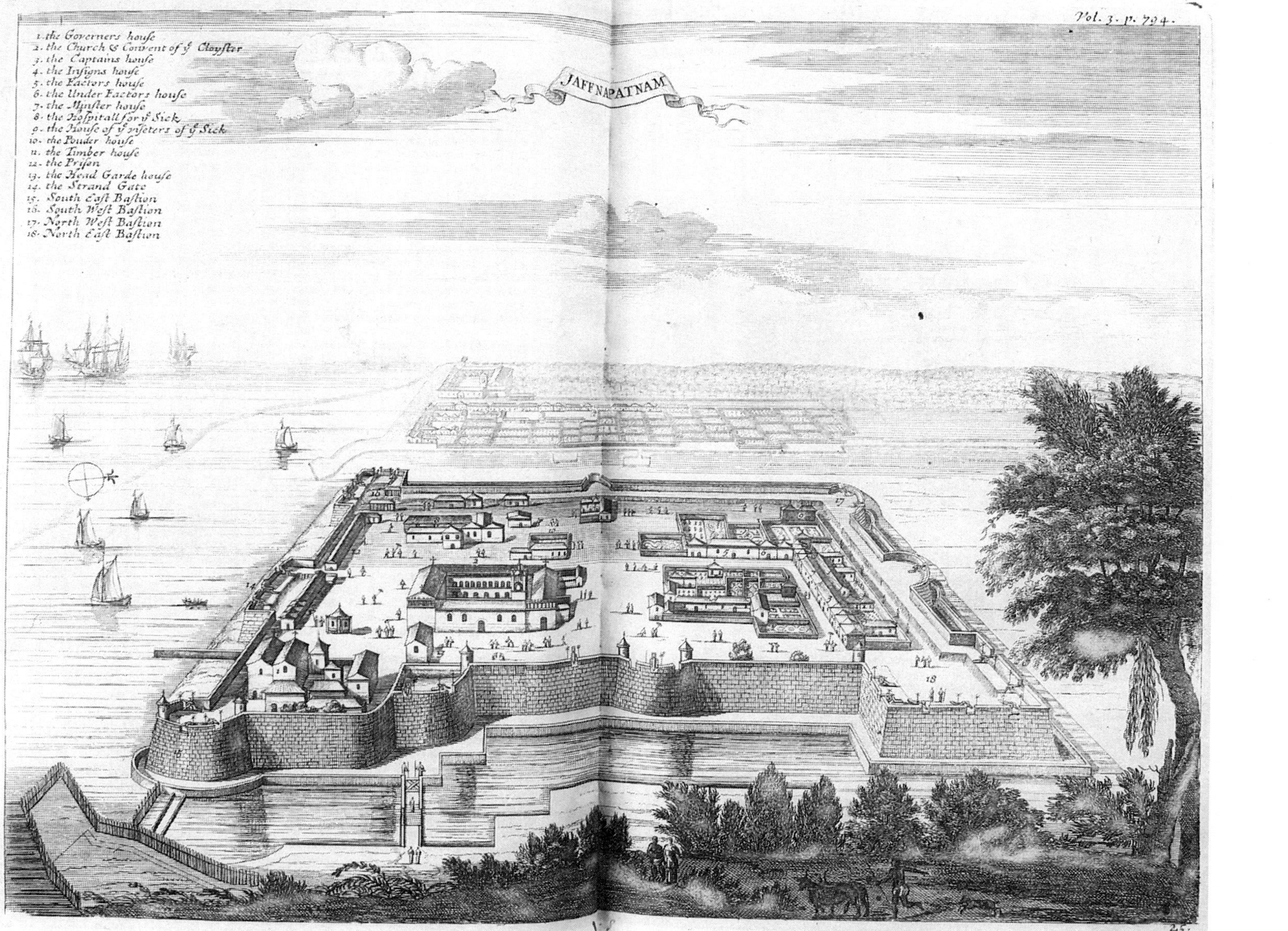
JAFFNAPATNAM
1. the Governers house
2. the Church & Convent of y Cloyster
3. the Captains house
4. the Insigns house
5. the Factors house
6. the Under Factors house
7. the Minster house
8. the Hospitall for y Sick
9. the House of y visiters of y Sick
10. the Pouder house
11. the Timber house
12. the Prison
13. the Head Garde house
14. the Strand Gate
15. South East Bastion
16. South West Bastion
17. North West Bastion
18. North East Bastion
25.

Baldæus.

to retreat to the Castle, which they did in great disorder, many of the Inhabitants of the Country thronging in among the *Portugueses*, so that the Castle was so crowded with People that they had not room enough to dispose them to any advantage.

But the better to straiten the Castle of *Jafnapatnam*, and take away from the Garison all hopes of relief, it was thought necessary to attack a certain Outwork or Redoubt, built upon a small Isle in the middle of the River, not far from its Entrance, which it commands. This Fort was built by *Anthonio Amiral de Menezes*, and may justly be call'd the Key of *Jafnapatnam*; and if such another were made on the Point of *Calmom*, no Vessel could approach the Castle without leave.

Accordingly we detatch'd a good Body of Men to the Isle of *Ourature*, in order to attack the said Fort, in which at that time commanded one *Hieronimo de Paiva* with a good Garison. The Isle of *Ourature* (where formerly the *Portugueses* had a Castle, the Ruins of which are yet to be seen) lying at some distance from this Water-Fort, we were forc'd to raise our Batteries against it upon the Isle of *Caradiva*: But finding that by reason of the distance betwixt us and them, and the strength of the Wall, we could make no Breach in it, it was resolv'd to assault the place by the help of certain Vessels provided with Breast-works and Cannon. But before we thought fit to venture at so desperate an Attempt, it was resolved to send the following Summons to the Commander of the Fort.

The Fort Cays summon'd to a Surrender.

" IT having pleased Almighty God to " bless our Arms with such Success, " that there is no possibility left for you " to resist us, or defend your self against " our Attacks: It is therefore that we " have thought fit to let you know " (as is usual upon such occasions) that " we are come to summon the Fort of " *Cays*, in the Name of the States-" General of the *United Provinces*, of the " Governors of the *East-India* Compa-" ny, and his Excellency *John Maatzuyker* Governor-General, and the " Council of the *Indies*; as by these Pre-" sents I summon the said Fort, not

Baldæus.

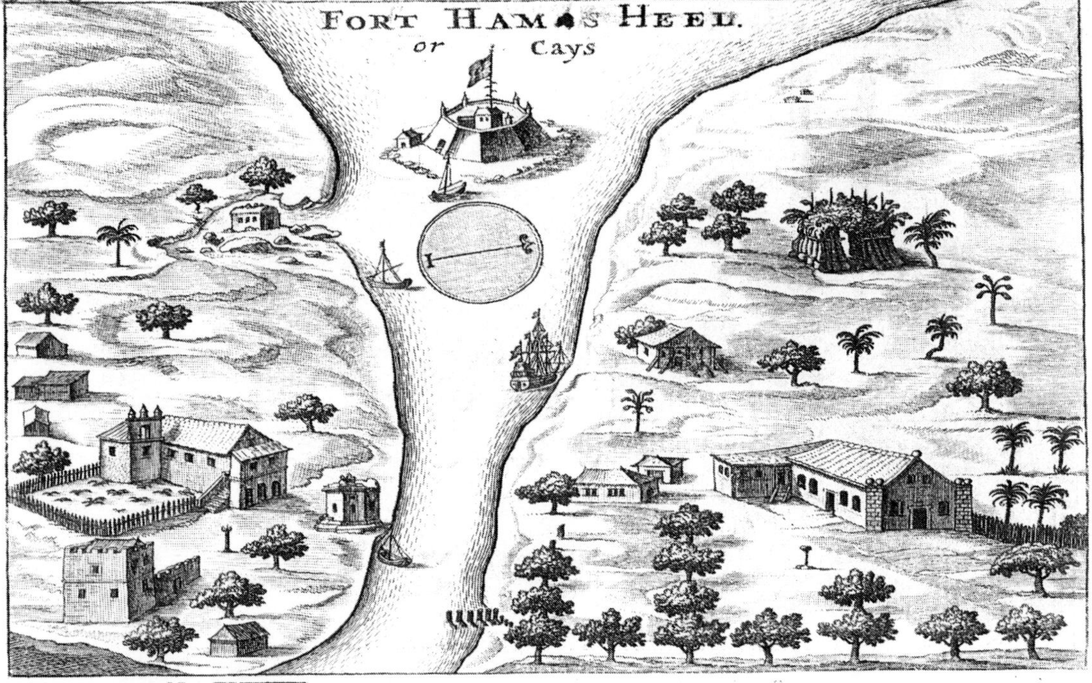

" queſtioning but that after you have " given ſufficient Proofs of your Courage, you will now conſider how unable you are to reſiſt our Force. " Don't therefore obſtinately reſiſt God's " Will, and our Strength, ſince we " offer you ſuch Conditions as are generally allow'd to brave Soldiers. " But in caſe you will be obſtinate in " making trial of our Strength, we proteſt before God and the Chriſtian " World, that we are innocent of all " the fatal Conſequences and Miſeries " that are likely to befal you; being " reſolved on our ſide (if God grants " us Victory) to treat you after the " ſevereſt manner, according to the " Cuſtom of War, and not to hearken " to any Conditions. You have given " ſufficient Proofs of your Courage to " admiration; it is time therefore you " ſhould now act with Prudence, and " conſult your ſafety. We expect your " poſitive Anſwer within three hours " by the Bearer of this, or whom " your Excellency ſhall think fit to " ſend to us, who ſhall return ſafely " upon our Word and Honour: Subſcribing my ſelf (as you think fit) " either your Friend or Enemy.

From the Camp, 10 *April* 1658.

The Admiral and General of the *Dutch* Forces, both by Sea and Land.

This Letter being tranſlated into *Portugueſe*, was ſent into the Fort; the Commander whereof remembring the old Verſe,

Fiſtula dulce canit, volucrem dum decipit auceps,

ſent the following Anſwer.

The Anſwer thereupon.

" That the Fort belonging to nobody, " but to the King of *Portugal* his Maſter, " he was oblig'd to maintain the ſame " for his Majeſty till the laſt drop of " his Blood. That he could do no " more than what pleaſed God to permit him, but neither he nor his Men " were to be terrified by Threats.

* This

REGNUM
JAFNAPATNAM,
cum
INSULIS ADJACENTIBUS.
Vol. 3. p. 797.
26.
Menes
Septentrio
Oriens
Occidens
WANNJAS PROUJN CJÆ PARS
Chette Cou lang.
Peringali
Manaer Insula
Manaers kil
Tellemanaer
Pieters kerk
Adams brugh
Hoorn
Enckhuysen
Delft
Middelburgh
I. Bramines
I. Dona Clara
Iª Deserta
Leyden
Jafnapatnam
Colombourt
Calmone
Palicoura
Passod Catchay
Pomery
Patiarapalli
JAFNAPATNAM REGN.
Provincia
Tenmarache Provincia
Billegam patte
Waddemarache Provincia
I. Amsterdam Olim I. Caradiva
Moelea Willypatte
Duytsche mylen
Spaensche Leagues
Eng and French Leagues

This bold Answer made us think of nothing else but Force, so that we were preparing every thing for an Assault, which would have cost us many a brave Fellow, had not the want of Fresh Water in the Fort oblig'd them to come to a Capitulation. For having no other fresh Water in the Fort, but what was preserved in a large Wooden Cistern, part whereof was taken away by the Ships, that transported some Women of Quality with their Riches from *Jafnapatnam* to *Negapatnam*, and the rest being spoil'd by our Bombs, they were glad to accept such Articles as we were willing to give them, which however were very honourable, the Soldiers being allow'd to march out with all the Marks of Honour, and to be transported into *Europe*. The Commander who had a Wife and Children, was permitted to go to the *Indian* Coast, or that of *Coromandel*. The 28*th* of *April* I preach'd the Thanksgiving-Sermon for this Surrender, upon the Text out of the 48*th Psalm*, *ver.* 8. Upon this Occasion Captain *Cornelius Rob* the younger (who died two Years after at *Amsterdam*) Captain *Peter Wash* (who was kill'd afterwards before *Cochin*) and Mr. *Van der Rheede*, gave most signal Proofs of their Courage. Since that time divers Vaults for fresh Water have been made in this Fort and in *Manaar*.

Baldæus. The Fort surrendred.

CHAP. XLV.

Continuation of the Siege of Jafnapatnam. *Sea-fight before* Goa. *Divers Engagements betwixt the* Dutch *and* Portugueses. Jafnapatnam *surrendred. Some* Portugueses *living among the* Hollanders *there plot against them, are betrayed by a* Topas. *The Provinces and Churches of* Jafnapatnam.

Strength of the Castle of Jafnapatnam.

But it is time to return to the Castle of *Jafnapatnam*, which being built upon a Rock, and surrounded with a strong triple Wall, seem'd to defy both our Mines and Cannon, especially since we were not so well provided with Gunpowder as we should have been; wherefore we thought it our safest way to expect that from Time, which Force was not likely to procure, resolving in the mean while to annoy the Enemy as much as possibly we could with our Bombs, which kill'd them abundance of Men.

The Portugueses endeavour in vain to fetch Provisions.

The Enemy finding themselves in a little time reduc'd to great Straits, sent out divers Boats to fetch some fresh Provisions from the Islands, but were always forc'd to return without Success. Upon this occasion *Ysbrand Gotskens* born at the *Hague*, then Director of the Company in *Persia*, and *Barent Clebont*, then a Lieutenant, since a Captain at *Jafnapatnam*, behaved themselves bravely, being both wounded, one near the Mouth, the other in the Knee.

A Topas comes over to us with a Letter.

The *Portugueses* in the mean while living in hopes of Succours from *Goa*, sent a Letter by a certain *Topas* from *Trinquemale*, named *Ignatio Feras*, to their Admiral; but this Negro coming over to us with the Letter, we sent a good Body of our best Forces to prevent their Landing, but we heard of none.

The Dutch worst the Portugueses at Sea.

On the other hand we received the joyful News, that Commodore *Adrian Roothaus*, had *March* 23. in an Engagement with the *Portugueses* near *Goa*, burnt one of their biggest Galeons call'd the St. *Thomas*, and had so disabled the rest, that they had but little hopes left of relieving *Jafnapatnam*. For which Victory we gave publick Thanks to God the 26*th* of *May* 1658. the Text was taken out of *Exod.* 15. 9.

Several Sea-Engagements betwixt them.

About the same time I received a Letter from the Reverend *Theodoro Sas* (since Minister at *Malacca*) then in the *Dutch* Fleet before *Goa*, intimating that the 20*th* of *Jan.* in the same Year 1658. the *Portugueses* attack'd us with 10 Galeons and some Frigats; the Engagements lasted till Night without any considerable Damage on our side. That on the 27*th* and 29*th* of the same Month another Combat ensued, without any great Loss on both sides. The 3*d* of *Febr.* the Enemy attack'd us once more, but were chased under their Castle. In all these three Engagements the *Dutch* had no more than 9 Men killed and a few wounded. The Letter was dated aboard the *Phenix*, cruising before the Bar of *Goa*, *Febr.* 11. 1658.

In the mean while our Forces having so closely surrounded the Castle of *Jafnapatnam* with their Lines and Works, that they

Baldæus. they could not stir even with the least Boat, without being taken or sunk; and being now destitute of all hopes of Relief, they hung out the white Flag, *June* 21. on the South East Bastion. The Capitulation was agreed upon the next following Day, under these Conditions: That the Garison should march out with their Arms, Colours flying, Drums beating, *&c.* and take along with them one piece of Cannon, and to be transported to *Europe*; the Head Officers shall be civilly treated, and to be conducted to one or other of their Forts, and the Ecclesiasticks to the Coast of *Coromandel.* All Gold, Silver and other Precious Moveables, shall be left to the Disposal of the Conquerors; the Inhabitants shall likewise be transported to what part of the *Indies* they like best, most of whom went afterwards by the way of *Malacca* to *Batavia.*

Jafnapatnam *surrendred.*

The Conditions.

They march out.

Accordingly *John de Melo Leonardo d' Oliveiro, Viador de Fazendas*, and *Anthonio Mendes d' Aranha* march'd out of the Castle with the rest of the Head Officers, *Rodrigo Boralho* delivering the Keys at the same time to Major *John van der Laan*; but they were so weak, that they did not think fit to carry along with them their piece of Cannon, tho they spent two whole days in marching out. A considerable Number of Soldiers laid down their Arms and Colours before the Standard of the Company, as did many of the Inhabitants (among whom was *Caspar Figeiro* the Scourge of the *Cingaleses)* with their Wives and Children, Negroes, 40 or 50 Ecclesiasticks, *Franciscans, Jesuits*, and *Dominicans*; notwithstanding that during the Siege (which lasted 3½ Months) they had lost near 1600 Men by the Sword and Mortality.

Immediately after Commodore *Peter de Bitter* was sent to *Batavia*, by the way of *Malacca*, to bring this joyful News to Mr. *John Maatzuyker* our General, and the Council of the *Indies.* The 23*d* of *Jun.* I preach'd a Thanksgiving-Sermon out of *Exod.* 17. 15. which was continued every Year on the same Day.

When we entred the Castle, we found it all battered to pieces by our Bombs; and such was the stench, that for sometime no body could abide there. We took care to have the Springs clear'd, the Dung removed, the Churches, Houses and Walls repair'd; 300 Coco-Trees were also to be planted, and many Houses, that stood too near the Ditch of the Castle, to be broken down; and to encourage the Inhabitants of the Country to settle here, the Custom upon Tobacco was taken off, and *Jacob Rhee* our Head Factor, a very understanding Person, constituted *pro tempore* Commander in Chief here.

The Castle repaired.

Things being thus disposed, our Forces were soon after transported to the Coast of *Coromandel*, in order to reduce the City of *Negapatnam*: We left but a slender Garison at *Jafnapatnam*, compos'd for the most part of *Portugueses*, who had taken Service among us; besides which there was a considerable Number of Prisoners in the Castle.

A treacherous Design formed against the Dutch at Jafnapatnam.

These in conjunction with some of the Natives (not without the Consent of *Raja Singa)* fram'd a Plot against us: Their Design was, to murder all the Officers in the Castle, whilst I was preaching in *Portuguese* in the City; which done, certain Persons of their Gang should attack and kill the Guard, and thus to make themselves Masters of the Castle.

It happen'd by accident that whilst I was preaching, *Don Manoel Andrado*, one of our *Cingalese* Captains and *Modliar*, coming with 18 of his Followers (who generally attended him) to the Church, remain'd in the Porch, where he could hear as well as within the Church. He was not a little surpriz'd (as he himself told me afterwards) to see the *Portugueses* remain standing likewise without the Church-door, and laying their Hands upon their Swords; yet not being able to guess the true reason thereof, this Treachery was not discover'd till some days after, when the whole Design being laid open to Mr. *Jacob van der Rhee*, he took care to double the Guards, to shut the Castle-gates, and to secure all such as had a hand in the Plot. The next thing was to send for me by a Letter (I being then visiting the Churches in the Country) upon the receipt whereof I return'd immediately to the Castle, where with great Astonishment I had an account given me of the whole Design, how it had been discover'd, and the Traytors secured. For which Delivery I preach'd a solemn Thanksgiving-Sermon in *Low-Dutch*, the 15*th* of *Septemb.* 1658. out of the Book of *Esther, Chap.* 9. 20——24.

Is discovered.

Not long after most of the Traitors having confessed their Crimes, some were condemn'd to be hang'd, others to be beheaded, and some to be laid upon the Wheel. The three chief Heads of this Conspiracy were, a certain Inhabitant of *Manaar*, one *Don Louys*, and another *Portuguese*; these three were laid upon the Wheel or a Cross, and after they had received

Baldæus.

The Traytors exeted. ceiv'd a Stroke with the Ax in the Neck and on the Breast, had their Entrails taken out, and the Heart laid upon the Mouth.

A certain Jesuit nam'd *Caldero*, a Native of *Malacca*, was beheaded. This unfortunate Person being prevented by Sickness from going along with the rest of the *Portuguese* Clergymen, had not been concern'd in this treacherous Design, much less given his Consent to it. But some of the Traytors having given notice thereof to him by Letters, wherein they stiled him the *Father of their Souls*; he was unwilling to betray his Countrymen, for which he paid now with his Head: eleven more were hanged, and afterwards exposed in the open Country on Trees; but the Heads of the Ringleaders were fix'd upon Poles in the Market-place.

The Castle of *Jasnapatnam* is of a Quadrangular Figure, and strongly fortified with very high and thick Walls; it is bigger in Circuit than the Castle of *Batavia*, being the Capital City of the whole Kingdom. *Philippo de Olivero*, after having defeated the *Cingaleses* near *Achiavelli*, not far from the great *Pagode* (the Ruins whereof are to be seen to this day) took the same from the Emperor of *Ceylon*. *The Portugeses conquer Jasnapatnam.* Hard by this *Pagode* is to be seen a most miraculous Spring, 24 Rods in Circumference, cut out of an entire Rock, or, as the Inhabitants will have it, open'd by a Thunderbolt, of which more hereafter, when we shall treat of the Isles of *Jasnapatnam*: *A miraculous Spring.* we took it after it had been 40 Years in the possession of the *Portugueses*.

Bigness of Jasnapatnam. *Jasnapatnam* is divided into four Provinces, which are very populous; its whole Length is about 6 *German* Leagues, and its Breadth 3, being well inhabited and adorned with Villages and Churches. The whole Number of the Villages amounts to 159, of their own Churches 34, besides the *Dutch* and *Portuguese* Churches. *Jasnapatnam* is on the Northside wash'd by the Gulph of *Bengale*, and borders to the South of a River, which makes it a kind of an Island, and exonerates it self in two different Channels into the Sea.

Provinces of Jasnapatnam. The Provinces of *Jasnapatnam* are *Belligamme*, *Tenmarache*, *Waddemarache* and

Baldæus. *The Church Telipole.* and *Patchiarapalle.* The Province of *Belligamme* has 14 Churches, the chief whereof is *Telipole* a large Structure, with a double row of Pillars; the House thereunto belonging is the Work of the Jesuits, beautifyed with a pleasant Garden, handsome Court and most delicious Vineyards, affording most sorts of *Indian* Fruits, and water'd with several Springs.

In *August* 1658, the Reform'd Religion was the first time (as in all other Churches of *Jafnapatnam* and *Manaar*) introduced and taught here by me. The 12*th* of *Jan.* 1661. the holy Sacrament was the first time administred to 12 Communicants of the Natives. The 19*th* of *April* in the same Year their Number encreased to 15, and before my Departure to 30. In the Year 1665, we had above 1000 Schoolboys, among whom were 480 who could answer all the Questions relating to the chief Points of our Religion. I have sometimes had no less than 2000 Auditors in this Church. *The Sacrament first administred to the Indians here.*

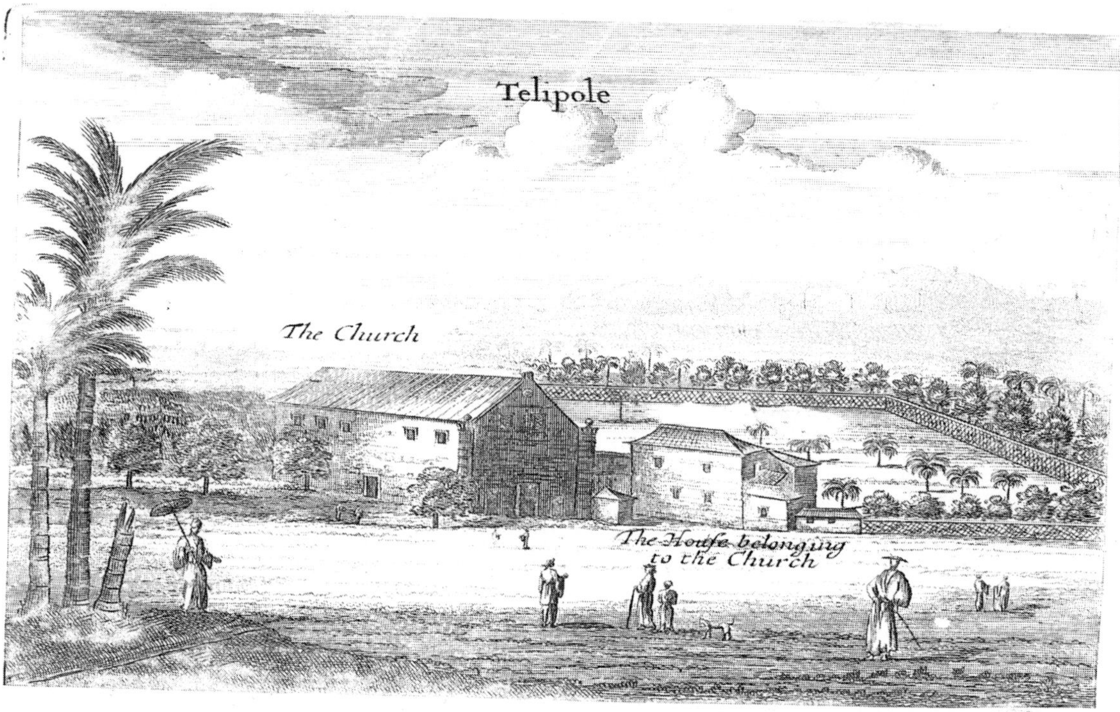

A certain *Indian* named *Michael Fonseca*, ask'd me once a very odd Question, *viz. When* John *baptized Christ, whether he baptized him in the Name of God the Father, the Son and the Holy Ghost*; and being answer'd *Yes*, he reply'd that thus *Jesus Christ* was baptiz'd in his own Name, which he could not well comprehend. I told him, there was not the least Absurdity in the matter, since *Jesus Christ* was not baptized upon his own account, or as God alone, nor as a bare Man, but as being endowed both with the Divine and Human Nature. That the *Son of God* could not be baptized otherwise but in the Name of God; and that under the Word *God*, was not only comprehended the *Father*, but also the *Son* and *Holy Ghost*; that *Jesus Christ* was the same in essence with the Father and the Holy Ghost; and that there were no degrees in the *Deity*, for tho the *Father* was the first, yet were the Son as well and truly *God* as the *Father* and *Holy Ghost*: wherewith he was well satisfy'd. For the *Indians* being generally very ingenious, they will ask many acute Questions, as concerning the *Creation and End of the World, the Immortality of the Soul, Hell*, and such like.

Most of the Churches here have certain Scaffolds or Theaters near them, especially *Theaters near the Churches.*

Mallagam .
The House belonging to ye Church
The Church

Mayletti .
The Church
The Church House

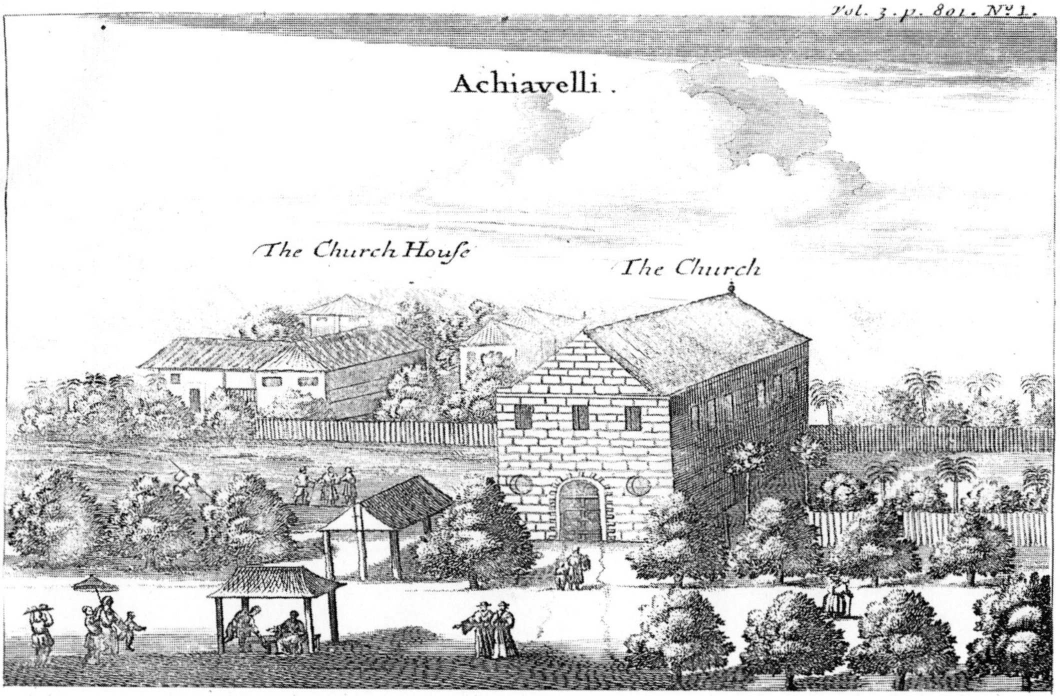
Achiavelli.
The Church House
The Church

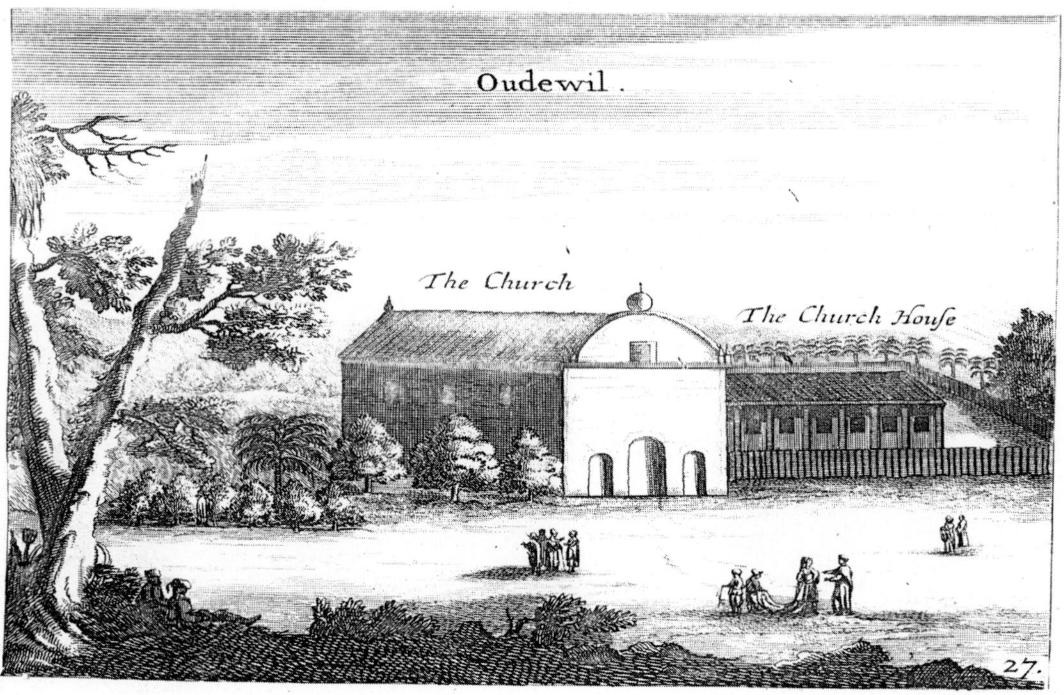
Oudewil.
The Church
The Church House
27.

pecially that of *Telipole*, where the Jesuits used to represent certain Histories of the Bible to the People on Holidays.

The Church Mallagam. About half an Hour thence stands the Church *Mallagam* of good Brickwork, with an adjacent House built upon two Arches, and a handsom pair of Stairs leading to the top of it. The Church was begun by the *Portugueses*, but finish'd by the *Dutch*. It has 200 School-boys, but not above 600 Auditors.

The Church Mayletti. The Church *Mayletti* is about 5 Quarters of an Hour from *Telipole*. Here are 750 Schoolboys, all taught by one Master, who has more work than the two at *Telipole*: the Auditors of this Church amount to 1500 or 1600. The Church is a large Structure of Stone; the House belonging to it is lofty, with a Balcony on the top of it, affording a very fine Prospect into the main Sea, so that it may well deserve the Name of *Belle videre*. The Church is not above half a Mile from the Sea-side. They abound here in Fish, such as Crabs, Soles, Plaice, *&c.* as likewise in Hares and Partridges.

Church Achiavelli. The Church *Achiavelli* lies about two Hours from *Telipole*, it is a large and lofty Structure built of Stone, capable of containing 2000 Persons; it was not finish'd till in our time. The Village lies extremely pleasant among the Woods, stor'd with vast Quantities of Turtle-Doves, which cue at certain Hours three times a day, and serve the Inhabitants instead of a Clock, to know the time of the Day. They have also Plenty of Hares, Stags and Wild-Boars, but are also annoyed by the Serpents. *Baldæus.* *Pleasantness of the Village.*

As divers old *Brahmans* live in this Place, so were the Inhabitants not so forward in embracing the Christian Religion; the antient *Brahman*, named *Philippo*, does not want the Knowledg of the Fundamentals of our Religion, but is more inclin'd to the Historical, than the Doctrinal part. Among others there lived here a certain *Brahman*, a Learned Person, with whom I used to have frequent Conversation, whilst I liv'd at *Achiavelli*; he was baptized at last in the *46th* Year of his Age, and afterwards writ the *History of the Life and Passion of our Saviour*, in a lofty Poetical Stile, in the *Latin Malabar*, call'd *Hanscreet*, which is quite different from the common *Mala-*

Baldæus.

bar Characters. The School here has about 4 or 500 Boys, and the Church 7, 8 or 900 Auditors.

The Church Ondewil. About an Hour from *Telipole* stands the Church *Ondewil*, in a great Plain, with an adjacent large Stone-house, formerly the Habitation of a *Franciscan* Fryar. The Soil is very luscious here and fertile in Rice, *Naceny*, and other Eatables. The Schoolboys amount to 600, and the Auditors to 900 or 1000.

The Church Batecotte. Two hours distant from the Castle is the Church *Batecotte*, with a lofty adjacent House, flat on the top, and adorn'd with a pleasant Garden, well stor'd with Trees; the Fields round about it are extremely fruitful. It is seated near the *Salt River*, and abounds in Fish and all manner of other Provisions. Of Schoolboys they have here about 8 or 900, and of Auditors in the Church near 2000.

The Church Paneteripou. About half an hour from *Batecotte* is the Church *Paneteripou*, a neat and magnificent Edifice of Stone, with a pleasant House near it built upon Arches, with two spacious Rooms and a Gallery, fine Gardens, and a delicious Fishpond or Cistern. The School is frequented by 600 Boys, who in my time had made such considerable Progress, that they could refute the *Popish* Errors concerning Purgatory, the Mass, Indulgences, Auricular Confession, &c. Mr. *Andrew* the Schoolmaster and his Usher, being Persons very diligent in their Stations. The Inhabitants are very devout here, and at Sermon-time seldom less than 12 or 1300 come to Church.

The Church Changane. The Church *Changane* is not above a good Mile from *Paneteripou*, lying with this and *Batecotte* in a Triangle, almost at an equal distance from one another. Both the Church and adjacent House are built of Stone, as is also *Paneteripou*: They are very conveniently built with a Court before, surrounded by a Brick Wall; behind is an Orchard of *Cocoe* and *Portuguese* Fig-Trees, besides *Potatoes*, *Bananaes*, &c. The School is frequented by 700 Boys, who are carefully instructed by their Schoolmaster nam'd *Ambrosio*. The Inhabitants flock to Church with so much Zeal, that there is scarce room to contain them all.

The Church Manipay. Two hours from *Jafnapatnam*, and one from *Changane*, stands the Church *Ma-*

nipay,

Paneteripou
The Church
The Church house

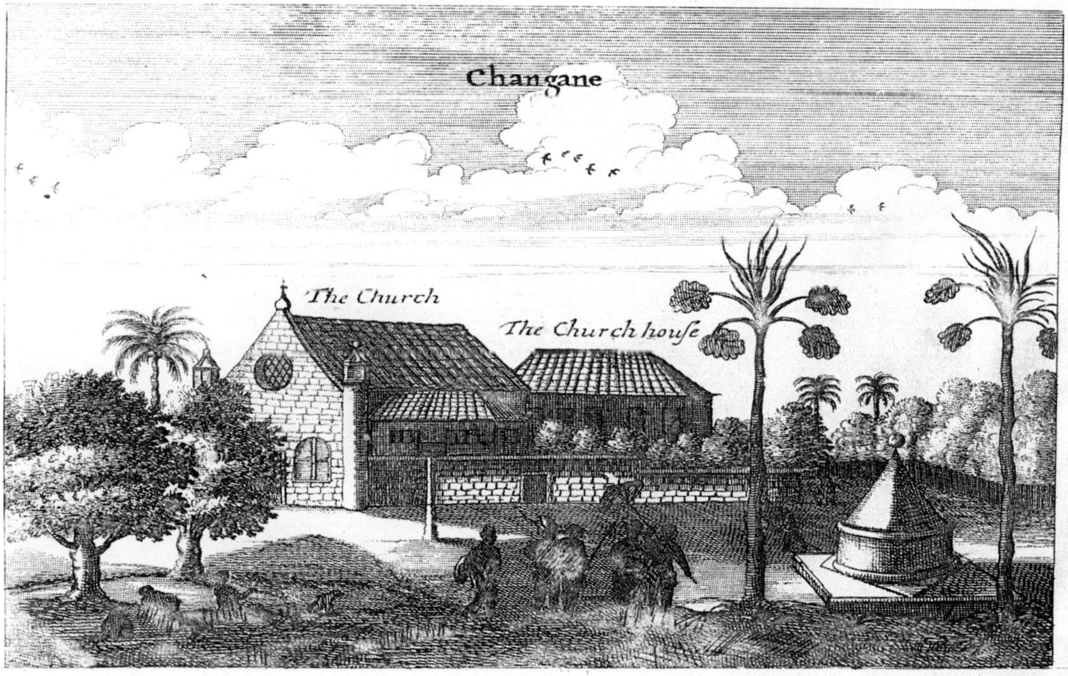
Changane
The Church
The Church house

Manipay
The Church
The Church house

Vanarpone
The Church
28.

Baldæus.

nipay. About 560 Children are educated in this School. It is scarce to be imagined, that at so small a distance there should be so great a difference betwixt the People, the Inhabitants here being a malicious Generation, superstitious, and still much inclin'd to Paganism. The Church is big enough to contain 2000 Souls, but seldom above 7 or 800 come to hear the Sermons. The House is built only of Clay, and cover'd with Palm-tree-Leaves. Just before the Church is a fine Pond or Cistern with fresh Water, near which stood formerly one of their *Pagodes*. This Place is inhabited by several of the Family of *Madapoli*, who were concern'd in the Plot (lately mention'd) with *Don Louys*.

The Church Vanarpone.

The Church *Vanarpone* stands just under the Castle of *Jafnapatnam*, most inhabited by Washers; *Vanar* signifying as much as a Washer in the *Malabar*. It is not very big, nor has a House belonging to it. The Schoolboys amount to 200, and the Auditors in the Church to about 5 or 600 Souls.

The Church Nalour.

Just by *Vanarpone* is the Church *Nalour*, built only of Clay, and slenderly cover'd. Here also stood formerly a *Pagode*. The School is frequented by about 590 Children, who are not so well versed in the Points of the Christian Religion as most of the rest, the People here retaining still a strong Inclination to Paganism, especially since some Years ago about 100 Printers of Callicoes were transplanted hither from the Coast of *Coromandel*, to the no small Prejudice of the Christian Religion, tho the Company were no great Gainers by it; since it is evident, that for want of good Water at *Jafnapatnam*, the same can't be brought to their true Perfection, and therefore are much better bought and transported from the Coast of *Coromandel*.

This is certain, that this Generation is very mischievous to the Christians here, it being frequent to see them appear in publick painted with *Cinza* or Ashes (accounted holy among them) and to carry their Beads; besides that the *Moors* have their publick Schools allow'd them of late Years. I must confess that whilst Mr. *Anthony Pavilioen* (at the time of my being there) was Governor of *Jafnapatnam*, he did all in him lay to assist me (at

*

 my

Baldæus. my request) in stopping the Progress of the Pagan Superstitions, and was not well pleased to see the Callico Printers introduc'd here, it being (not without reason) to be fear'd that in time they may (by promiscuous Marriages) increase to such a number as may endanger both the Church and State, especially if they are allowed the burning of their Dead, and some other Pagan Ceremonies they much insist upon.

It is further to be fear'd, that in time there may be a promiscuous Copulation betwixt the Christians and Pagans, which must needs produce direful Effects in the Church. It may be objected, that severe Punishments will put a stop to that Evil (some having already been punish'd with Death upon that account) but this does not altogether remove the Danger; besides, that it ought to be consider'd whether such a Severity be consonant to the Word of God or not.

The Church Sundecouli. The last Church not far from the City, is call'd *Sundecouli*, belonging to the *Civias*, or Chair-men and Water-Carriers. The Church is a neat Structure, but the Inhabitants an idle and base Generation. About 450 Children belong to the School, but seldom frequent it, because they generally go abroad a fishing with their Parents. Seldom above 400 come to Church, whereas there are about 1500 Inhabitants. It is a pleasant place, deliciously seated among Trees of a considerable bigness. Thus far we have spoken of the Province *Belligamme*, and its Churches, unto which belong likewise *Copay* and *Pontour*, containing about 800 School-boys, and 2000 Souls. The Children in these Schools are distinguish'd into several Forms, according to their respective degrees of Proficiency; so that those who have learn'd (for instance) the *Creed*, and *Our Father*, teach those that scarce know to say *Our Father*. Among these Boys, they have some they call *Merinhos*, who take an account of such as are absent, and return them to the Master, or the Head *Merinho*.

CHAP. XLVI.

The second, third and fourth Provinces, with their respective Churches, belonging to Jafnapatnam. *The Isles of* Jafnapatnam. *Vast number of Christians. The Author's Zeal in promoting the Christian Religion.*

THE second Province of *Jafnapatnam* is *Tenmarache*, which contains five Churches, with the Villages thereunto belonging. The first is the Church *Navacouli*, seated in a pleasant Plain abounding in Cattel and Fruit; as the Woods afford great store of Apes and Monkys, and all sorts of Venison and Wild Fowl. Both the Church and adjacent House are only of Clay, and cover'd with Palm-leaves. The School is frequented by 400 Children, and the Church by 7 or 800 Auditors.

The Church Navacouli.

The Church of Chavagatzery. An hour from *Navacouli* stands the Church of *Chavagatzery*, the biggest of the whole Province, and the adjacent House, very strong and well-built, having a pleasant Prospect towards the Sea, with fine Gardens, well stor'd with all sorts of *Indian* Fruits. They abound in Fish, for they live upon Husbandry and Fishing. The School is frequented by 1000 Children, who are instructed by two Masters and an Usher, and the Church by betwixt 2 and 3000 Souls.

The Church Cathay. The Church *Cathay* is an hour from *Chavagatzery*, through sandy and difficult Ways, but full of Ponds stor'd with Wild-ducks; besides which they abound in Snipes, Herns, *Indian* Ravens, and all sorts of small Birds. The Church and House are only of Clay, and cover'd with Leaves, like that of *Navacouli*. The School has 550 Children, and the Church 11 or 1200 Auditors.

The Church Waranni. Betwixt *Cathay* and the Church *Waranni* are sandy and difficult Ways. The Church stands in the midst of a small Wood of *Areek*, *Coco*, *Palm*, *Banano's*, *Mango's*, *Cajou* and *Guiavo*-Trees. This place affords, besides the ordinary Melons, the most delicious Water-Melons in the *Indies*. The Church is but slenderly built, and enclosed with a Wall of Earth, as is likewise the House; yet has it divers spacious Apartments, and a handsome Entrance. The School has about 800 Children, and the Church 2500 Auditors.

The Church Illondi Matual. The last Church of *Tenmarache* is that of *Illondi Matual*, unto which belongs the Village of *Nagar Kojel*, famous for a large *Pagode* that stood there formerly. The Church is only of Clay, but the adja-

Kopay
The Church
The Church House

Navacouli
The Church House
The Church

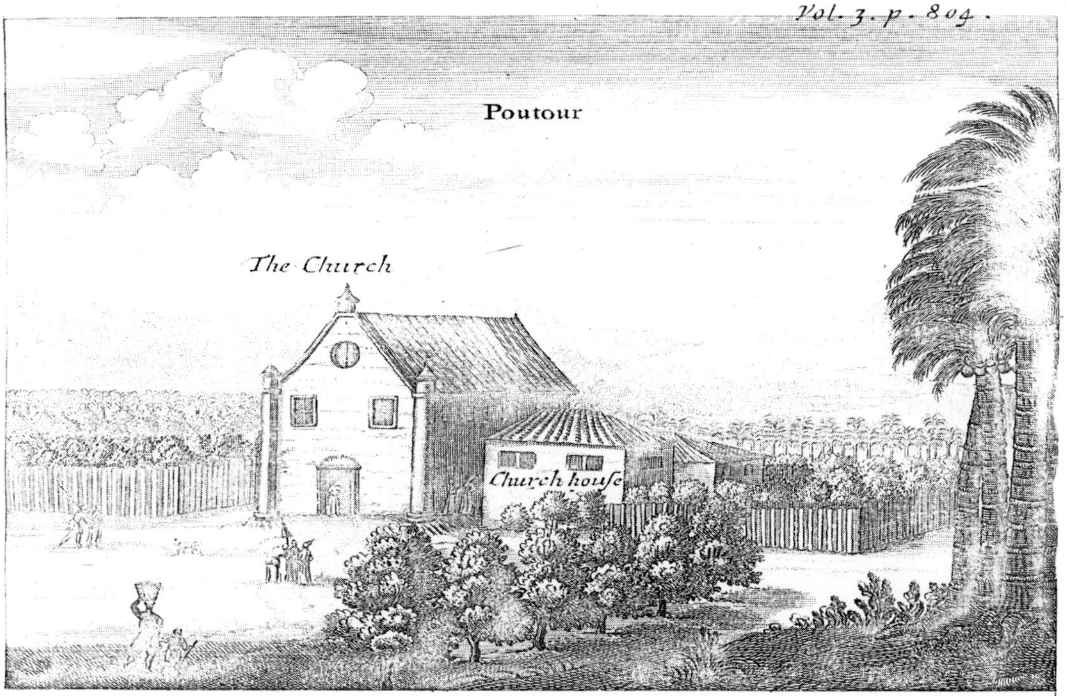
Poutour
The Church
Church house

Chavagatzeri
The Church
The Church House

29.

Cathay
The Church house
The Church

Waranni
The Church
The House

Baldæus. adjacent House of Stone, unto which you ascend by steps; it has three large Apartments, a neat Entrance, and a fair Prospect. Hereabouts are great numbers of Peacocks, and sometimes they see some Elephants in this Tract of Land. The Company also maintains here some tame Elephants, as in divers other places, they being separated at some distance for the better conveniency of their Fodder. Unto this School belong about 650 Children, and to the Church 1100 or 1200 Auditors.

The Province Waddemarache.

The third Province is call'd *Waddemarache*, having only three Churches. It affords such plenty of Pasture, of Cows, Sheep, Goats, Fowl, Pigeons, and Partridges, that you may buy a Sheep for 8 *d.* or 10 *d.* 60 Eggs for 3 *d.* and four good Pullets for a *Fanam*, or 5 *d.*

The Church Catavelli.

The first Church is call'd *Catavelli*; the Church and adjacent House are both of Brick, the last having a Summer-house on the top of it, from whence you have a delightful Prospect into the Plain. The School has 600 Children, and the Church 1000 or 1200 Auditors.

The second Church is *Vreputti*; the Village is inhabited by a set of Vagabonds and Thieves, of the Family of the *Nalloas*, not much inclin'd to Religion. The School is frequented by 690 Children, and the Church by 8 or 900 Auditors less or more. The Children are taught here to make their Letters in the Sand.

The Church Paretiture.

The Church *Paretiture* is the finest and largest of this Province, call'd by the *Portugueses*, *Punta das Pedras*, or the *Rocky Point*. *Paretiture* signifies in the *Malabar* Tongue as much as *Cottons Harbour*, from the great quantity of Cotton that grows thereabouts on small Trees. Not long ago, whilst we were engag'd in War with the *English*, a Fort was order'd to be erected here. During the War with *Portugal*, the *Dutch* carried off from hence one of their Priests, and plunder'd *Manaar* at the same time. Hereabouts also happen'd a smart Engagement betwixt the *Portugueses* and us, wherein we were hard put to it, and lost among others Capt. *John Hooghsaten*. During the Siege of *Jafnapatnam* the *Portugueses* expected the landing of their Succours in this place.

A smart Skirmish betwixt the Portugueses *and* Dutch *in this place.*

The Road is so good here, that Ships

A Large Tamerind tree under the shade whereof they frequently hear Sermons.

May

Illondi Matual
The Church
The House

Catavelli
The House
The Church

Ureputti
The Church
The House

Paretiture
The Church
The Church house

A good Road. may ride safe at Anchor for 7 or 8 Months, but they must take care to depart before the Northern *Mousson*, which renders this Shore very dangerous: So soon as any Ships are discover'd at Sea, a Flag is put out on a long Pole for their Direction. The Church was much decay'd, but has been repair'd of late. *Great number of Christians at* Pareticure. Just before the Church stands a tall Tamarin Tree, which affording a very agreeable Shadow in the heat of the day, the People are often instructed by the Minister to the number of 3000. The School has about 1000 Children. *Baldæus.*

The last and furthermost Province is call'd *Patchiarapalle*, which has four Churches, and as many Schools. This Province is very sandy and unwholesom, wants good Water, and is much infested by the Elephants, by reason of the vast quantity of wild Palm-Trees that grow here, and afford Food to the poorer sort of Inhabitants, tho the Elephants throw down some hundreds every year, being

The Elephants throwing down y Palm trees

The Province of Patchiarapalle *unwholesom.* very greedy after the Fruit when it comes to Maturity. At a certain season of the year the Children are seiz'd here with a certain Swelling in the Belly and Groin, which sweeps away a good number of them. They are also afflicted with certain Fevers (like those of *Manaar*) which regulate their Fits according to the Moon, and kill in a little time. The Itch and Small-pox are also very common here: The Inhabitants being very poor, and feeding most generally upon unwholesom Diet, such as dry'd Fish, *Pounates*, *Kelenges*, and a little Rice. As this Province borders upon *Raja Singa*'s Country, so they are subject to the Incursions of the *Cingaleses*, which is the reason that the House belonging to the Church of *Poelepolay* (the first in this Province) is surrounded with a high Wall with Port-holes in the nature of a Redoubt. *The Church* Poelepolay. The School has about 300 Children, and the Church 600 Auditors. Here are certain Women who have a way to play upon Earthern Vessels or Mugs (call'd *Callangs*) by blowing into them as into a Trumpet. This Province affords a kind of Wood call'd *Jagers-Wood* (or *Hunters-wood*) which for its goodness is transported to the Coast of *Coromandel*.

* Two

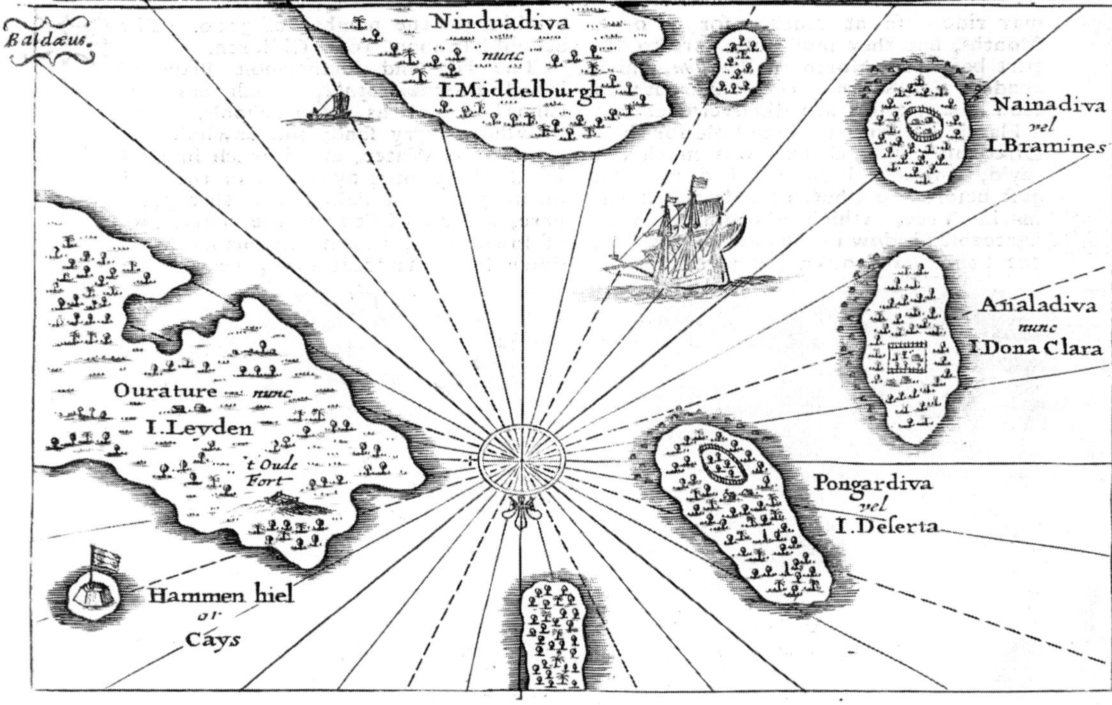

The Church Mogommale.

Two good hours from *Poelepolay* stands the Church of *Mogommale* in a Wood, with an adjacent House, both well built; the School has about 450 Children, and the Church 500 Auditors.

The Church Tambamme.

The Church *Tambamme* is the largest and best seated in the whole Province. The School has 500 Children, and the Church 900 Auditors.

The Church Mulipatto.

Mulipatto is the last Church, about a day's Journy from *Jafnapatnam*, near the Head of the River call'd *Passo Seco*, or the *Dry Passage*; where we have a *Palenka* guarded by some Soldiers. The Church-House is provided with Port-holes for its Defence, but the Church is mean and small. The School has no more than 215 Children, and the Church scarce 350 Auditors.

Thus far of *Jafnapatnam*, and its Provinces, Churches and Schools. We will now pass over into the adjacent Isles, which are six in number.

Ourature *the first Isle of* Jafnapatnam.

The first of these Isles is *Ourature*, which has three Churches, *viz. Aleputti, Wolane* and *S. John*, or *Ourature*, all which have together about 800 School-boys, and 2600 Auditors. This Isle has been subject to great Floods, both before and in the time of the *Portugueses*, to such a degree that the People were forced to save themselves on the tops of the Trees. Of this we saw an Instance in the year 1658. when a most furious Tempest, accompanied by a Hurrican, raised the Waters beyond the Shore to such a height, that it broke into the Water-Gate of the Castle, throwing down every thing that stood in the way; the Tiles were all blown from the Houses, the Trees tore up by the Roots, and unspeakable damage done both to Men and Cattle. After the fury of the Tempest was somewhat allay'd, several Fishes were taken in the Church-porch, which had been carried along with the Water over the Cortin. This Isle has plenty of Fish and Stags: It produces also a certain small Root call'd *Saye*, us'd by the Dyers to dye Red Cloths. They make also very good Butter here, and have store of Larks and some Sea-gulls.

An instance of a Flood.

The Products of this Isle.

The Isle of Caradiva.

The Isle of *Ourature* and *Caradiva* are separated by the River, in the midst whereof lies the Fort *Cays* (or *Hamsheel*) of which we have spoken before.

From

The Church Poelepoly
The House

The Church Tambamme
The House

The Church House
The Church Mogomma le.
The foot of ye Cross

The House
The Church Mulipatto.

Baldæus.

From this Isle the Elephants are embark'd by means of a Bridg, and transported to *Coromandel* and *Bengale*. This Isle is supposed to produce the best *Saye* in the *Indies*. It has a well built Church and House belonging to it of Stone; the Church was finish'd in my time, as was that of *Ourature*, which was set on fire by the *Portugueses*. The School is frequented by 490 Children, and the Church by 1000 or 1100 Persons.

Somewhat further into the Sea to the right as you sail to the Isle *Pongardiva*, lies a little Island call'd *Ilha Deserta*, i. e. the *Desert Island*, by the *Portugueses*. This Isle as well as that of *Carativa*, abounds in Serpents, and furnishes our Ships with Fuel.

The Desert Island.

Pongardiva.

Pongardiva is a large Isle, but the Ground being rocky, produces but little for the sustenance of Mankind, except Stags, Hares and Peacocks in great quantities; they abound also in Fish, and especially in large Oisters, which are better to stew than to be eaten raw. The Men are generally much taller here than in any other part of the *Indies*. The School has 200 Children, and the Church 800 Auditors.

Analativa, *or* D.Clara.

The Isle *Analativa* is small, but produces vast plenty of Oisters. The Inhabitants of both Sexes amount to about 800, and 200 Children. It has a little Church and convenient House near it. It was formerly call'd *Donna Clara*, from a certain Lady that liv'd there, and was Mistress of it in the time of the *Portugueses*. They still shew there a Chair wherein she used to sit, which is big enough to hold conveniently two Persons at once.

Nainativa.

The Island *Nainativa* has got its Name from the great number of *Jackals* that are found there; of which more anon. It is very small, and inhabited by *Brabmans* turn'd Christians, who lead very sober Lives. The School has 70 Children, and the Church 300 Auditors. The Church is very small, yet has an adjacent House fit to lodg Strangers in.

Nindundiva, *or* Ilha das Vacas.

Nindundiva, or the *Long Isle*, from its length, which is about six Leagues, is call'd *Ilha das Vacas*, i. e. the *Cow Island*, by the *Portugueses*, because abundance of

Baldæus.

Abounds in Cattel.

Cattel are transported thither from Tonday, which makes Cattel so cheap there that you may buy a good Cow for four *Dutch* Shillings (or half a Rixdollar) but their Oxen and Cows are not near so big as those on the Continent of *Jafnapatnam*. Oftentimes a Mortality happens among the Cattel, because the Ground being hot and dry, produces divers venomous Herbs, which they feed upon. The Inhabitants are very poor, and live upon miserable Diet: I remember that being once eight days in this Isle, I and my Company could scarce get Provisions for our Sustenance. The Isle is of difficult access, because the Shore is rocky, and has no Bays, but only a few narrow Creeks, where there is no coming in except in very calm Weather; otherwise the Sea beats with such violence against the Rocks, that there is no coming near them, tho there be sometimes five or six fathom Water. For which reason there is no coming at it except in the calm Seasons, which happen twice a year at the change of the *Moussons*: For the South-wind forces you upon the Rocks, and with the North-wind the Shore is too shallow to approach it. The *Portugueses* had formerly a Fort here, the Ruins whereof are to be seen to this day. They also brought some Horses into this Isle, which multiplying in time produc'd a certain kind of Horses that are very small, but hardy and very fit to travel on stony and rocky grounds: They live in the Wilderness, and are taken by forcing them unto the Bank of a River or Pond, where they catch them in Snares or Ropes. This Isle produces also a certain kind of Goats, out of which they take Bezoar Stones, but they are none of the best. It has about 900 Inhabitants, and 170 Children.

Great Mortality among them.

A remarkable Spring.

It is very remarkable that there is no fresh Water in all this Isle, except what is found in one place among the Rocks, being above half a mile in Circuit. If we may credit the Inhabitants, these Rocks were split by a Thunderbolt, which occasion'd these Springs, some whereof have not above half a foot, others a foot deep Water: The entire Rocks arising betwixt these Springs have often cast Men and Beasts down the Precipices.

There are some other Islands near this Shore, but being very small and not inhabited (as the *Paletiva*, and the two Brothers, since call'd *Hoorn* and *Enchuysen*) are not worth our particular Observation.

Christians in the Wannias and Manaar.

In the year 1663. I and my Collegue Mr. *John à Breyl* sent the following account to Mr. *Maatzuyker*, General of the *Indies* for our Company, *viz.* That in *Jafnapatnam* were at that time 15012 Children under the Tuition of the respective School-masters there, being all Natives; not reckoning those of *Manaar* and the Country of the *Wannias*, where in my Visitation 1665. in *March* and *April*, I found in those of *Poenery*, *Polveraincatti*, *Peringale*, *Mantotte*, *Nanatam*, and *Aripou*, all Churches belonging to the *Wannias*, and in the Churches of *Manaar*, viz. *Totavalli*, *Karsel*, *Irkelampatti*, *Tellemanaar*, *Peixale*, the Fishers and City Churches, 1315 Children of the Natives. Such as were come to Age of maturity amounted in the *Wannias* to 4533, and in the Isle of *Manaar* to 3520, not including 214 Slaves lately converted, who had already learn'd certain forms of Prayers. According to the Church-Registers (call'd here *Patolas*) in the year 1663. there were of Christian Men and Women in the Kingdom of *Jafnapatnam* 62558, not including the Slaves, whereof there were 2587. The number of the baptiz'd Children from 1658, till 1661, *viz.* in three years and a half, in the Churches of *Jafnapatnam* amounted to 5799 Children, and 36 that were come to Age of Maturity. During that time were married 2158 Couples, not reckoning those baptiz'd and married in the *Low-Dutch* and *Portuguese* Churches. At the time of my departure the number of the Children in the Schools was risen to 18000, and that of the baptized Children in 1663 to 12387. From the year 1658, till 1661. the whole burden of visiting all the before-mention'd Churches lay upon my Shoulders, till Mr. *Breyl* was join'd with me, who dying in his return to *Holland* (his Corps being inter'd at the *Cape of Good Hope*) 1665. Mr. *Bartholomew Heyne* succeeded in his place.

Number of Christians in Jafnapatnam.

How the Religious Worship is perform'd.

In the Churches of *Jafnapatnam* the Ten Commandments written in large *Malabar* Characters, are hung up on a Table, on both sides whereof are the *Our Father*, and the *Creed*. Every Sunday the People come to Church about Ten a Clock, and after they have sung a Psalm, the School-master reads a Sermon in the *Malabar* Language, for which purpose a certain number of Sermons are allotted to each Church, to be read in the absence of the Minister. This done, they conclude with singing another Psalm.

But

Vol. 3. p. 810.
The Catching of Horses in Jafnapatnam.
32.

But the greatest Trouble that belongs to a Minister in these parts, is the Instruction to be given both to young and old by way of mouth, which is best done by way of Question and Answer, which makes the deepest Impression into the Minds of these tender Christians. Besides, as the *Malabar* Tongue is so difficult to attain to, that none of our Ministers dare pretend to the Perfection of it; so on the other hand, they may learn without much trouble, as much as is requisite for the instructing them in the main Points of our Religion. Add to this, that our Ministers undergo much more Fatigue in their Stations than the *Romish* Ecclesiasticks, who preach very seldom; and each Church having its peculiar Attendant, they are not oblig'd to travel from place to place as we do. Besides, that they bring the *Portuguese* Language commonly along with them, which ours are forc'd to learn upon the spot, not without great difficulty; not to mention several other Disadvantages on our side, sufficient to convince those who extol the Merits of the *Romish* Clergy upon that score, and vilify ours: these I would have consider, that at this time there are no more than two or three Ministers belonging to all these Churches, which had no less than forty in the time of the *Portugueses*; and we have three Sermons every Sunday, and one in the Week; besides the constant Visitations of the Churches in the Country.

The Dutch *Ministers in the* Indies *undergo more Difficulties than the* Romanists.

Before my departure, I took care to have the next following Pieces translated (the same being revis'd by me before) out of the *Portuguese* into the *Malabar*, by *Francis de Fonseca*, a Member of the Reform'd Churches.

" The Gospel of St. *Matthew*. The " Lesser Catechism. Instructions for " Communicants. Questions and Answers out of the New Testament. " Short Questions and Answers concerning the chief Matters contain'd in the " Old Testament. (This was not quite perfected at the time of my departure.) " Consolations for the Sick. Formulary " of Baptism, both for Children and others. Morning and Evening Prayers, " as also Devotions to be used both before " and after Sermons, and before and after " Meals. Prayers for Rain and a fruitful " Season. Thanksgivings on account of " Victories obtain'd against our Enemies. " Prayers to be us'd in the Army before an " Engagement. Prayers for Criminals " before Execution. Formulary and Prayers of Marriage. Some Psalms of " *David* set in Metre after the *Malabar* " fashion. Some Sermons, *viz.* upon the " Nativity of Christ, upon his Passion, and " Death, Resurrection and Ascension; " upon the sending of the Holy Ghost, " the Circumcision of our Saviour, the " History of the Wise Men of the East, " the Resurrection and Day of last Judgment; upon Charity due from one " Christian to another, out of *Luke* 10. " Who is our Neighbour? the rejoycing " of the Angels in Heaven for the Conversion of a Sinner, upon the Question " of the Pharisees, *Mat.* 12. *v.* 38. and " such like.

Baldæus.

I had abundance of other Sermons by me in the *Portuguese* Language, but for want of a good Interpreter (whom I mention'd before, having his hands full with the rest) the same was fain to be defer'd till another opportunity, tho at the same time I never thought it convenient to overcharge these People with many Books, pursuant to the Opinion of Mr. *John Maatzuyker* our General, in his Letter sent to me from *Batavia*, Sept. 18. 1662.

" I Could not without an extreme Satisfaction understand the happy Condition of the Churches in *Jafnapatnam*, and the Effects of your Industry. " God Almighty bless your Endeavours " and Zeal to the honour of his holy " Name, and the Salvation of many " thousand Souls. Being in great want " of Books for the Churches and Schools " of this Country, it is impossible to " gratify your desire, especially since " many of these Books are very ill manag'd by some People. I hope you are " pretty well provided by this time, " that your good Intentions may not be " disappointed for want of them. Tho " in my opinion Reading and Writing are " things not so absolutely necessary for the " Edification of these poor Wretches, as " that they may be instructed in the " Fundamentals of Religion, which consists in few Points. For in case we " pretend to propagate Christianity by " reading and writing, I am afraid it " will prove both tedious and chargeable " to the Company. To promote this " holy Work we have sent three Ministers, whereof two are gone with the " Ships to *Malabar*, and the third is lately arriv'd with the Yacht the *Achilles*: " they are all three young Men, and " not long ago came from *Holland*, and " consequently most likely to do considerable Service for a long time, provi-

Baldæus. " ded they are indued with due Zeal, as " I hope they are, for the benefit of the " Isle of *Ceylon*, and the places there- " unto belonging. We have also sent a " Minister to *Negapatnam*: so recom- " mending you to the Protection of " Almighty God, I rest

From the Castle of *Batavia* 18 Sept. 1662.

Your affectionate Friend,

John Maatzuyker.

CHAP. XLVII.

The Nature and Qualifications of the Inhabitants of Jafnapatnam. *The* Bellales, *and their manner of living. The* Brahmans, *their Doctrines shewn and refuted.*

Qualifications of the Inhabitants of Jafnapatnam.

IT is time to say some thing of the Inhabitants of *Jafnapatnam*; which done, we will return to *Batecalo*, and so leaving the Isle we will turn our selves another way.

In *Ceylon* are divers Clans, or Families, as well as on the Coast of *Coromandel*. The Generation of the *Bellales* is the chiefest here since Christianity has been introduc'd, the *Brahmans* challenging the first rank among the Pagans.

The Habit of the Bellales.

The *Bellales* wear a kind of Garment from above the Navel, turning betwixt the Legs like a pair of Drawers. They also make use of *Seripous* (or Soles) tied to the bottom of the feet with Leather Straps, the upper part of the feet being bare, to prevent their sweating. Upon the Belly they have a kind of a Bag (call'd *Maddi*) being part of their Garment roll'd together, wherein they keep their *Areek* and *Betel*, and some Paper to make use of upon occasion. On the right side they carry a kind of a Knife in a Sheaf, and an Iron Pen pointed with Silver, as is likewise the Sheath, in which they keep also a piece of Steel to sharpen their Knife upon. They make holes in their Ears from their Infancy, which being adorn'd with Golden Pendants, draw them down to their Shoulders. They live upon Husbandry, and are rich in Cattel, such as Cows, Oxen for the Plow, Sheep, Goats and Bufflers. Their Habitations are both convenient and neat, with pleasant Gardens, well planted with *Betel*, and furnish'd with excellent Springs, which furnish them (during the dry Summer Season) with Water for the watering of the Gardens. Their Harvest is in *January* and *February*; their Winter, or rainy Season being in *November* and *December*. In some places, *viz.* in the low marshy Grounds, they have Harvest twice a year: They thresh their Corn (after the manner of the *Israelites*) with Oxen, not muffled; these tread the Seed out of the Ears.

Are rich in Cattel.

Their manner of threshing the Corn.

During the rainy Season it rains with such violence, that the Fields are all overflown; and I remember that in my time a considerable part of the *Cortin* of the Castle was wash'd away by the Rains. This continues for two months, and it happens oftentimes, that for eight months after it rains not above three times, which is the reason that they are oblig'd even to water the Coco-Trees till they are six years old. If you dig about two foot deep you meet with rocky ground, so that if you will have a Spring you must cut them out of the Rocks with vast Charge.

Great Rains.

The Ground rocky.

The before-mention'd *Bellales* make likewise Butter, but not after the same manner as we do in *Holland*. They take a kind of a Mill made like a Star at the bottom, this they roll betwixt both hands (as we do with our Chocolate) till the Butter comes. Some of our *Dutch* Women make also good Cheese, but it is not regarded among the Inhabitants; but Butter is in great esteem among them as well as among the *Moors*, nay the Family of *Commety* use Butter like Drink. Milk turn'd to Curds (call'd by them *Tayr*) is also in great request with them, and used like a cooling Medicine in Fevers, and the Small-Pox, which are very frequent here.

Their way of making Butter.

Their Cattel they keep both day and night in the Field, tho towards night they drive them into a certain Enclosure: They are never hous'd in the Winter, but feed in the Grounds where the Corn first sprouts forth, and afterwards are fed with Hay till Harvest time. If the Cattel happen to break into a Neighbour's Field, the Owner is oblig'd to make good the Damage. The *Bellales* are generally the richest of the Country; they don't marry except in their own Family, and com-

How they manage their Cattel.

commonly in the Spring; as the *Romans* did formerly in *May*, and the *Persians* in the Spring: if it happens to be a fruitful Year, they are the more inclined to marry. *Are litigious.* They are very litigious, and will go to Law for a Trifle, because they are constantly envious at one another.

The Brahmans. The *Brahmans* living in *Jafnapatnam*, or any other part of the *Indies*, are for the most part Men of great Morality, sober, clean, industrious, civil, obliging, and very moderate both in eating and drinking; they use no strong Liquors, wash or bathe twice a day, eat nothing that has had or may have Life, yet are much addicted (like all the rest of the *Indians*) to Pleasure. Notwithstanding they are Christians, they carry still certain Beads, and (as *Rogerius* observes, *fol.* 71.) like those of *Coromandel*, never marry out of their Families, but frequently their Brothers and Sisters Children; tho else they are great Enemies to Incest, but excuse this near Alliance by the great Value they put upon their Generation, which they deduce from *Bramma*, and *From whence descended.* some Learned Men from *Abraham* and *Ketura*, whose Children, according to *Gen.* 25. v. 6. *went into the Eastern Country.*

Tho they bear the Name of Christians, and know how to discourse rationally of the Ten Commandments, and the other Points of the Christian Doctrine, they still retain many of their Pagan Superstitions. *Retain some Pagan Superstition.* If you tell them of the Christian Liberty in Victuals and Drinks, they reply, that they are not ignorant of it, but as the Essence of Christianity does not consist in eating and drinking, so they did not think themselves oblig'd to feed upon such things as are contrary to their Nature and Education, being from their Infancy used to much tenderer Food, which agrees best with their Constitution, and makes them generally live to a great Age.

They are not ignorant in the Course of the Stars, in calculating the Eclipses of *Their reasons for it.* the Sun and Moon, know the *seven Stars*, which they call *Arramien*, i. e. *Six-fishes*, because, say they, we see no more than six. They understand also the Names of the Planets, and chiefest of the fixed Stars, but this must be understood from the most Learned among them.

*

Tho

Tho we shall treat in particular hereafter of the Errors of the Pagans, yet can I not pass by here in silence, what I have observ'd my self concerning their Opinion of *the Creation of the World, its Age,* and *Transmigration of the Soul.* In the Year 1665, after I had catechiz'd the People after Sermon in the Church of *Paretiture*, happening to discourse concerning the *Creation* and *Age* of the World; some of the *Indians* affirm'd that the World had stood 4864 Years since their *Kaligam* or fourth Period. For they have four Periods, the first called *Creitagam*, the second *Treitagam*, the third *Dwaparugam*, and the fourth *Kaligam*. And whereas the *Indians* in *Coromandel* did in the Year 1639, compute no more than 4739 Years since the Creation of the World, I told 'em that they follow'd the Footsteps of the *Chineses*, who in their Computations made no great account of 100 Years less or more, which made 'em smile. I told 'em further, that there was no certain Computation from the beginning of the World, except what was founded upon the Holy Scripture; and that in the Year 1665 (according to the *Jewish* Computation) the World had stood 5425 Years. Concerning the Origin of the Soul, I found them of the same Opinion with the Great *Rabbi*, viz. *That all Souls were created in the beginning, and kept till they were to be communicated to certain Bodies.* Unto which they have added the *Pythagorean* Tradition of the *Transmigration of the Soul.*

Their Belief concerning the beginning of the World.

Their Belief concerning the beginning of the Souls.

I remember that at a certain time, as I was walking with some of them, and endeavouring to refute this Opinion; they objected that it was impossible for a Child to be born Blind, Dumb or Lame, without having receiv'd a Soul that had been guilty of very gross Sins. For, said they, since the Child has not committed any Sins, and God does not punish any Body without sinning, this must be attributed to the Sins committed by the Soul whilst yet in another Body, and now entred into the Child. Unto which I reply'd in our Saviour's Words, out of *John* 9. 1. when his Disciples ask'd him concerning the blind Man from his Birth, *Neither had this Man sinned nor his Parents, but that the Works of God should be made manifest in him.* Whence it seems that the *Jews* were somewhat infected with this Tradition, mention whereof is also made by *Joseph. Antiq. l.* 18. *c.* 11. and *de Bello Judaico, l.* 2. *c.* 8. The Words of *Herod, Mat.* 14. 2. when he says concerning Christ, *This is* John *the Baptist, he is risen from the Dead*, intimate the same; as likewise what the *Jews* said concerning Christ, *Mat.* 16. 13, 14. some that he was *John the Baptist*, some *Elias*, and others *Jeremias*. Hence *Elias* (commonly call'd *Levita*) in his Book *Tisbi*, and the other Cabalists of the *Jews* were of Opinion, that the Souls pass thro three distinct Bodies, which they pretend to evince from the Words of *Job* 33. 29. *Lo! all these things worketh God twice or thrice thro one Man.* Thus the *Jews* affirm that the Soul of *Adam* was translated into the Body of *David*, and afterwards into that of the *Messiah*; which Error having been introduced into *Palestine* by *Antiochus*'s Philosophers, the *Jewish* Doctors did not stick to maintain that *the Souls of sinful Men did transmigrate into the Bodies of Beasts, according to the degrees or heinousness of their Crimes*; whereas it is manifest, that a rational Soul can't fix its Habitation but in the Body instructed with proper Organs, whereby it exerts its Operations; and the Scripture tells us expresly, that the *Soul and Spirit returns to God who gave it*; besides many other Arguments I alledged to them upon this Head against their Opinion.

Error among the Jews, concerning the Transmigration of the Soul.

Baldæus.

The learned *Vossius* is of opinion, that this Error took its beginning from the true Tradition of the Resurrection of the Dead, which was spread even among the *Druids* in *Gaul*, according to *Cæsar, lib.* 6. with this difference however, that the *Pythagoreans* affirm the Souls to transmigrate even into the Bodies of Beasts; whereas the first restrain it only to the Bodies of Men, which made them face Death with an undaunted Courage, according to *Lucan. lib.* 1.

This Opinion receiv'd among the Druids.

Felices errore suo, quos ille timorum
Maximus haud urget lethi metus, inde ruendi
In ferrum mens prona viris, animæque capaces
Mortis, & ignavum est rediturae parcere vitæ.

Appian says of the antient *Germans* among other things, that they despised Death in hopes of another Life; and *Thomas Aviot* an *Englishman* assures us, that the same had been found in *Virginia*. *Joseph Acosta* says the same of *Peru* and *Mexico*; and the same is related of *Guinea*, of the *Chineses*, the antient *Egyptians* and *Getes*. The *Pythagoreans* say of *Athalides*, that his Soul before it entred the Body of *Pythagoras*, transmigrated into three several other Bodies, first into that of

Eu-

Baldæus. *Euphorbus*, the Son of *Pantbus* in the *Trojan* War, afterwards into *Pyrrbus*, next into *Eleus*, and then into *Pythagoras*. All the *Indian* Pagans are infected with this erroneous Opinion, as we shall see more at large hereafter: but what is more surprizing is, that the *Sadduces* among the *Jews*, who had so much Veneration for the Books of *Moses*, should deny the *Immortality of the Soul*; when it is said in *Gen.* 1. 16. *That the Soul of Man was not created*, like material Substances, but was part of the *Spirit of God.* The same say all the *Gentiles*, as *Hermes*, *Zoroaster*, *Chalcidius* and *Epicharmis*. *Cicero in Somnio Scip.* says, *There is a near Relation betwixt God and our Souls*. *Seneca* in his Letter to *Lucilius* tells him, That *the Souls are in Heaven*; and speaking of the deceased Son of *Marcia*, he says, *in meliori Statu est*, he is *in a better State*. The *Turks*, and *Persians*, and *Mahomet* in his *Alcoran* acknowledg the *Immortality of the Soul*; which put these Christians to the blush, who affirm that *the Souls of the Wicked are annihilated*, or what others assert, *That the Souls rest in the Matter till the Day of Judgment*.

CHAP. XLVIII.

Marriages of the Bellales *and* Brahmans. *Divers Circumstances observed upon that account. Families, Degrees, and Handicraftsmen of* Jafnapatnam. *The Taking and Description of* Trinquenemale.

IN the preceding Chapter we told you concerning the Marriages of the *Bellales*, and how the *Brahmans* often marry their Brothers and Sisters Children. *Marriage-Customs.* Among some of the Christians in *Ceylon* obtains a certain Custom to this day, to tye the *Tali* or Bracelet of the Bride about the Bridegroom's Neck, a thing introduced by the *Pagans*, and imitated by the Christians: for as *Rogerius* observes, the Inhabitants of the Coast of *Coromandel* look upon it as a Ceremony so necessary towards the Confirmation of the Marriage, that whenever the Husband dies, the *Tali* he wore about his Neck on his Marriage-Day is to be burnt with him.

As Maidens without a good Portion are a very bad Commodity here, hence it is that frequent Collections are made to help the poorer sort to Husbands. They are of Opinion, that a single Man is but half a Man; nay that those who neglect or lose any time in propagating their own Kind, are not far different from a Murderer and a Destroyer of Human Kind (according to the opinion of *Plato*, which was likewise encourag'd among the *Athenians* and *Romans*) which is the reason they often marry their Daughters at 10 and 11 Years of Age, and nothing is more frequent than to see them bring forth Children at 13 or 14.

Weddings. After they have been three times proclaimed from the Pulpit, the Marriage Ceremony is perform'd by the Minister; the House where the Wedding is kept being generally adorn'd with a kind of Triumphal Arch raised without Doors, made of Fig-tree Branches, Flowers, Pomegranates, and such like. The richer sort seldom fail to give a good Entertainment to their Friends, of Venison, Hares, Partridges, Fish, Fruits, Preserves, *&c.* and the Evening is spent in dancing, singing, and divers other Diversions. However strong Liquors are never made use of on such Occasions, unless the *Hollanders* (who can't well be merry without them) bring some along with them. These Marriage-Diversions continue sometimes four or five days successively.

I remember that during my Residence here, sometimes Children of eight or nine Years of Age would have engaged in mutual Promises of Marriage, in mine and their Friends Presence; which I always opposed, fearing, not without reason, that they might repent their Bargain, before they came to a marriageable Age. For the rest they constantly observe this Custom, that the Female is younger than the Bridegroom; nay they seldom will chuse a Maid, that has already had her Monthly Times: this Custom is so strictly observed on the Coast of *Coromandel*, that if a *Brahman*'s Daughter remains unmarried till that time, she must lay aside all hopes of it for the future. *They marry very young.*

The learned *Selden* shews out of *Rabbi Moses Maimonides*, that the *Jewish* High Priests were not allow'd to marry a Maiden, unless she was under 12 Years of Age; and the antient *Romans* commonly married their Daughters at 10, 11 or 12 Years *The same practised by the* Jews *and* Romans.

Years of Age. It is sufficiently known what *Moses* says, in relation to the Marks of Virginity, *Deut.* 12. 17. which to this day is followed by the *Moors* of *Fez* and *Morocco*. If they happen to die without Issue, the Mother's Portion returns to her Friends, the rest to the Husband's. One laudable Custom they have, which is, that scarce ever Children marry here without the consent of their Parents; a Custom not only agreeable to the express Command of God, express'd in divers Places of the Scripture, and the Practice of all Ages even among the *Pagans*, but also consonant to the Civil Constitutions, and the Decrees of the Council of *Lateran* and other Councils, which declare a Marriage betwixt *Raptorem* and *Raptam* invalid in it self.

Children never marry without the Consent of their Parents.

Divers Tribes. The Tribe of the Chivias.

The Tribe or Family of the *Chivias*, use formerly to attend the Service of the King of *Jafnapatnam*, but now do all sorts of Drudgery, as carrying of Water and Wood for the *Dutch* Inhabitants; they make use also of them for Littermen, 10 or 12 of them being sometimes employed at a time, to carry a good bulky *Hollander*, 10, 20, nay 30 Leagues in a Litter. However as they are descended from Courtiers, so they are too proud to carry any ordinary Person, who must be contented to be carried by the ordinary *Coelys* or Labourers, who live all over the Country; whereas the *Chivias* inhabit in the District of the Church of *Chundecouli*.

Of the Parruas.

Those of the Tribe of the *Parruas* do not live in such great Numbers in *Jafnapatnam*, as they do about *Tutecoryn*; they apply themselves to the Sea, and especially in diving for Sea-Horse Teeth and Pearls. They generally speak *Portuguese*, and are an active sort of People.

Of the Chittiis.

The *Chittiis* live for the most part upon the Linen Manufacture and Traffick, the word *Chitty* signifying as much as a Merchant; they are a crafty Generation. Each of these Tribes does not marry into any other, besides their own, nay commonly in the same Family. Besides which, each Handicraftsman educates his Son to the same Trade he is of; thus a Weaver's Son follows the Weaving-Trade, as the Smith's Son does that of a Smith.

Of the Carreas.

The Tribe of the *Carreas* live upon Fishing, which they perform with monstrous large Nets; they inhabit near the Sea-shore of *Jafnapatnam*, and the Banks of the *Salt-River*. Those of the Tribe of the *Mokkuas* are likewise Fishermen.

Of the Nallouas.

The *Nallouas* are generally Slaves to the *Bellales*, and much blacker than the rest. Their Business is to gather the Liquor that flows out of the Coco-Trees, call'd *Suyri* and *Euwak* by the *Indians*, to dig the Ground, tend the Cattel, water the Trees, and such like Drudgeries, as is commonly done also by the *Coelys* or ordinary Labourers. They are a nasty Generation, you may smell them at a good distance, not unlike the *Hottentots* on the Cape of *Good Hope*.

Baldæus.

Of the Parreas.

The *Parreas* are the most despicable of all, their Employment being to carry out Dung and such like filthy things, they feed upon Rats and Mice.

Great Difference in the degrees of their Tribes.

It is observable, that the Tribes of the higher Rank look upon the inferiour Ones with a great deal of Scorn, these being obliged to salute the others in the Streets with deep Reverence, and other Ceremonies to shew their Submission. On the other hand, all the Men of what Rank or Quality soever, exercise a great Authority over their Wives, whom they rarely honour so far as to eat with them, but commonly dine alone. None of all these Tribes eat Cows Flesh, which is the reason that no Cows are killed but by the *Dutch*, the Cow being look'd upon among the rest as a Sacred Creature, as it was formerly among the *Egyptians* *, of which more hereafter.

**See* Exo. 8. 26. & Gen. 43. 32.

Tho their Tribes are very numerous, yet do they relate to some few Families, from whence they take their Original, like the Branches from the Stem of a Tree. The same was practised among the antient *Egyptians*, who distinguish'd their Nation into four Head Tribes, *viz.* the *Priests*, the *Soldiers*, the *Artisans* and *Handicraftsmen*, and the Sheep and Cowherds. Just as now-a-days some of the *European* Nations are distinguish'd into four Estates, *viz. Noblemen*, *Patricians* or *Gentlemen*, *Citizens*, and the Common People.

For the rest, the generality of the Inhabitants of the Kingdom of *Jafnapatnam* are naturally ingenious, and have a strong Memory; they are very sober and moderate in their Diet, and (except the *Nallouas* and *Parreas*) very clean in their Apparel, not quarrelsom, but very free with their Tongue.

The Inhabitants of Jafnapatnam.

Their general Vice is Fornication and Adultery, especially among the young Men, as the old Ones are much addicted to Superstitions, as to the choice of certain Days (whereof something was said before concerning *Raja Singa*) the Cries of Birds, and such like things used among the antient *Romans*. Hence it is that the *Portugueses* in those Parts have a Proverb to this day, *I know*

Baldæus. *not what unfortunate Sight* (Rosto Mosinho) *did come in my way this day.*

Their Superstition. Thus on the Coast of *Coromandel*, they look upon it as fortunate, if they see a certain red Bird, with a white Ring about his Neck. *John van Twist* in his Description of *Gusuratte*, tells us of the Natives there, that they look upon it as a good Sign, if they meet an Elephant or Camel loaden or unloaden, a Horse without a Burden, or a Cow or Buffler with Water on their Backs, for without a Load they were accounted unfortunate; a Ram or Dog with a piece of Meat in his Mouth, a Cat passing to the right hand of them: they also reckon it fortunate, if they meet any Body that carries Meat, Milk and Butter, or if a Cock crosses the way.

It is certain, that the Observations of the Cries and Flights of the Birds have not only been usual among the antient *Romans*, but also the *Jews*, with several other such like Superstitions, Predictions, asking Advice from the Devil, the finding out of stolen or lost Goods, &c. for *Necromancy* was forbid, *Isa.* 8. 19. Incantations, *Acts* 19. 19. Observations of the Cries of the Birds, *Ezek.* 21. 21. the choice of certain Days, *Esth.* 3.7. & 9. 24. the consulting of Woods, *Hos.* 4. 12. besides which, the Predictions from the different Appearance of the Water, Air, Fire and Earth, out of certain Union of Characters or Numbers (called *Cabala*) Chiromancy, Astrology, Inspections into the Magic Glass, and such like Diabolical Illusions, described more at large by *Peucerus* in his Treatise, *de variis Divinationum generibus.*

Besides the Artisans and Handicraftsmen, whereof there is great Plenty in *Jafnapatnam*, they have certain Persons who apply themselves to the Law; and in the high Court of Justice, composed of *Hollanders* and *Indians*, were set always (besides the *Modeliars*) a certain Person well versed in the Laws and Constitutions of his Native Country. They have also their Advocates, who make very long Speeches in their Pleadings.

Lawyers in Jafnapatnam.

Their Physicians. Neither are they destitute of Physicians, such as they are; for to speak Truth they are more than Empiricks, who practise according to certain Books and Traditions, transmitted to them by their Ancestors, and confirm'd to them by their own Experience. They know not what Anatomy is, and very little of the nature of purging Medicines, which are not often used in this hot Climate: However when a Purge is to be given (whether a Potion or Pills) the Composition is always made of fresh Herbs; and if it works too strong, they mix some poudered Pepper with Water, and apply it to the Navel in the nature of an Ointment. I can tell it by my own experience, that it is a good Remedy against the Belly-ach and Looseness.

Surgeons and Barbers. They have also good Store of Surgeons and Barbers, the last carry always a small Looking-glass along with them, their Rasors are thicker on the back than ours; they not only shave your Beard and Head, but also pare your Hand and Toe Nails, and cleanse your Ears.

Weavers. Weavers are here in abundance. These sit flat upon the Ground, their Feet being plac'd in a Hole dug for that purpose, whilst they are at work.

Painters. Callico-Printers or Painters are numberless here, who have a way of preparing their Colours, that they never go out by washing, tho those printed at *Jafnapatnam* are not near so good as those of the Coast of *Coromandel*, and especially those done at *Masulipatan*.

They are excellent Workmen in Ivory and Ebony Wood, as likewise in Gold and Silver, and will come with their Tools (which are but few) to work in the Houses of the *Dutch*. They are exactly well versed in the essaying of Gold.

Other Handicraftsmen. They are as well provided with Smiths, Carpenters and Bricklayers, as most Places in *Europe*, tho a Carpenter or Bricklayer gets not above five or six Pence a day.

Having thus given you a full account of the Kingdom of *Jafnapatnam*, we will now go from thence along the Seashore to *Trinquenemale*, taken 1639 by Mr. *Anthony Caan*, which might have been done before whilst Mr. *Adam Westerwold* was in *Ceylon* (there being no more than 50 Men in Garison) had not *Raja Singa* bent his Thoughts upon *Batecalo*, or as some will have it upon *Matecalo*. *Trinquenemale* has a most excellent Harbour, (as you may see by the Draught) nay to speak the Truth, the best and largest in the whole Isle of *Ceylon*, there being more secure riding at anchor here, than in the Harbours of *Belligamme*, *Gale* or *Columbo*.

Trinquenemale. This Place was several times relinquish'd and rebuilt by our Company, especially during our War with the *English*, it being not thought convenient to leave so good a Harbour, and so conveniently seated for the interrupting all Correspondence betwixt Foreigners and *Raja Singa*, to the Discretion of an Enemy;

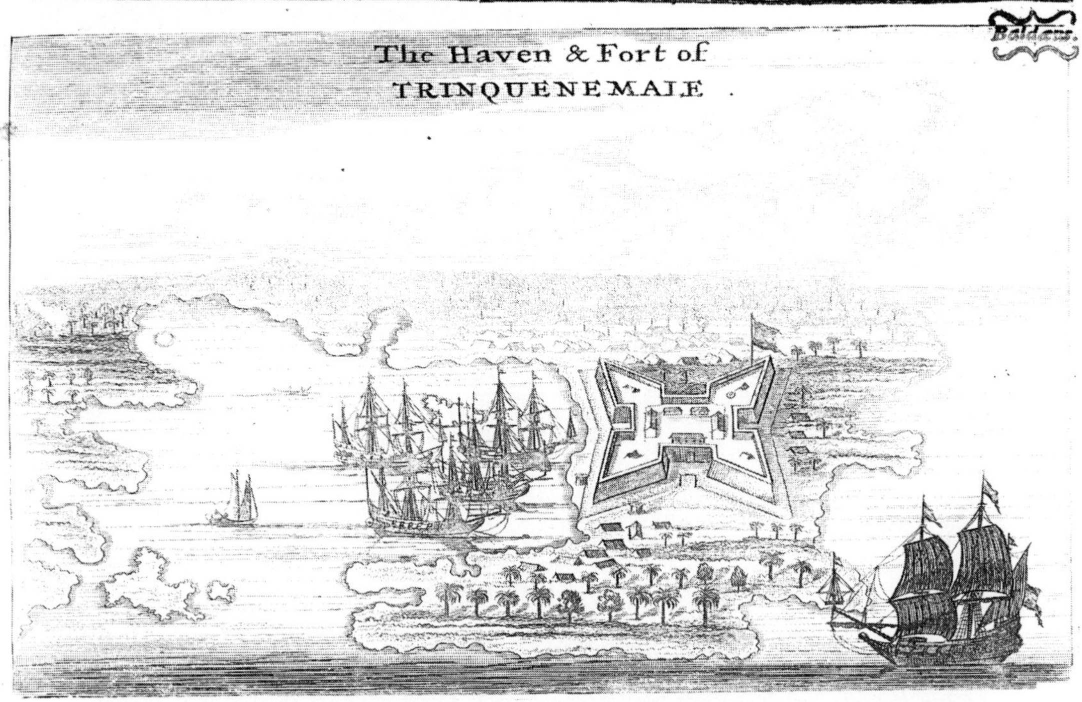

nemy; tho the repairing of it (during my stay in *Ceylon*) under Captain *Peter Wash*, cost us abundance of People, that were swept away by a Phrensical Distemper, which made them drown themselves in the Sea. Some of their Bodies being open'd, certain Worms were found in the Substance of the Brains, occasion'd questionless by the Violence of the Heat, the continual Labour, Watching, and the feeding upon Salt-Provisions; but more especially by the cold Night-Fogs. After which time it was strengthened with some additional Fortifications, as appears by Captain *Peter du Pon*'s Letter, dated the 5th of *Octob.* 1667. from *Macassar* in the Isle of *Celebes*.

Strengthened with additional Fortifications.

" I was once more order'd to sail with " some Forces to *Trinquenemale*, to take " once more possession of that Harbour " and Bay for our Company, which I " did accordingly with good Success; " and having refortify'd the Place with " four Bastions, and reduc'd the circum-" jacent Inhabitants to our Subjection, I " left a sufficient Garison there, and so " return'd to *Columbo*.

From *Trinquenemale* you travel by the way of *Capello* to *Batecalo*, the first place conquer'd by the *Dutch* in this Island, whereof we have given you the best account we were able, not questioning but that in case we should once live in Peace with the King of *Candy* (who is very old, almost doting, and much addicted to strong Liquor) our Countrymen will be much better acquainted with the Inland Countries than they have been hitherto.

According to the last Letter I receiv'd from *Tutecoryn*, dated *Decemb.* 20. 1668. there had been lately an Insurrection in the Isle of *Ceylon*, so that they were forced to draw their Forces together out of *Saffragam* and *Mannekewarre*, but was appeased since, tho the Forces were not as yet dismissed.

Baldæus.

CHAP. XLIX.

Natural History of Ceylon. *Their* Pagodes, *Convents, Monks. Manners, Habit and Oeconomy of the* Cingaleses.

HAving hitherto taken a view of those Places of *Ceylon* that are under the Jurisdiction of the *Dutch* Company, we will now take a turn to *Candy*, the Imperial Residence, as the most proper place to be inform'd concerning the real Constitution of this Isle, and its Inhabitants.

The City of Candy. The City of *Candy* is seated about 30 Leagues from the Sea-side, and 9 from *Vintane* up the River of *Trinquenemale*, about 21 Leagues by Land from *Matecalo*, and 9 from the Sea-shore, where the Emperor has his Docks for building and refitting his Ships and Gallies. The other Cities of *Ceylon* being not described in any Books, we must also pass by in silence here. All over the Isle you see abundance of very splendid *Pagodes*. The Foundation of that of *Vintane* has no less than 130 foot in Circumference; it is of a great height, and gilt on the top; it is oval on the bottom, and arises into a four-corner'd Point like a Pyramid. The *Great Pagode* betwixt *Gale* and *Matecalo* is also much celebrated, serving for a Light-house to Ships as well as that of *Trinquenemale*. *Their Temples.* In the large high *Pagode* before-mention'd stands an Idol representing a Man with a naked Sword in his hand, lifting up his Arm, as if he were ready to strike. To this Idol the *Cingaleses* pay their Reverence, and offer their Sacrifices upon all Emergencies, or in time of Sickness; for which reason they keep a Basket in every House, wherein they gather such Provisions as they are to sacrifice. They believe that the World will not have an end so long as that *Pagode* stands. Some worship an *Elephant's Head* of Wood or Stone, to obtain Wisdom. *And Idols.* They adorn their Idols with Flowers. These Elephants Heads are plac'd sometimes on Trees in the High-ways, sometimes in little Brick Houses or Chappels. You see also frequently in the high Road certain heaps of Stones, Earth or Dung, upon which each Passenger throws something as he passes by.

Just by *Belligamme* I saw the Figure of a Man at least six Yards high, cut in a Rock about half a yard deep, who us'd to be worship'd by the *Cingaleses*.

Near it is a high-peak'd Mountain, accounted the highest in the *Indies*, call'd *Pico de Adam*, or *Adam's Peak*; because *Adam's Mountain.* they are of opinion, that here stood formerly the Paradise, where *Adam* was created: they also tell you, that the Print of the Foot of *Adam* is to be seen to this day in the Rock, the Draught whereof is kept in the Imperial Court. Unto this Rock a vast number of People flock from far distant places, to see this sacred Relick, tho the Mountain is of very difficult access, nay (if we may credit *Maffæus* the Jesuit) quite inaccessible, unless by means of certain Iron Chains and Iron Spikes fastened to the Rocks.

Some are of opinion that they reverence the Chamberlain of the Queen *Candace* in this place, who according to some Historians, but especially *Dorothæus* Bishop of *Tyrus* (a Man equally famous for his Learning and Sanctity under *Constantine* the Great) preach'd the Gospel in the *Happy Arabia, Erythræa* and *Taprobana*.

There are also divers Convents in *Convents and Monks of* Ceylon. *Ceylon*, and a great number of *Brahmans* and Priests, who are in great Veneration among the common People; they never eat any thing that has been living, or is capable of producing any living Substance, as Eggs, *&c.* Their Friers wear yellow Habits, with their Heads shaven all over, for which reason they never appear in the Streets without Umbrello's, and Beads in their hands, muttering out certain Prayers as they go along. Their Convents have divers Galleries and Chappels, wherein are placed the Statutes of several Men and Women, who, as they say, have led holy Lives. These are adorn'd with Gold and Silver Apparel, and attended with burning Lamps and Wax-Candles day and night, plac'd upon Altars: The Candlesticks being supported by naked Boys artificially carved. The Friers have their certain hours for Prayers, which they perform in these Chappels.

Their Processions. They have also their publick Processions: The Head or Abbot of the Convent being mounted on a fine Elephant, sumptuously harnessed with an Umbrello over his Head, marches along the Street in great Pomp, under the sound of Horns, Trumpets, and other such

Baldæus.

The Indian Procession.

such sort of Musick, making an odd kind of Harmony, accompany'd by a great number of Men, Women and Children; the Maidens of Quality dance all along before the Elephant naked down to the middle, their Heads, Arms and Ears adorn'd with Golden Bracelets and Jewels; the Garments which cover their under parts are of different Colours. They pay their daily Devotions to a certain Idol call'd *Sambaja*, by prostrating themselves upon the ground, and afterwards clasping their hands together over their Heads. But concerning the Religious Worship of the *Cingaleses* we shall have occasion to say more in the following Treatise, which in effect differs very little from the *Malabars* and those of *Coromandel*, except that they are not altogether such Bigots, the Emperor of *Ceylon* allowing Liberty of Conscience to all Nations. The *Cingaleses* are not so stubborn, but that many of them have been without much difficulty converted to the *Roman* Faith, and since that to the Reformed Religion.

The Genius of the Cingaleses. For the rest the *Cingaleses* are naturally active and ingenious, and good Workmen in Gold, Silver, Ivory, Ebony, Iron Works, *&c.* Arms inlaid with Silver, eloquent, nimble, courageous, fit for Warlike Exploits, sober and watchful. They march one single Man after another, by reason of the many narrow Lanes in this Country; their Arms are a Half-pike, their Drums are small, but make a great noise, which may be heard at three Leagues distance in the Mountains; they are best in the pursuit of a routed Enemy. Since they have conversed so much with the *Portugueses* and other *European* Nations, they are grown so cunning that they must not be too much trusted, nor despised.

Incest is so common a Vice among them, that when Husbands have occasion to leave their Wives for some time, they recommend the Conjugal Duty to be perform'd by their own Brothers. I remember a certain Woman at *Gale*, who had Confidence enough to complain of the want of Duty in her Husband's Brother upon that account. The like happen'd in my time at *Jafnapatnam*, which had been likely to be punish'd with Death, had not at my Intercession, and in

Baldæus.

in regard of the tender beginnings of Christianity, the same been pass'd by for that time.

The Habits.

The *Cingaleses* are in Shape and Manners not unlike the *Malabars*, with long hanging Ears, but not so black. The Dress of the Men is a Vest call'd *Ropillo*, of Woolen or Linen Cloth; their under Garment is a piece of Linen wrapt about the middle, and drawn through both their Legs, like a pair of Breeches: On their Heads they wear a kind of red Caps, such as we call *Rock* Caps, which they look upon as a singular Ornament, and in their Ears Rings and precious Stones. The Hilts of their Swords or Scymeters are commonly of Silver, Ivory, or Gold, with flaming Blades.

The common People appear for the most part naked, having only a piece of Cloth wrapt round the middle to cover their Privy Parts. The Women go with their Breasts uncover'd, being generally well limb'd: Instead of a Head-dress they have a way of tying their Hair together like a Cap. They wear Golden or Silver Necklaces about their Necks, and Rings on their Fingers and Toes.

The *Cingaleses* as well as the *Malabars* are much addicted to Idleness and Pleasures, and insist much upon their Pedigree. They marry as many Wives as they think fit, as well as the *Mahometans*, of which there live a considerable number in this Isle. They marry their Daughters at 10 or 11 years of Age, a Custom not to be rooted out among them, they being very fond of the Virginity of their Wives. They bury their Dead after the manner of the Pagans.

Their Oeconomy.

In their Houses they are excessive neat, use instead of Trenchards and Table-Cloths the Leaves of Fig-trees; their Spoons are made of *Coco* Nutshells, and their drinking Vessels of Earth, with hollow Pipes, through which they pour (like the *Moors*) the Drink into the Mouth without touching their Lips; for as the *Cingaleses* and *Malabars* insist much upon their Noble Descent, so they will neither eat nor drink with those of an inferior Rank; nay many of them are so proud as not to eat with their own Wives.

Their Coin.

The most current Coin here are the Silver *Laryns*, each whereof is worth about 10 *d.* a *Fanam* is only 5 *d.* tho they have Golden and Silver *Fanams*; a *Pagode* was formerly no more than 84 *Stivers*, but is since raised to 120, or six *Dutch* Gilders; as well in *Ceylon* as *Malabar*, two Golden *Fanams* at 5 *d.* a piece make a *Laryn*.

CHAP. L.

Fertility of Ceylon. *A Description of the Cinnamon and Snakewood. A strange Tree.*

Fertility of Ceylon.

THE Isle of *Ceylon* is very fertile in Rice, and all sorts of Fruits, as *Ananas*, *Cocoes*, the best Oranges, Lemmons, and Citrons, exceeding by far those of *Spain* and *Portugal*; Fig-trees, *Cajouves*, Grapes, Potato's, *Quiavos*, *Papajes* and Pomgranats. You have here fresh Grapes the whole year round, except in the three Winter or rainy Months. It abounds also in Sugar-reeds, and Mulberry-trees, which produce a good quantity of Silk; as in Ginger, Pepper, Cardamum, Tobacco, wild Palm-trees, affording vast quantities of a kind of Sugar, and the Juice call'd *Suyri* their ordinary Drink. They are stor'd also with *Calabass* Trees, *Cotton* Trees, *Areek* Trees, *Portuguese* Figs, *Mangos* of divers sorts, long Pepper, Melons, Water-Melons, Onions, and Garlick. Since the settling of the *Dutch* here, they have also propagated with good success Cabbages, Asparagas, Carrots and Radishes: But the *Helen* or the Bride in Contest of this Isle is the finest and purest Cinnamon, which growing only in this Island, no wonder if we have disputed the entire Possession thereof for so many years with the *Portuguese*.

A Description of the Cinnamon, and the Tree.

This precious Spice is call'd by the *Cingaleses* *Cureneo potto*, and the Tree *Curindo-gas*, some of which are of a great bulk, their Leaves resembling those of the Lemmon Trees, but not quite so broad; the Blossom is white and of an agreeable scent, which produces a yellowish Fruit, not unlike a small Olive, out of which the Inhabitants press an Oil not much differing both in Colour and Virtue from that of Nutmegs, but in smell like the Cinnamon it self.

The Manner of peeling Cinnmon.

Baldæus.

The Cinnamon-Tree has a double Bark, the outward Bark being taken off with a crooked Knife; the inward Rind is cut with a Knife first round the Tree, and then in length, which being expos'd to the Sun-beams in the Fields, shrinks together into such small Rolls as we see them in *Europe*. The Trees that are thus peel'd perish, instead whereof the Fruits that fall upon the Ground produce other Cinnamon-Trees. The Wood is very white, and used by the Inhabitants for building. It is observable that these Cinnamon-Trees don't grow all over *Ceylon*, but only in some certain places: For in the whole Kingdom of *Jafnapatnam*, and the Isle of *Manaar*, none of these Trees are to be seen, but only beyond the River *Chilau*, in the Country about *Negumbo*, and the Inland Countries, as likewise near *Gale*. These Trees seldom grow together, but are generally seen in Woods mixt with other Trees. Whilst I was Minister at *Gale*, some of my Slaves us'd now and then to bring some Cinnamon Wood among the rest into the Kitchin, which when put into the Fire emitted a very odoriferous scent.

It is further worth taking notice of, that whereas according to the Judgment of the Naturalists and Physicians, the Cinnamon is very hot, yet does the Root of the Tree produce not only a Water smelling exactly like Camphyr, but also the strongest scented Camphyr it self: I have several pieces of it, which smell so strong that I am scarce able to endure it. Out of the Cinnamon Wood, whilst yet green, they distil a Water of an agreeable smell, and very wholesom to our Bodies. The Natives make out of the outward Bark of these Trees curious Cabinets: I have such a one by me of a considerable bigness, which was presented me by Major *Peter du Pon* 1665. just upon my departure from *Ceylon*.

Three sorts of Cinnamon.

The *East-Indies* produce three different sorts of Cinnamon. 1. Is the finest Cinnamon call'd *Canel Fino* by the *Portugueses*, being the same that is taken from very young, or at least not very old Trees. 2. The coarse Cinnamon call'd *Canel Grosso* by the *Portugueses*, taken from very thick and old Trees. And, 3. The *Canel de Mato*, or wild Cinnamon, which grows likewise on the Coast of *Malabar*, but is in no esteem; for whereas a *Baar* of *Ceylonese* Cinnamon is sold for 50 or 60 *Rixdollars*, the wild Cinnamon yields not above 10 or 12. Tho I have heard some of the most ingenious of the Natives affirm, that the wild Cinnamon might be much meliorated, and made fit for use. The *Dutch* Company is now, through God's Blessing, in the possession of the Cinnamon of all kinds, as likewise of all the Spices, *viz*. of the Nutmegs, Mace and Cloves, except the Pepper, which grows in several places.

The Snake-wood.

The *Snake-wood* or *Lignum Colubrinum*, grows most frequently in the Isle of *Ceylon*; it is white inclining to yellow, very hard, and of a bitter taste; it is in great request among the *Indians*, and accounted a good Remedy against several Distempers: They pouder it, and rub the whole Body with it to cure the Itch. They also take an Ounce of pouder'd *Snake-wood* in Water or Wine against the Colick, burning Fevers, and other Distempers, but especially against the Stings of the Serpents, of which there are many in this Island.

Its use among the Indians.

How first discover'd.

The *Cingalese* Naturalists say that the Virtue of the *Snake-wood* was first discover'd by a certain small Creature call'd *Quil*, or *Quirpele*, by the *Portugueses*, being of the bigness of our *Ferrets*, wherewith we catch the Rabbets; of this kind the *Indians* keep many in their Houses, partly for Sport, partly to catch Rats and Mice with. This Creature having a natural Antipathy against the Snakes and Serpents, whenever it is stung by them runs to the *Snake-wood*, and after having eaten of it, is cur'd of its Wound. *Marcellus de Boschhouwer*, a Person in great esteem in *Ceylon*, relates, that he has several times seen this *Quirpele* engag'd with Snakes, and among the rest one that vanquish'd a Serpent; but being wounded run to the next Wood, and having eaten some of this *Snake-wood*, return'd in half an hour to the place, where its vanquish'd Enemy lay extended dead upon the ground. The *Cingaleses* call the Root of this Tree *Nay Lelli*, unto which they attribute a singular Virtue for the Cure of divers Distempers.

Antipathy betwixt the Quirpele and the Serpent.

There grows a strange Tree in the Isle of *Ceylon* call'd the *Root-tree*, because its Branches turn to the ground like Ropes, where taking Root again, they produce a Tree that spreads in a short time over a spacious Tract of Ground. *Ceylon* produces also *Tamarind*-Trees of a considerable bulk, the Fruit whereof is accounted an excellent Remedy against the Scurvy and Dropsy. There grows another Tree in *Ceylon* like our *Noli me tangere*; for if you go to touch it, it moves backwards, and gives way to your hand.

For the rest, *Ceylon* is sufficiently provided with Medicinal Herbs, and they

Vol. 3. p. 825.

The Catching of Eliphants on the Island of CEYLON. 33.

cure all their Distempers with green Herbs, in the use whereof their Physicians are better vers'd (by Experience) than many of our pretending Chyrurgeons; God Almighty having provided Remedies sutable to the Distempers of each Country. *Baldæus.*

CHAP. LI.

Great number of Elephants in Ceylon: *Are very pernicious. Divers Instances of it. How they take the Elephants. Their Bufflers, Tygers, Bears, Birds, Fishes, Crocodiles and Porcupines, or Sea-hogs.*

THE Isle of *Ceylon* abounds in all sorts of four-leg'd Creatures, Birds, Fishes, Stones and certain Products of the Sea, of each whereof we must say something.

Elephants of Ceylon. Among the four-leg'd Beasts the *Elephant* challenges the first Rank; of these there are great numbers here, and so pernicious, that it is not safe travelling without some Soldiers with their Drums and Kettles, the noise whereof frightens these Creatures: They are most dangerous towards Evening when they are hungry; for the *Coleys* or Littermen often run away at the sight of an Elephant, leaving those they carry to shift for themselves.

I remember that in my time, a *Portuguese* Reform'd Minister, nam'd *John Fereira d'Almeyda*, travelling with his Wife from *Gale* to *Columbo*, the Litter-Carriers (according to their Custom) ran away at the sight of an Elephant, who did however not the least harm, but laying his Trunk upon the Woman's *Palankin* or Litter, went away: But things of that nature happen not always alike.

I observ'd once as I was travelling from *Manaar* to *Jafnapatnam*, that the Elephants had done considerable mischief hereabouts, and during the rainy Season had render'd the Ways almost unpassable. We had the good fortune to escape narrowly the danger of an Elephant who kill'd a certain Negro, one of the Commanders of the Elephant-Hunters, in a place we had pass'd not long before.

At *Mature* are vast Stables, where the wild Elephants are tam'd, and afterwards sold to the *Moors* of *Bengale* and *Coromandel*. They take the Elephants near *Mature* in the following manner: They fix abundance of large Stakes or Trunks of Trees in the ground, so as to leave the Entrance wide enough, but growing narrower within by degrees; in these they have certain Traps, and the wild Elephants being decoy'd by the tame ones into these Enclosures, are catch'd in the Traps or Snares, like as we do in our decoying Ponds. They are very hard to be tam'd, and require sometimes four whole Months before they can be brought to lie down: All this while they must be carried twice a day to some River or other to swim. This is done by putting a wild Elephant betwixt two tame ones, who take such care of the other, that they hit him from both sides with their Trunks, till they make him pliable, and at last quite tame. *How they take and tame the Elephants.*

It often happens that the young Elephants are taken in following the old ones. These are very unlucky: I remember, that one time as several of us were talking together, one of these young Elephants came slily and push'd with his back-side against one of our Company, that he was ready to fall upon his Nose.

They feed upon green Herbs and Leaves of Fig-trees, *Coco*, and other Trees; neither do they refuse *Areek* and Sugar. At a certain time of the year an Oil issues out of the Heads of the old Elephants when they run mad, and oftentimes kill their *Carnak* or Guides. The *Ceylonese* Elephants are accounted the largest and best in the *Indies*, and, if you will believe the Natives, are ador'd by the other Elephants.

Horses. Horses (great Enemies of the Elephants) were first brought from abroad into this Isle. The *Portugueses* having some years since sent Horses into the Isle *de Vacas*, they are multiply'd to such a degree, that you may see them feed in Herds of 60, 70, 80, or 100.

Bufflers. Of Bufflers they have a great store in *Ceylon*; I have seen whole Herds of them of 100 and more feeding in the Countries of *Chilau* and *Madampe*, which were but indifferently peopled at that time. They have also Hedg-Hogs, Oxen, Cows, Bulls, Sheep, Goats, Stags, Does,

Baldæus. Elks, tame and wild Boars, Hares and Partridges, Peacocks and Apes in abundance.

Tygers and Bears. The Woods here produce also some ravenous Beasts, as Tygers, tho I never saw any, but had a Grey-hound given me by a *Portuguese*, who bore the marks of a Tyger's Claws on his Buttocks. Bears I have seen both in *Jafnapatnam* and *Manaar*; I saw once five or six young ones drowned in *Manaar* by the Inhabitants, who had found them at *Mantotte*, and thought fit to take this course with them to prevent their increase.

Jackals. They abound also in *Jackals*, a Creature very greedy after Mens Flesh, for which reason they cover their Graves with great Stones; they sometimes take them with Grey-hounds, but when they are hard put to it, they piss, which emits so nauseous a scent that the Hounds can't endure it. The Flesh of the *Jackals* is given with good success by the Physicians of the Country to cure the Consumption. Towards the Evening the *Jackals* meet and make a most dreadful noise, and will some times fall upon Passengers. In my time a *Caffer* who was in drink had his Teeth eaten out by the *Jackals*. The *Jackal* is not unlike a Fox, and has exactly such a Tail. The *Malabars* call the *Jackals Adiviis*. I saw but one Leopard in the Isle of *Ceylon*, and not one Unicorn or Rhinoceros.

Ceylon affords vast quantities of Birds, call'd by the Inhabitants by peculiar Names.

Crows. Crows you shall see by thousands about Noon upon the Houses, but they are so cunning as not easily to be shot except through a hole or small Window. Towards night they leave the Towns, and retire to the Trees in the Country, and in the morning early look about for Prey. If one of them happens to be kill'd, the rest make a most terrible Outcry.

All sorts of Fowl and Birds. There are certain Birds in *Ceylon* call'd *Minbotos* by the *Portugueses*, who often make bold with the young Chickens; they have also Owls that make a dreadful noise in the night-time. They abound in Geese, Herons, wild and tame Ducks, Peacocks, Pigeons, Turtles, Partridges, Parrocets, of most delicious colours; Peewits, Swallows, Bats, &c. Among the rest here is a certain Bird which builds his Nest hanging on the Branches of the Trees: They have also abundance of fine singing Birds, Nightingals and Larks in abundance, Sea-gulls, Water-snipes, Bees, Fire-flies, Gnats and Locusts.

Fishes. *Ceylon* produces great plenty of Fish, as *Cacap*, Plaice, Crabs, Pikes, *King-fishes*, *Sail-fishes*, Craw-fishes, Haddocks, *Galleon-fishes*, Sharks, *Orados*, *Sardins*, large Smelts, *Bat-fishes*, Seals, Oisters, Muscles, Shrimps, *Pampus*, Barbels, *Bomtos*, *Corquados*, &c.

Crocodile. Among the Amphibious Creatures, the *Kaiman* or Crocodile, call'd *Lagarto* by the *Portugueses*, is very frequent here; some of which are 18 foot long. They have four Feet with crooked Claws, their Skin cover'd with Scales, which are so hard upon the Back, that they are Musquet proof; so that they are not vulnerable except in the Belly and Eyes: Their under Jaws are unmovable, but they have sharp Teeth: Their Back-bones being without Joints, they can't turn short, whence the best way to escape them, is to get away from them by many windings and turnings. 'Tis generally believ'd here that the Crocodile has a Stone or rather Bone in the Head, which given in Pouder is an excellent Remedy against the Stone. The Bones of the Sharks are accounted very good against the same Distemper.

Mr. *Rochefort* says, that in some of the Rivers of the Isles of *America* are certain Crocodiles that smell like Musque. I have with amazement seen Crocodiles lying upon the Water like Logs of Wood, with their Eyes shut; and if they happen to meet with a Prey, they leap at it on a sudden, like an Arrow from the Bow.

Vincent le Blanc tells us a story of a Burgermaster's Servant of *Alexandria*, who passing near the River-side was devour'd by a Crocodile which he took for a Log of Wood swimming upon the Water. They say that they have a white Fat, which is an excellent Remedy against sharp Humours that settle in any part of the Body. In *Jafnapatnam* there are many Crocodiles in the Fens, Ponds and Lakes, which if they happen to dry up in the Summer, they dig holes to live in; we were often visited by them in our Camp before *Jafnapatnam*, but they did no mischief. The *Chineses* make a dainty Dish of the young Crocodiles.

Porcupines. In the Isle of *Manaar* are great numbers of very large *Porcupines*, or Sea-hogs; they have very sharp Teeth, and their Flesh is fit for Food; the Females have Breasts and Milk, they come often ashore and feed upon Herbs.

* CHAP.

Baldæus.

CHAP. LII.

Serpents of Ceylon. *Remedies against their Stings. An odd Story of a Serpent-Catcher. Precious Stones, Products of the Sea. Amber-Grease, its Goodness.*

Serpents. SErpents are very common all over the Isle of *Ceylon*: The *Sea-Serpents* are sometimes 8, 9, or 10 yards long. The Land-Serpents call'd *Ratcatchers* are also very large, live on the tops of the Houses, but are harmless Creatures. The most dangerous are those call'd *Cobres Capellos* by the *Portugueses*, which frequently used to kill People whilst I liv'd in *Jafnapatnam*. So soon as any body is stung or wounded by these Serpents, they apply the *Adder-stone* to the Wound, and give the Patient some Milk. Our Chyrurgeon *Albert van Lambergen* writ to me 1666. that being stung by a Serpent, he became blind, but after some time recover'd his sight. A Parishioner belonging to the Church of *Manipay*, as he was mending the top of the Church, happen'd to be wounded by a Serpent that lay hid among a heap of Leaves, and died soon after. I saw once two Serpents twisted round one another sporting under the Wall of the same Church, which I order'd to be cut to pieces by a Soldier. Such of the Inhabitants as retain still some Remnants of Paganism, will not allow the Serpents to be kill'd.

Remedies against their Sting.

The *Malabars* call the Serpents *Pambo* and *Naga*, and give their Cattel and Children their Names; nay they feed them because they should do them no harm. The Serpents come frequently into the Houses, especially in the rainy season. During my Abode at *Jafnapatnam* two Dogs were stung to death in the House, and I have seen them sometimes pass up stairs over the Beds. Another time a Serpent pass'd so near my Wife in the House, that he touch'd her Leg with the Tail, and was afterwards kill'd by the Servants.

There is also here a kind of Adders call'd *Vipers* by the *Portugueses*, they are speckled and very venomous. Whilst I liv'd at *Jafnapatnam*, a certain High-*German* Sol-

Baldæus. dier belonging to the Garison (commonly known by the Name of the *Serpent-Catcher*) being sent for by Mr. *Anthony Pavilion* Governor of *Coromandel*, to take a certain *Cobre Capel*, that was in his Lodging-room; he came accordingly, and with his Hat only before his Face, laid hold with his other hand of the Serpent, without receiving the least harm; he did handle the Creature afterwards in our Presence, and not only carried it away in his Snapsack, but also used to sleep near it. I suspecting some Witchcraft in the matter, talk'd to him seriously about it; but he assured me, that nothing was done but by natural means, and that he always carried the Head and Heart of a Serpent about him: wherewith I was forced to rest satisfy'd, he being not willing to discover the whole Mystery.

An odd Story of a Serpent-catcher.

Among the Inhabitants of the Coast of *Coromandel*, and the *Cingaleses* and *Malabars*, are certain Fellows, who have an Art of making the Serpents stand upright and dance before them, which they perform by certain enchanting Songs. Those that are to take an Oath in those parts, put one of their Hands into an Earthern Vessel, wherein is a Serpent: if they escape without being wounded, they are supposed to swear true; but if not, on the contrary.

Remedies against the Stings of Serpents.

Upon this Occasion I can't forget to mention some Remedys used against the Stings of Serpents. First of all it is requisite to bind the affected Part above and below the Wound, to prevent the Poison from being communicated to the Mass of Blood, and afterwards hold it over or as near to the Flame as it is possible. I would have every body that goes to the *East-Indies*, to provide himself with some *Orvietan*, *Theriac*, *Mithridate*, Confection of *Alkermes*, Balsam of *Peru*, *Rue*, *Scordium*, *Scorzonera*, *Angelic*, and *Contrabierva* Roots, these being great Cordials and Antidotes.

They must keep to a cooling Diet, and avoid purging and bleeding, but instead thereof make use of bathing to open the Pores of the Body. The Peel of Lemons or Citrons taken fresh from the Tree, is accounted an excellent Remedy, and fasting Spittle applied to the Wound. If you can take the Serpent that has given the Wound, bruise the Head, and apply it to the affected part. However the *Adderstone* surpasses all the rest, but is often adulterated. The right one raises no Bubbles upon the Water, and sticks close to the Lips, if put to the Mouth.

The Serpents of *Ceylon* are not altogether so large as those of *Java* and *Banda*: at *Batavia* there was once taken a Serpent, which had swallowed an entire Stag of a large Size; and one taken at *Banda* had done the same with a Negro Woman.

Besides these Serpents, *Ceylon* produces several sorts of other crawling Creatures, as *Thousand Feet*, called *Millepie* by the *Portugueses*, which are sometimes 7 Inches long; Scorpions, Spiders of a prodigious Bigness, Frogs, Tortoises, Toads, &c. *Ceylon* also affords divers precious Stones, as *Saphirs*, *Rubies*, *Topazes*, *Granats*, &c. Some say it also produces Gold, Silver, Iron, and other Metals, but that their Kings will not allow these Mines to be dug. This seems not improbable, it being certain that Iron has been bought out of the Country. It affords also Chrystal in abundance. The Commodities chiefly vented here by the *Portugueses*, were colour'd Stuffs of all sorts, Velvets, Silks, Red Caps, Porcelain Spices, *Amfira* or *Opium*, *China* Root, Camphyr, Musk, Sandel wood, Lead, Copper, Tin, Saltpeter, Brimstone, gilt Looking-Glasses, glass Bottles, painted Callicoes of *Suratte* and *Coromandel*, all which are still in vogue here.

Precious Stones.

Commodities sold here.

The Isle of *Ceylon* has besides Fish, several Products of the Sea. Of the Pearls and Pearl-fishery we have spoken before, in the Description of *Tutecoryn*. *Ambergreese* is found here sometimes near the Sea-shore, in good large pieces and of the best kind: they call it *Panahambar* in the *Maldive* Islands. This precious Drug was altogether unknown to *Hippocrates*, *Dioscorides* and *Galen*, and to this day its true Origin is a Riddle to us; tho some will have it to be the Seed of the Whales, others a certain fine Earth, others a certain Pitch or Rosin, growing at the bottom of the Sea, and forced thence to the Shore by Tempests. Certain it is, that it is generally found after stormy Weather. Mr. *John Huygan van Linschoten* mentions a piece of *Ambergreese*, taken up near the *Cape Comoryn*, 1555, which weighed 30 Quintals. It's said, that the Birds are very fond of the Scent of it, and the Prints of the Bills of Birds have sometimes been perceived in the *Amber*, and is accounted a certain Sign of its Goodness.

Ambergreese.

Its Origin.

Mr. *Rocheford* in his *Natural History* of the *American Islands*, says, that the *Amber* there, when first taken, has so nauseous a Scent, that the Birds are drawn towards it as by the Smell of a Carrion: He says, it smells like rank Bacon.

* The

Difference. The *Amber* is of different kinds; the black (the worst of all) is found near the Isle of *Mauritius*; next is the *White*, and the *Grey* the best of all. In some parts of *America* there is a kind of *Amber*, they call the *foxed Amber*, because it is swallowed and vomited up again by the Foxes without any Alteration, except that it loses something of its Scent. The best *Ambergreese* is of an Ash Colour, like Ashes mix'd with Wax. It is adulterated with Wax, Rosin and Pitch; to know the real Goodness of it, you must thrust a hot Needle into it, and by the Smell of the Moisture that adheres to it, you may judg of its Goodness: You may also lay a small quantity of Amber upon a hot Knife; if it be good, it will melt immediately like Wax; and provided the Knife be very hot, it will quite evaporate without leaving the least Dregs behind. *Scaliger*, *Garcias*, *Monard*, *Fernandes Lopes*, *Clusius*, and *Rocheford* have written of the *Ambergreese*, its Medicinal Virtues we will leave to the Judgment of the Physicians.

Goodness how to be tryed.

Baldæus.

The Sea about *Ceylon* produces likewise whole Coral Trees, some Branches whereof curiously grown I preserve in my Study. It affords also certain Horns of Sea-Horses, called *Chankos*, which are frequently transported to *Bengale*, besides divers other sorts of Horns and Shells (but not so curiously twisted as those of *Amboyna*) *Sea-Apples*, *Sea-Stars*, and such like.

THE

THE IDOLATRY OF THE East-India Pagans,

Giving a true and full Account of the Religious Worship of the *Indosthans*, the Inhabitants of *Coromandel*, the *Malabars* and *Ceyloneses*; with a Description of their Idols.

PART I.

CHAP. I.

The general Consent of all Nations concerning the Existence of God. Divers Sects of the Brahmans. *Their Opinion concerning the Creation. The Idols* Ixora *and* Quivelinga.

The Existence of a God.

THE Existence of a God or supreme Being, is so firmly rooted in the Heart of Mankind, that there is no Nation in the World but what has acknowledged the same. What is alledged to the contrary by some, of the *Chileses*, *Tapujars*, *Brasilians*, *Madagascarians*, as also of the Inhabitants of *Florida*, the *Caribee* Islands, and especially of the *Cape of Good Hope*, must rather be attributed to the want of Knowledg of those Authors, than real Truth. Of this I was sufficiently convinced 1666. when I tarried three Months at the *Cape of Good Hope*, where I found these Barbarians to perform their Religious Service in the Night time, which I had no Opportunity to observe in 1665, when I came that way before. What is said of *Diagoras*, *Theodorus*, *Cyrenaicus*, *Bion*, *Evemerus*, *Lucianus*, *Epicurus*, and especially of *Protagoras*, *Abderites* and *Socrates*, and their Denial of the Existence of God, being to be understood only of the Plurality of Gods, which was always rejected by the wiser sort among the Pagans; whence it is that we meet with the Titles of *Ens Entium*, *the Being of all Beings*, *Ens primum*, *the first Being*, *Primus motor & vis motrix*, *the first moving Cause and Substance*, in their Writings.

This being laid down as a fundamental Rule, we will proceed to give an account of the Idolatry of the Pagans inhabiting the Coast of *Malabar* and the *Indies*, on both sides of the Cape *Comoryn*, viz. at *Tutecoryn*, *Trevanor*, *Coulang*, Co-

Calecoulang, *Cochin*, *Cranganor*, *Calecut*, *Canänor*, as also on the Coast of *Coromandel*, and the Isle of *Ceylon*. According to *Rogerius*, the *Brahmans* are distinguish'd into six Sects, *viz. Weistnouwas*, *Sciria*, *Smaerta*, *Schaerwaeka*, *Pasenda* and *Tschectea*; and the *Benjans* of *Gusuratte* into no less than 63: but in the forementioned parts, the *Brahmans* are divided into four head Sects.

Sects of the Brahmans.

The first are the *Cenrawack*, who use neither Fire, nor Candles, nor cold Water, for fear it should contain some living Creatures; they don't pass the Streets unless they be swept before with a Broom, which they always carry with them, for fear of treading upon any thing that is living. They believe neither God nor Providence, but that all things are produced by Chance.

The second Sect is called *Samaraeth*, they actually believe a God.

The third *Bisnou*, who call their God *Ram*. They have a Fast which begins in *August*, and holds 40 days.

The fourth Sect is that of the *Goegii*, who have no Habitations of their own, but sleep in the Night-time in the Churches; they walk generally naked, having only a Cloth to cover their Privities, and besmear themselves all over with Ashes. They believe a God (whom they call *Bruyn*) the Creator of the Universe, who is in every thing, whether Man or Beast (tho he can't be seen by the Creature) gives Light to Sun and Moon, and annihilates what and when he pleases. They say, that such as die in their Faith, go directly to their God *Bruyn*: they do not burn, but bury their dead. Whoever embraces their Sect, is obliged to take near a Pound of Cowdung every day among his ordinary Food, for six Months successively, the Cow being accounted sacred, and her Dung the purest thing among them. They are very superstitious: a Cart, Buffler or Ass without a Load, a Dog empty mouth'd, a Hegoat, Ape, a Goldsmith, Carpenter, Barber, Taylor, Smith, Cottonweaver, a Widow, a Burial, or some body going to a Burial, are altogether ill Omens to them; as an Elephant, Camel, an Horse without a Burden, a Cow, an Ox and Buffler laden with Water, pretends good Luck in their Opinion. Some acknowledg one *Vistnou* for their supreme God, but the most one *Ixora*; we will first treat of *Ixora*, and afterwards of *Vistnou* and *Bramma*.

See Rogerius, Texeira, Carolino, John van Twist, &c.

The *Brahmans* have a very odd Opinion of the Creation of the World (of which more hereafter) They say that this World will diminish by degrees, till it comes to a Drop of Water, which is the *Ixoretta* or *Divinity* it self: After that it shall encrease again, when *Ixoretta* crying out aloud, *Quen, quen*, will make it turn again into a single drop of Dew; this will make it revive again, first into a Mustard-Seed Corn, then turn to a Pearl, and lastly into an Egg, containing the five Elements. This Egg they say is to have seven distinct Shells or Partitions like an Onion, whence will break forth the Fire and Air upwards, and the others downwards; and, the Egg being thereby broken into two pieces, the upper part produced the Heavens, as the under part did the Earth; and because the Egg had seven Shells, which by the Division thereof made 14 half ones, the seven uppermost Parts furnished the matter for seven Heavens, as the seven undermost did for as many Worlds. An unpardonable Contradiction, when they themselves acknowledg their *Bramma*, and implore him as *the Creator of Heavens and Earth*; and how incongruous is it, to make the *Ixoretta* or Divinity subject to decrease?

Baldæus.

Opinion of the Brahmans concerning the Creation of the World.

They further add, that at the opening of the beforesaid Egg, there appear'd a Thred drawn all along the middle, which join'd the 14 upper and under Worlds: *Ixoretta* then taking his Place in the highest Sphere of the Heavens, there arose at the same time a Mountain on the Earth, named *Calaja*, on the top of which stood a Triangular Substance (*Tricona Sacra*) which produced a round Substance, called *Quivelinga*, i. e. *the Members of Generation of both Sexes*; which *Quivelinga* they say, is *Ixoretta* or the Divinity: for finding that all living Creatures were procreated by the carnal Copulation of Men and Women, they reverenced this *Quivelinga*, as the Original of all created things, and adorned him in their Temples with the best sweet Herbs and Flowers. They have a certain religious Order called *Jogiis*, who wear the Figure of this *Quivelinga*, either of Wood or Copper, about the Neck, and offer him daily the best of their Victuals. *Rogerius* speaks to the same purpose of the *Lingam*, i. e. *Membrum virile in Muliebri*, as the *Ixora* or *Eswara* is represented in their *Pagodes*.

What Quivelinga was.

St. *Austin* * tells us something like this of the *Priapus*, which used to be carried in Procession in Honour of *Bacchus*, thro the Cities of *Italy*, and that the Matrons used to crown his *Membrum virile*

*L. 7. c. 21. de Civitate Dei.

Baldæus.

virile with Garlands. I have read in several Authors of known Integrity, and speak it upon the Credit of divers People yet living, that the *Canarins*, and Inhabitants about *Goa*, do carry their Brides to such a *Priapus*, in order to deliver them of their Virginity. The whole matter whereof I will for Modesties sake relate in Latin: *Sponsa magno comitatu multaque cum pompa inter plausus ac sonos musicos ducitur ad Idolum, quod ænea virga vel ferrea, vel eburnea prominente præditum conspicitur, & ad hanc nudata visit: Sponsa a Matre vel a proximis Consanguineis vehementer impellitur, quod cum absque gravi dolore fieri nequeat, illi qui adsunt, cantando & saltando sponsæ flebiles voces opprimant, si quæ est, quæ dolorem immensum verita, hoc modo Virginitate privari recusat, blandis Consanguineorum verbis ad Idolum paulatim adducitur, atque ad id a Matre tamdiu (invita quamvis) adigitur, donec Virginitatem amiserit; postea Sponsa domum redens Sponso traditur, qui de hoc præ se susceptoLabore sibi maximopere gratulatur.*

Canarins *offer their Brides to* Priapus.

Baal Phegor seems to have been the *Priapus* of the *Jews*. *Jerom* in his Commentary upon the Prophet *Hosea*, says, That the *Jewish* Women worshipped *Baal Phegor*, *ob obscæni magnitudinem Membri, quem nos* Priapum *possumus appellare.*

The *Brahmans* will indeed not allow of this Interpretation, alledging that they adore under this, the Circular Figure which is infinite, whereas the Signification of the word sufficiently contradicts them. *Quivelinga* being composed out of the word *Linga* or *Lingam*, i. e. the *Manly Yard*, and *Quiven*, the same with *Ixora*; and the Figure carried by the *Jogii*, expresly represents the Conjunction of the Members of both Sexes.

Quivelinga then (as we said before) is of a Circular Figure, which being enclosed in three distinct Rinds or Shells, which they say are transmuted into three Gods, *viz. Bramma*, *Vistnum* and *Quiven*; the first and hardest produces *Bramma*, the second *Vistnum*, and the innermost *Quiven*. *Quivelinga* being thus despoil'd of his Shells, was burnt to Ashes by Fire, and fix'd in the Triangle: *Quivelinga* being thereby become a thing without Sense or Motion, it was requisite it should be guarded by some body; which *Bramma* and *Vistnum* refusing to do, *Quiven* undertook the Task, and constantly attending *Quivelinga* with Prayers and Sacrifices of Flowers, deserved thereby to be ranked above his Brothers, and obtain'd the Title of the *Great God*, as their Poets call him. The *Brahmans* say, that *Bramma*, *Vistnum*, and *Quiven* or *Ixora*, are commissioned by the *First Being* to rule the World in the Nature of his Viceroys. They say *Ixora* resides in *Calaja*, *Vistnum* in the *Milk-Sea*, and *Bramma* in *Sattialogam*, or the highest Place in Heaven, of which more hereafter.

CHAP. II.

A Description of Ixora, *his Wives. Abstinency of the* Brahmans. *Divers sorts of Eunuchs.*

A Description of Ixora.

IXORA is as bright and white as Milk, with three Eyes, two whereof are plac'd as those of other Men, and the third in the Front, being so full of Fire, that it consumes every thing it looks upon. His Stature is immense; for *Bramma* being desirous to see his Head, soar'd up high into the Earth, but could not reach it. *Vistnum* (whom they call the God of Inventions and Changes) having the same Curiosity to see his Feet, which reach'd deep into the Ground, transformed himself into a Hog, the better to dig up the Earth, but could likewise not obtain his Wish. For, say they, *Ixora* is of so vast an extent, that the Serpent *Bategu* (which is so long as to compass the seven Worlds and the seven Seas) was not big enough to serve him for a Bracelet. I heard a Pagan once ridicule a *Brahman*, because he put the Figure of *Ixora* in his Chamber; whereas according to their Opinion, it was much larger than the Serpent *Bategu*.

His Bigness.

This Pan *was anciently represented with Horns reaching up to the Clouds.*

Ixora has no less than 16 Hands, wherewith he holds the following things, *A Heart*, a *Chain*, a *Fiddle*, * a *Bell*, *Porcellain Bason*, *Capalla*, i. e. *Bramma*'s *Head*, a *Trident*, a *Rope*, an *Ax*, *Fire*, *Gold*, a *Drum*, *Beads*, a *Staff*, an *Iron Wheel*, a *Serpent*, with a Crescent or half Moon on his Forehead. His Apparel is a *Tygers* Skin, his Cloke the Hide of an Elephant, surrounded with Serpents †. He wears about his Neck a Collar of the Skin of a certain Creature, called *Maudega*,

* *As* Pan *had his Flute.*

† Pan *wore the Skin of a Panther, the Spots whereof intimated the variety of Nature in Stars, Flowers, Isles, &c.*

dega, on which is fastened a Bell, such as our Oxen or Sheep commonly have about their Necks.

He has also about his Neck three Chains, one whereof being intermix'd with Roses and other Flowers, affords an odoriferous Scent. The second is made of the Heads of *Bramma*; for they say, that *Bramma* dies and revives every year, and that *Ixora* gathering his Heads as often as he dies, had made this Chain of it. The third is made of the Bones of *Baldæus.*

The Idol Ixora

Chatti, one of *Ixora*'s Wives. For it is to be known that he has two Wives, one named *Grienga* or the *Goddess of the Seas*, whom he always carries in his Hairlocks; the other this *Chatti*, otherwise called *Paramesceri*, who they say dies and revives once a Year; and as often as she dies, he takes one of her Bones, which are put into this Chain. He carries also the same Beads as the *Brahmans* do, his whole Body being besmear'd with Ashes, and thus rides in Triumph thro *Calaja*, upon an Ox named *Irixapatan*, unto whom they offer certain Sacrifices.

His Attendants are called *Pudas*, *Pixaros* and *Pes*. *Pudas* is represented like a fat and short Person, with a large Paunch, without a Beard, having Serpents hanging down with their Tails from his Head. He wears a Bracelet on his left Arm, and two others about his Thighs, made of Serpents, and a Staff in his Right Hand. The *Pes* and *Pixaros* are represented much taller, with burning Torches in their Hands in the Night-time.

They say that *Bramma* has created the Universe, *Vistnum* governs it, and *Ixora* kills and puts a Period to every thing. They further add, that *Ixora* has communicated part of his Substance to his Wife *Paramesceri*, alias *Parvati*, and she again to him; so that they are both Hermaphrodites, and *Ixora* is sometimes represented as such; and *Rogerius*, *lib.* 2. says, that the *Brahmans* call their *Ixora*, *Ardhanari*, i. e. a *Manwife*. There are however a certain sort of *Brahmans* called *Tirimimpi*, who are so far different from the rest, that they won't as much as cast an Eye upon a Woman; for which reason as often as they pass thro the Streets, they have certain Persons, who bid the Women go out of the way. Thus the *Hierophantes* of *Athens*, and the Priests of the Goddess *Cybele* among the *Ro-* *A strict sort of Brahmans.*

Baldæus. *Romans*, used to deny themselves the use of Venery, the first by castrating themselves, the others by certain Drugs. The *Jews* distinguish betwixt *Eunuchs made by God*, and those made by Men, the last are believed to owe their Original to the *Persians*; and among the *Jews* they had certain Persons, called *Impingentes*, because they used to run against Posts and Doors, rather than to look upon a Woman.

Divers sorts of Eunuchs.

Rogerius * mentions another sort of *Brahmans*, called *Sausiazii*, who renounce all Worldly Pleasures, abstain from Women, and even the *Betel* (tho generally used all over the *Indies*) eat but once a day, have no fix'd Habitations, use nothing but earthen Vessels, and live upon Alms. The fundamental Rules of their Sect being to withstand *Lust*, *Anger*, *Covetousness*, *Pride*, the *Pleasures of the World*, and *Revenge*.

* L. 2. c. 4.

CHAP. III.

Contest betwixt Bramma, Vistnum *and* Ixora, *who is obliged to be a Mendicant twelve Years. A Child produced out of the Blood of* Vistnum, *occasions new Differences.*

THE Residence of *Ixora* is upon the Silver Mount *Calaja*, to the South of the famous Mountain *Mahameru*, being a most delicious Place, planted with all sorts of Trees, that bear Fruit all the Year round. The Roses and other Flowers send forth a most odoriferous Scent, and the Pond at the Foot of the Mount is enclosed with pleasant Walks of Trees, that afford an agreeable Shade, whilst the Peacocks and divers other Birds entertain the Ear with their Harmonious Noise, as the Beautiful Women do the Eyes. The circumjacent Woods are inhabited by a certain People, called *Mumis* or *Rixis*, who avoiding the Conversation of others, spend their time in offering daily Sacrifices to their God.

It is observable, that tho these Pagans are generally black themselves, yet do they represent these *Rixis* to be of a fair Complexion, with long white Beards, and long Garments hanging crosswise, from about the Neck down over the Breast. They are in such esteem among them, that they believe, that whom they bless are blessed, and whom they curse are cursed.

Within the Mountain lives another Generation, call'd *Jexaquinnera* and *Quendra*, who are free from all Troubles, spend their Days in continual Contemplations, Praises and Prayers to God. Round about the Mountain stand 7 Ladders, by which you ascend to a spacious Plain, in the middle whereof is a Bell of Silver, and a square Table, surrounded with nine precious Stones of divers Colours. Upon this Table lies a Silver Rose called *Tamara Pua*, which contains two Women as bright and fair as a Pearl; one is called *Brigasiri*, i. e. *the Lady of the Mouth*, the other *Tarasiri*, i. e. *the Lady of the Tongue*, because they praise God with the Mouth and Tongue. In the Center of this Rose is the *Triangle*, (mentioned in the 1*st Chap.*) of *Quivelinga*, which they say is the permanent Residence of God.

Ixora being one time diverting himself in this *Cajala* or *Paradise*, with *Pudas*, *Pes* and *Pixajos*, let fall some Words, intimating him to be the greatest in all the World; which *Bramma* and *Vistnum* not able to brook, a Contest arose about the Precedency, to decide which *Ixora* told them, that which of the two could take a full view of him from Head to Foot, should be accounted the Greatest.

Contest betwixt Ixora, Bramma *and* Vistnum.

Bramma hereupon got upon his Bird *Annam* (whereof more anon) and passed up into the Air, to get Sight of *Ixora*'s Head, whilst *Vistnum* transforming himself into a Hog, dug into the Ground, to come at his Feet: whilst he was thus employed, meeting with a most poisonous Serpent, he was so startled at it, that he desisted from his Enterprize. This Story is related more at large by several of the *Malabar* Poets.

Bramma on the other hand, resolute in his Designs, soared very high into the Air, when being met by three Flowers, they ask'd him whither he was a going; he replied, to get sight of the Head of *Ixora*; they told him, *his Labour was in vain*, by reason of the vast distance, which made *Bramma* change his Resolution: but at the same time desired the Flowers to tell *Ixora*, that he was prevented from coming so high as his Head, by a sudden Giddiness in his Brains, which

which they promised, and did accordingly; but *Ixora* being sensible of the Deceit, did with his *Chacra* or Scymeter, cut off one of the four Heads of *Bramma*, and cursed the Flowers. Out of the Blood of *Bramma*'s Head, came forth a Man with 500 Heads and 1000 Hands, named *Sagatracavaxen*. The day on which *Bramma*'s Head was cut off, was ever after looked upon as ominous, and named *Pongalacha*, i. e. *Dies infestus*; whence arose the Proverb of a thing that is never to be done, *It shall be at Pongalacha*.

One of Bramma's *Heads cut off by* Ixora.

The three Flowers were cursed, *viz.* That one of them should grow upon a Dunghil, and be cut down there; the other to be turn'd into a Crow, and the third into a Cow.

The *Brahmans* further say, That *Ixora* to expiate the Crime he had committed by cutting off the Head of *Bramma*, turned Mendicant as the *Jogii* do, with *Bramma*'s Skull in his Hand, till the same should be filled with Alms; whence arose that Custom practised to this Day, that he who kills a *Brahman*, must beg Alms for 12 years in the Skull of the *Brahman* killed by his Hands. *Ixora* therefore beg'd Alms for 12 Years; for tho he receiv'd sufficient Alms, yet by the fiery Rays that darted from his Eye in his Forehead, it was all consumed and turned to Ashes in an Instant.

One day as he was gathering Alms among the beforesaid *Mumis*, their Wives came running with whole Ladles of Blood to fill the Skull; but not being able to sustain the Glance of his Eyes, they were so surpriz'd, that they let slip not only their Ladles, but also their Clothes. The *Mumis* seeing their Wives naked, did fall Pellmell upon *Ixora*; one attack'd him with an Ax, which he seized and got up into the Air; another would have killed him with a Serpent, which he took in his Hands, without receiving any harm. Then they brought a furious Tyger to devour him, this he killed and flee'd, and made a Garment of the Skin; then they set upon him a wild Elephant, who underwent the same Fate, his Hide serving him afterwards for a Cloke; this *Ax*, *Serpent*, *Tyger*, and *Elephant*, are the same Trophies he holds in his Hands.

Ixora *attacked by the* Mumis.

Baldæus.

Vistnum willing to deliver *Ixora*, appear'd to the *Mumis* in the shape of a most beautiful Virgin, which occasion'd such a Surprize to them, that the Men (as their Wives had done before) fell into a Trance, and *Ixora* spill'd his Seed upon the Ground, which *Vistnum* with his Hand form'd into a Child.

Ixora being towards the end of the 12*th* year, quite tired with his Mendicant Life, had recourse to *Vistnum*, who commiserating his Condition, put out the fiery Eye, that consumed all the Alms in the Skull; which done, *Vistnum* wounded himself in one of his Fingers, and fill'd the Skull with the Blood, which put an end to his Pilgrimage, but gave birth to the Order of the *Jogii*, who in the Memory of *Ixora*'s Pilgrimage, lead a Mendicant Life to this Day.

Relieved by Vistnum

Out of the Blood of *Vistnum* a Child was procreated, called *Vareu*, which occasion'd new Contests, *Bramma* challenging it as his own, because it was begot in his Skull, *Vistnum* because it came forth out of his Blood, and *Ixora* because it came out of his Hands. To reconcile this Difference, *Devaindra*, a King of the aerial Spirits, persuaded them to relinquish their Pretensions by joint Consent; which they having consented to, *Devaindra* educated the Child at *Devalogam*, where becoming a famous Bowman, he protected that Place against *Sagatracavagem*, who, as we told before, being the Product of *Bramma*'s Head, had 500 Heads and 1000 Hands. Afterwards *Ixora* returned to *Calaja* his former Residence.

Another Contest.

It is observable, that if one of their Kings dies, they tie his Hands and Feet, when certain Soldiers come to threaten him with their Sticks; which Affront, they believe is a means to expiate the Trespasses committed by him in his Lifetime against his Subjects.

CHAP. IV.

The Children of Ixora; *the Nativity and Constitution of* Quenavady. *The Origin of* Sura. Quenavady *castrated. Contest betwixt him and* Superbennia. *His Habitation and Gluttony. Funeral Feasts of the* Malabars.

Children of Ixora.

IXORA had three Sons and one Daughter, the eldest resembling an Elephant, the second an Ape, the third had 6 Faces and 12 Hands. The Daughter, who was as black as a Coal, had the Face of a Hog. The eldest Son named *Quenevady*,

Baldæus.

navady was born in the Wood by *Piragu*, with an Elephant's Head and Face, the rest of his Body being like other Men. For *Ixora* walking one time with his Lady *Paramesceri* towards the Wood *Piragu*, she saw an Elephant sporting with a Female of the same kind, and so raised her Appetite, that she desir'd *Ixora* to be both transform'd into Elephants; which being done accordingly, they ate of a certain Fruit in the Wood, which made them quite frenzical, so that they made the same noise, overturn'd the Trees, threw up the Sand with their Trunks, and did all the other Actions of Elephants, not excepting even their Copulation. The

Quenevady's Original.

Female having conceiv'd immediately, brought forth this Child with the Elephant's Head and Face, and soon after they resumed their own Shape. *Paramesceri* tried to give suck to this young Monster, but being in danger of having her Breast torn in pieces by it, she deliver'd it up to *Ixora*, who had it brought up in *Calaja*.

A Description of him.

This *Quenevady* had the Hand, Teeth and Face of an Elephant, with large hanging Ears, and ugly Lips, with red Pimples all over the Face: His Hair is long (like his Father's) tied about with a Serpent or Adder, with a Crescent or Half-moon on his Fore-head, and four Hands, besides the Trunk; the rest of his Body like other Men, but shining like Gold, with a large Paunch tied about with a red piece of Stuff: He wears also the Girdle of the *Brahmans*, and on his Feet divers Gold Rings and Bells.

A Story of Ixora.

They tell you another Story of *Ixora*, *viz.* That being one time inebriated with the *Sury*, or Juice of the *Coco*-Tree, and having Carnal Copulation with *Paramesceri*, a small quantity of *Ixora*'s Seed was spilt upon the ground, and afterwards cover'd with Earth by *Paramesceri*; this produc'd a Palm-tree. *Ixora* coming soon after into the Wood, and seeing the young Tree, cut off the top thereof with his *Chacra*, or Weapon. The Liquor which issued thence so well pleased *Ixora*, that he took a good quantity of it in his Cup he always carried along with him, and having drank his full share, ty'd up the Tree, and so return'd to *Calaja*. He repeated this so often, that *Paramesceri* finding him always return in Drink from

*

from the Wood, took the next opportunity to follow him thither, and finding the Juice very acceptable, she tasted so long of it, till she was also inebriated. *Ixora* when he first espy'd his Wife behind him, cry'd out to her, *Calli*, that is, you *she-Thief*: whereupon she answering, *Calla*, i. e. *Thief*; the *Malabars* to this day call the said Juice *Calla*. *Ixora* being well pleas'd with the young Tree, he stretch'd it with his hand higher and higher, and so turn'd it into a Palm-tree.

It seems somewhat odd, that the *Brahmans* who pretend so much to Sobriety, should make their *Supreme God* a Drunkard, when they are so nice in this Point, that they will never make use of our Ink, for fear there should be some Wine in it. Thus the *Samoryn* of *Calecut* kill'd his own Brother-in-law because he was drunk, and the King of *Cochin* did the same to a Company of drunken *Nairos*.

The Brahmans *averse to Drunkenness.*

They further tell us of this *Ixora*, that he caus'd his Son *Quenavady* to be castrated, because he once, whilst yet in his Mother's Arms, touch'd her Privy-Parts with his Trunk: others say he actually enjoy'd her; which is the reason the *Malabars* say that the Elephants have no Testicles.

Quenavady *castrated.*

It is to this *Quenavady* the Pagan Artisans, Workmen, *&c.* offer the first-fruits of their Labour. After they have reverenced and offer'd Sacrifices to him for 12 years, he moves one of his Ears, as a sign that they must continue the same; which being done 12 other years, he shakes the other Ear, to give them to understand that he requires still more at their hands; if they hold on 12 years longer, he opens his Eyes and grants their Requests.

How worshipp'd.

Ixora being at a certain time desirous to try the Agility of his two Sons *Quenavady* and *Superbennia*, offer'd a very fine Fig as a Reward to him who should carry the day. *Quenavady* having a very thick Skin, and riding only upon a Mouse, whereas *Superbennia* had 6 Faces and 12 Arms, and rid upon a Peacock, being sufficiently convinc'd that his Brother would carry the Prize, took his opportunity whilst the other was riding round the *Calaja*, to turn short and so lay hold of the Fig. *Superbennia* having taken his turn, pursuant to the Wager, and not finding the Fig, did fall upon *Quenavady* so furiously, that he beat out one of his Teeth: But *Ixora* giving *Superbennia* another Fig, the difference was soon ended. But not knowing what to do with the Tooth, he gave it to *Vistnou*, desiring him to restore it to *Quenavady*, which he did accordingly by putting it into a Fig which he gave to his Nephew, who as he was going to eat the Fig found the Tooth, which he turn'd into a nice writing Pen, and kept it to write his Poetry with.

Difference betwixt Quenavady *and* Superbennia.

Baldæus.

For the rest *Quenavady* is represented as very voracious, for they say he could devour the whole World; nor is he to be satiated but in the *Sugar-Sea* call'd *Jexucadhil*, which is of a vast extent, and always boiling-hot, having in the midst a Mount compos'd of 9 very fine Stones, with a Plain on the top, deliciously seated, in the Center whereof stands the Tree *Luola*, inclosed with a row of precious Stones curiously wrought. In this Enclosure is a Structure of the finest red Coral, cover'd with precious Stones: The Doors whereof, as well as the Avenues to the place, are guarded by a good force of the *Pudas*, who spend their time in holy Meditations and Prayers in the Company of a good number of Women, who sing to the Praise of God. Close about the Tree *Luola* are Seats of Gold, and a Table made of the most precious Stone call'd *Bairacalle*, upon which stand a bright shining Mouse, and a Rose, in the Leaves whereof are written 14 Letters or Characters. This is the Residence of *Quenavady*, who rides upon the said Mouse.

The Sugar-Sea.

He has on each side of him a most beautiful Woman, who are continually employ'd to lade Sugar mixt with Hony into his Mouth; and for fear he should be tir'd with the same Diet, good store of *Affes* (*Indian* Cakes) fried in Butter-milk, Butter, and divers other Provisions, stand always before him. The Hills near it afford also Figs, Grapes, *Coco* Nuts, and all other sorts of the best Fruits, as well as Roses and other Flowers; the Musicians that attend divert him with Fiddles, Trumpets, Flutes, Hautboys, and other Musical Instruments, as many Women are employ'd to make rich Incenses, and to anoint his Body with Sandal Wood, Civet, Musk, and to offer all sorts of odoriferous Flowers.

The *Malabars* celebrate yearly the Memory of their deceased Friends with great Pomp and vast Charge, according to their Abilities. The Kings upon this occasion entertain the *Brahmans* (who are in high esteem there, as being the Interpreters of their *Vedam* or Law-book) magnificently, and distribute Mony after the Feast. And because in the

Funeral Feasts of the Malabars.

Indies,

Baldæus. *Indies*, but especially on the Coast of *Malabar*, there are many petty Kings, as those of *Trevancor*, *Coulang*, *Calecoulang*, *Porca*, *Cochin*, *Cranganor*, *Cananor*, &c. these Feasts are frequent in those parts, and the *Brahmans* will be sure to partake of them, tho they travel sometimes 10, 15, nay 20 Leagues for it, and take their full share; for tho they value themselves much for abstaining from Flesh, Fish, Eggs, Wine and other strong Liquors, yet will they make themselves a full amends with such Victuals as are allowable by their Constitution.

CHAP. V.

Of the other Children of Ixora. *A Coco-Nut in the Head of an Ape.* Siri Hanuman *born an Ape. Reviv'd from the dead. Combat betwixt* Superbennia *and* Quenavady. *His cursing of the Moon.*

THE next to *Quenavady*, is stiled *Egasourubum*, or the *true God*, represented with an Elephant's Head, and 11 Hands. He is only to be worship'd by the *Brahmans*, tho others also sacrifice to him, but must at the same time abstain from Flesh, Fish, Eggs and Wine. Next to him comes *Ceuxi*, whose Origin is related thus: *Paramesceri Ixora*'s Spouse having anointed her Body with Oil and Saffron, and washing her self in a Pond, did form from the Impuritys of her Body a living Man; *Ixora* seeing him at a distance, and believing him to be her Lover, hastned thither, and struck with his Weapon his Head off at the foot of the Mountain *Calaja*, which was turn'd into a *Coco*-Tree, whence it is that the *Indians* say, that the print of a Man's Face was fix'd in the *Coco*-Nut. *Paramesceri* being sorely afflicted at her Son's Death, *Ixora* pleaded his Ignorance, and to comfort her in her Affliction, cut off the Head of a white Elephant, which he put upon the Shoulders of her dead Son, and so restor'd him to life again. He is represented with an Elephant's Head and two Hands.

Why the Coco-Nut has the print of a Mans Face.

Ixora had also another Son, named *Siri Hanuman*, by *Paramesceri*, which was born an Ape. *Ixora* it seems was a most celebrated Dancer, and used frequently to shew his Activity in the presence of the Celestial Spirits, as well as his Spouse *Paramesceri*, who was so active in dancing, that one time when she had lost her Ear-Jewel out of one Ear, she took it up with two Toes of her Feet, and put it in her Ear again, to the incredible surprize of the Spectators. Hence perhaps arose the Custom used among the Ladies of the *Nairos*, who whilst they are dancing at a certain Feast celebrated in honour of one their Idols, let on a sudden slip all their Clothes, and remain naked. But to return to *Ixora*: Having invited many of the Celestial Spirits to see him dance, *Paramesceri* happen'd to see two Apes sport together in the adjacent Wood; she desir'd *Ixora* to transform both her and him into Apes, which done, they leapt about in the Wood till coming to a *Bambo*-Tree, *Paramesceri* then conceiv'd an Ape. In the mean time the Celestial Spirits being come, according to invitation, and among them *Jecxa*, *Quinnera* and *Quendra*, and finding their Host abroad, they sent the *Wind* (as the nimblest of all) to find out *Ixora*, who having told him his Errand, they both resum'd their former shapes.

The Wives of the Nairos slip off their Clothes in dancing.

Paramesceri being now asham'd of her Burden, requested the *Wind* to convey the Ape into the Womb of *Anhema*, one of the Ladies of the Celestial Spirits; and so they return'd home, where *Ixora* danc'd to the admiration of the whole Assembly. *Anhema* afterwards brought forth an Ape as white as *Ixora* himself, who being endow'd with peculiar Virtues by his Father, performed many noted Exploits; of which more hereafter in the History of *Siri Rama*.

Two odd Stories they tell of this Ape: First, That being one time very hungry, and taking the Sun for a dainty bit, he was endeavouring to leap up towards it, but was beat back by the Iron Weapon of *Ixora*, who gave him a good knock on the Pate, but without any harm, whence he got the Name of *Hanuman*. The other is, That meeting one time with a white Elephant call'd *Acrapadia*, on which was mounted *Devaindra* King of the Celestial Spirits, a Quarrel arose betwixt them, in which *Hanuman* was slain: His Father the *Wind* being afflicted at his Death, hid his Face under ground, so that the Inhabitants of the Earth being ready to perish for want of Air in the

Odd Stories of the Ape Siri Hanuman.

extremity of Heat, they address'd themselves to *Ixora*, who restor'd *Hanuman* to life, and recal'd the Wind above ground.

Thus the Wind was ador'd as a God both by the *Greeks* and *Romans*. The *Athenians* erected a Temple to the Wind, as *Augustus* did in *France*; the *Phenicians* did the same. This Ape has divers celebrated *Pagodes* erected to him by the *Indians*. We read in the *Portuguese* Histories, that in 1554, when they plunder'd the famous Pagode upon the *Adams Mount* in *Ceylon*, they found an *Ape*'s Tooth, (the most sacred Relick of the Pagans of *Pegu*, *Ceylon*, *Malabar*, *Bengale*, *Coromandel* and *Bisnagar*) enclosed in a Box set with precious Stones, which they carried to *Goa*; some of the *Indian* Princes offer'd 700000 Ducats to redeem it, but it was not accepted of, by reason the Bishop of *Goa* opposed it.

Another Son of *Ixora* was call'd *Superbennia*, with 6 Faces and 12 Hands, the occasion whereof happened thus: *Paramesceri* being one day employ'd in washing her self in a Cistern, 6 Weavers happen'd to pass by, who inflam'd with Lust, look'd very wishfully at her; this having the same effect upon her, she conceiv'd the same instant: but fearing *Ixora*'s Anger, she threw it out with her Spittle upon the ground, which turning in an instant into a Child with 6 Faces and 12 Hands, much resembling in all other respects the 6 Weavers, they took it along with them, and educated it in all manner of Accomplishments. One time being ingag'd in a Dispute with *Ixora*, he was so taken with his Wit, that he receiv'd him for his Son, assign'd him a Place at *Calaja*, and presented him with a Peacock to ride upon.

A Conception by fancy.

Baldæus.

Before I conclude this Chapter, I must tell you one thing more of *Quenavady*. Returning one day pretty late at night from a Banquet, when the Moon was not very light, it being only the 4*th* day after the New Moon in *August*, with his Umbrella in one hand, in the other a Poem, and some Cakes under his Arm, he ran unwarily against a Post with such violence, that he fell upon the ground and dropt not only his Umbrella, but also his Poems and Cakes: As he was most concern'd for the last, so he took a good bite or two of them before he rose again, or look'd for his Book and Umbrella. The Moon seeing this pleasant Spectacle, could not forbear laughing; which *Quenavady* perceiving, broke out into this Curse, *Who ever, O Moon, shall see thee for the future upon this day in* August, *shall be dammify'd in his Privities.* Hence it is that the Pagans will not stir abroad the 4*th* of *August* after Sun-set, nay even not on the 5*th*, for fear of partaking of this Curse; and if any one is oblig'd to stay without doors, he covers his Face, and even will not look into the Water for fear of seeing the Moon, tho they see the St. *Thomas* Christians, the *Jews* and *Mahometans* look upon it at the same time without the least detriment.

Quenavady *curses the Moon.*

CHAP. VI.

Ixora's *Daughter, and the Origin of the Small-Pox: Fear of the* Malabars *of that Distemper. Their* Pagode Amadyri *plunder'd by the King of* Cochin. *She comes to* Coulang.

A Certain Giant named *Racxada* (of which more anon) having liv'd 12 years with *Bramma*, he receiv'd among many other Presents a Book from him, and some Bracelets, as also the Virtue of being invulnerable. The Natives of *Coromandel* believe these Giants to have been Children of the *Brahman Cassiopa* by his Wife *Aditi*, just as the *Jews* say that *Lilith* brought forth Devils begotten by *Adam*. *Darida* finding himself thus plac'd above the common rank of Men, by his Strength bestow'd upon him by *Bramma*, would needs challenge *Ixora*, who knowing his Strength sent against him a certain Female named *Sorga*, who cut off one of his Heads (for besides his true Head, he had many others, but only in appearance) but *Darida* returning the next day, reiterated his Boasts, when *Ixora* engag'd five holy Women, call'd *Chamundigal* by the *Malabars*, in his Quarrel, who cut off his false Heads; but all to no purpose, so that *Darida* persisting in his Insolence, *Ixora* consulted with *Vistnum*, what to do in this exigency. Whilst they were debating the matter, *Vistnum* sent forth from his Body a certain matter (call'd *Bixa* by the *Malabars*) which entring that of *Ixora*, pass'd again thro the Eye on his Front,

Darida.

Baldæus.

Front, and falling upon the ground produc'd in an instant a Female, which *Ixora* acknowledging for his Daughter, gave her the Name of *Patragali Pagode*.

A Description of Ixora's Daughter.

This Daughter had 8 Faces, 16 Hands as black as a Coal, with large round Eyes, her Teeth like the Tusks of a Boar: In lieu of Pendants she has two Elephants in her Ears, and Serpents about her Body instead of a Garment; her Hair-locks are Peacocks Tails, in her Hand she carries a Sword, a Trident, a large Porcellain Bason, another Vessel call'd *Capala* by the *Malabars*, a Scymiter call'd *Mautegam*, a Hanger call'd *Carutela*, an Arrow, a Weapon call'd *Cona*, a Rope, an Ape with an Iron Wheel.

This Monster was no sooner born, but she went to revenge her Father's Quarrel, and fighting for seven days successively, she cut off 7 of his imaginary Heads; but finding all her Endeavours in vain, and that *Darida* was not vulnerable as long as he kept the Book and Bracelets given him by *Bramma*, she apply'd her self to *Sorga*, intreating her to take upon her the Habit of a Beggar, and by that means endeavour to get the beforesaid things into her hands. Accordingly *Sorga* took the opportunity to ask Alms of *Darida*, when he was at some distance from his House, who told her, that if she would go to his House his Wife would answer her desire, which if she did not, he would do it himself. *Sorga* then went to his House, and ask'd his Wife for the Bracelets and Book in her Husband's Name, who freely delivering the same, she brought them instantly to *Patragali*. *Darida* having thus lost his best Treasures, wherein *Bramma* had enclosed all his Happiness, and thereby being bereav'd of his former Strength, was soon after engag'd again, and had his true Head cut off by *Patragali*.

Being much exalted by this Victory, she came strait to *Ixora*, who being then just undress'd leapt into a Cistern, for fear of being seen by *Patragali*, from whence he gave her some Flesh and Blood; but finding her not satisfied thus, he order'd her to hold out her Bason, and cutting off one of his Fingers he fill'd it with his own Blood; but *Patragali* continuing still unsatisfied, took one of her Golden Chains (composed of small pieces like Pepper Corns) and threw it into his Face, which raising in his Face great numbers of Pimples, or small Ulcers, he cry'd out with great surprize, *Basuri*, i. e. *O you revengeful Woman!* and desiring her to desist, created two young Men named *Birapatrem* and *Quetraquele*, whom he bestow'd upon her, and thus pacified her Anger; but to rid his hand of her for the future, he presented her with a Vessel of Sandal Wood, ordering her to go with it into the World, and to reside (tho unknown) among the Mortals, and to require Vows and Sacrifices at their hands.

Opinion of the Pagans about the Small-pox.

The Pagans therefore imagining that it is *Patragali* sends the Small-Pox among the People, leave the Patient so soon as he is seiz'd with it; and hence perhaps it is, that they have a certain Idol representing a Female, with a Child laying his Arms about her Neck, and imploring her Assistance. They deliver up these Patients to the care of the *Comaras*, a Fraternity belonging to the *Pagode* of *Patragali*; these offer the Blood of some Cocks and other Sacrifices to the Goddess in behalf of the Sick; and for the rest give them only some *Cansies*, or Rice boil'd in Water; and leaving them for the rest to their own disposal, more die for want of good looking after, than by the Violence of the Distemper; nay sometimes are kill'd by *Comaras*, who inherit all their Moveables.

We told you before, that *Ixora* call'd his Daughter *Basuri*, which to this day signifies the *Small-Pox* among the *Malabars*, which they say is the Sword of *Patragali*, and for that reason endeavour to mitigate her Wrath by Sacrifices, wherein they follow the footsteps of the antient *Greeks*.

The Pagode of Patragali in Cranganor.

They say that *Patragali* has her chief Residence in the *Great Pagode* of *Cranganor*, call'd the *Pagode* of Pilgrims, from the vast number of Zealots that flock thither; and as this brings in a Revenue of many thousand *Fanams* to the King of *Cranganor*, so the King of *Cochin*, who fain would have had a share in the Booty, did post some Forces on the Passes, who rob'd and plunder'd the Pilgrims, intending by this means to oblige them to resort to the *Pagode* built in the Kingdom of *Palurti* under his Jurisdiction.

The King of Cochin robs a famous Pagode.

Thus the old King of *Cochin* did plunder and rob the famous *Pagode* of *Ammadiri*, of all its Treasure, at the head of a Body of 10000 Men, and afterwards laugh'd at them into the bargain, saying that he had taken it only as his Inheritance, as being the Son and Heir of the Idol; just as *Dionysius* the *Sicilian* Tyrant did with *Jupiter* and *Æsculapius*.

Adventures of Patragali after she left Ixora.

But to return to *Patragali*; she was no sooner got out into the Main with her Vessel of Sandal-wood, but being attack'd by by some Fisher-men and Ape-Hunters, was forc'd to return to *Calaja*, where finding *Ixora* overwhelm'd with Sleep, she overturn'd his Bedstead, which awakening him, she told him her Disaster; whereupon being endow'd with new Vigor by *Ixora*, she return'd to her Vessel, and having defeated the *Ape-Hunters*, and landed safely on the South-side of *Coulang* (a City of *Malabar*) the Queen thereof sent for her to Court, and entertain'd her there for 12 years as her own Daughter.

The Lord of *Couleta* (a Country 7 Leagues to the North of *Calecut*) then desiring *Patragali* in Marriage for his Son, the same was concluded, and she taken home, where she liv'd for 12 years without ever cohabiting with her Husband, as boasting her self to be the Daughter of *Ixora*. *Mendoza* speaks of a certain Idol in *China* with a Child hanging about her Neck, which the Jesuits would fain perswade the World to have been intended for the Virgin *Mary*, tho it seems much more probable, that it was intended for this *Patragali*. What Mr. *Le Blanc* tells us of the Female Idol of *Calecut*, seems very suspicious to me. *Baldæus*

CHAP. VII.

Patragali's *Father and Mother suffer Shipwrack. She sends her Husband to sell her Jewels, and goes in quest after him. Nine several Adventures which happen to her. The rest of* Ixora *his Children, their Adventures. What further becomes of* Paramesceri.

AFterwards *Patragali*'s Father and Mother-in-law being embark'd aboard a Ship with all their Riches, in order to traffick with them in Foreign Countries, they were attack'd at Sea by the *Ape-hunters*, who sinking their Ships, they lost all their Riches. *Patragali* then gave her Golden Foot-rings to her Husband to sell them, who departed accordingly, but meeting upon the Road a Goldsmith (a Highway-man of *Pandy*) he under pretence of viewing the Rings, entertain'd the Husband, till by several By-ways they brought him to *Pandy*. Here the pretended Goldsmith (who had not long before stoln just such Rings from the Queen of *Pandy*) accused *Patragali* of the Robbery, who was put in Prison, and afterwards empal'd alive on a Palm-tree. The Goldsmith's Wife having an aversion to so foul a Fact, upbraided her Husband with it, who kill'd and buried her near a Well.

Patragali's *Husband executed.*

Patragali having staid six days without hearing any News from her Husband, resolv'd to go in search after him.

Patragali's *Adventures whilst she goes in quest of her Husband.*

The first thing she met with was a Pigeon, which she ask'd, *whether she had seen her Husband?* The Pigeon reply'd, she had seen him go that way, but not return. In recompence whereof *Patragali* gave her this Blessing, That she should never want Water in *February* (being the driest season here) and presented her with a piece of her Chain, which she threw about her Neck, (the Turtles have such a Ring about the Neck.)

Patragali following the way shewn her by the Pigeon, met with another Bird, of whom having enquir'd as she did before of the Pigeon, she receiv'd the same Answer, which made her bestow a Tuft upon his Head, being perhaps the same we call the *Piewet* in our Country, call'd *Carpenteiro* by the *Portugueses*.

Afterwards *Patragali* coming to a *Mango*-Tree, she ask'd the same Question; but receiving no Answer, she curst it, that for the future the dead Corps should be burnt with no other Wood, and that all Vessels built of that Wood, should rot and be worm-eaten at Sea.

Meeting next a Cow, she was kick'd by her hindermost Legs; which she resented so ill, that she gave her this Curse, That of her four Teats one should be for the use of the *Pagode*, the other for the Prince of the Country, the third for the Owner, and the fourth only for her Calf; that they should make Drums of her Skin, and that consequently she should be subject to Blows both dead and alive.

The fifth she met with being a *Nairo*, or Soldier of *Malabar*, this Fellow had dug a hole, and having cover'd the same with some Twigs and Sand, *Patragali* fell into it as she pass'd along; she gave him this Curse, that he should be call'd Coward all his life-time.

The next was a *Naira*, or a *Nairo*'s Daughter, who being ask'd by her, whether she had not seen her Husband? she clapt

Baldæus.

clapt her Hands, ſaying in ſcornful tone, What are you running after your Huſband? I have not ſeen him. She gave him this Curſe, That ſhe ſhould be married to a *Nairo*, a Coward, who as ſoon as he turn'd Soldier ſhould leave her in 40 days after.

She then coming to a *Jaquo*-Tree, ſhe ask'd after her Husband again: the Tree bowing its Twigs, furniſhed her with ſome of its Milky Liquor (as this Tree does if you cut any of its Twigs) ſhe beſtow'd this Bleſſing upon it, That its Fruits ſhould be highly eſteem'd by the Kings and Princes, and that tho its Stem might corrupt, it ſhould continue to bear Fruit (as in effect it does) and that they ſhould employ its Wood in making their Cymbals call'd *Tabelyne*, and the Statues of their Idols.

The eighth ſhe met with was a *Polia*, a Man of mean Extraction, who not going out of her way (as they uſually do) ſhe told him, that he ſhould not be admitted into the Houſes of Perſons of Quality from *October* till *February*.

The laſt ſhe met with was a *Parrea*, likewiſe a Perſon of low Birth; but having paid her the uſual Reverence, ſhe admir'd at his Civility, which made her ask him, Whether he did know her? He reply'd, that he took notice of her Swines Tusks, and the Elephants in her Ears; which ſo pleaſed her, that ſhe told him, he ſhould drink of the Liquor of the Palm-tree (which in effect they do when they gather it) and that he and his Family ſhould feed upon Cow's Fleſh. Then tracing the way ſhew'd her by the *Parrea*, ſhe found her Husband empal'd upon the Palm-tree; which being too high for her, ſhe obtain'd by her Prayers that the Palm-tree broke, and ſo deliver'd her Huſband, whom ſhe brought to Life again.

Patragali now burning of Revenge to puniſh the Murderers of her Husband, addreſs'd her ſelf to *Ixora*, who having furniſh'd her with a ſtrong Body of *Raxaxos*, or Devils (having been wicked Men in their life-time) ſhe enter'd the Territories of *Pandy*, and at laſt kill'd the King and the Goldſmith. His Wife ſhe reviv'd from the dead, who having brought forth a Son, ſhe granted him a Privilege to work in the *Pagodes*, and to receive to himſelf the tenth part of all the Gold he ſhould make uſe of, the fourth in 10 of what he ſhould work for the King, and as much as he could get from private Perſons.

Patragali revenges her Husband's Death.

We told you before of the *Pagode* of *Patragali* in *Cranganor*, where beſides her Statue ſtands that of a large Man in Marble, which the *Brahmans* knock every day with Hammers upon the Head, to keep it from growing too big.

Thus much of *Ixora*'s Children, who were, properly ſpeaking, only four in number (*Superbennia* being only an adopted Son) we muſt alſo go on in the Story of *Parameſceri* his Spouſe and her Origin. *Jecxa Pajava* King of the *Peringales* had four Daughters, the eldeſt whereof was *Parameſceri*, otherwiſe call'd *Parvati*; *Saroſſodi* and *Gojatris* the ſecond and third being married to *Bramma*, and *Pagode Siri* to *Viſtnum*. Their Father being deſirous to ſee his Daughters in their full Glory, invited *Bramma* and *Viſtnum* to a moſt magnificent Feaſt. *Viſtnum* asking him whether he had invited *Ixora*, he anſwer'd, No, (*Ixora* being then in his Mendicant State) but afterwards conſidering the matter, he invited him at laſt, which *Ixora* took ſo hainouſly, that he reſolv'd to ſpoil the Feaſt.

Pedegree of Parameſceri.

The Day appointed for the Feaſt being come, *Siri Pagode* came in great Pomp in a ſtately Chariot made of nine moſt precious Stones, moſt artificially wrought, her ſelf being adorn'd with numberleſs Jewels and Pearls, and attended by a ſplendid Retinue of Servants and Muſicians: *Saroſſodi* and *Gojatris* the other two Siſters appear'd with the ſame Splendor. *Parameſceri* in the mean while having obtain'd leave to go to the Feaſt from *Ixora*, he order'd her to put on her beſt Apparel, and gave her his Serpents, his Umbrella of Peacocks Tails, his Chain of Bones, his Tygers Skin, and Elephants Hide; thus equipp'd ſhe mounted upon an Ox, and with a large Attendance of Drummers, and *Pudas* and *Pixares*, came to her Father's Palace, where being met at the Gates by her Siſters and the other Gueſts, theſe ſeeing her Equipage much below what they expected, inſtead of welcoming her as they ought to have done, burſt out into laughter, which ſo vexed *Parameſceri*, that without more ado ſhe return'd to *Calaja*, where ſhe gave an account of what Treatment ſhe had met with, becauſe *her Siſters appear'd at the Feaſt in a moſt ſumptuous Equipage, their Apparel being cover'd all over with precious Stones and Pearls, whereas ſhe who was the eldeſt Siſter, and married to* Ixora, *had been deſpis'd for her mean Appearance.*

Rogerius gives a ſomewhat different Relation.

Ixora mov'd at the juſt Complaints of his Spouſe, ſent his Son *Quenavady* to ſpoil the Feaſt. *Viſtnum* being well acquainted with *Quenavady*'s Temper, order'd good ſtore of Cakes to be ſet before

him

him in the Hall, which pleased him so well, that he soon forgot his Father's Orders. *Ixora* wondering at *Quenevady*'s long stay, sent his Brother *Superbennia* upon the same Errand; *Vistnum* knowing him not to be diverted with Trifles, sent out to him some ingenious Persons, who entertain'd him so well with subtile Discourses and Arguments, that he likewise neglected his Father's Commands.

At last *Ixora* finding both his Sons to stay behind, order'd his Daughter *Patragali* thither; *Vistnum* no sooner heard of her coming, but he commanded a most delicious Banquet to be set before her in the Hall, through which she was to pass, which so diverted her Senses, that she soon forgot what she came about.

Ixora finding all these Endeavours to prove ineffectual, resolved to go thither in Person; which *Vistnum* no sooner got notice of, but he told King *Jecxa Prajava* his Father-in-law, that not being able to cope with *Ixora*, he would retire with his Wife; and *Bramma* doing the same, the *Sun* and the *Moon* (two of the Guests) staid only behind: *Ixora* coming to his Father-in-law's Palace, upbraided him with the Contempt he had put upon him and his Wife *Paramesceri*, and so taking him by the Hair full of Anger, there came forth at the same instant a stout Warrior arm'd *Cap-a-pee* (like the *Mars* of the antient Pagans) call'd *Virapatren* by the *Malabars*, who cut off *Jecxa Prajava*'s Head, the Hands of the *God of the Fire*, and beat out the Teeth of the *Sun*. What *Rogerius* says concerning *Jecxa Prajava*'s having got a Goats Head instead of the other, and that the *Moon* also got a good banging, I could never learn either from these Pagans themselves, or from the *Portuguese* Histories.

Baldæus.

PART II.

CHAP. I.

The Idol Vistnum, *and his Transformation into a Fish.* Mats *Altar. Another Transformation of* Vistnum. *An Account of the Milk-Sea.* Cauram's *Altar.*

Vistnum's Descent and Residence.

Vistnum the second in rank among the Gods next to *Ixora*, is also descended from *Quivelinga*. He is of a black Colour, with one Head, and four Hands; he resides on the Sugar-Sea, and governs the World sleeping. Instead of a Bed, he reposes upon a noted Serpent call'd *Annatan*, with five Heads; two whereof serve him for Pillars, one for a Bolster, and two under his Hands. This Serpent, as they say, being once in the humour to try the Power of *Vistnum*, got a sixth Head, which *Vistnum* no sooner saw, but he got another Hand to lay upon the Head, and the Serpent having got a seventh Head, he got likewise another Hand; so that, as the Serpents Heads did grow to the number of a thousand, his Hands encreased in proportion; whence it is that they look upon the Serpents as Celestial Spirits, keep them in great Veneration, and never kill them, tho they are often hurt by them. Thus the Serpents were reckoned by the antient *Lithuanians*, *Samogitians*, *Prussians* and *Egyptians*.

Wears a Print on his Breast.

They tell us further, that *Vistnum* wears the Print of a Foot upon his Breast: For one *Ricxi Sirwelstena* being desirous to know which of the three was the most *Potent God*, came to *Calaja*, and gave *Ixora* a good Box on the Ear, who transform'd him into a Stone; but having after 12 years recover'd his Life, he did the same to *Bramma*, who let him go without doing him any harm. Then coming to *Vistnum*, and finding him upon his Bed, he set his foot upon his Breast, which *Vistnum* fix'd there, so that he was forced to continue there 100 years.

Vistnum's Wives.

Vistnum had two Wives, one call'd *Leximi* alias *Laetzemi*, and *Siri Pagode* before-mention'd. The first *Vistnum* found in the *Milk-Sea*, in a Rose of 108 large and 1008 lesser Leaves; her chief business is to scratch his Head. The

Baldæus.

other is call'd *Pumi Divi*, i. e. the *Goddeſs of Heaven*, in whoſe Lap he lays his Feet, which ſhe is to rub with her Hands.

They attribute no leſs than ten ſeveral Transformations to *Viſtnum*, nine whereof they ſay are accompliſh'd already, but the tenth is to come. Father *Kircher* the Jeſuit * mentions the ſame to have been related to him by Father *Hen. Roth* an *Auſtin* Frier; and *Rogerius* ſays likewiſe ſomething of them: but as under theſe ten Transformations are hid the chief Myſteries of the Pagan Religion on both ſides of the *Ganges*, ſo we will treat of them at large with this Precaution, that theſe Pagans often give divers Names to the ſame God, by reaſon of the great difference betwixt the Languages of the *Ben-*

Viſtnum ten times transform'd.

* China Illuſtr. Part 3. Ed. 6.

jans,

jans, *Gentives* and *Malabars*: So, tho they acknowledg the same *Ixora*, *Bramma* and *Vistnum*, some of them call'd *Ixora Mahex*, or *Mahadeuw*, *Bramma*, *Bruma* or *Ram*, and *Vistnum Bexuo*, &c. which seems to intimate as if they had a certain respect to the Trinity; just as the *Chineses* worship three Divine Attributes under the Name of *Pussa*, and the *Greeks* placed the three *Charities* near the Throne of *Jupiter*; and if the Modern *Jews* were not quite obstinate in their denial of the Trinity, they might be convinc'd by their own *Rabbies*, *Rabbi Isaac*, *Rabbi Judas Nagi*, and *Rabbi Simeon*.

The first Transformation was into a Fish. The first Transformation was into a Fish, occasion'd by *Raxiaxa* alias *Adirem*, who having carried away the Law-book of the inferiour Gods call'd *Devagal* or *Dewetas*, hid himself at the bottom of the Sea. The inferior Gods making their Complaints to *Vistnum*, he transform'd himself into that ravenous Fish the *Shark*, and thus diving to the bottom of the Sea, laid hold of *Raxiaxa*, otherwise call'd *Seremiaxen*, and *Sancasoor* by the *Benjans*, kill'd him, and seiz'd the Law-book, divided into four parts; the first whereof treated of the Souls of the Blessed, the second of the vagabond Souls, the third of good Works, the fourth of bad Works. But what *Rogerius* says, *l.* 1. *c.* 5. *viz.* that the fourth part is lost, I could never be convinc'd of. The Fish is call'd *Mat* or *Mathia*, tho the *Malabars* and *Benjans* call it *Zecxis*. The *Benjans* tell us, that these Books were stoln from *Bramma*, but the *Malabars* from the *Dewetas*, or inferiour Gods. The *Benjans* say that *Bramma* was transform'd into a Fish, whereas the *Malabars* ascribe it to *Vistnum*. The *Benjans* call these Transmutations *Altars*; so that according to their supposition *Mats* Altar being the first, has now stood 2500 years.

Upon this occasion I must agree with *Rogerius*, when he says, *l.* 2. *c.* 3. that he could not dive into the Mysteries of the Transformations, because I am certain that it cost me a great deal of trouble before I could attain to the knowledg thereof, and that not without the Assistance of a certain *Brahman*, who coming from *Bengale* settled at *Jafnapatnam*; and as I frequently convers'd with him, so I often used to discourse with him concerning the Animadversions made upon this Head by *Rogerius*: He being afterwards converted to the Christian Faith, and baptized in the Church of *Vanarpone*, and our Discourse running upon the Transformations of *Vistnum*, he told me that this *Vedam*, or Law-book, being inclosed in a *Chanke*, or Sea-horse's Horn, the same was found out by *Vistnum*; whence it is that they say the Prints of the Fingers are to be seen in these Horns to this day; and that they have put the *Saccaram* or Sword, and the *Chanki* or Horn into his Hands, as you see in the proceding Draught, tho some ascribe the same to *Bramma*. *Baldæus.*

But before we enter further upon the Description of the Transmutations, we must add certain Preliminaries as tending to the Explanation thereof.

Four remarkable Divisions of Time. All these Transformations were perform'd in four different times or spaces: The first call'd *Kortesinge* by the *Benjans*, they say continued 1728000 years. The second *Tretasinge* 1296000 years: The third *Duapersinge* 8064000 years: The fourth *Kallisinge* 4032000 years, being the same term of time we now live in; so that according to their Computation at *Suratte* there were in 1657, at least 4758 years elapsed of this last term of Time. For it is to be known, that the *Benjans*, and most other Pagans, *Egyptians*, *Chineses* and *Japoneses*, differ several 1000 of years in their Computations from ours. And to convince you that the *Benjans* have the same years with ours, it is to be observ'd, that they as well as we divide their Years into 12 Months, amounting in the whole to 360 days in the year; and to make amends for our odd days, they have thirteen Months in every fourth Year, yet so that the 13*th* Month hath no more than 16 days. And it is further their opinion, that after the expiration of this last term of Time of 4032000 years, the World shall be renew'd. In which Point they follow in some measure the Footsteps of *Plato*, who allow'd no less than 36000 years before the Sun could pass through the 360 deg. of the *Zodiack*; tho they make their *Annus magnus*, as the antient Pagans call'd it,

> *Interea magnum Sol circumvolvitur Annum* *.

* Virgil. l. 3. Æneid.

The Pagans on the Coast of *Coromandel* and *Malabar* call these four terms of time, *Critagom*, *Treitagom*, *Dwaparugom*, and *Kaligom*; where it is to be observ'd, that according to the Computation of the Pagans, and the *Gentives* of *Suratte*, there are in this year 1670 elapsed 4771. whereas those of *Coromandel* compute 4770, being only one year's difference: but finding in 1665. that the Inhabitants of *Jafnapatnam* computed then the 4864*th* year

Baldæus.

year of the last Term; I told them that they did not stand for 100 years less or more, whereat they smiled.

The second Transformation of Vistnum.

But it is time we should now proceed to the second Transformation. The 33 Gods and the *Adires* held an Assembly in the *Milk-Sea*, to consult how to get into their possession the *Ambrosia*, call'd by some *Amurtam* and *Amortam*, by others *Amratam*. Some say that *Ixora* and *Vistnum* having call'd together all the good and evil Spirits, enter'd upon a Debate, how to find out something endu'd with such a Virtue as to make Men live without Victuals or Drink, and without danger of Death, or being tir'd. Whereupon it being agreed, that they should turn the Mount *Mahameru* (call'd *Merouwa* by *Rogerius*) like the Turners do, and instead of a Rope make use of the Serpent *Harugu*, call'd *Sescha* by the *Brahmans*, being of so vast a bulk, as to enclose the seven Worlds and Seas; accordingly they began their Turners-work, but finding the Mount immovable, they addrefs'd themselves to a noted Ape call'd *Baly* (of whom more anon in the History of *Siri Rama*) by whose Assistance the Mount began to stir; and meeting at the same time with a beautiful Woman named *Dara*, they bestow'd her upon *Baly* as a Reward for his Services. But continuing their Work, the Mount by turning round tumbl'd into the Sea; so that being destitute of all means to recover it thence, they were forced to have recourse to *Vistnum*, who taking the shape of a *Tortoise*, dived to the bottom, and brought the Mount up on his Back. Here it was that *Vistnum* met with the beautiful *Macha Lecxemi*, whom he married afterwards. But the Mount being exceeding high, *Vistnum* took the shape of a Bird, and flew round about it, till it was brought lower. This Story seems to have some relation to the Fable of Mount *Atlas*, and what is said *Heb.* 1. *that God bears up the World.*

The Gods and the *Adires* then continuing their Work, did light upon some Poison, which being too strong for them they sent to *Ixora*, but were still in pursuit after the *Ambrosia*, which they intended to present to their Great King *Deva Indra* (who was then very sick) sirnamed *Quiera Navam*, because his whole Body was cover'd with *Manly Yards*, in revenge of the Adultery he committed with the Wife of the Great *Rixi Quendama*: For *Deva Indra* being extremely in love with the said Lady, transform'd himself into a Cock, and coming to her House in the night-time, began to crow most briskly. *Rixi* thinking it had been near break of Day, got out of his Bed, and whilst he was going to an adjacent Pond to perform his usual Devotions, *Deva Indra* took the opportunity to enjoy his Wife. *Rixi* returning from his Devotion, and perceiving the Cheat, transmuted his Wife into a Stone, and laid the other Punishment upon her Lover.

By this time the *Adires* having seiz'd upon the *Ambrosia* without giving a share to the Gods, these made their Applications to *Vistnum*, who thereupon taking the shape of a most beautiful Nymph, sat down at Table with the *Adires*, when their Attendants were just ready to distribute the *Ambrosia* among them. Being all extremely enamour'd with her Beauty, every one courted her for his Spouse. To decide the matter she told them, that they should put the *Ambrosia* into her Hand, and with their Eyes shut and Hands ty'd behind them, but their Mouths open, receive every one their share of the *Ambrosia*; and that he upon whom she should pitch for her Husband, should be the last. This being done accordingly, she seiz'd upon the *Ambrosia*, and carried it to the Gods. But whilst they were all opening their Mouths to receive the said *Ambrosia*, *Ravaben* (who had assum'd the shape of one of the Gods) shew'd his Boars Tusks, which *Vistnum* seeing gave him such a powerful Blow, that his Head flew from his Shoulders; whence the *Adires*, whatever shape they assume, always retain their Tusks. However *Vistnum* throwing the Body and Head into the Air, the same were transform'd into two Planets, call'd *Rahu* and *Quendaum*. *Rogerius* calls them, *Ragou* and *Ketou*, which in the *Malabar* signifies as much as *Caput* and *Cauda*, or the *Dragon's Head* and *Tail*. But here the *Brahmans* commit an Error in Astronomy, for they have no Planets, but a fixed *Sidus* consisting of 31 Stars on the North-side without the *Zodiac*; where the Moon passing from South to North, and again from the North to South, goes through this *Ecliptick-Line*, being the same the Sun passes through every year, and the Moon every Month in the year; for when she takes her Course from South to North, the place where she passes through the Ecliptick Line is call'd the *Dragon's Head*, as the place of the said Line through which she passes in her return from North to South is call'd the *Dragon's Tail*; hence it is, that (according to *Rogerius*) these Pagans say that there is an Antipathy betwixt Sun and Moon, and *Ragou* and *Ketou*, and when they see an Eclipse of the Sun or Moon, that they are fighting with *Ragou* and *Ketou*, or that they are devour'd by them.

The inferiour Gods employ part of the *Ambrosia* they had got in restoring their Great God to Health, and removing the *Manly Members* from his Body, instead whereof he got as many Eyes. *Baldæus.*

The before-mentioned Poison taken out of the Mount *Mahameru*, being so virulent, that whatever it touch'd was consum'd to Ashes, was given to *Ixora* in the presence of *Paramesceri* his Spouse,

who

Baldæus. who dreading the Effects thereof, clapt her Hand to his Throat to prevent him from swallowing it, and laying the other Hand upon his Mouth for fear he should spue it out again and set the World on fire, mingling at the same time her Prayers (*Nila candamtre acxeram*) with her Endeavours, the Poison forc'd its way through *Ixora*'s Ear, and was in an instant transform'd into a Devil, call'd *Canda Carna Pixaxo.* The Prints of *Paramesceri*'s Finger left three black spots on *Ixora*'s Throat, whence he got the Sirname of *Nili Candaon*, i. e. *Black Throat*, or *Black Head.*

Different Relation of the Benjans *and* Gentives *of the second Transformation.* The *Benjans* and *Gentives* give a different Relation of this second Transformation. They say that the Sea being swoln with Pride, broke out in these words; *Who is it that can compare with the Riches contain'd in my Azure Marble Vaults? Here it is the Moon has fix'd her Habitation; the Water of* Tammarith, *which renders those that drink it immortal, is inclosed in my Bosom. The Elephant with his seven Trunks, and the seven-headed Horse dwell in the Depths, which produce black, white and red Coral in vast quantity.* The *Great God of Heaven* being exasperated at this Vanity, commanded the Giant and the four-headed God *Bramma* to go to the River *Siam Boerwetty*, near which lies the Golden Mount *Meeperwat* seated in the Center of the Earth, and 40000 Leagues high, and to remove the said Mount into the Sea, by winding the Serpent *Signage* about it, and thereby force the Sea to cast out her Treasure, which had render'd her so vainglorious. This being put in Execution accordingly, the Sea cast out the following fourteen things. 1. The Mony call'd *Lecsemy.* 2. The most precious Jewel *Consenchmany*, or the Carbuncle, which carries a Lustre like the Full-Moon. 3. The Tree *Paertsatig.* 4. The Vessel *Silxeren*, with the Water of *Sora.* 5. *Doctor Dannewanter.* 6. *Indemademaen.* 7. The white Cow of Plenty call'd *Camdoga.* 8. The immortal Water call'd *Amarith.* 9. The Elephant with seven Trunks, *Hiera Wannesty.* 10. The beauteous Female Dancer, *Remba.* 11. The seven-headed Horse *Exmognora.* 12. The Bow *Dennok.* 13. The Horn *Chiank.* And, 14. The Poison *Sabar.* This done, the Sea began to abate of its Pride, the Mount and Serpent had their peculiar places assign'd them, and the Treasures of the Sea were distributed to different Places and Persons. Thus far of the second Transformation, containing 2500 years of the first term of Time.

CHAP. II.

Vistnum *transform'd into a Hog:* Waras *his Altar. Some Reflections upon the Fables of the Pagans.* Vistnum's *fourth Transformation into half a Man, and half a Lion.*

The third Transformation. A Certain *Adiren*, named *Renniacxem*, was of such vast length, that taking up the Earth he roll'd it together like an Anchor-Cable, and carried it upon his Shoulders to the infernal places call'd *Padalas*, whilst *Vistnum* was asleep in his Bed. He no sooner heard of the Presumption of this *Adiren*, but he assum'd the shape of a Hog, and digging with his Snout through the Earth, till he came to the *Padalas*, kill'd the Robber, and taking the Earth upon his Tusks, fix'd it in its former place. Hence it is, that in the *Pagode* call'd *Adi Warraha*, in the City of *Trimottam*, not far from *Sinzi*, there is to be seen the *Head* of a *Hog*, which the *Brahmans* say was the Product of the Earth, and is reverenc'd as the true Idol of *Vistnum* in memory of this Transformation.

The *Benjans* and *Gentives* of *Indostan* and *Suratte* give us the following account of it. During the first term of Time, say they, the World was so over-burden'd with Sin, that the Serpent of 1000 Heads unable to bear the weight thereof any longer, withdrew her self from underneath it, whereby the World, together with Men and Beasts, were cast into and perish'd in the depth of the Sea. *Bramma* addressing himself to the Great God, desir'd him to retrieve the World out of the Abyss of the Sea, which he willingly granted. Whereupon *Vistnum* assum'd the shape of a Boar's Head, with Tusks as big as an Elephant's Trunk, white all over his Body, with four Arms and Hands, having in one Hand a great Sword call'd *Godda*, and in the other a Book, as likewise a Horn and round *Tsicker.* Thus transform'd, he threw himself into the Sea, being at first no bigger than a Man's Finger, but increas'd before he reach'd the bottom to such a degree, that in case the Earth had been plac'd on the surface of the Water, and he stood upon it, his Head would have touch'd the Stars. Coming to the bottom of the Sea, he kill'd the dreadful Giant *Hirnaks*, whose Blood ting'd the whole Sea with red. *Vistnum* having trampled him under his Feet, lifted with his Tusks the Earth out of the Sea, and placing the Tortoise upon the Water, and the Serpent with a thousand Heads upon the Tortoise, he retir'd to his Residence, and *Bramma* with one word created a new Generation of Men. This Transformation comprehends 2700 years, in the first Period of time. *Baldæus.*

This Story seems to intimate, that these Pagans have heard something of the Deluge, considering especially that

*

Baldæus. the *Benjans* do live nearer to the Borders of *Persia* and *Armenia* than the rest of the *Indians*; there being also mention made of the Giants, *Gen.* 6. 4. and it is very probable, that the antient Pagans were not quite ignorant of the History of the Deluge, which they afterwards ushered into the World, under divers peculiar Deluges, as for instance the *Diluvium Ogygicum*, which happen'd in *Attica*, and *Deucalion's Deluge* in *Thessaly*; and the *Prometheus* of the antient Pagans, is by most Criticks taken for the same with *Noah*.

But we come to the fourth Transformation; yet before we enter upon the Particulars thereof, we must add something more relating to the third Transformation. The Earth being restored to its former Station, *Vistnum* upon an exact view found it something inclining to the *South*, which *Vistnum* not being able to remedy, he addressed himself to a certain Saint of very low Stature, nam'd *Rixi Agassia* (*Rogerius* * calls him *Agastea*) who having laid his holy Book upon that part inclining to the South, put it into a just Equilibrium.

* l. 2. c. 19.

Vistnum walking with this *Agassia* near the Seaside, the Sea asked *Vistnum*, *Who it was that walked with him?* Vistnum replied, *He is a Saint who is going to restore the Earth to its true Ballance.* Whereupon the Sea, scorning his low Stature (he being not above the height of a joint of a Finger) wetted him with its Waves; which Affront being highly resented by *Agassia*, he took some of the Seawater in his hand, and beginning to drink, did not desist till he had drunk up the whole Sea: *Dewetas* and *Rixiis* seeing the Sea thus exhausted, interceded with *Agassia* not to rob the World of so singular a Benefit, and prevailed upon him so far, that he pissed out again all the Water he had drunken before; and this is the reason their Philosophers alledg for the Saltness of the Sea.

Agassia after having restored the ballance of the Earth, took his leave of *Vistnum*, who to prevent the like for the future, order'd the *Great Serpent* to wind herself about the seven Worlds and seven Seas; and for more Securities sake, appointed 8 Guardians to watch over it, called in the *Malabar* by the following Names: 1. *Indra* the King of the Celestial Spirits. 2. *Vanni* the God of Fire. 3. *Padurpati* King of the evil Spirits. 4. *Nirurdi* King of the infernal Spirits. 5. *Varunna* the God of the Sea. 6. *Maril* the God of the Winds. 7. *Cubera* the God of Riches, called otherwise *Bassironnem*. 8. *Ixananam* or *Ixora* himself; hence it is that you see frequently eight Stones placed at the Entrance of, and about their *Pagódes*.

The fourth Transformation into half a Lion and half a Man was occasioned thus: During the first Period of Time, a certain Gyant *Hirrenkessep* (as the *Benjans* call him, but the *Malabars Reniacxen*) having been forced to abscond for 12 years on the account of *Bramma*, afterwards made the following Request to him: *Most Potent* Bramma, *grant me the Favour to make me a great Monarch upon Earth, and bestow this further Blessing upon me, that I may not be killed either by Day or by Night, either within or without my House, either by Heaven, Earth, Sun or Moon, by Thunder, Lightning, Stars or Comets, neither by Clouds, Winds, Hail, Snow or Rains, or Birds, Beasts, Men, Devils, Fishes or Water; not by Serpents, Adders, Poison, Sword, Arrows or any other Weapons.* Bramma having granted the Gyant's request, he soon made himself Master of the whole Earth, and overcome with Pride at his Success, issued out a Mandate, that no body should be adored but himself, under the forfeiture of the Lives of such as should contravene it. Things continuing in this State for some Years, the *Brahmans* began to murmur, that they should be *obliged to adore any terrestrial Power, tho never so great, to the prejudice of the celestial Spirits*; they resolved therefore to make their Supplications to *Vistnum*, imploring him *to deliver them from the Oppressions of this Tyrant*, who gave them for answer, *That the Giant should have shortly a Son born, who should be their Deliverer, and till then they must have Patience.*

The fourth Transformation.

Within 10 Months after *Naecksen*, the Giants Wife, brought forth a Son named *Prellade*, who when he was five years old was put to a Schoolmaster; being one time sent for by his Father, his Master instructed him how to pronounce his Father's Name in short writing, which was *Irenia*, but instead thereof the Boy said *Ary*, being the abbreviated Name of *Vistnum*. The Master astonished put his Hand upon his Mouth, bidding him to forbear, for fear of being the occasion of his own Death; but the more he forbid him, the more the Boy persisted in saying *Ary*, *Ary*, instead of *Irenia*.

The Schoolmaster not knowing what to do, brought him to his Father, telling him, *That his Son would not pronounce his Name, which he had taken so much pains to teach him.* The Father asking him the reason,

reason, the Boy answered, *Your Name is not the true Name, but the other is the Truth it self.* His Father asking further, *What is Truth?* The Son answered, *Vistnum who fills the 14 Worlds is the Truth. What Benefit,* said the Father, *do you receive from* Vistnum? *And what Benefit,* replied the Son, *shall I receive by yours?* The Giant told him, *Whoever repeats my Name, shall be blessed with Riches, Honour, Dignities and Life. How,* says the Son, *can you give Life and Riches? Yes I can,* replied the Giant, *and will convince you immediately, it being in my Power to take away your Life. That will scarce happen,* answered the Son, *according to your Providence and Discretion. What is Providence and Discretion?* asked the Giant. Baldæus.

The Idol of Vistnum transformed into half a Man & half a Lyon.

 That

Baldæus. *That is the Eternal Divine Name of* Vistnum, replied the Son, *the Creator of the* 14 *Worlds*. The Father asking him, *Where is this Name to be found?* The Son answered, *In every thing both in Heaven and Earth, every thing being filled with* Vistnum. *What*, replied the Father, *and is* Vistnum *also in this Pillar? Yes*, replied the Son, *and likewise in you and me*. The Giant not longer able to contain himself, told him, *Boy, because thou insistest thus upon the Name of* Vistnum, *I will beat your Brains out with this Stick; but if thou wilt pronounce my Name, thou shalt neither die, neither be beaten. That won't be*, says the Boy, *for your Names sake, because God has ordered it otherwise. But I will spoil that Ordinance*, replied the Giant, and with that struck with his golden Staff at the Boy, who, hiding himself behind the Pillar, implor'd the Name of *Vistnum*. The Giant turning again with more Fury than ever against the Son, struck with such Violence that the Pillar burst and produced a Monster, *half a Man, half a Lion*, an Hermaphrodite, with Breasts both above and below, breathing Fire and Flames out of its Nostrils.

The *Benjans* say, that the Giant did erect a red hot Pillar to tie his Son to, telling him at the same time, *Let us see who can deliver you out of my Hands*. The Son then invoking the assistance of *Vistnum*, the Pillar burst, and forth came the Monster. All the Standers by were amazed at this Spectacle, and the Giant himself trembled for fear. *Vistnum* resolving to revenge his own Quarrel, and at the same time not to break the Promise made by *Bramma* to the Giant, laid hold of the Giant, and hurrying him under Ground directly under the Threshold of his own House, and keeping him there till Sunset, tore his Body in pieces, thereby fulfilling *Bramma*'s Promise, that he should not be killed *within nor without his House, neither in Heaven nor upon Earth, neither by Beasts, Birds, Sword, Wind, Rain, Hail*. The Giant's Son succeeding his Father in the Empire, ruled with great applause for many succeeding years.

Thus ended the fourth Transformation of the first Period of time, called *Kortesinge* by the *Benjans*, comprehending in all 1728000 years; for tho all these Transformations were transacted within the time of 7700 years and three days, the rest, *viz.* 1720000 years, 360 days, must be supposed to have been the Intervals of these Transactions.

CHAP. III.

The fifth Transformation of Vistnum *into a* Brahman. *Great Plenty under* Mavaly. *The Request of the transformed* Vistnum. Prassaram*'s Altar and Birth. He kills* Reneca *his Mother.* Raja Inder*'s Cow of Plenty.* Prassaram*'s great Actions.*

WHilst *Mavaly* (called *Belragie* by the *Benjans* and *Gentives*) ruled the World, the Inhabitants thereof were so plentifully provided with every thing by his Bounty, that Poverty was a thing unknown among human Race. *Vistnum* perceiving that as the case then stood, there were no different degrees, nor any dependance in the World either on God or Man, resolved to divest *Mavaly* (by Fraud) of the Government of the World.

With this Intention *Vistnum* assumed the Shape of a *Brahman*, and appearing in a Mendicant Posture before *Mavaly*, he asked him, *who he was*, and upon what Errand he came? The pretended *Brahman* replyed, *Having heard of your Charity I am come to crave some Alms.* Mavaly answer'd, *I who have granted the Requests of many Kings and Princes, will not deny thee, let it be what it will, whether Kingdoms, Money, Honours, or whatever else you can ask.* The *Brahman* replied, my aim is not at such mighty things, but after all, for fear of Denial, I beg of you to promise me, without exception to grant my Request. *Mavaly* answering that he would, the *Brahman* begged him to confirm it with an Oath.

Mavaly being just upon the point of confirming it by Oath, the Planet *Venus* (who stood just by) told him, *And is it customary to swear to the giving of Alms?* which *Mavaly* being not in the least moved at, swore to the *Brahman*, who told him, *I am not covetous of Kingdoms or Provinces, my Desire is confined to three Foot of Ground, where I may erect a Hut, where to lay up my Books, Umbrella and Drinking-Cup;*

Cup; I beg you therefore to pour some of your Water upon the Ground. For it is a custom among these Pagans, that whenever they dispose of or sell any thing, they confirm their Promise or Bargain, by pouring some Water upon the Ground, part whereof the Buyer catches with his Hands and drinks, in confirmation of the Bargain; just as *Jacob* desired *Joseph* to lay his Hand under his Hips, when he was going to make him his Promise upon Oath, *Gen.* 47. 29. & 24. 2. where the Hips (according to some Interpreters) are taken *pro partibus generationis, in quibus circumcisionis signum dabatur.*

Baldæus.

Mavaly told him, *Ask a Kingdom and I will grant it.* The *Brahman* replied, *Were I a King, I must punish Criminals,*

which

Baldæus. *which I could not do without trespassing the Rules of the Order of the* Brahmans; *wherefore I desire no more than three Foot of Ground.* Mavaly replied, *that will not be enough to build you a House upon. I want no House,* said the *Brahman, having neither Wife nor Children, I desire only three Foot of Ground, which you can't refuse without being perjured. Mavaly* telling the *Brahman* that he never broke his Promise, and ordering *Venus* to bring him some Water, she desired him not to pour the Water upon the *Brahman,* whom she looked upon as an Impostor. *Mavaly* replied, *Of what consequence can three Foot of Ground be? Take heed,* answered *Venus, for this is* Vistnum *himself, who is come in disguise to deceive you.* Mavaly return'd, *I have not sinned against* Vistnum, *and therefore have no reason to fear him.* Notwithstanding which *Venus* continued to persuade him by many Arguments, not to trust him: But *Mavaly* persisting in his Resolution, told her, *Let come on it what will, if it should cost me my Life, I will not break my Oath.* Then taking the Vessel with the Water, he bid the *Brahman* to hold up his Hands, which *Venus* perceiving, she held *Mavaly*'s Arms, desiring him not to pour out the Water; but *Mavaly* pushing back her Hand, bid the *Brahman* a second time to hold up his Hands. *Venus* then changing her Shape, stopp'd the Pipe of the Vessel, which *Mavaly* endeavouring to loosen with a Twig, he hurt *Venus*'s one Eye, whence she got the Name of *Chueren.* Then Water coming out of the Spout of the Vessel, the *Brahman* did drink. This done, *Mavaly* order'd him to measure the three Foot of ground where he pleased. *Vistnum* having by this time reassumed his own Shape, he covered the whole Earth with one of his Feet, and with the other the Paradise called *Sorgalogam.* Whilst *Vistnum* was extending his Foot, *Bramma* poured Water upon it, which produced the River *Ganges,* so highly celebrated among the *Indians* and other Pagans. *Vistnum* having thus measured two Foot, *Mavaly* told him, he might also take the third, which he did by measuring the inferiour Region, called *Padalas,* and thus became Master of the whole World.

Vistnum *Master of the World.*

The *Gentives* add, that this *Brahman* (whom they call *Vanam,* i. e. *a black Dwarf,* and *Rogerius* calls him *Barmasari,* i. e. a young *Brahman,* by the Name of *Wamara* *) set his Left Foot upon *Mavaly*'s Breast or Head, and thus kick'd him thro the Ground into the infernal Region, whereof he made him King. But *Mavaly*'s Wife upbraiding *Vistnum* with Ingratitude, he carried her to her Husband, and as a Reward of his Piety bestowed upon him the Government of the place of Darkness, *Vistnum* himself remaining with him nine days to guard the Entrance thereof. *Rogerius* calls this *Mavaly* a Devil, named *Belli,* and says, that whilst the Waters of the *Ganges* were flowing from above over *Ixora*'s Head, and risen out of the Hip of a Saint, 60000 Men were brought to Life. This Fable had questionless its Origin from the want of Knowledg of the true source of the River *Ganges,* for which reason they generally stile it the *Heavenly River.*

* l. 2 c. 19.

Mavaly being not satisfy'd with his present Station, made his Complaint to *Vistnum,* who told him, that in regard he had been a charitable Person, a Man of Truth and without Sin, he would constitute him King of the Paradise. *Mavaly* making a deep Reverence (called by them *Sambaja*) returned for answer, It is not my ambition to reign, being only affected with the Hardships of my former Subjects, who have no body now to provide them with Necessaries, as I used to do. *Vistnum* replied, The poor shall serve the rich, and be maintained by them; so that he that will work, shall want for nothing. I will also constitute you the Doorkeeper of the Paradise, so that no body shall enter there without thy Knowledg. But replied *Mavaly,* how shall I then be able to judg at such a distance, how you deal with Mankind upon Earth? I will, answered *Vistnum,* assign you a certain Place in Heaven, from whence you may overlook the Earth; and so made him Doorkeeper of the Paradise.

Accordingly *Vistnum* distinguished Mankind into three sorts, Rich, Poor and Middle-sized, which were to have a Reciprocal Dependance on one another, That such as had lived piously and done Acts of Charity should be received after their Death, and live in Plenty and Splendor; but such as did otherwise, should after their Decease be transform'd again into Slaves and Drudges, to do Penance for their former Sins, till by their good Works they should merit Paradise, which they were not to enter however without *Mavaly*'s Consent. He also constituted a Feast (called *Ona* by the *Malabars*) to be celebrated yearly in *August,* when they spend several days together in feasting and other sorts of Di-

3 sorts of People.

Diversions, and appear in all their best Apparel.

The sixth Transformation. The sixth Transformation happened thus: After the appearing of *Hanumans* mentioned in the 5*th Chap. Part* 1. one *Braman* and *Bramani* being joined in Wedlock, did for a considerable time lead a pious and contented Life near the River *Bewa*; but the Woman being barren (a thing much despised among the *Benjans*) they resolved to retire into some Desart, there to implore God's Assistance. Having thus for some time led a Vagabond Life, they came to a certain *Pagode* built in a Forest, near which stood a very fine Tree, under the Shade whereof they reposed themselves for some time, and sent forth their Prayers upon their bended Knees. After some time finding their Prayers ineffectual, the Woman told her Husband, that they ought to leave this shady Place, and in lieu thereof to expose themselves to the Injuries of the Sun, Rains and Storms, to try whether perhaps by this Humiliation and Penance, God might be prevailed upon to bless them with Children. They persevered in this Austerity and continual Prayers for some longer time, but in vain; the Woman growing beyond all Patience, told her Husband, that being quite weary of Life, she desired him to fast with her, till thereby they could put a Period to their miserable Life. Accordingly having spent nine days without eating or drinking, *Vistnum* appear'd to them in the Shape of a Child, asking them, what was the occasion of their Mortification and fervent Prayers. The Woman answered, All our Prayers are directed to *Vistnum*, to bless me with such a handsome Child as thee. *Vistnum* replied, And do you instead of Gold and Silver desire Children, who commonly prove the Toils of Life? *Bramani* answered, all the Riches and Pleasures of this World are not so valuable to me, as a Son of my own, so well shap'd as thy self. *Vistnum* replied, Your Prayers are heard, and as you have three several times mortify'd your Bodies, so three Sons shall be born thee successively; and so he vanished.

Being both exhausted with Fasting, they died soon after; but the Soul of *Bramani* was infused into the Body of the new-born *Reneca*, and that of *Braman* into the Body of the new-born *Braman*, sirnamed *Siamdichemi*, who being come to their riper Years, were join'd together in Marriage; *Reneca*'s Sister being at the same time married to the Great *Raja Sestraarsum*, who had 1000 Arms. *Baldæus.*

Siamdichemi retir'd with *Reneca* to a Solitude, near the River *Ganges*, where they built a Hut of Straw, with an Intention to live upon the Fruits of the Earth, and pass their time in praying to *Vistnum*.

It was not long before *Reneca* (pursuant to the Promise made by *Vistnum*) brought forth a beautiful Son, unto whom she gave the Name of *Prassaram*, who being carefully educated under the Tuition of his Father, did in his 12*th* year interpret the most abstruse Characters that could be laid before him. His Mother having received a certain Cloth from *Vistnum*, which keeping Water as well as any Earthen Vessel, *Reneca* going to fetch Water one time out of the River *Ganges*, she happen'd to see the great *Raja Sestraarsum* with his Spouse (her Sister) a hunting near the River-side. *Reneca* asked one of his Attendants, who it was, and being answered, that it was *Raja Sestraarsum* with his Queen, she advanced towards them; but finding that her Sister took no notice of her, she sat down in a very melancholy Posture upon the Bank of the *Ganges*, complaining of the vast difference there was betwixt her Sister and her. Prassaram *the Son of* Reneca.

Alas, said she, *she is a Queen, and I a poor* Brahman's *Wife*; *she is possessed of Riches, Honour and Plenty, and I know nothing but Want and Misery.*

She was then a going to fill her Cloth with Water, but found it, to her great Astonishment, leaky; and being afraid to return home, staid abroad till after Sunset. *Siamdichemi* surpriz'd at her long stay, look'd out at the Doors, and finding her sitting in a melancholy Posture, ask'd her whether she had brought no Water; but she answering, she had not, and giving him the reason for it, he told her, that he was certain she had uttered some Expressions contrary to his Zeal and Piety; and being exasperated to the highest degree, commanded his Son *Prassaram* to cut off his Mother's Head with an Ax. *Prassaram* would have excused himself, but finding his Father resolute, he was forced to obey, and cut off his Mother's Neck. The Father being highly taken with the Obedience of his Son, told him, that he should ask him what he pleased, and it should be granted him. *Then*, said the Son, *resuscitate my Mother from the Dead*; the Father then taking some of the sanctified Wa- Reneca *killed.*

Baldæus. *And revived.* Water of the *Ganges*, besprinkled the Body with it, and muttering out certain Prayers, restored it to Life again.

Reneca could not forbear to make her Complaints concerning the harsh usage of her Husband, occasion'd only by some Weaknesses and Reflections upon her Sister's good Fortune, representing to him her Piety, Fidelity and Obedience she had shown upon all Occasions. These Reasons were so prevailing with the Husband, that he received her into his Arms, and banished all Revenge from his Thoughts.

Prassaram (tho not above 12 years of Age) being by this time advanced so far in the Knowledg of the Law, that he was past his Father's teaching, was ad- Prassaram *goes to* Raja Inder.

vised

vised by him to apply himself to *Raja Inder*, King of the *blessed Souls*, for his further Accomplishment, which the Son did accordingly; so soon as the Son had left him, he resolved to pay his Devotions to *Vistnum* for 12 years successively, sitting cross-leg'd without Intermission upon the Ground (a thing much practised among these Pagans) Thus 1659. I saw a certain *Jogy*, or Mendicant, at *Columbo*, whose Arms were grown together over his Head, by sitting in that Posture.

Soon after it happen'd, that the before-mention'd King *Raja Sestraarsum*, coming to give a Visit to his Brother-in-law with a great Retinue, he was so fast asleep, that all the noise of the Hounds, Horns and Drums could not awaken him: his Wife *Reneca* therefore having rouzed her Husband, by sprinkling some warm Water upon his Head, he arose; when

Raja Sestraarsum *visits the* Brahman.

Raja saluting the *Brahman*, told him, that the Fame of his Piety had induced him and his Retinue to come to sup, and to take a Nights Lodging with him.

The *Brahman Siamdichemi*, being much concern'd how to provide for so many 1000 Persons, at last consider'd of the *white Cow*, called *Camdoga*, belonging

The Cow of Plenty.

to *Raja Inder*, which furnishes those that have her in their possession with every thing they wish for. Having therefore desired *Inder* to send him the said Cow, he granted his Request; and the Cow being sent down, the *Brahman* desired *Raja* and his Attendants to sit down at Supper, which was served with such Variety and Plenty, that *Raja*, who was come upon no other account than to ridicule his Brother in Law's-Poverty, stood amazed thereat; and further to try his Ability, ask'd him, to present him with some Jewels; which the *Brahman* having presented him with (much beyond what could be expected) *Raja* ask'd him for some Clothes and Money for his People, which being likewise brought him by his Brother-in-law, he resolved also to stay the next day; and being served at Table with the same Plenty as before,

Raja *plentifully entertained.*

he stayed also the third day; when meeting with the same Entertainment, he was amazed to find out whence all this Plenty of Provisions, Clothes and Riches could come in a place, where he expected so little, especially since he observed that all was brought out of the *Brahman*'s Hut, which was not big enough to hold half the quantity. This made him order some of his Spies to take particular notice, whether there was not a Vault underground, from whence these things were brought. The Spies watching all Opportunities to satisfy their Master's Curiosity, found at last that a slender white Cow did bring forth all these things (which she threw out of her Stomach) whereof immediate notice was given to *Raja*.

Baldæus.

The next Morning as he was taking his Leave from the *Brahman*, being ask'd by him, whether he was desirous of any thing else, he told him, that he wanted nothing more, but only the white Cow he had seen in his Hut; the *Brahman* replied, that being not his own, she was not in his disposal. *And*, said *Raja*, *will you deny me so small a Request, after you have heaped so many Obligations upon me before? What I did before*, said the *Brahman*, *was in my own Power, but this is not. How*, replied *Raja*, *don't you know that it is in my Power to take her against your Will?* and then calling to some of his Followers, he commanded them to fetch the white Cow out of the Hut. The *Brahman* seeing this beloved white Cow thus snatched from him, told her at parting, *Dear* Camdoga, *must I thus leave you, how can I answer this to* Raja Inder *your Master? revenge thyself at once both of thine and mine Enemies.* The Cow

Raja's *People defeated by the white Cow.*

Camdoga no sooner heard these Words, but assuming a shape three times bigger than her own, she laid about her with her Horns to that degree, that she kill'd and trod under Foot several thousand of *Raja*'s People; which done, she flew like Lightning up into the Air to her

Siamdichemi *murdered.*

own Master. *Raja* exasperated at the Slaughter of his Men, and burning with Revenge, returned to the Hut of the *Brahman*, where they kill'd and left him wallowing in his Blood. The unfortunate *Reneca*, unwilling to outlive her Husband, set fire to the Hut, and burnt herself with his dead Carcase.

Reneca *burns herself with his Corps, whence the Custom of burning the Dead.*

Camdoga in the mean while meeting with *Prassaram* not far from her Master's House, told him what had happen'd, who declar'd he would revenge the same 21 times upon all the *Ketteriis* (a wicked Generation) and thus making the best of his way with his *Perzy*, Bow and Arrow, he penetrated into the middle of *Raja*'s Troops, and kill'd him with all his

Prassaram *revenges their Death.*

Guards; thence travelling through the World, he kill'd all the *Ketteriis* he met with, but could not do it so effectually, but that some escap'd his Fury, who multiplying by degrees, he was forc'd to renew his Revenge against them, which he did 21 times, till they were quite rooted out from the face of the Earth.

Baldæus. By this time *Vistnum* remembring his Promise made to *Prassaram*'s Parents, *viz.* that they were to be blest with three Sons, he commanded *Bramba* (the God with four Heads) to send down from Heaven the Souls of *Siamdichemi* and *Reneca*, and to convey them into the Bodies of *Ragia d'Asserat*, and his Wife *Couzila* (slain among the *Ketteriis*) unto whom he had made a Promise of exalting their Posterity.

Bramba finding by the Celestial Records, that their time was expir'd (for these Pagans believe that nothing is done without Divine Providence, and that the Fate of Men is written in *Bramba*'s Hand) infused the Soul of *Reneca* into the Body of *Couzila*, and the Spirit of *Siamdichemi* into that of *Ragia*, which brought forth a Son named *Ram*. This *Ram* having marry'd *Sytha*, and making his publick Entry into the City (according to the Custom of the *Benjans*) was met by *Prassaram*, who being inform'd that he was descended of the Race of the *Ketteriis*, did let fly at him, which *Ram* perceiving did the same from his Elephant on which he was mounted; but their Arrows hitting against one another in the Air did no mischief, except that all the strength of *Prassaram*'s Arrow being lodg'd in that of *Ram*, he was thereby bereav'd of all his Advantage, being no more than a common *Brahman* for ever after, whereas *Ram* encreased every day in Power.

The Story of Ram.

Prassaram *endeavours to kill* Ram.

The *Malabars* say that this Transformation was made by *Vistnum* in the shape of *Siri Parexi Rama*. For the *Rixi* living in the Desarts, being no longer able to endure the Oppressions from the Neighbouring Kings, offer'd their Sacrifices to *Vistnum*, desiring his Assistance against them. A certain famous *Rixi* named *Para Jara*, sacrificing one day to *Vistnum*, he appear'd in the shape of a Child, and assisted at the Ceremony of the Sacrifice; which done, *Parexi Rama* took up an Ax and kill'd 44 Kings, who used to infest the *Rixi*, and put them into the Possession of their Territories. *Siri Parexi Rama* being afterwards desirous to erect certain Temples, and not finding sufficient room for that purpose (because the Sea then touch'd the Mount *Gatte*) he offer'd his Sacrifice, when a Sieve appearing to him (such as they use to cleanse the Rice with) he found that as often as he did shake it, the Sea retreated backwards from the Shore; but whilst he was doing it a third time, *Varrinem* the God of the Sea, having transform'd himself into Pismires (call'd by them *Carreas*) gnaw'd the Sieve in pieces. However *Siri Rama* built 108 Temples, and erected as many Stones near them, from *Mangalor* to the Cape *Comoryn*, much reverenc'd to this day by the *Indians*.

The Malabars *account of this Transformation.*

In the mean while the Fishermen of that Coast making their Complaints to *Parexi Rama*, that by this means they had been bereav'd of their Subsistence, he constituted them his Guards of the Temples he had built, with a sufficient allowance for their Maintenance; so that these Fishermen being thus become *Brahmans*, they used always to wear a Thred of a Fishing-Net about their Necks whilst they were performing their Sacrifices, and introduc'd that Custom among the Pagans, for a new-married Couple to go a fishing with a Linen Cloth instead of a Net.

Parexi Rama being one time employ'd in his Solitude in sacrificing to the Gods, *Siri Rama* (or *Vistnum*) appear'd in the shape of a Man; which *Parexi Rama* taking notice of, his Jealousy was raised to such a height, that he would needs enter into a single Combat with him; but being prevented by the *Rixii*, they discover'd themselves to one another, and entring into a strict Friendship, *Parexi Rama* presented his Bow to *Siri Rama*, who return'd to the *Milk-Sea*.

The Origin of the Brahmans.

CHAP. IV.

The seventh Transformation of Vistnum *into* Rama. *His Birth. He gains his Bride* Sytha *by shooting. Beauty of* Lekeman. *His meeting with* Soupenekhia. Rawan *takes away* Sytha; *performs Wonders.* Ram *and* Lekeman *go in quest of* Sytha. Hanuman*'s great Actions in* Ceylon.

I*Xora* being reverenc'd by all the World, but especially by one *Rawan*, (call'd *Rawana* by *Rogerius*, who makes him a Son of the *Brahman Kassiopa*) who for 300 years offer'd him 100 Flowers every day; *Ixora* having one time a mind to try

The Story of Rama *or* Siri Rama *is so famous in the* Indies, *that Kings and Princes paint it upon their Arms and Palaces.*

try his Sincerity, took away one of the Flowers, and afterwards charged him with want of Duty; *Rawan* ignorant of the Deceit, counted his Flowers, and finding no more than 99, would have torn out one of his Eyes to compleat the number of 100. But *Ixora* stopping his Hand, told him, that having now had a sufficient proof of his Integrity, he should ask what he pleased and he would be sure to grant it: *Rawan* then asked a share with *Ixora* in the Government of the World; which being granted him by *Ixora*, *Rawan* nevertheless continued his daily Devotions, and being ask'd the reason by *Ixora*, he told him, that he would not desist from his Prayers, till he had given him 10 Heads and 20 Arms, which being likewise granted by *Ixora*, he fix'd his Residence in the Country of *Lanka*, in the famous Isle of *Ceylon*, call'd by others *Sanka*, who also say that he built seven Palaces there of Gold, Silver, Steel, Iron, and other Metals.

Having thus rul'd for some thousand years over all the Neighbouring Kings, he became so proud, as to force his Subjects to worship him instead of *Ixora*; which they were forced to do for 25 years, till being quite tir'd out of all Patience by his Tyrannys, they emplor'd *Ixora* to deliver them from *Rawan*, that so they might recover their former freedom of adoring him.

About that time there liv'd a certain *Ragie* named *Dasserat*, or *Desseratha*, or *Decxareda*. This King having three Wives, one of them named *Cousila*, after some time brought forth a Son named *Ram* by the *Brahman Wissiroe*, who encreased daily in Wisdom and Understanding, beyond what could be expected from his tender years. His second Wife *Keggy* (call'd *Kaicta* by the *Malabars*) brought forth another Son named *Barrat*; and *Somettery*, or *Somittra*, the third Wife, *Lekeman* and *Setteroukan*. The *Malabars* say, that these four Sons were born from these three Women by the means of four Pills.

Vistnum being thus brought into the World in the shape of a *Ram*, was educated by the *Brahmans* in all manner of Wisdom and Knowledg. There happen'd to live at that time a certain *Ragie* named *Sannek*, in the Country of *Siannak*, who having fix'd a prodigious strong Bow in a certain Enclosure made for that purpose, issued his Proclamation, to encourage all such as would venture to draw and break the said Bow, offering his Daughter *Sytha* with a great Portion as a Reward to him who should accomplish it. This being likewise come to the Ears of the *Brahmans*, *Ram* sollicited his Tutor to let him try his Strength, which the Master not without some Reluctancy having consented to, he went along with him under the Notion of his Servant, and coming to *Rag. Sannek's* Court heard him offer the same Reward to any one that could manage and break the Bow, telling them, that he who would enter the List should take the Vessel with *Betel*, which was offer'd by his own hand.

How Ram *got his Bride* Sytha.

Bendaons. The Malabars say, that Brawa going to sacrifice, and invited the Brahmans *to oppose the Demons, that sometimes used to disturb those Ceremonies.*

Immediately after he saw the beforementioned *Rawan* with 10 Heads take the *Betel*, and boasting of his Strength, told them that no body but him should pretend to *Sytha*: then drawing the Bow with his utmost Strength, he let slip the Sinew, which striking his Thumb off he fell into a Sound. Divers other *Ragies* try'd to mange the same Bow, but finding their Strength fail them were forced to desist.

The *Betel* being next brought to the *Brahmans*, among whom stood *Ram*, he at last obtain'd leave from his Master to accept of the *Betel*, which he did accordingly, and entring the List, found a tall Mast or Poll fix'd in the Center of the Court, on the top whereof was a Fish, and at the bottom a Cistern with Water, wherein plainly appear'd the shade of the Fish. *Ram* then drew the Bow with such violence, that he not only shot the Fish into several parts, but also broke the Bow to pieces.

The Bride rejoic'd at his Success, presented him with a whole Dish full of Jewels, as did all the rest there present proportionable to their Abilities: His Parents being also sent for to partake of the Honours done to their Son, they came with their other three Sons, who married the three Daughters of *Raja Sannek*, viz. *Barrat* married *Onnemela*, *Lekeman Sekhy*, and *Setteroukan Lila*.

Ram then desir'd to return to his Native Country; which being granted, not without great reluctancy, he went back with his Father, Mother and three Brothres, with their Wives, where his Father deliver'd up the Kingdom to him; but having receiv'd a Wound in his Thumb, which prov'd very painful to him, it was healed at last by his Wife, in acknowledgment of which Benefit he told her, that he would grant her whatever she would ask: She then desir'd her Husband to send his three Sons, *Ram*, *Lekeman* (call'd otherwise *Laatsmana*, and

Baldæus.

and *Settrugna*) and *Setteroukan* for 12 years into Foreign Countries, and to surrender the Kingdom to her Son *Barrat* (call'd *Baratha* and *Pareda* by the *Malabars*); *Barrat* on the other hand was unwilling to accept of this Offer, notwithstanding which *Ram* departed with his Family and two Brothers to the Village of *Baratpery* 12 *Cos* from *Asonti*, but leaving a pair of his Slippers behind, *Barrat* who still refus'd to encroach upon his eldest Brother's Right, used to sacrifice Flowers, Sandal-wood and Saffron to them in his absence.

Ram *travels along the* Ganges.

Ram in the mean while travelling along the River *Ganges* to *Pousouwattivan*, where after a month's stay, whilst the Brothers were busy in erecting the Huts, *Lekeman* used to go every day to gather Fruit for their Subsistence; he being a very handsom Person, and got upon a Tree to gather some Fruits, was espy'd by a certain Woman named *Souppenekhia* (and *Churpanaga* by the *Malabars*) the Sister of *Rawan*, and Widow of one *Vivali* (kill'd in *Rawan*'s Service) who being come to wash her self in the *Ganges*, told him, That *she looking upon him as the handsomest Person in the World, she must be miserable for ever unless he would vouchsafe to love her, which if he refused, she would turn her Love into Hatred, when he must prepare to engage with her in single Combat.* Lekeman reply'd, That *his Love being fix'd in another place, he could not oblige her, and that to fight with her would not turn to his Honour. O unfortunate Man!* cry'd she, *how little beest thou acquainted with my Strength! if I can't enjoy thee, I will have thy Life before I part from this place.* *Lekeman* then considering whom he had to do with, told her, that tho he was willing, it was not in his power, she being of the Family of the *Rachee*, and he of the Tribe of the *Bram-Ketterijs*; but that if she would go to his Brother *Ram*'s Hut, which was not far thence, and obtain his Consent, he would not be backward to gratify her desire. She no sooner came to *Ram*'s Hut, but he knew her at first sight, and looking upon this as a fit opportunity to revenge the Affront he had receiv'd of *Rawan*, he gave her a Letter directed to his Brother *Lekeman*, wherein he order'd him to cut off those Parts in which her Strength was lodg'd. Thus she left *Ram* well satisfied, hastening to her pretended Bridegroom, whom she found busy in gathering of Fruit, and delivering the Letter to him, bid him read his Brother's Consent. But *Lekeman* understanding his Brother's Intention, run towards her, and under pretence of taking her up in his Arms, cut off her Nose and Ears, wherein her Strength was lodg'd.

Rawan's *Sister in love with* Lekeman.

He cuts off her Nose and Ears.

Thus mortified she went away, threatning Revenge to the two Brothers, and making the best of her way to her Brother *Rawan*'s Palace; but lighting by chance upon an Uncle's House of hers named *Char*, who commanded 10000 Horse, she stop'd there, and being ask'd how she came so defac'd, she told them that some Robbers near the *Ganges* had treated her in this manner.

The youngest of her Uncles order'd immediately 300 Horse to be in readiness to march with him to the *Ganges*, where they attack'd *Ram*'s Habitation with such fury, that *Lekeman* was put under no small Consternation; but *Ram* defended his Habitation so courageously, that he kill'd most of the Horse-men with his Bow call'd *Diennoekbaanne*, with their Leader. *Char* had no sooner receiv'd Intelligence of this Defeat, but putting himself at the head of the remaining 9700 Horse, he march'd to the same place, but with no better success, being slain by *Ram* with all his Forces.

10000 *Horse-men kill'd by* Ram.

Souppenekhia having been an Eye-witness of this Defeat at a distance, made all the haste could to come to her Brother *Rawan*, who having ask'd her the reason, she told him, that meeting with a very beauteous Woman near the River *Ganges*, she endeavour'd to perswade her to come along with her, with an intention to present her to him; but being overtaken by her Husband and his Brother, they had so mortify'd her in that manner as they now saw her. *Rawan* highly exasperated at this usage, bid her to shew him the place where it happen'd, which she did accordingly, and at the same time gave him an account of what had happen'd to her Uncle and the 10000 Horsemen.

Rawan thus fore-warn'd, assum'd the shape of a Stag with two Heads, and so did feed near *Ram*'s Hut, the better to surprize him with the first opportunity; but being espy'd by *Sytha Ram*'s Wife, she was so much taken with his bright Skin, that she desir'd her Husband to shoot him, and to make her a Vest of his Skin. *Ram* told her that the same could not be done without danger; but she persisting in her Intreaties, he consented, yet under Condition, that she and his Brother *Lekeman* should not pass three certain Circles he made with Chalk cross the Hut. He no sooner got into the field, but the two-headed Stag set up his heels, and being pursued

Rawan *transform'd into a Stag.*

Baldæus.

Is shot by Ram. pursued by *Ram* for 3 *Cos* was shot with an Arrow in the Breast.

Rawan's Ghost at the same time entering into the Body of a *Fakier*, he went straitways to *Ram*'s Hut, and with a doleful Voice cry'd out to *Lekeman* to succour his Brother, who was in danger of perishing by his Enemies Hands. *Sytha* Thunder-struck at this Voice, beg'd *Lekeman* to succour her Husband, who told her, that he believ'd this Voice to be fictitious, as not questioning that his Brother,

Baldæus. ther, who had so lately slain 10000 Men, could be in a condition to cope with one. But *Sytha* imploring his Assistance with a flood of Tears, he went accordingly.

In the mean time the *Fakier* endow'd with *Rawan*'s Spirit, having assum'd the shape of a Beggar, came to beg some Alms of *Sytha*, who excus'd the matter, yet at last was prevail'd upon to give him some Fruit that were left the day before; but as she was extending Arm towards the Beggar, he catch'd hold of her Hand, and pulling her over the Circle (under pretence of bringing her to the place where her Husband was engag'd) he carried her to the Country of *Lanka* in the Isle of *Ceylon*.

He carries away Sytha.

As he was carrying her along he met with the Giant *Siettank*, of the Tribe of the *Raches*, who beg'd some Victuals of him in a threatning tone. *Rawan* having no Provisions to give him, took up a Stone, which he rubbing against his Thigh, made a large hole, the Blood whereof turn'd the Stone into Meat, which he gave the Giant, who had no sooner eat it, but it turn'd to a Stone again in his Stomach, and oppress'd him to such a degree that he was not able to stir or move.

Then *Rawan* pursuing his Journy came to the Mountain *Resmokperwat*, where he met with the Apes with Bears Heads, call'd *Hanuman*, *Suckerige*, *Anget* and *Siamboemt*; and *Sytha* dropping her Ring, the same was taken up by *Hanuman*.

Places her in a Garden in Ceylon.

Rawan coming into *Ceylon*, and not daring to bring *Sytha* into his House, plac'd her in a Garden under a certain Tree call'd *Sysem*, and having appointed her a Guard of twelve Giants, he daily made his Courtship to her, but she refused all his Offers.

In the mean time *Ram* returning homewards, and meeting with his Brother *Lekeman* by the way, they both came to the Hut, but to their great surprize found *Sytha* gone. *Ram* in a most violent Rage upbraided his Brother with leaving the Hut, but having understood the reason they resolv'd to go in quest of *Sytha*.

Ram and Lekeman go in quest of Sytha.

As they were passing through a very long subterraneous Passage, they met with a certain Giant at his Devotion, who being surpriz'd to see them, *Ram* told him, that the desire of finding out his Spouse had brought him through this dangerous place, asking him, whether he had not heard any thing of her: He answer'd, that he had seen a Giant flying through the Air, holding a Woman upon his Hand. *Ram* further enquiring what way they were gone, he answer'd, towards the Country of *Dekendesa*.

Ram verily believing this to be *Sytha*, bless'd the Giant, and pursuing his Journy to the Mount *Resmokperwat*, met with the before-mention'd Apes with Bears Heads, where *Hanuman* prostrating himself at his Feet, ask'd him, What brought him to this remote part of the World? *Ram* answer'd, To look after his Spouse. *Hanuman* reply'd, I saw a Giant pass through the Air with a Woman sitting upon his Hand, who drop'd this Earring. *Ram* infinitely rejoyc'd at the sight thereof (knowing it to be his Wife's) ask'd him, what way they had taken? *Hanuman* reply'd, To the Country of *Lanka* in the Isle of *Ceylon*; and at the same time offering his Service for the recovery of his Spouse, he entreated the Ape *Suckerige* to assist him in this Enterprize; promising him, that in case they succeeded, *Ram* should restore to him his Wife and his Estate in the Valley of *Kieckenda*, taken from him by his Brother *Bael*: But *Suckerige* remember'd his Brother's Strength, how he had worsted the Giant *Rawan*, and held his Head two Months under his Arms (before the Government of the World was committed to him by *Vistnum*) besides several other Giants told him, that *Ram* being only of a middle Stature, was not likely to conquer him.

Hanuman gives an account to Ram of Sytha.

Hanuman however persisting in his Persuasions, and extolling the Power of *Ram*, *Suckerige* asked a Token, *viz.* that he should shoot his Arrow thro some of the Branches of the Trees, whilst they were agitated by the Wind. *Lekeman* having understood his Request, spoke to his Brother *Ram*, who bidding them shut their Eyes, he shot at once with his Arrow thro seven Trees, and at the same time order'd *Suckerige* to challenge his Brother *Bael* in his Name; which being done accordingly, *Bael* appear'd, and in a scornful Tone told *Ram*, that he would cut off his Head at one Stroke; whereat *Ram* being exasperated to the highest degree, he drew his Bow, sent his Arrow through his Body, and restor'd the Valley of *Kieckenda* to *Suckerige*, and with it his Wife.

Ram kills Bael.

Ram having now taken a Resolution to stay with his Brother in the Mountain, sent *Hanuman*, *Anget*, *Suckerige* and *Sucking*, Chieftains of the Apes, into the Valley of *Quicxinta* (as the *Malabars* call it) not far from the Valley of *Kieckenda*, in quest of his Spouse. *Hanuman* being ready to depart with his Company, gave him his

Ring as a token to shew to his Spouse *Sytha:* Accordingly they set out on their Journy, taking two different Roads, two and two together; but not meeting with *Sytha*, they met at a certain place near the Sea-side full of Despair at their ill success. However *Hanuman* bid them have a good Heart, telling them, that *Ceylon* lying opposite to them cross the Seas, he would according to the Power granted him by *Vistnum* fly over the Sea into *Ceylon*, where *Rawan* kept his Residence.

Hanuman *flies into* Ceylon. *Hanuman* being at last in disguise, arriv'd in the Isle of *Ceylon*, met with ten Female Giants that were appointed her Guard by *Rawan* in the Air: These refusing him Passage, he assum'd the shape of a Fly, and thus escaping their Hands, advanced to the Shore of *Ceylon*; but being there met by a huge Giant who stopt his Passage, was forc'd to reassume his own Body of an Ape, and so to engage the Giant, who seeing him to fight so courageously, commended his Bravery, telling him, that he should succeed in what he desir'd. *Hanuman* answering, that he came only to look for his Master *Ram*'s Wife: The Giant reply'd, *She is kept by the most Potent* Rawan *in a Garden under a Sysem-Tree.* *Hears from* Sytha.

Hanuman then pursuing his Journy, and being extremely tir'd, did fall into a swound upon the Sea-shore; where having slept 18 hours, and forgotten the Name of the place assign'd him by the Giant, he transform'd himself into a Cat, and running through all the Houses and Corners of *Ceylon*, but without success, at last happen'd to light upon the top of *Rawan*'s House, from whence espying the Tree where *Sytha* was kept, he advanced towards it; but whilst he was in doubt whether it were *Sytha* or not, he saw *Rawan* coming towards her, and renewing his Courtship, offering all his Territories and Treasures in case she would consent to be his Wife; but *Sytha* reply'd, that being *Ram*'s alone, she would never encourage his Addresses, threatning to consume him by Fire if he persisted in his Demands.

Rawan was no sooner gone, but *Hanuman* dropt the Ring given him by *Ram* into *Sytha*'s Lap, who burst out into Tears, imagining that *Ram* had been kill'd by some of the Giants; but *Hanuman* throwing himself at her Feet, told her that *Ram* was in good health, and had sent him to look after her. *Sytha* still questioning the truth, *Hanuman* told her that the Ring was given him as a token to her, yet not with an intention to bring her to him, but only to learn News of her. Then haste away, reply'd she, and desire *Ram* to deliver me out of the hands of the Tyrant *Rawan*. *Baldæus.*

Hanuman went his way, but considering with himself, he would not forsake *Lanka* without leaving behind him some Remembrances of his having been there, he return'd to *Sytha*, asking her leave to gather some Fruits, which she deny'd, telling him, that he would be unfortunate in his Enterprize, if he fed upon any other Fruit but what he found upon the ground: Well, said *Hanuman*, and so laying hold of the next Fruit-Tree, and tearing it up by the root he eat the Fruit, the same he did to most of the other Trees in the Garden, except that where *Sytha* was plac'd. The Gardiner seeing the next Morning what havock *Hanuman* had made, told his Master what happen'd, who being incensed to the highest degree, order'd 10000 Giants to kill this Ape. *Hanuman* seeing them advancing against him, laid hold of one of the biggest Trees, and made such havock among these Giants, that scarce one of them escap'd. Hanuman's *Actions at* Ceylon.

Rawan no sooner heard of this Defeat, but he sent 25000 more to revenge the Quarrel of their Comrades; but these having undergone the same fate, he sent his youngest Son at the head of 12000 of the choicest Giants, who put *Hanuman* so hard to it, that they made him reel several times; but his Strength being continually renew'd by *Ram*'s care, he at first slew *Rawan*'s youngest Son, and at last the whole Army. *Great Slaughter of the Giants.*

Mandory Rawan's Spouse did all that lay in her power to perswade her Husband to deliver up *Sytha* to *Ram*, for fear of losing his whole Estate; but *Rawan* was so far from hearkening to her Counsel, that he issued a Proclamation, that he who thought himself the strongest Man in the Isle of *Ceylon* should engage with the Ape: But there being no body who durst compare for Strength with *Rawan*'s eldest Son, named *Indersiet*, (who formerly had vanquish'd *Raja Inder*) he order'd him, that whenever he was a going to shoot his Arrow, he should utter certain words taught him by *Bramma*, which had that effect as to turn the Arrow into a Serpent, and to entangle his Adversary.

Indersiet thus bold with hopes, advanc'd at the head of his Giants against *Hanuman*, who laid so bravely about him, that he made the Giants shrink, which *Indersiet* per-

Baldæus. perceiving, let fly his Arrow against *Hanuman*, which being in an instant transform'd into a Serpent, was tore to pieces by *Hanuman*; which *Indersiet* seeing, he flew like Lightning thro the Air to the holy *Bramma*, upbraided him with Deceitfulness, and threatning him with no less than the loss of his Life, unless he shew'd him the right way of vanquishing his Enemy.

Indersiet *makes use of a bewitched Arrow.*

Bramma being put to such a *nonplus*, hastned to *Hanuman*, and casting himself at his Feet beg'd of him not to oppose *Indersict*'s Arrow, as wanting not means to protect himself against his Attempts by divers other ways. *Hanuman* taking Compassion of *Bramma* granted his Request, who then told *Indersiet*, that by his Charms he had so order'd the matter as to render his Arrow more effectual than before. *Indersiet* encourag'd by his Promise, sent forth his Arrow against *Hanuman* a second time, which turning into a Serpent stuck so close to his Limbs, that the Giants had sufficient opportunity to exercise their Weapons upon him, tho he receiv'd no more harm by it than if he had been touch'd with a Feather. However they carried him before the ten headed *Rawan*, who ask'd him by what means he was become invulnerable: *Hanuman* reply'd, By *Ram*'s Blessing, whose Wife thou hast carried away, which if thou dost not restore forthwith, thy whole Country shall be laid desolate.

This Story seems to have some relation to that of Sampson.

Rawan exasperated at this Answer, commanded 10000 Giants to kill him, but finding their Endeavours prove unsuccessful, he ask'd *Hanuman* by what means he might be bereav'd of his Strength: He reply'd, If you dip my Tail in Oil, wrap it in Cotton, and then set it on fire, all my Strength will vanish in an instant. *Rawan* believing the matter, put it in Execution, notwithstanding which *Hanuman* pull'd the Serpent to pieces like a piece of Thred, kill'd most of the Giants, and set fire to the Houses. This done, he took his leave of *Sytha*, who gave him one of her Bracelets as a token, to shew *Ram* that he had seen her, charging him at the same time not to look back till he had past the Seas, else he would be in great danger. *Hanuman* strictly observ'd this Rule till he came to the Sea-shore, when approaching on a sudden to a great Flame, he look'd back, and the Flame reaching his Tail, he was glad to run into the Sea to extinguish the Fire.

Then taking his course through the Air, he pass'd the Seas, and meeting with his Comrades, told them what had happen'd, who thence made the best of their way to the Mountain *Resmokperwat*; and having shew'd *Sytha*'s Bracelets to *Ram*, who immediately order'd *Suckery*, Lord of the Valley of *Kieckenda*, to summon all the Apes under his Jurisdiction to arm against *Rawan*, he accordingly appear'd under their 18 Kings, each whereof appear'd at the head of 20000 Apes, amounting in all to 360000 Apes.

Ram and his Brother *Lekeman* march'd at the head of this powerful Army to the Sea-side directly opposite to the Isle of *Ceylon*, where *Ram* having spent three days in fasting and praying, to open a Passage for his Forces through the Sea, but in vain, he drew his Bow threatning the Sea to reduce it into such narrow Bounds, that where then was nothing to be seen but Water, the Terrestial Creatures should sport upon the pleasant Sands without danger. The Waves of the Sea thereupon humbling themselves before *Ram*, told him, that to open him a Passage through the depth could not be done without a total Destruction of a vast number of Fishes, but that there was in his Army a certain Ape call'd *Sichem*, endow'd with such a Quality by his Master the holy *Narsy*, that whatever Stone he should only touch, would swim on the surface of the Water like Wood. Accordingly *Ram* order'd a vast quantity of Stones to be brought from the neighbouring Mountains, which being only touch'd by *Sichem*, and then thrown into the Sea, did swim upon the Surface thereof, and making a Bridg of 100 Leagues in length, afforded an easy Passage for his whole Army.

A Stone Bridg of a hundred Leagues cross the Sea.

The Inhabitants of *Lanka* or *Ceylon* being soon alarum'd by the noise of their Drums, and other Warlike Instruments, *Rawan*'s Wife intreated her Husband to take a view of that prodigious Army from the top of his House, whom *Ram* no sooner spy'd at a distance, but with his Arrow he shot off his ten Crowns from his ten Heads. His Wife laying hold of this opportunity, exhorted him once more to deliver up *Sytha* to *Ram*, who, says she, can with the same Arrow which took off your ten Crowns, also take off your ten Heads.

But *Rawan* persisting in his Resolution not to part with *Sytha*, *Ram* told his Brother *Lekeman*, that to leave nothing unattempted to reduce *Rawan* to Reason, they would dispatch the Ape *Anget* to him to demand *Sytha*, and in case of refusal, to tell him now, that they were

were come to destroy all with Fire and Sword.

Rawan being advertis'd of his arrival, call'd together all his Giants, (among whom was his Brother *Bebickhem*) and having caused 10 Statues to be made with 10 Heads like himself, he took his place in the midst of them: *Anget* coming boldly into the Room, ask'd what Monsters these were, and which of them was *Rawan* himself? Whereat *Rawan* being highly exasperated, ask'd who it was that dares affront him thus, threatning to make him repent his boldness. *Anget* reply'd, Were I not here in the quality of an Ambassador, I would try my Strength with thee, being sent by *Ram* to let thee know, that he did not come with this Army to destroy thy Subjects, but to recover his Wife *Sytha*; which if thou refusest to do, he declares himself innocent of all the Effusion of Blood that shall ensue. But *Rawan* answering, that he was resolv'd not to deliver her; *Anget* brought this Answer to *Ram*.

Rawan's *Brother comes over to* Ram. At the same time *Rawan*'s Brother, with five of his chief Counsellors, finding him not in a capacity to cope with so powerful an Army, assum'd the shape of Apes, and throwing themselves at the Feet of *Ram*, crav'd his Mercy and Protection.

The Apes of *Ram*'s Army taking them for Spies, handled them very roughly at first coming into the Camp; and *Hanuman* or *Hanneman* especially, would have disswaded him from having the least concern with them, but were appeased by *Ram*, when he told them that he knew them to be Men of Honour and Probity.

By this time *Rawan* had arm'd 10000 of his boldest Giants to attack *Ram*'s Camp; but these being soon defeated, he sent 18000 more, who having undergone the same fate, he sent 30000 more; and these also succeeding no better, he sent 50000 more, who were all routed like the rest. Rawan's *Obstinacy.*

Then *Rawan*'s eldest Son entreating his Father to let him engage alone against the whole Camp of *Ram*, he could not consent to his Request; but having convinced his Father of the Advantages he had lately got by the Instructions of *Bramma*, he put him at the head of 10000 of his choicest Giants. With these Troops being advanc'd to *Ram*'s Camp, he encourag'd them to fight bravely, whilst he soaring up into the Air did hide himself behind one of the Wheels of the Chariot of the Sun, till coming directly over *Ram*'s Camp, he sent forth one of his Magical Arrows, which turning immediately into a Serpent, sent forth such a vast number of other Serpents among the Apes, that their Arms and Legs being quite entangled, they were knock'd down on all sides by the Giants. *Baldæus.*

Ram not a little surpriz'd at this Disaster, ask'd *Rawan*'s Brother what was best to be done; who told him, that if he would send for his wing'd *Garroude*, the Serpents would vanish in an instant. *Ram* following his Advice, *Garroude* no sooner appear'd but the Serpents vanish'd, and the Apes fought it out bravely with the Giants.

In the mean while *Ram* having advis'd with his Council how to attack *Indersiet*, *Rawan*'s eldest Son in the Air, and *Lekeman* having offer'd his Service, he got upon *Hanuman*'s Back, who carrying him up into the Air, *Indersiet* sent a shower of Arrows against him; but these being repulsed by *Lekeman*'s Shield, and *Indersiet* seeing him advance towards him, threw away his Bow and Arrows, and laying hold likewise of his Sword and Buckler, a most furious Combat ensued, which remain'd dubious for some time, till *Lekeman* giving him a Blow on his Neck cut off his Head at one stroke, which dropt down before his Father's Feet. *Mandory* his Mother burst out into a most violent Passion for the loss of her beloved Son, tearing her Hair and Breasts with her Nails, and upbraiding her Husband with Cruelty, Injustice and Lasciviousness, but to little purpose, *Rawan* persisting in her Resolution of not delivering *Sytha*. Rawan's *eldest Son slain.*

Being resolv'd to make his utmost Efforts, he crav'd the Assistance of his Brother, a most famous Giant, nam'd *Coukeringh* (or *Kompacarna*, as *Rogerius* * calls him after the *Malabars*) this Giant used to spend his whole Life in sleeping, except one day when he appear'd in his full Activity, and to spend his time in filling his Belly with Victuals for the whole succeeding year. It being then in the third Month of his sleep, *Rawan* call'd to him aloud, Brother *Coukeringh*, rouze, rouze, and come to my Assistance, or else we are lost! *Coukeringh* asking him half asleep, what was the matter? *Rawan* told him, that being attack'd by a vast Body of Apes under the Command of one *Ram*, who had kill'd two of his Sons, and no less than seven Generals, with 200000 Giants, he had no other means left to reprieve himself and his Subjects from Destruction, but to implore his Aid. The Giant reply'd, Thou beest

* C. 3.

He seeks for Assistance by his Brother.

Baldæus. unfortunate, *Rawan*, to have entangl'd thy ſelf in an unjuſt War againſt an Army headed by the Divine *Ram*; I have foreſeen it in my Sleep, that the ſame will turn to the Deſtruction of thy ſelf and thy Country.

Rawan ſtood amaz'd, but full of Deſpair, told his Brother, That if it was his fate (written in his Forehead) to die by the hands of *Ram*, it was in vain to avoid it, deſiring once more his Aſſiſtance. The Giant reply'd, My Life is at your Service, and ſo ordering his Chariot drawn by ten pair of Aſſes to be got ready, put himſelf at the head of *Rawan*'s Army compos'd of Giants. *Ram* in the mean while underſtanding that the great Giant was coming againſt him, he appointed ſome thouſand of Apes to throw upon him the tops of the Rocks, which they did accordingly, tho in vain, the Giant piercing the Mount that was thrown upon him with his Arrow, notwithſtanding it had 100 Leagues in compaſs.

This made *Ram* ask *Bebickhem*, *Rawan*'s Brother, by what means the Giant *Coukeringh* might be vanquiſh'd. *Bebickhem* reply'd, You muſt retreat three Paces backwards; that can't be, anſwer'd *Ram*, becauſe I am deſcended of the Race of the *Ketteriis*, who dare not retreat under pain of Baniſhment. But there is no other Remedy, return'd *Bebickhem*; but the beſt Advice I can give you is, to deſcend from your Chariot, and let the ſame be carried three Paces backwards. This being approv'd by *Ram*, was done accordingly, ſo that whilſt the Giant was making a moſt horrid ſlaughter among

The Giant Coukeringh ſlain. the Apes, he ſhot his Head off, which falling upon the ground ſhook the Earth as if a whole Mountain had tumbled down, a whole River of Blood as black as Pitch guſhing out of his Veins.

Notwithſtanding this the Trunk of his Body continued to make a great ſlaughter among the Apes; ſo that *Ram* being again oblig'd to have recourſe to *Rawan*'s Brother, he told him, that if he ſent out a Party of Apes to get a blue Cloth died with Indigo, and therewith cover'd the Body, it would become immovable. In the mean while the Trunk of the Giant continued to make great havock among the Apes, but to little purpoſe, they being reviv'd (by the Aſpect of *Ram*) as faſt as they were kill'd.

By this time the blue Cloth being brought was thrown upon the Trunk, which in an inſtant remain'd as unmovable as a Stone in the Field. *Rawan* ſeeing himſelf thus reduc'd to deſpair, had recourſe to the Goddeſs *Bowanni*, unto whom he offer'd a Sacrifice of freſh Butter, Sandalwood, Flowers and Spices, imploring her Aid againſt *Ram* with ſuch fervency, that it is believ'd he would have obtain'd his Requeſt, had not the Ape *Hanuman* defiled the Sacrifice by throwing one of the dead Carcaſes of the ſlain Giants upon the Altar, erected in a deep hole for this Sacrifice. *Rawan's laſt Sacrifice.*

Rawan thus drove to the laſt extremity, put himſelf again at the head of his Forces, and like a deſperate Perſon ſlew all the Apes he met in his way, forcing all the Hills before him the Apes threw in his way, till *Ram* drawing his Bow ſhot off nine of his Heads; and then calling to him aloud, *Rawan* ſaid he, deſiſt from Bloodſhed, return me my *Sytha*, and I will heal thy Wounds, and reſtore thee thy Heads and Kingdom, without which thou wilt certainly loſe all. But *Rawan* replying, that if Fate had ſo ordain'd it, he would rather loſe his 10 Heads alſo than *Sytha*. *Ram* ſhot likewiſe his tenth Head off: But perceiving that the Headleſs Body laid ſtill about him with its 24 Arms, he threw ſome Water upon it, and muttering out certain words, made it as immoveable as a Stone. *Rawan ſlain by Ram.*

Mandory was no ſooner inform'd of her Husband's Death, but ſhe threw her ſelf at *Ram*'s Feet, bewailing his Obſtinacy, notwithſtanding the many forebodes of his Fall, an unfortunate Raven and a doleful Owl having ſettled upon his Houſe, with very dreadful Lamentations and Outcries, the fore-runners of his Misfortune. As I have, added ſhe, been innocent of what has happen'd, ſo I hope you won't deny me my Protection: *Ram* bid her be ſatiſfied, ordering her at the ſame time to paſs ſeven times through the ſmoke of the Fire kept at *Tchie*, to purify her ſelf, and renew her Virginity, which done he would marry her to her Husband's Brother *Bebickhem*, who accordingly was put into *Rawan*'s place. *His Wife married to his Brother.* Then *Ram* being carried in his *Roſe Litter* to the Tree *Syſem*, where *Sytha* was kept a Priſoner, ſhe embrac'd him, returning him a million of Thanks for her Deliverance. *Ram meets again with Sytha.* The next thing *Ram* did, was to revive his Apes ſlain in the late Engagement; and ſo march'd back over the ſame Bridg that had carried him into *Ceylon*. Being come to the oppoſite Shore, he order'd the Stones to be carried to the place whence they had been taken, and marching to the Valley of *Kieckenda*, he would there have taken his leave of *Suckery*; but he refuſing

Returns home. refusing to part with him thus, would needs accompany him with all his Forces as far as the Village of *Baratpoeri*, where *Ram* was receiv'd by his Father, Mother and Brother, with great Demonstrations of Joy, the sweet-scented Rose-Water, Saffron, Betel, and other Perfumes, being lavishly bestow'd upon him and all those that had attended him home.

Ram having bestow'd his Blessing upon *Suckery* he return'd home, but *Hanuman* staid with him. He reign'd in Peace 11 years after his return, and begat two Sons, *Lan* and *Chus*. Then taking his opportunity when he had sent *Hanuman* out of the way, he ascended into Heaven with the Inhabitants of the Earth, except his two Sons.

The *Malabars* say, that *Ram* being jealous of *Sytba*, would have murder'd her, had she not cleared her self by the Fire and a solemn Oath. Another time being again seiz'd with a Jealousy, because she had *Rawan*'s Picture drawn upon a piece of Board, she purg'd her self by putting her Hand into a Vessel fill'd with Serpents. *Baldæus.*

They further add, That her Husband being become extreme jealous, caus'd her to be thrown before the Elephants, and afterwards before the Tygers, but she escaped without the least harm. They say, that when *Hanuman* saw *Ram* ascend into Heaven, he cry'd aloud to him, O Divine *Ram!* what have I done, that you will leave me behind! *Ram* answer'd, *Hanuman*, be not dissatisfied, thou shalt never die, and many Pagodes shall be erected to thy Memory. Farewel.

Thus ended the second Period of Time, which, according to the Computation of the *Benjans*, contains a Million and 296000, whereof *Ram* reign'd 2000. This second Period is call'd *Treitagom* by the *Malabars*, and *Tretanike* by the *Benjans*.

CHAP. V.

The eighth Altar. The Parents, Birth and Education of Kisna. *His miraculous Deliverance.* Ragia Kans *endeavours to murder him.* Kisna *turns a Shepherd, and flys with his Company to* Goggel.

The eighth Transformation the most remarkable. AS the eighth Transformation of *Vistnum* is accounted of the greatest moment above the rest; for, say the Pagans, in all the others *Vistnum* appear'd in the World with some part of his Divinity, but in this he carried along with him the whole Substance of it, so that he left his place vacant in Heaven: This Transformation happen'd with the beginning of the third Period of Time; and, according to the relation of the *Benjans*, was thus.

One *Ragia Kans* living in the City of *Mottera*, 25 *Cos* from *Agra*, upon the River *Siemmena*, had a young Sister named *Deuki*. About 3 *Cos* higher up the same River liv'd a certain *Brabman* named *Wassendeuw* in the City of *Goggel*. The said *Deuki* being arriv'd to a marriageable Age, her Brother *Ragia Kans* look'd out for a Husband for her; but meeting with none for his purpose in that City, he sent to the City of *Goggel*, where his Messenger hearing of the Worth and Piety of *Wassendeuw*, the same was at his Recommendation married to him when he was only 19, and she no more than 12 years of Age.

The said *Ragia* having understood that there was among his Subjects a certain *Brabman*, named *Narret*, well skill'd in Chiromancy (a thing in high esteem among the Pagans *) he sent for him, desiring him to look into his Sister's Hands, and to foretel, without dissembling the matter, what good or bad Fortune was like to befal her. The *Brabman* having view'd her Hand, told the King, that according to the Lines of her Hand she was to bring forth six Sons, and one Daughter, the youngest of whom will not only take away thy Kingdom, but also thy Life.

* See Vossius l. 2. Idol. c. 47. & Pucer. de Divin.

The King being not a little surpriz'd at this Prophecy, order'd the said *Deuki* and her Husband to be imprisoned in a strong Castle, and that all the Children begotten upon her Body should be kill'd immediately. Accordingly the Midwife brought the new-born Babes to her Brother, who beat out the Brains of six of them (*viz.* five Sons and one Daughter) against a Stone. Afterwards understanding that she was with Child with the seventh, he enclosed her in a Room with Iron Doors, and appointed her a Guard of 100 Soldiers, with strict Orders that the Child as soon as it was born should be brought to him. Upon this occa-

Baldæus.

occaſion I can't but obſerve, that this as well as the enſuing part of the Story of *Kiſna* ſeems to have a near relation to the Hiſtory of the Birth of our Saviour, his flight into *Egypt*, the Murder of the innocent Children by *Herod*, Chriſt's Miracles and Aſcenſion, *&c.*

The time of her Reckoning being expir'd on the day * *Aetben*, of the Month *Souwanne*, this unfortunate Lady being overwhelm'd with Grief, ſhe brought forth a Son about Midnight without the leaſt Pain, whoſe Face was as bright as the Full Moon; but as ſhe had occaſion to rejoice at the Birth of ſo fine a Child, his Fate put her into incredible Affliction: But *Viſtnum* (whoſe Divine Virtue was infuſed into this Child) comforted his

* *The* 8th *day of the decreaſing Moon.*

Mother,

Mother, telling her, that he would find means to escape the hands of his Uncle, and deliver her out of her Prison. Then speaking to his Father, Pray, says he, carry me to *Goggel* on the other side of the River *Siemmena* to the *Brahman Nen*, whose Wife being lately brought to Bed of a Daughter, exchange me for her, and leave the rest to my disposal.

Wassendeuw answer'd, how is it possible to remove thee out of a Chamber so closely guarded and kept, that not the least thing could pass in or out? *Kisna* (this was the Child's Name) reply'd, the Doors shall be open'd to thee, and the Guards so overcome with Sleep, that nothing shall stop thy free Passage; he had no sooner spoken these words but the seven Doors open'd themselves, so that *Wassendeuw* took the Child and carried him off without the least hinderance. But coming to the River *Siemmena* directly opposite to *Goggel*, *Kisna*'s Father perceiving the Current to be very strong (it being in the midst of the rainy Season) and not knowing which way to pass it, *Kisna* commanded the Water to give way on both sides to his Father, who accordingly pass'd dry-footed cross the River, being all the way guarded by a Serpent that held her Head over the Child to serve it instead of an Umbrella. The *Benjans* call this Serpent *Sickenasy*. Coming to the *Brahman*'s House, the Door open'd it self, and finding the *Brahman* and his Wife asleep, he exchang'd his Son for their Daughter, which he carried along with him to the Castle. In short, the Water afforded him once more a free Passage, and finding the Doors of the Castle open, and the Guards asleep, he lock'd them after him, and deliver'd the Girl to his Wife.

The Guards hearing the Child cry soon after, enter'd the Chamber, snatch'd it from the unfortunate Parents, and brought it to *Ragia Kans*, who finding it a Girl, upbraided the *Brahman* with want of Skill, yet for fear of the worst, was going to strike the Head against a Stone; but the Child slipping out of his hands flew up into the Air, and told him, *It was in vain to attempt to murder her, since he that was to take away his Head and his Kingdom, to revenge the Death of his five Brothers and a Sister, was safe at* Goggel. This said, it flew up high into the Air, where it was turn'd into *Lightning* by *Vistnum*, a thing never seen before in the World.

Ragia Kans not a little surpriz'd at this Accident, consulted all his Friends what he had best to do in this Emergency; but none being able to advise him to any purpose, whilst he was very melancholy and ruminating upon the oddness of the thing, he understood that the pious *Brahman Nen* who liv'd at *Goggel*, had a most beautiful Son, which put it into his head, whether it might not perhaps be he who was to take Revenge of him for his Tyrannies. At last, to make sure work, he resolv'd to have the Child kill'd; but not thinking it safe to undertake so hainous a thing bare-fac'd (for fear of the common People) he made his Applications to his eldest Sister *Poetena*, enjoyning her as she tender'd his Life, to go with some Presents to this *Brahman*'s House, and to endeavour to kill this Child, by anointing her Teats with Poison.

Accordingly coming with considerable Presents to the Child's Mother at *Goggel*, she wish'd her much Joy, and taking the Child in her Lap, she gave ample Recommendations of its Beauty, and then kissing and playing with the Child, laid it to her Breast: But this Child being proof against all Poison, did suck away not only all her Milk, but likewise the Blood out of her Veins, till she dropt down dead upon the spot.

Ragia sorely afflicted with this News, releas'd his Sister *Deuki* and her Husband, asking his Sister's Pardon for his having pretended to thwart the immutable Decrees of Destiny, and desiring that all past things might be buried in Oblivion. However, as the Child at *Goggel* lay constantly in his Head, he advis'd with his *Vizier*, or Chief Minister, upon the matter: He told him, that there liv'd a certain Giant named *Sectasor* at *Mottera*, who had the Gift of transforming himself into a Cart and Oxen, by which means he might carry the Child into the Air and murder it. The King pursuant to his Advice, sent for the said *Sectasor*, who at his request crossing the River *Siemmena*, when he came near the City of *Goggel*, transform'd himself into a little neat Cart, drawn by two white Oxen with gilt Horns; and passing thus through the Streets of the City, at last stop'd near the *Brahman Nen* his Door. One of the neighbouring Women having just at that time *Kisna* in her Arms at the Door, set the Child upon the said Cart, which was no sooner done, but *Sectasor* flew with the Child up into the Air. The Mother amaz'd at this Spectacle, cry'd out aloud, *O* Vistnum *protect my Child!* Her Prayers were heard; for *Kisna*, when he saw himself high in the Air, assum'd the shape and strength of a Giant, and

gave

Baldæus. gave ſuch a Blow near the Giant's Heart, that he beat the Breath out of his Body; then reaſſuming his former ſhape of a Child, got upon his dead Carcaſe, and ſo fell down with it upon the ground. His Parents being Eye-witneſſes of the Deliverance of their ſuppoſed Son, were ſo ſurpriz'd thereat, that looking upon him as ſomething extraordinary ſent them from Heaven, they ſacrificed to the Gods, and gave abundance of Alms to the Poor.

Ragia Kans finding himſelf diſappointed in his hopes, had recourſe once more to his moſt truſty Counſellors: one of them told him, that there was a certain *Deyt*, or Giant, named *Turnawent*, who being endow'd with the Virtue of transforming himſelf into a Whirlwind, the King engag'd him on his ſide, in order to carry the Child into the Air. *Kiſna*, who heard the Whirlwind rolling croſs the River *Siemmena* towards the City of *Goggel*, being then in his Mother's Lap at the Door, roll'd down upon the ground; whence the Whirlwind ſnatching him up into the Air, his Parents ſtood amaz'd at ſo ſtrange a Spectacle, imploring *Viſtnum* for his Aſſiſtance.

Kiſna being carried to a vaſt height by the Wind, aſſum'd the ſhape of a Man, and taking the Giant *Turnawent* by the Throat, turn'd his Neck round; and then reaſſuming his former ſhape, got upon the dead Carcaſe of the Giant, and fell down along with it upon the ground juſt before his Parents Door, to the great Amazement of the Inhabitants of *Goggel*, who could not but look upon this Accident as miraculous, or that had ſomething of Divine in it.

Kiſna in the mean while remaining upon the Giant's Back, cry'd moſt vehemently; his Mother laid him to her Breaſt, but he not ceaſing to cry, ſhe laid him in a hanging Cradle; notwithſtanding which he continued crying, till his Mother having recounted to him the Story of *Ram* (as related before) he leap'd out of the Cradle, and taking the ſhape of *Ram* with his Bow and Arrow, he cry'd out, *Lekeman*, let us go after *Rawan* and deliver *Sytha*. His Mother being ready to proſtrate her ſelf at his Feet, he ſoon reaſſum'd his former ſhape, and encreaſed miraculouſly both in Strength and Wiſdom.

It happen'd one time that his Mother did bring upon the Table a Golden Diſh with Rice Milk, and ſome Herbs dreſs'd after the way of the *Benjans*, which *Kiſna* ſeeing, he told her he could not eat it unleſs theſe things were all mix'd together, which ſhe did accordingly: but *Kiſna* taſting it, deſir'd her to ſeparate them again; his Mother anſwering him that it was not in human Power ſo to do, he laid his Hand over the Diſh and ſeparated them immediately, to the aſtoniſhment of his Parents.

His Father being a *Brahman* of the Cowherds, maintain'd his Family by breeding of Cattel, which, ſince the bringing of *Kiſna* into the Houſe, was encreaſed to 900000.

His Mother being one time buſy in churming, he ask'd her for a little Butter: ſhe gave him a little, but not thinking that enough, he ask'd for more, which ſhe refuſing, he took the opportunity whilſt ſhe was gone out of the way to take away ſome. His Mother returning ask'd *Kiſna* what was become of the Butter? He anſwer'd, that the Cats and Rats had eat it. But the Mother not thus ſatisfied, look'd into *Kiſna*'s Mouth, where ſhe had a view of the whole World with its Waters, Foreſts, Mountains, *&c.* encloſ'd in a blue Circle. The Mother aſtoniſh'd at ſo ſtrange a Spectacle, yet ſoon recover'd her ſelf, when ſhe ſaw *Kiſna* return to his Childiſh Shape and Game again; ſo taking up a Twig, threaten'd to ſtrike him, but he running out of the Town ſhe purſu'd him, but not being able to overtake him, he ſtood ſtill at laſt, when ſhe gave him three or four Blows, urging him ſtill to tell her what was become of the Butter; he perſiſted in his former ſtory, that the Cats and Rats had eaten it. She took all the Ropes belonging to the 199000 Cows, endeavouring to tie them together in Knots; but notwithſtanding all her Endeavours, the Knots would not tie, till *Kiſna* finding her much out of humour at this Diſappointment, he permitted the Ropes to be knotted, and himſelf to be ty'd with the Ropes; but his Mother finding him cry bitterly, ſhe releas'd him ſoon after.

Another time his Mother being gone to milk the Cows, order'd him to hold a Stick in his hand to make the Cows ſtand ſtill whilſt ſhe was a milking; but finding ſhe had left her Braſs Veſſel, wherein ſhe uſed to gather her Milk behind, and not daring to ſend *Kiſna*, he told her he would ſoon find a way to fetch the Veſſel without ſtirring from the place, and ſo extending one of his Arms ſo far as to reach the Veſſel, he gave it to his Mother, and ſo reaſſum'd the ſhape of a Child.

In the mean while *Ragia Kans* being

inform'd that the Inhabitants of *Goggel* increas'd considerably in Riches (for *Kisna*'s sake) he order'd his Governor to load them with heavy Taxes; which being done accordingly with the utmost Severity, they advis'd with *Kisna* whether they had not best remove with their Cattel to the fertile Valleys of the Mountain of *Perwet*. *Kisna* approving their Proposition, perswaded his Parents to do the same, so that they transported all their Moveables and Cattel to the most fertile Vallies about the Mount *Perwet*, or *Ooden Perwet*, near the River *Siemmera*; here they fix'd their Habitations in a certain Village call'd *Brindawink*, seated in the midst of most pleasant Pasturages, planted with Trees, and so abounding in Grass, that those vast Herds of Cattel were not able to consume it. *Kisna* was so well pleas'd with the place, that he clad himself after their fashion, with a Garland of Peacocks Feathers upon his Woolen Cap, and a Flute to play away the rest of the Cowherds.

CHAP. VI.

Further Designs of Ragia Kans *against* Kisna *by the means of certain Giants,* Raja Inder *and* Bramha. Kisna *produces a Pearl-Tree, and is made a King of the Cowherds.*

Ragia Kans highly exasperated at this removal of his Subjects, summon'd a certain Giant nam'd *Bacassar*, who having the virtue of transforming himself into a Hern, he sent him to carry away *Kisna*, which he did accordingly; and having carry'd him up into the Air, endeavour'd to swallow him, but *Kisna* transforming himself into a fiery Flame burnt the Hern to Ashes, and he return'd to his Parents without receiving the least harm. The News thereof having soon reach'd the Ears of *Ragia Kans*, he sent another Giant nam'd *Wickeraak*, who transforming himself into the shape of a Boy, came to *Kisna* as he was looking after the Cattel in the field, and engag'd in a wrestling Match among the other Boys, not questioning by this means but to draw *Kisna* into the Game, and so make an end of him: But *Kisna* (who was not ignorant of his Design) challeng'd him, and as they were wrestling gave him such a kick upon his Breast, that he tumbl'd down dead upon the spot.

Ragia Kans finding himself once more disappointed in his Aim, sent the dreadful Giant *Agasor*, whose Entrails were all Fire. This Giant having laid himself close to the Cowherds Huts, open'd his dreadful Jaws, so that the uppermost reach'd up to the Skies, his Teeth representing like Coco-trees, and his Throat like the Entrance of the Huts. *Kisna* knowing the Deceit, drove his Cattel to his own Stables, but the rest went straitways with their Cattel into the Giant's Throat; which the Giant no sooner perceiv'd, but he shut his Teeth, so that the poor Wretches finding themselves in the midst of Fire and Flames, apply'd themselves to *Kisna*, who was got among them on purpose to make himself an Instrument of their Deliverance: he bid them not to despair, and then extending himself with all his might, made the Giant to burst in pieces, and thus open'd a Passage for the rest to escape the Flames.

This miraculous Deliverance being soon spread all over the neighbouring Country, *Ragia Kans* entreated the Giant *Dawanneel* (who had the power of transmuting himself into a Flame) to destroy *Kisna*: Accordingly he came to the place where *Kisna* and his Companions were feeding the Cattel, and setting all (not excecpting even the Trees and Grass) into a light Flame, the Cowherds fled to *Kisna* (who was at some distance) for help, which he promis'd them in an instant, and so advancing towards the Giant, took and held him round the middle, till he forc'd him to swallow all the Fire again.

Ragia Kans almost reduc'd to despair, had recourse to the Giant *Kasep*, who having assum'd the shape of an Ass of a prodigious bigness, advanc'd towards the Cowherds with a dreadful Countenance; who being terrified at so dreadful an Aspect, left *Kisna* alone, who was so far from being surpriz'd at this monstrous sight, that he laid by his Pipe, and advancing towards the Ass, who came openmouth'd upon him, endeavour'd to take him by one of his hindermost heels, but the Ass gave him so terrible a kick with his

Baldæus.

his Foot, that he threw him 8 or 10 yards high into the Air. *Kisna* finding himself thus roughly handled, thought fit to assume the shape of a Giant, and so taking the Ass by the hinder Leg, did swing him three or four times about his Head, and then throwing him against the ground squeez'd the Breath out of his Body.

The God *Bramba* being not ignorant of what had pass'd, and curious to know whether *Kisna* was not endow'd with some Divine Virtue, took his opportunity, and carried off all the Cattel belonging to *Kisna* and the other Cowherds; who running to *Kisna* and imploring his Assistance, he bid them shut their Eyes, which they had no sooner done, but he produc'd the same number of Cattel they had lost. *Brahma* came about a year after and brought back all the Cattel, asking his Pardon for what was past. *Kisna* told *Brahma* that he had better keep within his own bounds; and causing the Cattel he had produc'd to vanish immediately, he kept them brought back by *Brahma*.

Another time, all the Cattel just after they had been drinking about Noon out of the River *Siemmena*, fell dead on a sudden upon the ground: *Kisna* surpriz'd at this Accident, and knowing that *Garroude* having lately dislodg'd the monstrous Serpent *Kallinaegh* from her Dam call'd *Rammane Drepek*, he shrewdly suspected that she had taken to this River, and infected the same with her Venom: Then getting upon a Palm-tree, he assum'd his white and black Skin, and two more Arms and Hands; and sending for *Garroude*, order'd him to go to *Bramba*, and to demand of him the things taken out of the Sea in the times of *Couram*, and left in his Custody till his return. *Garroude* hastening to *Brahma*, brought back to *Kisna* the *Chianko*, or Horn, the beauteous Woman *Leksemy*, and the Jewel *Consenkmany*. This done, he took the Horn in one hand, a piece of Iron in the second, another Weapon in the third, and a Flower in the fourth hand. Thus equipp'd, he leapt into the River in the presence of his Companions, and diving to the bottom, met with the Wife of some of the Attendants belonging to the Serpent *Kallinaegh*, who ask'd him what had brought him thither, fore-warning him to retreat in time, before he should be seen by the Serpent, which questionless would devour him in an instant. *Kisna* reply'd, that being come on purpose to find out the Serpent, he desir'd he might be shew'd him; which they refusing to do, he turn'd his Eyes on all sides, and at last espying the Serpent he awaken'd him out of his sleep, bidding him to leave this River unless he would pay for it with Death. The Serpent *Kallinaegh* swelling with Rage flew upon *Kisna*, and beat him backwards; but he recovering himself, squeez'd the Serpent's Head to that degree, that not knowing what to do he twisted himself about his Body: but *Kisna* encreas'd the bulk of Body in such a manner, that the Serpent ready to burst, was forc'd to let go his hold, being ready to drop down dead for want of Strength. *Kisna* then got on the top of his Neck, and putting an Awl through his Nostrils, rid upon him as if he had been on horse-back. The Wife and Attendants of the Serpent finding him quite out of breath, intreated *Kisna* to spare his Life, promising to quit the River immediately. But *Kallinaegh* not willing to consent to what they had offer'd, still endeavour'd to get rid of *Kisna*; but finding all his Endeavours in vain, and that *Kisna*'s Body increas'd every minute in weight, he was glad to approve of what had been offer'd by his Wife. *Kisna* having pardon'd his Offence, told him, that he would double his Strength (because he had been engag'd against a God) and that *Garroude* should not any more disturb him in his Den, provided he would leave this River, and for the future never hurt either Men or Beasts.

The Serpent with his Wife and Attendants having paid their Reverence three times to *Kisna*, left the River *Siemmena*; and *Kisna* arising on a sudden above the surface of the Water, reassum'd his own shape, and coming ashore blew his Horn, by the sound whereof all the Cattel were in an instant restor'd to Life.

All these Miracles wrought by *Kisna* had such an influence upon the Cowherds, that they consulted all possible means to pay him due Reverence. One among the rest told him, You know that *Raja Inder*, the King of Heavens and the blessed Souls, keeps an annual Feast in the Mountain of *Ooden Perwet* with the Believers; and since we have no less Obligations to *Kisna*, let us make also a Feast to his Honour, and invite him to the said Mountain. This being approv'd of by a general Consent, they prepar'd a most splendid Feast, which they celebrated with such demonstrations of Joy, that the Noise thereof coming to *Inder*'s Ears, and looking upon it with a jealous Eye, call'd together the Rains (disposed in twelve peculiar places) ordering them to pour down their Waters upon the Fields and Cottages of these Cowherds: They were ready to obey, and pour'd forth such prodigious showers of Rain, that the Fields being all laid under Water, Men and Beasts were upon the point of being drown'd. The Cowherds highly surpriz'd at the oddness of the thing (it being in the dry *Mousson*) had once more recourse to *Kisna*, who order'd them to get up to the top of the Mount *Ooden Perwet* till the Rains ceased; and they had no sooner obey'd his Orders, but he took the whole Mountain, with Cattel, Men and all upon his little Finger, and lifted them up seven times higher than the Waters could rise.

The Rains finding their Endeavours frustrated, return'd to *Inder*, and told him, that they had pour'd down their Waters seven days and nights without intermission, but in vain, there being a certain Person in those parts who could lift the whole Mountain with his little Finger into the Air. *Raja Inder* then perceiving his Error, came to *Kisna* to make his Excuse, and dismounting from his Elephant, beg'd forgiveness for having attempted any thing against him, pleading his ignorance, and as a token of his Repentance, presented him with the *Camdoga*, or Cow of Plenty, which *Kisna* was pleas'd to accept of, and pardon'd his fault.

Not long after *Kisna* coming home one day, found his Mother busy in putting some Pearls on a String; he ask'd her from what Tree she had gather'd them; but she answering, that she never knew Pearls to grow on Trees, but only in Oister-shells, *Kisna* took one of the biggest, which he had no sooner put into the ground, but they saw a Pearl-Tree sprout forth full of the most exquisite Pearls. The Mother standing amaz'd, and ready to worship him, he caus'd the Tree to vanish immediately.

Kisna produces a Pearl-tree.

Soon after some of the Cowherds and their Wives as they were walking in the Forest, agreed to wash themselves in the River; *Kisna* espying them at a distance, secretly got all their Clothes, and getting upon an adjacent Palm-tree, had his sport to see them coming naked out of the Water without being able to find their Clothes: They were not a little surpriz'd at first, but looking up and seeing *Kisna* in the Palm-tree, they desir'd him to restore their Clothes, which he told them (to try the Modesty of the Women) he would, provided they would come underneath the Tree; but they excusing the matter, he threw the Women their Clothes.

Makes sport with the Women.

Baldæus.

At a certain time *Kisna* taking a walk with the other Cowherds, they chose him their King, and every one had his place assign'd him under the new King. There liv'd among them a certain charitable *Brahman*, whose Wife (without the knowledg of her Husband) paid her daily Devotions to *Kisna*, who sent two of his Messengers to let her know, that being disposed to make merry at her House with some of his Companions, she should provide something for their Entertainment. The Messengers meeting with the *Brahman* told him the Message, who told them, that he knew nothing of *Kisna*, neither would he make any Entertainment for him. With this Answer they return'd to *Kisna*, who chiding them for their mistake, bid them speak to the Woman; which being done accordingly, she no sooner heard the Name of *Kisna*, but making a low Reverence, to work she went, and having dress'd five or six good Dishes with a handsom Desert, she carried them her self to *Kisna*, begging him to accept of what she was unworthy to offer, which he did, and gave her his Blessing; that as long as she liv'd she should want for nothing, and that after her Decease her Soul should not transmigrate * into another Body; but that being purified by him, she should go directly to Heaven.

Is chosen King.

**These Pagans look upon it as a singular Blessing when their Souls are not to enter into other Bodies.*

Kisna with his Companions having feasted plentifully upon what the *Brahman*'s Wife had brought them, as they were returning home met with some Milkmaids, unto whom *Kisna* told, that they must not pass by without paying Toll to him, who was King of the Place. The Maids not thinking he had been in earnest went on their ways; but *Kisna* with his Stick breaking their Milk Vessels, one of them was so exasperated thereat, that she made Complaint thereof to his Mother, who calling him to an account for this Outrage, he deny'd the matter; but his Mother believing the contrary told him, that he had broken the Peace, and that if it should come to *Ragia*'s Ear, he might be punish'd for it: He reply'd, I did not know I had done them any wrong; but as for *Ragia Kan*'s Anger I don't fear it, tho he knew it to morrow.

It happen'd not long after, that in a certain Moonshiny Night in the Month *Alsoor* (in which begins the New Year)

Baldæus. *Kisna* with some of his Companions were diverting themselves with their Pipes in an adjacent Wood; and *Kisna* especially play'd so charmingly upon his Flute, that the Women in the Village being awaken'd by the sound of this Harmony, came running into the Wood to partake of their Divertisements. *Kisna* ask'd them whether they were not afraid to come into the Wood at that time of night? They answer'd, That their Ears and Hearts had been so touch'd with his melodious Harmony, that they were not able to stay at home: So *Kisna* gave them a Tune or two, which so surpriz'd them, that most of them stood amaz'd, gazing all the while at his Beauty, whilst others past their time in dancing. This they continued till midnight, when having bestow'd his Blessing upon the Women he sent them home, he and his Companions passing their time in the same Jollities all night till break of day.

CHAP. VII.

A further account of the Designs of Ragia Kans, *who is kill'd at last by* Kisna. *New Decrees against* Kisna, *which prove ineffectual. His other Miracles.*

RAgia Kans being more and more alarm'd at these Miracles, sent for his chief Minister named *Panjewello*, and his two chief Generals nam'd *Siannoor* and *Mostik*, to consult with them how to rid his hands of *Kisna*: *Panjewello* told him, that all clandestine means having prov'd to no purpose hitherto, he knew no other way than to engage the strongest of all the Giants (named *Keby*) against him.

Ragia approving his Advice, sent accordingly the said Giant, who meeting with *Kisna*, ask'd him where he was going? Where I please, reply'd *Kisna*: Ho ho, answer'd the Giant *Keby*, I will take care of that, and so was going to lay his great Paws upon him; but *Kisna* taking him by the Throat, did not let go his hold till he had squeez'd the Breath out of his Body; which done, *Kisna* put his Hand into his Throat, and pulling his Heart out, first laid it upon his Mouth, and afterwards threw it to the Ravens.

Ragia Kans being now put to the last shift, a certain *Brahman* named *Naret*, advis'd the King to invite *Kisna* with his Followers to a Feast, and so to have him kill'd at Table. *Ragia* approving his Counsel, sent Messengers to invite them accordingly, but they were so far from granting their request, that they desir'd *Kisna*'s Parents not to let him go, who with Tears in their Eyes beg'd him to stay at home; but *Kisna* refusing to hearken to their Advice, order'd his Chariot to be got ready, and taking his Father, his eldest Brother and Mother along with him, went forward to *Goggel* upon the River *Siemmena* opposite to *Mottera*.

Here it was that *Akeroer* one of the King's Messengers, bathing himself in the River, and diving three times successively (after the manner of the *Benjans*) saw *Kisna* under Water seated upon his Throne; which Apparition being seen by him again in the same state above Water, he could not forbear to break out into these words: *O holy* Kisna! *thou beest truly God in human Shape, because thou appearest both under and above Water; a sign thou beest present in all places, a Quality belonging only to the Gods! Pardon me for having invited thee to this Feast.* *Kisna* told him he was sensible it was not his fault, and din'd with him the same day in a Garden *Akeroer* had just near the Bank of the River.

After Dinner they pass'd the River, but had not gone far before they met the King's Washerman with a pack of Clothes on his Back; some of the Company of *Kisna* having a mind to divert themselves, push'd one another against the Washerman, who giving them foul Language, *Kisna* bid his Companions to thresh him handsomly, which they did.

Ragia Kans exasperated to the highest degree at this usage of his Servant, resolv'd to declare open Enmity against *Kisna*. Not long after *Kisna* meeting upon the Road a Barber, he presented him (according to the Custom of that Country) a Looking-glass to look in, and pair'd his Nails; the Barbers in the Eastern Countries always pairing the Nails on the Hands and Toes after they have shav'd the Beard. *Kisna* gave him his Blessing, telling him, that his Soul should directly go to God without being transplanted into another Body.

As

As they were entring the City they were met by a Gardiner's Wife, who used to serve *Ragia Kans* with Flowers: This Woman prostrating her self at *Kisna*'s Feet, said, *O Divine Man! having never seen any thing so beautiful as thy self, I offer to thee these Flowers design'd for* Ragia Kans, *thinking my self much more oblig'd to your Divinity than his Majesty, entreating thee not to despise my Cottage, but to take up thy Lodging there for this night.* Then presenting *Kisna* with a Garland of Flowers, he took up his Lodgings in the House, being welcom'd by the Husband in the most devout manner in the World, who declar'd himself unworthy of receiving so great a Guest, and serv'd *Kisna* and his Company at Table, who at parting bestow'd his Blessing upon him, *viz.* That they should never want, and their Souls go directly to Heaven.

Being advanc'd a little further, they met a poor Cripple or lame Woman, having a Vessel fill'd with Spices, sweet-scented Oils, Sandel-wood, Saffron, Civet and other Perfumes. *Kisna* making a halt, she made a certain sign with her Finger on his Forehead, casting the rest upon his Head. *Kisna* asking her what it was she would ask him? The Woman reply'd, Nothing but the use of my Limbs. *Kisna* then setting his Foot upon hers, and taking her by the hand, raised her from the ground, and not only restor'd her Limbs, but also renew'd her Age, so that instead of a wrinkly tawny Skin, she got a fresh and fair one in an instant. At her request *Kisna* and his Company lodg'd the following night in her House.

Kisna *breaks the strong Arrow of* Mottera.

The next following day *Kisna* and his Company walking through the Streets of *Mottera*, they were shew'd the strong Bow, which none of the Giants had been able to manage; but *Kisna* broke the String of it at the first pull. Thence they walk'd towards the Court, where the Courtiers were expecting the coming of the King: these seeing a whole Troop of Country Fellows, would not allow them Entrance into the Court; but pushing *Kisna* back roughly, he struck 10 of them (among whom were two Colonels) down to the ground, so that they expir'd at his Feet, and their Souls were convey'd immediately to Heaven, a Favour he bestow'd upon the Souls of all such as were slain by his hands.

Kills 10 Courtiers.

Ragia Kans being inform'd of all these Transactions, and almost reduc'd to despair, order'd a Turret to be erected upon the Back of an Elephant, furnish'd with two Warlike Engines, to be manag'd by as many Men. He order'd the Guide of the Elephant, that as soon as he saw *Kisna* coming to the Castle, he should send out the Elephant to trample him under feet, or else endeavour to kill him by the means of the Engines.

Baldæus.

The following day *Kisna* going towards the Court, the Guides set loose the Elephant upon him; but *Kisna* not only stopt him in his full Career, but also putting his Foot against his Trunk, pull'd out both of his Teeth; afterwards seizing him by the Tail, swung him three or four times round his Head, and then dash'd his Head against the Stones. *Ragia* now finding himself reduc'd to the last extremity, and enrag'd with Anger, address'd himself to his two renown'd Generals *Kansjamdoor* and *Mostik*, telling them, that since they had eaten his Bread so many years, it was now time to shew their Fidelity and Bravery, and to deliver him from his mortal Enemy.

Kills an Elephant.

Accordingly they having sent a Challenge to *Kisna*, he appear'd at the appointed time and place, where a most fierce Combat ensu'd, which remain'd dubious for three hours, till at last *Kisna* threw them (one after another) with such a prodigious force to the ground, that the Blood, and with it their Souls, gush'd out of their Mouths.

Kills two Generals.

During the Combat *Ragia Kans* happening to look over the Wall of the Castle, no sooner saw *Kisna*, but he thought he heard a Voice telling him, that he was the Person who should at once take away his Life and his Crown. He was scarce return'd into his Apartment, when News being brought him of the death of his two Generals, he commanded every one to betake themselves to their Arms, to fight against *Kisna*, offering a great Reward to any that could deliver him up into his hands either dead or alive. Accordingly the whole City rose in Arms, and engag'd *Kisna* without the Castle Gates, but were not able to conquer this invincible Hero.

Routs a whole Body of Men.

For *Ragia Kans* having in the mean while order'd *Kisna*'s Parents to be whipt with *Siambokken*, or brass Scourges in his presence: *Kisna* (according to his Omnisciency) being not ignorant of the matter, leap'd over the Wall into the Palace, where finding *Ragia Kans* sitting upon his Throne, he got hold of his Head, and press'd it to the ground till he broke his Neck, and to consummate the matter, gave him three or four terrible Blows which beat out his Brains.

Kills Ragia Kans.

The

Baldæus.

The next thing he did, was to send his eldest Brother to deliver their Parents from their Captivity, who finding the Guards fled, brought them to *Kisna*, where they receiv'd one another with mutual Embraces; *Kisna* declaring his Sorrow for their Sufferings upon his account, and these declaring themselves amply rewarded with the sight of his Person. *Kisna* having put *Ongeseen Ragia Kan's* Father in his stead, return'd with his Parents, Brothers and Companions to their usual Habitations, where he put himself under the Tuition of a certain learned *Brahman*, having chosen a certain poor Scholar named *Sedamnia* for his Attendant at School to carry his Books and Writings.

Kisna under the Tuition of a Brahman.

There liv'd at that time at *Mottera* a certain Merchant, a Relation of *Kisna's* Mother, whose Daughter call'd *Conta* being married to *Ragia Dandou*, King of *Essenapour*, had brought forth five Sons; the First-born whereof his Father had obtain'd by his Prayers to *Inder* the King of the Celestial Spirits, the second from *Bramma*, the third from the Wind, and the two last from the famous Hero *Essonocomaer*.

The five Brothers did at a certain time undertake a Journy with their Mother to *Mottera*, to visit their Grandfather, where they contracted something of Acquaintance with *Kisna*, and frequently reverenced him. About the same time the Women of *Goggel*, and of the Village inhabited by the Cowherds, were very earnest in their Sollicitations for *Kisna's* return, without which they said they neither could nor would eat or drink.

In the mean while the five Brothers having receiv'd the unwelcome News of their Father's Illness, were forc'd to return to *Essenapour*; and the fatal *Exit* of *Ragia Kans* and so many of his Giants being come to the Ears of *Jerasjanda* his Brother-in-law, he resolv'd to revenge the same to the utmost of his Power. Accordingly having gather'd a Body of 95000 chosen Horse, he laid Siege to *Mottera*; but *Kisna* having by his frequent Sallies quite ruin'd his Army, took him Prisoner at last, but knowing that he had by his constant Prayers obtain'd from *Bramma* that he should live 100 years, and at last be kill'd by one *Rhijm*, he released his Prisoner, who having soon gather'd another Army, besieg'd *Mottera* a second time, and was worsted again as before by *Kisna*. The same he continued to do sixteen times, till all his People being slain in the Wars, he passed through all the Corners of the World to raise new Forces, and meeting with the famous Giant *Sialinder*, he put him at the head of his Forces, and so forc'd the Siege of *Mottera* a 17th time.

Jerasjanda resolves to revenge Ragia Kans Death.

Is sixteen times worsted by Kisna.

The situation of *Kisna's* House was such as to be plainly discover'd in the Camp, as from thence he had a full Prospect of their Army. *Kisna* having posted his Brother at the Entrance of his House, he happen'd to be seen by the Enemy's General, who mistaking him for *Kisna*, advanced towards the House: *Kisna* who saw him coming at a distance, considering with himself, that in case he should fall by his hands, his Soul must go straitways to Heaven (a favour he thought him unworthy of) run out of the back-door, making the best of his way to a Cave of a certain *Brahman* about 4 *Cos* from *Mottera*; this Man had by his continued Prayers obtain'd from *Bramma*, that if any one should disturb him in his Devotions, the same should be consumed to Ashes. *Kisna* being not ignorant of this, and seeing his Adversary pursuing him, enter'd the said Cave, and throwing a piece of Cloth over the *Brahman's* Head shelter'd himself behind it. The Giant who follow'd his Footsteps, soon after enter'd the Cave, and finding the *Brahman* cover'd with with a piece of Cloth, gave him two or three sound Boxes on the Ear, telling him, that he should take that as a Reward for his care in hiding *Kisna* in his Cave. *Retreat, Retreat*, said the *Brahman*, *before I uncover my Face, unless thou wilt be consumed by Fire*. Then taking away the Cloth, the Giant was immediately in a Flame, and burnt to Ashes. *Kisna* return'd to *Mottera*, and having routed *Ragia Kans* Brother's Forces, he took him Prisoner; but in respect of *Bramma's* Promise, dismiss'd him soon after.

Kisna in the mean while considering that *Jerasjanda* was to live 100 years, and that consequently he would not lay aside his Designs against *Mottera*, it happen'd that *Wissuchre* the Son of *Bramma* being come from Heaven to give *Kisna* a Visit, and asking him what it was he would request of him? He answer'd, Build me a City in all respects like that of *Mottera*; which he did accordingly the same night in an adjacent Island, being altogether like that of *Mottera*, except that this was of Gold instead of Stone. *Kisna* being inform'd thereof by *Wissuchre* himself, over-whelm'd the Inhabi-

Another Miracle of Kisna.

habitants of *Mottera* with so heavy a Sleep, that (unknown to them) he carried them with all their Cattel, and *Ragia Ongescen* their King to this new City, unto which he gave the Name of *Davarca*, leaving *Sedamma* his old School-fellow and Attendant behind him in a certain Village, which since has got the Name *Sedammapoer*; which done, he return'd with his Brother to *Mottera*.

By this time the Giant *Sialinder* having gather'd a vast Army, sat down before *Mottera*; but *Kisna* and his Brother after having kill'd a great number of the Enemy, feigning a Retreat were pursu'd by *Sialinder*'s Forces, till coming to a high Mountain they vanish'd, and retir'd to the City *Davarca*; and *Sialinder* being thereby become Master of *Mottera*, settled his Residence there.

In the mean while *Kisna*'s School-fellow being married was grown so poor, that he was forced to sell his Clothes to buy Victuals. Being almost reduc'd to despair, his Wife advis'd him to take a Journy to his old School-fellow *Kisna*, who she did not question would commiserate his Condition. How is this possible, reply'd the Husband, being quite naked and not fit to appear before any body? *Kisna*, answer'd the Wife, does not despise the poor, go and take a handful of *Kam* * along with thee for a Present.

* *A certain Seed.*

The Husband follow'd his Wife's Advice, and went to *Davarca*, who was no sooner enter'd the Street where *Kisna* liv'd, but being discover'd by him from a Window, he came out to meet and embrace him, and carrying him into his House order'd him to be wash'd and provided with new Clothes. *Kisna* ask'd him whether he had brought him any Presents. *Being a poor Man*, reply'd *Sedamma*, *I had nothing to give but this, which my Wife sent to thee, in hopes that the Gods would not refuse the meanest Present.* *Kisna* receiv'd it kindly, and put it in a Corner of a Cottage belonging to one of his Neighbours; and at the same instant *Sedamma*'s Cottage was turn'd into a spacious Palace: His Wife was much surpriz'd at this change, but imagining that it was done by *Kisna*, she search'd all the Corners of the House, and where-ever she turn'd her Face found such a vast quantity of Gold and Silver, and of *Ropias*, that she had sufficient wherewithal to provide her self with Servants, Provisions and every thing in proportion to the Grandeur of her Palace. *Sedamma* being ignorant of what had happen'd, return'd full of Melancholy from *Kisna*, ruminating upon the Road whether he had not best leave his Wife and Children; but soon recollecting himself, that he ought not to lay the whole Burden upon his Wife's Shoulders, and despair of God's Mercy, he made the best of his way homeward: but approaching the Village, he was amaz'd to see the Change that had happen'd since his departure, which made him suspect he had miss'd his way; but finding by some undeniable Circumstances that he was in the right, he went into the Village, where finding instead of a Cottage of Straw a Royal Palace, he stood astonish'd, not knowing which way to turn, till being discover'd by his Wife out of a Window, she sent one of the Servants to desire him to enter; which he did, and being kindly receiv'd by his Wife and Children, he ask'd the exact time of this sudden Change, which happening (as far as they could guess) precisely at the same time he presented the Seed, they paid their Devotions to *Kisna*, distributed Alms among the Poor, and liv'd in great Plenty for a long time after.

Baldæus.

CHAP. VIII.

A King's Daughter in love with Kisna, *sends him word of it.* Kisna *delivers 16000 Royal Virgins, and cures the Leprosy.*

SOmetime after *Ragia Bhiemeck* King of *Poercp* had a Son and Daughter born him, the first named *Rochemeya*, the other *Rochemy*, who being grown up, the Father was very desirous to have his Daughter well match'd before his Death. Among others he consulted with upon this matter, there was a certain *Brahman* named *Naret*, much celebrated for his Wisdom and Learning, who being desir'd by the King to inspect his Daughter's Hands, and to foretel him by the Art of Chiromancy, who should be her Husband; *Naret* having taken a full view of the Lineaments of her Right-hand, told her, *Blessed Virgin! who beest ordain'd to*

Baldæus. *to be the Spouse of the holy* Kisna. The Father rejoic'd thereat to the highest degree, told this good News to his Son, who being of a contrary Sentiment, reply'd, that he would never suffer so beautiful a Creature to be married to a Country Clown.

Rochemy design'd for Kisna. It is to be observ'd, that the Soul of *Sytha*, *Ram*'s Spouse, being transplanted into the Body of this Virgin, in order to be espoused to *Kisna*; this young Lady was not insensible thereof, for which reason she had resolv'd to think of no body else but *Kisna*: which her Brother being *Is oppos'd by her Brother.* resolv'd to prevent, he sent to the Giant the King of *Mottera*, that in case he was inclin'd to marry his Sister he should come with all speed, his Father intending to marry her to *Kisna*. The Giant ravish'd at this joyful News, order'd a most magnificent Equipage of Elephants, Camels, Horses, Oxen and Chariots to be got ready, and attended with Trumpets, Hautboys, Kettledrums, and other Musical Instruments, and a numerous Retinue, set out from *Mottera*.

No sooner were they come within two days Journy to *Rochemy*'s Father's Residence, when she, not knowing what to do in this Exigency, thought fit to give notice thereof to *Kisna* by a Letter, which she order'd one of her Servants to deliver to the first *Brahman* she met, in order to carry it to *Kisna*; the Contents whereof were as follows.

Rochemy's Letter to Kisna. "HOly *Kisna!* worthy to be belov'd "of me and all the World: Be"ing resolv'd to be nobody's but only "yours as long as I have Breath to draw, "I thought fit to let you know, that my "old Father likewise wishes nothing "more than to see that happy day; but "my Brother, who has more Ambition "than Piety, having sent for the Giant "of *Mottera* to marry me, and being "come within two days Journy of our "Residence, I desire you to provide a"gainst their Attempts, nothing being "able to resist your Divine Powe.

Your Highness's always devoted,

ROCHEMY.

The Servant having brought a *Brahman* to the Princess, she by a Present of a Golden Dish fill'd with *Ropias*, and a promise of more if he perform'd his Errand, engag'd him to undertake the Task: Accordingly he went full speed for 5 *Cos*, when being somewhat tir'd he sat down under a shady Tree, to refresh himself with a draught of cool Water, and falling asleep, was carried by *Kisna* to *Davarca*. The *Brahman* awaking out of his sleep, and finding himself at *Davarca*, soon guess'd the truth, and going strait to *Kisna*'s House, deliver'd the Letter at his Feet. *Kisna* had no sooner read the Letter, but assuming the shape of a Man with four Arms, and taking his Bow and Arrow, he got upon his Cow with the *Brahman*, and so set out on their Journy from *Davarca*.

In the mean time the Giant approaching to the Residence of his pretended Spouse, was met by her Brother, and conducted into the Palace; and *Kisna* arriving soon after near the City, rested himself under the shade of a Tree near a Pagode, whence he sent the *Brahman* to *Rochemy* to give notice of his arrival, who rewarded him with vast Presents for his Fidelity.

Rochemy knowing that her Brother was in the Evening to make a Cavalcade with her pretended Bridegroom through the City (according to the Custom of the *Benjans*) she resolved to lay hold of this opportunity to escape their hands: For this purpose she entreated her Father, that being now arrived to the Age of nine years, she might offer her Sacrifice to the Goddess *Robani*. The Father having granted her Request, she took a Dish full of Pearls, and with two of her Attendants went towards the Pagode, whither her pretended Bridegroom and her Brother would needs accompany her, but staid without the Temple whilst she perform'd her Sacrifice; which done, she came out of the Temple near the Door, where she knew *Kisna* had plac'd himself, who no sooner saw her appear, but he took her up and carried her away.

At the Outcry of her Maids the pretended Bridegroom came with his whole Attendants to snatch her from him, but *Kisna* receiv'd them so couragiously with his Bow and Arrows, that they were forced to retreat with the loss of several thousands of their best Men. *Rochemy*'s Brother seeing the Bridegroom defeated, would nevertheless try his Strength with *Kisna*, and coming up with him was a going to cleave his Head with his Scymeter; but *Kisna* having disarm'd him threw him upon the ground, and after having given him some Blows, ty'd him Neck and Heels together under his Cart, and so made his Entry into *Davarca*, where he was receiv'd with all imaginable Demonstrations of Joy. *Rochemy*'s Brother *Rochemy deliver'd by Kisna.*

was

was releas'd at her request, and *Kisna* consummated his Marriage with great Pomp in the City of *Davarca.*

Sometime after it happen'd, that a very strong Elephant being seiz'd by a Crocodile in a certain Cistern or Pond where the Elephants us'd to drink, a furious Combat ensu'd, which put all the Elephants that were Spectators thereof into no small Confusion. At last seeing they were not able to assist their Companions, and press'd with Hunger, they went away, and left the poor Elephant in the lurch. He seeing himself thus destitute kept on struggling with the Crocodile, sending up at the same time his Prayers to *Vistnum* to deliver him from the Jaws of the Crocodile.

Kisna delivers an *Elephant from a Crocodile.*

But it being then the time of *Kisna*'s appearing upon Earth, he heard his Prayers after 20 days, and sending for *Garroude* to carry him immediately to the Pond, he threw his Weapon at the Crocodile, and cutting off his Neck releas'd the Elephant, who kneeling before *Kisna*, he told him he should ask what he pleas'd, and it should be granted him. Nothing, reply'd the Elephant, but that I may go immediately to Heaven, being quite weary of this World. *Kisna* granting his Request, took him into his *Palankin*, or Litter, and carrying him to Heaven, order'd *Garroude* to convey him immediately back to *Davarca.*

About the same time one *Ragia Boettaenpat* having two Wives named *Somuta* and *Surisa*, the first brought forth a Son named *Droe*, and the other one named *Rasepoeter*; but *Surisa* being most belov'd by her Husband, *Somuta* when her Son *Droe* was about five years of Age, sent him very neatly dress'd to pay his Respect to his Father, who being extremely delighted with him, highly caress'd and set him in his Lap. *Surisa* having got notice thereof, sent immediately her Son to the King, whilst she remain'd at some distance to observe what pass'd. But the King being so much taken with *Droe*, that he scarce look'd at the other; *Surisa* enter'd the Room, and upbraiding him with Ingratitude, made him send away *Droe* and take her Son in his Lap.

Droe exasperated to the highest degree at this Affront, went away without making his Reverence; and making his Complaint to his Mother, told her, that he was resolved to retire into a Desert to spend his time in Prayers. The Mother did all she could to disswade him from it, but in vain; for taking the next opportunity of his Mother's absence, he got privately out of the House. He had scarce travell'd 2 *Cos* from the City, when being met by the Learned *Brahman Naret*, he ask'd him whither he was going? He answer'd, As young as I am, I have taken a Resolution to retire from the World, where I find there remains nothing but Malice and Envy: Then relating all that happen'd to him, he told him, that he was resolv'd to pass his days in the Desert. *Baldæus.*

Go on my Son, reply'd *Naret*, thou wilt be heard by *Kisna:* Then going forward, he came to a Forest, where seeing a *Mango*-Tree, he repos'd himself under its shade, and spent three days and nights in Tears, Prayers and Fasting. *Kisna* mov'd with Compassion at his tender Age, appear'd to him, asking what made him pray with so much Fervency? *Droe* prostrating himself at the feet of *Kisna* said, O Divine *Kisna!* my Request to thee is, "That the Affront given me "by *Surisa* may turn upon their Heads, "that she may be a Slave to my Mother, that I may succeed my Father in "the Kingdom, and after my Death be "plac'd in some pleasant place you shall "choose for me.

Kisna answer'd, Thy Prayer is granted, go return to thy Parents, *Surisa* shall live a Slave to thy Mother, thou shalt succeed thy Father in the Throne, and after thy Death I will place thee in the Heavens in the form of a Star, that shall remain for ever in the Firmament, and serve the Mariners for a Guide. *Droe* having paid his Reverence to *Kisna*, return'd full of Joy to his Father's Palace. The old King, who had been almost distracted at his absence, receiv'd him with more than ordinary Satisfaction, and for ever after shew'd so much Affection to his Mother, that *Surisa* was in comparison of her no more than a Slave, and after some years surrender'd the Kingdom to him. He rul'd very fortunately for many years, and after his Death was plac'd among the Stars, being the same the *Benjans* call to this day *Droe Katara*, i. e. *Stella Polaris*, or the *North-Star.* Droe, *or the North-Star.*

It happen'd some time after, that *Ragia Nerkaseur*, a most Potent Monarch, having conquer'd 16000 Kings, kept them close Prisoners with their Wives and Daughters; these offer'd their constant Prayers to *Kisna* for their delivery from this Oppression. *Kisna* considering that they having spent these three years in Prayer, it would be high time to deliver them, sent for *Garroude*, whom he order'd to carry him to *Nietskanda*, where he

was

Baldæus. was no sooner arriv'd, but he told the King *Nerkaseur*, that unless he released the Royal Captives, he must pay for it with his Head. The King answering *Kisna* with Threats, they prepar'd both sides for a Combat: For *Kisna* having kill'd those that were sent against him, the King himself at the head of a strong Troop, attack'd *Kisna* with great fury, who kill'd every Man of them except the *Ragia*, who persisting in his Obstinacy, had at last his Head cut off by *Kisna*, who releas'd all the Prisoners in an instant, and among them 16000 Royal Virgins, who prostrating themselves at his feet, he gave them leave to return to their Parents, or where else they pleas'd: But they desir'd to stay with him, imploring his Protection, which being granted by *Kisna*, he carried them to *Devarca*, where he built a Seraglio for their Reception, wherein each Lady had her own Apartment.

Kisna *delivers 16000 Captives.*

In the Country of *Ammaramo* liv'd a certain zealous *Ragia* named *Amarich*, who having publish'd a general Fast by beat of Drum (according to the Custom of that Country) the same was observ'd with the utmost Strictness. It happen'd that the *Brahman Doerwassa* passing that way the same day, he was invited by the said King to stay there till the next day after the Fast-day.

The *Brahman* complying with the King's Request, he sent for some of his chief *Brahmans* to know the exact hour when they might begin to eat: These having consulted their Books, and told the King, that the just time would be two hours after Sun-rising; he invited the beforemention'd *Brahman* against that time to a Collation. But the *Brahman* missing the appointed hour, the King went to the River to wash himself; but finding after his return, that the *Brahman* was not come yet, he advised with four of his *Brahmans* what was best to be done, who told him, that if he let slip this lucky hour all his Fasting would avail him nothing, advising him at the same time to take only a little Water and a Leaf of the *Tully*-Tree, till the *Brahman* should come.

This *Brahman Doerwassa* having a Prophetick Spirit, was not ignorant that the King had eaten something in his absence, and therefore went to the King, asking him why he had put such an Affront upon him? The *Ragia* was for excusing the matter, but to no purpose; for the *Brahman* going out of the doors gave him this Curse, That he might from head to foot be cover'd with Boils and the Leprosy; which being fulfill'd in an instant upon the unfortunate King, he pray'd to *Kisna* to deliver him from this Evil, but in vain, his Evil encreasing every day, so that at last being quite tir'd with Life, he resolv'd to put a Period to it by Fire. Every thing being got in readiness for this purpose, *Kisna* appear'd to him, asking what was his Request? He reply'd, to be freed from my Distemper. *Kisna* cur'd him not only of his Leprosy, but also turn'd the same into a Fiery Wheel, which following the *Brahman Doerwassa* where ever he went, put him into such a fright, that he offer'd his Prayers to *Ragia Inder* to deliver him of this Fire: but *Ragia Inder* telling him, that he must apply himself to him who was the Author thereof, he made his Applications to *Bramma*, from whom having receiv'd the same Answer, he implor'd the Assistance of *Kisna*, begging him to pardon his sudden Passion, and to deliver him from the Evil he had been pleased to lay upon him. *Kisna* chiding him for his unruly Passion, advis'd him to lay the same aside for the future, and then deliver'd him from the Plague of the Fiery Wheel.

Kisna *cures the Leprosy.*

CHAP. IX.

The Origin and Qualifications of Droepeti. *She binds up the Wound of* Kisna. Sussuster *forc'd out of his Kingdom.* Droepeti *exil'd with her Brothers, and fed by the Sun. They come to Court. Their further Transactions.*

In the Country of *Estenapour* liv'd a certain *Ragia* named *Pandouw*, whose Wife was call'd *Droendy*: His Brother nam'd *Deuderaes* being blind, had a Wife call'd *Sendary*, and by her a hundred Sons, the eldest whereof was named *Dersiende*. In the Country of *Ransiaandoes* liv'd at the same time a certain King nam'd *Droepet*, whose Daughter was reputed the most beautiful Woman that ever was seen. *Ragia Pandouw* happening to die left behind him five Sons, the eldest of which

which succeeding him in the Throne, one of the other four was put to School to a certain *Brabman*, to be instructed in all matters relating to their Divinity. The Daughter of *Ragia Droepeti* being now come to a marriageable Age, her Father was not a little sollicitous how to bestow his Daughter to the best advantage: For this purpose he sent his Messengers to invite the neighbouring Kings and the chiefest *Brabmans* to a great Feast, and caus'd a long Poll to be erected, with a strong Bow underneath, and a Fish on the top, in the same manner as we have mentioned before in the Story of *Ram*.

Kisna appearing here among the rest, yet would not attempt the Bow, having promised his Assistance (upon this account) to a certain *Brabman* named *Aerssing*, he manag'd the Bow with that dexterity, that he shot down the Fish, and receiv'd a fine Necklace of Pearl from the hands of his Bride.

Aerssing *gains* Droepeti *by shooting.*

One time *Droepeti* seeing a Cow pass through the Fields with five Bulls following her, she stood amaz'd at the Novelty of the thing, as she thought; this coming to the Ears of *Camdoga* the *Cow of Plenty*, she was so offended thereat, that she told her she would make her to be thus pursu'd by five Men. The King entertain'd his Guests with a splendid Feast, but the Bridegroom having made a Vow not to enjoy his Bride till after his return home, they came no sooner to his own House-door, but being met by his Mother, he told her that he had brought something along with him: Then, reply'd the Mother, your two Brothers must each have his share: That can't be, return'd *Aerssing*, for it is a Woman. That signifies nothing, answer'd the Mother, what I have once said is impossible to be recall'd. *Aerssing* full of Grief told his Brothers what had happen'd, who abominating the matter, communicated the same to *Droepeti*.

Camdoga's *Curse.*

It happen'd afterwards, that *Kisna* having invited the *Panspendaons* with her Mother, and *Droepeti* to dine with him at *Davarca*, as they were walking after Dinner in the Field, *Kisna* had a mind to cut some Sugar-Reeds; but cutting his Finger, all the Standers-by call'd for some Linen Rags to tie it up: But *Droepeti* immediately tearing a piece of her Golden Brocado'd Gown, she ty'd it about his Finger. *Kisna* (according to his Omnisciency) knowing how many Threds there were in the piece she had torn off, *viz.* 999. he told her that she should have as many Garments of Cloth of Gold as there were Threds in it. They then took their leave, and tho *Kisna* knew well that *Droepeti* was still a Virgin, yet he took notice of it.

Kisna's *Finger ty'd up with a piece of Golden Stuff.*

After their return home, one *Senbem*, Brother-in-law to *Droepeti*, began to be much out of humour, alledging, that *Sussuster* was not the rightful Heir of the Throne; for, said he, tho *Deuteraes* by reason of his Blindness might be incapable of the Government, and therefore *Pandouw* was put in his stead, yet after his Decease *Sussuster* his Son could not succeed him, the right of Inheritance of the Crown belonging to the eldest of the hundred Sons of *Deuteraes*, and consequently to *Dersiende* his eldest Son. This gave occasion to pitch upon some way to restore *Dersiende* to his right; and knowing that *Sussuster* was much addicted to play at Dice, they look'd upon this as the best means to encompass their Design: *Sussuster* having been for some time a Favourite of *Kisna*, grew so ambitious as to despise him at last. *Kisna* remembring this Affront, whilst he was playing with *Dersiende*, so order'd the matter that *Sussuster* lost all his ready Mony, whereby being egg'd on more and more to recover his loss, he at last threw at all, and lost his Estate and Kingdom.

Sussuster *and* Dersiende *play for the Crown.*

It had happen'd some time before, that *Dersiende* being in *Sussuster*'s Palace, look'd into *Droepeti* her Apartment, which being pav'd with Glass (a thing he never had seen before) he took it for Water, and would not venture to go in. *Droepeti* perceiving his Error, told him, *How, Are the Sons like the Father? Is the whole Family blind?* which put *Dersiende* into such a rage, that he swore he would revenge it with the first opportunity.

Dersiende remembring his Oath, whilst they were at play purposed to set as much Mony against *Droepeti* as he would desire; which being agreed to, *Dersiende* won that Stake likewise. Things being come to this pass, he propos'd to *Sussuster* that he would lay all he had got of him at one Stake, provided he would engage, that in case he did win it, he would choose a voluntary Exile for 12 years. *Sussuster* in hopes of better fortune, consenting to the Proposition, they threw the Dice, but Fortune frowning again upon *Sussuster*, *Dersiende* remain'd in Possession of all.

By this time *Dersiende* remembring the Affront *Droepeti* put upon him in her Apartment, order'd her to be stripp'd stark naked, and to expose her to the view

Droepeti *order'd to be stripp'd.*

Baldæus. view of his Servants. The distressed *Droepeti* reduc'd to this extremity, implor'd *Kisna*'s Assistance to relieve her from the shame she was likely to undergo, putting him in mind of his Bounty after she had torn her Garments for his sake. In the mean time the Servants being employ'd in undressing *Droepeti*, they had no sooner pull'd off one of her Garments, but another succeeded in an instant; which continuing thus 999 times, they were seiz'd with such an Astonishment, that they entreated *Dersiende* to desist, lest *Kisna* should give him some severe proofs of his Anger; which had such an influence upon *Dersiende*, that he dismiss'd her without any further harm.

Is deliver'd by Kisna.

They go into Exile.

The time of the appointed Exile now approaching, the five Brothers with their Mother *Sendary* and *Droepeti* left their Native Country; but beginning to want Provision upon the Road, *Droepeti* paid her Devotions to the Sun to supply their Wants. The Sun commiserating their Condition, fill'd them every morning a Vessel with Victuals, sufficient to feed 1000 Men. At last coming to a certain Village call'd *Widoenougan*, they lodg'd in the House of one *Widoenougarre*, where she left her Mother, who was grown so decrepit, that she was not able to follow them.

Thence wandring through vast Deserts without meeting either with Man or Beast, they at last came to a pleasant River, where whilst they were reposing themselves, they saw a certain famous and learned *Brahman* named *Derwasa*, walking along the Bank of it at the head of 1000 *Brahmans* his Followers; who being not ignorant (by his Skill) who they were, after the usual Salute immediately address'd himself to *Sussuster*, telling him, that he and his Company had a mind to take a Dinner with him, which *Sussuster* approving (trusting to the Bounty of the Sun, and the *Brahmans* Piety) he desir'd them to come, which they promised to do as soon as they had wash'd themselves in the River.

Droepeti understanding what had happen'd, had recourse to the Vessel, but finding it empty, knew not what to do, but advis'd them to have recourse to *Kisna*'s Bounty: Accordingly they sent forth their joint and fervent Prayers to *Kisna*, but finding no relief, and the time of the *Brahmans* coming being near at hand, they resolv'd rather than to be expos'd to such Shame and Confusion as this, to make a large Wood Fire, and therein to put a Period to their miserable Life. They went to work immediately, and having gather'd a sufficient quantity of Wood, *Droepeti* was shewing the rest the way, and these following to tread in her footsteps.

Kisna then seeing their Constancy stopt them, and asking what was their Grievance? *Sussuster* reply'd, O *Kisna!* who knowest every thing, thou canst not be ignorant of what has happen'd to us to day! *Kisna* answer'd, Let me see the Vessel that was presented you by the Sun; which being produc'd, *Kisna* view'd it on all sides, and finding a Grain of Rice on the brim he eat it, and by its multiplying Power gave it such a Virtue, that it not only satisfied him, but also the *Brahman* and his 1000 Followers, who thank'd *Naccod*, the youngest Brother of *Sussuster* (who was sent to bring them to Dinner) that tho they had not the least Appetite to eat since they had been washing in the River, yet they thank'd his Brother for his good Intentions.

This unfortunate Company having thus wander'd for nine years through the Deserts, at last resolv'd to try their fortune at the Court of King *Weraart*, of the Tribe of the *Ketterijs* in the Country of *Messedees*. *Sussuster* being the first that went to King *Weraart*, being demanded who he was? he ask'd the King whether he had not heard of the five Brothers *Panspendaons*? The King replying, he had; he told the King, that he had serv'd them as their Historian, and that if the King would receive him in the same Station, he would relate to him the Adventures of that King, how he had lost his Kingdom at Dice, &c. The King pleas'd with his Proposition, order'd him to stay at Court. The second Brother encourag'd by his Success, address'd himself likewise to the King, telling him that he had serv'd *Sussuster* in the quality of a Cook, who ordering him to dress a Dish of Meat, he did it accordingly, and pleas'd the King so well, that he made him his head Cook. *They leave the Deserts.*

The third, who was an excellent Bowman, thought fit to lay his Bow and Arrows aside; and appearing in the Presence of the King without any Weapon, told him, that he had serv'd *Sussuster* in his Prosperity in the quality of a *Brahman*, but being now forced to bear his share in the Misfortunes of his Master, he came to shelter himself under his Royal Protection. The King being taken with his Discourse, receiv'd him into his Service. The fourth, after having paid his Reverence to the King, told him, that

that he had been Gentleman of the Horse to *Suſſuſter*, in which Station he was receiv'd by the King. The fifth Brother not knowing what to ſay in his own behalf, told the King, that he had been Shepherd to him, in which Station he was likewiſe receiv'd by King *Weraart*.

Droepeti being now alone, made likewiſe her Applications to the King, alledging that having ſerv'd in the quality of a Maid of Honour in the Court of *Suſſuſter*, ſhe hoped to be receiv'd among the Ladies of the Court, which was willingly granted her. Having thus continued two years in their reſpective Stations, they began to revive their hopes of ſeeing their Native Country again, there being but one year more to the end of their Exile.

But *Derſiende* finding the time of their Exile near expiring, ſent out certain famous Wreſtlers to try their Skill with them. Theſe paſſing through ſeveral Countries, had vanquiſh'd many of the *Ragias*, and in ſcorn carried their Pictures ty'd to their Knees: Coming at laſt to King *Weraart*'s Court, they challeng'd and kill'd the King's Brother-in-law, and were for doing the ſame to the King, who rather than hazard his Perſon, offer'd them his Picture to be carried in Triumph upon their Knees. But *Suſſuſter* being inform'd of the matter, told him, that ſuch a piece of Cowardice being unworthy of the Name of the *Ketteriis*, he adviſ'd him to match him with his head Cook, whom, as he ſaid, he had often ſeen wreſtle ſtoutly at the Court of *Suſſuſter*. The King extremely pleas'd at this Propoſition, ask'd the Cook, whether he durſt engage with one of theſe famous Wreſtlers; who having anſwer'd, Yes, and the appointed time being come, they went to it bravely, and held it for a conſiderable time with equal Advantage, till at laſt the Cook found means to twiſt his Arms back, and ſetting his Foot againſt his Rump, threw him backwards, and kill'd him upon the ſpot.

Derſiende had no ſooner heard this unwelcome News, but he ſent his Uncle with 200000 Horſe into King *Weraart*'s Country, to drive away all the Cattel; which being done accordingly, and notice thereof given to King *Weraart*, he put himſelf at the head of 600000 Horſe, and overtaking the Enemy in a great Plain, a bloody Battel enſued, but his Forces being routed he was taken Priſoner by the Enemy.

The Prince overwhelm'd with Tears, engag'd the Cook who had ſo lately obtain'd the Victory, to go in purſuit of the Enemy, who coming in ſight of them cry'd aloud, Halt you Robbers, releaſe the King, or this day ſhall be your laſt; they laugh'd at this madneſs, till ſeeing him lay about him with his Weapons amongſt the hindermoſt, they turn'd their Arms againſt him; but the Cook aſſiſted by *Kiſna*'s Strength, ſlew the whole Army, except one whom he ſent to *Derſiende* to carry him the News of this Defeat. *Baldæus.*

He had no ſooner receiv'd theſe diſmal Tidings, but he told him, certainly theſe are the *Panſpendaons*, go and put thy ſelf at the head of 6000 choſen Horſe to revenge our Quarrel: Accordingly he enter'd King *Weraart*'s Territories, making great havock among Men and Beaſts, without the leaſt oppoſition, *Weraart* not daring to oppoſe his Forces (that conſiſted only of 200 Horſe) to ſo powerful an Enemy. *Suſſuſter* vex'd at his Cowardice, told him, that if he did not think fit to hazard his Perſon, he ſhould give leave to the Prince and his Governour the *Brahman*, to go along with what Forces he had in queſt of the Enemy; which the King not refuſing, the Prince and the *Brahman* went after the Enemy in their Chariot; and finding them in Battel array ready to receive them, the Prince was ſo frighten'd thereat, that the *Brahman* was forc'd to tie him in the Chariot, and cover him with a Cloth: Then the *Brahman* attack'd the Enemy with ſuch fury, that notwithſtanding the inequality of their number, he ſlew them all (after a bloody Engagement) upon the ſpot, except their General, who being made a Priſoner, the *Brahman* gave him three or four ſound boxes on the Ear, telling him, that he ſhould go to his King to carry him the good News, but have a care how he ever came there again. The *Brahman* was ſo humble as to beſtow both all the Honour of the Victory, and the Booty upon the Prince, who willing enough to accept of the ſame, made his Entry in a triumphant manner into the City.

Not long after King *Weraart* playing at Tables with one of his Nobles, made his boaſt of the late Victory obtain'd by his Son, which *Suſſuſter* not able to brook, told the King, *That what he boaſted of did not belong to his Son, but to the* Brahman. The King hearing him ſay theſe words, threw the Dice with ſuch violence into the Tables, that one of them flew into

Baldæus. *Sussuster*'s Face, and drew some Blood from him: *Sussuster* highly exasperated at this Affront, consulted with his Brothers and Sister to leave the Court secretly, and return to their Native Country, the time of their Banishment being near expir'd, which they did accordingly.

The Prince no sooner understood their departure, but he went immediately to the King, telling him, he was sorry the King had taken so ill what *Sussuster* had told him, it being nothing but the bare truth; for, said he, it was not I, but the *Brahman* that obtain'd the Victory, and it were they who have twice deliver'd our Country and your self from Destruction. I advise you to take care what you do, for I assure you they are the *Panspendaons* themselves.

The King stood amaz'd at these words; And is it possible, said he, that I who am but a Petty King should be served by them? And so ordering all his Elephants, Horses and Chariots to be got ready, he follow'd them with all possible speed; and having overtaken them at last, he prostrated himself before *Sussuster*, saying, "Most Potent King! whom I am unworthy to serve, pardon me for having receiv'd Services from you, contrary to my knowledg; pray return along with me, that we may not take our leave without a merry Cup. I will afterwards provide you with Camels, Elephants, Horses, Chariots, and what else shall be requisite for your Journy. *Sussuster* being prevail'd upon to return with the King to the City, they took their mutual leaves at a most solemn Feast, with mutual demonstrations of Friendship; and being provided with all Necessaries for their Journy, return'd towards their Native Country.

Sussuster prays to Kisna. But whilst they were upon the Road, *Sussuster* repenting of his former Pride, frequently sent his Prayers to *Kisna*, acknowledging his Crime, for which he own'd he had been deservedly punish'd by him: But the time of his 12 years Banishment being now expir'd, he promis'd to serve him with all humility, if by his Assistance he and his Brothers might be restor'd to their Native Country. *Kisna* well satisfi'd with this Acknowledgment, appear'd to them, asking what was their request? *Sussuster* answer'd, That *Dersiende* may be put out of the Throne, and I be plac'd there in his stead. *Is heard by him.* *Kisna* having promis'd him his Assistance, said that they had best send a certain Poet (who stood hard by) to demand the Kingdom of him. The Poet went accordingly, demanding the Kingdom to be restor'd to the true Owners, the term of the 12 years Banishment being now expir'd. But *Dersiende* answer'd, that he did not know the *Panspendaons*, and was resolv'd to keep his Crown in spite of them; and so bid the Poet to go out of his Presence. *Dersiende refuses to restore the Kingdom.* *Kisna* understanding this Answer, told them, Perhaps he has taken it amiss, that we have not sent to him a Person of a higher rank. The *Panspendaons* reply'd, that they were ready to throw themselves at his feet, if they thought he would grant their Request; which being approv'd of, *Kisna* promis'd to go along with them in Person.

CHAP. X.

Kisna *lodges with a* Brahman: *Goes to the Court of* Dersiende, *who engages in a bloody Battel with* Sussuster, *and is routed.* Droepeti *is enjoy'd by five Brothers.* Kisna *visits divers wicked Kings. The Conclusion of his Reign.*

At *Estenapour* liv'd a *Brahman* named *Widder*, who fed upon Alms; his Wife was call'd *Prediwette*, both Persons very zealous in their Devotions to *Kisna*; who being not ignorant of their Zeal, resolv'd to bless them with a Visit. Accordingly he came to the Cottage of the poor *Brahman*, who after having prostrated themselves at his Feet, brought some Rock Water (according to the Custom of the Country) to wash his Feet. *Kisna* told them I intend to dine with you, and so laying himself down pretended to sleep, with an intention to observe all that pass'd in the Cottage. *Kisna visits a poor Brahman.*

Ragia Dersiende hearing of the coming of *Kisna* to this poor Cottage, before he had visited his Court, forbid all the Inhabitants under pain of death, to furnish the poor *Brahman* that day either with Mony or Provisions. The *Brahman* being in great necessity would fain have pawn'd his Brass Kettle and Fryingpan, but nobody daring to lend him any Mony, or or give the least Provisions, he return'd in a very melancholy Posture. His Wife bid him not despair, telling him, that *Kisna* knowing their Poverty, would accept the Will for the Deed; and so ordering him to go into the Garden to gather such Herbs as were there, and allow'd them to eat (for the *Brahmans* dare not eat all sorts of Herbs or Roots, as for instance, the Beets, because they are red, and resemble Blood) which being done, she dress'd them, and having awaken'd *Kisna*, offer'd it to him upon a *Pysang* Leaf; *Kisna* ask'd them, Have you nothing else? I suppos'd you would have made some Cakes: The Woman answer'd, that their Poverty being such as not to permit them to do it; *Kisna* bid her look backwards, where seeing in a Corner a fine Basket of Fruits and Sweetmeats, she prostrated her self at his Feet.

Thus feasting together, *Kisna* ask'd them after Dinner, what they requested of him? The *Brahman* reply'd, "Nothing, but that I may serve and love thee with a sincere Heart, that I may never cease to pray to thee, and that when my Soul and Body must be parted, my Zeal for thee may nevertheless continue with me. *Kisna* reply'd, All this shall be granted thee, and because thou hast prefer'd Piety before Riches, you shall likewise have your full share of them. He had no sooner spoken these words, but the *Brahman*'s Cottage was in an instant chang'd into a magnificent Structure; and *Kisna* presented them with as much Gold as was sufficient to maintain them in great plenty all their life-time.

Blesses him with Riches.

Kisna after having once more imparted his Blessing to his Host, departed, taking his way towards the Castle of *Dersiende*, it being then just three hours before Sunset, the usual time for the Kings in the Eastern Countries to give Audience to their Subjects. *Kisna* was receiv'd with a great deal of Reverence by some of the Court; but the King looking upon him with an indifferent Eye, ask'd him, When he came into the City, and why he would not pay him a Visit before the poor *Brahman*? *Kisna* reply'd, Riches are of no value to me, the meanest Cottage of a Believer I prefer before the most sumptuous Palace of a King: And why then, said the King, would you come to Court? I did come, reply'd *Kisna*, in the Name of the *Panspendaons*, to demand thy Kingdom, their 12 years Exile being now expir'd. The King answer'd, I know them not, neither will I deliver the Kingdom. *Kisna* told him, that if he would not, he should at least allot a Village for their Maintenance: I will not give them the breadth of a foot, answer'd *Dersiende*; then prepare your self, said *Kisna*, you must fight for it.

Kisna goes to the Court of Dersiende.

Baldæus.

The *Panspendaons* hearing this Answer, prepar'd for a vigorous War; and having engag'd King *Weraart*, and the potent *Ragia Droepet* (*Droepeti*'s Father) in their Quarrel, with four other Kings, they attack'd *Dersiende*, who having drawn up his Horse in a great Plain, a fierce Battel ensu'd, which lasted 18 days, *Kisna* fighting in a Chariot drawn by Oxen.

A Battel fought for 18 days.

In *Dersiende* his Army was a famous Warrior named *Caran*, who having (by his constant Prayers) obtain'd a prodigious Strength from *Kisna*, did perform Wonders in his Chariot: *Kisna* espying him at some distance, order'd *Ersiende* (who sat with him in the same Chariot) to break the Wheel of *Caran*'s Chariot, which being done accordingly by a strong Arrow, *Caran* came down out of his Chariot, but whilst he was busy in mending the Wheel, was by the same *Ersiende* shot with an Arrow into the Breast: He drawing the Arrow out of the Wound, cry'd out to *Kisna*, And is this the Reward thou givest me for so many Offerings? *Kisna* answer'd, Have Patience; my Will is to deliver thee out of this troublesom World, and to allow thee a place in Heaven, whither I am going to meet all the Believers (my time upon Earth being almost expir'd) after I have purged the World of the wicked. *Caran* was no sooner slain, but the Victory declar'd against *Dersiende*, whose Forces were all slain upon the spot (as were King *Weraart*, and King *Droepet* on the other side) and among them *Dersiende* himself, with his 99 Brothers. Thus the *Panspendaons* being restor'd to the Kingdom, they pay'd their constant Devotions to *Kisna*, who from thence return'd to *Davarca*.

The Giant Caran *kill'd.*

All this while *Droepeti* had liv'd without the knowledg of any Man; but Peace and Quietness being now restor'd in the Kingdom, the five Brothers were concerting all possible means how to enjoy *Droepeti*, without Incest. At last a certain *Brahman* named *Wissumna*, propos'd the following Expedient. The Year, said he, has 360 days, which divided into five equal parts, each amounts to two Months and 12 days: And it being your Mother's Will that the five Brothers should have an equal share in

Droepeti,

Baldæus.

Droepeti, *Suſſuſter* muſt cohabit with her the firſt two Months and 12 days; and the other four Brothers ſucceſſively each his two Months and 12 days: But to wipe off the ſtain of Inceſt, *Droepeti* muſt after the Expiration of each reſpective term of two Months and 12 days purify her ſelf three times by the Fire; whence it is evident, that the Pagans aſcribed to the Fire a purifying Quality; from whom the *Jews* queſtionleſs took that Doctrine, and the *Roman* Catholicks their Purgatory. This being approv'd of by the joint Conſent of the five Brothers, it was further agreed, That he who ſhould tranſgreſs his limited time, ſhould be baniſh'd for 12 years. But *Suſſuſter* willing to appeaſe the Gods by Sacrifices, in conſideration of the great Effuſion of Blood occaſion'd by his Reſtauration, conſulted the *Goegys* (a certain Order of the *Brahmans*) who adviſ'd him to inſtitute a ſolemn Feaſt, offer Sacrifices, be liberal to the Poor, and to maintain a certain number of learned *Brahmans*, to read and explain their holy Writings. *Suſſuſter* obey'd, and perform'd every thing with all imaginable exactneſs, ordering a Hole to be dig'd, which he fill'd with Sugar, Butter, Sandelwood, Milk, Rice and Betel, and offer'd Roſes, Flowers, Spices, and other rich Incenſe.

Suſſuſter's *Sacrifice.*

This done, he invited *Kiſna* to a ſumptuous Feaſt; and asking him, what Acknowledgment he was able to pay him for the many Favours he had receiv'd at his hands, *Kiſna* anſwer'd, Take a white Horſe with black Ears and a yellow Tail, and faſten a Paper on his Head with the following Lines written in Golden Characters: "Whoever meets me and "lets me paſs unmoleſted, ſhall worſhip "me and *Kiſna*, who will reward their "Piety; but whoever ſtops me, let him "prepare to fight. He further told him, that he ſhould give him his Brother *Erſiende* for his Companion, his intention being to purge the World of the wicked, during that ſhort time he had to ſtay as yet upon Earth. The King obey'd, and having preſented his Brother with a Chariot, and put him at the head of a good Body of Horſe, he took his leave of *Kiſna*, who went his way, the Horſe leading the Van without a Guide.

Kiſna *viſits the World, to purge it from the wicked.*

This Horſe paſs'd through many Kingdoms, where every one that did read the Inſcription, pay'd Reverence to *Kiſna*: But coming into the Territories of *Sindera*, who having receiv'd ſeveral ſignal Obligations from *Kiſna*, ſeiz'd upon the Horſe, by that means to engage *Kiſna* to come to his Court: Accordingly *Kiſna* (who knew his Intention) viſited him in his Court, where being reverenced and preſented by the King, he gave him his Bleſſing, and ſo ſet forward again to the King of *Sudannewa*.

He [illegible] Sindera.

This King ſtopping the Horſe worſhipp'd *Kiſna*, alledging, that he did not do it to engage with *Kiſna*, but to try his Strength againſt *Erſiende*: *Kiſna* accepting his Excuſe, *Erſiende* drew his Bow and ſhot an Arrow into his Breaſt. The King lifting up his Eyes unto Heaven, and tearing the Arrow out of his Wound, cry'd, O *Kiſna!* doſt thou thus reward thy Adorers! My Soul muſt now tranſmigrate into another Body. No, anſwer'd *Kiſna*, thy Soul ſhall aſcend to Heaven in an inſtant, and enjoy eternal Bliſs.

Comes to Sudannewa, *who is kill'd by* Erſiende.

Hence he travell'd to the impious King *Anſſalauw*, who ſtopping the Horſe, and bringing his Forces to fight againſt him, were all ſlain upon the ſpot. Next coming to King *Sallauw*, he follow'd the footſteps of *Anſſalauw*, and had the ſame Fate. Afterwards they came to *Mottera*, the Reſidence of the famous Giant *Ragia Jeraſingh*, who had been formerly defeated no leſs than 18 times by *Kiſna*. This Giant having fortified *Mottera* with high and ſtrong Walls, drew out his Forces into the Field, himſelf being cover'd with a Cuiraſs, or Armour, that was both Sword and Shot-proof. Both Armies engag'd one another with ſuch fury, that the like had never been ſeen before, with ſuch various Succeſs, that it remain'd dubious who was likely to be the Vanquiſher, the Night putting an end to the Battel for that time.

Comes to and vanquiſhes ſeveral Kings.

Kiſna being ſenſible that it would be a hard task to kill this Giant as long as he made uſe of this Armour, got with *Erſiende* over the City Walls, having transform'd both himſelf and *Erſiende* into the ſhape of two old and tall *Brahmans*. In this poſture they ſeated themſelves near the *Pagode*, where the Giant us'd to waſh himſelf, who coming thither ask'd them, *What is it you two devout Men deſire? ask and you ſhall have it, be it what it will.* *Kiſna* reply'd, That Kings were apt to promiſe much more than they intended to perform. The Giant anſwer'd, that was never his Cuſtom, deſiring them to ask what they pleaſ'd, it ſhould be granted: The diſguiſ'd *Kiſna* then ask'd the King to give him his Hand as a token of his Sincerity, which the King having done accordingly, *All that we ask of thee*, ſaid he,

He leaps over the Walls of Mottera.

he, *is, that whenever thou engagest again against* Kisna, *thou shalt not put on thy shot-free Armour.* The King (tho suspecting the matter) answer'd, Well, since I have given my word it shall be done, provided that he who engages in a single Combat with me shall bring no Bow and Arrow; but if he will fight with a *Gors* *, or try his Skill with me in wrestling, I am ready to answer him.

* *A kind of* Indian *Weapon.*

Kisna and *Ersiende* disappear'd without answering one word, and *Ersiende*'s Skill lying chiefly in his Bow, he engag'd *Ersiende*'s Brother (a famous Wrestler) in his stead. The Combat was so equal, that the night parting them they refer'd the whole Decision of the Quarrel till next day; being both equally tir'd with wrestling, they fought with the *Gors* the next day; they engag'd most furiously all the day, giving one another most terrible Blows, but with equal advantage, so that night approaching, they were forced to defer the final Decision till the third day: Then it was that the Giant exerting all his Force, gave such frequent and terrible Blows to *Rhijm Ersienden*'s Brother, that being ready to faint, he was knock'd down several times: But imploring *Kisna*'s Assistance, he was endow'd with new Vigor, so that recovering his Strength, he attack'd the Giant *Jerasingh* afresh, and at last laying hold on his Legs, tore him asunder, with his Entrails hanging down upon the ground. *Kisna*'s Forces seeing this Spectacle, attack'd his Army, and slew them all upon the spot.

The Giant Jerasingh *kill'd.*

Kisna in his return being met by *Sussuster*, was entertain'd by him in a Garden without the City, *Ersiende* at the same time presenting him with a Garland of Flowers. *Kisna* being highly satisfied with him, said, *Desire what you think fit.* But *Ersiende* excusing himself, *Kisna* told him, *That his time upon Earth being near expir'd, he intended to grant him whatever request he could make.* Then, reply'd *Ersiende*, bestow one of your Wives upon me. *Kisna* answer'd, Take my Chariot and go to *Davarca*, visit all the Chambers of my *Seraglio*, and which of the Ladies thou findest without me, take her for thy own. *Ersiende* went instantly to the *Seraglio* at *Devarca*, and entring the first Chamber found *Kisna* talking with the Lady; then going to the second, he found him there likewise; and so in the third, fourth, and all the rest: Being struck with Amazement, he return'd to the Garden where he had left *Kisna*, and prostrating himself, said, *O* Kisna, *thou brest the true God, and present every where, pardon my Errors!* *Kisna* giving him his Blessing, told him, he should persevere in his Prayers, and so return'd to *Davarca*.

Baldæus.

Kisna afterwards seeing the Cowherds multiply to 56 *Karool* (each *Karool* making 100 *Lak*, each whereof is 100000) or 560000000 living Souls, and that they had encreas'd as well in Iniquity as well as in Number, he was highly incens'd against them, declaring that he would root them out, not by his or other Mens hands, but their own.

Vast Increase of the Cowherds.

It happen'd that a great number of them being invited to a Feast where *Kisna* was also present, they were so full of wantonness, as to stamp upon the precious Flowers call'd *Massiou* and *Cassomba* (affording a most delicious Tincture for dying) with their Feet. Not contented thus, it being a Moonshiny Night, they contriv'd to ridicule the famous Prophet *Ruchi*, whom they saw sitting very thoughtfully under a Tree. For this purpose they put a Basket under a certain Man's Clothes, dress'd like a Woman, and carrying her to *Ruchi*, ask'd him, whether this Woman was to bring forth a Male or Female Child? He not minding them the first time, they pull'd him by the Arm, and ask'd him the same Question in a very rude manner a second time; when being as it were awaken'd out of his Pensiveness, he told them, he should bring forth an Iron Bar which should break all their Skulls. He had no sooner said these words, but the disguis'd Man was seiz'd with most intolerable Pains, which did not cease till he had brought forth an Iron Bar. Being amaz'd at so odd an Accident, they had recourse to *Kisna*, who order'd them to go to the Village of *Perwatspatang*, seated upon the River, where they should find a Stone, wherewith they must rub the Iron Bar till it was reduc'd to Pouder, and then throw it into the River. They did as they were order'd, but no sooner had they thrown the Pouder of the Iron into the Water, but the whole River was fill'd with Reeds or small Canes, as if it had been a Forest: They gave an account of it to *Kisna*, who told them it was well.

It happen'd upon another Festival, that the young Tribe being merry together, one of the Company took up one of these Reeds from the ground, and striking another over the Head in jest, he saw him drop down dead before his Feet: The Friends of the deceased taking up another such Reed, struck the other young Fellow over the Head, who likewise

Baldæus. wise falling down dead, his Friends did the same to them, and so one to another, till they were all kill'd, according to the Prediction of *Ruchi* the *Brahman.*

Kisna having now fulfill'd his Office in rooting out Wickedness among Man, sent for the *Panspendaons* and *Droepeti*, and their Mother to *Davarca*, where he told them, that having selected them as well as his Wives from the rest, he would have them go to the Mount *Hemaatsiel Perwet*, whence they should be taken up into Heaven. Accordingly they went with *Kisna*'s 16000 Wives to the said Mount, the Peak whereof nobody could reach but *Suffuster*; however they were all together drawn up insensibly through the Air into Heaven.

Kisna knowing that his time was come to leave the Earth, he took a handful of Dust, and throwing it over the City, their Golden Streets and Houses were in an instant transmuted into Straw, Dirt, Wood and Stones; which done, he ascended strait to Heaven. *Kisna ascends to Heaven.* The Pagans are unanimously of opinion, that in case the whole Sea was fill'd with Ink, and the Earth made of Paper, and all the Inhabitants of the Terrestrial Globe were only imploy'd in writing, they would not be sufficient to give an exact account of all the Miracles wrought by *Kisna* in 100 years time, in the third Period of the World call'd *Duapersinge*, containing 864000 Years. *The same is said of Christ, Joh. 21. 25.*

CHAP. XI.

The ninth Appearance of Vistnum *in the shape of* Boudha *or* Bodhe. *His tenth Transformation into a flying Horse, call'd* Kallenkyn. *The Origin and Actions of* Bramma.

The ninth Appearance. THE *Benjans* tell us of *Bodhe*, that he has neither Father nor Mother, that he is invisible, but whenever he appears it is with four Arms: He spends his whole time in praying with a dejected Countenance to the Great God (call'd *Mahadeuw* by the *Benjans*) and that after having continued 26430 years without performing any Miracles, his time is expir'd upon Earth, being the time we now live in, according to the Computation of the Pagans. For pursuant to the Computation of the *Benjans* at *Suratte*, there were in the year of Christ 1649, pass'd 4750 years, and consequently 21680 years to come.

What is said of this Idol concerning his being born without Father and Mother, and his Invisibility, seems to have some relation to what they may perhaps have heard of Christ, as his four Arms intimate his Power, a thing frequently attributed to the Pagan Gods; just as the antient Poets made their Giants with a hundred Hands. The Jesuit *Kircher* attributes likewise four Heads (but erroneously) to this *Bodhe* (call'd *Bhavani* by others) and says, that by his four Arms they would represent the four Elements. What the said Jesuit relates of *Ramtzander* the Son of *Bal*, who came from Heaven to deliver his People from the Oppression of the Giants and Tyrants, seems to be a Confirmation of what we said before concerning some obscure Remnants of Knowledg among these Pagans of Christ.

The tenth Transformation. The *Benjans* tell us, that *Kallenkyn* is a white wing'd Horse, standing upon three feet only in Heaven, holding one of the foremost Legs up without intermission. They say, that at the beginning of this Transformation the *Benjans* shall live piously and happily, but by degrees turn to all manner of Impiety and Wickedness for 40570 years: Then, say they, this Horse is to trample upon the Earth with his right fore Leg with such a force, that the Serpent *Signagie* being no longer able to bear the World, the *Tortoise* finding the whole Burden laid on her Back, will run to the Sea and drown the World, which is to be the Conclusion of the last Period of the World; after which the first is to begin again: For it is observable, that all the Eastern Pagans believe the Eternity of the World, allowing only some Changes from one time to another.

The Whiteness of this Horse intimates the Cleanness, its Wings the Activity and Agility, and the Horse it self the Strength of the God *Vistnum*; it being certain, that tho most of the *Indian* Pagans, and especially the *Malabars*, are black themselves, yet they have a peculiar esteem for the white Colour, as may be seen in the White Cow of Plenty, call'd *Camdo-*

The Idol Bodhe.

Camdoga, and the famous White Elephant of the King of *Siam*, mention'd in the first Book. Thus *Virgil* describes *Turnus* his Horse to be white *; and of the Strength, Activity and Excellency of a Horse there are many Passages to be found both in sacred and profane History. The Wings attributed to this Horse seem to be done in imitation of the *Pegasus* of the antient Pagans, which was plac'd by them likewise among the Stars. What they say of the World's being cast into the Sea by the Tortoise, appears to have some relation to *Noah*'s Flood: And it is observable, that according to the Doctrine of the *Malabars*, before the last Metamorphosis of things, there shall be such disorders in the World, that the

* L. 9. Æn.

the whole Race of Families and Tribes ſhall be confounded. They ſay there ſhall but two pious Kings be remaining upon Earth at that time, *viz.* the Kings of *Vappi*, and of *Aſari*.

Thus much of the God *Ixora* and *Viſtnum*; we muſt alſo ſay ſomething of the third, *viz.* *Bramma*, who owes his Origin to *Quivelinga*. *Rogerius* deduces his Origin from a Flower-pot, but the Commentator upon *Rogerius* had ſufficiently ſhewn that *Tamara* is quite another thing. Tho this Opinion ſeems to agree in ſome reſpect with what Father *Kircher* ſays in the *9th* Transformation of *Viſtnum*, *viz.* that he was transform'd into *Lotum*, being a certain Product of the Sea, and the opinion of the *Egyptians*, of

Origin of Bramma.

Thales

Thales and the *Stoicks*, who acknowledg'd the Water either the Principal or the Nourisher of every thing.

The Creator of the World. The chief things attributed to *Bramma* by these Pagans are, that he has not only created the World, but also determines the Duration and Times of all created Matters: And as they also acknowledg him the Son of God, and the Supreme Governor of Angels, nay even ascribe to him a human Nature; so it is evident, that these Attributes must have their Origin from what they have heard (tho perhaps confusedly) of Jesus Christ the Son of God.

They represent it with four Heads, but say he lost one by *Ixora*'s means to punish his Pride. Hence it is that the *Brahmans* now adays have no more than three Books of the *Vedam*, the fourth which treated of God being lost.

For the first of these Books treated of God, and of the Origin and Beginning of the Universe. The second, of those who have the Government and Management thereof. The third, of Morality and true Virtue. The fourth of the Ceremonials in their Temples, and Sacrifices. These four Books of the *Vedam* are by them call'd *Roggo Vedam*, *Jadura Vedam*, *Sama Vedam*, and *Tarawana Vedam*; and by the *Malabars*, *Icca*, *Icciyxa*, *Saman*, and *Adaravan*. The loss of this first Part is highly lamented by the *Brahmans*. They also attribute to him the Preservation of all created things; whence the modern *Brahmans* ascribe all the good or bad Fortune which befals Mortals here upon Earth to the Direction of *Brahma*, who they say has also prefix'd every living Creature his time of Life and Drath.

They further say, that not only the several Worlds, but also the different Families and Tribes have their Origin from *Bramma*. *The Origin of the 14 Worlds.* The *Super-aereal* World they say came out of his Brains or Face; for these Pagans acknowledg certain *Celestial Orbs*, with *Aristotle*. The second World they say did come out of his Eyes; the third out of his Mouth, the fourth out of his left Ear, the fifth out of his Tongue and Gums; the sixth out of his Heart, the 7*th* out of his Belly, the 8*th* out of his Privy Parts, the 9*th* out of his left Thigh, the 10*th* out of his Knees, the 11*th* out of his Heels, the 12*th* out of the Toes of his right Foot, the 13*th* out of the Ball of his left Foot, and the 14*th* out of the Air that surrounded him.

The *Brahmans* say they are the Product of his Brains, and the *Nairos* or Soldiers, of his Feet; as the *Exastri* (a sort of Kings) are out of his Arm, *Baldæus.* which is the reason that they never make the same low Bows before their Kings as their other Subjects, but have the Privilege of sitting down in their Presence. Unto these 14 Worlds as many divers *14 sorts of People.* sorts of People attribute their Origin: 1. Such as are endow'd with Wisdom. 2. Those that are provident in their Actions. 3. Those that are eloquent. 4. Such as are cunning and designing. 5. Drunkards and Gluttons. 6. The Generous and Brave. 7. The Idle and Lazy. 8. Whore-masters and voluptuous Persons. 9. Labourers, Artisans, and Handicrafts Men. 10 Peasants and Gardiners. 11. The *Parreas*, and other sorts of nasty People, who they say came out of the Heels of *Bramma*. 12. Thieves, Murderers and Robbers. 13. Those that oppress the Poor. 14. Those endow'd with peculiar Qualities, and an active Spirit. They further say, that they can judg by the Physiognomy of a Person, what part of *Bramma* he was come from. Of the Worlds and the seven Seas we shall say more presently.

The *Malabars* say, *Bramma* has two Wives, *Sarossody* and *Quiatry*, who are both barren. The first being his own Daughter, has given occasion to a Proverb among the *Malabars*, You must not do like *Bramma*. The Equipage, or rather Carriage of *Bramma* is a certain Bird, call'd *Annam* by the *Malabars*; for these Pagans attribute to every one of their Gods a certain Horse or Carriage call'd *Wahanam*, which carries them from place to place. They further say, that this Bird *Annam*, if Milk mix'd with Water be set before him, he will drink the Milk without touching the Water, an Emblem of such as know how to distinguish Good from Evil.

They relate many other fabulous things, as for instance, That *Bramma* after a Period of many Ages, is to die and be reviv'd; that he he has certain Deputies or Assistants, the chief of whom is *Dewendra*, the Head of all the Governors of the seven Worlds which are beyond our World, met below the Heavens, or *Bramma*'s Residence: In these Worlds (say they) the Believers live after their Death. They allow that some things of lesser moment, such as Herbs, Cucumbers, &c. have been created by others, but that all things of moment owe their Origin to *Bramma*, who lost one of his four Heads, because he had told a Lie to *Ixora*, and several such Absurdities more.

Baldæus.

CHAP. XII.

Of the Creation, Quality and Division of the World, according to the Opinion of the Learned Heathens.

THE *Benjans* and *Malabars* constitute God the Creator of the Universe, for they frequently give God the Title of *Creator of Heaven and Earth.* We told you in the preceding Chapter, that they attribute the Creation of the World to *Bramma*; whereunto we will now add, that they say, the Power of creating the World was communicated to him by *Vistnum.* They believe with *Epicurus* and *Metrodorus*, more than one World, of which before; besides which they make seven great Seas. 1. The *Water-Sea.* 2. The *Milk-Sea.* 3. The *Cream-Sea.* 4. The *Butter-Sea.* 5. The *Salt-Sea.* 6. The *Sugar-Sea.* 7. The *Wine-Sea.* The Paradise they place in the *Water-Sea*; the Priests and *Jogyes* belong to the *Milk-Sea*; the Voluptuous in the *Cream-Sea*; the Fortunate and Blessed in the *Butter-Sea*; the Merciful in the *Salt-Sea*; those who are Liberal in giving Alms in the *Sugar-Sea*, and those that live in great Plenty in the *Wine-Sea.*

7 Seas.

Notwithstanding this general Opinion, the *Brahmans* maintain, that the World was produc'd from an Egg; of which opinion it seems were also the antient *Egyptians*, the *Thebeans*, *Orpheus*, *Plato*, and the *Persians.*

The *Malabars* look for the Origin of all things in the Privy Member of their God, which being too large, he could not enjoy his Wife *Chatti*, wherefore he was forced to cut it into 18 pieces, which turn'd into divers sorts of Arms; but the Blood which issued thence produc'd the Sun, Moon, and Stars; and some few drops falling upon the ground, the Roses, and other sorts of Flowers: But all living Creatures, both rational and irrational, were brought forth by *Ixora*'s cohabiting with *Chatti.*

The *Brahmans* further are infected with a ridiculous Opinion, that the World is not round but flat; and that consequently the Terrestrial Globe is not enclos'd in, or surrounded by the Air, but limit its Extent by the Horizon that is obvious to our sight; for they maintain, that the Heavens are the uppermost half, and the Earth the lowermost of the Egg-shell; whence it is that they consider the Heavens as immovable, and the Motion of the Sun, Moon and Stars (unto whom they attribute peculiar Souls) to be like the Fishes at Sea in the day from East to West, and in the night from the West (not below but along the edg of the Horizon) to the North, and so again to the East. If you object, that according to their Supposition, the Sun must never cease to shine: They answer, that to the North there is a vast ridg of Mountains call'd *Mahameru* or *Merouma*, behind which the Sun, Moon and Stars withdraw from our sight. They add, that the World rests upon an Ox, who when he has a mind to ease himself, he throws the World from one of his Horns to the other, which occasions what we call Earthquakes.

Ridiculous Opinion of the Brahmans concerning the Figure of the World.

They are also grosly mistaken in the Computation of the Extent of the Earth, which the *Brahmans* say, is from North to South 100000 *Joxenas*; whereas it is beyond all doubt, that the whole Circumference of the Globe amounts to no more than 5400 *Germ.* Miles, reckoning 15 of these Miles to a Degree, of which there are 360. They also constitute no less than five Elements, adding the Heavens to the rest; in which point they follow the footsteps of *Aristotle*, who calls the Heavens the first Element. These five Elements both the *Brahmans* and *Benjans* reverence like Gods, because, say they, they enter into the Composition of every thing upon Earth; whence they allot every one of them his peculiar *Wahanam*, or Horse. They have also invented no less than seven *Padallas*, as they call them, or subterranean places (not unlike the Purgatory and *Limbus Patrum* of our Modern *Roman* Catholicks) which inferior Worlds are known among them by these following Names, *Adela*, *Bidela*, *Sudela*, *Taladelam*, *Sadelam*, *Mahadelam* and *Padelam*; and are inhabited by Men who receive no other Light but what certain Serpents carrying very bright Stones on their Heads afford them.

As also concerning its Magnitude.

CHAP.

Baldæus.

CHAP. XIII.

The Opinion of these Pagans concerning the Soul, and its Transmigration. The Form, Structure, Splendour and Revenues of their Pagodes *or Temples. Of the Ceremony of washing of these Pagans.*

THE modern *Brahmans*, in imitation of the antient *Egyptians*, *Thracians*, *Druids* and *Germans*, believe, that the Souls were not such from Eternity, but created by God, and kept as part of his Essence, till after the Creation of the Earth, they were infus'd either into Men or Beasts. Concerning the *Pythagorean* Doctrine of the Transmigration of Souls (so generally receiv'd among the modern Pagans) we have had occasion to speak before in the Description of *Ceylon*; we will only add in this Place, that the *Malabars* say on this Head, They are of opinion, that this Transmigration of the Souls from one Body into another is instituted by God as a Punishment for our Sins, which continues till they are either conveyed into Heaven or Hell; they say, there is a certain Judg, nam'd *Chitra Putta*, who judges of the Actions of Mankind when they lie upon their Deathbed, and determines according to their past Actions, whether the Soul of the deceas'd shall transmigrate into a Dog, Cat, Crow, Cow, King, Brahman, Serpent, *&c.* So that in case a Person in his Life-time has done a notorious Injustice to another, his Soul shall be transplanted into the Body of a Slave of the offended Party. The Reason why they abstain with so much Strictness from all sorts of Meat, is no other, than that they are afraid, as *Tertullian* expresses it, that in feeding upon a piece of Beef, they may eat a piece of their Father or Grandfather.

The Pythagorean *Transmigration of the Souls.*

These Pagans have their *Pagodes* or Temples erected to the Honour of their Idols; in the choice of the Places, and manner of the Building, they follow rather their Instinct or pretended Inspiration, than any general Rule or Method. These *Pagodes* are on the Coast of *Malabar* most commonly built of Marble, and on the Coast of *Coromandel* of very large square Stone; such is the most celebrated *Pagode* at *Rammanakojel*, a vast Structure, and endow'd with vast Revenues, by the great conflux of Pilgrims that continually resort thither, of which I have been an eye-witness my self.

The Building of their Pagodes.

The *Pagodes* of the *Malabars* are generally cover'd with Copper, adorn'd with Balls gilt on the top; within and without stand their Idols with many Heads and Arms, surrounded on all sides with Serpents. The *Pagode* is enclosed by a Brick-wall, for the Reception of the People, who don't enter the *Pagode*, but perform their Worship in the Court, as the *Jews* did in the Hall of *Solomon*. Hence it is that the Gates are well guarded, being commonly either of Marble or covered with Brass, with the Figures of Elephants, Tygres, Bears and Lyons upon them; and on the Frontispiece many dreadful Heads of Lions with Hogs Tusks, representing the Idol *Patagali*, *Ixora*'s Daughter.

These *Pagodes* are not only maintain'd by the Presents that are constantly made, but have also a constant Revenue from the Customs of all Commodities bought or sold, an exact account whereof may be seen in *Rogerius*, *l.* 2. *c.* 10. These Pagans have also a great Reverence for their *Pagodes*; whence it is that they will not enter a *Pagode* with their *Seripous* or Slippers: and they always have their Cisterns at the Entrance of the *Pagodes* to cleanse themselves before they enter; just as the same is practised among the modern *Mahometans* in their *Mosques*, and as the *Jews* had the *Brass Sea* belonging to the Temple for the *Levites* to wash themselves in. *Linscoten* mentions, that the *Pagan* Priests in *Calecut* besprinkle those that are entering the *Pagode* with *Holy Water*, like our *Roman Catholicks*. The Pagans in *Coromandel* have abundance of small *Pagodes* on those Places, where they burn their dead, whereof I took particular notice at *Negapatan*; and in *Bantam* the richer sort maintain frequently small Chappels for their private use. Of the *Pagodes* in *Pegu*, see *Casp. Balbi*; of those of *Japan*, *Caron* and *Almeyda*; and of those of *China Ferdinand Pintho*.

Their Revenues.

Reverence for their Pagodes.

Their Custom of washing themselves daily, seems not only to be introduced for the cleansing and cooling of their Bodies, but chiefly for the purifying of 'em from their Sins; for as these Pagans make a Distinction betwixt *venial* and *mortal* Sins, they regulate their washing accordingly. The first they are cleansed

Their Washing.

Baldæus.

sed of by dipping the Head under Water, whereas to purify themselves of the others (*viz.* such as include the Loss of Life or Family, and fall under the Cognizance of the Civil Magistrates) they dive the whole Body under Water: Their Constitutions (being to them the same as our ten Commandments) are:

1. That those of an inferiour Rank must not touch those of a superiour Quality, and the greater the Difference the more is the Distance; whence the inferiour People cry out in the Streets *Tintelas*, i. e. *don't make your self unclean*, and those of superiour Rank *Popo*, *Give way*; for if any of the common sort happen to touch a Person of a high Rank, he becomes unclean, and must wash himself with Water.

2. Those that touch a dead Carcase, nay even any of the deceased Kindred, within fifteen days after, become unclean.

3. Those that touch a Woman in Childbed, or the Child;

4. Or a Woman that has her Monthly Times, till the fourth day.

5. All such as are become unclean, if they touch another he becomes so likewise.

6. If one that is unclean eats Rice before he has cleansed himself, he loses the Advantage of his Family, and commits a mortal Sin.

7. Persons of Quality commit a mortal Sin, if they eat Rice boil'd by one of an inferiour Rank.

8. The same it is, if he lies with a Woman of a low extraction.

9. The *Brahmans*, tho all of the same Tribe, yet are not permitted to eat with one another; thus if any one touches with his Right Hand (wherewith he eats) his Neighbour, it is a venial Sin, because that Hand is unclean by touching the Rice; the same it is, if the Figleaf (which they use instead of a Twine thred) touches his that sits next to him: but if but one single Grain of Rice should happen to fall upon the Figleaf of the others, he must not eat it, without committing a mortal Sin.

10. Immediately after Dinner or Supper, they take away the Figleaves, and the least Grain of Rice that perhaps may be fallen upon the Ground, which is laid up together in a certain place, because all the Remnants are unclean. The Place where they have eaten, they purify with Cows Dung; and if the least Grain of Rice should be left behind, he that touches it, becomes unclean immediately on that part of his Body which touch'd it, which must be purify'd by Water. Thus if any body puts his Finger into the Mouth, nay if two Persons of a different Rank meet at a Cistern, if but one Drop of Water that has touch'd the Body of him that is of an inferiour Degree, happens to fall upon him of a superiour Rank, he becomes unclean, and is guilty of a venial Sin.

Cowdung used for purifying.

Their Ceremonies in washing.

Their Ceremonies observ'd in washing are: First of all they fancy, that the Stone on the edg of the Cistern is *Bramma*, the Place where they wash is *Vistnum*, and the Cistern it self *Ixora*. They enter the Cistern quite naked (their Privities being cover'd only with a Leaf) and write with their Fingers the Syllable *om* in the Water, and then with three Fingers cast up a little Water into the Air, intimating, that *Ixora*, *Vistnum* and *Bramma* have bathed themselves there; at the same time pronouncing these Words, *Tottum quenca bitten pava*, i. e. *By the touching of this Water I have cast away my Sin.* Then parting the Water with both their Hands, they dip their Hands in it, and thereby believe themselves cleansed from all their Sins committed by touching. Afterwards they cast some Water with both Hands towards the 8 parts of the World, as a Sacrifice to the eight Guardians thereof, say the *Siri Pagode*, wash their Faces three times successively, saying, *Purify me*; this done, they throw likewise some Water towards Heaven, as a Sacrifice to the Sun; and having wash'd their Hands and Feet, take a small Quantity of the Ashes of Cowdung in the left Hand, which being mix'd with a little Water, they say *Sudamaga*, i. e. *be clean.* Furthermore, as they suppose the Left Hand to be the Earth, and the Right the Heavens, and the inside of the Hand the Place of Propagation; they lay the Right Hand close upon the Left, saying, *Let this be the end of the World*; and as they believe that at the end of the World, *Ixoretta* is to be transformed into an Egg, they imagine that the Concavity betwixt their two Hands represents the said Egg, whence (after having paused a while) they take away the Right Hand, saying, *Heaven and Earth are separated*; and then write with the Forefinger of the Right Hand in the Ashes contain'd in the Left, the two Syllables *ja ra*, intimating the Contest betwixt the Fire and Air in the Egg, in carrying the Heavens to the top, and the Earth underneath. This done, they lay their Hands below the

Navel, on the upper orifice of the Stomach, upon the Breast, Front, Head, and Crown of the Head, and afterwards upon the inferiour Parts of the Body; they likewise touch the Eyes, Ears, Feet and Heels with their Fingers, extending now and then their Hands, as if they were going to give something: they likewise shew their empty Hands to the eight *Guardians of the World*; and afterwards besmearing themselves with Ashes with three Fingers of the Right Hand (in honour of *Bramma*, *Vistnum* and *Ixora*) on the Breast, Front and Shoulders, they then reckon themselves clear and purified of all their Sins. If you ask them, what makes them use all these Ceremonies, they give for answer, That they have two different Laws, *viz.* the *Carma* and *Nbana*, one whereof contains Instructions for the inward Service of God, the other for the exteriour or Ceremonial part. They add, that *Paraxi Rama*, when he made the Sea recede from the Coast of *Malabar*, did recommend in a most peculiar manner the observance of the *Carma* to the *Malabars*, whence *Malabar* to this day retains the Name of *Carma pumi*, i. e. *the Country of Carma*. *Baldæus.*

CHAP. XIV.

Of the Holy Ashes used in anointing themselves, and of their Festivals.

THE Ashes of Cowdung are a thing in such request among the *Indian*-Pagans, that they with it besmear every Morning, their Front, Breast and Shoulders; every King maintains in his Court a certain Person, who every day early in the Morning exposes a good quantity of these Ashes upon a Fig-leaf in the Market-place, when every one that pleases comes and takes some part thereof for his use; of these Ashes they also offer daily Sacrifices to their Gods. The *Jogyes* attend constantly near the *Pagodes*, with a whole Bag full of these Ashes, which they distribute to the People, who in return give them some Alms. They always appear besmear'd with these Ashes, in which consists a great part of their Holiness, their God *Ixora* being also bedaub'd with these Ashes; the reason whereof, as they relate it, is this.

Why the Ashes of Cowdung is sacred with 'em. We told you before, that *Ixora* or *Quiven*, having undertaken to keep *Quivelinga*, the Ashes which settled within the Shell, render'd *Ixora* immortal. *Vistnum* being desirous to enjoy the same Prerogative, seiz'd upon a Cow, and carrying her to *Calaja*, *Ixora*'s Residence, he snatch'd away some of these Ashes; which *Ixora* perceiving, he struck out several of her Teeth by a Blow he gave her, which falling upon the Earth, produc'd a kind of large Water Melons, call'd *Abobacus* by the *Portugueses*. However *Vistnum* keeping close behind his Cow, he gather'd the next Dung, and burnt it to Ashes; whence it is that to this day these Pagans have so great a Veneration for the Cowdung, that they believe it purifies every thing upon Earth. The said Cow brought forth a Bull-calf, unto which *Ixora* gave the Name of *Irixipaten*, and used him instead of a Horse. The *Malabar* Women, tho otherwise pretty cleanly, yet are so intoxicated to this Superstition, that they cleanse their Chambers and their Cisterns with Cowdung.

How the King of Calecut purifies himself. The *Samoryn* or King of *Calecut* washes himself every day before Dinner; and when he goes to the *Pagode*, the way from the Cistern to the *Pagode* is cover'd with Cow-dung, upon which they strow Roses and other Flowers; besides that two Women each with a Pot of Cowdung mix'd with Water, walk just before him; and the Place where he dines is afterwards constantly cleansed with Cow-dung. They relate farther of the Cow, that *Quenevady* and *Superbennia* did sit betwixt her Horns, the Sun and Moon in her Eyes, *Bramma*'s two Wives in her Ears, *Ixora* in her Nose, *Vistnum* in her Tongue, in her Thighs the *Rixii*, the four Books of the *Vedam* in her four Legs; that her Milk is the true *Ambrosia* or *Amortam*, and her Piss the *Tirtam*, or the Water fit to purify themselves from their Sins: whence it is, that when they see a Cow ready to piss, they catch it with their Hands, drink a little of it, and with the rest wash their Faces. As these Pagan Kings claim the Patronage of Cows, so the *Samoryn* of *Calecut* is attended every Morning early by six Boys, all over besmear'd with fresh Cow-dung, with Garlands of Flowers on their Heads; as soon as the *Samoryn* rises, they pay

Baldæus. pay him Reverence, who orders them immediately to give the Flowers to the Cows, which they do.

They have not the ſame regard for the Bulls and Oxen, tho they make a Bull the Father or Author of the Royal Family of the *Exaſtri*, from whence the Kings of *Cochin*, *Cranganor*, *Cananor*, and others are deſcended; they relate, that all the Males of this Family being extinct, a Woman of the ſame Tribe being begot with Child by a Bull, revived the ſaid Family.

Opinion of the Malabars *of the Cowdung.* The *Malabars* alledg the following reaſon for the Aſhes of the Cow-dung; They ſay that the *Lingam* (i.e. *membrum virile*) of *Ixora*, before it was cut in pieces, being ſo long that it reach'd up to his Forehead, let fly ſome few Drops of Seed, which happening to light into his fiery eye in the Front, was burnt to Aſhes immediately. Hence it is that in *Canara*, betwixt *Cananor* and *Mangalor*, there are to be found a certain Order of pretended holy religious Men, living conſtantly in the *Pagodes*. Theſe appear in the Streets quite naked, and making a noiſe by the ringing of a Bell they carry along with them, the Women (without diſtinction of Age or Quality, even to the Queens) come running out to touch their Privy Members.

That the *Egyptians*, and after them the *Jews*, had a peculiar Veneration for Cows and Calves, is ſufficiently evident from many Paſſages in the Scripture; and *the Aſhes of the Red Cow* are mention'd, *Heb.* 9. 13. & *Numb. ch.* 19.

Beſides this Purification, theſe Pagans have alſo their meritorious Acts of Piety; ſome of the *Jogiis* carry Iron Collars about their Necks, walk conſtantly with Iron Fetters and Chains, and have Iron Nails with the Points inwards in their wooden Slippers or Sandels. Some have been known to ty themſelves with Ropes to a Tree, till they expired in great Torments.

I ſaw 1657, one of theſe *Jogys* at *Columbo*, whoſe Arms were grown together over his Head, a Poſture he had choſen out of Devotion. Others of this Order never ſleep, but pray inceſſantly; of this kind are alſo to be found in *Japan* and *China*.

Another meritorious Act of the Pagans is the viſiting their celebrated *Pagodes* and other holy Places (like the Pilgrimages of the Romaniſts) as the famous *Pagode Rammanakojel*, the *Adams* Mountain in *Ceylon*, and divers other Places at *Suratte*, *Davarca*, *Mottera*, *Caſi*, *Bengale*, and *Ayotia*, 12 Leagues from *Caſi*; for which reaſon it is, that the rich erect *Pagodes*, Jans (call'd *Ammalams*) and Ciſterns for the Conveniency of the travelling Men and Beaſts.

The *Malabars* have a peculiar way to merit the forgiving of their Sins; there grows a certain Stone call'd *Talagramma* on one ſide of the Mount *Mahameru*, near a Riverſide (which the *Jogys* always carry about them) ſome whereof contain Gold, and are then called *Jerenia Querpam*; one of theſe carry'd in a Veſſel, and in another the five following things belonging to the Cow, *viz.* the *Cream*, *Milk*, *Butter*, *Piſs*, and *Dung* mix'd together, call'd by them *Panchaviam* Wine, and afterwards put into the other Veſſel, wherein lies the *Talagramma*, and given to any Perſon whilſt he recites the *Vedamantiram* (a Prayer of five words) purchaſes Pardon for all Sins, deſtroys his Enemies, reconciles him to his Friends, and procures Riches. This Prayer is in high Veneration among the *Brahmans*, which they uſe conſtantly when they are ſitting down to eat, but no body dares to ſay it in the Streets: The five Words are *Paneſua*, *Apaneſua*, *Vineſua*, *Udaneſua*, and *Sumaneſua*; the firſt ſignifies the *Soul* or *Spirit*, the ſecond the Poſteriors, where the Excrements are diſcharg'd; the third the *Hearing*; the fourth *Seeing*; the fifth the *Smelling*.

They have alſo their Feſtivals: one of the moſt remarkable Feſtivals of theſe Pagans, is celebrated in Honour of *Viſtnum* or *Ixora*; tho the *Malabars* ſolemnize certain Feſtivals, as that in Honour of *Ixora's* Spouſes, which are not regarded by other *Brahmans*, which beginning the 8*th* of *Jan.* continues for nine days, the Ceremonies may be ſeen in *Rogerius*, *l.* 2. *c.* 12. The Feaſts celebrated in Honour of *Ixora* and *Viſtnum*, are call'd *Trenaca* and *Panduga*. The *Gentives*, *Malabars*, and Inhabitants of *Coromandel* alſo ſolemnize a Feaſt to the Memory of the Nativity of *Viſtnum*, and his Transformation into *Kiſna* in *Auguſt*, when they adorn their Houſes with all ſorts of Greens, which ſeems to have ſome Reſemblance to our Chriſtmaſs: They alſo uſe another Feaſt to the Honour of *Viſtnum*, in remembrance of the 16000 Virgins; it begins the eighth day after the Full Moon in *Oct.* They have alſo a Feaſt in Honour of *Viſtnum's* Spouſe, call'd *Laſceni* by thoſe of *Coromandel*; this is celebrated by the *Brahmans* Wives in *September*, for nine days, when they *Their Feſtivals.* pray

pray for the long Life of their Husbands, and to obtain Riches. They have also two other Feasts in *July* and *November*. They observe besides this certain days, as Sacred and Fortunate, as the First day of every Month, the day of the Solstice, when the Sun turns from the North to the South.

They pay every Morning their Reverence to the Sun, and having wash'd themselves three times, they threw the Water with their Hands upwards, to prevent (as they say) the evil Spirits from keeping the Sun betwixt the Mountains. The New Year they begin with the New Moon in *April*, as the modern *Jews* in the Month *Abib*. They call the New Years Feast *Samwatsaradi Panduga*, *Panduga* signifying as much as a Feast, and *Samwatsaram* a Year, as *Adi* is the first day of the Month; for they have twelve Months in the Year, *viz.* April call'd *Thestram*, May *Weiwiacam*, June *Jestam*, July *Ajadam*, August *Spawanam*, September *Badrapadam*, October *Aswyam*, November *Carticam*, December *Margisaram*, January *Ponjam*, February *Magam*, March *Paelgouwan*. And because these 12 Months are not equivalent to the Months of the Sun, they have every third Year a Leap-year, consisting of 13 Months, which we have only once every four Years.

Baldæus.

Besides the Names of every Month, and of every day in the Week, the *Malabars* have a peculiar Name for each day in every Month. They have also peculiar Names for each Year, as far as sixty Years, unto which they add the Word *Samwatsaram*, signifying a Year, which however is often left out for Brevities sake; then they say *Prabawa* the *First*, *Pinawa* the *Second*, &c. *Tsaja* the sixtieth, meaning the *Samwatsaram* or Year. They compute by 60 years, just as the *Greeks* do by their *Olympiads*; they also name the Days of every Week (like the antient Pagans) after the Planets; thus *Suria* signifies to them the Sun, and *Jendra* the *Moon*, whence they call *Suria Waram* the *Sunday*, and the *Monday Jendra Waram*.

They divide each day into 30 Hours, just as the *Gentives* divide their Day and Night into 60 Hours, some whereof they account fortunate, and some unfortunate. Of the Pagan Feasts you may consult *Carolinus*, *chap.* 22.

CHAP. XV.

Of the Fastdays of the Pagans, and their Origin. Their Marriages and solemn Oaths; Ceremonies used with their Sick and Dead.

As the Pagans pray constantly thrice a day, *viz.* in the Morning, about Noon (when they repose themselves) and in the Evening, so they have their solemn Fastdays; one of these is call'd *Egadexi*, which Word (in their Learned Language, call'd *Samoscrad*, or *Hanscret*, as *Kircher* stiles it, which is in the same esteem among the *Malabars*, as the *Latin* in *Europe*) signifies as much as *eleven*, or *the eleventh*, because it is kept the eleventh day after the full Moon, and again the eleventh day after the new Moon; so that they have two of these Fasts every Month, *viz.* one every 15 days, when they abstain from eating all the day long, or at least till four or five a Clock in the Afternoon, when they must not feed upon Flesh, or Fish, or Rice, but only upon Fruits, Pease, Beans, Milk, and such like, and not drink the least strong Liquor.

The Origin of this Fast-day is ridiculous enough. They tell you, that a young Fellow much addicted to Venery, going one night very late to visit his Mistress, could not light on a Boat to ferry him over the River; however, being resolv'd not to depart, he staid there all night, and did fall asleep, without having eaten any thing all that day: Next morning early passing the River, as he was going to his Mistress's House, he met with a Camel just at Sun-rising, at which throwing a Stone it hit accidentally upon some Flowers, and cast them from the Stalks upon the ground, and so he came to his Mistress.

Origin of the first Fastday of these Pagans.

After some years happening to die, and being carried before *Chitraputren*, he could not produce any good Works he had perform'd in his Life-time to intitle himself to the Paradise, except this his accidental fasting, and the throwing down of the Flowers at Sun-rising, which he interpreted as a Sacrifice intended for the Sun. *Chitraputren* after a long hearing condemned him to the infernal Regions;

Baldæus. gions; yet in consideration of his fasting on the 11*th* day after the Full-Moon, having the favour granted him of abiding for some days in the Paradise, he was ask'd, what Paradise he would choose? He answer'd, The *Woman's Paradise.* Being convey'd thither accordingly, as he was in Bed the next night with one of the Ladies, he broke out into most dreadful Ejulations; and being ask'd by his Bedfellow the reason, he reply'd, *Because I have so short a time to stay in this Paradise.* The Woman who had taken a liking to him, told him, that he should rise early in the Morning, wash himself all over, and at the Gate watch the coming of the Servants of *Ixora*, who were then going into the *Wood of Roses*, to gather Flowers for their Master; she bad him to crowd in among them, and having gather'd the most odoriferous Flowers he could find, offer them as a Present to *Ixora.* He follow'd the Woman's Advice, and having gather'd the most sweet-scented Flowers he could, offer'd them to *Ixora*, who extremely pleas'd with this Present, ask'd *Chitraputren* who this young Man was? he told him, he was a Person condemn'd to the infernal Punishments: But *Ixora* order'd him to remain in Paradise with the same Woman, and to gather Flowers for him. Now because this young Man got into Paradise by his fasting, the Pagans fast upon the before-mention'd 11*th* day.

The second Fast. They have another Fast call'd *Quiverasiri*, which deduces its Origin from *Quiven* (the same as *Ixora*) and *Rasiri*, *i. e.* the Night, signifying as much as a *Night-fast*, or *Quivens* night: It falls out in *February*, and being one of their establish'd Fasts, is kept with a great deal of strictness, they being forbid either to eat or drink, or to sleep all that night, which they spend in rehearsing the Fictions of their Gods, and walking round the Pagodes till Day-break, when they sacrifice to the Idol, and give Alms to the Poor; which done, the Fast is ended.

Its Origin. The Origin of this Fast they ascribe to one *Beri*, a famous Hunter, who going one Evening abroad to shoot some Birds, got upon a certain Tree near a Cistern, call'd *Cuola*, the Leaves whereof smell as sweet as Flowers: Being very eager at the sport, he tarried upon the Tree all night, and to pass away his time without sleeping, he pull'd off constantly the Flowers of the Tree, which he throwing one after another upon the ground, one of them did fall upon *Quivelinga*, who happen'd just to lie under the Tree without *Beri*'s knowledg, who return'd to his own home the next Morning.

Some years after the said *Beri* happening to die, and being carried before *Chitrapoutren* the Judg of the dead, he found upon Examination, that having committed many Crimes in his Life-time by killing the wild Beasts, he was condemned to the infernal Regions. But as *Jewen* or *Jamma* the Chieftain of the Devils and his Company were hurrying him along, they were met by *Ixora*, who being inform'd of his fasting all the night long upon the Tree *Cuola*, and his offering of the Flowers to *Quivelinga*, he deliver'd him immediately out of the Devil's hands, aad sent him into Paradise.

Some tell a different Story upon this head, *viz.* That *Beri* perceiving a Tyger under the Tree, was forced to remain upon the Tree all night without eating any Victuals: They also tell you the Dialogue betwixt *Beri* and the Tyger; *Beri* it seems told the Tyger, that whereas he was not able to fast above three days, he desir'd him to let him go unmolested to his House, where he would take leave of his Wife and return again. The Tyger reply'd, No; for, said he, if I let thee come down safely, thou wilt certainly kill me with thy Bow and Arrow, which thou didst leave under the Tree whilst thou wast climbing up to fetch a Pigeon thou hadst shot before. But *Beri* taking an Oath by *Ixora* that he would return, the Tyger let him pass. *Beri* being return'd home, told his Wife what had happen'd, and that he must return to the Tree where the Tyger staid for his coming: The Woman offer'd to go in his stead, and so did his Children to be devour'd by the Tyger, alledging, that without him they should be depriv'd of all Subsistance. But *Beri* not approving their choice, they went all together to the Tyger, unto whom *Beri* said, Pursuant to his Oath he was come to be devour'd by him: But the Woman entreating the Tyger to devour her in his stead, as not being able to subsist without him, and the Children making the same Petition to him, the Tyger was put to such a Nonplus, that he did not know what to choose; but whilst he was ruminating upon the matter, *Ixora* threw a Net over them, and so drew them all into Paradise.

The third Fast call'd *Tirinadira*, is kept only by the Women, having got its Name from the 27*th* day of the 9*th* Month; on which day *Canteven* the *God of Love*, being kill'd by *Ixora*, the Women were so griev'd thereat, that they would *The third Fast.* *Its Origin.*

would not touch the least Eatables all that day; and ever since keep a Fast on the 27th of *December* in memory of this Disaster, being much about the same time we celebrate the Feast of our Saviour's Nativity. They say the reason why *Ixora* kill'd this *Canteven*, or *Cupid*, was because the last was fallen in love with *Paramesceri*, *Ixora*'s Spouse, for which reason he burnt him to Ashes with his fiery Eye on the Forehead. But the *Brahmans* say that *Ixora* being for a considerable time employ'd in holy matters, and thereby become forgetful of *Paramesceri*, she addrest herself to *Canteven*, to infuse into her Husband fresh Sentiments of Love; but she afterwards no sooner understood his Death, than she died for Grief: Being however brought to Life at the Foot of the Mount *Timana* (where she staid for sometime after to do Penance, and thence got the Name of the Daughter of the Mount *Timana*) *Ixora* appear'd to her, promising to continue his Conjugal Love hereafter. *Paramesceri* took this Opportunity to desire *Ixora* to revive *Cupid* from the Dead, with this addition, that he should remain immortal for ever after; whence they say, that *Cupid* reigns all over the World by the Strength of Imagination in both Sexes; by which they seem to intimate, that as the Inclination to Love ceases in old Persons, it is constantly reviv'd in the young ones, and so will continue as long as the World stands.

Why the God of Love was killed by Ixora.

The fourth Fast.

They have another famous Fast, called *Masaupasa*, from the Word *Masa* (which in the high *Malabar* Tongue signifies a Mouth) and *Upada* a Fast, being the most sacred of all their Fasts, beginning with the last day of *October*.

Such as keep this Fast, having first wash'd and dress'd themselves very clean, repair to the Pagode of *Vistnum*; and the next day being the 19th of *Novemb.* after having chang'd their Clothes, go round the said Temple early in the Morning 101 times, and the most devoted 1001 times. The same they repeat every day during the whole *November* and *December*, muttering all the while by themselves the Words *Naraina* and *Aquanama*, Sirnames belonging to *Vistnum*. All this while they must eat nothing but Milk and Figs, neither look upon a Woman, and think or speak of nothing but what relates unto *Vistnum*. The next following year they take the same course, beginning with the 1st day of *Decemb.* and continuing till the 10th of *Jan.* in all 40 Days. The third Year they begin with the 1st of *Jan.* and continue the same Devotions till the 10th of *Feb.* and thus the same successively for nine years longer, till the Number of 12 years being compleated, they obtain a general Pardon for all their Trespasses.

Baldæus.

Their Marriages.

Concerning their Marriages, *Polygamy* and some other matters relating to this purpose, we have had occasion to say something already in the Description of *Ceylon*: we will now give an account of such things as were not mention'd, or at least not circumstantially in that Place. The first is, that the *Brahmans* are not only at liberty to marry as many Wives as they think fit (a Privilege they always enjoy'd, as may be seen out of their antient Records, call'd *Poranes*) but also may choose their Wives out of four different Tribes, just as the *Levites* enjoy'd the Privilege of marrying in what Tribe they thought fit among the *Jews*.

As to their Marriage Ceremonies, some precede the Marriage it self, some are concomitant to it, and the rest follow it.

Marriage-Ceremonies.

The first thing they observe is, to consult an Astrologer about the Position of the Planets, and the Time or Hour, when it is fortunate for the Bride to be married; for which reason they also consult on what day of the Month, and under what Conjunction the Bridegroom is born. Next they apply themselves to a *Brahman* or Priest, who for four days successively before the Wedding, burns a little Rice and Butter mix'd with Eggs for a Sacrifice. The time of the solemn Promise or Engagement approaching, they light a large Waxcandle, and put some Rice upon the Table of *Quenevady*, the huge devouring Elephant beforemention'd. This done, the Bridegroom throws a Necklace or *Taly*, with some Gold fasten'd to it, about the Bride's Neck, as a Token that the Engagement is now made; whence the *Malabars* call Marriage *Quitha*, i. e. an *Obligation*. The Wife after the Death of her Husband, always breaks this Necklace, as a Token that the *Obligation* is dissolv'd, after which the Bride fasts 15 days.

After the Copulation is perform'd, they entertain their Friends at a Feast; but the young Couple are not bedded till about eight or ten days after: for before they can actually cohabit, they must attend a fortunate Conjunction of the Planets; and before they enter the Bedchamber, perform their Prayers at the Door, in the Company of a Priest, who gives them his Blessing. The next fol-

Baldæus. following day, the new married Couple take a piece of Cloth, cut at one end, wherewith they go a fishing in a River; the first Fish they take, they touch on the Head with a great deal of Reverence, and according as they take more or less Fishes, they shall have few or more Children; if they catch nothing, the Woman is to prove barren.

As the chief reason why they marry so young among the *Brahmans*, is their Fondness of a Maidenhead, so on the other hand nothing is more despicable among them than a Maiden come to a full Age, which has introduc'd the Custom of begging Portions for Maidens that they may be married in time.

The *Indian* Kings that are not *Brahmans* never marry, but only keep certain Mistresses, whose Children don't inherit, nay can't as much as challenge the least Prerogative, in respect of their Nobility; so that here obtains the Axiom, *Fructus sequitur ventrem.* The Kings Sisters are generally marry'd to some other Sovereign Princes, who must fast 15 days before Marriage. The *Nairos* have likewise no settled Marriages, whence their Wives are stiled *Parasceri*, i. e. *Women for many.* The *Brahmans* take as much care to couple a Bull and a Cow together, as other People do in marrying their Children.

Their manner of taking an Oath. These Pagans perform their solemn Oaths near a *Pagode*, and the *Brahmans* of *Coromandel* in the Presence of a Priest, near a holy Fire, just as the *Romans* use to do in the Presence of their Priests, the *Athenians* before the Altar, and the *Arcadians* during the Sacrifice. These Pagans being ready to take an Oath near the *Pagode*, they put three Fingers of the Right Hand, *viz.* the *Thumb*, the *next*, and the *Middle Finger*, into an Earthen Vessel fill'd with melted Butter; this done, they put a Leaf into the same Butter, which they tie close round their three Fingers: after three days the said Leaf is taken off in the Presence of the King or Prince of the Country; if his Fingers are not burnt, his Adversary suffers Punishment, but if he proves hurt, he is sure to be punish'd.

They have another way of taking an Oath, no less dangerous than the former; he that takes the Oath is oblig'd to swim cross the River betwixt *Cochin* and *Cranganor*, which is full of Crocodiles; and if he that has taken the Oath escapes without hurt, he is supposed to have taken a just Oath.

In *Canara* they have another way, for they put some Adders and a Lemon into an Earthen Vessel; and if he that takes the Oath, takes the Citron out of the Vessel, without receiving any harm, he has truly sworn. The Inhabitants of *Formosa* when they take an Oath, break only a Straw to pieces.

What Ceremonies they use with their Dead and Sick. Whenever any body falls sick, the Patient need not fear to be disturb'd with much Physick, Bleeding, Clysters, and such like, their chief Remedy consisting in Fasting, sometimes more than is convenient. They also send forth continual Prayers, to obtain a happy Transmigration of the Soul, and exhort the Patient to rehearse continually the Name of God, and when his Strength fails, his Friends repeat the same in his Presence; because the *Brahmans* are of opinion, that he who dies with the Name of God in his Mouth, goes directly to the Paradise: For the same reason they also distribute Alms to the Poor. If they give the Patient any Medicines, they are generally Laxatives of fresh Herbs, a little Milk *Cansie* (or Rice and Water boil'd together) a little Saffron, Ginger, or Leeks.

When the Patient is near expiring, they reiterate their Prayers, besprinkling them with Holy Water of the River *Ganges*; for they say, that the infernal Judg sends his Servants to torment them at that time, and that they send forth their Prayers to *Vistnum*, to send one of his Servants to deliver the dying Person out of their Clutches.

After their Decease they wash the Corps, afterwards shave his Beard, stop his Mouth with *Betel* and Lime, wrap him in a Shrowd, and last of all close his Eyes. Of the burning of their Dead we have spoken before, in the Description of the Funeral Ceremony of the Prince of *Ceylon*, and *Rogerius* * has given a more ample account of the whole matter. Some of these Pagans bury their Dead near their Habitations, and without the Cities (like the *Athenians* and *Romans*) and cover them with great Stones, for fear the *Jackalls* and other Wild Beasts, should dig them up and devour them.

* l. 1. c. 10.

They fast and shave their Heads for their deceas'd Friends; and if they be of Royal Extraction, all the Subjects are obliged to have their Heads shav'd. In *Malabar* the next Relations don't stir out of Doors for 15 days, sleep only on Mats upon the Ground, and don't assist at the usual Sacrifices. When I mention Fasting, I mean that they only eat a little Rice at Noon. After 7 days they send for

for the Barber, who having cleans'd the House with Milk and Cowpiss, and the Persons belonging to it, they gather up the Ashes of the deceas'd Person, after the Expiration of the 15 days; and having put the same into an Urn, they throw it with great Lamentations into the River, the Sea, or any other Water: This done, they purify the Place where the Corps was burnt, and plant there a Fig-tree. Afterwards changing their Clothes, and being cleans'd by repeated Washings, they put an end to the Mourning, except the next Heir, who continues in Mourning a whole Year, during which he abstains from Flesh, Fish, Eggs, Wine, nay even from their beloved *Betel.* No Person must touch his Head, neither must he cohabit with his Wife: Besides which, he is obliged to perform daily the following Ceremony; He takes a small quantity of boil'd Rice, made up in form of a little Ball, this he lays upon a Figleaf spread upon the Ground without the House-door, and taking part of another Figleaf, he bends it together, fancying all the while, that the Deceas'd is there present to eat the Riceball; then taking a little Rice mix'd with Butter in both his Hands, he turns his Face about, as if he were looking to put it into the Mouth of the deceas'd Person. This done, the Standers by clap their Hands together, a Signal to the Crows (of which there are vast Numbers in *Malabar*) to come to take the Ball of Rice, prepar'd for the deceas'd Person; which if the Crows do, the Heir is at Liberty to go to his Dinner, but if they don't, it is look'd upon as an ill Omen, and the whole Ceremony consider'd as fruitless. *Baldæus.*

At the Conclusion of the Mourning, the Relations of the deceas'd are invited to a splendid Feast, where however they must not eat either Flesh, Fish or Eggs, and none but the richer sort are invited to partake of it. This they repeat once a Year, on the same day the deceas'd died, to the Memory of their Friend. I will not enlarge my self in this Place upon that most barbarous Custom of some of these Pagans, for the Wives to burn themselves alive with the dead Carcases of their Husbands, a thing still practis'd in the most populous City of *Pandi*; for when the Funeral Ceremony of *Vinepi Naigne*, the Prince of the Country, was solemniz'd with great Pomp, 300 of his Wives did precipitate themselves alive (under the Sound of Drums and Trumpets) into the same Hole fill'd with burning Oil, Butter, and other combustible Matter, which burn'd both his and their Bodies to Ashes. We conclude with a hearty Wish, that these poor Wretches, quite entangled in the Darkness of Paganism, may thro his Mercy, and with the Assistance of such Magistrates as ought to keep a watchful eye over their Actions, be in time brought to the true Knowledg of the Gospel.

FINIS.

THE
INDEX
TO THE
Third Volume.

A.

ABissines, 640
Abuses of English Seamen, 215. How to redress them, 216.
Abuses in the Queen's Ships, 216. How to reform them, 217.
Abuses in the King's Service at Sea, and how to reform them, 370.
Account of Discoveries in the West Indies, 414.
Achiavelli Church and pleasant Village, 801.
Aconcagua River in Chile, 18.
Acunha sent to Diu takes Arabian Vessels, 599.
Adam's Bridg, and the print of his Foot, 650.
Adam's Mountain in Ceylon, 820.
Admonition to Gentlemen to beware how they are drawn into Expeditions at Sea, 314.
Advantages of the Commerce between Chile and the Philippine Islands, 56. Of keeping a Fleet on the Coast of Spain in time of War, 213. Of the Peace after Queen Elizabeth's Death, 229.
Advice of Sir William Monson for suppressing the Argierines, 252. His Advice to Subjects to comply with the King, 298. To Great Persons and unexperienc'd Generals at Sea, 303. For a King to elect Generals, Counsellors, and Governors, 304.
Advice to plant the Island of Madagascar, 449.
Aerssin gains Droepeti by shooting, 881.
Affront offer'd by the Dutch to the English Embassadors, 242.
Agat Stone, 657.
Agra City and Castle, 577.
Agreement between Philip Mascarenhas and Cornelius van Sanen, 620.
Albacoras Fish in Chile, 36.
Alliance betwixt the Emperor of Ceylon and the Dutch, 713.
Allowance of Victuals in the King's Ships at Sea, 347.
Allowance of Victuals in the King of Spain's Galleys, 351.
Almagro and Pizarro fall out, 111.
Almagro beheaded by Order of the Pizarros, 116.
Almagro assists to conquer Peru, 406.
Almeyda the Viceroy of India's Death, 588.
Almonds in Chile, 9.
Alucan leaves Diu, 594.
Amadabat City describ'd, 566.
Amazons River discover'd, 104. Navigated up to Quito, and down again to the Sea, 105.
Amazons River, 419.
Amber, 657.
Amber-greece, 828. Different kinds of it, the Goodness how to be try'd, 829.
America by whom first peopled, 64. What Light of it among antient Philosophers, 85. What in Scripture, 86. Discovery of it, and by what means, 89. Discover'd by Columbus, 403.
Amethist Stone, 656.
Ammenam an Indian Measure, 729.
Amoks desperate Villains, 644.

Ana-

Analativa *Isle*, 809.
Anchediva *Island, the* Portuguese *Fort there demolish'd by the* Dutch, 621.
Anchorage *paid at* Mocha, 576.
Angol *City founded, its Situation, Description, and Character of the Natives*, 142.
Angretotte *Fort lost by the* Dutch, 788.
Animals *in* Chile *describ'd*, 11, *and* 43.
Ann *Royal Ship lost*, 299.
Answers *to the Resolutions of Queen* Elizabeth's *Council about making a defensive War against* Spain, 225.
Answer *to a Project of the* Dutch *for surprizing* Canaria *and* St. Thome, 483.
Antony de Meneses *taken with Letters*, 726.
Antony de Abreu *sent to* Goa *to give an Account of the Condition of* Columbo, 763.
Apahames *Officers of note in* Ceylon, 720.
Apavicoras *Shell-fish in* Chile, 35.
Apostles *River in* Chile, 124.
Appendix *to Sir* William Monson's *sixth Book*, 553.
Araucanos *resolve to revolt*, 142. *They revolt, aud raise a numerous Army*, 143. *Send an Embassador to treat with the new* Spanish *Governor*, 150.
Arauco *River in* Chile, 20.
Areek *an* Indian *Fruit*, 729.
Arguments *against fishing answer'd*, 521.
Armenians, 640.
Arms *of* Chileses, 60.
Arroba *is twenty five pounds weight*, 37.
Articles *propos'd by the* Dutch *to the* Great Mogul, *and the Answers*, 569.
Artificers *but few in* Chile, 74.
Ashes *of Cow-dung, why it is sacred among the Pagan* Indians, 894.
Atagualpa Inga *designs to surprize and destroy the* Spaniards. *Is summon'd by a Friar, and taken Prisoner*, 109.
Athenians *reject Advice, because not just*, 306.
Augustus Cæsar's *Advice to Governors*, 307.

B.

Babylon, 426.
Badur *King of* Cambaia *his warlike Preparations*, 591. *Takes* Citor; *offers the* Portugueses *a Place to build a Fort*, 592. *Is kill'd*, 593.
Ballen *a River in* Chile, 24.
Basket-work *that will hold Water*, 80.
Batecale *Kingdom*, 621.
Batecale *describ'd*, 713.
Batecotte, 802.
Battel *fought for eighteen days, a Fable*, 885.
Bazaim, 601.
Beasts *in* Ceylon, 826.
Bellares, *their Habit, Wealth in Cattel, manner of treading their Corn, way of making Butter, how they manage their Cattel*, 812. *They are litigious*, 814.
Besorus *King of* Egypt *the first that us'd Discipline in War*, 308.
Best *Cities in* Peru *next to* Lima, 113.
Betel *Island taken by the* Portugueses, 589.
Bezoar *Stones in* Chile, 37. *In* Malabar, 622.
Bezoar *Stone Oriental and Occidental*, 658.
Biobio *River in* Chile, 20.
Birds *in* Chile, 37. *In* Ceylon, 826.
Bishop *supreme in Ecclesiastical Affairs in* Chile, 124.
Bishop *comes to* Cochin, 635.
Bloodstone, 657.
Boatswain *his Duty*, 326. *His Office*, 342.
Boatswain *of the Yard his Duty*, 326.
Boldness *of* Chilenians *to avoid Slavery*, 76.
Bombay, 602.
Book *of the Proceedings in the Expedition to* Cadiz *under K.* Charles *I. and the Answer to it*, 268.
Boy *taken as a Spy*, 738.
Brahmans *whence descended, their Pagan Superstition, and Reasons for it*, 814. *Their Belief concerning the Beginning of the World, and of Souls*, 815. *Their Marriage Customs, they marry young*, 816. *A strict sort of them*, 833. *They are averse to Drunkenness*, 837. *Their Origin*, 858.
Brama Indian *God, one of his Heads cut off by* Ixora, 835. *His Origin*, 890.
Bravery *of a Servant*, 593. *Of* Portugueses, 628.
Bread *in* Cuyo, 82.
Bridg *of the* Ingas, 17.
Brochia *City*, 574.
Buenos Ayres *founded*, 104.
Buffaloes *in* Ceylon, 825.
Building *of Ships*, 357.
Bull *of Indulgence*, 636.
Burning *Mountains in* Chile, 13.

C.

Cachopoa *River in* Chile, 19.
Cadiz *Expedition by the Earl of* Sussex, 184. *Ships taken and burnt there*, 187. *Quitted again*, 188.
Cafres *Blacks of the South of* Africk, 717.
Calecut *Kingdom*, 625.
Calecut *City*, 627.
Caleture *Town*, 654. *Invested by the* Dutch, 717. *Surrender'd*, 718.
Cambaia *Province, its Limits and Fertility*, 565. *Its Extent*, 566.
Cambaia *City describ'd*, 566.
Cambra *River*, 425.
Camdoga's *Curse*, 881.
Campana *River in* Chile, 24.

Cananor,

Index *to the Third Volume.*

Cananor, 622. *Taken by the* Dutch, p. 624
Canary *Islands*, 484
Canarines *offer their Brides to* Priapus, 832
Candea *conquer'd by* Raja Singa, 669
Cannon, their Names, Weight, Charge, &c. 342
Canoes *of Whalebone*, 79
Capiapo Indians *revenge the Death of their* Cacique, *are overcome by Capt.* Francis de Aquirre, 136
Capoulican *General of the* Araucanos, *makes* Lautaro *his Lieutenant. His Character*, 146. *He designs to besiege the City Imperial, but is miraculously prevented*, 148. *Is betray'd by one of his own Men, and taken by the* Spaniards, 153. *His Speech, he is baptiz'd and executed*, 154
Captains of Privateers, 337
Caradiva *Island*, 808
Caran *Giant*, 885
Caravans *of* Aleppo, *and* Alexandria, 576
Caravel *taken by Stratagem*, 497
Carcal *Town*, 652
Caren *Fountain in* Chile, 27
Carnatica *Kingdom*, 654
Carnero *Port in* Chile, 33
Carpenters Office, 345
Carracks, *their Navigation to the* East-Indies, 395
Carreas *a Tribe of* Indians, 817
Carthagena *founded, its Situation, Buildings*, 104
Carthagena, 416
Caspian *Sea*, 424
Castro *Viceroy of* India, *relieves* Diu, 599
Cat no Indian *Animal*, 111
Catavelli, 806
Catechism introduc'd among the Indians *not to be alter'd*, 793
Cathay *Church*, 804
Catherine *made Queen of* Candea, *remov'd from* Manaar, *her Superstition, and Reception at* Candea, 673. *Is crown'd*, 674. *Her Reflections on a Murder committed by the* Portugueses, 675. *Falls sick and dies.* 692
Catseyes *Stones*, 657
Cattel great Product of Chile, 9
Cavendish's *Voyage round the World*, 401
Cauquenes *River in* Chile, 19
Cienuvieraat *murders Prince* Ouve, *clears himself, and marries Queen* Catherine *of* Ceylon, 682. *Convenes the States, and what was concluded*, 687. *Besieges* Walena, *raises the Siege*, 691. *Falls sick, assembles the States, his Speech*, 693. *Declares the Administrators of the Empire, and settles it*, 694. *Delivers his Children to them*, 695
Ceremonies of Pagan Indians *in washing*, 894
Ceremonies with their sick and dead, p. 900
Cessares Indians *suppos'd to be* Spaniards *originally*, 59
Ceylon *Island its extent and discovery*, 667. *Arrival of* Portugueses *there*, 668. *Its Fertility*, 822
Ceyloneses *their Temples, Idols, Convents and Religious Men, their Processions*, 820. *Their* Genius, 821. *Their Habit, Oeconomy, Coin*, 822
Cezimbra *Town on the Coast of* Portugal, 199
Chalbin *River in* Chile, 24
Chambaronigo *River in* Chile, 19
Changane, 803
Chapter of Santiago *in* Chile *chosen by the King*, 124
Chatham *its Conveniency for the Navy*, 454. *Exceptions against it*, 455
Chavagatzeri, 804
Chaul, 601
Chengier *City*, 652
Chico, *River in* Chile, 24
Child, *Bird in* Chile, 39
Children in Ceylon *never marry without their Parents Consent*, 817
Chile *Kingdom, its Situation and Climate*, 1. *Its Division, Temperateness, is free from Lightning*. 2. *From poisonous Creatures, and Bugs, its Climate and Soil like* Europe, 3. *Etymology of the Name of* Chile, 30. *Its vast Riches*, 115
Chiloe, *Islands of* Chile, 50
Chittijs, *a Tribe of* Indians, 817
Chivias, *a Tribe of* Indians, 817
Chom, *or Road of* Sohali, 573
Chono, *Islands of* Chile, 51
Choros *Shell-fish in* Chile, 34
Christians of St. Thomas *decay'd and restor'd, had their own Bishops, acknowledg the Jurisdiction of* Rome, 638. *Where they inhabit, their Doctrine*, 639
Christians in the Wannias, *and* Manaar, 810
Chuapa, *River in* Chile, 18
Cibil, *Herb, its Virtues*, 82
Cingalese *and* Malabar *Tongue both us'd in* Ceylon, 792
Cingaleses *go over to their Emperor*, 780. *Attack'd in vain*, 785. *Routed*, 701
Cinnamon *Tree in* Chile, 47
Cinnamon *and its Tree describ'd*, 822. *Three sorts of it*, 824
Civil War betwixt the Heirs of the Empire of Peru, 109
Clerk of the Navy, his Duty, 325
Clerk of the Survey at Chatham, *his Duty*, 325
Clerk of the Rope-yard, his Duty, 326
Clerks of the Check, their Duty, 325
Clothing of the Chilenian *Islanders*, 78

*

Cochin

Cochin *City, Christians and* Mahometans *liv'd in it, not wholesom, but plentiful,* 631. *Its Churches and Monasteries; an unsuccessful Assault upon it,* 634. *Besieg'd a second time by the* Dutch, 632. *Surrender'd to them,* 635

Coxswain and his Mate their Office, 348

Coco *Islands,* 54

Coco-*Nuts in* Chile, 9

Coco-*Nut, why it has the Print of a Man's Face,* 838

Colcura *River in* Chile, 20

Colderon *Town,* 652

Colina *River in* Chile, 19

Columbo *reliev'd,* 668. *Besieg'd by the* Dutch, 702. *Furiously ply'd with great Cannon,* 721. *Assaulted by Sea and Land with ill Success,* 724. *Want in the Town,* 726. *Sally with* 200 *Blacks,* 727. *More Particulars of the Siege,*728. *Famine in the Town,* 732. *They fire briskly upon the Besiegers,* 733. *False Attack upon it,* 736. *The* Dutch *assault and enter the City, but are repulsed to the Bastion of* St. John, *their slain and wounded in the Assault; Cannon planted by them on the Bastion to play into the City,* 757. *Articles of Surrender propos'd by the Besieged,* 758. *Articles granted them,* 759. *The City surrender'd,* 760. *What was found in it,* 779

Columbo *its Siege according to the* Portugueses *account. Number of People in the City,* 763. *Conduct of the Governor, the City summon'd,* 764. *General Assault, the* Dutch *repulsed,* 765. *The Governor's Son kill'd, Blacks turn'd out of the City,* 768. *The City neglected by those of* Goa, *Famine increases, Deserters hang'd, Messengers come with Letters from* Raja Singa, 769. *Cats and Dogs sold at a great rate,* 770. *Extremity of Want,* 771. *Mortality,* 772. *Successful Sally, the City enter'd by the* Dutch, 773. *Hot Engagement in the City,* 775. *It is surrender'd, only* 190 *marching out,* 776. *Origin of the City,* 777

Columbus *offers his discovery to several Kings and Princes, and is rejected; the* Queen *of* Spain *imbraces it; he sails upon his discovery,* 90. *Had but* 90 *Men in his Ships,* 91. *Lands, and takes Possession,* 92. *Is put in Irons, his Expressions thereupon,* 94. *He dies at* Valladolid, 95

Combat of Elephants, 578

Commodities sold in Ceylon, 826

Commotion in Candea *appeas'd by the Empress,* 682

Comparison betwixt the times under Q. Elizabeth *and* K. Charles I. 293. *Betwixt the antient Trade and the new,* 437. *Betwixt the* West-India *Trade and our Fishery,* 515

Competition between France *and* Spain *by Sea.* 383

Composition of the Serpents Stone, 657

Conception, *City and Bay in* Chile, 19,20

Conception *City in* Chile *founded,* 138. *Its Situation, Latitude, and Character of its Inhabitants,* 139. *Rebuilt,* 148

Conception by fancy, 839

Conchalli *Spring in* Chile, 28

Conditions of the Truce betwixt the Dutch *and* Portugueses *in* India, 617

Considerations offer'd to the Ministry of England *by Sir* Will. Monson, 557

Constellations of Chile, 42

Constitutions of Pagan Indians, 894

Contest betwixt the Indian *Gods* Ixora, Brama, *and* Vistnum, 835

Consultation about the Dutch *General's going to* Raja Singa, 742

Contents of a Letter sent to Raja Singa, 783

Contra-Rotulator *of the Admiralty,* 323

Contributions under Q. Elizabeth *to carry on the War against* Spain, 293

Contrivance of Portugueses, 701

*Conveniency of a Lecture of Navigation,*435

Conversion of Indians, 606

Cook of a Ship, his Office, 348

Cooper at Sea, his Office, 348

Copiapo *River in* Chile, 17

Copiapo *Port in* Chile, 33

Copiapo *Valley describ'd,* 119

Copties, 640

Coquimbo *Port in* Chile, 33

Coquimbo, *or* La Serena *City founded in* Chile, 134. *It abounds in rich Metals, its advantageous Situation,* 135

Cordage and Tackling for Ships, and Match for Fire-Arms in Chile, 9

Cordellera *Mountain in* Chile *describ'd,* 10

Coronados *River in* Chile, 24

Corporal his Office, 348

Correspondence with the Eastern Christians necessary, 642

Cortes *goes to discover* Mexico, 104. *His Exploits,* 411

Cois *an* Indian *Mile, half a* Dutch *League,* 573

Coucon *Port in* Chile, 33

Coukering *the Giant slain,* 866

Coulan *its Air wholesom,* 643. *The Natives treacherous; besieg'd a second time by the* Dutch, 644

Countries whence India *Commodities are brought,* 395

Coutinho *succeeds* Almeyda *as Viceroy of* India, 588

Cow of Plenty, 857. *Cow-dung us'd for purifying,* 894

Coypo *River in* Chile, 20

Cranganor *City and River*, 629. *The City taken by the* Dutch, *was an Archbishoprick, and had a College of Jesuits, and one call'd of* Chanotte, p. 630
Creator of the World, 891
Creed in the Malabar *Language*, 665
Crocodiles *in* Ceylon, 826
Cross found in the Ruins of Goa, 606
Crowing of a Cock admir'd by the Indians, 107
Cuba, 93, *and* 415
Cubagua, 419
Cudagua *Lake in* Chile, 19
Cumana, 419
Curavara *River in* Chile, 20
Cuyes *small tame Rabbets in* Chile, 44
Cuyo *Province of* Chile, *Remarks on it, and Inland Country*, 60. *Its Situation*, 62
Cuyo Indians *of a Copper Colour*, 80. *More hairy than the* Chilenians. *Their Women paint their Faces green. Proof of their Agility. They pretend to an Instinct in finding things lost; build no Houses*, 81. *Love to be Independent*, 82

D.

Daman, 601
Danes *sail to* Ceylon, *are rejected, and return to* Denmark. 700
Danger in attempting to take Argier, 254
Dangers to Ships upon accidental meeting with Whales, 535
Darida, 839
Darien, 416
Daughters in Chile *are Riches to their Parents*, 77
Decan *Kingdom its limits*,
Delightful Prospect, 28
Delora *River in* Chile, 19
Demonstrative Proof of the Wealth of Chile, 133
Desert Island, 869
Deserters, 721, 734, 735, 736, 780
Desperate old Indian, 77
Diamonds, 655
Difference betwixt the Countries on the East and West-side of the Mountains of Chile, 25
Difference betwixt the King of Shain's *Ships formerly and now*, 350
Difference betwixt Spaniards *and* Portugueses *about the* East-Indies, 398
Difference among Portuguese *Generals*, 629
Differences with the Dutch *at* Suratte *about Customs*, 566. *Betwixt* Almeyda *and* Albuquerque, 588. *Betwixt two Brothers in* Ceylon, *fomented by the* Portugueses, 779. *Betwixt* Badur *and the* Portugueses, 592
Different Seasons on the North and South sides of the Mountains in India, 649
Directions of an Admiral to his Ships if they lose Company, p. 332
Disaster of K. Henry *the* 8th's *Ships*, 221
Discouragement to Seamen, 330
Discovery of America *prosecuted*, 95
Discovery of several Countries, 389
Discovery of the Hollanders *Trade, and their circumventing us therein, and how to reduce the fishing into our hands*, 514
Discourse of the Shipping of England, *and Officers of the King's Ships*, 328
Discourse of the North-West Passage, 426
Dissave, *a Governor in* Ceylon, 720
Distances from Port to Port round America, 420
Betwixt Jafnapatan *and* Columbo, 790
Between Ports in the North-Sea, 492
Distinction of the strength of Ships, 350
Diu *City describ'd. Its Origin*, 584. *Attack'd by the* Portugueses, 587
Diu *Island taken by the* Portugueses, 593. *Besieg'd and reliev'd*, 594. *Reliev'd again*, 598
Division of Limits between Dutch *and* Portugueses *in* Ceylon, 619. *Among great Men in* Ceylon, 681
Dog frights the Indians, 99
Dominick Correa *deserts to the* Indians, *is made General, and is murder'd*, 677
Drake's *Voyage to the* West-Indies, *and Actions there*, 169. *His Voyage to the Road of* Cadiz *and* Terzera *Islands*, 170. *His Voyage with* Hawkins *to the* West-Indies, *where both dy'd*, 182. *He was vain-glorious*, 399. *His Voyage round the World*, 400
Drink, which most proper in India, 660
Droe *the North-star*, 879
Droepeti's *Origin and Qualities, order'd to be stripp'd*, 881. *Deliver'd by* Kisna, *goes into Exile*, &c. 882
Dutch *Admiral refuses to take in his Flag to the* English, 242
Dutch *that have pass'd the Straits of* Magellan *to little purpose*, 402
Dutch *their Character*, 445, 559
Dutch *Ship taken by Stratagem*, 497
Dutch *Fleet in danger of being lost*, 644. *Sails to* Cochin, 645
Dutch *invited into* Ceylon *by the Emperor*, 703
Dutch *Envoys sent to* Ceylon, *have Audience of the Emperor*, 705. *Their Proceedings and Dispatch*, 706
Dutch *Squadron sent to* Ceylon, 710. *Arrives there*, 711
Dutch *Ships sent to* Goa, 730
Dutch *Ships arrive at* Suratte, 731
Dutch *General presented with an* Elk *by the Emperor of* Ceylon, 735
Dutch *receive Intelligence of* Portuguese *Succours coming to* Columbo, 748

Dutch *Prisoners eight sent out of* Columbo, 755
Dutch *Interpreter escapes from the Emperor of* Ceylon's *Camp*, 784
Dutch *pass the River* Alicaon, *and beat the* Portugueses, 789
Dutch *march from* Manaar *to* Jafnapatan; *Their Passage over the River, they take that City*, 794. *They worst the* Portugueses *at Sea*, 797

E.

Earl *of* Cumberland's *Expedition with 7 Ships*, 176. *His next Expedition with* 8 *Ships*, 179. *Again to the Coast of* Spain, 181. *His Voyage to* Puerto Rico, 207. *His Design, his Error in the Voyage*, 208. *Exception against his Enterprize*, 209. *Takes the Town and Fort*, 211
Earl of Essex's *Voyage to the Islands to little or no effect*, 189
Earl of Northumberland's *Voyage*, 299
Eastern Churches deny the Supremacy of the Roman *See*, 641
East-Indies, *the beginning of the* English *resort thither*, 382
Edgar *King of* England *maintains the Prerogative of the Seas*, 297
Election of an Admiral, his Qualifications, and Duty, 330
Elephants of Ceylon, *how taken and tam'd*, 825
Emanuel Diaz *deceives the* Portugueses, 678
Emeralds, 656
Emperor of Ceylon *joins with the* Cingaleses, 701. *Dies*, 702
Encouragement to Merchants in Chile, 10
Engagement between the Emperor of Ceylon *and the Rebels*, 697. *Betwixt the* Dutch *and* Portugueses, 788
English *that attempted to pass the Straits of* Magellan, *and fail'd*, 402
Envoys sent by the Emperor of Ceylon, *view the place where the* Dutch *General was kill'd*, 748
Epistle of Sir Will. Monson *to all Sea-Officers and Sailors*,
Error of Transmigration of Souls among Jews *and* Druids, 815
Errors of the Earl of Northumberland's *Voyage*, 300
Errors in the Attempt upon Argier *under King* James *the First*, 256
Errors in the Expedition to the Isle of Ree *under King* Charles *the First*, 266
Esperanca *River in* Chile, 24
Estimate of Ships for carrying Fish abroad, 530
Eunuchs, divers sorts of them, 834
Euxine *Sea*, 424
Examples of the Goodness of Generals towards Enemies, 309
Examples of great Men who have refus'd to take base Advantages of their Enemies, 310
Excellent Pastures in Chile, 25
Excessive Cold, a remarkable instance of it, 114
Exhalations and other Meteors, 12
Exhortation to pay Ship mony, and contribute to curb the Insolencies of the Dutch, 286
Existence of God, 830
Expedition of the English *to* Portugal, 174
Expences at Sea how to be sav'd, 312
Exploits of Portugueses *at* Adem, *and other places*, 395
Eyou *River in* Chile, 20

F.

Factories *of* Dutch *in* India, 609
Famous Robber taken, 721
Fasts of the Indian *Pagans, their Original*, 897
Feather Beds not us'd in India, 661
Fertility of the Coast of Chile, 34
Festivals of the Mogul, 578
Of the Malabars, 896
Fight at Sea with Ships how to be manag'd, 356, 358
Fight of Galleys, 359
Fights betwixt the Dutch *and* Portugueses, 707, 719
Figueira *routed, and Consternation on that account at* Columbo, 762
Fine Island in Chile, 51
Fire Engine of the Turks *burnt by the* Portugueses, 594
Fireship burnt, 596
Fish on the Coast of Chile, 35. *In* Ceylon, 826
How to be vented in England, *and abroad*, 522
Fishermen taken by the Dutch, 739
Fishing upon several Coasts to the Southward, 531. *To the Northward*, 532. *In* Newfoundland, 533
Five Portuguese *Galleys engage three* Dutch *Vessels*, 788
Flag, the Ceremony of wearing it, and Use made of it, 364
Flamencos *Birds in* Chile, 39
Flavio Amalphy *first found the use of the Loadstone at Sea*, 340
Fleet of England *in the* Downs, *and nothing done*, 195
Fleet of 1100 *Sail under King* Edward *the Third*, 281
Fleet of Portugueses *cast away*, 728
Fleets that have been lost, and that have pass'd the Straits of Magellan, 59
Fleets of Spain *and* England *at Sea*, 178
Florida, 415
Flying Fish, 36
Flowers in Chile, 7

Forbisher's *Expedition at Sea*, 180. *Again to* Breſt, p. 182
Formoſa *Iſland its miſerable Condition*, 634
Fort built at Cananor *by the* Portugueſes, 623. *Beſieg'd and diſtreſs'd by the* Indians, *but not taken*, 624
Forts of the Chilenians, 70
Fountains, Springs and Brooks in the Mountains of Chile, 15
Fountains of Chile, 27
Four principal Officers of the Navy, what ſort of Men they muſt be, 327
Four remarkable Diviſions of Time, 845
Francolines *Fowl in* Chile, 39
French *debar'd fiſhing on the* Engliſh *Coaſt*, 239
Fruits of Chile *deſcrib'd*, 7
Funeral Feaſts of Malabars, 837

G.

GAle *deſcrib'd*, 717
Gallegos *River in* Chile, 24
Gaſlinaſas *Birds in* Chile, 38
Galleys, how they may be us'd in England, 361. *Their uſe in time of War*, 362. *The beſt place in* England *for them*, 363
Gama's *Reception at the* Samorin's *Court*, 625. *His Speech to that King, and his Anſwer*, 626. *Gets aboard, his Letter and the King's Anſwer*, 627
Ganges *River*, 661
D. Garcia *new Governor of* Chile *lands at* Quiriquina, 150. *Lands on the Continent and raiſes a Fort, beats the* Indians *that attack him; is reinforc'd, gives* Caupolican *Battel, and beats him*, 151. *Raiſes another Fort, and again beats the* Indians, 152
Garcia de Noronha *Viceroy of* India, *agrees with* Mamud, 595
Garzolas *Birds in* Chile, 39
Gaſca *ſent from* Spain *to quell the Rebellion in* Peru, 409
Geldria Dutch *Fort*, 653
Generous Wine in Chile, 8
Georgians, 639
Giants among the Chilenian *Iſlanders*, 78
Gigantes *River in* Chile, 24
Goa, *its Air, taken by* Albuquerque, 603. *Loſt again*, 604. *Retaken*, 605. *Its Inhabitants*, 608. *How to be block'd up by Sea*, 609. *Block'd up by the* Dutch, 610
God of Love kill'd by Ixora, 899
Goga *City*, 574
Gold great plenty in Chile, 8. *More of it than Silver*, 9
Gold Mines in Chile *wrought*, 132
Good Rowers among the Chilenians, 79
Goodneſs of the Iſle of Ceylon, 790
Gors *an* Indian *Weapon*, 887
Grain of Chile, 7
Granate *Stone*, p. 657
Grand Pilot, his Duty, 325
Great Snows, 26
Great Oppoſition made by the Indians *of* Chile, 116
Great Rains, 812
Greeks, 639. *They us'd five days before Eaſter to excommunicate the Pope*, 641
Guaſcar Inga *taken Priſoner*, 109. *Is put to death by order of* Ataguálpa, 110
Guaſco *River in* Chile, 18
Guaſco *Port there*, 33
Guayac *Tree in* Chile, 47
Gunners Duty, 326. *His Office*, 343
Gunners of Sconces their Duty, 326
Guzarat, *its Extent*, 573. *Its Traffick*, 574

H.

HAneraed *Governor of* Harcipore *conſpires with the* Portugueſes, *is routed, try'd and executed*, 696
Hanuman *gives an account to* Ram *of* Sytha, 862. *Flies into* Ceylon, *bears of* Sytha, *his Actions in* Ceylon, 863
Haraties Serpents *in* Ceylon, 720
Harbours of England, 376
Of Wales *and* Scotland, 377
Of Ireland, 378
Of Holland, Zealand, Flanders, 466
Of Biſcay, Galicia, Portugal, 469
Of Algarve, Andaluzia, Barbary, 470
Hardſhips the Spaniards *endur'd in* Chile, 114
Hartſtone, 657
Havana *Port in* Cuba, 95
Hawkins *and* Forbiſher's *Voyage to the Coaſt of* Spain, 177
Herradura *Port in* Chile, 33
Hebrides *Iſlands, uſe to be made of them*, 558
High-ways in Chile *of great note*, 11
Hogs Stone, 657
Holy Kings Iſland, 56
Holy Week celebrated in Chile, 129
Holy Water, 650
Honduras, 416
Horſes in Ceylon, 825
Houſekeeper at Chatham-*Hill his Duty*, 326
How to work the Sun at Sea, 340
Hulſt, Dutch *General, in danger of being kill'd*, 738. *His Journey to the Emperor of* Ceylon, *and Reception*, 742. *Deſigns to return*, 743. *His Entry*, 744. *His Audience and Speech; what paſs'd betwixt him and the Emperor; Honour done him, Propoſitions made by him*, 745. *Is preſented with a Garter, takes leave, returns to the Camp, views the Works, is wounded*, 746. *Dies. His Character*, 748. *His Corps carry'd to* Gale, 748
Hunting and Hawking in Chile, 40
Hunting in Cuyo, 62

Husband-

Husbandmen and Fishermen the Support of Commonwealths, p. 537
Hyacinth *Stone,* 656

I.

JAcobites, 639
Jafnapatan *City taken by the* Dutch, 794. *Its Castle summon'd,* 797. *The Besieged endeavour in vain to get Provisions,* 797. *Is surrender'd, and repair'd,* 798. *Its Description, how gain'd by the* Portugueses, 799
Jamaica, 415
James Botelho *his bold Enterprize,* 592
Janiere *usurps the Crown of* Ceylon, 671. *Seeks Assistance from the* Portugueses, 672. *Is murder'd,* 675
Jasper *Stone,* 656
Jazy *of* Diu *joins in Confederacy with* Mir Hazem *the* Turk, 584. *Plays the Hypocrite with the* Portugueses, *and is discover'd,* 588. *Fortifies himself,* 589
Jeresjanda *resolves to revenge* Ragia Kan's *Death, is sixteen times worsted by* Kisna, 876
Jerasingh *the Giant kill'd,* 887
Jews *and* Romans *married young,* 816
Ill Management of Spanish *Ships,* 349
Illondi Matual, 804
Impaling of Indians, 713
Imperial River in Chile, 20
Imperial City in Chile *founded, and its situation,* 140
Imperial Prince of Ceylon's *Death,* 688
Increase and Traffick of Goa, 608
Increase of Cowherds fabulous, 887
Indersiet *makes use of a bewitch'd Arrow,* 864
India, *its Bounds and Division,* 565
Indian *Stratagem,* 143
Indian *Pagans look upon it as a great Blessing when their Souls are not to enter into other Bodies,* 873
Indians *conceal their Treasure from Foreign Nations,* 14. *All of them surpriz'd at the sight of Horses,* 109
Indians *of* Chile *their Courage and Boldness,* 67. *Their State Assemblies, manner of their meeting, and choice of a General,* 60. *Their Nobility examin'd,* ib. *Their Temper, Make, they are good Horsemen, their Numbers and Habitations, Houses, Fidelity to one another, Furniture,* 71. *Their Diet and Bread,* 72. *Their Clothing, Finery, Dancing, Wind Instruments,* 73. *Their way of keeping account, their Hardiness against Wet and Cold, they bear Wounds better than the* Spaniards, 75. *Their Complexion; they have no red Hair, speak* Spanish *perfectly, bear their years well, live long, have good Teeth, cannot endure to leave their own Country,* 76. *Their Marriages, how they manage Poligamy,* 77. *They go to War without Pay, are very brave, and want Iron,* 78
Indigo, 658. *Its Goodness.* Indigo Laura. *Trial of it. Good made in* Coromandel, 959
Inhabitants of Jafnapatan *their Qualifications,* 812. *Their Vices,* 817. *Their Superstition, Lawyers, Physicians, Surgeons, Barbers, Weavers, Painters, and other Handicrafts,* 818
Insolencies of the Dutch, 240. & sequent. 553
Inspiration on the Clergy and Laity in Chile, *to sing,* 131
Instance of a Flood, 808
Instructions from an Admiral to his Vice and Rear Admirals and Captains, 332
Instructions given by the Earl of Lindsey, 333
Instructions given by a Spanish *Admiral,* 353
Instructions to Gaspar Figueiro, 719. *His welcome at* Columbo, 721
Instructions for a general Assault upon Columbo, 723, 753
Intelligence how to be got in Spain, 218. *How in the* Tercera *Islands,* 219
Intolerable Cold on the Mountains of Chile, 26
Introduction to the Earl of Northumberland's *Voyage,* 292
To Sir Tho. Drake's *Voyage round the World,* 399
Inventor of the Sea-Needle, 89
John *Emperor of* Ceylon *drives the* Portugueses *from* Gannoor, 670. *Is routed, and retreats to the Deserts,* 672. *In a Beggars Disguise, burns Houses in* Candea, *but is forc'd to fly,* 674. *Is restor'd to his Kingdom, and marries Queen* Catherine, 676. *Revenges the Death of his General,* 677. *Falls sick, and dies; his Character,* 681
Joris Spilbergen *comes to* Ceylon, 679. *His Funeral, place of Burial, his Corps burnt,* 690
Journy in search of Mines remarkable, 14
Island of Providence, 451
Islands of Chile, 50. *Of* Salomon, 53. *Of* St. Laurence *and* St. Stephen, 56. *Of* Angels, 56. *Of* Chile *and the Straits of* Magellan *peopled by Savages,* 79
Isle of S. Paul, 53
Isle of Patagones, 56
Itata *River in* Chile, 19
Juan Ferriandez *Islands of* Chile, 51
Ixora Indian *God describ'd, his Bigness,* 832. *Attack'd by the* Mummies, *reliev'd by* Vistnum, *his Children,* 835. *A Story of him,* 836. *His Daughter describ'd,* 840

K.

Keeper of the great Stores of the Navy his Duty, p. 324
Kidney Stone, 657
King of Aden *forc'd aboard a* Turkish *Ship, and hang'd,* 600
King of Panane *joins with the* Portugueses, *appears at Court and is accus'd of Treason, committed to Prison; his Trial, Sentence, Execution, Behaviour, Speech and Successor,* 691
King of Cochin *robs a famous Pagode,* 841
King of Calecut *how he purifies himself,* 895
King's Merchant belonging to the Navy, his Duty, 325
Kisna *an* Indian *God, his Parents,* 867. *His Birth,* 868. *His Deliverance,* 869. *Turns Shepherd,* 870. *Produces a Pearl-Tree, makes sport with Women, is chosen King,* 873. *Breaks the strong Arrow of* Mottera, *kills ten Courtiers, an Elephant, two Generals, and* Ragia Kan, *and routs a whole Body of Men,* 875. *Is under the Tuition of* Brahma, 876. *A Miracle of his,* 877. *Delivers an Elephant from a Crocodile,* 879. *Delivers* 16000 *Captives, cures the Leprosy,* 880. *His Finger ty'd up with a piece of Gold Stuff,* 881. *Visits a poor* Brahman, 884. *Blesses him with Riches, goes to the Court of* Dersiende, 885. *Visits the World to purge it from the wicked. Blesses* Sindera, *comes to* Sudanewa, *routs several Kings, leaps over the Walls of* Mottera, 886. *Ascends up to Heaven,* 888

L.

Ladies River in Chile, 21
Lakes in Chile, 29
La Riga *River in* Chile, 18
Lampa *River in* Chile, 19
Lands in the same Latitude with Chile, *yet differing in Temperature,* 3
Langotama *River in* Chile, 18
Language in which the Eastern Christians worship God, 641
Lascarines *Soldiers in* Ceylon, 720
La Serena, *vid.* Coquimbo.
Lavapie *River in* Chile, 20
Lautaro, *an* Indian, *Page to* Valdivia, *his Treachery, and Speech to his Countrymen,* 144. *He enters and sacks the City of the* Conception, 147. *Takes it a second time,* 148. *Marches to besiege* Santiago, *is kill'd with an Arrow,* 149
Laws of K. Richard *the First for punishing Offenders at Sea,* 367
League betwixt the Dutch *and* Samorin, 627
Leagues to answer a Degree, 340
Length and Breadth of Europe, Asia, *and* Africk, 421. *Of Days,* 340
Letters from the Dutch *General to the Viceroy of* Goa, 615. *From K.* John *of* Portugal *to D.* John de Castro *Viceroy of* India, 646. *From the States General to the Emperor of* Ceylon, 683. *From Prince* Maurice *to the same,* 684. *From the Governor of* Palicate *to the same,* 705. *From the* Dutch *Admiral to the same,* 710. *From the Emperor of* Ceylon *to General* Hulst, 721, 725, 731, 732, 736, 741, 743, 749, 751, 755, 756, 780. *From the* Dutch *General to the Governour of* Columbo, *and his Answer,* 722, 732. *Intercepted by the* Dutch, 726, 729, 734. *From a Spy at* Goa, 730. *From the* Dutch *General to the Emperor of* Ceylon, 734, 741, 743. *From the Governor of* Columbo *to the Emperor of* Ceylon, *and from the Citizens of that place to him,* 735
Levo *River in* Chile, 20
Lewis *the* 2d *K. of* Hungary *lost through his Subjects refusing him Supplies,* 295
Lewis *Island, what is requisite for planting of it,* 525. *Its use,* 558
Lewson (*Sir* Richard) *his Voyage to the Islands to no purpose,* 196. *His Voyage to* Ireland, *where he destroy'd some* Spanish *Ships,* 197. *His Voyage with Sir* Will. Monson *to the Coast of* Spain, 198. *Takes two Easterlings,* 199. *Attacks a Carrack and eleven Galleys at* Cezimbra, 200. *Takes the Carrack,* 201. *Burns two Galleys,* 202. *He and Sir* Will. *in the Narrow Seas, where is no Action,* 206
Lima *in* Peru *founded by* Pizarro, *its Situation delicious, it never rains there,* 112
Limari *River in* Chile, 18
Lion-fish, 36
List of Portugueses *Ships for relief of* Columbo, 729
Lope de Souza *Governor of* Diu, 595
Lord's Prayer in the Malabar *Language,* 665
Lucayos *Islands,* 414

M.

Machis, *or* Indian *Doctors, their Character,* 5.
Madrastapatan *Town,* 653
Magalhaens, *or* Magellan *first attempted to sail round the World,* 396. *His Death,* 397
Magellan *offers to discover the Strait of his Name,* 101. *Sails upon his Discovery, his Men mutiny; leaves the Mutineers ashore, passes the Straits in* 20 *days, is kill'd,* 102
Mague *Tree in* Chile, 48
Mahometan *Religion,* 580

Mahometans *in* India, *their Circumcision, Washing, Sabbath, Mosques, Orders, Tenets of Religion*, 581. *Their Paradise, Rules to attain Eternal Bliss, Manners and Customs, Tokens of being marriageable, Marriages*, 582. *Their Divorces, Food, Habitations, Clothing*, 583. *Their Burials*, 584
Mahomet's *Origin*, 580
Maiz *or* Indian *Wheat*, 72
Malabar *Language an Introduction to it*, 663. *Rules for learning of it*, 664
Malabar *its Extent and Rivers*, 621. *The Climate, Seasons, Product*, 622
Malabars *Enemies to the* Portugueses, 573
Mallangam, 801
Mallua *River in* Chile, 19
Mamadabath *City*, 574
Mamud *King of* Cambaja, 593. *Is repuls'd at* Diu, 597
Man *an* Indian *Weight*, 622
Manaar *Island taken by the* Dutch, 790. *Reasons of its Name, its Situation, Churches, Pearl-fishery, Inhabitants, who speak* Portuguese, 792. *Has plenty of Fish, one sort peculiar*, 793
Manegues *Shell-fish in* Chile, 34
Manipay, 802
Mankind naturally hardy, 80
Manner of travelling in Cuyo, 62
Manner of living of the Dutch *in* India, 660
Manufactures of the Islands of Chile, 51
Mapocho *Valley describ'd*, 119. *Inhabited by* 80000 Indians, 120
Mapocho *River in* Chile, 18, 28
Marcellus Boschouter *sent to* Ceylon, 684. *His Treaty and Agreement with that Emperor*, 689. *He desires to be dismiss'd*, 686. *Has great Favours bestow'd on him*, 687. *Is sent Embassador, comes to* Bantam, *thence into* Holland, *engages with the* Danes, *sails for* Ceylon, *and dies*, 699
Maronites, 640
Marriages and Christenings celebrated with much Pomp in Chile, 131
Marriages of Pagan Indians, 899
Martin Alfonso de Souza *attacks* Daman, *takes and demolishes it*, 591
Martires *River in* Chile, 24
Mascarenhas *Governour of* Diu, *his Speech to his Souldiers*, 598
Masquerade of great Expence, 131
Mass of Silver brought from America, 89
Masters Attendants of the Navy their Duty, 325
Master Shipwrights their Duty, 325
Masting of a Ship, 346
Masulipatan, 655
Matthias de Albuquerque *his Bravery*, 768
Maule *River in* Chile, 19
Mayletti, 801
Maypo *River in* Chile, 18
Mayten *Fountain in* Chile, 28
Mecca, 424
Medicinal Herbs in Chile *describ'd*, 6
Medicinal Fountain in Chile, 29
Medina Sidonia *Duke, Admiral of the* Spanish *Fleet, engag'd by the* English, 171
Mediterranean *Sea*, 424
Melchites, 639
Men how to be preserv'd in fight, 358
Mendoga *River*, 24
Messengers of the Navy their Duty, 327
Metaquito *River in* Chile, 19
Method for Conversion of Indians, 790
Military Exhortations of the Chilenians, 70
Mine blows up 100 Portugueses; *another* 300 Indians, 598
Ministers beheaded by the Chineses, 634
Miraculous Spring, 799
Miserable state of the Portugueses, 595
Misfortune of D. Diego Lobo *a* Spanish *Captain*. 202
Mocha *City describ'd, its Encrease and Trade*, 575. *Its Riches, Trade of the* Portugueses *there, Water and Fuel scarce*, 576
Mogul's *Letter in favour of the* Dutch, 572. *His Court and Religion*, 580
Mogommal *Church*, 808
Monasteries of Men not so full as Nunneries in Chile, 129
Monson (*Sir* William) *his Dedication to his eldest Son*, 163. *His Dedication to his Friends*, 168. *His Voyage to the Coast of* Spain, 204. *Attempts a Galeon, but is repuls'd*, 203. *His Farewel to the Gentlemen he dedicates his Book to*, 231. *His Epistle to his second Son*, 233. *His Epistles to the Commanders in Queen* Elizabeth's *Wars*, 236. *The several Capacities he serv'd in at Sea*, 239. *His Justification*, Ibid. *His Voyage about* England, Scotland *and* Ireland, 246. *His contrivance to draw the Pyrates within his reach. His Reception, being taken for a Pyrate*, 248. *He takes a Pyrate*, 251. *His Opinion of the Expedition of* Cadiz *under K.* Charles *the First*, 258. *His further Opinion upon the News of taking a Fort there*, 265. *More about keeping of* Cadiz, *when taken*, 266. *His Epistle to Projectors*, 453. *Several Passages of his Life*, 502. & sequent. *His Epistle to the King*, 512. *To the Gentlemen that read his Discourses*, 513
Moussons *when they blow in the* East-Indies, 340
Moors *obstruct the* Portugueses *settling at* Calicut, 626
Moorish *Vessel gives Advice of the Condition of* Gale, 735
Mortality of Cattle, 810

Mount Libanus *inhabited by the* Maronites, p. 641
Mules in Chile, 9
Mulipatto *Church*, 808
Murder committed in the presence of the Mogul, 577
Martilla *Tree in* Chile, 48
Muster of Ships and Mariners in England *in Q.* Elizabeth's *days*, 279
Mutiny among the Portugueses, 598
Mutiny at Columbo *against the Governor*, 787
Muxillones *Island of* Chile, 50

N.

NAel *Stream, a Whirlpool on the Coast of* Norway, 535
Naicks Indian *Lords*, 654
Nainativa *Island*, 809
Naires, 644. *Four hundred of them slain*, 632
Naked People in a very cold Country, 78
Nalloras, *a Tribe of* Indians, 817
Nalour, 803
Names of Ships left by Q. Elizabeth *at her Death*, 214
Of Ships Sir Will. Monson *serv'd in*, 251
Of Timber and Planks in a Ship, 346
Of the Governours of Hispaniola, 414
Natural Obedience of Chilenians *to their* Caciques, 78
Navacouli, 804
Navy set out by K. Charles *the First*, an. 1635. 290
Negapatan *City master'd by the* Dutch, *Protestant Religion there, miserable condition of it*, 651
Negumbo *taken a second time by the* Dutch, *the* Portugueses *attempt in vain to recover it*, 787
Nestorians, 639
New Guinea *Islands*, 53
New Granada, 416
New Viceroy of Goa, 790
Nile *River*, 425. *Its source*, 661
Nindundiva, *or* Ilha das Vacas, 809
Nombre de Dios, 416
Nuble *River in* Chile, 20
Number of Christians in Jafnapatan, 810
Nunho d' Acunha *goes for* Goa, *his Rendevouz, assaults* Diu *in vain. His Design against* Bazaim, 590. *Attacks and takes it*, 591. *Sails again for* Diu, *is visited by* Badur, 592. *His Death*, 595

O.

O*Ath, manner of taking it by the Pagan* Indians, 900
Observations on the Harbours of England, Scotland *and* Ireland, 378
Observations of Sir William Monson, 221. *On the* Dutch, 298
Old Stories, 77, 838
Offer of exchanging Prisoners at Columbo, 754
Office of the Admiralty in England, 318
Office of the Master of one of the King's Ships, 339
Officers of the Admiralty their Allowance, 319
Officers in constant Pay belonging to Ships, their Pay, 320
Officers of the Admiralty, their Duty, 321
Officers Assistants of the Navy, their Duty, 324
Ojos de Agua, *a remarkable Spring in* Chile, 16
Ondewijl, 802
Onor *Kingdom*, 621
Ophir *said to be* Hispaniola, 86
Opinion concerning the strength of Columbo, 785
Opinion of Malabars *concerning Cow-dung*, 896
Order of Battel of the Chilenians, 70
Orders of the Dutch *relating to their Affairs at* Suratte, 567
Given by the Dutch *General at* Cochin, 635
Orellana, 419
Origin of 14 *Worlds*, 891
Of the first Fast-day of the Indian *Pagans*, 897. *Of the second and third*, 898. *Of the fourth*, 899
Oversight of the Ship the Saphir, 785
Ourature *first Isle of* Jafnapatan, 808
Outrages committed by the Lascarines, 784
Oysters of Chile, 34

P.

P*Acifick Sea*, 31
Pacudo *Port in* Chile, 33
Pagan Temple plunder'd, 644
Pagodes in India, *their Revenues and Reverence paid them*, 893
Palicate *City and its Road*, 653
Palm-Tree in Chile, 47
Pan *represented with Horns, his Flute and Panther's Skin*, 132
Panama *on the South Sea founded*, 103
Panane *Town*, 625. *Attack'd by the* Portugueses, *and taken*, 627
Pancteripou, 802
Panuco, 415
Paper affix'd to a Tree, charging the Dutch *with breach of Faith*, 783
Paragua *Tree in* Chile, 47
Paramesceri's *Pedegree*, 842
Paretiture, 806
Parras 50 *Pound weight in* India, 717
Parreas, *a Tribe of* Indians, 817
Particulars concerning the East-Indies, 392
Parvas, *a Nation, their Conversion*, 645. *Their constancy in the* Roman *Religion*, 647
Parvas, *a Tribe of* Indians, 817

Index *to the Third Volume.*

Pastene, *a* Genoese, *sent from* Peru *with Succours to* Chile, 133. *His joyful Reception*, 134. *Is disappointed of a second Supply in* Peru, *and returns to* Chile, 135
Patamars, *what they are*, 740
Patchiarapalle *Province of* Jafnapatan, 807
Patragali *Pagode in* Cangranor, 841
Patragali's *Adventures*, 842, 843. *Revenges her Husband's Death*, 844
Pattapatane *City*, 574
Paxáros *River in* Chile, 24
Paxaro Carpentero *the Woodpecker in* Chile, 39
Paxaros *Island of* Chile, 50
Peace with Spain *after Q.* Elizabeth's *death*, 237
Betwixt Portugueses *and* Badur, 591
Pearl-fishing, 99, 648
Pearls of a prodigious bigness, 99
Pedegree of the King of Ceylon, 668
Pegus *a sort of wild Rabbets in* Chile, 44
Pejerreyes *Fish in* Chile, 37
Pengu *Tree in* Chile, 48
Penguin *Islands*, 56
Penna *Town*, 654
People of Chile *very patient*, 75
People of 14 *sorts*, 891
Pepper, 622
Pericos *Shell-fish in* Chile, 35
Paricotes *Rats in* Chile, 44
Persecution of Christians at Manaar, 792
Persian *Gulph*, 426
Peru *how nam'd*, 86. *Its discovery first attempted*, 106
Petapouli *Town*, 654
Peterroa *River in* Chile, 19
Petition of the Dutch *to the Great* Mogul, 566
Philip *made King of* Candea, *poison'd by his Brother*, 670
Phlebotomy, or bleeding in Chile, 72
Picos *the* Papagayos *Shell-fish in* Chile, 35
Pilot and Coaster his Office, 341
Pimienta *Harbour*, 55
Pinguedas *Birds in* Chile, 39
Pizarro *left with only thirteen* Spaniards *and a* Mulatto *in the Island* Gorgona. *Is reliev'd by a Ship from* Panama, 107. *Returns to* Panama, *and thence into* Spain, *then persues his Conquest of* Peru, 108. *He revolts*, 135. *His Actions*, 405. *His Death*, 408
Places impassable in the Mountains of Chile, 15
Places taken by the English *in Q.* Elizabeth's *time of little or no consequence*, 211
Plantations of the French, 446
Plants in Chile, 5
Plato's *Advice to Governours*, 307
Poanque *River in* Chile, 18
Poelepolay *Church*, p. 807
Pongardive *Isle*, 809
Popes Bull for Dominicans *and Jesuits to confer Degrees in* Chile, 127
Porca *Kingdom, its Air unwholesom, Factory of the* English *there*, 643
Porcupines, 826
Porters at the Ship-Yards their Duty, 326
Portland *Race*, 536
Porto Novo, 652
Portuguese *Discoverys in* Africk *and* India, 390
Portuguese *Fleet at* Chaul *engages* Mir Hazem, 585. *Advise their Admiral, who rejects it, is cast upon a Rock, and kill'd*, 586
Portuguese *Fort near* Diu, 592
Portuguese *Embassadors at* Batavia, 610. *Their Reception, Credentials, Age, Train, their Audiences*, 611. *Fourth Audience*, 612. *One of them returns to* Goa, 614
Portuguese *Fort at* Calicut *besieg'd*, 628. *Reliev'd*, 629
Portuguese *account of the Siege of* Columbo, 761
Portuguese *Squadron gets clear of the* Dutch, 785
Portuguese *Merchant comes into the* Dutch *Camp*, 740
Portugueses *receive Succours*, 597. *Their way of living in* India, *their Character and Distempers*, 608. *Massacred at* Calicut, *and their Death reveng'd*, 628. *Side with the* Zingaleses, 669. *Commit great Insolences in* Ceylon, *fall out with* Janiere, *resolve on his Death*, 674. *They leave* Candea, *and are routed*, 676. *March to* Jafnapatan, *and are beaten*, 688. *They surprize the Emperor's Camp, offer Peace*, 697. *Are rejected, propose a Truce, march towards* Candea, *surprize* 500 Candeneses, 698. *Erect a new Fort, rout the* Malabars, *build two more Forts, make Peace with the Emperor*, 700. *They take the Field, plunder* Badule, 701. *Are attack'd in their March, and routed*, 702. *They make War on the Emperor, are beaten, make Peace*, 702. *They endeavour to render the* Dutch *suspected in* Ceylon, 707. *Are put to a great* Nonplus, *march towards* Candea, *take and burn it, are routed by the* Cingaleses, 711. *Rout the* Cingaleses, 777. *Force their King to pay a yearly Tribute, which is resented, surprize* Columbo, *are besieg'd in the Fort*, 776. *Make a vigorous Sally and raise the Siege*, 779. *Defeated at Sea*, 789
Poverty, falsly pretended, to refuse K. Charles *the First Supplies*, 294
Poverty of England *caus'd by the* Dutch, 553

Pran, an Indian Spy, forms a Design against the Spaniards, but it turns to the ruin of the Indians, p. 153
Prassaram the Son of Reneca, 855. He endeavours to kill Ram, 858
Precious Stones in Ceylon, 828
Precedents of Princes defending their Prerogatives on their Seas, 284
Pretences for not relieving of Columbo, 776
Princes, Embassadors, and others transported by Sir Will. Monson, 250
Prizes taken in the War in Q. Elizabeth's time, 112
Prizes taken, how divided, 338
Processions in Chile, their Magnificence, 128
Prodigious Ransom, 110
Project for the security of the English Navy, 452. To prevent the French landing in England, 457. To prevent the French and Dutch Fleets joining, 458. To war upon Holland, 461. To get Possession of the Island of Wakerland, 464. To make War upon Spain, 466. To increase 200 Sail of Ships, 470. For settling in Guinea, 471. Of a Voyage to the East-Indies to settle there, 474. To intercept the Ships of Cambaia trading to the Red-Sea, 479. Of the Genoeses, to bring the East-India Commodities to Muscovy by Land, 480. To come to Tombagatu and Gago in Africk for Gold, 480. For a private Voyage to Guinea, 482. To trade to the West-Indies with the King of Spain's Consent, 482. To ruin Spain with the Assistance of Holland, 487. For the Spaniards to annoy the Dutch in their Trade, 490
Promocaes River in Chile, 19
Proposition of Sir Will. Monson to the Parliament concerning the Navy, 380
Protestation of the Dutch General against the Portugueses in India, 616
Provinces of Jafnapatan, 799
Provisions to maintain the King's Labourers, and the Labour they shall be put to Winter and Summer, 362
Punishments at Sea, 330
Puntagale besieg'd by the Dutch, 715. Taken by Storm, 716
Puren Lake in Chile, 20, 29
Purser's Duty, 326. His Office, 347
Pyramid of Heads, 711
Pyrats in the North of Scotland and Ireland, 247
Pyrats of Malabar, 622

Q.

Qualities of the Natives of Chile, 75
Quantity of Fish vented in other Countries, 516
Quartermasters at Sea their Office, 348
Queen Elizabeth's Death, 229
Queen of Cochin taken by the Dutch, 632
Quenavadi, Indian God, his Original and Description, 836. Is castrated. How worshipp'd; difference betwixt him and Superbennia, 837. He curses the Moon, 839
Queule River in Chile, 21
Quicksilver and Lead little us'd in Chile, 8
Quillota Port in Chile, 33
Quintero Port in Chile, 33
Quirpele a Creature, an Enemy to Snakes, 824
Quiriquina Island of Chile, 33
Quito Province temperate, tho under the Line, 85
Quiveling what it was, 830

R.

Ragia Kans endeavours to kill Kisna, 870, 871. His further Designs against Kisna, 875
Raja Singa Enemy to the Portugueses, 668. His Message to D. John Emperor of Ceylon, is defeated, dies. His Murder of Pagan Priests, and Repentance, 671
Raja Singa dissatisfied with the Dutch, 780, 782. His Answer to their General, 784. He treats with the Portugueses, his Elephants seiz'd, 787. Makes a Diversion in favour of the Dutch, 788. His Troops routed, 789
Raja Sestraarsum visits the Brahman, is plentifully entertain'd; his People defeated by the white Cow, 857
Rainbow how it appears on the Mountains of Chile, 12
Ralemo River in Chile, 20
Ram the Story of him, 858. How he got his Bride Sytha, 859. He travels along the Ganges, 10000 Horsemen kill'd by him, 860. He and Lekeman go in quest of Sytha, he kills Bael, 862. Meets with Sytha, 866. Returns home, 867
Rama, or Siri Rama, 859
Rammanacoyel Island, 649
Ramon Fountain in Chile, 27
Rapel River in Chile, 19
Rapel Lake in Chile, 29
Rapid Rivers in Chile, 15
Rapid Tides, 98
Rates for Seamens Wages, 278
Ratification of a Truce betwixt Dutch and Portugueses in India, 615
Rawan transform'd into a Stag, 860. Is shot by Ram, 861. He carries away Sytha, and places her in a Garden in Ceylon, 862. His Obstinacy, his eldest Son slain, he seeks for Assistance by his Brother, 865. His last Sacrifice, he is slain by Ram, and his Wife married to his Brother, 866
Rawan's Sister in love with Lekeman, 860

Index *to the Third Volume.*

Rawan's *Brother comes over to* Ram, 865
Reasons against Salomon's *having discover'd* America, 88. *For not attacking the* Spanish *Ships in* Ferol, 193. *For* King Charles *the First's not resenting the Wrongs offer'd by the* Dutch *sooner, and for setting out his Fleet* an. 1635. 289. *Against the* India *Voyage answer'd*, 475. *Of the* Dutch *for continuing the War with the* Portugueses *in* India, 609. *Why the* Malabars *made War upon the* Portugueses, 623
Recital of Captains who were instrumental in the Conquest of Chile, 137
Recloma *a famous* Indian *Lady*, 22
Red Sea, 424
Reflections on the Dutch *Enterprize upon the* Canaries, 484. *On the ill management of the* English *with respect to* Holland, 554
Reinforcement sent to the Dutch *Fleet near* Tutecorin, 754
Religious Digression of Ovalle, 101
Religious Worship, magnificent and costly in Chile, 127
Religious Worship how perform'd in Jafnapatan, 810
Remarkable Cures perform'd by Chilenian *Doctors*, 5
Remarkable Spring, 810
Remarks upon the Trade of India, 575
Remedies against Serpents Stings, 827, 829
Reneca *kill'd and reviv'd*, 856. *Burns her self with* Siamdichemi's *Corps, whence the Custom of burning the dead*, 857
Report of Pigmies, 80
Reproof of the Spaniards *Covetousness*, 96
Resemblance betwixt Animals in Chile *and in* Europe, 4
Resolutions of the Chilenians, 114. *Of* Q. Elizabeth's *Council to make a defensive War against* Spain, 222. *How to hinder their landing, and fight if landed*, 223. *Of the* Dutch *Council of the* East-Indies, 704. *Of the* Dutch *Council of War*, 728
Rich Mines discover'd, 15
Riches of Chile, 8
Riches of Peru *not believ'd in* Spain, 108
Ridiculous Opinion of the Brahmans *concerning the Figure of the World, and its Magnitude*, 892
Riode Mendoza, 17
Riosin fondo *in* Chile, 24
River of Plate *discover'd, the Virtue of its Water, its fall*, 100, 420
Rivers of Chile, 17
Robbers punish'd, 785
Rochemy, *a Virgin, design'd for* Kisna, *her Love to him, she is deliver'd by him*, 878
Rock of Turky *Stones in* Chile, 119
Roupie *its Value*, 573
Rubies, 656
Rudder and Sails of Ships to be carried ashore at Mocha, 576
Rule to know the Age of the Moon, 340. *To know the Burden of a Ship*, 346
Rumecan *slain*, 599
Rumenstadt, 593. *Quitted by the* Portugueses, 594
Russians, 639

S.

SAbaio, *his Death*, 603
Sadrastapatan *Town*, 653
St. John's *River*, 24
S. John de Puerto Rico, *or* Boniquen, 414
S. Thomas *the Apostle's arrival in* India, *his several Voyages, one of his Miracles*, 637. *Another Miracle, his Death*, 638
S. Thomas's *Town*, 653
S. Vincent's *Port in* Chile, 33
S. Victorian's *River*, 24
Salt River in Chile, 17
Salt found on a Herb in Chile, 30
Salt and Cask for fishing, 527
Salutes at Sea how to be regulated, 368
Samorin *Sovereign of* Malabar, 622. *His Dress*, 625
Sandal, *or* Sander's *Tree in* Chile, 47
Sandwich, *the People base and ill affected*, 241. *Advantage the* Dutch *may take of it in a War with* England, 242. *More of their Villany*, 244
Santa Marta, 414
Santiago *City Capital of* Chile *describ'd, its Conveniences, a noble Street in it*, 120. *Its Town-House*, 121. *Church of* S. Dominick, Franciscans *Convent, Jesuits Church*, 122. *Its Government, Court of the Royal* Audiencia, 123. *This Court of great Advantage to the City*, 124. *Its Foundation, Riches, Militia*, 125. *Its vast Increase and Trade*, 126
Saphirs, 656
Sea of Chile, 30
Sea-Coasts, Ports and Havens of Chile, 32
Sea-Wolves, or Seals, 36
Seas beyond the Ocean discover'd, 424
Seasons in Chile, 4
Sebald de Weert *comes to* Ceylon, *differs with the Emperor, invites him aboard*, 680. *Speaks too boldly, which is the cause of his and his Companions Death*, 680
Sebastian Cabot *his Discoveries*, 445
Sebastian Cano, *a* Spaniard, *the first that sail'd round the World*, 397
Sects in the East, 639
Security to England, 468
Serpent-Catcher, 828
Serpents in Ceylon, 827
Serpent-Stone, 657
Sevaldo *Islands*, 56

Several

Several Sea-Engagements betwixt Portugueses *and* Dutch, 797
Sheathing of Ships, 346
Sheep of Chile, 44
Ships of the Bishop of Placentia *lost in the Straits of* Magellan, 59
Ships built by K. James *and K.* Charles *the First*, 277
Ships built in Spain *from* 1590 *to* 1600, 351
Ships burnt and destroy'd by the Portugueses *at* Diu, 587
Siamdichemi *murder'd*, 857
Siege of Cochin *rais'd*, 633
Siege of Batecalo, 712
Silveira *Governor of* Diu *prepares for his Defence*, 594
Simplicity of the Indians, 94
Siri Rama, 859
Skirmish betwixt Portugueses *and* Dutch, 806
Slaughter of Giants, 863
Small-pox, the Indians *opinion about them*, 840
Snakewood, its use, how first discover'd, 824
Snow on the Mountains of Chile, 13
Soboral *Island of* Chile, 50
Sofar *taken Prisoner*, 593. *His Treachery*, 595. *He attacks* Diu, 596. *Is kill'd*, 597
Solyman *lands and attacks the* Portugueses *at* Diu. *Retreats*, 594. *Renews the Siege, attacks the place, and is repulsed*, 594. *His Treachery with the King of* Aden, 600
Sovereignty of the Seas of England, 282
South Sea, remarks on its Navigation, 31. *When first heard of, and its Riches*, 96. *Its Discovery continu'd, and its Ports and Islands*, 99. *Discover'd by* Vasco Nunez de Balboa, 405
South-Wind most favourable in Chile, 30
Spain, *how to have been ruin'd by a Fleet*, 75
Spaniards *take* Atagualpa's *Ransom, and put him to death*, 110. *Drawn into an Ambush through Covetousness*, 134. *Beaten a second time by the* Araucanos. *Fly from the City of the* Conception, 147
Spanish *Fleet lost in the Straits of* Magellan, 59
Spanish *Ships sent safe from* Dover *to* Dunkirk *in spite of the* Dutch *by K.* James *the First*, 238
Special Duties of the Officers of the King's Ships at Sea, 336
Spilberg's *Observation of 25 Ports in the Straits of* Magellan. *He is assaulted by the* Indians, 32
Springs extremely cold, 16
Spies hang'd, 731
Stars of Chile, 41
State of Portugal *an.* 1625. p. 259. *Of the* Canaries, *and* Tercera *Islands*, 260. *Of* Andaluzia, Sevil, *and the Straits*, 263
State of the West-Indies, 263. *Of* Ireland *and* Scotland, 379. *Of the Harbours in* France, 460
Steward and his Mate their Office, 348
Stone-Bridg 100 *Leagues long across the Sea, a Fable*, 864
Story of a Chilenian, 75. *Of a Pilot said to have dy'd in the House of* Columbus, 90. *Of Sir* Will. Monson, *and a* Portuguese *at* Lisbon, 498. *Another of Sir* Will. *at* Villafranca, 501. *Of two Pirats*, 537. *One alluding to that of* Sampson, 864. *Others*, 502, 503
Strange Fish in the West-Indies, 533
Strange Escape, 771
Stratagems to be us'd at Sea, 492
Straits of Magellan *and S.* Vincent, 54
Successful Sally, 598
Succession in the Kingdom of Calicut, 625
Succours sent into Chile, 133. *Their joyful Reception*, 134
Sudden change of Air, 12
Sugar-Sea, 837
Summons sent by the Dutch *into* Columbo, *and the Answer*, 750
Sundecouli, 804
Supplies sent to the Dutch *in* Ceylon, 789
Suratte *City*, 566. *Description of it*, 572. *Its Trade*, 573
Surgeon of the Navy his Duty, 327. *His Office*, 348
Surveyor of the Victuals of the Navy his Duty, 325
Sussuster *and* Dersiende *play for a Crown*, 881
Sussuster *goes into Banishment*, 882. *Prays to* Kisna, *is heard*, 884. *His Sacrifice*, 886
Swabber and Lier their Office, 348
Syriack *Language propagated at* Rome, 631

T.

TAgataguas *Lake in* Chile, 29
Taltales *Birds in* Chile, 38
Tambamme *Church*, 808
Tea how prepar'd, 660
Tegnapaton *Town*, 652
Telipole *Church*, 800
Teno *River in* Chile, 19
Termapatan *City*, 623
Thorn-Bushes in Chile *affording plenty of Fuel*, 4
Three Portuguese *Frigats taken by the* Dutch, 782
Three sorts of People, 854
Tierra del fuego *on the* Magellan *Straits*, 52
Time of fishing to the Northward, 524
Tinguiritica *River in* Chile, 19
Tirepoplier *Town*, 652

Titles given by the Portugueses *to Persons serving in* India, 394. *Of the King of* Ceylon, 667. *Of Dukes and Earls introduc'd in* India *by the* Portugueses, 667. *Of the Kings of* Achem *and* Siam, 579
Toadstone, 658
Tolten *River in* Chile, 21
Tondy *on the Coast of* Coromandel, 650
Tongoy *River in* Chile, 18
Topas, *the Son of a* Portuguese *and an* Indian *Woman*, 717
Towns of Portugueses *in the* East-Indies, 394
Trade to Africk *and* Asia, 440. *To other parts nearer* England, 442. *To* Turky, 443. *To* Russia, 444. *Of the Red-Sea*, 573
Trades to be advanc'd by Fishing, 523
Trangebar, *a* Danish *Fort*, 652
Transmigration of Souls believ'd in India, 893
Treacherous Design against the Dutch *at* Jafnapatan *discover'd*, 798. *The Traitors executed*, 799
Treasurer of the Admiralty his Duty, 322
Treaty betwixt the Portugueses *and* Cingaleses *soon broken*, 777
Trees always green in Chile, 4
Trees of Chile, 46
Trevancor *Kingdom*, 645
Tribes of Indians, 817
Trinquenemale, 818. *Strengthen'd with additional Fortifications*, 819
Truce betwixt Dutch *and* Portugueses *in* India, 617. *Betwixt* Spaniards *and* Dutch, 683
Tumbez *discover'd*, 107
Tunny *Fish in* Chile, 36
Tutecorin *taken by the* Dutch, 648. *Its Climate*, 649
Two brave Exploits of Portugueses, 586

V.

VAldivia *conquers* Chile, 118. *Pursues his Conquest*, 134. *Marches to* Peru *to assist the King's Forces*, 135. *Is victorious, and returns to* Chile *with a Supply*, 136. *Pursues his Conquest*, 138. *Strengthens his Garisons, designs a Voyage for* Spain, 141. *Marches against the* Araucanos, *engages them*, 144. *Is taken by them, and kill'd, they make Flutes of his Bones*, 145
Valdivia *River and Port in* Chile, 21
Valdivia *City in* Chile *founded, and a Fort erected*, 141
Valparaiso *Port in* Chile, 33
Vanarpone, 803
Vander Meyden *succeeds* Hulst *as General at the Siege of* Columbo, 748
Van Teylin's *Letter about the Affairs of the* Dutch *at* Suratte, 567
Variety of Waters diverting, 16
Vasco Nunez *first sees the South Sea, and pursues the Discovery of it*, 97. *Is beheaded*, 98
Vast Riches of the first Conquerors of Peru, 111
Vaypin *Isle*, 631
Venetians *trading in* England, 442
Venezuela, 419
Viceroy of India *how declar'd by the* Portugueses, 394
Victuals carried to Sea, 521
Villagran *marches to revenge* Valdivia's *Death, and comes to a Battel with* Lautaro, 146
Villa Rica *City in* Chile *founded, and its Situation*, 141
Vinne Lamantia *rebels against* Raja Singa, 668. *Comes to a Composition with him, is betray'd and murder'd*, 669
Violent Tempest, 739
Visiapour *Kingdom subject to the* Mogul, *its Limits*, 602. *Its King willing to attack* Goa, 608
Vistnum's *Descent and Residence, wears a Print on his Breast, his Wives*, 843. *Is ten times transform'd*, 844. *Is Master of the World*, 854
Ultecueste *Root in* Chile, 34
Ungrateful Return, 133
University and rare Wits at Cordova *in* Tucuman, 100
Unsuccessful Attempt of the Dutch, 634
Voyage of Danes *to the* East-Indies, 699
Voyages set out by Q. Elizabeth, *and what Profit they turn'd to*, 315
Voycas *Birds in* Chile, 39

W.

WAddemarache, 806
Wannias *Country*, 793
War with Spain *resolv'd on under* K. Charles *the First*, 258
War with Scotland *how to be manag'd, if they proceed in Rebellion*, 311. *The same how to be done on the West of* Scotland, 313
Waranni, 804
Warlike Ornaments of Chileses, 70
Warrant-places granted by the L. *High Admiral*, 328
Washing of the Indian *Pagans*, 893
Way of registring Events in Chile, 74
Wealth and Strength of the Mogul, 578
Weapons a strange sort, 82
Westerwold *comes before* Batavia, 712
Whales on the Coast of Chile, 35
Whales and several sorts of monstrous Fishes, 534
White Wine in Chile, 8
Wives of the Nairos *slip off all their Clothes in dancing*, 838

Index *to the Third Volume.*

Wild Cows in Chile, 46
Wingurla *a Factory of the* Dutch, 602
Winter and Summer at once in several Parts of Ceylon, 794
Wise Repartee of an Indian, 99
Women in Chile *make the Bread*, 72. *Their Behaviour at Feasts, care of their Husbands and Dress*, 73. *They hate Head-Dresses and Paint*, 74. *Their hard Education*, 75. *Their manner of mourning*, 78
Wonderful Preservation, 133
Worlds, two undiscover'd, besides the four known, 422

X.

XAverius (*S.*Francis) *his Speech, Death, Body uncorrupted, Transportation to* Goa, 607. *His going to the* Indies, *and coming among the* Paruas, 645

Y.

YAnaconas, *what they are*, 113
Yarmouth *Men build Ships to sell to the* Dutch, 529
Youth of Chile *their Education*, 70
Ysbrand Gotsken's *account of his Negotiation*, 739. *He is sent to the Emperor of* Ceylon, *his Negotiation*, 753

Z.

ZEmbre *Lake*, 425
Zenobia *Queen her Character*, 305
Zenu *Island*, 418

FINIS.